"Jon Lang firmly situates urban design as a discipline and discerns with great clarity a compelling narrative about its influence as a practice in shaping our cities and their physical manifestations over the last 150 years. His argument foregrounds architecture at scale – its compulsions, ambitions as well as aspirations in understanding how it has historically propelled the protocols for Urban Design."

—*Rahul Mehrotra, Professor of Urban Design and Planning,*
Graduate School of Design, Harvard University

"This is a comprehensive book on the history and theory of urban design, focusing on the paradigms that have transformed the built environment, in a rich combination of theory and practice from around the world. It is written by a leading urban design scholar and would be valuable for all urban students."

—*Ali Madanipour, Professor of Urban Design, School of Architecture,*
Planning and Landscape, Newcastle University

"Focusing on urban design paradigms, Lang establishes the much-needed generative history of our discipline in the 20th and early 21st centuries, connecting urban design to its roots across space, time, and cultures. More than a historical narrative, Lang's critical perspective highlights the various ideologies that have shaped urban design practice and projects. This book should become a standard text for anyone interested in the contemporary built environments."

—*Ali Modarres, Director of Urban Studies and the Assistant Chancellor for*
Community Engagement at University of Washington Tacoma

The Routledge Companion to Twentieth and Early Twenty-First Century Urban Design

The Routledge Companion to Twentieth and Early Twenty-First Century Urban Design is a fully illustrated descriptive and explanatory history of the development of urban design ideas and paradigms of the past 150 years. The ideas and projects, hypothetical and built, range in scale from the city to the urban block level. The focus is on where the generic ideas originated, the projects that were designed following their precepts, the functions they address and/or afford, and what we can learn from them.

The morphology of a city—its built environment—evolves unselfconsciously as private and governmental investors self-consciously erect buildings and infrastructure in a pragmatic, piecemeal manner to meet their own ends. Philosophers, novelists, architects, and social scientists have produced myriad ideas about the nature of the built environment that they consider to be superior to those forms resulting from a laissez-faire attitude to urban development.

Rationalist theorists dream of ideal futures based on assumptions about what is good; empiricists draw inspirations from what they perceive to be working well in existing situations. Both groups have presented their advocacies in manifestoes and often in the form of generic solutions or illustrative designs. This book traces the history of these ideas and will become a standard reference for scholars and students interested in the history of urban spaces, including architects, planners, urban historians, urban geographers, and urban morphologists.

Jon Lang, Emeritus Professor, is the principal of his own consulting firm and formerly the director of urban design for ERG in Philadelphia, Pennsylvania. His consultancy work has taken him to all the continents of the world, except Antarctica. Born in India, he was educated in that country, England, South Africa, and the United States. He received his architectural degree from the University of the Witwatersrand and city planning from Cornell, where he also obtained his doctorate. Before settling in Australia in 1990, he headed the joint MArch/MCP Program in Urban Design at the University of Pennsylvania. At the University of New South Wales, he headed the School of Architecture and was the associate dean for research in the Faculty of the Built Environment in the 1990s and early 2000s. He has served as a visiting professor at universities in North and South America and Asia and has authored books on architectural theory, on urban design, and on modern architecture in India. His writings on urban design include *Urban Design: The American Experience* (1994), *Urban Design: A Typology of Procedures and Products* (2005; 2017), and, with Nancy Marshall, *Urban Squares as Places, Links, and Displays* (Routledge 2016). His book with Walter Moleski, *Functionalism Revisited* (2010), provides the intellectual basis for this endeavor. He has been a juror on several international urban design competitions. In 2010, he received the Reed and Malik Medal from the Institution of Civil Engineers in London.

The Routledge Companion to Twentieth and Early Twenty-First Century Urban Design

A History of Shifting Manifestoes, Paradigms, Generic Solutions, and Specific Designs

Jon Lang

NEW YORK AND LONDON

First published 2021
by Routledge
52 Vanderbilt Avenue, New York, NY 10017

and by Routledge
2 Park Square, Milton Park, Abingdon, Oxon, OX14 4RN

Routledge is an imprint of the Taylor & Francis Group, an informa business

© 2021 Taylor & Francis

The right of Jon Lang to be identified as author of this work has been asserted by him in accordance with sections 77 and 78 of the Copyright, Designs and Patents Act 1988.

All rights reserved. No part of this book may be reprinted or reproduced or utilised in any form or by any electronic, mechanical, or other means, now known or hereafter invented, including photocopying and recording, or in any information storage or retrieval system, without permission in writing from the publishers.

Trademark notice: Product or corporate names may be trademarks or registered trademarks, and are used only for identification and explanation without intent to infringe.

Library of Congress Cataloging-in-Publication Data
Names: Lang, Jon T., author.
Title: The Routledge companion to twentieth and early twenty-first century urban
   design : a history of shifting manifestoes, paradigms, generic solutions, and specific
   designs / Jon Lang.
Identifiers: LCCN 2020021400 (print) | LCCN 2020021401 (ebook) |
   ISBN 9780367860509 (hardback) | ISBN 9781003016670 (ebook)
Subjects: LCSH: City planning—History—20th century. | City planning—
   History—21st century. | Architecture—Environmental aspects. | Architecture
   and society.
Classification: LCC HT166 .L346 2020 (print) | LCC HT166 (ebook) |
   DDC 307.1/2160904—dc23
LC record available at https://lccn.loc.gov/2020021400
LC ebook record available at https://lccn.loc.gov/2020021401

ISBN: 9780367860509 (hbk)
ISBN: 9781003016670 (ebk)

Typeset in Bembo
by Apex CoVantage, LLC

Every effort has been made to contact copyright holders. Please advise the publisher of any errors or omissions, and these will be corrected in subsequent editions.

In memory of

Elsie M. Lang
Author of Literary London
(T. Werner Laurie 1906)
and
British Women in the Twentieth Century
(T. Werner Laurie 1929)
Whom I never met but who has been an inspiration to me

Jane Lang
Author of Rebuilding St Paul's after the Great Fire of London
(Oxford University Press 1956)
Who introduced me to the politics of architectural design

and

Elizabeth Bond
Who made my journey possible

HafenCity, Hamburg: A visualization of its future quality
Source: Lang (2017, 153); courtesy of HafenCity Hamburg GmBH/fotofrizz and Taylor & Francis

Failure is less frequently attributable to either insufficiency of means or impatience of labour than to a confused understanding of the thing to be actually done.
—John Ruskin in *The Seven Lamps of Architecture* (1849, 9)

Preface

A plethora of statements exist on the nature and purposes of urban design. They are often confusing and contradictory because they mix positions on the domain of urban design with manifestoes on what urban designers should be aiming to achieve: "Information overload increases the need for organizing frames of reference to integrate the mass of rapidly changing information" (Hall 1966, ix). The goal of this book is to provide one.

The consensus is that urban designers *design* projects, such as new towns, precincts of cities, and a few blocks of some human settlement. At an equally high level of generalization, the purpose of urban design is to create a better-built environment for a better social world. No statement says its purpose is to deliberately make life worse. This end has nevertheless too often been achieved not through malice but through a misunderstanding of how the built environment functions for people at different stages in their life cycles who have different competencies and who live in different cultural and geographical settings. The strengths and limitations of competing approaches to urban design are important to comprehend if urban design as a field of professional expertise or as a discipline is to make progress.

The Argument

The focus of attention in this book is on the self-consciously designed building projects that have shaped the morphology of cities and other human settlements. A sequence of often-coexisting urban design paradigms has specified how these schemes should be designed. Each paradigm addresses what are seen by its proponents as the current concerns of a society. What have been and what are these paradigms? How good have they been, and how good are they today? This book addresses these questions. Its goal is to inform students and professionals of the current ideological bases for urban design practice and the inherent partialities in their own work. Consciously or subconsciously, most urban design schemes are adaptations of generic ideas derived from a current design paradigm. The available paradigms form part of manifestoes presenting highly value-laden positions on what constitutes a good city.

Several studies of manifestoes and paradigms precede this work. They review the competing statements on what constitutes good architecture (e.g., Conrads 1970; Hayes 1998; Jencks and Kropf 2006; Mallgrave and Contandriopoulos 2008) and good landscape architecture (e.g., Swaffield 2002; Herrington 2016). Some of the statements presented address urban design (e.g., Hermansen Cordua 2010), but those that deal specifically with the topic are scattered in books and journals. The goal here is to provide a road map for accessing and assessing the diverse statements made during the twentieth century and now during the early twenty-first century by categorizing them according to an intellectual and chronological order.

xi

Preface

The first half of the twentieth century was particularly important in shaping our current thoughts on the city. During it, the world was turned upside down by a host of technological advances and sociopolitical changes in a manner that the world has not seen since. They spawned a diversity of views on the nature of a good city and good urban designs. The second half of the century witnessed the spread of these ideas across the world accompanying broad changes in the ways of life and values of the rapidly expanding middle classes. At the beginning of the twenty-first century, new concerns emerged that seize our attention. They are the basis for a fresh set of approaches to urban design. How sensitive are they? My concern is primarily with the European experience and the US experience but also with the way urban design concepts have been appropriated and developed in other parts of the globe, such as Singapore, China, and the Emirates.

The dozen new national capital cities of Latin America, Asia, and Africa built between 1950 and 1990 are all modernist ventures. Brasília has been the most influential. In Africa, Abuja, Dodoma, Lilongwe, and Gaborone are derivatives of the generic model of buildings set in green open space. Little of the space serves a function other than as being a symbol of prestige. Much of it has been and is still undergoing change. Whether anything paradigmatically unique has appeared in the application of the ideas discussed in this book in modernizing societies remains unclear (see the essays in Lu 2011). This observation does not negate the uniqueness of specific designs.

Objectives

Urban design projects come in many types. My effort to categorize them was presented in *Urban Design: A Typology of Procedures and Products*, published in 2005 and updated in 2017. That book presented a three-dimensional model into which, I argued, all urban designs can be slotted. The dimensions were *procedural type*, *product type*, and *paradigm type*. With that model as a basis, over fifty examples, or case studies, of projects were categorized by their procedural type, how they were brought into existence, or, in a minority of cases, how they were planned to be implemented. Among the product types described were new towns, central business districts, infrastructure elements, and housing estates. The design paradigms employed were mentioned in passing, but not categorized. The objective here is to fill in that gap by describing and explaining the urban design paradigms of the past century and a half.

My effort focuses on what the proponents of each paradigm identified as the problems that needed to be addressed and on the affordances of the built environment that they believed to be important in doing so. On the basis of an understanding of current paradigms and the criticism of past paradigms, it is possible to suggest a way forward. I have taken the liberty of doing so in the Epilogue.

The Outline of the Book

The book is divided into a prologue, four parts, and an epilogue. The purpose of *Prologue: The Nature of Urban Design* is to establish a foundation for the story developed in the book. It presents the position on what urban design is about that I accept. The intellectual antecedents of the urban design paradigms of the twentieth century are discussed in *Part One* of the book. *Part Two* covers the manifestoes, generic solutions, and specific design of the early twentieth century and *Part Three* how those ideas were developed in the post–World War Two era. The current paradigms that are competing for our attention are presented in *Part Four*. The *Epilogue* offers a critique of all these ideas and the position that I accept and advocate as the way forward.

xii

The introduction to each of the parts of the book describes the sociopolitical and economic context in which the paradigms of the period were developed. Each also describes the range of pragmatic urban development projects that were contemporaneously shaping the morphology of cities. It was the perceived limitations of these projects that gave impetus to the self-consciously developed manifestoes, design paradigms, and generic and illustrative designs that shaped specific schemes.

The definition of urban design given in the prologue crosses cultural boundaries. The distinctions among pragmatic, rationalist, and empiricist approaches to design explain much about the different manifestoes specifying the goals of urban design and the nature of the projects built. My understanding of these intellectual philosophies shapes the whole story, so providing it is an important task of the prologue. The term 'function' has fashioned much architectural discourse, so it is equally important to state at the outset the meaning given to the term in this book.

The chapters that form the central parts of the book, *Part One* to *Part Four*, have a common structure. No design paradigm is a complete departure from past ways of thought. They build on antecedent ideas. The chapters thus begin with a summary of those ideas. The manifestoes and the design paradigms that build on them follow. This review is followed by a description of the generic solutions and/or illustrative designs that provide an image of the intentions, explicit or implicit, of the design paradigms. Specific exemplary and hybrid designs that result from these modes of thought follow. Questions about their quality are largely left to the reader. I identify the functions that each design paradigm addresses, from the most basic one of shelter to the intellectual aesthetic ideas of the designers involved. My values are, no doubt, evident in my observations.

What can be learned from all these manifestoes and paradigms and the projects that have resulted from them? The epilogue presents the observations of social and behavioral scientists and of self-reflecting designers on what was accomplished during the twentieth century and has been in the early twenty-first. The book ends with my view of the major concerns facing societies in a changing world and their implications for the nature of cities and urban designs. It is by no means a unique view.

Acknowledgments

A host of city planners, architects, landscape architects, and those who boldly identify themselves as urban designers have aided me in my work. They have shared their knowledge, insights, and illustrations with me. They brought my attention to approaches to urban design and projects of which I was unaware. Initially, Wilfred Mallows at Witwatersrand and John Reps at Cornell stimulated my interest in cities and the qualities of the built environment that give them their character. My colleagues and the many students with whom I have worked over the years at schools of design in Australia, India, Indonesia, Puerto Rico, Singapore, Spain, Sri Lanka, the United States, and Venezuela have been continuous sources of challenge and inspiration.

In this book, I have relied heavily on secondary sources. Also, there is an Anglophone bias to the literature on which I have relied. The names of the scholars on whose studies I have drawn parade throughout this book and their works are listed in the references and bibliography at the end of it. The secondary sources have been challenged or corroborated by extensive on-location observations. I have, nevertheless, included some specific designs that I have not experienced firsthand.

Although my orientation is different, I have been influenced by and have built on the objectives of four books: *The Urban Pattern: City Planning and Design*, by Arthur B. Gallion and Simon Eisner (John Wiley 1993); *The History of the City*, by Leonardo Benevolo (MIT Press 1980);

Preface

The Elusive City, by Jonathan Barnett (Harper and Row 1986); and *Emerging Concepts in Urban Space Design*, by Geoffrey Broadbent (Van Nostrand Reinhold International 1990). Some of the ground that I cover has been covered not only by these four scholars but many others as well. The principle ones are Kevin Lynch in his book *A Theory of Good City Form* (MIT Press 1981), Jonathan Barnett in *City Design: Modernist, Traditional, Green and Systems Perspectives* (Routledge 2016), and Peter Hall in *Cities of Tomorrow: An Intellectual History of City Planning and Design in the Twentieth Century* (Basil Blackwell 1998). My effort is one of synthesis, of filling in the gaps and telling a different story. In doing so, Werner Hegemann and Elbert Peets's *The American Vitruvius: An Architect's Handbook of Civic Art* (The Architectural Book Publishing Co. 1922) has been a constant inspiration.

Unabashedly, I have mined my own previously published research. I have reused descriptions and photographs of urban design schemes that were included in *Functionalism Revisited* (Ashgate 2010), which I wrote with Walter Moleski; *Urban Squares as Places, Links and Displays*, which I coauthored with Nancy Marshall (Routledge 2016); and/or either the first or the second edition of *Urban Design: A Typology of Procedures and Products* (Architectural Press 2005; Routledge 2017).

I owe a considerable debt to the scholars who read the manuscript or parts of it and made suggestions on how to improve it. They include Olgu Çalişkan, Anemone Koh, Jusuck Koh, Scott Hawken, Nancy Marshall, and Arlene Segal. James Weirick gave me access to his slides on the history of urban design. All their contributions have been invaluable and very much appreciated. I am especially grateful for the help I received from scholars, such as Alexander Cuthbert, whose views on urban design differ from mine. Caroline Nute provided intellectual support, editorial assistance, and considerable aid in improving the character of the illustrations in this book. Her contribution throughout the creation of this work enhanced its quality.

Over the years, my research efforts have been enriched by field studies around the world. This work was possible only because of the generosity of university funding sources, private foundations, and public agencies. They include, in approximately chronological order, Cornell University, the R. K. Mellon Foundation, the University of Pennsylvania, the Philadelphia Foundation, the Ford Foundation, UNESCO, NATO, the Grosser Family Fund, the United States Education Fund in India, the American Institute of Indian Studies, the Australian Research Council, the Getty Foundation, and the City of Sydney. Completing this work would not have been possible without the continued use of the resources provided by the Faculty of the Built Environment at the University of New South Wales.

The Illustrations

Acquiring illustrations to illuminate the text of a book is a challenging task. I was assisted along the way by countless organizations and individuals. The list of credits appearing in the bibliography and references attest to my debt to others. The photographs, diagrams, and drawings, unless otherwise indicated, are my own; I am their copyright holder; their copyright has expired; and/or they are in the public domain. Every effort has been made to contact and credit the copyright holders of the other material I used. It has been extremely difficult to trace several of them. I have no record of the provenance of the illustrations identified as being part of the 'collection of the author.' If copyright proprietorship can be established for any work not specifically stated or erroneously attributed, please contact me at jonl@unsw.edu.au. I will be pleased to rectify errors.

Jon Lang,
Sydney, New South Wales,
March 2020

Contents

Preface   *xi*

  The Argument xi
  Objectives xii
  The Outline of the Book xii
  Acknowledgments xiii
    The Illustrations xiv

PROLOGUE
The Nature of Urban Design   2

  The Hierarchical Nature of the Functions of the Built Environment 3
    Basic Functions 4
    Advanced Functions 5
    Functions of the Built Environment and Design 5
  Urban Design 6
    Urban Design as Project Design and as Public Policy 7
  Manifestoes and Paradigms, Generic Concepts, Illustrative Designs, and Specific
    Designs 8
  The Philosophical Bases of Urban Design Manifestoes and Paradigms 9
    Pragmatism 9
    Rationalism 10
    Empiricism 12
  Observations 14
  Key References 14

PART I
Antecedents of Twentieth-Century Urban Design   16

  The Nineteenth Century 16
    The Industrial Revolution and the Victorian Era 17
    Urban Development and Design 17
    Project Types 19
  Pragmatic Urban Designs 19

Contents

The Outline of the Discussion 20
Key References 21

1 Religious Canons and Prescriptions   23
Antecedent Ideas 23
Manifestoes and Paradigms 24
Generic Concepts and Illustrative Designs 26
Specific Designs 29
    Exemplars of Canonical Designs 30
        Teotihuacán, Mexico (ca 100 BCE to 250 CE), and the Forbidden City,
            Beijing, China (1406–) 30
    Hybrid Examples 32
        Baghdad Now in Iraq (762–66); Jaipur, Rajasthan, India (1726);
            Salt Lake City, Utah, USA (1847); and Al Bastakiya (Al Fahidi
            Historical District), Dubai (1890s) 32
Commentary: The Functions Addressed 35
Observations 35
Key References 36

2 The Classical and Beaux Arts Tradition   37
Antecedent Ideas 37
Manifestoes and Paradigms 39
Generic Concepts and Illustrative Designs 41
Specific Designs 42
    Exemplars of Classical Urban Designs 45
        Zamość, Poland (1580–1600); Piazza del Popolo, Rome, Italy
            (1811–22); Napoléon III's Paris, France (1854–73); and Vienna,
            Austria, of Franz Joseph I (1880s) 45
    Hybrid Examples 48
        Washington, DC, USA (1791); Eixample, Barcelona, Spain (1856);
            and the Hobrecht Plan for Berlin, Germany (1858–62) 48
Commentary: The Functions Addressed 51
Observations 52
Key References 53

3 Social and Philanthropic Urban Design   54
Antecedent Ideas 54
Manifestoes and Paradigms 55
Generic Concepts and Illustrative Designs 56
Specific Designs 58
    Exemplars of Model Industrial Towns 59
        Saltaire, Yorkshire, England, UK (1851–76), and the Krupp brothers'
            Villages at Essen, Germany (1850–1903) 59
    Hybrid Models 61

*Le Familistère de Guise, France (1856), and Echota, New York,
USA (1893)* 61
Commentary: The Functions Addressed 63
Observations 64
Key References 64

4 The Garden Suburb 65

Antecedent Ideas 65
Manifestoes and Paradigms 67
Generic Concepts and Illustrative Designs 68
Specific Designs 69
  Exemplars of the Garden Suburb 69
    *Riverside, Illinois, USA (1869–); Hampstead Garden Suburb, London,
England, UK (1906–); and Die Gardenstadt Perlach, Near Munich,
Germany (1909–)* 69
  Hybrid Examples 72
    *The Civil Lines, Delhi, India (1858–); Margarethenhöhe, Essen,
Germany (1915–); and Forest Hills Gardens, Long Island, New York,
USA (1909–)* 72
Commentary: The Functions Addressed 74
Observations 75
Key References 76

5 The Urbanist Tradition 77

Antecedent Ideas 78
Manifestoes and Paradigms 79
Generic Concepts and Illustrative Designs 80
Specific Designs 82
  An Exemplar of Sitte's Ideas on the City 82
    Central Vienna, Austria (ca 1890) 82
  Hybrid Examples 83
    *Bagaregården, Gothenburg, Sweden (1926), and Louvain-la-Neuve,
Belgium (1969–90)* 83
Commentary: The Functions Addressed 85
Observations 85
Key References 86

PART II
Early-Twentieth-Century Manifestoes, Paradigms, Generic Concepts, and Specific Designs 88

Urban Development and Pragmatic Urban Designs 90
*Changes in Architectural and Urban
Design Paradigms* 92

Contents

The Outline of the Discussion 92
Key References 93

6 The City Beautiful   95
Antecedent Ideas 95
Manifestoes and Paradigms 97
Generic Concepts and Illustrative Designs 98
Specific Designs 99
    Exemplars of the City Beautiful 100
        The McMillan Plan, Washington DC, USA (1902); Louisiana
            Purchase Exposition, St. Louis, Missouri, USA (1904); The Plan
            of Chicago, USA (1909); the University of Texas at Austin, Texas,
            USA (1913); and Germania, Berlin, Germany (1936–43) 100
    Hybrid Examples 103
        Canberra, Australia (1913); New Delhi, India (1914); and Thessaloniki,
            Greece (1917) 103
    Commentary: The Functions Addressed 107
    Observations 107
    Key References 109

7 Modern Empiricism   110
Antecedent Ideas 110
Manifestoes and Paradigms 112
Generic Concepts and Illustrative Designs 116
Specific Designs 119
    Exemplars of Empiricist Design 120
        Wekerletelep, Budapest, Hungary (1908–); Welwyn Garden
            City, England, UK (1920–); Radburn, New Jersey,
            USA (1929); Rockefeller Center, New York, New York, USA
            (1928–34); and Belrampur, Madras (Now Chennai), India
            (1917) 120
    Hybrid Examples 125
        Hufeisensiedlung, Britz, Berlin, Germany (1925) and Tel Aviv, Palestine,
            Now Israel (1925) 125
    Commentary: The Functions Addressed 127
    Observations 128
    Key References 130

8 The Rationalist Response   131
Antecedent Ideas 131
Manifestoes and Paradigms 133
Generic Concepts and Illustrative Designs 138
Specific Designs 143
    Exemplars of Rationalist Design 144

*Le Corbusier's Plans for Paris, France (1924), Antwerp, Belgium
(1933), and Algiers, Algeria (1931); Narkomfin, Moscow, Russia
(1928–30); Derzhprom, Kharkiv, Ukraine (1926–28); Magnitogorsk,
Chelyabinsk, Russia (1929–); the Housing Estates (1927–40); the
MARS Plan for London, England, UK (1942); and the Illinois
Institute of Technology, Chicago, Illinois, USA (1943–56) 144*

Hybrid Examples 154

*Amsterdam South, the Netherlands (1914); Les Quartiers Modernes
Frugès, Pessac, France (1924); Le Quartier de Gratte-ciel,
Villeurbanne, Lyon, France (1924–34); and Karl-Marx-Hof,
Vienna, Austria (1927–30) 154*

Commentary: The Functions Addressed 157

Observations 159

Key References 160

PART III
Post–World War Two Pragmatic Urban Design and
the Rationalist and Empiricist Responses · 162

The Postwar Years 162

Pragmatic Urban Designs 164

The Outline of the Discussion 170

Key References 170

9   The Post–World War Two Rationalists · 171

Antecedent Ideas 171

Manifestoes and Paradigms 172

Generic Concepts and Illustrative Designs 177

Specific Designs 181

Exemplars of Rationalist Designs 186

*Civic Center Proposals (1940s to 1970s); Punjab University,
Chandigarh, India (1958–); the Pilot Plan, Brasília, Brazil (1956);
Lafayette Park, Detroit, Michigan, USA (1960); La Grande Motte,
Occitanie, France (1960s); the Work of Team 10 (1960s); Arcosanti,
Scottsdale, Arizona, USA (Late 1960s but Continuing); and the Work
of the Metabolists in Japan (1970s) 186*

Hybrid Examples 194

*Universidad Nacional Autónoma de México, Mexico City, Mexico
(1952–); Barbican Estate, London, England, UK (1959–82);
La Défense, Haut-de-Seine, France (1958–); Empire State Plaza,
Albany, New York, USA (1959); and the Work of the Tendenza
Movement (1965–85) 194*

Commentary: The Functions Addressed 200

Observations 201

Key References 203

xix

Contents

10 The Post–World War Two Empiricists 204
Antecedent Ideas 204
Manifestoes and Paradigms 206
Generic Concepts and Illustrative Designs 213
Specific Designs 219
  Exemplars of Empiricist Designs 222
    *Columbia, Maryland, USA (1962–2014); Port Grimaud, Var, France
    (1963–70–); Rector Place Battery Park City, New York, New York,
    USA (1979–2012); Village Homes, Davis, California, USA
    (1960–72); and Arumbakkam, Madras (Now Chennai),
    India (1973–80) 222*
  Hybrid Examples 226
    *Runcorn, Merseyside, England, UK (1965–); Ciudad Guasare Proposal,
    Zulia, Venezuela (1981); Superblocks, Pedestrian Malls, and
    Transit-Oriented Developments; and Auroville, Tamil Nadu,
    India (1965–) 226*
Commentary: The Functions Addressed 230
Observations 232
Key References 233

11 The Postmodernist and the Deconstructivist Response 234
Antecedent Ideas 234
Manifestoes and Paradigms 236
Generic Concepts and Illustrative Designs 238
Specific Designs 240
  *Exemplars of Postmodern and an Exemplar of Deconstructivist Urban
  Design 243*
    *Quartier Antigone, Montpelier, France (1979–); Place de Toscane,
    Marne-la-Valée, France (2006–); Plaza d'Italia, New Orleans,
    Louisiana, USA (1975–78); and Parc de la Villette, Paris, France
    (1982–83) 243*
  Hybrid Examples 247
    *M. S. Ramaiah Medical College, Bengaluru, Karnataka, India (1979);
    Tsukuba Civic Center, Tsukuba, Japan (1980–3); Richmond
    Riverside, London, England, UK (1984–); and Federation Square,
    Melbourne, Australia (1996–2002) 247*
Commentary: The Functions Addressed 250
Observations 251
Key References 252

PART IV
Urban Design in an Age of Corporate Financial Capital 254
Neoliberalism 255
Neoliberalism and Urban Design 255

Contents

Project Types 257
Urban Development and Pragmatic Urban Design 258
The Outline of the Discussion 260
Key References 261

12 Modernist, Neo-modernist, and Hyper-modernist Urban Design 263
Antecedent Ideas 263
Manifestoes and Paradigms 264
Generic Concepts and Illustrative Designs 266
Specific Designs 267
   Exemplars of Modernist, Neo-modernist, and Hyper-modernist Urban
    Design 270
    The One, Hangzhou, Zhejiang, China (2016); Wohnpark Neue Danau,
     Vienna, Austria (1993–98); Hudson Yards, New York, New York,
     USA (2010–24); the Central Business District, Beijing, China
     (2000–); and Nur-Sultan, Kazakhstan (1997–) 270
   Hybrid Examples 275
    EuropaCity, Berlin, Germany (2008–25); The Interlace, Singapore
     (2007–15); Huangshan Mountain Village, Anhui, China (2017);
     and Namba Parks, Osaka, Japan (2003) 275
Commentary: The Functions Addressed 278
Observations 279
Key References 280

13 Hyper-modernism, Parametricism, and Urban Design 281
Antecedent Ideas 281
Manifestoes and Paradigms 283
Generic Concepts and Illustrative Designs 283
Specific Designs 284
   Exemplars of Parametric Urban Design 285
    Kartal Pendik, Istanbul, Turkey (2006–), and Longgang City Center,
     Shenzhen, China (2008) 285
   Hybrid Designs 286
    One North District, Singapore (2001–16); the 8150 Sunset Boulevard
     Proposal, Los Angeles, California, USA (2015); and the Center for
     Fulfillment, Knowledge, and Innovation, Detroit, Michigan, USA
     (2016) 286
Commentary: The Functions Addressed 290
Observations 291
Key References 292

14 The Empiricist Responses 293
Antecedent Ideas 293
Manifestoes and Paradigms 294

xxi

Contents

Generic Concepts and Illustrative Designs 296
Specific Designs 298
  Exemplars of the Empiricist Responses 300
    Celebration, Florida, USA (1990–2020); Rouse Hill Town Centre,
      Hills District, New South Wales, Australia (2000–07); and Legacy
      Town Center, Plano, Texas, USA (1998–2010) 300
  Hybrid Examples 303
    Ebbsfleet, Kent, England, UK (2012–); HafenCity, Hamburg, Germany
      (2008–30); Val d'Europe, Marne-la-Vallée, France (2000–16); and
      eThekwini, KwaZulu-Natal, South Africa (2017) 303
Commentary: The Functions Addressed 306
Observations 307
Key References 309

15 Sustainable Urbanism and Urban Design   310
Antecedent Ideas 310
Manifestoes and Paradigms 312
Generic Concepts and Illustrative Designs 314
Specific Designs 315
  Exemplars of Sustainable Urban Design 318
    Hammarby Sjöstad, Stockholm, Sweden (1990–2017); Alternative 20,
      Los Angeles River Restoration, California, USA (2014–); Masdar,
      Abu Dhabi, UAE (2007); Eco-City, Ras Al Khaimah, UAE (2007);
      Forest City, Cancun, Mexico, Proposal (2019); Downsview Park,
      Toronto, Ontario, Canada (2000–); and the Disaster Mitigation
      Proposal for New York City, New York, USA (2012–) 318
  Hybrid Examples 324
    Punggol 21-plus, Singapore (2007–); Meixi Lake Eco-City, proposal,
      Zhengdong New District, China (2009–); Liuzhou Forest City,
      China (2016–20); The Springs, Shanghai, China (2018–20); and
      High Line Park, New York, New York, USA (1999–2018) 324
Commentary: The Functions Addressed 328
Observations 329
Key References 330

16 Smart Cities and Urban Design   331
Antecedent Ideas 332
Manifestoes and Paradigms 332
Generic Concepts and Illustrative Designs 335
Specific Designs 335
  Exemplars of Smart Designs 336
    Karle Town Centre, Bengaluru, Karnataka, India (2019–), and Madrid,
      Spain (2011–) 336

Contents

A Hybrid Example 338
    Songdo International Business District, Korea (2003–) 338
Commentary: The Functions Addressed 339
Observations 340
Key References 340

EPILOGUE
Looking Back to Look Forward   **342**
The Pragmatic Future 342
The Outline of the Discussion 343
Key References 344

17 A Critique of Twentieth- and Early-Twenty-First-Century Urban Design   345
General Commentaries 345
The City Beautiful 347
The Modernists 348
    Rationalist Urban Design 349
    Empiricist Urban Design 352
        The Garden City 352
        A Note on Broadacre City 353
        New Urbanism and Smart Growth 354
Postmodernism 355
    Deconstruction 355
Parametric Urban Design 355
Sustainable Designs, Landscape Urbanism, and Agrarian Urbanism 356
Smart Cities 357
Commentary: The Functions Addressed 357
Observations 358
Key References 359

18 The Way Forward: Toward Compact Cities   360
Whereas 360
    Societal Issues Confronting Urban Designers 361
        Individual Rights of Property Developers 361
        Dealing With Complexity 361
        Sustainable Environments 362
        Population Growth and Demographic Changes 363
            Multiculturalism 364
            Designing for Declining Cities 364
        Income and Resource Disparities 364
        Competing Functions/Goals 365
        A Changing World 365
        Fiscal Responsibilities 366

xxiii

Contents

The Goal 366
    A Good City 367
    Compacting Cities as a Design Goal 370
Therefore 371
    An Agenda for the Next Generation of Urban Designs 371
    Piece-by-Piece Urban Design 371
    Plug-In Urban Design 372
    All-of-a-Piece Urban Design 373
    Total Urban Design 374
Conclusion 374
Key References 375

Bibliography and References	*376*
Credits	*403*
Index	*414*

Prologue

Tehran in 2012

The Nature of Urban Design

"Before one can study the history of something, the nature of that something needs to be defined; the subject matter of the domain needs to be identified" (Rapoport 1990, 1). This book is about urban design in the context of the changing morphology of cities and the images that architects have had and have of what constitutes a good city and a good built environment.

All cities have a physical form, a morphology, a design. The design is the result of the myriad decisions made by individuals and organizations seeking to maximize their own interests. Each decision, whatever its scale, may have been a self-conscious act, but their sum is an unselfconsciously designed city. These decisions are shaped by the *invisible web* of laws of a society that govern how the built environment is created (Lai 1988; Talen 2012; Carmona 2017) and the *capital web* of investment commitments (Crane 1960). In our modern world, they are made within encoded rules and property developers' perceptions of opportunities to make a profit on an investment and their attitudes toward risk taking. Societies differ in their tolerances for the degree that people can deviate from the rules, codified or simply understood. Few are totally honest; few are totally corrupt.

The morphology of a city can be represented in a figure-ground diagram showing its built forms against a background of its open spaces: roads, parks, squares, courtyards, and miscellaneous spaces between buildings. The 1748 study of Rome in Italy by Giambattista Nolli (1701–56) shows a very different morphology to that of the Dupont Circle area of Washington, DC in the United States. Rome's morphology resulted from many piecemeal decisions. Washington's street structure was *self-consciously* planned, whereas that of Rome emerged *unselfconsciously* from

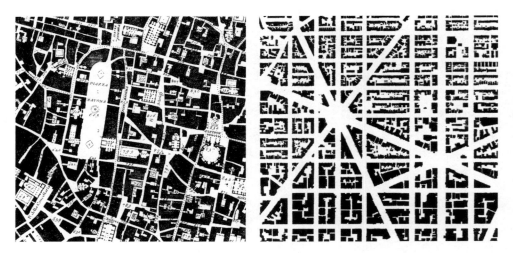

Figure 1 The morphology of areas of cities: The 1748 Nolli plan of Rome (left) and the 1791 layout of Washington as later built (right)

Credit line (left): Collection of the author.
Source (left): Lang and Marshall (2017, 3); courtesy of Taylor & Francis
Credit line (right): Redrawn from various sources by the author

many smaller self-conscious designs, such as those of its plazas and buildings. Both cities are a 'collage' of buildings, open spaces, and the street infrastructure that provides the armature on which the individual pieces hang (Rowe and Koetter 1979).

What is the best way to interpret this collage? It is as a place containing many places. Architects tend to call places activity sites; ecological psychologists call them behavior settings (Barker 1968; Schoggen 1989; Heft 2001). Behavior settings consist of a *standing*, or recurrent, activity that takes place within a configuration, or pattern, of built form, a *milieu*, that coexists for a *time*. The same pattern of built form may accommodate different activities at different times of the day, week, or season. It almost certainly affords activities that do not occur. Settlements consist of two contrasting types of behavior settings: those that are places of localized activities and those that serve as links. Localized settings often contain links and link places. Patterns of built form also possess aesthetic qualities whether or not they are consciously designed to do so.

Individuals and associations consciously seek to enhance the way the patterns of a place function for themselves, some other group of people, other species, or the natural environment. In the design fields, the term 'function' has generally been narrowly defined as the efficiency of the links between places and the cost-effectiveness of infrastructure constructions. But this view is insufficient.

The Hierarchical Nature of the Functions of the Built Environment

The built environment is artificially configured, unselfconsciously or self-consciously, to house activities and to be a display. The range of activities and types of display are vast. Some activities serve an instrumental end but many serve a multiplicity of other purposes. The ends must be seen in terms of the various species inhabiting it, those species' processes of perception and cognition, and their motivations and competencies. Animals, reptiles, and insects create their

Figure 2 The Za'atri refugee camp for Syrians, Jordan in 2013
Credit line: United Nations photograph by Mark Garten

own architectures by instinct to meet their needs (von Frisch 1974; Arndt 2014). For *Homo sapiens*, the potential functions of built form are diverse and complex, as can be observed in any human settlement. Some places are rich in behavioral opportunities and others less so, depending on their histories and the resources available to establish them, as can be seen in comparing two settlements in Syria. Damascus has the longest continued history of any city on Earth of being shaped by conscious and unselfconscious decisions. It is rich in behavior settings. Za'atri, a refugee camp for Syrians, is impoverished in comparison, although ad hoc developments have enlivened it since the photograph was taken.

Many efforts have been made to categorize the functions served by different configurations and materials of the built environment. The one that gives greatest clarity and explains the most is based on Abraham Maslow's model of human motivations (Maslow 1987). It is described in detail by Walter Moleski and me in *Functionalism Revisited* (2010). The synopsis presented here suffices for this book.

Maslow suggested that people have a hierarchy of needs, from the most basic (to survive) to the most abstract (to understand intellectual concepts). These needs trigger people's motivations to participate in or create specific behavior settings and to own valued objects. The motivations exist within a culturally defined moral and social order. The polar extremes of political order are represented by autocratic societies and democratic societies, although some societies appear to be anarchic. In the autocratic, decisions are centralized in the hands of an individual or a coterie of people; in the democratic, diverse people hold the power to make decisions; and in the anarchic, chaos seems to reign.

Basic Functions

The fundamental human motivation in Maslow's hierarchy is to survive. We need shelter, water, and clean air to breathe. Although people *survive* in highly polluted environments (air and water pollution), their lives are shortened. It is not only we humans who are motivated to survive but also other animate species and inanimate organisms. Humans may dominate, but the urban environment is full of animals: tame, wild, and feral, desirable and undesirable (Donovan 2015). The number of foxes in London, bears in Anchorage, boars in Barcelona, cougars on the edges of Los Angeles, and wallabies on the periphery of Sydney seems to be increasing. Vegetation and wild animals (to say nothing of pets) serve many purposes in defining a healthy world, but the functional requirements of human purposes often rule. Perhaps they should not.

Designing to shelter people from life-threatening conditions has been a self-conscious concern from prehistoric times. Some of these events, such as earthquakes, are natural phenomena, but crime and civil insurrections also shape many design considerations. We humans have purposefully destroyed cities in times of conflict, but many of our actions have simply been unselfconscious and careless. Our actions have contributed to alterations in climates worldwide, erratic weather conditions, and, more generally, a warmer planet. These changes present a major challenge that policymakers and designers must now face.

Providing for people's psychological sense of security involves their being part of kinship groups and communities, some local and others of common interest. Having appropriate levels of privacy in the behavior settings they inhabit and control over their social environments is also important (Altman 1973). Understanding where they are in a city and being able to find their way around it with ease are additional fundamental needs. The patterns that enable people to form a clear cognitive map of their surroundings help fulfill this need (Lynch 1960).

Once their survival and security needs have been sufficiently met, people strive to develop a sense of self-worth through living in desirable places and owning desirable objects. The patterns and materials of the built environment and the objects within it, their forms and coloring, and the way they are illuminated carry meanings based on learned associations and, possibly, as Carl Jung (1875–1961), the Swiss psychoanalyst, believed, some that are innate (Jung 1968). They reflect a person's and a people's identity, whether it be their social status or their cultural background. As the patterns act as a symbol of who we are, we are motivated to reconfigure them to better reflect what we perceive our status to be and the status to which we aspire. In some cultures, making the layout of the built environment accord with spiritual beliefs meets the need for mental security.

Cities and their precincts have images in their inhabitants' and outsiders' minds (Strauss 1961). Some places are port cities or industrial cities; others may be administrative and service centers. Some precincts in cities are business districts; others may be manufacturing areas. Certainly, some are residential neighborhoods that have their own character based on the status and culture(s) of the people who live there (or once lived there). Each neighborhood, over time, becomes identified with the people who live in it, as a result of their piecemeal acts.

The highest level in Maslow's hierarchy of basic needs is that for self-actualization—to be what one can be. How the built environment can function to serve such needs is unclear. Cognitive and aesthetic needs, however, have more understandable implications.

Advanced Functions

Cognitive and aesthetic needs are manifest throughout our lives. We need to be able to learn to survive as well as to make advances in life, so the ability to learn is present in achieving all our basic needs. An educative environment is one that is rich in the variety of people and activities from which one can learn as a participant or vicariously as an observer. They can also be challenging.

Aesthetic needs involve not only the symbolic meanings of the environment as they refer to status and aspirations but also for some people, the cognoscenti, understanding designers' expressions. Architectural critics tend to evaluate self-consciously designed places in terms of the originality of their designers' ideas. Their criticism is divorced from everyday life but important to members of the art community. Most people are concerned with the quality of the places they inhabit in meeting their needs from those of survival to the portraying of social status. This book is about the paradigms that urban designers have employed to better provide the places that they believed were needed for people to flourish.

Functions of the Built Environment and Design

Each element of the morphology of settlement, whether a building or part of the public realm, inevitably prioritizes meeting the needs of some people over others. In an era of globalization, some designs are perceived by clients as symbolically desirable because of what advertisers and the international media promote as fashionable. The yearning for what is internationally regarded as high-status imagery in the public realm of cities often means that the requirements of desired local activity patterns are overridden. The designs sought are those that enhance the self-image of the people with the power to influence decisions—the power elite of a nation or a city (Mills 1956). Often, however, the functional requirements of machines that serve human purposes rule because they have to work well.

Kiyo Izumi distinguished between those environments in which the needs of machines rule and those in which the human spirit rules. *Anthropozemic* environments consist of places such as the lanes for vehicles on streets and tank farms, whereas *anthropophilic* ones are the settings for everyday human life. This book is primarily about the latter, but even in *anthropozemic* environments, basic human needs must be met satisfactorily to enable machinery to function well (Izumi 1968).

The built environment is constantly being changed by human actions and weathering. In turn, buildings and urban design complexes create patterns that change the natural world. Hard surfaces create heat islands that change local climatic patterns. The movement of winds is affected by the texture of cities. Urban designers are only just beginning to be conscious of these matters, and in most localities, the political will to energetically deal with them has yet to emerge. What, then, do we mean by the term 'urban design'?

Urban Design

"Urban design is about creating a vision for an area" (Llewellyn-Davies 2000, 12). An urban design results from a self-conscious "act of will" (Bacon 1967a). Urban designers *design*. They make proposals for the four-dimensional layouts of new towns and suburbs and the redesign of precincts and the blocks of a city on behalf of a property developer, public or private. Their focus is on the design of the public domain of places and the way buildings frame them or stand as objects in open space.

Controversies arise over the scope of concern of urban design. To some commentators, urban design includes devising of the means for implementing any proposal by "deploying the skills and resources to realize that vision" (Llewellyn-Davies 2000, 12). How a proposed project is to be implemented is, indeed, often neglected by its proponents. Consequently, many proposals remain buried in reports. In exploratory urban designs, however, the objective is simply to produce ideas without worrying about how they might be implemented. The task is to make decision makers—property developers, public agencies, and politicians—think about possibilities.

Although "*Urban design* is a relatively new term for an activity of long standing" (Lang 1994, ix), it has an extensive history. Various people have long been interested in defining the nature of good cities and the places within them. The formal education of people interested specifically in seeking to create them is more recent, although students at the academies of Renaissance Italy and at the École nationale supérieure des Beaux-Arts in Paris from its origins in the seventeenth century produced many civic designs.

The first formal civic design program was founded in 1909. Headed by Stanley Adshead (1868–1946), it existed in the School of Architecture at the University of Liverpool. Adshead chose the term 'civic design' because it implied a focus on the architectural and aesthetic aspects of town planning. From its establishment, the program was concerned more broadly than its name suggests with urban life (see Adshead 1909). The same observation can be made about the studies at the University of Illinois at Champagne–Urbana. Charles Mulford Robinson (1869–1917) was appointed professor of civic design there in 1913.

The Liverpool civic design program was important because it recognized that the ability to design good buildings does not mean that a person can adequately consider the cultural, socio-political, and economic concerns of everyday life that urban designers must address. In 1950, a two-year master of civic design degree course was established at the university; it was open to nonarchitects in recognition of the variety of skills that are required in designing new towns, precincts, and building complexes.

Studies in civic design at Harvard University, influenced by Werner Hegemann, go back to the 1920s under the leadership of Joseph Hudnut (1886–1968). Hudnut established the Graduate School of Design (GSD) there in 1936 and a year later brought Walter Gropius to

Harvard, although he was opposed to Gropius's hard-line functionalism (Pearlman 2007). The rubric *urban design* replaced *civic design* in the post–World War Two years. It was a term bandied about in the early 1950s by Clarence Stein (1882–1975) and Lewis Mumford (1895–1990), but it was José Luis Sert (1902–83) who gave the term credence by organizing a conference on the subject at Harvard University in 1954, when he was dean of its GSD. He also established an urban design program with a strong rationalist intellectual orientation. He had been closely associated with the Congrès Internationaux d'Architecture Moderne (CIAM) in Europe during the 1930s and 1940s and brought its views with him to the United States (Sert and C.I.A.M. 1944). The irony is that the development of urban design as an intellectual field stems largely from the general, but not universal, shortcomings of CIAM's vision of good urban environments.

Urban design strengthened as a discipline and a unique field of professional endeavor in the 1960s, when many new buildings complexes that were highly praised by the architectural cognoscenti were seen by their inhabitants to have significant shortcomings as places to inhabit. In response, city planning as a discipline became political and social and less concerned with the quality of the morphology of cities; meanwhile, architecture as an endeavor turned a blind eye to the social issues that its work inevitably involved. It focused instead, with considerable success, on the visual aesthetic nature of individual buildings as objects, as art forms. The two fields traditionally concerned with the form of cities thus diverged, creating an intellectual and professional gap that was filled mainly by several architects but also some landscape architects and individuals from outside the design professions. They maintained their concern with the built quality of cities, building complexes and the spaces that form the public domain of places.

Urban Design as Project Design and as Public Policy

The design paradigms and generic solutions that are described in this book consist primarily of three types of projects: *total urban designs*, *all-of-a-piece urban designs*, and *plug-in urban designs*, with a focus on the first two. The first is composed of projects that are proposed and completed by a single team of developers and design firms. The second type involves the development of a conceptual design that is then parceled into several components and implemented by different developers and designed by their architects and others in accordance with specified design guidelines. *Plug-in urban design* refers to the insertion of an infrastructure item into the environment to have a catalytic effect on property development in its surroundings. The infrastructure element can be as varied as a school, a highway or rail connection, or a park. Museums have proven to be successful as catalysts in regenerating declining precincts of some cities (e.g., Bilbao in Spain). All new developments, intended or not, affect adjacent areas. The multiplier effects of a project generally refer to its positive impacts on its surroundings; side effects generally refer to the negative. The central purpose of plug-in urban designs is, however, to have a positive catalytic effect on further property development decisions and the quality of the public realm of a place (Lang 1994, 2005, 2017).

An alternative type of urban design deals with providing incentives for specific types of developments to be built in a district of a city. It is *piece-by-piece* urban design. It involves producing a general image for a precinct and designing the policies to achieve the built forms required to attain it, rather than creating a specific conceptual design and the guidelines to get it implemented. The goal may be to retain the character of an area or it may be to change it. It is "urban design as public policy" (Barnett 1974). Important as it is, it is discussed only in passing in this book. The focus here is on project design.

All the types of urban designs are created in a political, social, and economic environment. They exist in a geographic, technological, and cultural setting and contribute to its development. They are buffeted by the shifting economic fortunes of the countries and cities in which they are located. Political and administrative changes in urban governance affect perceptions of the goals of any property development and the means of implementing it. The history of urban design during the past sesquicentenary is also very much a story of changing technologies that have shaped the way people and goods are transported, how harsh climatic conditions can be ameliorated, and how everyday communications are conducted. At the time of writing, many new technological developments seem to be in the offing (Brynjolfson and Mcafee 2014). They are hinted at in *Part Four* of this book.

The twentieth century saw the rise and decline of the socialist state and accompanying changes in concepts of public welfare that changed the nature of urban designing and what is considered to be a well-designed scheme. In many parts of the world today, urban designs are being produced in a neoliberal economic context. All these changes are reflected in a series manifestoes prescribing the nature of good urban designs.

Manifestoes and Paradigms, Generic Concepts, Illustrative Designs, and Specific Designs

A manifesto is the public declaration of an individual's or a group's advocacies. Each manifesto is directed at changing the thoughts and deeds of other people. Implicit in the proposals and projects of every designer is a set of beliefs about how the world functions and how it ought to function. Putting the set into words and drawings reveals the writer's attitudes toward people and the natural world and which functions of built form are deemed important to address. The first part of the twentieth century abounded with manifestoes directly or indirectly promoting what were regarded as good future-built environments. Such periods are correlated with rapid developments in technologies, social upheavals, and political instability.

If urban design manifestoes consist of general statements on what constitutes a good world, socially, psychologically, and in built form, then paradigms are exemplars of good ways of working. Several urban design paradigms were developed during the twentieth century. A number coexisted and coexist to this day, each having proponents who argue for one or other from the basis of their beliefs about what constitutes a good person, good people, and a good world. A paradigm is replaced by a new one when its inconsistencies become clear or when there is a shift in a society's perception of the issues that need to be confronted.

Generic solutions are conceptual examples of what should be done to solve classes of standard, frequently occurring problems. Illustrative designs are proposals for hypothetical situations that illuminate the way forward on the basis of a specific paradigm. The changing history of urban design thought can be represented in the chronology of generic designs for cities, their precincts, the nature of streets, and other infrastructure elements that hold the morphology of the whole together. Manifestoes are thus the most general statements arguing for specific urban design directions; paradigms are statements of good practice based on them; and generic solutions and illustrative designs are the operational definitions of a paradigm. Generic solutions have the greatest impact on what is implemented, because the design process is primarily one in which the designers adapt generic solutions or illustrative designs to meet what they regard as the requirements of the situations that they face (Bazjanac 1974; Schön 1983; Lawson 1990; Francescato 1994). Thus, as paradigms and generic solutions change, so does what is built.

The Philosophical Bases of Urban Design Manifestoes and Paradigms

The dispute between two major philosophical positions—rationalism and empiricism—on the acquisition and use of knowledge plays out in the development of urban design manifestoes (Shane 1975; van Schaik 1985; Broadbent 1990). Rationalists assume that the knowledge of a subject is derived from innate processes of intuition and deductive reasoning, whereas empiricism stresses the role of experience and evidence in the formation and support of ideas (Garvey and Stangroom 2012). The former are idealists; the latter are realists.

An alternative to rationalism and empiricism is a purely pragmatic, laissez-faire attitude toward decision-making (Broadbent 1990; Tjallingii 1996; Turisi 1997). The approaches to urban design developed by those at the forefront of the field during the twentieth century and early twenty-first century have been a reaction to what they perceive to be the opportunity costs incurred by pragmatic designs. Those designs could have been done better.

Pragmatism

Pragmatic designs result from their creators' focusing on satisfactorily meeting the utilitarian functions of a project. To Jeremy Bentham (1748–1832), an English philosopher and social reformer, 'utilitarian' meant something sensible, realistic, and practical in narrow functional and economic terms. Many designs result from what property developers and their architects perceive to be a reasonable and logical method of serving a utilitarian function. The designs are based on beliefs about ends that are straightforward to accomplish and economically rewarding and that work well enough, rather than being based on self-conscious intellectual ideas and theories.

Pragmatists believe that actions should be judged solely on their consequences and not on idealistic grounds: "[All designs are] hypotheses to be worked out in practice and to be rejected,

Figure 3 Pragmatic designs, Nairobi: Self-conscious (above) and unselfconscious (below)
Credit line: Johnny Miller/Millefoto

corrected, and expanded as they fail or succeed in giving our present experience the guidance it needs" (John Dewey, cited in Tjallingii 1996, 92). Pragmatic urban designs are narrowly functional and fail to address the broad range of functions that a project may serve. They are satisficing (i.e., good enough) solutions to utilitarian functions and give a return on capital invested. Much is designed unselfconsciously by habit. The photograph of Nairobi shows two abutting pragmatic designs. A self-consciously designed gated middle-income neighborhood lies adjacent to a slum, largely unselfconsciously developed by many individuals in a piecemeal manner. Both rationalists and empiricists among urban designers have believed that they can do better for both the wealthy and the poor, but their proposals still needed to possess a pragmatic quality to be implemented. Neoliberals believe that the marketplace is the best arbiter of quality.

Rationalism

Rationalist thinking applied to urban design leads to outcomes based on assumptions on what is a good world and the type of built environment that best accommodates it. Such an attitude goes back to the Greek philosopher Plato (ca 427–348 BCE) and so is sometimes referred to as the Platonic approach to design. Rationalism today is, however, most closely associated with the ideology that is represented in the *Code Civil des Français* established under Napoléon I (1769–1821) in 1804. Known as the Napoleonic Code, it proposed a legal framework based on *ideals* not *precedents*. It had a profound impact on thinking throughout continental Europe and then in other countries striving to modernize (Lai 1988; Longworth 2015). It is often, shortsightedly, referred to as the continental European approach to design and the domain of progressive utopians (Boguslaw 1965; Tjallingii 1996).

Rationalist urban designs have a long history dating back to at least the fifth century BCE, when the Greek town of Miletus was rebuilt with a gridiron plan associated with Hippodamus

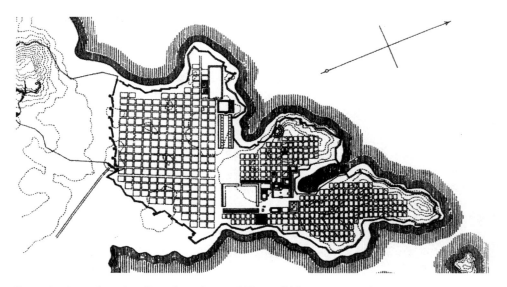

Figure 4 An early rationalist urban design: Miletus (fifth century BCE)
Source: Wikimedia Commons

(498–8 BCE). More importantly for subsequent urban design, Roman military camps had gridiron plans with each of their subareas rationally allocated to a specific activity. In more-recent European history, over 300 bastide towns were built for colonization and defense purposes in the Angevin region of France between 1220 and 1350. The *Laws of the Indies* of the Spanish developed in the sixteenth century prescribed 148 principles/directives for the planning of colonial cities (Rodriguez 2005). Rational though these designs were, they had a pragmatic component to them.

During the eighteenth and nineteenth centuries, diverse philosophers presented their views on what a new socioeconomic world should be like and the built environment in which it should occur. Among them were the French architect Claude-Nicolas Ledoux (1736–1806), Robert Owen (1771–1858), a Welsh social reformer and architect, and Charles Fourier (1772–1837), a French philosopher. The three had in common a belief in socialism as an ideal political system and the importance of the built environment in improving people's social lives and values.

Fourier's book *Théorie des Quatre Mouvements et des Destinées Générales* (1996; originally 1808), written soon after the 1789–99 French Revolution, is one of the founding documents in the history of socialism. Ledoux's manifesto and generic design ideas are presented in *L'Architecture considérée sous le rapport de l'art, des mœurs et de la législation* (*Architecture Considered in Relation to Art, Morals, and Legislation*), published in 1804. Architecture, in pure geometric forms, he argued, was the basis for enhancing society. Robert Owen's architectural views were more pragmatic.

Owen's *New View of Society; Essays on the Formation of the Human Character*, published in London in 1813, and other writings make up his manifesto advocating for a utopian socialist world. His approach to social and physical design is illustrated in his reform of industrial production methods at New Lanark in Scotland and his experimental communities in the United States (see Chapter 3). Radical design ideas were contemporaneously being brewed in Russia.

The Russian contribution to the formation of the intellectual background on which many urban design paradigms are based is exemplified by the writings of Apollinari Krasovsky. His 1851 book *Grazadanskaia Arkhitektura* (*Civil Architecture*) is a rationalist manifesto (Senkevitch

Figure 5 An eighteenth-century rationalist design: New Lanark, Scotland
Credit line: Photograph by Geert Koolen/Shutterstock.com

1974). Embracing new technologies and social tasks, his ideas later affected approaches to modern urban design through the early twentieth-century Russian schools of architecture and art—the VKHUTEMAS (State Higher Art and Technical Studios) and the INKHUK (Institute of Artistic Culture)—and then on to Germany and the Staatliches Bauhaus Weimer (1919–33), the most celebrated and most influential school of design the world has seen. The manifestoes produced by its staff (e.g., Hilberseimer 1925, 1927, 1944; Sert and C.I.A.M 1944; Gropius 1962) and its teachings set the agenda for much urban design in the post–World War Two years.

Similar institutions were founded in Japan, India, and Latin America. In India, for instance, Nobel laureate Rabindranath Tagore (1861–1941) sought a regional architecture in the face of globalizing forces at Shantiniketan. Such establishments had minor impacts on their own countries and almost none on the international scene. Only the Graduate School of Design at Harvard during the 1940s and 1950s, with its European émigrés, matched the Bauhaus' impact on modernist architecture and urban design.

The rationalists were and are a diverse set of people even though they have a common intellectual heritage. Their individual backgrounds and aspirations shaped their views on what constitutes good people and good environments.

Empiricism

Empiricist approaches to design are based on the belief that what works well should form the basis for new designs. It's a more pragmatic approach to design than that of the Rationalists, but one backed by a sense of idealism. The line of thinking is most closely associated with the spirit of English common law, which is founded on the application of precedents to current

Figure 6 Picturesque landscape design: West Wycombe grounds, England, designed primarily by Humphrey Repton (1752–1818) with a folly, and the Temple of Music, designed by Nicholas Revett (1721–1804)

situations (Lai 1988). Empiricists are considered to be regressive utopians because they draw their ideas from what exists and thus evidence, not idealistic dreams (Boguslaw 1965). It is often referred to as the Anglo and Anglo-American (or Anglo-Saxon by Le Corbusier) approach to design.

The empiricist view can be traced back to two philosophers of ancient Greece, Socrates (d. 399 BCE) and Aristotle (394–22 BCE), and to medieval Islamic philosophers such as Al Farabi (b. 951) and the Moorish Andalusian Muslim philosopher Abu Bakir ibn Tufail (1105–81). Empiricist thought in Europe can be traced from Thomas Aquinas (ca 1225–74), Leonardo da Vinci (1452–1519), and Galileo Galilei (1564–1642) to British intellectuals. *An Essay Concerning Human Knowledge* (1691) by John Locke (1632–1704) was a bold debunking of rationalist methods (Broadbent 1990; Garvey and Stangroom 2012).

The precedents on which the empiricist designers drew and draw were and are varied. The classical heritage has been an enduring one. In the nineteenth century, the classical and baroque drew the attention of many architects working on civic projects, as can be seen in the work associated with the École des Beaux-Arts in Paris (see Chapter 2). The picturesque has been equally influential. Landscape design in Britain was particularly influenced by empiricist philosophers. Although others preceded Lancelot 'Capability' Brown (1715–83), he was the most prolific practitioner of the picturesque. He favored simple landscape designs that replicated the 'natural' countryside, with the buildings as part of the composition (Phibbs 2017).

The empiricist urban design theorists and practitioners in Britain tended to favor country or small-town living as the precedent for ideal urban designs. In the early twentieth century, this attitude is seen in the advocacies of Ebenezer Howard (1850–1928) and the garden city movement. Much of the contemporary thinking in the United States had a similar bias that can be traced from Thomas Jefferson (1743–1826, third president of the United States) to Frank Lloyd Wright (1876–1959) (White and White 1964; Conn 2014). Empiricist approaches to urban design today rely heavily on learning from precedents that are believed to function well in localizing designs in their geographic and cultural context.

In Germany, the empiricist approach is represented in the urbanist work of Reinhard Baumeister (1833–1917). His *Stadterweiterungen in technischer, baupolizeilicher und Wirtschaftlicher Beziehung* (*Town Extensions: Their Links with Technical and Economic Concerns and with Building Regulations*), published in 1876, was an early textbook for city planning. Toward the end of the century, a strong empiricist approach to precinct design theory based on what makes the environment easy to understand and enjoyable developed in the country. It was bolstered by contemporary empirical psychological theories of perception.

The experimental studies on perception by Hermann von Helmholtz (1821–94) influenced the ideas and writings of Hermann Maertens (1877–1916) and Camillo Sitte (1843–1903) and the design of towns. Systematic research on the built environment, its place as part of natural ecosystems, and the relationship between human behavior and the layout of cities, their precincts, and their buildings began in the late nineteenth century but received a boost in the second half of the twentieth century with the rise of such organizations as the Environmental Design Research Association (EDRA), founded in the United States in 1969 and its European contemporary, IAPS (the International Association for People-Environment Studies). Because rationalist thinking is deeply embedded in much architectural thinking about cities, this body of knowledge is only slowly seeping into urban design practice. The exceptions to this generalization were those studies, such as that of Kevin Lynch (1960) on the cognitive images of cities, Oscar Newman (1972) on defensible space, and William Whyte (1980) on small urban spaces that had a more immediate impact. Their implications for design were immediately clear. Much urban design simply continues to be highly pragmatic.

Observations

European (Western) and Asian (Eastern) attitudes toward the universe, human behavior, aesthetic values, and thus urban design are often contrasted. Distinguishing between European liberalism (reputedly emphasizing tolerance) and Asian authoritarianism (reputedly emphasizing discipline and order) is, however, misleading. Depending on what aspects of their beliefs one examines, philosophers with a rationalist orientation, such as Plato and St. Augustine, along with Confucius and Kautilya, would be regarded as Asian and Eastern. In contrast, Ashoka, Akbar the Great, Lao-tzu, Mahatma Gandhi, and Sun Yat-Sen would be regarded as Western (Sen 2000). Rationalist and empiricist approaches to urban design compete for hegemony throughout the world and are neither Eastern nor Western, as can be seen in the examples of schemes included in this book.

Several designs are *exemplars* of a design paradigm in application. They closely follow the design paradigm's edicts. Few urban designs today are based purely on rationalist or empiricist philosophies. Few are purely pragmatic solutions. Many designs, while true to the general principles of a paradigm, draw on other ideas. They are *hybrid* examples. Robert Venturi (1925–2018), in *Complexity and Contradiction in Modern Architecture* (1966), regards them as more interesting and lively than pure types. They may also be hybrid examples because the ideas explicit in a generic solution are whittled away to meet building bylaws and property developers' demands. Examples of both exemplars and hybrids are presented in the coming chapters.

Key References

Broadbent, Geoffrey. 1990. *Emerging Concepts in Urban Space Design*. London: Van Nostrand Reinhold International.

Lai, Richard Tseng-yu. 1988. *Law in Urban Design and Planning: The Invisible Web*. New York: Van Nostrand Reinhold.

Shane, Grahame. 1975. "Contextualism." *Architectural Design* 46 (11): 676–70.

Tjallingii, Sybrand P. 1996. *Ecological Conditions, Strategies and Structures in Environmental Planning*. Wageningen: DLO Institute for Forestry and Nature Research.

van Schaik, Leon. 1985. "Rationalism and Contextualism." *Architecture SA* (May–June): 52–56.

Part I

Haussmann's Paris: Avenue de la Grande Armée
Credit line: Photograph by Balkorstat/Shutterstock.com

Antecedents of Twentieth-Century Urban Design

Self-conscious urban designs date back to the earliest civilizations on Earth. The settlement of Çatalhöyük (ca 7500 BCE) in Anatolia may have evolved piece by piece unselfconsciously, but the Bronze Age towns of Harappa and Mohenjo-Daro in the Indus Valley were clearly preplanned. Vedic and Chinese texts prescribing settlement patterns were written as early as 4000 BCE. The story in this book may begin there, but its focus is on the modern era of Western European thought and its impact on the world. The restructuring of our concept of the universe by the Polish mathematician-astronomer Nicolaus Copernicus (1473–1543) initiated the era: The earth was no longer considered to be the center of the solar system. Curiosity in the search for knowledge and its explorations of the globe led to Europe's displacing Asia as the world's economic powerhouse. The development of notions of group and individual rights helped.

Our concepts of individual rights began with the *Magna Carta Libertatum* (1215) and its defining them under the monarchy in England and later the Protestant Reformation with the posting of *The Ninety-Five Theses* by Martin Luther (1483–1546) in Wittenberg in 1517. The posting heralded the Protestant belief that rewards after death come from hard work and not simply by doing good deeds. In Britain, the overthrow of King James II (1633–1701) during the Glorious Revolution of 1688 led to the formulation of a Bill of Rights in 1689 and the establishment of parliamentary democracy. The American Revolution (1765–83), in which patriots won independence from Great Britain, led to the 1791 US Bill of Rights, establishing an individual's right to the freedom of religion, speech, and ownership of private property. It also placed limitations on the power of the government. Soon afterward, the French Revolution (1789–99) and the future development and propagation of rational thought and Cartesian philosophical ideas promoted concepts of liberty, constitutional government, and the separation of the powers of church and state. Contemporary southeastern Europe was under the control of the Islamic Ottoman Empire (1453–1922). Asia remained conservative; Hinduism, Confucianism, Buddhism, and Islam prevailed as intellectual traditions.

The Nineteenth Century

The nineteenth century was "the best of times" and "the worst of times," as Charles Dickens noted in the opening words of *The Tale of Two Cities* (Dickens 1859, 1). It was an age of enlightenment and of suppression (Osterhammal 2014). In Britain, Adam Smith produced *An Inquiry into the Nature of the Wealth of Nations* in 1776. He argued that competition among the users of resources was the path for success of firms and industries. In France, the ideas embedded in *Code Civil des Français* (1804) became an intellectual force delivered across Europe by Napoleonic conquests and globally in the French Empire. In Britain, North America, and the British colonies, the concepts of English common law held sway. The view of God (or gods) as the creator of the universe was challenged by the texts of Charles Darwin (1809–82). Although Alfred Russell Wallace (1823–1913) had already published works on evolutionary theory, Darwin's *On the Origins of Species by Means of Natural Selection* (1859) and the *Descent of Man* (1871) changed the way people began to think about the world as much as Copernicus had earlier.

The century was also an era of colonization by the European powers, furthering the globalization of the international economy and the spread of Eurocentric design ideas across the world. The East India companies of the Dutch and British became major multinational corporations. Slaves from Africa worked in large numbers on the cotton fields of the United States and the cane fields of the Caribbean (Carey, Ellis, and Salih 2004). The slave rebellion in Haiti (1791–1804) eventually led to the end of the slave trade. Britain abolished slavery in 1834, and the United States in 1865. Brazil followed in 1888. Racist stereotypes that justified slavery nevertheless persisted. Tsar Alexander II's emancipation reform ended serfdom in Russia in 1861. Strivings against colonial rule began to appear in India with the founding of the Indian National Congress in 1885. In China, the Society of Righteous and Harmonious Fists, known as 'The Boxers,' rebelled against colonial forces (1899–1901).

Important as all these events were in stirring up intellectual endeavors, the technological advances created by the Industrial Revolution in Europe led to comprehensive changes in the ways of life and livelihoods of people throughout the world and the habitat of many other species, animate and inanimate.

The Industrial Revolution and the Victorian Era

The middle of the eighteenth century saw the introduction of machinery to replace human hands in labor. The year of the American declaration of independence and the publication of *The Wealth of Nations*—1776—was also year that the first prefabricated iron bridge was built in England's Severn Valley. The Industrial Revolution soon spread across the country to Scotland, continental Europe, and the United States (Allen 2017). Japan's industrialization began after the Meiji Restoration of imperial rule in 1868.

A second phase of the revolution began around 1850 with the development of steam-powered trains and ships. They provided the first major advances in transportation modes in centuries. The electric relay was developed in 1835; the telegraph that used Morse code followed in 1837. The first telephone call was made in 1876. Thomas Edison (1847–1931) created an efficient electric light bulb in 1878. Toward the century's end, the gasoline-powered automobile was developed in Germany. Of all the nineteenth-century inventions, it, along with the telephone and refrigeration, had the greatest impact on the morphology of cities in the twentieth century.

The new technologies, military and civil, aided the expansion of the British, French, German, and Russian Empires and led to the demise of the Spanish and the Napoleonic in Europe and the Mughal in South Asia. Colonial cities saw major projects' being implemented in the image of good cities of the colonizers. The colonized countries were dramatically changed by their conquerors, but the colonizers were, in turn, affected by their colonial experiences. Several urban design ideas were first implemented abroad before being applied 'at home.'

In Great Britain and Ireland, Queen Victoria reigned from 1837 until her death in 1901, giving her name to an era. It was a time of strict moral codes and norms of behavior, manners, and modesty, on the surface at least, for the upper and middle classes. Workers, including young children, labored in the industries and mines of Europe. Their wretched state in capitalist England was described by Friedrich Engels (1820–95) in 1845 and by Karl Marx (1813–83) with Engels in their influential 1848 pamphlet *The Manifesto of the Communist Party*.

Urban Development and Design

The population of the world doubled during the nineteenth century; people flocked to cities in search of better lives. The change in the mode of transportation from foot and horse to trains facilitated rapid urban expansion. London grew from a compact town into the world's largest metropolis, sprawling into its hinterland. Living conditions for the poor were abysmal but better than in the countryside (L. Mumford 1961). Slums were overcrowded; sanitation conditions were deplorable. In London, the River Thames became an open sewer. In 1858, the 'great stink' of the river was accompanied by a renewed outbreak of cholera, leading to many deaths. Paris, held in high esteem for its cultural advances, was even worse (Olsen 1986). The desire for more-salubrious living conditions led to the building of major sewer systems, significant social reforms, and new ideas about what the city should be like.

Urban areas around the world were reshaped by urban renewal projects. The aristocracy built palaces for themselves; property developers built large houses for the wealthy and slums for the poor. The demolishing of city walls in places such as Vienna and Barcelona provided new development opportunities. Regency London (1795–1820), with the designs of John Nash (1752–1835), who was much influenced by contemporary picturesque landscapes, gave the heart of that metropolis much of its present-day character. Paris was reshaped for Napoléon III under the direction of Baron Georges-Eugène Haussmann (1809–1891). The Belgian, French, and British colonial powers used the wealth obtained from the exploitation of their colonies to build grand civic complexes in the hearts of Brussels, Paris, and London. The power of the Austro-Hungarian Empire (1867–1918) in central Europe led to similar grand schemes in Vienna and Budapest.

The disparity in the quality of living conditions of the wealthy, the middle classes, and the poor was vast and obvious. The wealthy lived in highly desirable urban locales or in the countryside, and middle-class people emulated them to the best of their ability. In London, the wealthy might be living adjacent to one of the city's garden squares developed in the late eighteenth and early nineteenth centuries or near one of the city's parks. Lowly workers lived in crowded hovels. Cholera, measles, scarlet fever, and diphtheria were regular scourges. Rickets, especially in children, led to fractures and skeletal deformities.

The etchings of Gustave Doré (1832–83) present a powerful image of the poverty-stricken areas of London that he saw in his wanderings around the city with Blanchard Jerrold (1826–84),

Figure 1 Wealth and poverty in nineteenth-century New York: The interior of a middle-class home (left) and slum accommodation as photographed by Jacob Riis (right)

Credit line (left): Collection of the author
Credit line (right): Photograph by Jacob Riis
Source (right): Riis (1890)

a journalist (Doré and Jerrold 1868). The photographs of Jacob Riis (1849–1914) published in *How the Other Half Lives* (1890) do the same for New York. The development of photography enabled many observers to capture penetrating images of both elegant and deplorable urban scenes. A concern for the improvement of working and housing conditions as well as the desire to beautify cities led to questioning what urban design projects were needed and what they should be like.

Project Types

A wide range of project types built during the nineteenth century set precedents for twentieth-century urban design. Many were initiated to accommodate the swelling population of cities. The most comprehensive were the new towns. They varied from company towns associated with industries or mines to private developer–initiated schemes driven by the desire to create profits, but they also included the efforts of reformers to establish ideal settlements.

The *Eixample*, an extension to Barcelona (1855–), designed by Ildefons Cerdà i Sunyer (1815–76), was one of many developed for the expansion of cities. Urban renewal schemes were also carried out, some on a massive scale. The most influential was the redevelopment of Paris under the direction of Haussmann. While many soon-to-become slums were being built, some urban renewal schemes were targeted at slum clearance. Housing projects were built in the inner city to provide good housing options for the poor. World's fairs from London (1851) to Chicago (1893) displayed the new technological marvels of the era to many people. Carefully designed suburbs demonstrated what could be done to provide safe and pleasant settings for family life (Stern and Massengale 1981; Fishman 1987; Galinou 2010; Stern, Fishman, and Tilove 2013).

Several completely new project types were introduced during the nineteenth century. They varied from industrial complexes to university campuses, a particularly US idea that spread as an urban design type throughout the world (Turner 1984). In rural areas, farm complexes resulting from the mechanization of agriculture were new types. Some of these developments were given much thought, but others were pragmatic solutions that sufficed in responding to immediate utilitarian demands.

Pragmatic Urban Designs

During the nineteenth century, property developers established formulae for building highly profitable towns and commercial and residential areas. In the United States, entrepreneurs founded new towns as the country expanded westward. By midcentury, they were aided by the expansion of the railroad network. Railway companies invested in lines stretching out from the city. Land was bought, a gridiron plan was laid out, and the site was subdivided into parcels and sold as speculative ventures to contractors and citizens. The size of the plots correlated with the income level of purchasers. The companies made a greater profit from the sale of land around the stations than in the operation of trains. Newly founded cities grew slowly at first; Chicago housed only 5,000 people in 1840, but because of its locational advantages, it had 100,000 just two decades later.

While nineteenth-century pragmatic designs ranged across all project types, the ones that had the greatest impact on the development of urban design ideologies were the housing developments associated with the 'dark satanic mills' of the song *Jerusalem*, by the English poet William Bake (1757–1827). The accommodation for workers in the narrow row houses or tenements of the industrial cities of Britain, continental Europe, and the United States was cramped and lacking in ventilation and sunlight. Sanitation and drainage were poor, and dampness penetrated

Antecedents of Twentieth-Century Design

Figure 2 Pragmatic urban designs: Central Chicago in 1890 (left) and cotton mills in Preston, England, on a clear, non-working winter day (right)
Credit line (left): Library of Congress, Geography and Map Division
Credit line (right): Collection of the Ewing Galloway Agency, Syracuse University

the interiors of houses. Hot in summer and cold in winter, they provided a minimum level of shelter. Families were large and dwelling units overcrowded. The backyards of the houses were tiny and accommodated rudimentary toilet facilities. The streets served as filthy playgrounds for children. Profitable for landlords, it was the type of housing that angered Friedrich Engels (Engels 1845).

In England and Wales, workhouse complexes were built to provide labor, accommodation, sustenance, and healthcare for the unemployed. Children received some education. Living conditions were meant to be harsh, to deter people from entering the workhouses unless they were destitute. Contemporary pragmatic suburban developments for the middle class were substantially more salubrious and spacious.

The generic suburban type for middle-class people was laid out in a gridiron pattern of tree-lined streets. Each plot contained a single house. In the United States, the plots were unfenced in the front of the houses and enclosed at the rear. In many other English-speaking countries, they were enclosed in the front and rear by low walls or fences. Common facilities grew up near the stations where commuters left for work each morning and returned home in the evening. Many such places were much sought after as places to live, but social reformers and designers believed that they could be better.

The Outline of the Discussion

The interwoven threads of thought that underlie the development of twentieth-century urban design paradigms can be divided into five major strands. They have in common a desire to remake the city into, at least, a salubrious and safe living environment. The first strand, discussed in Chapter 1, has its roots deep in the past. Specific urban geometrical patterns were and are associated with spiritual well-being based on cosmologies and/or religious beliefs. Separating this strand from the four that follow does not deny the spiritual ideas implicit either in classical urban designs or in the motivations of leaders of the social and philanthropic movement. The chapter simply emphasizes the impact of formal, religion-based, spiritually significant geometric canons on the design of human settlements. In several societies today, elements of spiritual concerns linger on in the formulation of urban designs.

The second of these interwoven strands is the classical work of the Beaux Arts that had its antecedents in the ideas of the Renaissance architects and further back in the buildings of Rome and Greece. The enemy was the tightly packed medieval city. The image of a good city was, in contrast, one of grand axes formed by boulevards terminating at focal buildings and/or point elements in the cityscape. The tradition's descendant was the City Beautiful movement of the twentieth century and the classical designs of this century.

The third strand, which is covered in Chapter 3, is that of the social and philanthropic movement led by advocates for the provision of good laboring and living conditions for the workers of the industrial city. While paternalistic, it produced several progressive urban design ideas based on strong social agendas. The desire to improve living conditions in the city is reflected in most of the urban design ideas of the twentieth century. On the empiricist side, the garden city movement was given its form by Ebenezer Howard. On the idealistic, rationalist side, architects such as Tony Garnier (1869–1948) and later Le Corbusier and CIAM led the way.

The fourth strand deals primarily with suburban designs for the middle class on the periphery of cities in North America, the British Isles, continental Europe, and the colonists' neighborhoods in the cities of subjugated nations. They were a direct antecedent of the garden city movement and the pragmatic suburban designs of twentieth-century cities around the world. Today, many people desire to live in such suburban environments of primarily single-family homes; they are regarded as good places for family life.

The scholars and designers of the fifth and final strand of antecedents to twentieth-century urban design discussed here, unlike the others, assumed that there were lessons to be learned from the medieval city and from the classical city. The designers who examined the old cities were urbanists rather than anti-urbanists; they did not want to demolish the existing city and start again. They wished to understand what made medieval urban environments behaviorally and visually interesting. Such places also contained a richness of behavior settings that many contemporary urban designs lacked. The townscape movement of the mid twentieth century was its natural descendant.

Other, although less significant, strands of thought also exist. Their presence will become clear as the discussion of the development of urban design ideas proceeds through the book.

Key References

Allen, Robert C. 2017. *The Industrial Revolution: A Very Short History*. Oxford: Oxford University Press.

Carey, Brycchan, Markham Ellis, and Sara Salih, eds. 2004. *Discourses of Slavery and Abolition: Britain and its Colonies, 1760–1838*. Gordonsville, VA: Palgrave Macmillan.

Mumford, Lewis. 1961. *The City in History, Its Origins, Its Transformations, and Its Prospects*. London: Secker & Warburg.

Olsen, Donald J. 1986. *The City as a Work of Art: London, Paris, Vienna*. New Haven and London: Yale University Press.

Osterhammal, Jürgen. 2014. *The Transformation of the World: A Global History*. Translated from the German by Patrick Camiller. New York: Princeton University Press.

1

Religious Canons and Prescriptions

Several architects' practices in the early twenty-first century are based on religious canons or cosmologies (e.g., Bubbar 2005). Several urban design projects following cosmological principles were built during the twentieth century; many buildings, especially in South and East Asia, still are. The history of such designs is lengthy.

Early Chinese texts and early Hindu texts clearly show that divine design percepts were derived from the perceived working of the cosmos. There also appears to be much that was pragmatic about them. For Muslims, sharia law stems from the directives that Prophet Muhammad (570–632) received from Allah. For nonbelievers, it seems more likely that they were empirically based on what he saw was working and not working around him and what he wished to promote. Christian ideas about cities can be traced to the Bible. Different sects have drawn on contrasting passages to ensure that by following their strictures, believers would achieve everlasting life after death on Earth. During the nineteenth century, many new utopian settlements were designed to have behavior settings that would cater to a sect's prescribed ways of life and aesthetic values (Hayden 1976). Where did all these ideas come from?

Antecedent Ideas

The earliest design canons were handed down orally from master to apprentice and were given religious significance to ensure that they would be followed. They responded to the spiritual need to make sense of the world and reasons for life on it. Oral traditions specified ways of life, including religious rituals, and the auspicious layout of buildings and settlements to ensure good lives. The similarity of many prescriptions suggests that certain patterns hold archetypical meanings buried in the unconscious mind of everybody. Some patterns, squares, and circles, in particular, appear repeatedly in the art, myths, and religions of members of widely dispersed cultures (Jung 1968). The swastika, for instance, although understood in much of the world today as a symbol of Nazi Germany, is a sign of good luck in many places, from Asia to South America, that had no known contact with each other.

Ritual structures based on cosmological beliefs were built by hunter-gatherers before human settlements had formed. Göbekli Tepe in southern Turkey dates to about 9500 BCE. Stonehenge in England, the best known of such ritual sites, came much later, in 2500 BCE, well after

23

self-consciously designed settlements based on a belief in the talismanic power of geometric forms had already been built. Such settlements exist on all the inhabited continents of the world (Harari 2011). Towns in China based on cosmologies date from 4000 BCE. The Egyptian Pharaonic settlements, those in Mesoamerica, and the Etruscans in what is modern day Italy are others that date back to before our common era. We understand some of them because they are explained in writings; others, such as Göbekli Tepe and the Mesoamerican settlements, remain a mystery.

Manifestoes and Paradigms

The best-known ancient texts that clearly describe the relationship between the divine and urban geometries are principally of Chinese and Indian origin. Islamic statements are based more on an interpretation of urban forms in Arabia and Northern Africa than on any single manifesto. Renaissance texts are concerned primarily with use of geometries to attain a sense of beauty based on proportional systems related to nature and the human body. The *Ten Books on Architecture* of the Roman author Vitruvius (Marcus Vitruvius Pollio, ca 80 to 20 BCE) were the inspiration. While there are references to ideal cities in the Christian Bible, few statements relate specific geometric patterns directly to the divine.

The pre-Colombian bases for the design of cities in Central America are largely conjectural. The *Popol Vuh* is a myth history of the K'iche' people of present-day Guatemala. It had not been transferred from the oral form to the written form until 1550. It survived the purges of the Spanish conquistadores by being translated into Spanish in 1701. It had informed the ways of life of the Mayan and thus influenced the building of cities such as Tulum, Chichén Itza, and Uxmal. The Mayans had a profound interest in astronomy, but its links to the design of settlements are unclear. The Indian and Chinese mythologies set themselves apart from others in that they are specific and have, or once had, an empirical basis (M. Smith 2011).

Indo-Aryan town planning requirements were prescribed in the *Shilpa Shastras* but also, in passing, in the *Puranas*, which provide broader treatises on life. The two are the great epics on Indian urban mythology and show the close connection between cosmic geometries and stipulations for town layouts that avoid harmful outcomes for their inhabitants. Several recent texts pick up on their themes. The basic proposition is that when space is enclosed, it acquires spiritual qualities based on its shape, size, orientation, and location on Earth due to magnetic lines of energy that pass between the poles. This argument is meticulously presented by Darshan Bubbar in *The Spirit of Indian Architecture: Vendetic Wisdom for Building Harmonious Spaces*. He notes, "The mandala system encompasses all that is in the universe. It is a process of connecting man with the universe. Man and nature follow the same laws" (Bubbar 2005, 24).

The mandala, a square with its sides oriented toward the cardinal points of the compass, is the unequivocal form of the absolute. The spirit of a site is said to be pressed prone to the earth within the square. The locations of the limbs specify the appropriate use of each part of a site, whether for a town or for a dwelling. The most general subdivision of the mandala is into nine squares that may be again divided into nine squares. Each such square is devoted to a god. The central one is allocated to the god Brahma, the creator. Ideal town layouts are based on it.

The *Shilpa Shastras* consist of sixty-four treatises specifying the requirements of different types of cities and villages from their plans to the locations of their various components down to architectural details of columns and brackets (Acharya 1930). In a new town, the space for a temple had to be allocated first and then areas to caste groups according to their status. The social stratification was represented by plot dimensions and building size, height, and color.

Religious Canons and Prescriptions

The mandala pattern is also a central design schema in Chinese cosmology. The cosmology's concern is with the energy forces that connect people, Earth, and heaven. Its implications are encapsulated in the feng shui edicts for city and building design. The requirements are illustrated in the *Book of Rites*, a collection of writings that set out the social forms, administration, and ceremonial rites of the Zhou dynasty (1046–256 BCE). The *Rites of Zhou*, the *Book of Etiquette and Rites*, and the *Book of Rights* together form the *Three Li* that codified the propitious place for the location of new settlements and how their form should model the cosmic field. These writings provided diagrams on which the Chinese imperial cities were based (Scranton 2014). If the edicts were not followed, dire consequences, it was predicted, would follow.

The ancient Indian and Chinese design decrees seem arbitrary today, and indeed, feng shui was banned by the Chinese government under Mao Zedong (1893–1976) during the country's Cultural Revolution for being based on superstitions. The original empirical bases for the design principles may have been lost, but the forms are still regarded by many people as auspicious. The Islamic decrees differ in nature; they do not guarantee auspicious designs but ones that afford correct behavior.

No unified statement on the design of cities and their precincts appears in the Quran, but sharia law provides a template for how the lives of Muslims should be conducted and thus norms of behavior. It provides prescriptions for respecting what has already been built, the need for privacy, and the utilitarian functions of streets (AlSayyad 1991). Privacy requirements, for instance, resulted in design guidelines that prevent the overlooking of private spaces and the distance that one can see down a street before it should be bent (Hakim 1986). Historically, before the development of the automobile, streets in North African Islamic cities had to be wide enough to allow for two fully loaded camels to pass each other. Such stipulations later legitimized local authorities' building and urban designs codes. Christian religious texts, in contrast,

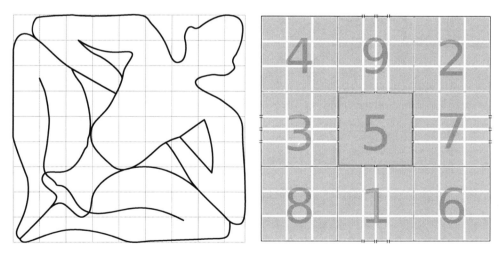

Figure 1.1 The mandala form in India and China: The *Vastu-Purusha mandala* (left) and the conceptual plan for the city of Chengzhou (right), where the numbers indicate the appropriate building types for each square

Source (left): Lang, Desai, and Desai (1997); courtesy of CEPT University Press
Credit line (right): Gurdjieff at en.wikipedia

provide no specific design rules. The inspiration for making good cities and for improving city life is, nevertheless, deeply imbedded in Christian philosophy.

Many designs ideas have been imbued with the ideas of creating a kingdom of God on Earth. The only description of New Jerusalem in the Christian Bible appears in chapter 21 of the Book of Revelation. The city is huge. It is square and enclosed by 65-meter-thick (200-foot-thick) walls. Each wall has three gates inscribed with a name of one of the twelve tribes of Israel. The city is 2,200 kilometers (1,380 miles) on its sides and built of precious metals and gems. Its streets are paved with gold as transparent as glass. Its impact on urban designing seems minimal, but its geometry is interesting. It is a square. Certain Christian denominations have been more down-to-earth in their concept of a good city plan. The Mormon city is one.

The Mormon prophet, Joseph Smith (1805–44), presented a concept for city plans based on Moses's arrangement of the camps of the tribes of Israel (J. Smith 1833). At their center was the Tabernacle, a portable temple. Smith's goal was to emphasize religious unity so that people would always know where the temple in a city is. The extent to which his plan for the 'City of Zion' was inspired by religion and the degree to which it was simply a pragmatic method for subdividing a site is unclear. The idea of Zion may be a reference to the image of Jerusalem or any group of people who are pure of heart (Ostler 2011).

Generic Concepts and Illustrative Designs

Several generic designs are described in ancient Chinese texts and ancient Indian texts. Some are drawn in detail, and others remain highly general, but they have attributes in common. The most obvious are their relationship to the cardinal points of the compass, their grid pattern of streets, and their symmetry.

In Chinese cosmology, a city should have a symmetrical, rectangular plan with three gates on each side, with streets linking those on one side to those directly opposite, as shown in Figure 1.1 (right). Royal quarters were at the center. Feng shui masters would select the site for the city, to ensure that it would be healthy and bring good luck (Steinhardt 1990). One prescription for a city reads as follows:

> Each side is 9 *li* (~3 km) in length with three gates; 9 longitudinal and 9 latitudinal lines divide the interior of the city with north to south roads 9 times the carriage gauge in width, the ancestral temple is on the left (of the palace city in the middle) and Sheji altars for the god of land and the god of grains on the right side; the palace faces the imperial court and backed against the market and the court and market are both one hundred *mu*.
>
> *(He 2007)*

The geometry of the plan of New Jerusalem presented in the Christian Bible is remarkably similar. The Indian Shastras present designs that also have a resemblance.

The Shastras state that a village should have 12, 24, 50, 108, 300, or even more houses, provided that the number is based on a cosmological order. It should have a grid pattern of streets and be walled for defense. It should have a temple for Shiva, the destroyer, and an east-facing temple for Vishnu, the preserver, with a tank (artificial water body) in front of it. The Shastras also specify the requirements for forty-eight types of structures, including palaces and cowsheds. Two types of Brahmin villages are illustrated here—the Dandaia and the Padamia. The Padamia, as shown, is only one of five permutations of the type (Acharya 1933). Other urban forms are derived from the *Vastu-Purusha Mandala*. Conformity to the edicts gives a place an identity and

Religious Canons and Prescriptions

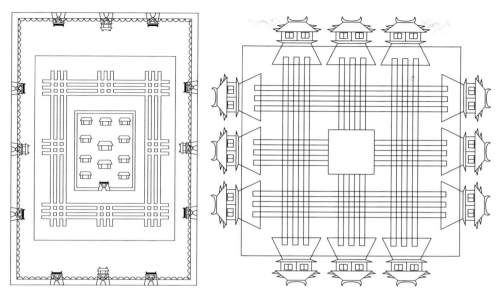

Figure 1.2 Cosmological diagrams for Chinese cities: The generic plan for an imperial city (left) and an ideal plan, based on a square subdivided into nine squares (right)
Credit line (left): Collection of the author
Credit line (right): Wheatley (1971); courtesy of Edinburgh University Press

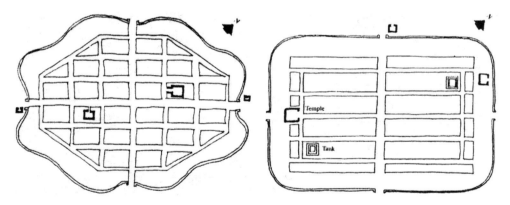

Figure 1.3 Two of nine generic town forms in the Shilpa Shastras: Dandaia (left) and Padamia (right)
Source (left and right): Lang, Desai, and Desai (1997, 29); courtesy of CEPT University Press

its inhabitants a clear position in the caste hierarchy and thus a feeling of economic security. The Hindu edicts are clearly highly prescriptive; Islamic sharia law is concerned more with procedural responsibilities.

The layout of the traditional Islamic city is not prescribed but rather results from following a series of performance guidelines. The generic characteristics of a medieval Islamic

Antecedents of Twentieth-Century Design

city as it evolved is shown in Figure 1.4 (left). The citadel is the bastion from which a city's circumferential defensive wall is laid out. The great mosque is at the city's heart with the bazaar around it. The city is divided into sectors, each with its own center containing a mosque, local bazaar, and baths, much as in the twentieth-century neighborhood unit concept. Rural markets and cemeteries are located outside the city walls (Aziz undated; Saoud 2010).

The houses are designed to ensure the safety, security, and privacy of the female members of a household. Visual privacy is ensured by having walled compounds, by restricted building heights, by the high placement and small size of windows, and by balconies' being located so that they do not overlook neighbors. A law of precedence decreed that new buildings had to be built without intruding in any way on those already built. In twentieth-century terms, they had to be designed with a sense of decorum. Doors and windows of different buildings, for instance, must not directly face each other. The streets must be narrow for climatic purposes in hot, arid climates but also to ensure that people meet face to face when passing each other. They should be wide enough to handle camel traffic. The outward appearance of the houses must be modest and not be a display of individual economic or social status. Many of these edicts are ignored today.

Of all the religion-based settlement ideas in Europe and in the United States, the Mormon proposition is presented here as an example of one Christian sect's approach. Joseph Smith's concept of a city was presented in his plan for the 'City of Zion' (Jackson 1992). Smith's 1883 generic plan was for a city of 15,000 to 20,000 inhabitants. When it had its full complement of people, a new settlement would be developed. The plan was a 1-mile (1,600-meter) square

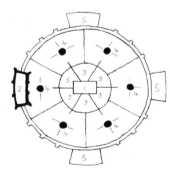

1. great mosque
2. citadel
3. bazaar
4. minor center (with mosque, local bazaar, hammam, etc.)
5. cemetery

Figure 1.4 The generic Islamic city: The overall layout (left) and a typical residential area pattern (right)

Credit line (left): Drawing based on several sources by the author
Credit line (right): Photograph by M. Khebra/Shutterstock.com

divided in a gridiron pattern of square blocks formed by 132-foot-wide (40-meter-wide) streets with the houses set back from the street. Smith wrote,

> No one lot, in this city, is to contain more than one house, and that to be built twenty-five feet back from the street, leaving a small yard in front, to be planted in a grove, according to the taste of the builder; the rest of the lot for gardens; all the houses are to be built of brick and stone
> *(Joseph Smith,* Plat of the City of Zion, *1833, cited by Jackson 1992).*

The central blocks of the plan would be for temples, schools, and other public facilities. Farms were to be located on the outskirts of the city but close enough to it for rural families to avail themselves of the town's social and educational amenities. The plan made no comment on governmental buildings such as town halls.

Specific Designs

Examples of the self-consciously designed cities and precincts based on religious canons abound. Temple complexes in Mesopotamia (e.g., Ur), Egypt (Thebes), Central America (Teotihuacán), Cambodia (Angkor Wat), Indonesia (Borobudur), and cities, including imperial capitals in China, were based specifically on some cosmic principles (Lynch 1981; Madeddu and Zhang 2017). Square city plans with gridiron layouts for cities in China go back, at least, to the Shang dynasty (ca 1700–1027 BCE). The plan for Xi'an created during the Tang dynasty (618–907) is relatively recent. Its design had both pragmatic and cosmological bases. Xi'an was an antecedent of other cities not only in China but elsewhere; Kyoto in Japan is one.

Some of these cities are exemplars of the application of generic ideas to specific designs. Teotihuacán, to the extent that we understand it, and the Forbidden City in Beijing are two

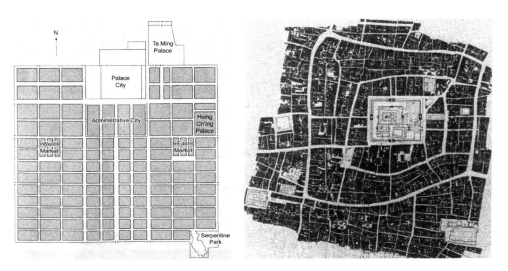

Figure 1.5 Cities based on a representation of the cosmos: A regular example, Chang-an, China (left), and a distorted one, Madurai, India (right)

Source (left): Madeddu and Zhang (2017, 719); courtesy of Taylor & Francis
Source (right): Lynch (1981, 76); courtesy of Julian Smith and MIT Press

Antecedents of Twentieth-Century Design

very different ones. Others borrowed from various antecedents or became distorted, over time, by pragmatic considerations, as in Madurai in south India. It is not the only example of a hybrid design.

Baghdad has cosmological overtones but owes much to the study of the geometry of Euclid, the fourth century BCE Greek mathematician, by the city's founder/builder Abbasid caliph al-Mansur (754–75). Al-Mansur sought a geometrically pure city that would be based on astrological readings (Marozzi 2016). Jaipur's geometry, though having a cosmological basis, was deformed by the necessities of its site and European influences. Salt Lake City in the United States deviates from Joseph Smith's ideal form, for topographic reasons. Unlike these two examples, which were based on prescriptive guidelines, Dubai's Al Bastakiya was shaped by performance guidelines.

Exemplars of Canonical Designs

Teotihuacán, Mexico (ca 100 BCE to 250 CE), and the Forbidden City, Beijing, China (1406–)

Teotihuacán exemplifies the Mesoamerican tradition of planning settlements as a model of the universe. Housing 125,000 people at its peak, the city's plan consists of a great ceremonial axis—the Avenue of the Dead—and rectangular compounds for thirty to one hundred people. Along the axis are pyramids to the sun and the moon, palatial dwellings, and, at the southern end, the citadel with the Temple of the Feathered Serpents. The axis is tilted 15.5° east of north as in other contemporaneous Mesoamerican plans. That direction faces the sunset on August 11, the beginning of the Mayan Long Count calendar that is based on the creation date of 3114 BCE (in the proleptic Gregorian calendar) (Millon 1973; Lynch 1981). Much about the layout remains in the realm of speculation. The application of a cosmological mode is clearer in the layout of Beijing's Forbidden city.

The Forbidden City (Zijin Cheng) was the Chinese imperial palace from the Ming dynasty (1368–1644) to the Qing dynasty (1644–1912). It lies at the center of the walled city of Beijing, surrounded by the Imperial City and the Inner City. Enclosed by a 7.9-meter-high (26-foot-high) wall surrounded by a 52-meter-wide (171-foot-wide) moat, the city is a rectangle: 961 meters (3,153 feet) in the north–south direction and 753 meters (2,470 feet) east to west (Yu 1984; Steinhardt 1990).

The symmetrical plan of the city is a cosmogram based on an arrangement of groups of three—the shape of the Qian trigram—representing heaven. This pattern is seen in the sequence of spaces of the buildings of the Outer and Inner Courts. The residences of the Inner Court are, however, arranged in groups of six—the Kun trigram—representing Earth. The relationship of the buildings to each other follows the rules laid down in the *Book of Rites*. Ancestral temples are in front of the palace, storage areas are in the palace forecourts, and residences are at the back. The use of red and yellow was determined by the status of the use and users of a building. Red exemplifies happiness and yellow the earth. The latter, an auspicious color, was reserved for the buildings of the royal family. One exception is the library, which has black tiles that were associated with water and fire prevention, and another is the Crown Prince's residences, which have green tiles. Green is the color associated with wood and thus growth (Yu 1984).

The line of statuettes that decorate the sloping ridges of each building is another reflection of the status of the building's users or its purpose. The line consists of a man riding a phoenix followed by an imperial dragon. A minor building might have three or five statuettes. The Hall

30

Religious Canons and Prescriptions

Figure 1.6 Teotihuacán: A view down the Avenue of the Dead
Credit line: Photograph by Christian Andries/Shutterstock.com

Figure 1.7 Forbidden City, Beijing: A general view from the south
Credit line: Photograph by Serge Ruddick/Shutterstock.com

of Supreme Harmony has ten. A *Hangshi* or 'ranked tenth,' is found only on this one building in the Forbidden City. The interior layout of the buildings, like their relationship to each other, is as prescribed in the *Book of Rites*. The symbolic aesthetic qualities of the complex are clearly intelligible and meaningful to those who understand the rules.

Antecedents of Twentieth-Century Design

Hybrid Examples

Baghdad Now in Iraq (762–66); Jaipur, Rajasthan, India (1726); Salt Lake City, Utah, USA (1847); and Al Bastakiya (Al Fahidi Historical District), Dubai (1890s)

The round city of Baghdad was a total urban design. Al-Mansur founded it to be the seat of the Islamic Empire, although its site was selected as auspicious by Nestorian monks, a Christian sect. Its design is based on a mixture of astrological interpretations, Islamic principles, and the search for a perfect geometry. The plan is a circle, about four miles (6.4 kilometers) in circumference, formed by 80-foot-high (24-meter-high) castled walls. The walls are penetrated by four gates, through which the streets lead in a straight line to the center of the city. The gates have domed gatehouses above them. At the center of the city is a grand mosque and the Golden Gate Palace, the home of the caliph. It was surrounded by vegetation and a circle of the houses of his children and others associated with the palace. The work on the city began on July 30, a date that astrologers determined was auspicious, and completed in four years (Marozzi 2016). Jaipur came much later and still thrives.

Jaipur was established by Maharaja Jai Singh II (1644–1743) to house a population of 35,000 people. He wished to relocate his capital from nearby Amber to a site spacious enough to both house a growing population and lie closer to a good water supply. He selected Vidyadhar Bhattacharya (1693–1751), a Bengali auditor, to design it. The city, located in a hot, semi-arid, area, was planned following the principles of the *Vastu Shastra* and the *Shilpa Shastra*. The two dictated the overall configuration of the city, the location of its main streets, and their three-dimensional design.

The streets of the grid plan are broad and have diagonal squares at their intersections, a modern (to Jai Singh) European feature. The spaces between the planned streets were built pragmatically following a subconsciously developed hierarchy of lanes leading to private cul-de-sacs. The resulting block pattern is akin to those produced by Islamic guidelines. The central square of Jaipur contains the palace. The main temples are to the north. Each part of the town was reserved for an occupational/caste group, as dictated by the *Vastu-vidya*.

Figure 1.8 Abbasid Baghdad: A simulated reconstruction of its design in the tenth century
Source: Jean Scott/Look at Science/Science Photo Library

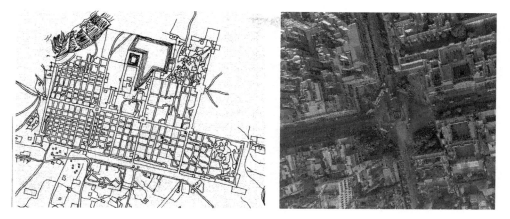

Figure 1.9 Jaipur: The plan (left) and an image of the intersection of the main streets (right)
Source (left): Lang, Desai, and Desai (1997, 48); courtesy of CEPT University Press
Credit line (right): Courtesy of Airpano

Façade controls on the main streets specified the color, materials, and nature of the arcades and terraces along them. Over time, these prescriptive guidelines have been poorly enforced, so a unity in appearance has been largely lost. Known today as the Pink City, the color was not part of the original design but was applied for a late-nineteenth-century visit from the Prince of Wales, later King Edward VII (1841–1910).

While the plan of Jaipur is based on the nine-square mandala, one square is displaced to the southeast. The city's layout was constrained by a hill on the northwest and swamps to the east. In addition, the orientation of the plan is to the northeast rather than strictly to the north, possibly because of astrological considerations (the city is the location of one of Jai Singh's observatories, the Jantar Mantar), as well as the necessity of including an existing palace in the overall scheme. The squares of the plan are unevenly divided so that its geometry departs from the ideal. Such departures are acceptable in the Shilpa Shastra (Sachdev and Tillotson 2002). The Salt Lake City plan also shows deviations from the ideal layout for Zion as established by Joseph Smith.

Salt Lake City was not based on a cosmology but rather on the interpretation of an instruction that Joseph Smith said he received from God. The city was laid out by Brigham Young (1801–77), president of the Church of Jesus Christ of Latter-day Saints, and other Mormon leaders in 1847, after the assassination of Joseph Smith, in 1844. "The Lord commanded that the city should be built beginning at the temple lot" (Ostler 2011). Young selected the site for the city from a viewpoint in the foothills of the valley. It was one where the saints could make a covenant with God.

Several pragmatic changes were made to the ideal design. The overall square pattern was distorted, as in Jaipur, by the intrusion of the adjacent foothills into the valley. The lot sizes were larger too, being 1.25 acres (0.5 hectares) in size, not 0.5 acres (0.2 hectares). The streets were wider than those in the Zion plat: 172 feet (52.5 meters) across, not 132 feet (40 meters). Given these larger dimensions, more than one house could be built on a single lot (Hamilton 1995; Ostler 2011). The restricted square layout of Zion was soon abandoned; the city has expanded into the metropolis that it is today. The religious basis for the design gave way to pragmatic property development requirements.

Antecedents of Twentieth-Century Design

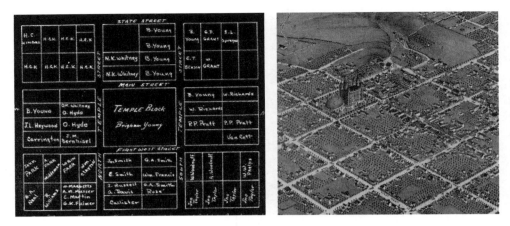

Figure 1.10 Salt Lake City: the original layout and the allocation of building lots (left) and an 1870 view of the city (right)

Credit line (left): Collection of the author

Credit line (right): Adapted from an 1870 drawing by Augustus Koch

Figure 1.11 Al Bastakiya, Dubai: The layout in 1981 (left) and a recent view (right)

Credit line (left): Drawing based on several sources by the author

Al Bastakiya (now known as Al Fahidi Historic District) in Dubai exemplifies a precinct based on sharia law. It exists today after having been restored and renovated and after its use changed to serve as a tourist attraction. It is also an example of the impact that an authoritative figure can have on the survival of historic areas of cities. Al Bastakiya had been slated for demolition by the Dubai municipality in 1989, to make way for the construction of office buildings. The village was restored in 2005 as a result of a visit by Charles, Prince of Wales (b. 1948), at the instigation of a British architect, Rayner Otto, who had made his home in a restored unit there.

34

Al Bastakiya is a small village consisting of only sixty residences. Located on Dubai Creek, it was built by wealthy Persian textile and pearl traders from Bastik in present-day Iran. They were attracted to the location by its generous trading tariffs. The built pattern reflects sharia law's principles, establishing the relationships between public and private spaces and between individual residents and the community. The walls between properties and the street are higher than a person sitting on a camel can see over, and the streets are wide enough for a laden camel to be passed by another going in the opposite direction or one being unloaded. The mosque lies in the prominent position, and the open space adjacent to it is a marketplace. The architecture of the buildings is uniform in character and modest in outward appearance. A prominent feature of the village is the traditional Persian wind towers used to draw air down over wet mats into the houses to cool them.

Commentary: The Functions Addressed

Some religious canons deal in detail with the operational functions of water supply and drainage, sanitation, and other requirements for a healthy life for a place's people. The most important function of urban designs that follow religious canons is, however, that they give their inhabitants a sense of security by supporting their belief that the layout ensures their good health and success in life. Designs following religious edicts fulfill what Amos Rapaport calls the *high-level meaning* of built forms—the cosmological and supernatural symbolism that is encoded in specific geometries. He contrasts this level with the *middle-level meaning*, where messages about the identity and status of the inhabitants of a settlement are communicated through the form and color of their residences. Both sets of meanings are encoded in the Chinese and Indian prescriptions, but not in the Islamic. The exterior appearance of the houses in historic Muslim settlements was largely uniform and hid status differences. A *low-level* meaning describes how the built environment affords the behavior and movement patterns of people—the meaning of function held by the modernists (Rapoport 1990). Directly or indirectly, the religious canons address all three concerns.

The lack of political success of Mahatma Gandhi (1869–1944) in striving for India's independence from Britain during the 1930s while living at the Sevagram Mission in Maharashtra has been ascribed to the layout of the community. It did not follow the guidelines of the Shilpa Shastras. Gouru Tirupati Reddy has taken a deterministic position on the consequences of a settlement's not complying with the Shastras: "Death by electrocution [*sic*] or fire, election defeats, women not having sons," and so on (Reddy 1994).

For people who believe in the stipulations of the canons, satisfying them is necessary for these people's piece of mind. It gives them confidence that everything in life will go well. Today many people who regard the canons as superstitions consider it better to follow them 'just in case.' The same observation applies to those Muslim people whose beliefs in sharia law are not wholehearted or for those who have moved into existing neighborhoods laid out on the basis of others' ways of life.

Observations

The approach to design described in this chapter still has relevance in some cultures. Several recent designs are based on cosmologies. Auroville (1968–) in India and Maharishi Vedic City in Iowa founded in 2001 are examples (see Chapter 10). Arcosanti (see Chapter 9) in Arizona designed by Paolo Soleri (1919–2013) is a more abstract example (see Chapter 8). Soleri's design is rationalist in nature, but it was inspired, in part, by the cosmology of Pierre Teilhard de Chardin (1881–1955), who portrayed the evolution of humanity from matter to ultimately a reunion with Christ. Some observers consider Arcosanti to be a Christian 'City of God' for another reason—Soleri's concept of archology—a combination of architecture and ecology.

The Jaipur plan was a precedent for the unimplemented Vidyadhar Nagar designed by B. V. Doshi (b. 1927), the 2018 Pritzker Prize winner. Doshi was, however, using the design to establish a continuity of a sense of place rather than for its divine intentions. The relevance of the mandala as the basis for design is nevertheless strongly supported by several architects and writers today, although others dismiss it. Darshan Bubbar (b. 1937) falls in the former camp.

Bubbar argues that the Shastras have an empirical basis because of the magnetic forces that govern our well-being. He shows how the design principles inherent in the mandala should be applied to modern buildings, whether they be residences, office buildings, or religious edifices. In urban design, he is a proponent for the utility and benefits of the grid street pattern for settlements on cosmological grounds and more-utilitarian grounds (Bubbar 2005).

Feng shui principles are now applied across the world by adherents to its beliefs. The failure to apply the principles in design is given as a reason for the existence of some of the recently developed ghost towns in China, although other similar designs in the country seem to be happily inhabited. Property developers use compliance with feng shui or, in India, Vastu, as a marketing device, thus showing the commercialization of the values on which building designs can be based (Madeddu and Zhang 2017).

Urban designs must now deal with the turning and parking requirements of automobiles. They also need to deal with the new communications technologies and even the technologies that we now take for granted that have led to changes in most people's ways of life. The loss of concern for the divine meanings inherent in geometries is regarded by some observers as an impoverishment of our contemporary cultures.

Key References

AlSayyad, Nezar. 1991. *Cities and Caliphs: On the Genesis of Arab Muslim Urbanism.* Westport, CT: Greenwood Press.

Bubbar, D. K. 2005. *The Spirit of Indian Architecture, Vedantic Wisdom for Building Harmonious Spaces and Life.* New Delhi: Rupa.

Sachdev, Vibhuti and Giles Tillotson. 2002. *Building Jaipur: The Making of an Indian City.* London: Reaktion Books.

Smith, Michael E. 2011. "Cosmograms, Sociograms, and Cities Built as Images." *Wide Urban World* (April 4). http://wideurbanworld.blogspot.com.au/2011/04/cosmograms-sociograms-and-cities-built.html accessed November 19, 2016.

Steinhardt, Nancy S. 1990. *Chinese Imperial City Planning.* Honolulu: University of Hawaii Press.

Yu Zhuoyun. 1984. *Palaces of the Forbidden City.* New York: Viking.

2
The Classical and Beaux Arts Tradition

The search for impressive, bold, and beautiful urban design concepts in Europe is closely associated with the Renaissance. From the fifteenth century, a renewed interest in the architecture of classical Greece and the civic centers of ancient Roman cities has spurred thoughts on what makes an ideal city design. Grecian and Roman ruins could be observed, admired, and closely analyzed to derive organization principles for new schemes. They still can be and still are in the twenty-first century, but it is the schemes built in the nineteenth century that continue to inspire. Classical architecture is considered to be timeless.

Classical designs, utopian and pragmatic, built from the mid fifteenth century, have had a profound influence on subsequent urban design thought. Most importantly, their principles were absorbed by the École nationale supérieure des Beaux Arts in Paris during the period of its peak influence between the 1850s and the first decade of the 1900s. The staff and graduates of the École were well-connected to the powerful elite of France, so they shaped the projects carried out in the country. The school's reputation and high admission standards attracted students from around the world who took its ideas of good design back with them to their homelands.

Antecedent Ideas

The consideration of idealized city plans with unified geometries has a long history, as the previous chapter indicated. Some such designs were transferred into reality. Baghdad was one. However, the explorations of Renaissance architects have had a major impact on subsequent urban design thought in Europe and then elsewhere. Christian beliefs underpinned some designs proposed as ideal, but the percepts of Euclidean geometry were given form in many Renaissance schemes. The plan for Sforzinda in Poland, for instance, while it drew on images of vice and virtue that derived from an interpretation of *The City of God Against the Pagans* (426) by St. Augustine (354–430), was much inspired by the architecture of Greece and Rome and the writings of Plato and Vitruvius.

Plato gave strict instructions for the layout of cities but little information on what their urban design qualities should be, apart from "temples are to be placed all around the agora" (cited in L. Mumford 1961, 179). For civic building complexes, the Roman forums were a direct source of inspiration for Renaissance architects and through them to the École des Beaux Arts in the nineteenth century. The forums had their antecedents in the Grecian agora, a paved open space surrounded by temples, public buildings, and colonnades, many of which contained shops.

The most influential Roman design was the Forum Romanum. Dating from the seventh century BCE, it was the central meeting place of the city. Surrounded by buildings, porticos, and colonnades, the forum was the physical manifestation of the corporate life of the city. The buildings consisted of temples, basilicas, and shops. The open space was enriched by statues, pillars, and arched victory gateways. The impressive axial plans of the temples such as those at Baalbek (131–61 CE) were also influential. However, later designs had a more immediate impact on urban design thinking. The Rome of Pope Sixtus V (1521–90) is probably the most important example.

Sixtus V sought direct visual links between the major churches of Rome then hidden as separate elements in the intricate medieval street pattern of the city. His objective was to make pilgrimages from one to another easier. His architect, Domenico Fontana (1543–1607), in creating bold vistas toward the churches, made the street something more than a way of providing easy access between churches. Straight and lined by buildings, they appeared monumental. Where they crossed, Fontana placed focal points such as fountains (Bacon 1967b; Benevolo 1980). The idea of axially linking places became a common feature of many later schemes.

Classical urban designs had architecturally unified buildings lining streets. If they were not the work of a single design team, getting a visual unity relied on the architects of the individual components of a scheme designing with a sense of decorum or being required to so design by prescriptive guidelines established by those in authority. Such guidelines go to back to ancient Persia, but those established in 1802 by Charles Percier (1764–1839) and Pierre Léonard Fontaine (1762–1853) for the buildings that line Paris' Rue de Rivoli (named after the 1797 military victory of Napoléon Bonaparte [1769–1821]) set a precedent not only for classical designs but for many twenty- and twenty-first-century urban designs.

Figure 2.1 An antecedent of Renaissance and Beaux Arts designs: A reconstructed view of the Forum Romanum, Rome (ca 0 CE)

Source: Fletcher (1954, 143); courtesy of Pavilion Books

The Classical and Beaux Arts Tradition

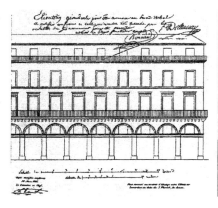

Figure 2.2 Rue de Rivoli, Paris: The 1802 guidelines (left) and the street today (right)
Source (left): Hegemann and Peets (1922, 175)
Source (right): Lang (2017, 132); courtesy of Taylor & Francis

With the classical architecture as an underpinning, Renaissance architects produced several treatises on what constitutes good buildings and good urban designs. Johannes Guttenberg's development of the printing press in the 1430s enabled them to be widely disseminated.

Manifestoes and Paradigms

The writings of Leon Batista Alberti (1404–72) are the exemplar of Renaissance architectural thought, but other philosophers also described imaginary ideal societies and the types of urban environments required to accommodate them. Their books include *Utopia* (1516), by Thomas More; *The City of the Sun* (1602), by Thomas Campenella; and *New Atlantis* (1627), by Francis Bacon. These works portray worlds of enlightenment, public spirit, and civic splendor. In the nineteenth century, the works of Samuel Butler (*Erewhon*, 1872) and William Morris (*News from Nowhere*, 1890) continued in the same vein. Alberti nevertheless had the greatest impact on architectural and urban design thought (Argan 1970).

Alberti's *De re Aedifactoria* (*On the Art of Building*), published in 1452, was *the* contemporary manifesto on urban design, despite its primary focus on individual buildings. Although he considered many patterns of the medieval city could be reapplied to the design of small towns, many of his ideas were a reaction to its density. He sought a spacious, geometrically well-ordered city of straight streets and palatial squares (Pearson 2011). Alberti addressed concepts of civic order and governance, public health through clean water supplies, sanitation and drainage, and the nature of the city's circulation system via thoroughfares and streets. He recognized the importance of privacy and being part of a community in people's lives. He argued for nature and built form to be integrated in order to create unified wholes.

Alberti's design ideas are portrayed in an illustration believed to be by one of his sometime collaborators, Luciano Laurana (1420–79), and in a contemporary portrayal with the same title by Fra Carnevale (1420–84). They show idealized people-free urban spaces. Each has a foreground feature—a prominent element—with the other buildings forming a framing backdrop.

Antecedents of Twentieth-Century Design

The architecture is primarily that of ancient Rome but integrated with contemporary up-to-date design ideas (Argan 1970).

Several other influential Italian architects presented their ideas for ideal cities in treatises. Pietro Cataneo (ca 1510–74) wrote four books, *I Quattro Libro di Architectura* (1554), the first of which presented ideas for fortified cities. His work was cited by Andrea Palladio (1508–80) and influenced that of Vicenzo Scamozzi (1548–1616). Scamozzi offered his view of architecture and urban design in *L'idea dell'architectura Universale* in 1615. The proposals presented in these books share star-shaped fortifications, a central plaza, and a hierarchical ordering of streets. These images soon spread across Europe.

But tastes change. In the seventeenth and eighteenth centuries, architects sought spectacular urban designs displaying the power of those in authority. Radial streets converged at points in the city. A central square, the location of government, became part of a hierarchy of spaces. The sense of enclosure was obtained more by point elements or colonnades than by buildings lining open spaces. Further changes took place in the nineteenth century with the impact of the Industrial Revolution on city life. Idelfons Cerdà i Sunyer (1815–76), a wealthy and politically well-placed Catalan civil engineer, was an early recognizer of its potential effects on city life and the need to design accordingly.

Cerdà presented inclusive views of city planning and urban design in two books. *Teoria de la Construcción de las Ciudades* (1859, *Theory of City Construction*) and *Teoria de la Viabilidada Urbana y Reforma de la de Madrid* (1861, *Theory of Urban Road Space and Reform of that of Madrid*). They show the influence of the Sanitation Movement on Cerdà's proposals for the development of a city's public health infrastructure (Melosi 2000) and the Renaissance ideals in his advocacy for an efficient city with baroque architectural qualities. Cerdà argued for the integration of road- and waterborne transportation systems with urban railroads, something unknown at the time. The Eixample that he devised for Barcelona consisted of square blocks laid out in a grid manner crossed by long straight diagonal streets (see Figure 2.15) (Soria y Puig 1999).

The promotion of the Baroque, an ornate classicism, is better exemplified by the civic designs being produced at the École des Beaux Arts. The school advocated for the application of the French and Italian baroque and Rococo to both new urban designs and buildings. Because the École's students came from several countries, classical schemes based on baroque principles began to appear in early-twentieth-century United States and Latin America, particularly in Buenos Aires (Carthian 1979). In Europe, the situation was somewhat different. Otto Wagner (1841–1910), while retaining the ideas of axiality and symmetry in his design proposals for

Figure 2.3 The ideal Renaissance city: *La Città Ideale*, late fifteenth century, usually attributed to Luciano Laurana but possibly by Pierro della Francesca

Credit line: Collection of the Urbino National Gallery
Source: Wikimedia Commons

Vienna, abandoned historical eclecticism for more modern ideas. He argued for the use of up-to-date technology in his architecture. His article 'The development of a great city' (1912) was a shock to his contemporaries. He blazed the trail for what was to come.

Generic Concepts and Illustrative Designs

An ideal Renaissance urban design consisted of straight streets lined with buildings that had a continuous horizontal roof line. In Alberti's generic design, all the buildings along a street are of uniform height and have the same door designs to make streets nobler. Luciano Laurano's illustration of an ideal city space with a foreground element and the adjacent buildings as background not only illuminate Alberti's ideas but also was produced to attract design commissions. Due to the unsettled nature of the times, the ideal town designs had fortified walls around them (D. Friedman 1988).

The generic fortified town designs of the period were star shaped with either gridiron or axial plans. They stand in strong contrast to the intricate, unselfconscious layouts of the medieval city. They were also precedents for proposals that well illustrate the generic classical ideas. The 1667 plan prepared by Christopher Wren (1632–1723) for London after the Great Fire of 1666 illustrates the fundamental design principles being advocated. It has been highly influential.

The Great Fire destroyed most of the walled city. Wren's design cut through the medieval pattern of London's landholdings to create a grand vision for the city's future. It consisted of large squares from which axial boulevards and avenues radiate. At its heart was a new, classical, centrally planned domed St. Paul's cathedral. It was to replace the gothic structure destroyed in the fire. A contemporarily modern classical edifice was built, but the form of Wren's original proposal was dismissed as too 'popish.' In Wren's proposal for the city, he strove "to combine grandeur . . . with the needs of a predominantly mercantile community" (Jane Lang 1956, 23).

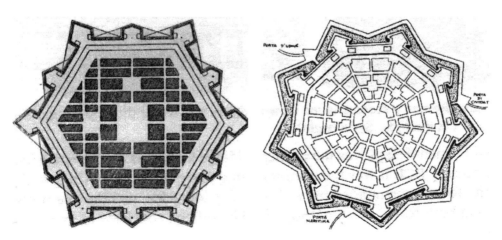

Figure 2.4 Ideal Renaissance new town plans: A grid layout proposed by Pietro di Giacomo Cataneo (left) and a radial design by Vincenzo Scamozzi (right)

Credit line (left): Collection of the author.
Original source (left): Cataneo (1554)
Credit line (right): Collection of the author.
Original source (right): Scamozzi (1615)

Antecedents of Twentieth-Century Design

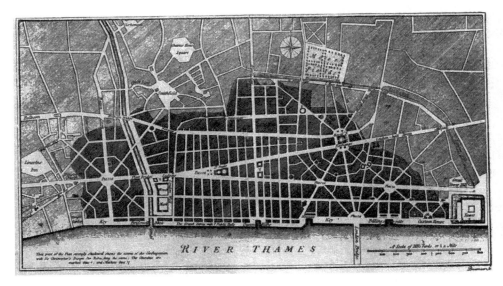

Figure 2.5 Sir Christopher Wren's plan for London
Source (left): Wikimedia Commons

The acquisition of land to implement the proposal would have required autocratic powers. Neither the contemporary parliament nor King Charles II had them. Baron Georges-Eugène Haussmann (1809–91), who worked for Napoléon III in France two centuries later, did.

In the nineteenth century, the École des Beaux Arts proposals were primarily for civic building complexes. The focus of attention was on creating impressive symmetrical axial plans. The generic design is simple in its composition: It consisted of wide boulevards lined with trees and four- or five-story buildings. The boulevards provided grand vistas terminated by major buildings facing squares with central features of fountains, statues, or obelisks. A characteristic of a generic Beaux Arts layout is the 'crow's foot,' a place where three or more avenues start at a central point and fan out from it to give long vistas through a city.

Buildings often enclosed a square at the end of a vista. They were five stories in height, symmetrical and flat roofed and often had rusticated façades. Grand staircases led to large pedimented entrance doors. The façades of the buildings were adorned with sculptures, bas-reliefs, and classical over-scaled details. Ideally, the plans of the buildings were also symmetrical, starting from large entrance halls with grand staircases to more-utilitarian spaces. Colors were subdued and polychrome (Drexler 1977). The overall unity of the design made building complexes imposing.

Specific Designs

Many Renaissance urban designs proposals remained just that. The unimplemented plan for Sforzinda by Filarete (Antonio di Pietro, ca 1400–69) was one of the earliest designs produced for a specific site. It consisted of an eight-point star surrounded by a circular moat. Towers were to be located at the points of the stars and gates at the inner angles. The radial streets met at a central square. A square onto which the palace would face and another for a market were also contained in the plan. Canals for transporting goods were located along every second street.

They were linked to the outside world by a river. The design was based on the belief in the deterministic power of perfect forms to create a perfect society (Rosenau 1959). Palmanova, implemented over a century later in 1593 by the Venetians, is a fine example of a late-sixteenth-century Renaissance plan that is the manifestation of Scamozzi's idea.

Several specific designs were particularly important in the development of twentieth-century urban designs. Versailles (1671) founded by Louis XIV (1638–1715) and Karlsruhe (1715) are among those that have grand axial plans. Louis XIV and Karl III Wilhelm von Baden-Durlach (1679–1738) had the absolute power necessary to ensure that their projects were built. The plan for Versailles has its roads focusing on the Place d'Armees in front of the royal palace. The Karlsruhe scheme is Versailles on a truly grand scale; it has thirty-two streets and avenues radiating out from the palace.

Other seventeenth- and eighteenth-century designs for squares such as the Place Royale (now Place des Vosges, 1605) and the Palais de Luxembourg (1611) and streets such as the

Figure 2.6 An implemented Renaissance new town design: Palmanova
Credit line: Photograph by pio3/Shutterstock.com

Figure 2.7 A Renaissance town design: Bundesverfassungsgericht, Karlsruhe
Source: Biom/Getty Images

Antecedents of Twentieth-Century Design

Avenue de Champs-Élysées (1667) in Paris established many of the design principles that architects followed in the eighteenth and early nineteenth centuries. The Baixa Pombalina plan prepared by Manuel da Maia (1677–1768) and others for Lisbon after the earthquake of 1755 superimposed a gridiron plan starting from the Praça do Comércio on the medieval city. In the early nineteenth century, the Arc de Triomphe at the Place Etoile (1806–36) in Paris designed by Jean Chalgrin (1739–1811) was another precedent for later schemes and was later incorporated by Haussmann into his scheme for the city.

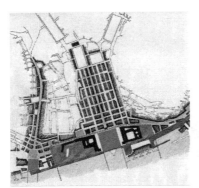 

Figure 2.8 The Baxia Pombalina plan (left) with the Praça do Comércio on the waterfront (right)

Credit line (left): Courtesy of Pedro Ferreira/Bruno Soares Arquitectos
Credit line (right): Photograph by TTstudio/Shutterstock.com

Figure 2.9 Classical St. Petersburg
Credit line: Courtesy of Airpano

In contemporary Russia, the classical design of Saint Petersburg was built during the modernizing efforts of Peter the Great (1672–1725, reigned 1682–1725) and more so during the reign of Catherine the Great (1729–96; empress 1762–96). The planning and architecture were carried out by a succession of international architects, but it was ultimately led primarily by Italian-born Carlo di Giovanni Rossi (1779–1849). St. Petersburg illustrates the grandeur and simplicity of classical designs. The streets and squares have a clear geometrical unity in building height and the pattern of fenestration. The buildings line the streets with their façades, broken only by cross streets (Lavrov and Perov 2016).

Several designs could be chosen as exemplars of classical and baroque design. Those described first (next) are among them. Others that are a hybrid mixture of ideas but are generally regarded as classical designs follow. They are presented in approximately chronological order.

Exemplars of Classical Urban Designs

Zamość, Poland (1580–1600); Piazza del Popolo, Rome, Italy (1811–22); Napoléon III's Paris, France (1854–73); and Vienna, Austria, of Franz Joseph I (1880s)

Zamość, a fortified new town, received World Heritage status in the 1990s as an outstanding example of a planned Renaissance design. It was built for Jan Zamoyski (1542–1605), a wealthy aristocrat, who wished to create a fortress to avoid paying taxes to the Polish royal court. Erected between 1580 and 1600, the town was designed by Bernado Morando (1540–1600) from Padua in Italy. It retains its fortifications (in some places, the walls are 7 meters thick), central square, and many buildings. Later, new towns such as Citadelle Vauban de Neuf-Brisach (1697) in Alsace, France, had much bolder fortifications, due to advances in artillery power. Such fortifications endured until they served no defensive purpose.

Morando, later mayor of the town, created a hexagonal plan for Zamość on a 75-hectare (185-acre) site with a 200-hectare (almost 500-acre) buffer zone around it. The design has two parts: in the west is a precinct for the nobility and in the east, the town proper. It has, like

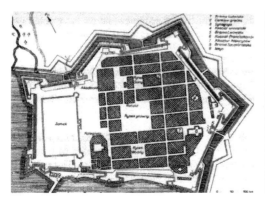 

Figure 2.10 A fortified Renaissance town—Zamość: The plan (left) and an aerial view of the center today with the fortifications beyond (right)

Source (left): Wikimedia Commons
Credit line (right): Photograph by Daniel Jedzura/Shutterstock.com

Antecedents of Twentieth-Century Design

Pietro Cataneo's illustrative proposal (Figure 2.4 left), a grid plan with a square at its center. The buildings around the square were for the burghers of the city. They, along with the palace, arsenal, church, and town hall, were designed by Morando. They reflect pre-baroque, mannerist architectural norms but incorporated central European features such as the sheltering arcaded galleries surrounding the square. Piazza del Popolo, built two centuries later, is closer to the baroque in character.

The Piazza was constructed before the arrival of railroads to Rome. Built inside the Aurelian walls, it functioned as a grand welcoming point for visitors coming from the north. Designed by Giuseppe Valadier (1762–1839), the piazza is reminiscent of Bernini's plan for St. Peter's Square (1656–58). The oval piazza required the demolition of several buildings: a fountain, a trapezoidal square, and some screening walls. It is not a true oval but rather two semi-circles separated by a rectangular area. At its center is a granite Egyptian obelisk of the reign of Seti I (died 1279 BCE). Trees are important, enclosing elements at the two ends of the piazza. ('Popolo' originally meant 'poplar,' not 'people.') Three streets branch out from the piazza into the city, forming the 'trident' (*il Tridente*) or a 'crow's foot.' Twin churches—Santa Maria dei Miracoli (1681) and Santa Maria in Montesanto (1679)—frame the junction of the roads. The churches are similar but are not the same as they would have been in a pure classical design (Fletcher 1954; Giedion 1963; Moore 2016).

Piazza del Popolo was a significant urban renewal project, but it is small in comparison to the redevelopment of Paris under the guidance of Baron Georges-Eugène Haussmann (1809–91) from forty years later. The Industrial Revolution was well underway by then, and migrants were flocking into the city from rural areas. Central Paris was overcrowded, filthy, and crime ridden. The city's streets were described as narrow, disorderly, and monotonous. They stank. British visitors used to the stench of London were horrified to find conditions in Paris, a rich and cultivated metropolis, even worse (Olsen 1986, 37). On top of everything, the city was prone to civil unrest and rioting.

Figure 2.11 Piazza del Popolo, Rome: The plan (left) and a view from the Terrazza del Pincio (right)

Source (left): Wikimedia Commons
Credit line (right): Photograph by Wolfgang M.
Source (right): Wikimedia Commons

The Classical and Beaux Arts Tradition

The rebuilding of Paris began after the street fighting of 1848. Napoléon III (1808–73), when head of the Second French Empire, appointed Haussmann to be prefect of the Seine and instructed him to bring light and air into the heart of Paris and to beautify the city. The design was also to "slash the belly of the center of revolutions" (Haussmann, cited by Hegemann and Peets 1922, 245). The French Senate simplified the laws of expropriation, making property acquisition straightforward. Haussmann was responsible only to Napoléon III and not to Parliament for his actions. The resulting scheme demonstrates the nature of the Beaux Arts approach to urban design on a grand scale. The designs for the Rue de Rivoli and the Champs-Élysées were direct antecedents. Washington, DC, was another precedent on which Haussmann could draw, but its design lacked the purity of character that Haussmann sought.

Haussmann's design necessitated a significant demolition of buildings and the creation of wide new boulevards that, like Pope Sixtus V's Rome, connected key points of the city. The best known of such points is Étoile around the Arc de Triomphe. The boulevards were designed to be pleasant promenades lined with shops, restaurants, theaters, and arcades. Their straight lines also enabled soldiers to control mobs more easily.

Although the individual buildings along the boulevards were developed by different entrepreneurs, the whole composition was unified by building design guidelines. They specified the height of buildings, the proportions of elements in their façades, the mansard roofs with dormer windows, and the use of cream-colored stone (Pinkney 1958). The creation of the street pattern and buildings aligning them were accompanied by major public work projects. The building of sewers transformed Paris as much as they transformed the boulevards. The redesign of Paris had a catalytic effect on property values in the center of the city because it became a pleasanter place to be; they soared. Meanwhile, Vienna was similarly undergoing major redevelopment.

Franz Joseph I (1830–1916), emperor of the Austro-Hungarian Empire (1867–1916), led the building of institutions, open spaces, and residences that provided a grand environment for the lives of Vienna's wealthy (Olsen 1986, 58–81). A major square, Heldenplatz lies in front of the Hofburg, the erstwhile imperial palace. It is a large, classical, green-centered space designed by Pietro Nobile (1774–1854). The Maria-Thereseien-Platz created in 1889 lies adjacent to it.

Figure 2.12 Haussmann's Paris: Etoile (now Place Charles de Gaulle) in 1931 (left) and the Place de l'Opéra, with the opera designed by Charles Garnier (1825–98) (right)

Credit line (left): Photograph by Manselli/Getty Images

Antecedents of Twentieth-Century Design

Figure 2.13   Franz Joseph's Vienna: Heldenplatz with the Imperial Palace extension

It is flanked by two almost identical museums, both designed according to plans by Gottfried Semper (1803–79) and Karl Freiherr von Hosenauer (1833–1894). At the center of the space is a statue of Empress Maria Theresa.

The medieval fortification walls and moats of Vienna were replaced by the Ringstrasse, encircling the city. The boulevard, although it has a somewhat broken character is lined by trees and buildings built to the property line. Gardens and a series of linked formal squares formed by classical buildings replaced the bastions of the fortifications. Designed following guidelines, the buildings were built for the nobility by many of the city's foremost master builders. By the late 1890s, Viennese Art Nouveau, came to the fore as the favored architectural design paradigm; ostentatious pomp and splendor were rejected.

The Heldenplatz, Maria-Thereseien-Platz and the Ringstrasse and the buildings that align them were designed to symbolize the glory of the Hapsburg Empire. Ringstrasse was as much an urban beautification effort as a helpful traffic arterial (Olsen 1986). Consequently, the parallel Lastenstrasse was built outside the former city walls to aid traffic movement. It still does.

Hybrid Examples

Washington, DC, USA (1791); Eixample, Barcelona, Spain (1856); and the Hobrecht Plan for Berlin, Germany (1858–62)

When the idea of a new capital for the United States was first mooted, French Major Pierre Charles L'Enfant (1754–1825), who had fought in the American Revolution, wrote to George Washington (1732–99), the country's wartime general and first president, seeking the commission to design the city. He succeeded despite his letter's being written before Congress's passing the 1800 Residency Act that established the site of the city and the appointment of three commissioners to oversee its planning and the erection of the buildings required for the federal government. L'Enfant assumed his charge was to create a three-dimensional design for the city, but he was responsible only for its plan.

L'Enfant's plan is a combination of a gridiron and axial street pattern. In the center of his scheme is a 400-foot-wide (122-meter-wide), 1-mile-long (1.6-kilometer-long) grand avenue that is now the National Mall. A narrower diagonal avenue, later named Pennsylvania Avenue, links the Capitol (formerly Congress House) and the White House (President's House). Despite its fragmented character, it has become Washington's grand avenue. L'Enfant's plan also contained a canal that passes in front of the Congress and the President's Houses (Reps 1991). The design had a direct antecedent in Karlsruhe, a town sketched by Thomas Jefferson (1743–1826), one of the United States' founders. He passed the drawings on to L'Enfant.

L'Enfant's disagreements with Congress led to the design's being revised by Andrew Ellicott (1754–1820), who eliminated the canal. The design of the US Capitol building was completed in 1800 but was much altered until about 1850, when the current grand neoclassical building was completed (Reps 1991; Reed 2005). Except for the road structure, the Capitol, and the White House, the rest has been built piece by piece over time, controlled by generic zoning codes and various building guidelines. The Eixample in Barcelona, in contrast, was a complete three-dimensional design.

The defensive walls of Barcelona, long obsolete, were demolished in the 1840s, enabling the expansion of the city. The old city housed 187,000 people in squalid, disease-rife conditions at

Figure 2.14 Washington, DC: L'Enfant's plan
Source: Wikimedia Commons

Antecedents of Twentieth-Century Design

a density of 856 people per hectare (contemporary odorous Paris was 400 people per hectare). A design competition held for the city's extension was won by its chief architect, Antonio Rovira i Trias (1816–89), with a radial scheme (Urbano 2016). The central government in Madrid intervened and appointed Cerdà to design the extension, the Eixample.

Cerdà regarded the provision of sunlight, ventilation, access to greenery, and good sewage systems as a basis for urban design. He also understood the importance of a city's having an efficient and coordinated transportation system. He created a design of long straight streets, a gridiron road plan, and diagonal streets. He proposed peripheral blocks with chamfered corners to allow drivers of horse-drawn vehicles to easily see around them. His was an egalitarian plan that catered to all classes of people. Local architects attacked the design as monotonously American with communist-like squares, but the bourgeoisie commissioned leading architects such as Antonio Gaudi i Cornet (1852–1926) to build them houses there (Soria y Puig 1999). The gardens in the center of the blocks were never implemented, and the Eixample's design became more developer friendly.

A more comprehensive approach to city planning and urban design is embedded in the contemporary plan for Berlin prepared in 1862 under the direction of James Hobrecht (1825–1902), a civil engineer. The *Bebauungsplan der Umbebugen Berlins* (*Binding Land Use Plan for the Environs of Berlin*) represented an effort to modernize Berlin. Much attention was paid to the development of the sewerage system, as had been done in London and Paris. The plan, beginning at the regional scale, included two large ring roads, off which arterial roads led into Berlin.

Like Haussmann's plan for Paris, the Hobrecht plan consisted of wide streets and city squares (Bernet 2004), but it lacked an overall coordinating idea. The areas between the axes were divided into rectangular spaces of dense perimeter blocks (the *hinterhof* now a generic type

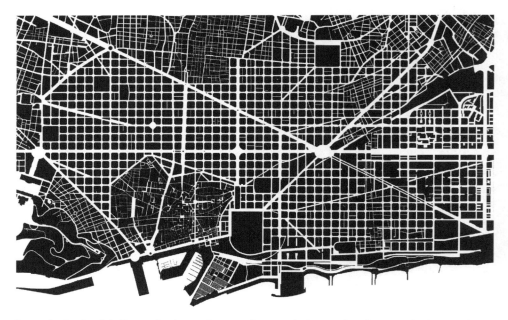

Figure 2.15   Cerdà's Eixample design for Barcelona with the medieval city in the lower left
Credit line: Drawing by psynovec/Shutterstock.com

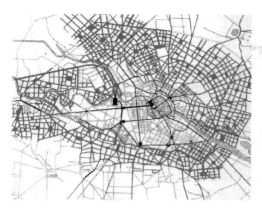 

Figure 2.16 Berlin (1900): The Hobrecht plan (left) and the street forms (right)
Source (left): Bodenschatz (2012, 35); courtesy of DOM Publishers
Credit line (right): Photograph by Claudio Divizia/Shutterstock.com

known as the Berlin block) of mixed-use buildings with minimal setbacks from the streets. The fronts of the blocks facing the street were for the middle class, whereas the interiors were for low-income residents. The interiors soon became overcrowded and, receiving little sunlight, were poor living environments that rapidly deteriorated. The large 160-meter by 200-meter blocks formed long dreary street fronts. It was the type of housing that the German garden city advocates and later architects such as Bruno Taut (1880–1938) argued against. Taut described them as housing of stone that "turned hearts to stone" (Wiedenhoeft (1985, 105).

The block type has proven to be resilient. Many blocks were damaged by Allied bombing during World War Two but were gentrified in the 1990s. The barren streets were planted with trees to enrich the scene, and the blocks adapted to the needs of Berlin's changing population of various socioeconomic levels and ethnic backgrounds. Their potential affordances for a high-quality urban life have been recognized.

Commentary: The Functions Addressed

Classical urban designs from the Renaissance onward were an antidote to what philosophers, civil engineers, and architects saw as the negative characteristics of the medieval city. Although Alberti recognized the positive aspects of the tight, intricate, narrow street pattern of the old cities, their limited exposure to sunlight and their poor sanitary conditions needed to be eliminated. The classical designs and baroque designs opened the city to light and air and thus promoted the health of their populations and their self-esteem.

The impact of the industrial revolution, the massive movement of migrants into cities, and the ravages of cholera and typhoid meant that by the mid nineteenth century, the sewers in cities were totally inadequate. People's poor health had reached a critical level. In addition, the development of the water closet increased the need for better sewerage systems. The work of Joseph Bazalgette (1819–91) in London, Haussmann in Paris, and Hobrecht in Berlin in developing the sewerage systems of those cities substantially improved the health of their citizens and of the major rivers flowing through them. Many other urban renewal schemes in European and US cities of the period were accompanied by new water supply, sewerage, and drainage systems (Melosi 2000).

Antecedents of Twentieth-Century Design

The function of the new designs to promote a sense of security from external military threats decreased as time progressed. In the early Renaissance, defense against cannon shots was a major preoccupation, as can be seen in the design of Zamość. The fortifications took up substantially more space than the town itself did. As military technology advanced, the walled fortifications became redundant. Tearing them down in Barcelona, Vienna, and Asian cities such as Baghdad gave municipal authorities modernizing development opportunities.

Designing for communal life was seldom an expressed concern during the period, but it implicitly underlay many design concepts. The provision of new squares to provide light into the dense city and to act as displays of the power of municipal authorities also provided places for formal gathering, such as markets and religious celebrations. They thus afforded opportunities for a sense of a communal public life and people's identification with a place to develop. Hobrecht assumed that the mixing of accommodations for different social classes within a single Berlin block would attain a degree of social cohesion, but the propinquity intensified the stratification.

The classical and baroque designs with their splendid axial and, often tree-lined, boulevards were both routes for vehicular movement and major aesthetic displays. They were prestigious, and the cities that possess them remain so. The boulevards and squares give a city its character and its citizens a sense of pride. The designs thus functioned in a twofold manner. First, they expressed, through their architecture and street pattern, that their cities were up-to-date, and second, they functioned as an expression of the power of those in control.

During the early Renaissance, the location of the palace was a central feature of any design. The power of the church was also expressed by its prominence on the central square of new developments. The expression of the individualism of a citizen was not a concern, except for the houses of the nobility. They had the wealth to commission distinctive houses for themselves within the framework of any city plan, whether it be the Eixample of Barcelona or the Ringstrasse of Vienna.

The projects gave their designers, often architects but sometimes civil servants or engineers, a mode of self-expression, even though the designs all followed a contemporary urban design paradigm. The urban design schemes are clearly associated with their designers. We talk of L'Enfant's Washington, Haussmann's Paris, Cerdà's Barcelona, and Hobrecht's Berlin. The projects also functioned to enhance the reputation of their sponsors. Sixtus V and Napoléon III, for instance, are remembered today for the projects they commissioned more than for anything else they accomplished.

Observations

Renaissance ideals attracted the attention of many designers and their patrons. The plans of Philadelphia in the United States (1682) and Adelaide in Australia (1837) are similar to Cataneo's model, but without its fortification. The idea that a new town with a central square or featured building to it gives it an identity and clear boundaries, even if not formed by a fortification but by an open greenbelt, is still with us today.

Implementing grand designs was, and still is, considerably easier on greenfield than brownfield sites. L'Enfant's plan for Washington was for a greenfield site; Haussmann's plan for Paris was an urban renewal project. There was little apart from the topography and the location of waterways to constrain the layout of the former; the latter had to be ruthlessly driven through medieval Paris.

Haussmann's Paris has been an inspiration for city planners and urban designers ever since it was implemented. Adaptations of generic classical and baroque urban plans can be found not

The Classical and Beaux Arts Tradition

Figure 2.17 The European Classical in Japanese hands: The 1932 Changchun plan (left) and Hsinking Avenue (right)
Credit line (left): Map by Shinkyō
Source (left): Wikimedia Commons
Source (right): Wikimedia Commons

only in France but also in the country's colonial cities, such as Hanoi and Beirut. Japanese planners produced several such plans for Chinese cities during Japan's occupation of China during the 1930s. The only one to be implemented was Changchun (Hsinking under the Japanese), the capital of Japan's puppet state of Manchukuo. It has grand axial boulevards and classical public buildings (Meyer 2015). More importantly, many cities have aspired to have a grand Haussmann boulevard. Andrássy út (1872) in Budapest, Kurfürstendamm (late 1800s) in Berlin, Avenida 9 de Julio in Buenos Aires (1912), the Boulevard of the Victory of Socialism in Bucharest (1970s), and the contemporaneous development of Pyongyang in North Korea are all Paris's descendants. In the United States, the principles of Haussmann's Paris formed the basis of the early-twentieth-century City Beautiful movement. Bold gestures though they are, none has captured Paris's elegance.

Key References

Argan, Giulio C. 1970. *The Renaissance City (Planning and Cities)*. New York: George Braziller.
Carthian, Jean Paul. 1979. "The Ecole des Beaux Arts: Modes and Manners." *Journal of Art Education* 33 (2): 7–17.
Drexler, Arthur, ed. 1977. *The Architecture of the École des Beaux-Arts*. New York: Museum of Modern Art.
Fletcher, Bannister. 1954. *A History of Architecture on the Comparative Method*. Sixteenth edition. London: Batsford.
Olsen, Donald J. 1986. *The City as a Work of Art: London, Paris, Vienna*. New Haven and London: Yale University Press.
Pinkney, David H. 1958. *Napoleon III and the Rebuilding of Paris*. Princeton, NJ: Princeton University Press.

3

Social and Philanthropic Urban Design

The Industrial Revolution and the accompanying philosophies of economic utilitarianism and materialism in Europe and the Americas led to cities' sprawling as their populations swelled. William Morris (1834–96) deplored, in his 1884 lecture "Art and Socialism," the way London was "swallowing up with loathsomeness field and wood and heath" (Morris 2012, 207). While the wealthy led sheltered lives, workers lived in congested, squalid, and polluted slums. As many as a dozen shared a room. Public houses were ubiquitous, and workers were seen to be consuming their wages in whiskey and gin. Crime was rampant. Diseases such as tuberculous and rickets were endemic; cholera was a regular visitor. The cities in Asia were comparatively hygienic.

The Conditions of the Working Class in England, written by Friedrich Engels in 1845, provided a bleak analysis of the degraded living condition of the workers in the north of England. Bradford was described in the following terms in its newspaper:

> There are scores of wretched hovels, unfurnished and unventilated, damp, filthy in the extreme and surrounded by stagnant pools of human excrement and everything offensive and disgusting to sight and smell. No sewers, no drainage, no ventilation. Nothing to be seen but squalid wretchedness on every side . . . all this is to be seen in the centre of this wealthy emporium of the worsted trade.
>
> *(Bradford Observer, October 16, 1845)*

No wonder civic reformers were horrified when comparing such scenes with their own more-salubrious homes. They sought change. Many twentieth-century urban designs ideas were imbued with the same spirit.

Antecedent Ideas

Philanthropic efforts to meet the housing needs of the poor have a long, if disjointed, history. The Fuggerei (1516) in Augsburg, Germany, founded by Jakob Fugger still exists. It was, however, the experimental communities of the eighteenth century that led to the major reform efforts of the industrializing nineteenth. An eighteenth-century example is the Royal Salt Works at Arc-et-Senans in France (1774–79) designed by Claude-Nicholas Ledoux (1726–1806), a

54

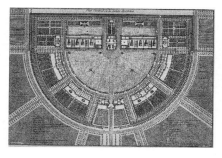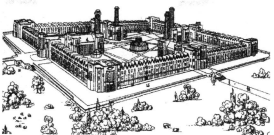

Figure 3.1 Experimental urban forms: The Salt Works at Arc-et-Senans (left) and the design for an Owenite community at Harmony, Indiana (right)

Source (left): Wikimedia Commons
Source (right): Wikimedia Commons

neoclassical architect. While not a philanthropic gesture, its design represents the search for ideal forms that also possessed operational efficiencies and housed workers well.

The town was circular, an ideal shape for Ledoux (as it was for al-Mansur when designing Baghdad). The form also recognized the functional hierarchy of the tasks involved in running a salt works. An entrance building is located on the circumference of the circle. On one side of it are guardrooms and a prison; on the other is a forge. Carpenters,' laborers,' marshals,' and coopers' quarters are also located on the perimeter. The director's house is situated at the center of the circle. Behind it are the stables, and on each side of it are the salt works (Gruson 2008). The scheme was regarded as too grand for the revolutionary spirit of the times, so little was built. Ledoux's idealistic concepts were exemplified in the model villages of the nineteenth century. Other utopian communities challenging conservative social norms were established in Europe and the United States during the eighteenth century (Hayden 1976).

Among the first religion-based communities in the United States were those of the Shakers (the United Society of Believers in Christ's Second Coming). Practicing celibacy, their failure to continuously recruit new members led to their demise, but their parsimonious designs are reflected in twentieth-century minimalist architecture. The Shakers' first settlement was Niskayuna (later named Watervliet) built in the 1780s. Better known ones, such as New Lebanon (1788), followed. Another important settlement was the financially successful communist sect of Rappites (named for their leader George Rapp [1757–1847]).

In the early nineteenth century, the Rappites built Harmony in Pennsylvania (1804), another Harmony (1814) in Indiana, and Economy (1824) in Pennsylvania. The towns much influenced Robert Owen, who bought the Pennsylvanian Harmony and renamed it New Harmony. In 1824, he proposed another Harmony for Indiana, this time designed by Thomas Stedman Whitwell (1784–1840). Many manifestoes stating what reformers were trying to achieve and the mechanisms for doing so were written in the eighteenth and nineteenth centuries. Only a few are mentioned here, to illustrate the spirit that drove much urban design thinking in the twentieth century.

Manifestoes and Paradigms

Those that give a picture of the attitudes that led to change away from purely pragmatic designs can be said to have begun with that of Mary Wollstonecraft (1759–97). An English philosopher

Antecedents of Twentieth-Century Design

and advocate for women's rights, she was an early seeker for a better quality of life for working people (Wollstonecraft 1796). In 1801, Thomas Spence published *The Constitution of Spensonia; A Country of Fairy-land situated between Utopia and Oceania*. Benjamin Disraeli (1804–81), twice prime minister of the United Kingdom, published his novel *Sybil* in 1845. In it, he describes a factory located in rural surroundings with an attractive village for workers adjoining it. Sir Benjamin Ward Robinson (1828–96) proposed *Hygeia* (1876), a city with an efficient sanitary system and well-spaced houses with gardens. It was, however, *The Manifesto of the Communist Party*, by Karl Marx and Friedrich Engels, published in 1848, that has had a profound and lasting effect on politics, social reform, housing movements, and art and art history. Their thesis was that societies develop through class struggles for control, between the bourgeoisie and the laboring classes. The two believed that the structural contradictions in capitalism would lead to socialist societies. Socialist ideas were already underpinning many designs, and they persisted well into the twentieth century.

The advocacies of some reformers had a direct influence on later urban design thought. Robert Owen, as already noted, believed that the social and built environment in which people lived, not their genetic qualities, governed their health and intellectual development. He argued that social and psychological concerns should be addressed first when thinking about how to improve people's lives. That idea remains central to progressive urban design thought. His ideal was the small industrial village/town established as a cooperative venture. Similar sentiments were expressed by Claude Henri de Saint-Simon (1760–1825) in France. While Saint-Simon believed that individual expertise and enterprise were the basis for human advancement, he nevertheless linked socialism with the notion of progress.

Activists for social reform, such as Octavia Hill (1836–1912), were strong advocates for building good housing for the poor. She opposed governments' providing such accommodations, arguing that they would be impersonal; she expected philanthropists to fund sound housing through social welfare organizations (Hill 1875). She also fought for more open space in working-class areas of cities and was largely responsible for keeping large tracts of land in London, such as Hampstead Heath, as parkland.

One of the most important movements that combined social goals with physical settings was the Settlement House Movement that began in the United Kingdom in 1884 but was particularly strong in the United States. Funded by wealthy philanthropists with the goal of raising the economic and moral well-being of the poor, the settlement houses had educational, health, and childcare facilities. The first was Toynbee Hall in London; in the United States, it was Hull House in Chicago. Paralleling these efforts, social activists were developing laws to improve the quality of the built environment of cities.

Zoning laws and building codes specifying how cities should be developed to ensure healthy living environments have a history stretching back to the Persian and Egyptian empires and the earlier developments in the Indus Valley. In the nineteenth century, beginning in Germany, they were strongly promoted by social reformers. The creation of zoning laws affected the height and form of buildings and the morphology of a city by restricting what can be built where and its shape (Talen 2012).

Generic Concepts and Illustrative Designs

Social reformers who produced illustrative designs of their vison of a good industrial town invariably placed them in the countryside. Two influential generic designs demonstrate the attitudes in much contemporary thinking. They are Owen's self-supporting industrial town and Victoria, a model temperance community, proposed by James Silk Buckingham (1786–1855).

Social and Philanthropic Urban Design

Owen's design, was for a self-sufficient community of about 1,200 people. Communal buildings were located at the center of an open space at the core of the development, with housing in large gardens around them. The factory was located outside a circumferential road. The agricultural belt around the settlement would provide food for it. Such communities, Owen suggested, should be located at a distance from each other. They could form a commonwealth safeguarding their mutual interests. Such ideas were picked up the garden city movement.

Buckingham presented a symmetrical and spacious village model, which like the Mormons' City of Zion, would be 1 square mile in size (Buckingham 1849). It would be a salubrious settlement with good drainage and exposure to sunlight and have clean air for its residents. The layout consists of a series of nested squares decreasing in size and becoming more prestigious toward the center. He accepted the contemporary socioeconomic hierarchy of society, so his plan showed no social reordering. The outer square would house 1,000 workers. Next toward the center would be an arcade for workshops, followed by larger houses, retail shops, and even larger houses closer to the center. At the settlement's core would be a park surrounded by large mansions and public buildings. Some suburban villas would be located outside the town. Also located in the countryside 0.5 miles (880 meters) outside the town would be the factory using the latest in steam technology. While Buckingham's model attracted some attention, only his proposal for an association to administer the development of new villages was taken up elsewhere. A more influential generic idea that had a major impact on twentieth-century design ideas was the early-nineteenth-century utopia the phalanstère, proposed by Charles Fourier (1772–1837) in France.

The phalanstère provided families with an acceptable minimum standard of life in a communal setting. A phalanstère would have 1,620 people living in a single structure. The traditional house, Fourier observed, was a place of oppression for women. Although families had private apartments, in a phalanstère, many activities, such as cooking and child-rearing, would be shared, an idea present not only in twentieth-century feminist design concepts but also in the cohousing movement (Durrett and McCamant 1988). Fourier proposed that 6 million phalanstères, loosely governed by a World Congress, be built in the world.

The proposed phalanstère comprised a central component and two lateral wings. The center was designed for quiet activities. It included dining rooms, meeting rooms, libraries, and study rooms. A lateral wing was designed for noisy activities, such as carpentry, hammering, and forging, and for childcare, because playing children are noisy. The other wing contained a

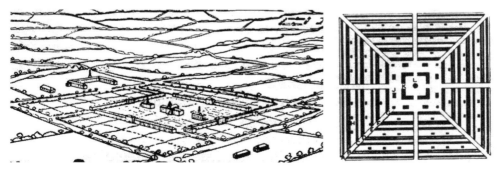

Figure 3.2 Model town proposals: Robert Owen's self-supporting industrial town (left) and Buckingham's Temperance Community (right)

Source (left and right): Gallion and Eisner (1993); courtesy of John Wiley & Sons

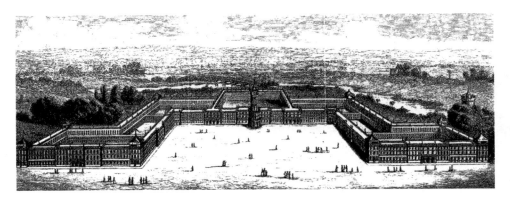

Figure 3.3 Fourier's phalanstère
Credit line: Drawing by Charles Fourier
Source: Wikimedia Commons

caravansary, ballrooms, and halls for meetings with outsiders who had to pay a fee to visit the community. This income was predicted to be sufficient to sustain the autarchic economy—one where the leaders have complete control—of the phalanstère.

Fourier inspired the work of Jean-Baptiste André Godin (1817–88) in Guise in France and the founding of several communities in the United States, such as the Phalanx in New Jersey. The US settlements were short-lived ventures, but Fourier's influence has been long-lasting and is seen most clearly in two different twentieth-century approaches to urban design, as represented in the proposals of Le Corbusier and the advocacies of Dolores Hayden (b. 1945; see Hayden 1984).

Specific Designs

The efforts of social reformers, accompanied by the interest of several industrialists, led to the building of model industrial communities. These "villages of vision" provided generous accommodations by contemporary standards and supporting facilities for workers and their families (Darley 1978). They were philanthropic gestures that enhanced the financial return on the industry owner's investments by increasing worker productivity. Many of the model towns were also based on strong moral convictions.

Two of the earliest towns were founded in Ireland. One was Portlaw (1826), founded by the Malcolmson family, members of the Society of Friends (the Quakers). Another Quaker, John Grubb Richardson (1813–91) established the linen-factory town of Bessbrook (1846). Its design brief was guided by three Ps: no public house and no pawn shop and consequently no need for police (Waterford County Museum 2010).

Sir Titus Salt (1803–1876), a nonconformist congregationalist, was an early British industrialist who provided a salubrious living environment for workers at Saltaire. In France were *Le Familistère* at Guise (1856), built by Jean-Baptiste André Godin (1817–88), and Noisiel-sur-Seine (1870), created around their chocolate works by the Menier family. In the Netherlands, Agnetapark (1888) in Delft was designed by Eugene Gugel (1832–1905) for Dutch industrialist Jacques Van Marken (1845–1906) and his wife, Agneta.

Port Sunlight in Merseyside, England, was built by the Lever brothers to house workers in their soap factory. Its civic center design has a baroque layout that Lewis Mumford suggests is of

Social and Philanthropic Urban Design

Figure 3.4 A model industrial village: Noisiel-sur-Seine, the factory (left) and Place des Pompes (right)
Credit line (left and right): Courtesy of Archives départementales de Seine-et-Marne

"comic precision" (Mumford 1961, Plate 41). Bournville outside Birmingham was built by the Quaker family of George Cadbury (1839–1922). New Earswick, near York, was developed by Joseph Rowntree (1836–1925), another Quaker. Designed by Raymond Unwin (1863–1940), it was a company town housing both managers and workers. In Germany, the Essen villages were developed by the Krupp brothers around their munitions factory. In the United States, Pullman, Illinois, was founded in the 1880s by George Pullman (1831–97) for his railcar company and Hershey by Milton Hershey (1857–1945), a Mennonite, for his chocolate works. Hershey differs from many model towns that favored row houses; it has tree-lined streets of individual houses. The goal was to avoid the perceived monotony of row houses. In Germany, the Krupp family built a succession of model villages associated with its factories.

Many of the industrial new towns were designed by leading architects or landscape architects. Frederick Law Olmsted (1822–1903) was the designer of Vandergrift, Pennsylvania (1895), for the Apollo Iron and Steel Company. Olmsted's middle-class suburban designs, such as Riverside, Illinois (see Chapter 4), served as precedents. The Güell family employed Antonio Gaudi i Cornet for the creation of Colònia Güell (1890s) south of Barcelona for their textile industry. McKim, Mead, and White designed Roanoke Rapids in North Carolina, Naugatuck in Connecticut, and Echota in New York (1894). Good housing, generous open spaces, and the segregation of commercial, manufacturing, and residential areas were common to all these model settlements.

Exemplars of Model Industrial Towns

Saltaire, Yorkshire, England, UK (1851–76), and the Krupp brothers' Villages at Essen, Germany (1850–1903)

Sir Titus Salt, influenced by the philanthropic employer in Disraeli's *Sybil*, developed the town of Saltaire outside Bradford. The town (a UNESCO World Heritage site) lies in the picturesque Aire River valley and is named after its founder and the river. At 25 acres (about 10 hectares) in size, Saltaire was also served by the Leeds and Liverpool Canal and by a railroad. The town's layout, the mill, and the church were designed by Henry Charles Lockwood (1811–78), a local architect (Banerjee undated). He favored an Italianate style for the buildings.

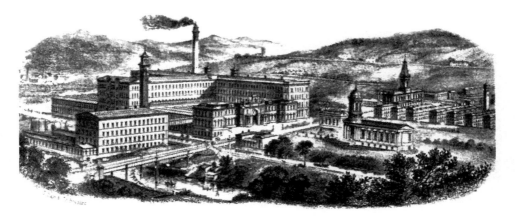

Figure 3.5 Saltaire: The spinning mill and town
Credit line: Courtesy of The Victorian Web

The spinning mill wove worsted from coarse Russian donskoi and Peruvian alpaca wools. It was originally water powered, but large steam engines soon replaced the water wheels. The mill is located at the head of the town adjacent to the railroad. Its 250-foot (76-meter) chimney, fitted with patented fuel economizers and pollution-reduction devices, towers over the building. Its design was based on Santa Maria Gloriosa dei Frari in Venice (Leach and Pevsner 2009). The mill itself is symmetrical and five stories and basement in height. The façade has two central arches with matching turrets topped with belvederes. Large windows provide light and ventilation to the interior. A warehouse stretches from it to the rail tracks.

The town is laid out in gridiron pattern. As can be seen in Figure 3.5, a main street, Victoria Road, crosses a bridge above a curving weir in the Aire and another bridge over the canal. The park and playing fields lie alongside it. The road goes past the office building, and the United Reformed Church with its tower topped by a cupola lies opposite it. On the other side of the railroad tracks is Victoria Hall and rows of workers' housing. Their layout is like that in the standard industrial towns of northern England that so enraged Engels, but the houses were larger and had efficient plumbing. More importantly, the workers could afford the rents. In total, the town has 850 houses and forty-five almshouses.

Designing for a communal life and a sense of community is a concern in much neighborhood design today. Salt, although not a teetotaler, prohibited public houses—the traditional gathering place in English villages—in the town. The Saltaire Club and Institute was the substitute. Although the United Reformed Church is prominent, Salt, unlike atheist Robert Owen, allowed workers to follow their own religious preferences. He provided building sites for Wesleyans, Primitive Baptists, and Roman Catholics as well as a room for Swedenborgians. Schools and an infirmary also formed part of the town. Allotments were provided for gardening. Salt, a benevolent autocrat, was held in high esteem. Reportedly, 100,000 people lined the route of his funeral cortège. The Krupps were similarly autocratic and respected.

The Krupp family involvement with arms production dates from the seventeenth century, but it only took off when Alfred F. A. Krupp (1818–87) took over the company at the age of fourteen, upon the death of his father in 1826. The invention of the patented spoon roller by his brother Hermann in 1841 enabled the steel mills to prosper. The company demanded highly skilled labor and total commitment from its workers (Manchester 2003). In return, Krupp

Social and Philanthropic Urban Design

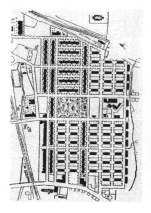

Figure 3.6 Kronenberg: The plan (left) and a view of the tenements in 1910 (right)
Credit line (left): Collection of the author
Credit line (right): Photographer unknown
Source (right): Wikimedia Commons

provided them with housing colonies replete with parks, sports facilities, and nondenominational schools (Benevolo 1971). He also provided social services, sick relief funds, pensions, and benefits for widows and children.

The first Krupp workers' colonies were laid out in a gridiron pattern with long barrack-like tenement blocks lined up in parallel rather like many twentieth-century modernist housing estates. Over time, the number of colonies was greatly expanded. Those neighborhoods built in Essen by Alfred Krupp were Arbeiterkolonie Westend, Stadtpark, and Kolonie Kronenberg, which is illustrated in Figure 3.6.

Later colonies, developed under the leadership of Friedrich Alfred Krupp (1854–1902), had picturesque houses in gardens. After 1903, new housing along the lines of garden suburbs were planned. The large Siedlung Margarethenhöhe (see Figure 4.8) illustrates the evolution of housing in the Krupp villages from tenement blocks to detached houses. The later towns were hybrids of vernacular, garden city, and modernist patterns. They are not the only hybrid examples.

Hybrid Models

Le Familistère de Guise, France (1856), and Echota, New York, USA (1893)

Several nineteenth-century model villages associated with industries were a mixture of ideas. Some were parts of existing towns and relied on them for many services. Le Familistère de Guise of Jean-Baptiste André Godin and Echota developed by the Niagara Falls Company in upstate New York are examples. The latter is close to being a standard suburban subdivision but one with communal facilities. In common, the two began as autocratic developments but became democratic in operation.

Godin was a manufacturer of cast-iron stoves and cookware. He began work on an industrial and residential enclave in the town of Guise in 1846, having decided to relocate his factory there to take advantage of a new railroad line. Planned for a population of about 1,600 people,

Antecedents of Twentieth-Century Design

its development paralleled Haussmann's work in Paris. Construction began soon after the 1848 workers' uprisings in France. Given that it was in an established town, Godin did not have to provide the amenities that the town already provided.

Built on a 7-hectare (18-acre) site, the complex consisted of the factory and the Familistère in three large buildings. The main building, where the families were housed, was formed by three large four-story rectangular structures joined at the corner. In the center of each building was a large hall surrounded by galleries, off which were the workers' accommodations. Each family had an apartment of three or four rooms. The hall was for children to play in all weathers and for communal gatherings. Opposite the main building was a theater and an infant school.

Although begun autocratically, Godin turned over the administration of the Familistère to a cooperative society in 1880. The factory continued to operate and was eventually bought by the conglomerate, Le Creuset, in the 1950s. The cooperative society was disbanded in 1968 and the apartments sold to individual investors. In the twenty-first century, the Familistère has undergone considerable rehabilitation. Echota had a much shorter life as a company village.

Echota village, built in 1894, is really a suburban development, not a new town. It was designed by Stanford White (1853–1906) of McKim, Mead, and White (Roth 1979). The Niagara Falls Power Company had already erected a power station, designed by White, nearby. The town, described as utopian, was laid out in a gridiron pattern by the company's engineers on an 84-acre (34-hectare) site. The company provided reticulated water and a sewerage system. The village consisted of sixty-seven single-family houses, some duplex units, and three- and four-story row houses. Shops, a railroad station, a fire station, and a school completed the neighborhood. The residential units were rented to the company's workers at nominal rates (Linnabery 2016).

The paved streets were lined with maple trees and elm trees, which gave a visual unity to the whole design. The houses, though small, were carefully planned to have efficient circulation patterns and good cross ventilation. They were clad in wooden shingles or clapboard and had the qualities that McKim, Mead, and White had perfected in the 1880s. The buildings were sparingly detailed with natural wood colors and white trim but became livelier when painted after the 1901 Pan-American exhibition in nearby Buffalo made bright colors fashionable. Unusual for its time, even for opulent neighborhoods, each house had indoor plumbing and

Figure 3.7 The Familistère at Guise; the factory lies across the river
Credit line: Courtesy of the Familistère at Guise

Social and Philanthropic Urban Design

Figure 3.8 Echota village: A typical street of single-family houses
Credit line: Courtesy of the Niagara County Historical Society

electricity (Crawford 1995; Linnabery 2016). In 1900, the company sold the units to their tenants, and in 1910, it sold the village; the area then began to decline before being rediscovered and revived by individual householders much later.

Commentary: The Functions Addressed

While the utilitarian function of the model industrial villages was to provide basic accommodations for workers, they were self-consciously designed to create a salubrious everyday living environment. The objective was to reduce absenteeism in the workforce and thus to increase the profitability of an enterprise by providing a decent standard of living to workers. The location of many of the villages in the countryside functioned to dissipate the smoke generated from the steam engines that were driving machinery and it afforded recreational opportunities for workers in clean rural air. Being close to nature was also expected to achieve spiritual benefits by bringing workers closer to God.

An additional design goal of the model villages was to uplift the spirits of workers and to obtain their loyalty. In return, they obtained job and residential security. Any sense of individuality was subjugated. While families may have had their individual quarters, each unit was the same as the others. Higher-ranked workers' status was indicated by their having larger units.

Symbolically, the model towns functioned as a demonstration of social reformers' and some industrialists' concern for the working classes. For many industrialists, providing these was a good deed that they hoped would lead to their own salvation after death (Darley 1978). They, along with politicians, also sought to stifle unrest among workers by enhancing their quality of life. This position was later reflected in the choice that Le Corbusier offered society: "Architecture or Revolution?" (Le Corbusier 1922, cited in Neil Leach 2009, 207).

The function of the facilities provided for the workers was to establish a sense of community bound together by a common cause. The goals were to enhance workers' moral well-being, to provide for their spiritual life, and to educate them in the manner that the company owners considered fit. Owen's Institute for the Formation of Character (1816) at New Lanark is an

Antecedents of Twentieth-Century Design

example of what the reformers were attempting to achieve, although, as an atheist, he was little concerned about the spiritual life of his workers.

Observations

An extraordinary number of industrial villages were built as model settlements (see Darley 1978, 273–311, for an extensive list of those in the United Kingdom and Ireland). The review in this chapter focused on the European and North American experience, because industrialization took place there first, but similar villages were founded in Latin America and Asia. In India, they were often associated with the development and maintenance of the railroads. Railway colonies, such as that at Kharagpur, remain in operation to this day. They were built according to British models and originally for higher-echelon British railroad workers, not peons.

All these towns can be seen either as an effort in social control or as an example of the thoughtfulness of industrialists. The same attitudes are reflected in many later-twentieth-century rationalist and empiricist designs.

Key References

Benevolo, Leonardo. 1971. *The Origins of Modern Town Planning*. Translated from the Italian by Judith Landry. Cambridge, MA: MIT Press.

Crawford, Margaret. 1995. *Building the Workingman's Paradise: The Design of American Company Towns*. London and New York: Verso.

Darley, Gillian. 1978. *Villages of Vision: A Study of Strange Utopias*. St. Albans: Granada.

Gallion, Arthur B. and Simon Eisner. 1993. *The Urban Pattern: City Planning and Design*. Sixth edition. Hoboken, NJ: John Wiley.

Hayden, Dolores. 1976. *Seven American Utopias: The Architecture of Communitarian Socialism*. Cambridge, MA: MIT Press.

Manchester, William. 2003. *The Arms of Krupp: 1587–1968: The Rise and Fall of the Industrial Dynasty That Armed Germany at War*. Boston, MA: Back Bay, Little, Brown, originally 1968.

Mumford, Lewis. 1961. *The City in History, Its Origins, Its Transformations, and Its Prospects*. London: Secker & Warburg.

4
The Garden Suburb

The image of suburbia is one of independent houses sitting in spacious gardens set in exurban surroundings. The first cities had such scattered developments on their fringes. Wealthy residents of ancient Rome sought refuge in the countryside, where they could breathe clean air and escape the diseases rife in the city. The growth of the scattered residences into coherent and denser suburbs during the nineteenth century served a similar purpose. People with the financial means to escape from the squalor and pollution of Coketown sought a cleaner, heatheir, and greener environment for themselves and their children. William Wilberforce (1759–1833), the abolitionist, for instance, moved with his family from London to Clapham, outside it. He was an early commuter. He wanted to escape the vices of the city while retaining his offices in it. In later life, he moved back to the city to take advantage of the range of offerings that Clapham lacked (Schlossberg 2000).

Many suburbs were pragmatically developed and designed. They were laid out without any central guiding idea behind their design other than to provide easy-to-sell houses and a handsome profit for their property developers. What, then, is a garden suburb? In everyday usage, often the only element that differentiates what is called a garden suburb from any suburban residential development is the amount of vegetation it flaunts. A true garden suburb has, however, a core area that provides the full range of amenities required for daily life and easy access to external employment opportunities.

Antecedent Ideas

The garden suburb, as it appeared in the mid nineteenth century as a development type in Britain, was inspired by several overlapping antecedents. One was the English village and a second the English country landscape. Villages were small in area and population but possessed the basic amenities of life: homes, a church, a tavern, and a grocer. It had a green, which served the dual purpose of flood control and a place for recreation. If large enough, a village might have a market square, although the green was often used for that purpose. The open countryside was nearby.

Some villages were self-consciously created as an entity by English estate owners who wanted to build or relocate settlements on their lands. An example is Milton Abbas in Dorset, a highly

Figure 4.1   A self-consciously designed English Village: Milton Abbas
Credit line: Photograph by Karen Balkin/Shutterstock.com

autocratic development. In 1780, its owner, Joseph Damer (1718–98), the earl of Dorchester, commissioned architect Sir William Chambers (1723–96) and Capability Brown to design a new village. He wished to remove housing that intruded on the view from his mansion. The existing village was demolished, the villagers relocated, and the site landscaped by Brown. Milton Abbas was built out of the earl's sight to contain thirty-six semi-detached thatched cottages set in rows on both sides of a central road, forming a unified composition. Each cottage has a lawn in front of it and had a horse chestnut tree planted between it and its neighbor. Built from cob, the cottages were painted yellow (although they are now white). It and similar villages were the inspiration for the garden suburb. The first garden suburbs in Britain were also shaped by a change in tastes.

The English landscape paradigm replaced the more formal baroque garden as the accepted landscape architectural type. It had two major antecedents: the paintings of rural landscapes by Claude Lorrain (1606–82) and Nicholas Poussin (1594–1665) in France and the Chinese garden, which had recently become known in Europe. The asymmetrical nature of the Chinese garden and the sweeping vistas portrayed in the paintings captured the imagination. The picturesque city parks also impressed. Birkenhead Park, an early publicly funded urban park, shaped the thoughts of Frederick Law Olmsted (1822–1903), the first major US landscape architect and the codesigner of Riverside in Illinois. He had visited it during his travels (Olmsted 1852).

The suburbs that appeared in Britain at the end of the eighteenth century to meet the aspirations of a growing prosperous merchant class formed a third antecedent of the garden suburb. A housing estate now swallowed up in London that might be regarded as a garden suburb was the development at St. John's Wood (Galinou 2010). The neighborhood was designed for people who sought a country environment but could not afford to build grand country

Figure 4.2 "Landscape with the Marriage of Isaac and Rebecca" (1648) by Claude Lorrain (left) and the Shanghai Yuyuan, Shanghai (right)

Source (left and right): Wikimedia Commons

Figure 4.3 Housing development types in London: A mansion in St John's Wood (left) and housing for the wealthy in Belgravia (right)

houses. They were members of the middle class, including returned nabobs who had made their, often-ill-gotten, fortunes in British India. An early plan (1803) by architect John Shaw (1776–1870) consisted of detached and semi-detached villas surrounded by gardens. Its design stood in sharp contrast to the row house development in areas such as Belgravia in contemporary London. Shaw's design had an inner circle of thirty-six residences and an outer of sixty-four semi-detached houses (M@ 2017). This layout gave way to a more pragmatic gridiron plan. The site was subdivided, and the plots were sold to developers, who built individual houses in a setting of gardens and tree-lined streets.

Manifestoes and Paradigms

The written arguments describing and explaining why its advocates considered the garden suburb to be a good idea and the characteristics that it should possess were not contemporary to its first development. They are largely from the twentieth century. Many manifestoes were presented in now largely forgotten pamphlets and essays (e.g., H. Barnett 1905). Other treatises are well known. *Town Planning in Practice: An Introduction to the Art of Designing Cities and Suburbs* (1909) by Raymond Unwin (1863–1943), a social and political radical, is one. Unwin believed that all urban planning should start with the creation of homes in pleasant surroundings. Hermann Muthesius (1861–1927), author of *The English House* (1904), argued for the adoption of the garden suburb as the ideal residential model for the middle class in Germany. Later, Lewis Mumford, the US historian and critic, promoted the type in his books *The Culture of Cities* (1938) and *The City in History* (1961). The boldest statement is even more recent: *Paradise Planned: The Garden Suburb and the Modern City* (Stern, Fishman, and Tilove 2013).

The garden suburb concept was developed as an alternative to the pragmatic residential developments that were taking place on the periphery of cities. Possessing all the necessary facilities for daily life other than employment, it was promoted as an ideal environment for family life close to both the countryside and the city. Advocates argued that it provided a safe environment and a sense of community in which neighbors looked out for each other. Children could roam independently throughout the suburb. In temperate climates, seasonal changes added to the enjoyment of adults and the vicarious education of children. The assumption was that the garden suburb would be populated by a socioeconomically homogenous group of people. Another assumption was that the man of the family would be the breadwinner and the woman the household manager.

Advocates stated that a suburb should have heart, a village center, places of worship, shops, and community facilities. The center is the place from where the suburb should be linked to the outside world; in the case of the railroad suburb, it would be by train. The layout should be based on the existing topography and natural features of a locale. Roads should be lined with trees and designed to form a unified composition. The goal was to create an effect of tranquility and peace. Such feelings, it was argued, are enhanced by the introduction of large areas of greenery and elements such as ponds with paths running between them. The interplay of light and shade was regarded as important in obtaining a feeling of tranquility. The combination, it was believed, would raise the spirits of the residents of such developments (Miller and Gray 1992; Galinou 2010).

Generic Concepts and Illustrative Designs

A garden suburb is usually located on the periphery of a city and linked to its center by some mode of transport. Several were built around new railroad stations as train lines spread out from the city. In the era of the streetcar, or tram, garden suburbs were streetcar developments. Others are automobile suburbs (Stern and Massengale 1981). A few were neighborhoods built within cities as sites became available for development.

Two basic types of layout patterns for garden suburbs can be found: the gridiron and the ruralistic. The former is the standard generic and more pragmatic model. The latter is the type to be employed on sloping sites so that the roads follow the contour lines of the topography. Often, however, the type has been employed simply to create a picturesque, romantic setting reminiscent of country roads. In contrast, the grid plan has been superimposed on sloping sites, sometimes steeply sloping, that automatically gives a suburb a picturesque appearance. In either case, but especially in the ruralistic garden suburb, there would be no sidewalks. In both the gridiron and ruralistic types, the houses are set back from the road. In the United Kingdom, the houses are surrounded by walls or hedges, but in North America, only the backyard of a house is likely to be enclosed (Stern, Fishman, and Tilove 2013). In Islamic countries, the walls surrounding a home are, ideally, high to maintain a household's privacy. The threshold to the house is at the sidewalk, not the front door.

The generic model of a garden suburb has a small park or square at its center. Around them are the requirements for community life: shops, a community hall, a religious building (or buildings), and a library. In the case of the railroad suburb, the train station is located on one side of the square. Historically, men would leave to go to work in the city from there in the morning and return home there in the evening. As ways of life have changed, so have commuting patterns and who does the commuting.

The aesthetic character of the garden suburbs and the type of the architecture sought represents the effort to reproduce the picturesque symbolism of paintings. In the generic ruralistic type, meandering paths shaping views toward specific objects set in a carefully re-created natural landscape became the model to replicate. Advocacies for such designs were somewhat marred by unsubstantiated claims that they would be less expensive to develop than would conventional pragmatic developments.

Specific Designs

Many garden suburbs were built in the late nineteenth century and even more in the twentieth. Almost uniformly, they were privately financed and constructed for the middle classes. Riverside, a suburb of Chicago, was begun in 1867. Bedford Park (1875) in west London is an early British example. Designed by Richard Norman Shaw (1831–1912), known for his design of country mansions, it consisted of large houses, a church, public halls, clubs, and shops (Greeves 1975). In the twentieth century, the houses were subdivided, and the area lost much of its glamor. Humberstone in England is an exception; it was developed by a workers' group but later in time (1909).

In the United States, Residence Park in New Rochelle, New York, was built in 1887 by New York financier Adrian Iselin (1818–1905). Great attention was paid in its design to the creation of public spaces in a natural setting to forge a village-like atmosphere. In continental Europe, garden suburbs were largely twentieth-century developments. Rheinisches Viertel (1910–14) designed by Paul Jatzow (1875–1940); Gartenstadt Staaken, the work of Paul Schmitthenner (1884–1972), a leader of the emerging German Garden Cities Association; and Gartenstadt Falkenberg estate, designed originally by Bruno Taut (1880–1938), are significant examples located on the periphery of Berlin. They influenced later modernist housing design in Germany of the Weimar Republic (1919–1933).

Six garden suburbs are described here. Chronologically, they begin with the Civil Lines in Delhi; Riverside, Illinois; and Hampstead Garden Suburb in London. Margarethenhöhe, a Krupp industrial village; and Forest Hills Gardens in New York are examples so late in their development that they could be regarded as examples of early-twentieth-century thinking about suburban design rather than as its precedents. The final example is Perlach near Munich in Germany another late design. In the last four examples, the buildings are an integral part of the design. Of the six, three can be regarded as exemplars of the type.

Exemplars of the Garden Suburb

Riverside, Illinois, USA (1869–); Hampstead Garden Suburb, London, England, UK (1906–); and Die Gardenstadt Perlach, Near Munich, Germany (1909–)

Riverside, Hampstead Garden Suburb, and Perlach illustrate the variety of forms that garden suburbs can take. Riverside is a suburban village made possible by the development in 1863 of the Burlington and Quincey Railroad heading out from Chicago. It is one of the earliest of the professionally planned communities designed for an upper-middle-class population. The 1,600-acre (650-hectare) site lies astride the Des Plaines River, about 9 miles (14 kilometers) from central Chicago. The design is often attributed solely to Frederick Law Olmsted but it was codesigned with Calvert Vaux (1824–95), an architect and landscape designer of British origin (Stern and Massengale 1982). They created the setting; the houses were individually built.

Riverside, as in the generic model, has a central village square surrounded by shops located at the train station. The road and landscape pattern creates the sought-after rustic environment. The suburb has an interconnected park system that functions as a scenic backdrop for the houses and provides recreational opportunities. The floodplain of the river and its banks form part of this system. The houses are individual single-family detached homes set well back from the road. No fences separate properties along the street fronts, but each house has a backyard. Unlike many such suburbs, it has sidewalks. Many of the houses were designed by leading architects such as Louis Sullivan (1856–1924), who designed the Babson House (1911) and Frank Lloyd Wright (1867–1959)—the Tomek (1905) and Coonley (1909) houses. The ups and downs of the US economy meant that Riverside was built out only in the 1940s. Times change. The station once bustling with commuters now has only a trickle of people boarding trains into Chicago's Loop each working day. Hampstead is also a railroad suburb, but much of it lies beyond easy walking distance from a station.

Hampstead Garden Suburb was founded by Henrietta Barnett (1851–1936), a social idealist who, with her husband, possessed a moral imperative to address the socioeconomic disparities in London's population. She first considered planning a suburb to do so in 1896, but nothing happened until she set up a trust in 1906 to acquire 243 acres (98 hectares) of land north of London. She appointed Raymond Unwin to be the planner. The two envisaged a development of 5,000 properties for a socially diverse population of 13,000 people (Darley 1978; Miller and Gray 1992). Barnett sought an environment where people of different social classes would mingle and form friendships. Economic realities have, however, made the suburb a middle-class world. The village-like atmosphere that she thought appropriate was easier to achieve. Hampstead Garden Suburb would be a village-like neighborhood with a sense of community (Darley 1978). It would be quiet; church bells were banned. Pubs would not be allowed, but tea shops would be located around a central square.

The plan is a modified grid with axes focusing on the spire of the main church. The streets are wide and lined with trees, and the houses are bounded by hedges not walls. The houses along

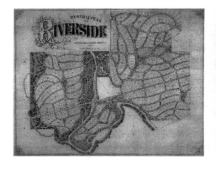 

Figure 4.4 Riverside, Illinois: The plan (left) and a typical street view (right)
Credit line (left): Collection of the author

the streets have different setbacks to avoid monotony. Their architecture has been described as being in the style of the Arts and Crafts movement (Miller and Gray 1992). Copartnerships built cottages, a hostel for working women, and apartments. Sir Edwin Lutyens (1869–1944) designed the central square on which two churches, one Anglican and the other a Free Church, and a Quaker Meeting House were built. Barnett wanted a small square as in the generic model, but Lutyens designed something grand. Unfortunately, it is lifeless center to the suburb in comparison to the commercial heart of Riverside. The school on the square that he designed in 1911 is a substantial building, but not one contributing to the square's being a community hub.

Perlach designed by the firm Berlepsch-Valendás, and von Hansen is a comparable contemporary development in Germany. The eastern portion of the development shows the nature of the curvilinear road pattern of the development. The individual houses had garden plots between them, and the scheme includes a church and an athletics field. At its center is a market square surrounded by arcaded buildings housing the neighborhood facilities (Berlepsch-Valendás 1910; Walter 2014). The architecture, like many of the garden suburbs, is regressive. It borrowed from local

Figure 4.5 Hampstead Garden Suburb: Typical houses (left) and the Henrietta Barnett School on the central green (right)

Figure 4.6 Perlach near Munich: The plan of the eastern portion (left) and an image of the market square (right)

Source (left): Berlepsch-Valendas (1910, 4)
Source (right): Berlepsch-Valendas (1910, 6)

traditions at a time when enthusiasm for modernist architecture was already rising in Germany. Architecture with which people are familiar had great popular appeal and was easily marketed.

Hybrid Examples

The Civil Lines, Delhi, India (1858–); Margarethenhöhe, Essen, Germany (1915–); and Forest Hills Gardens, Long Island, New York, USA (1909–)

The Civil Lines in Delhi may seem to be an unusual choice to include here, but it has many of the attributes of a garden suburb. It is, however, more pragmatic a design. It shows that design ideas exported from the colonial powers to their colonies were often later imported in a refined form. Its establishment precedes that of Riverside, Illinois, and that of Hampstead Garden Suburb. It was also more opulent.

Before the founding of New Delhi in 1913, Delhi consisted of three parts: Old Delhi (Shahjahanabad) of Mughal times, the cantonment of the military, and the Civil Lines. The Civil Lines was the residential area for British civil servants and business people built after the 1857 uprisings (also regarded as the First War of Independence) of the sepoys (Indian soldiers) of the Briton-officered Bengal Army of the East India Company. British families thereafter segregated themselves from the indigenous life of the old city and lived in their own residential areas with their own institutions, such as schools and clubs. As the nineteenth century progressed, the British residents were joined by wealthy Indian families, especially those whose respective heads were part of the administration of the colonial government of India.

The Civil Lines provided a way of life, made possible by large numbers of lowly paid Indian servants, that few of its residents could have afforded 'at home.' The suburb, designed by British military engineers, has a gridiron plan, in contrast to the contemporary hierarchal, twisted layout of the treeless streets and alleys of Delhi. The Civil Lines' streets are lined with trees, and the gardens are luxuriant. The houses are bungalows set in compounds enclosed by a low wall. Each compound had two entrances: one a major one for the family and the other a minor one

Figure 4.7 Old Delhi in 2012 (left) and a nineteenth-century Civil Lines bungalow in its compound in 2011 (right).

Credit line (left): Photograph by Mikladin/Shutterstock.com
Credit line (right): Courtesy of Miki Desai

for servants. Entrances in the wall facing the street were flanked by gateposts that acted as symbols of status. The driveway leads to a sheltering portico where the family members and guests alighted from their vehicles. The compound often contained a trellis for climbing plants, such as bougainvillea, a rose garden, fernery, a marble basin and fountains and, toward the end of the nineteenth century, a tennis or badminton court. The servants' quarters and kitchen, the stables, and the carriage and harness rooms were located behind the bungalow. Water was supplied from a well (Desai, Desai, and Lang 2012).

Margarethenhöhe, more obviously a company town, came later. Margarethenhöhe was owned by the Krupp Company; individuals did not own property in it as they did in the Civil Lines, Riverside, and Hampstead. The suburb stands on a 50-hectare (123.5-acre) site with the same amount of woodland—a greenbelt—surrounding it. It was developed by the Krupp Trust for a population of 15,000. Despite its being a company town, in 1915, fewer than half of its residents were Krupp employees. Designed by Georg Metzendorf (1874–1934), its layout is only marginally deviant from the ideal generic garden suburb model.

Margarethenhöhe has a central square around which are the community facilities. Narrow streets curve off it in a somewhat snail shell–like form. The village has a demarcated entrance, a school, a church, and nowadays a supermarket. Unlike most industrial villages, it had a tavern. A tramway took workers to the factory. Each house, as in the Civil Lines, stood in its own garden with space to raise rabbits and chickens. The architecture is regressive, drawing on elements of medieval German village buildings. By most measures, it has been a great success for the people who have chosen to live there. The same can be said of Forest Hill Gardens.

Forest Hills Gardens was begun in 1909, when Margaret Olivia Sage (1828–1918) bought 142 acres (57 hectares) of land from the Cord Meyer Development Company. Sage was founder of the Russell Sage Foundation, a philanthropic organization funding research in the social sciences with the objective, rather like those of Henrietta Barnett, of improving the social and living conditions of people in cities. The foundation also promoted direct actions; the building of Forest Hills Gardens is one of them. Sage appointed Grosvenor Atterbury (1869–1946), an architect specializing in designing homes for the wealthy, to design the community. Fredrick Law Olmsted Jr. (1870–1957) was the landscape architect. It was created to be a generic model

Figure 4.8   The Krupp village Margarethenhöhe
Credit line: Photographer unknown
Source: Wikimedia Commons

Antecedents of Twentieth-Century Design

Figure 4.9 Forest Hills Gardens: The general layout drawn by Grosvenor Atterbury (left) and a street scene (right)
Source (left and right): Lang (1994, 97); courtesy of John Wiley & Sons

for US suburban design (Klaus 2004). It was named 'Best Community' by *Cottage Living Magazine* in 2007.

Forest Hills Gardens is a railroad suburb, a fifteen-minute journey from Manhattan, on the then recently established Long Island Rail Road. The journey home from city to the railroad station and then through the suburb was regarded as a trip from a bustling urban environment to a cozy, domestic home. A square with arcaded sidewalks faces the station. Grand avenues branch out from it. The architecture of the 800 gabled roofed houses in the neighborhood is regressive. Many are in a semi-timbered Tudor style; others have Norman-style turrets.

The construction technique developed by Atterbury was, in contrast to the architecture, progressive (Zivkovic 2009). Each house was built from approximately 170 standardized concrete panels fabricated offsite and positioned by crane. Atterbury's system influenced the work of mid-1920s European modern architects like Ernst May (1886–1970), who used panelized prefab concrete systems in a number of the experimental housing projects in Frankfurt.

Until the 1970s, Forest Hill Gardens was subject to restrictive covenants. They prohibited the sale of homes to Jews, African Americans, and working-class people. Today it is a diverse community, but lower-paid workers are largely excluded due to financial constraints.

Commentary: The Functions Addressed

The garden suburb as a development type was a response to the perceived problems of the dense city and the low-density, pragmatic, piecemeal developments taking place haphazardly on the periphery of cities. It satisfies the basic needs of the people who choose to live in one. For those people who prefer an urban way of life, garden suburbs are nice places to visit, but they lack the bustle of everyday urban life.

As a model that provides a healthy environment for families away from the pollution and crime of the industrial city, the generic model functions well. Provided the houses are well designed, the garden suburb meets people's basic needs for health, comfort, and privacy. In doing so, it affords the meeting of their security needs; residents have a sense of safety and control over their immediate home territories. For many people, buying a place in a garden suburb is a good investment ensuring financial security and peace of mind in old age.

The nineteenth- and early-twentieth-century garden suburbs were connected to major city centers or employment opportunities by heavy- or light-rail transit systems, enabling them to function as dormitory suburbs. The nearness to shops and facilities for residents provided by the basic model was a major convenience in the pre-automobile era but less so with easy access by car to hyper-markets and shopping malls. The convenience remains important for the less mobile. In addition, designing for ease of walking to local destinations is said to encourage people to obtain some casual exercise. Garden suburbs afford children the opportunity to be free-ranging rather than battery-raised youngsters. They can roam throughout such suburbs independently on foot or on bicycles if they are so predisposed in an information technology–filled world and if their often hesitant, protective parents allow it.

Property developers advertise new garden suburbs as communities. The use of local facilities based on similar values does afford the growth of common interest links among the residents, especially at the child-raising stage of life. Households are, however, likely to be only members of a community of limited liability; they have some obligations at a local level, but not many (Suttles 1972). Children are likely to be the true local people, especially if they go to a school within walking distance of their homes.

The architecture works well in giving residents a sense of identity, of where they fit into a society's socioeconomic hierarchy. This sense is enhanced if the architectural character is unified. For individual identity, the houses need to be individually designed. In Riverside, they are. For the cognoscenti, knowing who the designer of the suburb is and the intellectual reasoning behind the design is a bonus.

Observations

The garden suburb may originally have been a peculiarly Anglo-Saxon idea but was soon the type of development sought by people across the world as cities grew into metropolises. The generic garden suburb model appears in many guises in different cultural contexts to this day. In late Imperial China and during the Republican period (1911–45), the housing in the international concessions—precincts within the cities controlled by foreign powers—reflect the garden suburbs of home. Now it is the type of residential environment sought after by the very wealthy. In Latin America, the designs by José Luis Cuevas (1881–1952) in Mexico City—Colonia Hipódromo Condesa and Lomas de Chapultepec—for instance, could serve as examples of the garden suburb, but they are developments of the 1920s and 1930s, when art deco architecture had widespread acceptance as a symbol of the machine age (Flores Garcia 2001).

Some important lessons can be learned from the specific suburban designs described here. Delhi's Civil Lines was a pragmatic response to the felt need of the British residents of India to feel at home and to obtain a sense of security through segregation from the indigenous city. The same attitude was evidenced in the United States with the middle-class 'white-flight' to the suburbs of the country's major metropolises after World War Two.

Hampstead Garden Suburb shows that however well-intentioned the social objectives of a project may be, human nature is not as adaptable as one may think. Trying to fly in the face of social and economic realities is difficult. Much can be achieved through the affordances of the built environment, but hoping to change social behavior patterns by changing physical design patterns is unrealistic unless the people involved are strongly predisposed to change.

The early garden suburbs set precedents for others to follow. The residential areas of imperial New Delhi located south of the capitol complex were designed by Sir Edwin Lutyens (1869–1944) following the same pattern of streets and bungalows as in Civil Lines, despite his disparaging remarks about the bungalow as a residential building type. It is now the type of environment sought after by the Indian elite. Riverside is frequently referred to as a precedent for good suburban design, especially by landscape architects who admire the way its layout defers to the topography of the land and the picturesque qualities of its design. Forest Hills Gardens, where Clarence Perry (1872–1944) once lived, is a precursor to his generic neighborhood unit model developed in 1927 (L. Mumford 1961).

Individual architects have taken the garden suburb ideas in different directions. Some remained garden suburb enthusiasts throughout the twentieth century. More importantly, the garden suburb of the nineteenth century was the antecedent of the garden city movement and indeed of many planned suburbs that afford more than a pragmatic design in the twenty–first century.

Key References

Galinou, Mireille. 2010. *Cottages and Villas: The Birth of the Garden Suburb*. New Haven: Yale University Press.

Miller, Mervyn and A. Stuart Gray. 1992. *Hampstead Garden Suburb. Arts and Crafts Utopia*. Chichester: Phillimore.

Mumford, Lewis. 1961. *The City in History, Its Origins, Its Transformations, and Its Prospects*. London: Secker & Warburg.

Stern, Robert A. M., David Fishman, and Jacob Tilove. 2013. *Paradise Planned: The Garden Suburb and the Modern City*. New York: Monacelli Press.

Unwin, Raymond. 1909. *Town Planning in Practice: An Introduction to the Art of Designing Cities and Suburbs*. London: T. Fisher Unwin.

5
The Urbanist Tradition

"Old cities and old streets have a peculiar charm for all who are not insensible to art impressions" (Camillo Sitte, cited in Collins and Collins 1965, 35). Although some medieval towns were partially self-consciously planned, their tightly knit character emerged in a piecemeal manner following accepted norms that varied from culture to culture. It was a worldwide phenomenon. For instance, in India cities such as Shahjahanabad (Old Delhi), following Islam traditions was begun in in 1639 by the Mughal emperor Shah Jahan (1592–1658). African cities as varied as Cairo and Timbuktu saw such intricate dense developments. Renaissance designs were largely a reaction to the European medieval city. In the twentieth century, many urban design ideas resulted from architects' love/hate attitude toward it. Its intricate designs attracted and repelled. What made them and the Renaissance response both visually attractive? The medieval city, it must be remembered while delighting the eye, could be "most powerfully offensive to the nostrils of a stranger" (Mawman 1805).

During the nineteenth century, much thought was given to what makes a good, salubrious urban environment. City planners and social reformers addressed issues of hygiene and transportation, the physiological needs of people, and intellectual aesthetics ideas, but few asked how the three- and four-dimensional quality of cities is experienced. Many designs ended up being impressive but unintentionally boring. A German scholar, Hermann Maertens (1877–1916), an Austrian architect and historian, Camillo Sitte (1843–1903), the head of the Museum of Applied Arts in Vienna, and Charles Buls (1837–1914), mayor of Brussels, explicitly focused on the core of urban design concerns: the experiencing and use of the urban spaces formed by buildings.

The three possessed two things in common: They were observers of the urban scene and they appreciated the forms of both the medieval city and classical and baroque designs. The three were unified in their opposition to the advocacies of the contemporary old guard of planning: Reinhard Baumeister (1833–1917) and Joseph Stübben (1845–1936). A nonconformist by religion, Sitte was particularly critical of the attempts to turn cities into classical monuments, as was happening in Vienna (Olsen 1986).

Baumeister's book *Stadterweiterungen in Technischer, Baupolizeilicher und Wirtschaftlicher Beziehung* (*Town Extensions: Their links with Technical and Economic Concerns and with Building Regulations*), published in 1876, presented city planning as a 'scientific' and quantifiable activity.

Figure 5.1   A medieval town: Carcassonne, France
Credit line: Photograph by Jay Si/Shutterstock.com

Baumeister addressed the technical aspects of traffic management, then still horse drawn, and sewerage and drainage systems. He also advocated for the segregation of the precincts of a city into a business sector, an industrial area, and residential neighborhoods. It was a progressive view but one that failed to consider the qualities that make cities interesting and lively places.

Sitte and Buls believed in social, economic, and technological progress but recognized the dislocation that many people felt in dealing with a rapidly changing world. They were thus interested in not only urban development schemes but also the preservation of noteworthy buildings and urban precincts as well as maintaining the quality of the rural villages that were being engulfed by urban growth. What distinguishes Buls from Maertens and Sitte was his interest in both suburban development and the redevelopment of city centers.

Antecedent Ideas

Maertens, Sitte, and Buls deplored contemporary city planning approaches. Their observations and prescriptions were a reaction to them. It may seem contradictory, but the immediate ancestor of Maertens and Sitte's ideas were those of Reinhard Baumeister, but their antecedents go back to classical Greece. Baumeister suggested that architects look at the ancient city anew and simultaneously at the way Renaissance architects had designed city squares. Sitte followed suit. Baumeister was also concerned with creating laws/rules based on empirical studies, although his focus of attention differed almost entirely from those of Maertens, Sitte, and Buls. The influence of classical Greece's interest, conscious or not, for the sequential unfolding of the cityscape as one moves through it, is clearest in Sitte's arguments.

It is not clear who influenced Maertens, but the theories of psychologist Hermann von Helmholtz (1821–94) on how observers scan the built environment gave Maertens's assertions their legitimacy. Sitte's discussion of the differences between Greek and Roman squares and his concern for the flushing effect of winds along streets picks up on Vitruvius's observations, with which Sitte was familiar (Collins and Collins 1965). Alberti, though not mentioned by Sitte, brought attention to the design of streets and the classification of plazas by type, akin to Sitte's studies. Buls claims not to have been familiar with the work of his contemporaries or those who had gone before him. He nevertheless drew on the ideas of German philosopher Arthur Schopenhauer (1788–1860).

Schopenhauer influenced Buls's attitude toward public art. His view that "beauty would strengthen the morals and uplift the population" and increase the intellectual level of a city's

The Urbanist Tradition

citizens underlies much of Buls's planning and design philosophy (Smets 1995, cited by Payre 1998, 3). Buls's recognition of the positive aspects of modernity but simultaneous desire to preserve the historical areas of towns can also be traced back to Schopenhauer.

Maertens, Sitte, and Buls shared a somewhat deterministic view of the impact of the quality of the built environment on social behavior. This view was, and still is, used to justify many design decisions that architects argue for.

Manifestoes and Paradigms

Maertens, Sitte, and Buls produced three major works advocating for an empiricist approach to understanding the aesthetic effect of urban patterns. The first is Hermann Maertens's *Der Optische Maaßstab oder die Theorie und Praxis des ästhetischen Sehens in den bildenden Künsten: Auf Grund der Lehre der Physiologischen Optik für Architekten, Maler, Bildhauer, Musterzeichner, Modelleure, Stukkateure, Möbelfabrikanten, Landschaftsgärtner und Kunstfreunde* (1877). The second is Camillo Sitte's *Der Städtebau nach Seinen Künstlerischen Grunsatzen* (*City Planning according to Artistic Principles*), which was published in Vienna in 1889. And the third is Charles Buls's *L'esthétique des Villes* (1839). In them, their authors argued that urban design principles should be based on how people experience the city and not solely on the intellectual aesthetic ideas of the cognoscenti.

Maertens, in his book, opposed monumental Beaux Arts planning and the creation of the large open spaces that dominated much civic design thinking in the nineteenth century. Making prestigious places in the eyes of the wealthy, he argued, should not be the sole focus of the attention of urban designers. Instead, drawing on the research of Helmholtz, he prepared measurements of how we view buildings and urban objects on the basis of the visual size of their components—the details of building façades and sculptures—for them to be clearly visible and contemplated from specific distances. He devised rules for the sizes of buildings and squares depending on what one can peruse at specific distances.

In *Der Städtebau*, Sitte argued that the network of public open spaces framed by buildings is the fundamental concern of urban design. Urban designers, Sitte stated, should focus on creating sequences of spaces that enrich the experience of people moving through a city. Controls should be placed, he reasoned, on the dimensions and details of buildings that form the three-dimensional nature of streets, squares, and other public open spaces. The design of the buildings should be left to private enterprise, as in the ancient cities, provided that they were based on what design controls specify (Sitte 1889; Broadbent 1990).

Beautiful buildings, Sitte believed, do not, by themselves, make an aesthetically interesting city, one that holds a viewer's attention. In Chapter 8—"The Meager and Unimaginative Character of Modern City Plans"—of his book, he opposed making open spaces geometrically pure by removing encroaching buildings and making key buildings visible all at once from a single point. Seeing a building emerge from behind occluding structures as one approached it, he stressed, is a more enriching visual experience than seeing it immediately all at once from afar. Moving through the medieval city provides a rhythmic, unselfconsciously choreographed sequence of experiences of the streets and squares that are the spaces of life in public. The three elements—streets, squares, and activities in public spaces—he argued, should be the focus of attention in urban designing. He thus presupposed the concept of behavior setting developed later by ecological psychologists such as Roger Barker (Barker 1968).

Sitte favored curving or irregular street alignments to provide ever-changing vistas for a person moving from one space to another, but he was aware that arbitrarily creating twisting streets can result in inauthentic designs (Collins and Collins 1963). After conducting extensive studies

79

of existing spaces in cities, Sitte concluded that while many people might agree on the beauty of specific places, nobody had done an analysis of why they thought them so. He believed that the principles that can be deduced from the places that people regard as beautiful can be applied to modern urban design. Although the focus of attention today when Sitte is discussed is on his appreciation for both the picturesque medieval and the classical city, he was also concerned with hygiene and was a strong proponent of urban parks as 'sanitary greens' that would provide lungs for the city (Sitte 1889). He shared this advocacy with Buls.

Buls's *L'esthétique des Villes* came later than Maertens's and Sitte's writings. He had by then become an ardent supporter of Sitte's positions. He believed that much could be learned from the medieval city, but for him, there was also a place in cities for grand designs of symmetrical complexes of important buildings. Buls was, nevertheless, opposed to the grandiose architectural schemes in Brussels such as the royal palace built in 1900 by King Leopold II (1835–1909) and funded by the king's brutal exploitation of his Congo colony. Buls fought for the preservation of the then threatened Grand Place, now a UNESCO World Heritage site, in the city.

Buls was an advocate for what might be called urban design through conservation. Despite the necessity for change in the urban fabric to develop the economic and social life of cities, architects and planners should, he recommended, remember that the citizens of a city take pride in the artifacts and places that reflect their history. Change "ought to be brought about with filial respect for all, that, without inconvenience, can be preserved of our old memories" (Buls 1899, III para. 3). He was also critical of designing cities from a bird's-eye view or simply as a plan; the patterns and details so created would, he feared, be devoid of interest (Payre 1995).

From today's perspective, Buls was against the globalization of urban design and architectural patterns. Brussels should not be like Paris. Each city has its own character, and that character should be retained. The suburbs, he thought, should also have their own personalities and should not be turned into mini-cities.

Generic Concepts and Illustrative Designs

According to Helmholtz, a person's range of vision on the vertical axis from a spot while they look ahead is 27 degrees. Maertens thus concluded that a building can best be contemplated at a distance of double its height. Its details, to be seen clearly, should be visible at a distance equivalent to its height (i.e., within a 45-degree angle of vision). At a distance of three times its height, a building can be seen in its context, the angle of vision being 18 degrees. A building's silhouette is clear from a distance of four to five times its height (Hegemann and Peets 1922; Moravánszky 2012). From these types of analysis, Maertens's established rules for giving a square a sense of enclosure, of being an outdoor room.

For Sitte, the generic city planning process should begin by establishing its armature consisting of a hierarchy of streets and a hierarchy of places. The principle places and street should have a sense of enclosure. The major streets should thus have buildings side by side along them. The street layout could either be picturesque or follow a Platonic geometrical layout. He was, however, against the gridiron plan, particularly as it was applied in US cities. Simultaneously, he opposed trying to replicate the plan of the medieval city that had evolved over time. He recognized that the 'organic plan' with its winding streets or its short straight stretches offered a pedestrian a lively sequence of new views. Such patterns should not, however, he believed, form the basis of new designs. The patterns were a product of history, and history cannot be established instantaneously. "Straight roads today are necessary" (Hegemann and Peets 1922, 18).

From his observations, Sitte, echoing Maerten's approach, concluded that the minimum dimension of a square should be equal to the height of the major building facing it, and the

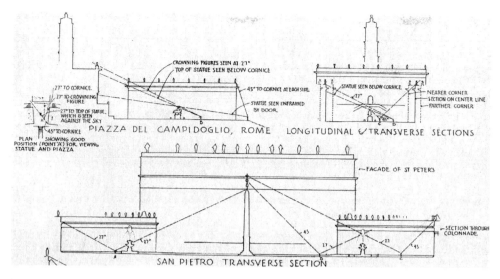

Figure 5.2 An analysis of viewing angles in Piazza del Campidoglio and Piazza San Pietro, Rome
Source: Hegemann and Peets (1922, 17)

square should be no large than twice that dimension, to give it a feeling of being a room. The square's length should not exceed double its width. In his book, Sitte provided examples of good and poor urban places. In doing so, he picked up on many of Maertens's ideas, although he does not mention Maertens in his writings. Maertens's ideas were so well known at the time that Sitte must have been aware of them.

Three squares that Sitte regarded as almost good are presented in Figure 5.3. The Kursaal in Wiesbaden faces a square with colonnades framing it on two sides. The combination forms a simple but powerful composition. The Place de la Trinité in Paris gets its life from being the crossing point of small streets. The space in front of the Église Catholique in Wiesbaden is of the correct size for the whole of the church to be seen from across the square without having to tilt one's head. Sitte believed that all three places would have been improved by entrances to the open spaces from adjacent streets being "partly eliminated or closed by arches and colonnades" (Hegemann and Peets 1922, 17). In general, he was opposed to placing statues and fountains in the center of a square, although he recognized that Greek and Roman squares often had them there to enhance the importance of both the statue and the square. He preferred objects to be located on the side of a space, to free up the center for public gatherings.

Buls believed that straight roads should generally "be closed by a prominent building at the 'eye line'" (Buls 1899, II para 10). Designers should not, he thought, hesitate to bend streets around historically important buildings. The sequential experiencing of vistas as one moves through a city adds to its meaningfulness. Streets and squares should be designed so that classical buildings can be seen from station points farther away than buildings, such as Gothic structures, rich in details. Large buildings should have small buildings nearby to give scale to a vista. A square should not be created simply to house a monument; it needs to serve a multiplicity of functions; otherwise, "it is an artificial creation lacking life" (Buls 1899, II para 9). Buls's model of a good street was one lined with trees. Similarly, he was for the preservation or planting of copses of trees to preserve the rural character of those villages being engulfed by urban expansion (Smets 1995). All these prescriptions must be seen in their geographic and cultural context.

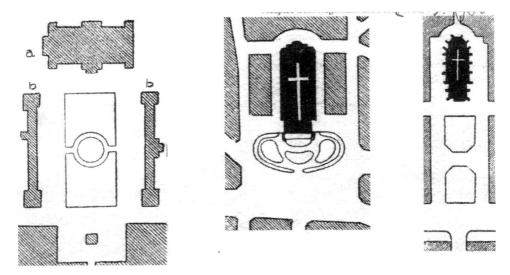

Figure 5.3 Three of the many places that Sitte studied: Kursaal in Wiesbaden (left); Place de la Trinité, Paris (center); and the Église Catholique, Wiesbaden (right)
Credit line: Adapted from Hegemann and Peets (1922, 21) by the author

Specific Designs

The examples of Maertens's designs are difficult to locate, and Buls's designs were products of the Brussels city administration, so it is not clear whether they illustrate his advocacies. Consequently, a proposal by Sitte for the heart of Vienna, even though never implemented, must suffice to illustrate what the group advocated for.

An Exemplar of Sitte's Ideas on the City

Central Vienna, Austria (ca 1890)

In Sitte's time, central Vienna consisted of a disparate set of important buildings surrounded by a dense cluster of medieval streets. His design proposed significant changes while attempting to retain the city's existing character. The city planning department in Vienna paid no attention to Sitte's advice. Its mind was firmly fixed on the prevailing Beaux Arts design paradigm and technical matters such as enhancing the movement of horse-drawn traffic.

Sitte's proposal consisted of a theater facing City Hall, a university building, and Parliament (IX) (see Figure 5.4). The composition left an open space too large for a square, so Sitte proposed reducing it in size, with new buildings that would create a small square between them (e.g., VI). This square would be linked to a square (VII) in front of the theater (f). Between the theater and its annex (g), he proposed putting another small square (VIII). The square (IX) in front of Parliament is enclosed by a colonnade and walls. A new building (k) sited to form a long square in front of the Palace of Justice gets rid of an odd-shaped open area. The Gothic Votivkirche (b) had a poorly shaped space in front of it. Sitte proposed to create a new square (III) enclosed by a colonnade. The square would act as an atrium to the church. In front of it would be a square (IV) with a monument (Hegemann and Peets 1922, 21; Broadbent 1990, 120).

This design shows Sitte's admiration of the Renaissance open spaces in cities rather than simply the picturesque odd-shaped spaces of the medieval city. The irregularities of Vienna's street and open space layout would be replaced by a sequence of regularly shaped squares arranged symmetrically around the forecourts of buildings. The buildings become both objects on display and space-making elements. Their relative sizes would meet Maerten's standards.

Sitte's opposed the proposal for the Ringstrasse created after the demolition of Vienna's city walls. Despite its being a ring road, he disliked the linearity of much of the boulevard. He instead proposed the forming of a sequence of new spaces along the way. He thus had different ideas for Vienna than did Otto Wagner (1841–1918; see Chapter 8).

Hybrid Examples

Bagaregården, Gothenburg, Sweden (1926), and Louvain-la-Neuve, Belgium (1969–90)

Sitte's *Der Städtebau* drew immediate interest in Austria, Germany, and Scandinavia. During the early twentieth century, his principles shaped the design of extensions to a number of cities. The internationally acclaimed design for Bagaregården is an example. It is a 125-hectare (309-acre) subdistrict of Gothenburg in Sweden. Designed by Albert Lilienberg (1879–1967), it was also much influenced by the garden city movement's ideals. Getting away from a gridiron plan that Sitte disliked, its sequences of spaces and tight design show the spatial arrangement that Sitte favored.

Another hybrid scheme that hearkens back to Sitte's enthusiasm for the sequential experience of opening and enclosing spaces as one walks through the medieval city is that of the post–World War Two new university town of Louvain-la-Neuve in Belgium. It was built after

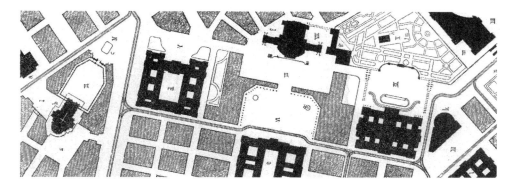

Figure 5.4 Sitte's proposal for central Vienna
Source: Hegemann and Peets (1922, 21)
Legend: a: Chemical Laboratory, b: Votivkirche, c: Plaza for a large monument, d: University, e: City Hall, f: Theatre, g: Proposed annex to the theatre, h: Temple of Theseus, j: Proposed Goethe memorial, k: Proposed new building, l: Palace of Justice, m: Part of the Imperial Forum, n: Triumphal Arch.

Antecedents of Twentieth-Century Design

Figure 5.5 Bagaregården: A typical street
Credit line: Photograph by Raphael Saulus
Source: Wikimedia Commons

Figure 5.6 Louvain-la-Neuve: The layout with university buildings in a dark shade (left) and a view of the central spine (right)
Source (left and right): Lang (2017, 135); courtesy of Taylor & Francis

the linguistic division of the country in 1962. A new university was deemed necessary south of the border to replace the French-medium component of the University of Louvain north of the border. In reaction to the lifelessness of the new universities being built in Belgium on modern rationalist lines, town and gown were to be an integrated unit in it rather than separate entities (LaConte 2009). The buildings of the university are linked through the center of the town by an east–west pedestrian spine that has kinks in it so that the vista changes as one walks along it. Small squares open off it; those facing south house cafés.

The design affords the activities characteristic of a lively university town very well with its clearly demarcated mix of public, semi-public, semi-private, and private spaces. During the university vacations, the pedestrian traffic through the center is much reduced (for a fuller description, see Lang 2017, 134–36). The outer neighborhoods, designed following garden suburb principles, are quieter. Recent developments on the fringes are largely pragmatic and automobile oriented.

Commentary: The Functions Addressed

It would be misleading to think that Maertens, Buls and Sitte were concerned only with the visual aesthetic function of patterns of the built environment, but that was the issue that they emphasized. Their attention was specifically on the visual impact of geometric forms rather than on their symbolic value—their associational meanings. The three did, however, recognize that urban open spaces also functioned as symbols of political power. What they identified was the fascination with one's surroundings created by the sequential experience obtained when walking through the medieval city. Sitte recognized that large city squares could be boring places and that if one of the functions of cities is to be aesthetically pleasing as part of everyday life, then they had to hold one's attention. They must be interesting. This assertion was corroborated in the research of psychologists such as Daniel Berlyne (1924–76) in the 1970s (Berlyne 1974).

Explicit and implicit in the concern of Maertens, Buls, and Sitte for the function of the open spaces in the city was their interest in what makes a healthy living environment. Like Aristotle, they were also concerned with how urban forms enable a city's inhabitants to achieve a sense of security. Perhaps the criticism that Sitte received from Josef Stübben and Baumeister, that he did not consider the street patterns in terms of their function as channels of movement of non-pedestrian traffic in his design proposals, is reasonable, but in much urban design, the pedestrian experience is neglected.

Observations

The empirical basis for Maertens's rules is clear, but applying them given the social and economic dynamics of the property market is difficult. The result is that his observations are almost entirely ignored. In the early twentieth century, German municipal authorities, however, responded positively to his theories; they provided rules for opening dense city precincts to light and air without destroying their character (Jerram 2007).

Maertens's and Sitte's concern for the quality of streets remains central to urban design. They considered streets to be the basic unit of design rather than the block surrounded by streets. Land is, however, bought and developed by blocks bounded by streets or by individual plots within a block. The quality of the street results from what is built independently on its sides unless designs controls are imposed to treat the street as a unit. The weakest part of Sitte's argument is his dismissal of the gridiron plan as laid out in New York. He denigrated its traffic-handling capacity, although he did so in the pre–traffic light era. New York is much admired, and the gridiron pattern and numbering of streets makes wayfinding straightforward.

Sitte's book was translated into French in 1902 and Spanish in 1926. It was not translated into English until 1946, although a detailed overview of his work was presented earlier by Werner Hegemann and Elbert Peets in their tome *The American Vitruvius* (Hegemann and Peets 1922). Hegemann and Theodore Goecke (1850–1919), a coeditor of Sitte's writings, were among his most ardent supporters. They drew attention to his admiration for the classical and the baroque when he was being dismissed as a romantic favoring only the picturesque because he recognized the positive aesthetic aspects of the medieval city.

Two sets of followers were inspired by Sitte's observations. One group picked up on his admiration for the picturesque medieval city. The difficulty is, however, to use the design principles that were derived from many unselfconscious decisions in a self-conscious design. The second group consisted of those who, like him, were learning from the squares and streets of the Renaissance and the baroque. In Britain, his intellectual descendants included Raymond Unwin and Patrick Abercrombie (1879–1957), while on the continent, they included Cornelius Gurlitt (1850–1938), an architect and art historian, and Albert Erich Brinckmann (1881–1958). Brinckmann continued to analyze cities as Sitte had done. In addition, his admiration for Maertens's work is clear in his *Platz und Monument. Untersuchungen zur Geschichte und Ästhetik der Stadtbaukunst in neuerer Zeit* (1908; Collins and Collins 1965). The concern with the sequential experiencing of urban spaces is seen later, in the work of Gordon Cullen (1914–94) and the townscape movement of the mid twentieth century (Cullen 1961) and the proposals of new urbanists later on in the century.

One of Sitte's most important contributions was his enthusiasm for planning the physical city in its three-dimensional form, as had been done by Haussmann. Later, Frank Lloyd Wright and Le Corbusier had a similar enthusiasm, but they, and other modernists, particularly those of the rationalist school, failed to heed any of Sitte's lessons. Le Corbusier dismissed Sitte's ideas as antiquated (Adshead 1930). Le Corbusier believed that people should lead the Calvinistic type of life in which he was raised. Enjoying life and what makes cities fun was not among his concerns. A humanitarian, Sitte believed that planners and designers had to make cities enjoyable.

Perhaps the greatest legacy of Maertens, Sitte, and Buls is that they drew conclusions about good urban forms after getting out and examining the built environment. They extracted principles from what they had seen. If Helmholtz was the basis for their ideas, then the twentieth century saw continued experimental research on optics, the interestingness and pleasurableness of visual forms in the experimental aesthetic studies of psychologists such as Daniel Berlyne.

Key References

Adshead, S. D. 1930. "Camillo Sitte and Le Corbusier." *Town Planning Review* 14 (2): 85–94.

Buls, Charles. 1899. "L'esthétique des Villes." *Municipal Affairs* 3 (December): 732–41. Translated from the author's *L'esthétique des Villes*. Bruxelles: Bruyland-Christophe, 1893.

Collins, George R. and Christiane Crasemann Collins. 1965. *Camillo Sitte and the Birth of Modern City Planning*. New York: Random House.

Hegemann, Werner and Elbert Peets. 1922. *The American Vitruvius: An Architects' Handbook of Civic Art*. New York: The Architectural Book Publishing Co.

Sitte, Camillo. 1889. *Der Städtebau nach Seinen Künstlerischen Grundsätzen*. Translated from the German by George R. Collins and Christiane Crasemann Collins as *City Planning According to Its Artistic Principles*. London: Phaidon Press, 1965.

Part II

Les Quartiers Modernes Frugès (Cité Frugès), Pessac, Bordeaux (1920–26)
Source: Lang (2017, 118); courtesy of Taylor & Francis

Early-Twentieth-Century Manifestoes, Paradigms, Generic Concepts, and Specific Designs

The urban design ideas that emerged during the first half of the twentieth need to be understood against the contemporary backdrop of political turmoil and technological advances. During the first decade of the century, the political world was turned upside down. The United States took control over the Philippines from Spain, and the Russo-Japanese War (1904–5) established Japan as a world power. The Russian Revolution of 1905 was a prelude to what was to come in 1917. The old order of the gentry/landowners in control of a serf/laboring population was severally challenged. Technological advances led to major changes in the ways of life of millions of people. Cities were taken from the age of the horse and train to that of the automobile.

Henry Ford (1863–1947) produced the first mass-produced automobile in 1903. By the beginning of World War One, an automobile had become a prerequisite for middle-class families in the United States and then rapidly elsewhere. Its mode of manufacture gave rise to the concept of Fordism—the cheap mass production of standardized products by workers. The efficiency movement, under the intellectual leadership of Frederick Winslow Taylor (1856–1915), author of *The Principles of Scientific Management* (1911), sought to streamline industrial production by making it better organized. The concept of efficiency and functionalism in manufacturing had a significant effect on design thinking during the "First Machine Age" (Banham 1960). Urban environments had to be efficient.

In technologically advanced societies, electricity became available to all homes and indoor plumbing to many. The first cinema opened in 1903; the massive Gaumont Palace cinema in Paris seating 6,420 began operation in 1911. The first air conditioner was also produced in 1903. It was the greatest invention of the twentieth century, according to Lee Kuan Yew (1923–2015), prime minster of Singapore from its independence in 1959 until 1990. It certainly made Singapore and Las Vegas as we know them possible. The first electric refrigerator for homes came onto the market in 1913. The automated telephone exchange appeared in the early 1900s; the first radio broadcast for entertainment took place in 1906 and television in the late 1930s. Of all the technological inventions, the development of the refrigerator, the telephone, and the automobile had, arguably, the greatest impact on daily life for masses of people. Other developments also changed the activities in which people engaged. Professional sport fixtures became mass events drawing large crowds. Advances in medical science meant that consulting a doctor was more likely than not to be beneficial.

Accompanying these developments was the collapse of artistic orthodoxy. Radical, not incremental, paradigm shifts occurred in many fields. At the beginning of the century, composers such as Igor Stravinsky (1882–1972) and artists such as Pablo Picasso (1881–1973) rebelled against classicism in the arts; authors like Henry James (1843–1916) and Marcel Proust (1871–1922) were exploring the human psyche in their novels. Jazz, originating in the African American areas of New Orleans in the United States, developed from its roots in blues and ragtime to form a new musical expression in the 1920s. In the fine arts, the exploration on the nature of light by the Impressionists and then on form by Picasso and Georges Braque (1882–1963) invaded architectural thought and had a deep impact on the rationalist school of architecture.

Early-Twentieth-Century Manifestoes

World War One heralded a new era. Its effects pushed many intellectual developments ahead rapidly (Roberts 1999; Streissguth 2016). The war, and afterward the Spanish flu pandemic (1918–20), had devastating social and psychological effects on Europe. The destruction of cities and villages and the deaths of soldiers and civilians during and after the war traumatized people for a generation, and its impacts on the human psyche linger. Socialism arose as a sociopolitical ideal. Authorities in Europe sought to improve housing conditions and educational opportunities for the people. The role of women in the life of several countries began to change. They had taken leading roles in politics and industry during the war years, and they continued to enter the workforce in increasing numbers afterward. More particularly, women began to play a greater role in public life. Women achieved the full right to vote in many self-governing countries during the war and immediate postwar years: Canada in 1917, the United Kingdom the following year, and the United States two years later. New Zealand had opted for universal suffrage in 1893 and Australia in 1902. Women's right to stand for parliament followed. These rights were not necessarily available to women of color, indigenous populations, and the poor.

The war's end saw the dissolution of the German, Austro-Hungarian, and Ottoman Empires. The British and French Empires had reached their greatest extent, but moves by colonized countries to obtain independence began to take effect. The Russian Revolution of 1917 led to the formation of the Union of Soviet Socialist Republics (USSR) in 1922 and later the Cold War between capitalist and socialist interests. With the psychological wounds of World War One still healing, the hardships of the Great Depression of the 1930s left a long-lasting mark on the peoples of Europe and the Americas (Freeman 2014). Many ideas about what cities should be like were forged during it. Frank Lloyd Wright's ideas were much affected by the Depression.

Figure 1 Ypres, Belgium in 1920
Credit line: Official photograph, UK government

More broadly, it encouraged a frugality of spirit that only the economic boom of the second half of the twentieth century began to dismiss (Roberts 1999).

The establishment and failure of the League of Nations, the collapse of democracy with the rise of aggressive authoritarian regimes in Germany and Italy, and Japanese aggression in Korea, China, and the Pacific brought about World War Two in 1939. The Spanish Civil War (1936–1939) was its prelude. The years between the two world wars were volatile ones in the fine arts too. Movements such as Dadaism and Surrealism were a response to the slaughter that took place during World War One. They made architects think too. Against the backdrop of the pragmatic development of cities, they produced many ideas about what physical form cities should take.

Urban Development and Pragmatic Urban Designs

During the nineteenth century, cities expanded considerably in their populations and the area of land that they occupied. London's population grew from 1 million people in 1800 to 6.7 million a century later. In 1939, it reached 8 million people, a figure it did not reach again until 2015. Many other well-established cities saw similar expansions in their populations due to natural increases and the immigration of people from rural areas and from poorer countries. The resulting demand for employment opportunities, housing, and services resulted in metropolitan areas suburbs' spreading farther out into the countryside.

The morphology of cities continued to be shaped upward and outward by major individual, self-conscious, grand gestures and a multitude of smaller pragmatic design decisions. New building technologies and the development of the safety elevator made the skyscraper possible, leading to changes in the skyline of cities. Horizontally, growth was shaped by the new technologies available. At the beginning of the twentieth century, the primary mode of transportation within the city was by horse-drawn vehicles and between cities and their suburbs by railroad. Although horse-drawn omnibus lines existed in European and North American cities starting in the 1820s, it was the electric rail-based trolley/tram system toward the end of the nineteenth century that changed the morphology of cities. Cities acquired streetcar suburbs and ribbon-shopping strips along transportation routes. The development of subway/underground rail systems from the 1860s but particularly after their electrification in the 1890s led to further changes in the distribution of economic activities and the types of built environments erected to accommodate them.

The new transportation developments tended to segregate the city into distinct components—a process that was supported by city planning precepts and zoning ordinances. The increasing use of individual automobiles from 1910 onward furthered the spread and segregation of land uses. It also eliminated the amount and stench of dung and dust (or mud if it had been raining) on streets and the dead horses that had to be removed from them. In 1916, 9,202 dead horses had to be removed from the streets of Chicago, even though cars were already in widespread use. No wonder the automobile was seen as a miracle pollution reducer. It was also cheaper to own a car than run a stable.

Most major cities of the economically developed world had central business districts surrounded by areas in transition, then inner-city neighborhoods, and suburbs on their fringes, but such generalizations need to be taken with caution. The whole was tied together by intraurban and suburban transportation lines. The urban neighborhoods were built for and inhabited by different socioeconomic groups, and the nature of buildings, religious institutions, and shops reflected it. In multicultural cities, neighborhoods were often inhabited by distinct ethnic groups. Much development was pragmatically piecemeal, haphazard, and uncoordinated,

Early-Twentieth-Century Manifestoes

Figure 2 The city in the first half of the twentieth century: Market Street, Sydney, in 1910 (above left); Broadway, New York, in the 1920s (above right); and the Bund, Shanghai, in 1936 (below)

Credit line (above left): Adapted from various sources by the author

Credit line (above right): American Studio

Source (above right): Wikimedia Commons

Credit line (below): Adapted from various sources by the author

leading to considerable opportunity costs. The new towns built between the two world wars were mostly pragmatic company towns of mining and industrial organizations. In some, the spirit of nineteenth-century philanthropy endured.

Overcrowding and the lack of affordable housing, traffic congestions, pollution, and the paucity of recreational opportunities persisted. Growing diseconomies of scale in cities due to

Early-Twentieth-Century Manifestoes

their aging infrastructure saw government-led plans for change either through direct action or by changes in taxation policies and the subsidization of types of development, particularly housing, that private developers were not building. The rationalists among urban designer saw cities as unmitigated sets of problems that could be solved only by total demolition and rebuilding on a massive scale. Empiricist approaches were more conservative, literally and figuratively.

Changes in Architectural and Urban Design Paradigms

The twentieth century began with the city beautiful design as the paradigm dominating the thinking of urban designers, but other thoughts about what makes a good city were emerging simultaneously. Much of what ensued had its roots in Germany. Reinhard Baumeister in *Stadterweiterungen in Technischer, Baupolizeilicher und Wirtschaftlicher Beziehung* (1876), already mentioned, and Josef Stübben in *Der Städebau* (1907) advocated procedures for controlling haphazard, pragmatic urban development. In Britain, *Town Planning in Practice: An Introduction to the Art of Designing Cities and Suburbs* by Raymond Unwin was published in 1909. These three works were based on a study of the existing city and what appeared to work well and what did not. They formed the basis of an empirical approach to urban design. The rationalists among modernists rejected this view; they were going to invent the future. The Bauhaus, founded in 1919, was imbued with this spirit. While often remembered for its development of a new architectural style, the Bauhaus' committed social concern was more important in shaping urban design in the pre–World War Two years. Contemporary developments in Russia had a similar influence (Banham 1960).

The Russian schools of architecture, particularly the VKHUTEMAS (an acronym for Higher Education and Technical Studios) founded in 1920 under the leadership of Moisei Ginzburg (1892–1946) and Nikolai Ladovsky (1881–1941) explored a rationalist and constructivist approach to design that revolutionized architectural thinking about the nature of cities and about urban design (Khazanova 1971; Senkevitch 1974). VKHUTEMAS was closed in 1931, when the Soviet state interceded and shifted the allowable architectural paradigm from constructivism to social realism. The consequent displacement of artists such as Paul Klee (1879–1940) and Wassily Kandinsky (1866–1944) to the Bauhaus led to the spread of revolutionary artistic ideas around the world (Wingler 1969).

Rationalist architects established CIAM in their efforts to achieve hegemony for their ideas. The empiricists among urban designers never formed such a strong coherent group but instead produced several manifestoes based on the worlds that inspired them. If the City Beautiful movement was a descendant of the nineteenth-century European Beaux Arts tradition, then both the empiricists and rationalists owed much to the spirit of the social and philanthropic movement. A religious fervor certainly underpinned their philosophies if not their designs.

The Outline of the Discussion

The objective of this part of the book is to describe and explain the richness of ideas that dominated the thinking of urban designers during the first half of the twentieth century. It begins with a look at the City Beautiful movement. Its goals and generic nature are described in Chapter 6. Grand and not-so-grand schemes following the percepts of the movement were built throughout the century in North America, European countries, Australia, and the colonies of the European powers and of Japan. Once dismissed out of hand as bombastic, many of the patterns of form that its proponents sought for cities appear in the thinking of both rationalists and empiricists.

92

The manifestoes, generic ideas, and designs of the rationalists and the empiricists were developed contemporaneously during the first half of the century. Describing the proposals of the empiricists before that of the rationalists is a somewhat-arbitrary decision, but many of the ideas of the latter were based on a rejection of those of the former; the rationalists wanted to totally break away from the status quo. The two chapters discussing empiricist and rationalist paradigms, in many ways, represent the heart of the discourse in this book.

As described in Chapter 7, the empiricists consist of two broad groups of advocates: the garden city proponents and the urbanists. Frank Lloyd Wright's Broadacre City is a deviant type; it fits in neither category neatly. It is hardly a city as we understand it, but implicit in the principles that form Wright's proposal is much that we can see in pragmatically designed suburbs today. The rationalists also provided urban designers with a varied set of generic and illustrative designs on which to draw. Chapter 8 begins with the description of a few of the many individual manifestoes prescribing what the city should be. Of them, the advocacies of the Bauhaus and CIAM are the most important because of the impact they had on what was subsequently built (Wingler 1969). The specific designs chosen to illustrate empiricist and rationalist thought are diverse and not neatly categorized. They nevertheless provide a broad survey of what was proposed during the years between the two world wars.

Key References

Banham, Reyner. 1960. *Theory and Design During the First Machine Age.* Cambridge, MA: MIT Press.
Freeman, Robert. 2014. *The Interwar Years.* London Kendall Lane.
Roberts, J. M. 1999. *Twentieth Century: The History of the World 1901–2000.* New York: Penguin.
Streissguth, Tom. 2016. *World War 1: Aftermath.* Minneapolis, MN: ABDO Publishing.
Wingler, Hans M. 1969. *The Bauhaus: Weimar Dessau Berlin Chicago.* Edited by Joseph Stein. Translated from the German by Wolfgang Jabs and Basil Gilbert. Cambridge, MA: MIT Press.

6

The City Beautiful

The City Beautiful movement developed in the United States at the end of the nineteenth century. Its ideals captured the imagination of people in the country at a time when immigrants from Europe and the countryside were pouring into cities across the nation. The designs proposed by the movement's advocates, like those of the 'villages of vision,' were antidotes to the industrial Coketown. Crowding, lack of open spaces for recreation, traffic congestion, and pollution from industries and from horses made cities dank places. The formulation of the paradigm occurred in Chicago, which was, because of its meatpacking industry, the 'slaughterhouse of the world.'

The city beautiful designs established a visible intellectual link to the European classical and Beaux Arts architecture held in high esteem by many of the US elite. As such, the movement's advocacies stood in sharp contrast to the contemporary architectural ideas of Louis Sullivan (1856–1924) and Frank Lloyd Wright, who sought a uniquely US approach to architecture and urban design.

Antecedent Ideas

The ancestors of the City Beautiful movement include the Rome of Pope Sixtus V, L'Enfant's plan for Washington, Rossi's work in the creation of classical St. Petersburg, and Haussmann's design for Paris. More immediately, the civic designs produced by academics and students at the École nationale supérieure des Beaux-Arts in Paris had an impact. Several architects who produced city beautiful schemes for US cities studied there or had worked for architects educated there. They had probably read Josef Stübben's *Der Städtebau*, advocating for broad boulevards radiating out from points in the city as the armature for urban developments. European urban and landscape designs were certainly important models for US architects (Peterson 1976).

The members of the Senate Park Commission, who were responsible for the early-twentieth-century McMillan plan for the Mall in Washington, toured Europe's important palace gardens and urban designs to get ideas. They were particularly impressed by Haussmann's design for Paris and the use of landscape elements such as trees to define spaces. They admired the gardens at the Château de Vaux-le-Vicomte (1658–61) (Figure 6.1), designed by Louis le Vau (1612–70) with André le Nôtre (1613–1700), and the Palace of Versailles. These gardens had their own antecedents in sixteenth-century designs, such as those at the Villa Lante, a mannerist design

Figure 6.1 An influential garden layout: Château de Vaux-le-Vicomte
Credit line: Photograph by Cynthia Liang/Shutterstock.com

Figure 6.2 World's Columbian Exposition: The Court of Honor with *The Republic* statue in the foreground and the administration building in the background
Credit line: Photograph by C. D. Arnold
Source: Wikimedia Commons

The City Beautiful

and at the Villa d'Este at Tivoli near Rome. These two gardens were famous for their terraces and fountains and their classical geometries.

The immediate ancestor of the city beautiful designs was the World's Columbian Exposition of 1893—held to celebrate the 400th anniversary of Christopher Columbus's arrival in 1492 in what was the New World to European explorers. The cruciform layout with a pool at its centerpiece was the work of John Wellborn Root (1850–1891), Daniel Burnham (1846–1912), Frederick Law Olmsted (1822–1903), and Charles B. Atwood (1849–1895). The composition was symmetrical, balanced, and rich in detail. The buildings, designed by several architects, were unified by strict design guidelines (Kostoff 1993). The exposition's site was 600 acres (240 hectares) in size and housed fourteen major neoclassical buildings and two hundred pavilions. Its scale and grandeur became a symbol for a Chicago's arising from the ashes of the Great Fire of 1871, which had destroyed much of the heart of the city. The white stucco generally used for the buildings' façades gave the exposition its nickname: The White City. Earlier World's Fairs in London and Paris had, in contrast, celebrated technological advances and been constructed of metals and glass.

Over 27 million visits were made to the Chicago exposition during its six-month run. Politicians, architects, and the public were impressed by the grandeur of the plan and the gleaming neoclassical architecture. Walter Burley Griffin (1876–1937) visited the exposition while it was being built and during its run. The image of the parliamentary building complex in the competition entry for Canberra by his wife, Marion Mahony Griffin (1871–1961), and him was similar in concept to that of the Court of Honor at the exposition.

Manifestoes and Paradigms

The aphorism attributed to Daniel Burnham by Charles Moore (1921, 147) to many observers is a hallmark of the attitudes of the advocates for the city beautiful paradigms. Burnham is reputed to have stated,

> Make no little plans. They have no magic to stir men's blood and probably themselves will not be realized. Make big plans; aim high in hope and work, remembering that a noble, logical diagram once recorded will never die, but long after we are gone will be a living thing, asserting itself with ever-growing insistency.
> *Attributed to Daniel Burnham by Charles Moore (Moore 1921, 147)*

Burnham, however, produced no major advocacy for city beautiful ideas. Three items written by Charles Mulford Robinson (1869–1917), a journalist and the first professor of civic design at the University of Illinois, strongly promoted the city beautiful model. They are the article "Improvements in city life: aesthetic progress" (1899) and two books, *The Improvement of Towns and Cities: Or the Practical Basis for Civic Aesthetics* (1901) and *Modern Civic Art: Or on the City Made Beautiful* (1903). Together, they can be regarded as *the* manifesto of the movement.

Robinson argued for a 'New Jerusalem,' full of light, parks, and bold streets. His vision was of a clean, imposing city, with underground sewerage and drainage systems and broad tree-lined boulevards. The boulevards, he believed, would enhance traffic flows as well as the aesthetic quality of the city. Special attention, Robinson argued, should be paid, as in Rome's Piazza del Popolo, to the point of arrival in the city from outside. At that time, the railroad station was the major portal to the city. Its central station, as in many European cities, should, Robinson argued, be grand and have a square in front of it to emphasize its importance. Waterfronts should be lined with quays, as in Paris, and have shaded promenades along them.

Robinson deemed diagonal streets to be necessary to ease traffic circulation. He advocated for the establishment of focal points where such streets cross. Public buildings should be located

Early-Twentieth-Century Manifestoes

at important points; they should not simply line a street. A city should have a civic center where the municipal buildings are clustered. The buildings should be unified in design that follows a single proportional module. In an existing city, if the buildings of the civic center are not adjacent to each other, they should be linked by arcades and colonnades or, if they are too far apart, by formal, tree-lined avenues.

Business districts should have broad thoroughfares for through traffic. They should have an open space, a square located at a main focal point from which streets should radiate out. Lateral and minor streets should be designed to serve local traffic needs. Minimum and maximum heights should be set for the buildings along streets so that they can be visually unified. Buildings should be designed with a sense of decorum rather than in competition with each other. Street furniture, lighting standards, and streets signs should have a unified character, as should any advertising. There should be no overhead wires apart from those serving tram/trolley lines. A generic design is implicit in these instructions.

Generic Concepts and Illustrative Designs

The generic city beautiful design is remarkably simple when presented in a two-dimensional diagram. Grand, broad boulevards spread out from focal points. These points are marked by statues or fountains and surrounded by major civic buildings such as town halls, libraries, and museums. The statues are allegorical representations of moral virtues, not memorials to prominent citizens. The buildings, built to the property line, give a sense of enclosure to the street; they make a street a longitudinal place rather than simply a link for the movement of vehicles. The generic architectural style of the buildings is classical but with baroque antecedents.

One of the many unimplemented designs illustrate the generic city beautiful concepts well. It is the plan for Chicago, which shows the desired patterns of diagonal streets laid across a standard city grid layout. As described next, the proposal features a bold, new, domed civic

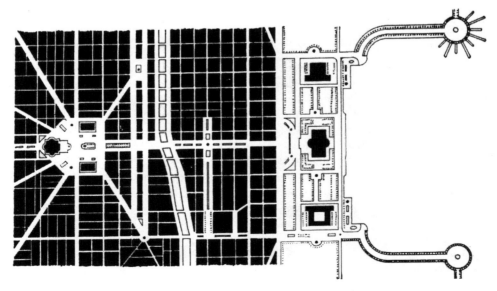

Figure 6.3 The generic city beautiful ideas as shown in the Chicago plan
Source: Gallion and Eisner (1993), courtesy of John Wiley & Sons

center where the axial streets come to a point, and the city hall is the focus of attention. The diagram represents the contemporary generic design idea for city administrations to follow.

Specific Designs

Specific city beautiful design proposals in the United States range in type from whole cities (e.g., San Francisco), to governmental building complexes (e.g., the Colorado state capitol in Denver), universities (e.g., the University of Minnesota) and suburbs (Yorkship Township, now Fairlawn, Camden, New Jersey, 1916), and projects as unexpected as an air force base (Barksdale, Bossier City, Louisiana, 1935). The implementation of many proposals was thwarted by political changes and the onset of wars; some were simply too difficult or expensive to implement because they necessitated the acquisition and demolition of whole tracts of cities.

One of the major designers of city beautiful schemes was Eliel Saarinen (1873–1950), a Finnish-American architect (Hallas-Murula 2005; Niemi 2016). His proposals coincided with stirring nationalisms not only in his native Finland but also in Hungary (Budapest in 1911), Ireland (Dublin in 1912), Estonia (Tallinn in 1912), and Australia, where he took second place in the competition to design Canberra (1913). Daniel Burnham, best known for his plan for Chicago (1909) with Edward H. Bennett (1874–1954), created plans for cities as varied as Cleveland (1903) and San Francisco (1904) in the United States and Manila and Baguio in the Philippines (1905). Due to economic and political vagaries, only bits and pieces of his proposals were built.

Design proposals for San Francisco and for Philadelphia saw only minor components of citywide designs implemented. The City Hall complex (1915) in San Francisco hints at what San Francisco would have looked like if Burnham's plan for the city had been implemented. The Benjamin Franklin Parkway (1917) in Philadelphia with one end dominated by the city hall and the other by the Museum of Art acts as the spine of the city's museum district (Brownlee 1989). In Greece, Thessaloniki's plan (1919) is another that had only minor parts built.

Boulevards influenced by Haussmann's Paris were built in several countries, but none of them has the architectural integrity of their Parisian antecedent. The extraordinarily wide Avenida 9 Julio in Buenos Aires (1916) is very different in character from any of the boulevards of Haussmann's Paris or the Avenue des Champs-Élysées. The buildings lining it are mixed in

Figure 6.4 Eliel Saarinen's city beautiful schemes: Tallinn, Estonia (left) and Munikkiniemi-Haaga, Finland (right)

Credit line (left): Courtesy of the Estonian Museum of Architecture
Source (right): Wikimedia Commons

height and character. Any sense of unity that the street has comes from the color of the structures and the trees lining it.

Of the many city beautiful urban design proposals, eight are described here. Three are city plans, and the remainder are precinct designs. They include two proposals that were not implemented, four that were partially implemented, and one that was completed.

Exemplars of the City Beautiful

The McMillan Plan, Washington DC, USA (1902); Louisiana Purchase Exposition, St. Louis, Missouri, USA (1904); The Plan of Chicago, USA (1909); the University of Texas at Austin, Texas, USA (1913); and Germania, Berlin, Germany (1936–43)

The first city beautiful plan of consequence was that prepared for the monumental core of Washington, DC. The plan was named after James McMillan (1838–1902), Republican senator for Michigan, who headed the Senate Parks Commission. The members of the commission included Burnham, landscape architect Frederick Law Olmsted Jr., and architect Charles F. McKim (1847–1909). Augustus Saint-Gaudens (1848–1907), a sculptor, later joined the commission at the behest of McKim. The plan was much influenced by Burnham and is seen as his. It eliminated the English landscape design of the mall created by Andrew Jackson Downing (1815–52) and implemented some unrealized aspects of L'Enfant's original plan (Kohler and Scott 2006).

The report proposed a north–south, east–west cruciform design for the Mall, with the United States Capitol building anchoring the Mall's eastern end of the east–west axis. At the other end would be West Potomac Park. The commission recommended that the just-authorized Lincoln Memorial be placed in the park to act as a significant termination to the axis. It also suggested that the memorial to Ulysses S. Grant, a hero of the Civil War (1861–65), be moved to a new plaza on the mall directly in front of the Capitol. A new East Potomac Park would anchor the southern end of the north–south axis with, possibly, a new memorial. The neoclassical Thomas Jefferson memorial (1939) now does just that.

The Mall was to remain an open vista of grass lined by trees but narrowed to 100 yards (91 meters). Behind the trees would be a row of public office buildings, museums, and cultural attractions. The plan included a low Beaux Arts bridge linking West Potomac Park with Arlington National Cemetery across the Potomac River and two new reflecting pools on the National Mall. One (cruciform in shape) would extend from West Potomac Park toward the Washington Monument, at the intersection of the two axes. The other would extend from East Potomac Park north to the Washington Monument (Reps 1991). For pragmatic foundation reasons, the Washington Monument was erected off the north–south axis.

The report suggested several changes to areas adjacent to the Mall. To the north of the Capitol, it was proposed that a new passenger railroad station be built to replace the Baltimore & Potomac Railroad Terminal then located on the National Mall. Union Station, designed by Daniel Burnham, was the result. Pennsylvania Avenue NW remained the link between the Capitol and the White House. The implementation of the plan was interrupted by World War One but resumed after peace had been re-established. It culminated in the construction of the Lincoln Memorial in 1922. Contemporary international expositions

The City Beautiful

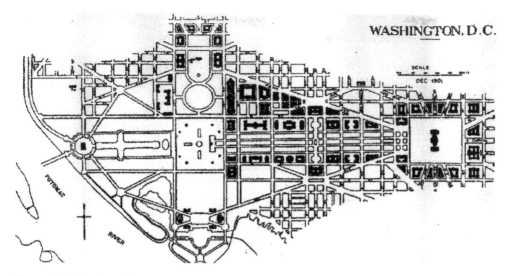

Figure 6.5 The McMillan plan for the National Mall, Washington
Source: Wikimedia Commons

held in the United States were closer in character to Chicago's 1893 White City than the Mall was.

The 1904 Louisiana Purchase Exposition, also known as the St. Louis World's Fair, is an example. It is a direct descendant of the 1893 Chicago Fair, as was the Pan-American Exposition in Buffalo (1901) that preceded it. The St. Louis World's Fair was an international exposition that ran from late April to December. Planning started in 1901, when the Louisiana Purchase Exposition Corporation selected a prominent St. Louis architect, Isaac S. Taylor (1850–1917), to be the chair of the Architectural Commission and the director of works for the exposition. The design of the fair's 1,200-acre (4.9-square kilometer) site plan was executed by George Kessler (1862–1923), a city planner and landscape architect. It consists of a cruciform of boulevards, where one axis is crescent shaped (Francis 1905).

Emmanuel Louis Masqueray (1862–1923) a Franco-American architect who had studied at the École des Beaux Arts, was Taylor's chief designer. He was responsible for the design of several of the fair's buildings. Other buildings were the work of prominent architects, apparently including, but unacknowledged, an African American. The United States government, forty-three of the forty-five states then in the union, plus fifty foreign nations had exhibitions. There were also over fifty concession-type educational and scientific displays. Almost 20 million visitors attended the fair. Celebrated though the fair was, it is *The Plan of Chicago* that has been the most influential of the city beautiful schemes.

A Daniel Burnham and Edward H. Bennett, another graduate of the École des Beaux-Arts, began work on the plan in 1906; it was published three years later. The Commercial Club of Chicago was its sponsor (Burnham and Bennett 1909). Its members had been impressed by the 1893 fair. Burnham, who donated his time working on the project, envisioned Chicago as Haussmann's Paris on the prairie.

101

Early-Twentieth-Century Manifestoes

Figure 6.6 The Louisiana Purchase Exposition: The government building at the end of the axis
Source: Wikimedia Commons

Axial boulevards radiating from a central domed foreground building were the central components of the design. The boulevards, cutting across existing property ownership lines, were supposed to be part of a network of grand avenues and focal points. The plan included an extensive yacht harbor on the Lake Michigan waterfront, quays along the river, and proposals for improved railroad terminals (Wilson 1989). Despite only minor components of *The Plan of Chicago* being implemented, its proposals set the standard for the early-twentieth-century civic centers built in the United States. It also influenced contemporary university campus designs.

The plan for the University of Texas at Austin was executed by Paul Cret (1876–1945), a 1903 graduate of the École des Beaux Arts. He was a consulting architect to the university, from 1930 until his death, and was responsible for the design of the Main Building on the campus and directly or indirectly the design of eighteen other buildings. The major feature of the campus design is the mall leading from the Main Building to the Littlefield Fountain and beyond down University Avenue to what is now Martin Luther King Jr. Boulevard. The buildings erected along the mall do not frame it to the extent shown in the original Cret design, but their design is in the simplified classical style of his oeuvre.

One of the architects much influenced by Cret was Albert Speer (1905–1981), creator of the design for Welthauptstadt (Germania), Adolf Hitler's vision for a rebuilding of Berlin. Speer, designated by Hitler as the "first architect of the Thousand Year Third Reich" also designed many of the buildings of the project in, at least, sketch form (L. Krier 1985).

Construction began with the demolition of parts of Berlin and the resettlement of 'Aryan' residents in alternative housing. In contrast, many wealthy Jews were left to live in squalid conditions. The forced labor of concentration camp inmates was used in the construction process (Moorhouse 2010). Between 1937 and 1943, some work on the project took place, but when World War Two turned against Germany, the project halted. The completed portions of the scheme include the great east–west city axis that involved broadening Charlottenburger

The City Beautiful

Figure 6.7 The Chicago plan: The view toward the municipal palace
Credit line: Courtesy of the Art Institute of Chicago/Art Resources NY

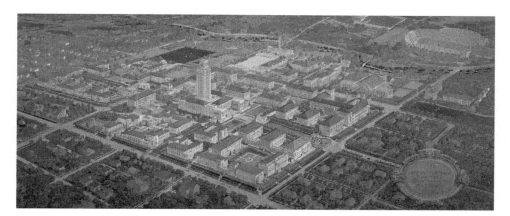

Figure 6.8 The University of Texas at Austin master plan
Credit line: Courtesy of the Architectural Archives, University of Texas at Austin

Chaussee (Straße des 17 Juni today) and placing the old Prussian Victory Column at its center. During the Nazi era, it was lined by flags displaying the swastika.

Hybrid Examples

Canberra, Australia (1913); New Delhi, India (1914); and Thessaloniki, Greece (1917)

The designs of Canberra and New Delhi, while essentially city beautiful schemes, have garden city attributes. The plan for Thessaloniki is a highly pragmatic solution to the situation that the city found itself in after the fire of 1917, which destroyed its heart. The design is nevertheless a fine example of what many cities aspired to be.

Early-Twentieth-Century Manifestoes

Figure 6.9   Germania: The Boulevard of Splendors
Credit line: Collection of the author

After the federation of the Australian colonies into a single nation in 1901, the country needed a new capital, because the rivalry between the country's two leading cities, Sydney and Melbourne, meant that neither was acceptable to the other as the location for the country's capital. Between 1899 and 1902, a parliamentary committee carried out the search for a suitable site. It ultimately selected a sheep station in the Molonglo Valley of New South Wales located between the rival cities to be the site.

In 1911, the prime minister of Australia, Andrew Fisher (1862–1928), initiated the competition for the design of the new capital city. It was won by US-American spouses Walter Burley Griffin (1876–1937) and Marion Mahony Griffin (1871–1961). Of the 137 entries received from around the world, all but a handful were city beautiful schemes (Reps 1997). The Griffins' design was, however, much more carefully worked out than those of the other competitors (Weirick 2006; Freestone 2007). It paid close attention to the land forms and climate of the area, even though the Griffins had not visited the site.

The design consisted of a geometric arrangement of axes, circles, and hexagons. Two axes were proposed. One, the land axis, visually runs from Mount Ainslie through Capital Hill to Bimberi Peak; the other, at right angles to it, the water axis, runs from Black Mountain along a proposed lake. The government buildings were arrayed on the land axis. The Griffins' plan proposed a central parliamentary triangle laid out on a series of terraces. At its apex was a building that the Griffins designated the Capitol, a temple for popular gatherings. The government buildings, including the bicameral Parliament House lying below the Capitol, were in this triangular area. Parliament House was to be the foreground building of the composition with those for administrative and judicial functions as a backdrop. The arrangement symbolized the Griffins' strong belief in constitutional democracy. They located the High Court of Australia next to the land axis and adjacent to the water axis close to a 'Water Gate' and a proposed central lake basin.

The buildings of the Parliamentary Triangle, however, have been situated in a modernist manner as individual objects in space. Their architecture also departs from what the Griffins intended. That shown in the competition entry drawings was influenced by the contemporary Art Deco and Art Moderne work in Europe. The first House of Parliament (designed by John

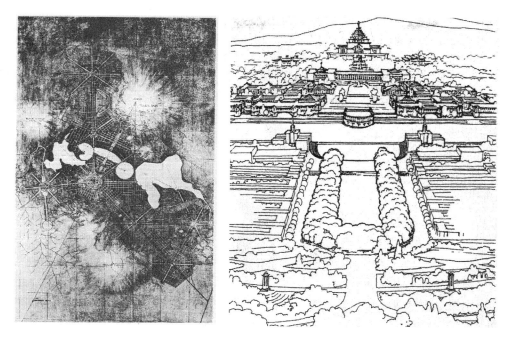

Figure 6.10 The Griffins' winning entry for the design of Canberra: The plan (left) and the conceptual design for the Parliamentary Triangle (right)

Credit line (left and right): Courtesy of the National Archives, Australia

Smith Murdoch, 1862–1945, and the Department of Public Works) and the administration buildings are in what might be called a British colonial modernism, while the Parliament building designed by Romaldo Giurgola (1920–2016) of Mitchell/Giurgola Architects is a highly symbolic building, both in its design and in its location. Opened in 1988, it is neo-modernist edifice topped by a steel structure from which the Australian flag flies. Its outline approximates that of the Capitol in the Griffin's sketch of the Parliamentary Triangle (Weirick 2006).

The plan for New Delhi came a year after that for Canberra. It was made necessary by the decision of the Government of India to move the capital of British India from Calcutta (now Kolkata) to the site of the old Mughal capital, Delhi. The action was taken partly on symbolic grounds but also because of the increasing agitation in Bengal for independence from British rule. The design of the town, located south of the existing old city of Delhi, was the work of the New Delhi Planning Committee, but it is attributed to Edwin Lutyens (1896–1944). The scheme consists of two axes that cross at right angles—the King's Way (now Rajpath) and Queen's Way (now Janpath)—and radiating axes, one of which links the Council House (now Parliament) and Connaught Place to Old Delhi. On a rise, the Raisina, at the head of King's Way is the Viceroy's House (now Rashtrapati Bhavan). On either side of the approach to the building are the Secretariat buildings (R. Irving 1981). At the other end of King's Way are the ruins of Purana Qila, the first great Mughal citadel, though the National Stadium now intervenes. The War Memorial (now India Gate) also designed by Lutyens and a cupola for a statue of George V were placed along the axis. The cupola now stands forlornly empty.

The Raisina obscures the view of the lower levels of the Rashtrapati Bhavan as one approaches from the east. This problem was the subject of an acrimonious debate between Lutyens and the designer of the Secretariat buildings, Herbert Baker (1862–1946). The Parliament building, also designed by Baker, sits uncomfortably on one side in a previously completed plan. It was added because of the 1919 reform of the Government of India.

The application of the city beautiful paradigm in New Delhi was designed to represent "the idea of peaceful domination and dignified rule . . . over the traditions and life of the British Raj" (Delhi Town Planning Committee 1913, 3). The irony is that it has come to symbolize freedom from that rule.

The design for Thessaloniki was more a pragmatic than a purely symbolic gesture. It was commissioned by the Greek prime minister, Eleftherios Venizelos (1864–1936), after the fire of 1917 destroyed much of the city. The plan was formulated by the French architect, archaeologist, and planner Ernest Hébrard (1877–1938), who was instructed by Venizelos to produce a 'modern plan' (Gerolympos 1995; Lagopoulos 2005). Hébrard later executed a similar scheme for Hanoi, the capital of French Indo-China (now Vietnam).

Hébrard's designs for Thessaloniki and Hanoi opened spaces in the dense city with boulevards and squares. The façades of buildings lining both were designed to make a grand impression.

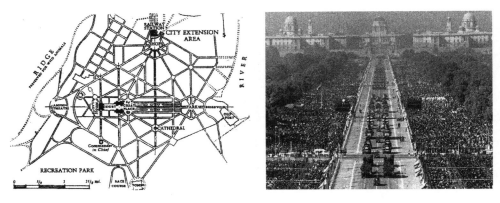

Figure 6.11 New Delhi: The plan of the government complex (left) and a view of the Republic Day Parade 1996 (right)

Credit line (left): Adapted from various sources by the author
Credit line (right): Photograph by R. K. Dayal
Source (right): Lang, Desai, and Desai (1997, frontispiece); courtesy of CEPT University Press

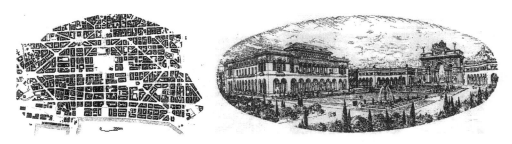

Figure 6.12 Thessaloniki: Hébrard's 1918 plan (left) and his proposal for a Place Civique (right)
Source (left and right): Wikimedia Commons

Only components of the designs were built, due to the lack of the funds required to complete them. The major design gesture in Thessaloniki was a grand boulevard leading from the seafront, where he designed Alexander the Great Square, to the city center. Civic Square (where the agora of the ancient city was subsequently found) was to have the town hall and other municipal buildings around it in accordance with the generic city beautiful model. The square that now exists at the seafront is named for Aristotle; it is a work of the 1950s.

Commentary: The Functions Addressed

City beautiful designs were carried out under the direction of authorities who wished their cities to be regarded as modern and culturally important in emulation of Paris. The designs thus functioned to fulfill the needs of civic leaders to raise their own self-esteem and to give a city a prestigious identity. In doing so, city beautiful designs have symbolized a variety of political ends—democratic and autocratic (Peterson 1976; Wilson 1989). They have come to represent political power, as in the 1970s and 1980s projects in Bucharest in Romania and Pyongyang in North Korea. The primary function of the schemes in both cities was to establish a prestigious place on the international scene and a sense of pride in the hearts of their citizens. That said, one of the major objectives of city beautiful schemes was certainly to open up space to make cities brighter places in which to reside and work.

A professed goal of wide axial boulevards was to enhance traffic flows. The intersections where diagonals cross a grid layout are, however, less than ideal for traffic movements. Wide streets do, however, enable sun to shine into them and have a sanitizing impact. Trees lined in rows give a visual order to the scene. They also help ameliorate climatic conditions, reduce pollution levels, and restrict the development of heat-island effects. In hot, arid climates, however, the city beautiful is not a wise paradigm to select as the basis for a design.

A catalytic effect of most of the implemented schemes mentioned here has been the increase in property value of adjacent areas. A side effect of the schemes has been that they have reinforced social inequalities. In the schemes built, it was often working-class residential neighborhoods that were demolished to make way for boulevards. Poor residents were displaced.

The projects are also associated with their designers, so they represent part of the oeuvre of a firm and the architects involved. In this way, the schemes function to fulfil a professional enterprise's need to have an identity not only to boost its self-esteem but to advertise its services. Burnham was clearly aware of this function when offering his services for free in developing the Chicago Plan with Bennett.

Observations

The application of the city beautiful as an architecture of display rather than as a creation of salubrious environments is what remains in people's minds. The widespread employment of the classic model in its city beautiful guise was mentioned in Chapter 2. After World War Two, the paradigm was applied, among other political purposes, to represent communist ideals. Haussmann's Paris was the precedent rather than the city beautiful as developed in the United States. The design of the Nowa Huta district of Kraków in Poland begun in the immediate postwar year of 1947 and funded by the Soviet Union is an example. It was designed to be a communist utopia. Like Magnitogorsk (see Chapter 9), with which it has some similarities, it is a steel works city. It now houses 200,000 people. Similarly, two dictators followed Hitler's efforts in Berlin, although again it was Paris that their designers had in mind. The development of Bucharest is a prime example, although the Pyongyang of Kim Il-sung (1912–94) and his son Kim Jong-il (1941–2011) rivals it.

Figure 6.13   Nowa Huta, Kraków
Credit line: Photograph by Piotr Tomaszewski-Gullion
Source: Wikimedia Commons

The Avenue of Victory of Socialism, built in Bucharest (1977–89), was the dream of a dictator, President Nicolae Ceauşescu (1918–89). He proclaimed,

> I am looking for a symbolic representation of the two decades of enlightenment we have lived through; I need something grand, something very grand, which reflects what we have already achieved.
>
> *(cited in Cavalcanti 1997, 72)*

Ceauşescu's chief architect, Dr. Alexandru Budişteanu, believed that monumental boulevards create a grand city. The Avenue of Victory of Socialism is Bucharest's central axis. Its lengthy vista celebrates President Ceauşescu. He had the political control to finance his idea, hire architects, and supervise the construction of the project. Unlike Haussmann's Paris or even Italian dictator Benito Mussolini's 1936 Via della Conciliazione's linking St. Peter's basilica to the heart of Rome, the overwhelming consideration in the design of the Avenue of the Victory of Socialism was Ceauşescu's desire to fulfill his own aesthetic ideals.

The city beautiful, as an urban design paradigm, still has utility as a model for the design of civic building complexes in cultures where public buildings are regarded as important. Implementing urban renewal schemes on a large scale in democratic societies is nigh impossible because of existing property holdings and the restriction on the power of eminent domain (i.e., the right of governments to take/purchase properties for projects in the public interest). Christopher Wren discovered that in the City of London after the Great Fire of 1666.

The City Beautiful

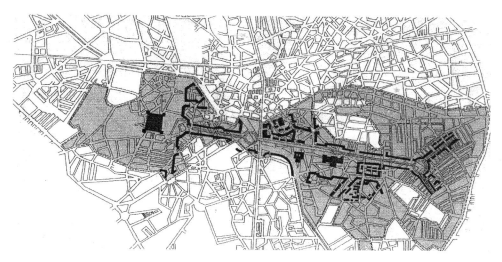

Figure 6.14 The Avenue of the Victory of Socialism, Bucharest, showing the area demolished for the boulevard
Credit line: Adapted from Calvacanti (1979) by Chao Wang
Source: Lang (2017, 126); courtesy of Taylor & Francis

Key References

Burnham, Daniel H. and Edward H. Bennett. 1909. *Plan of Chicago Prepared Under the Auspice of the Commercial Club During the Years MCMVI, MCMVII and MCMVIII*. Edited by Charles Moore. Chicago: The Commercial Club. Reprinted New York: De Capo Press, 1970.

Peterson, Jon A. 1976. "The City Beautiful Movement: Forgotten Origins and Lost Meanings." *Journal of Urban History* 2 (4): 415–34.

Reps, John W. 1997. *Canberra 1912: Plans and Planners of the Australian Capital Competition*. Carlton South, VIC: Melbourne University Press.

Robinson, Charles M. 1903. *Modern Civic Art: Or, the City Made Beautiful*. New York and London: G. P. Putnam's Sons.

Wilson, William H. 1989. *The City Beautiful Movement*. Baltimore and London: Johns Hopkins University Press.

7

Modern Empiricism

The urban problems and opportunities for change created by the Industrial Revolution were evident everywhere in Europe and the Americas at the beginning of the twentieth century. In response, the empiricists among urban designers looked at existing places that they admired for inspiration when devising schemes for the new century. Some were concerned with the nature of the metropolis; others with getting away from it. The former included Frank Lloyd Wright, during the early stage of his long career, and architects such as Francisco Mujica (b. 1889), celebrating the skyscraper city, and Patrick Geddes (1854–1932), advocating for urban renewal through 'conservative surgery.' This diverse group of people did not feel aghast at the high-density, pragmatically developing city. They had ideas for doing it better. Those trying to get away from that city and to start again included two important figures: Ebenezer Howard (1850–1928), a parliamentary stenographer, and Frank Lloyd Wright in a guise different from that of his earlier career.

Antecedent Ideas

It is easier to discern the intellectual antecedents of the garden city advocates than those of the urbanists. The nineteenth-century observations of urbanists such as Camillo Sitte and Josef Stübben, although well known, had only a little practical impact on architects' and civic reformers' thoughts about the city. Patrick Geddes's ideas were influenced by Hebert Spencer (1820–1903), a liberal politician, biologist, and anthropologist, and by Pierre Guillaume Frédéric le Play (1806–82), a French engineer and social scientist. From them, he developed his view that cities had to be understood and design proposals created to recognize the nature of their regional climatic and cultural context. The need to also see places within a market economy formed the basis of his design philosophy (Boardman 1978; Munshi 2000).

For many urban designers, as for the public, the environments of their childhoods shaped their values. Wright enjoyed the qualities of the valley near Spring Green, Wisconsin, where he spent his early childhood. He loved the way its houses were spread out among trees. He turned to this imagery after his efforts to deal with the high-rise city. He translated what he remembered of Spring Valley into the design of Broadacre City. He was also much influenced by progressive social ideas, such as those that the Wisconsin Progressive Party promulgated in

110

the United States during the Great Depression. The party's 1934 political platform was based on the belief that every family should own a home and that all utilities, education, and healthcare should be provided by public coffers. There would be agricultural and food cooperatives; banks and other lending institutions would be nationalized. This influence gave way to Wright's acceptance of a much more individualistic, self-reliant model of the adult human as the basis for his designs (White and White 1962; Secrest 1998; Huxtable 2004). Ebenezer Howard's ideas too were shaped by his early experiences.

Although born in London, Howard was educated in the rural counties outside the city. For two years, as a young adult, he lived in the United States, first, unsuccessfully, as a farmer and then as a journalist in Chicago, where he read the poetry of Walt Whitman (1819–92). Whitman's *Leaves of Grass* sympathetically addressed the severe impact that urbanization in the United States had on people. Howard also read the essays and poems of Ralph Waldo Emerson (1803–82), a champion of individualism. In combination, they shaped Howard's thoughts on socialism. Back in England, Howard was a recorder of the proceedings of British Parliament. That experience gave him a broad understanding of prevailing political attitudes in the United Kingdom.

Despite his love of London, Howard was overwhelmed by its miseries (Beevers 1988). His garden city idea had many direct antecedents, including the advocacies of Robert Owen, James Buckingham, and John Ruskin (1819–1900), an English art critic and philanthropist. To Ruskin, both the social form and the physical form of cities needed attention (Ruskin 1865). His proposed solution was to create clusters of houses in walled compounds on the village scale so they, as Howard later argued, combined the best that country life and urban life offer. More broadly, Howard was inspired by Henry George's *Progress and Poverty. An Inquiry into the Cause of Industrial Depression and of Increase of Want with the Increase of Wealth: The Remedy* (1879) and by Edward Bellamy's *Looking Backward: 2000–1887* (1888). Bellamy imagined a socialist utopia that eliminated the problems for the poor that he associated with capitalism. George, like Bellamy, believed that land should be held in common by all the members of a society.

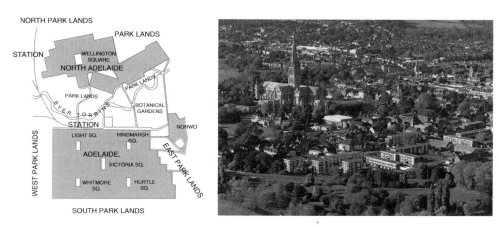

Figure 7.1 The garden city, antecedent models: The Adelaide plan (left) and Salisbury with its cathedral (right)

Source (left): Howard (1902, 129)

Credit line (right): Photograph by Alexey Fedorenko/Shutterstock.com

Early-Twentieth-Century Manifestoes

Howard admired English country towns, such as Salisbury, that provide a rich set of uncrowded behavior settings. He acknowledges the importance of the layout of Adelaide in South Australia, designed by Colonel William Light (1786–1889), in the formulation of his ideas (Howard 1902, 129). Surrounding the city with a greenbelt giving easy access to parkland, as in Adelaide, was a characteristic of the garden city idea. Howard's ideas were further rooted in the nineteenth-century garden suburb as developed by Olmstead and Vaux. Another important influence on Howard was the model industrial village or company town. They included Saltaire, Rowntree, Bournville, and Port Sunlight. Bournville was probably the most influential. (George Cadbury, the son of John Cadbury, Bournville's founder, hosted the first Garden City Association Conference in 1901).

Other developers of generic ideas drew on their own experiences. The neighborhood unit model of Clarence Perry (1872–1944) was influenced by his experience of living in Forest Hills Gardens. He made explicit, in conceptual form, the elements of life that he found rewarding while living there (L. Mumford 1961).

Manifestoes and Paradigms

The urbanists' ideological statements are less celebrated than those of the garden city proponents. A few early-twentieth-century architects did speculate on what the future city should/ would be like on the basis of their extrapolations of what they perceived to be trends in the technological developments of the time. They assumed that the metropolis would thrive and embrace the automobile.

As 'anticipatory design scientists,' they produced drawings of high-rise cities with segregated routes for vehicles and pedestrians. One of them, Harvey W. Corbett (1873–1954), who had studied at the École des Beaux Arts, was a strong proponent of the skyscraper city. He even predicted that individual airplanes would become part of the urban scene and that rooftops would require landing platforms. Architects, such as Mexican Francisco Mujica (b. 1899), produced designs based on an extrapolation of the utility of automobiles. Hugh Ferriss (1888–1962), a New York architect, is another who did.

Ferriss is better known for his drawings than for his designs, which were along the lines of those of Mujica and Corbett. In 1922, Corbett commissioned Ferriss to illustrate the impact of New York City's 1916 zoning laws on the profile of buildings. The laws specified how buildings should be set back at certain levels and their massing limited to ensure that sunlight reached street level. The legislation had an aesthetic impact on a building's design and thus the city's appearance, preventing buildings from occupying the whole of their lots and going straight up as high as practical. They began to be stepped back. Ferriss presented his own views on urban design in a 1929 book, *The Metropolis of Tomorrow*. Frank Lloyd Wright also had some ideas on how the existing city full of skyscrapers should be shaped and produced a thoughtful document in 1926 to illustrate them (Wright 1969).

After examining the hearts of Chicago and New York, Wright accepted the gridiron plan for the blocks of a city, but he proposed the vertical segregation of car, truck, and pedestrian movement channels. The image of the city that he drew was one of tunnels, bridges, and skyscrapers that would stand on planted landscaped podiums. Parking would be located below grade or within buildings above the second-floor level. The first-floor level was for shops. The second-floor level was for pedestrian circulation; there would be bridges over streets so that pedestrians could circulate freely and safely. The streets, he believed, should be wider than they were at the time, and they should have landscaped median strips. After this look at the skyscrapers of Chicago and New York, he drew the conclusion that existing cities were obsolete, cancerous

112

Figure 7.2 The extrapolation of perceived trends: A 1920s neo-American design by Francisco Mujica (left) and the predicted city of 'crowding towers' from Hugh Ferriss's *The Metropolis of Tomorrow*

Source (left): Mujica (1929, Plate CXXIV)
Source (right): Ferriss (1929, 63)

messes. He nevertheless produced a design of tightly packed high-rise buildings sitting on a multilevel car park, Crystal City, for Washington in 1939 (Duran 2017). Patrick Geddes's attitude to the city was different.

Geddes, a Scottish biologist and sociologist who had meandered into city planning, presented his ideas in two books: *City Development* (1904) and *Cities in Evolution* (1915). Although he was influenced by garden city ideals and was a strong advocate for the conservation of the natural environment, he did not automatically seek a green city. He developed his ideas while working professionally in Edinburgh and teaching sociology at the University of Bombay (now Mumbai) and studying the Indian City.

Geddes considered the purpose of city planning and, implicitly, urban design to be the fulfillment of physical, economic, and social needs based on a conservationist view of the design task. Like organisms, cities and/or their precincts, he thought, go through processes of growth, maturation, and decay. Geddes argued for the use of 'conservative surgery' in renewing the old cities of Europe and Asia, the two continents with which he was familiar. He opposed turning urban precincts into garden neighborhoods by demolishing them and building anew. Urban neighborhoods, he argued, should retain their existing street and building patterns but have their sanitary quality and service infrastructures improved (Tyrwhitt 1947; Mairet 1957; Boardman 1978). Wholesale demolition, he stressed, would destroy community networks. This observation was not heeded later in the century, resulting in urban renewal projects' severely dislocating many lives (Gans 1962).

Although Garden City on Long Island, New York, was initiated in 1869, it is a heavily planted pragmatic railroad suburb, not a garden city in Ebenezer Howard's terms. The garden city manifestoes began in 1896 with the advocacies of Thomas Fritsch (1853–1933). He considered the garden city to be the urban type for the future in *Die Stadt der Zukunft*. He was worried about the impact of industrialization and the loss of traditional values on German life. He is, however, remembered today for his antisemitism more than for his views on urban design. Ebenezer Howard's advocacies were more influential even in Germany.

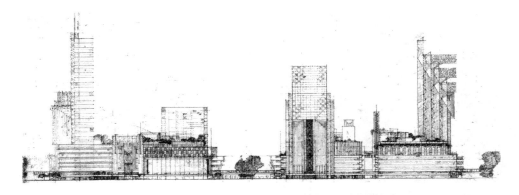

Figure 7.3 Frank Lloyd Wright's diagram for the skyscraper city (above) and his Crystal City proposal (below)

Credit line (above and below): 2020 Frank Lloyd Wright Foundation, Scottsdale, AZ; all rights reserved

Howard's ideas were developed when the railroad was still the major means of transport between the city and its hinterland and the horse-drawn vehicle for travel within it. His *Tomorrow: A Peaceful Path to Real Reform*, published in 1898, sold so well that it was revised and republished in 1902 as *Garden Cities of Tomorrow*. A related manifesto was written by Barry Parker (1867–1947) and Raymond Unwin (1863–1940), who collaborated in addressing the housing needs of the poor. Their book, *The Art of Building a Home* (1901), was part of the Arts and Crafts movement's effort to provide housing for laborers' families. Unwin and Parker argued that the poor should have individual houses, to avoid being stigmatized (Miller 1982).

Howard argued for the design of self-contained towns surrounded by a greenbelt. His garden city would marry the best aspects of the countryside with those of the city. The countryside may have clean air and nature's beauty, but it offered few opportunities for its people to develop their economic lives. It also possessed little variety in the way of amusements. The garden city that Howard proposed would have the qualities of a city in a clean, uncrowded, leafy environment.

He argued, like Robert Owen, for a necklace of satellite new towns around a metropolis. Each should have separate areas for industries, commercial activities, residences, recreational facilities, and parks. Each would be largely self-sufficient. Employment opportunities would be available in industries located on the town's periphery or in the institutions and services required to administer the city. The adjacent countryside would produce the food necessary for it; goods not available locally could be imported, whereas goods manufactured locally could be exported via the railroad.

While commuting to the metropolis for work would be unnecessary, Howard recognized that only a metropolis can support major museums, art galleries, and theaters and that the residents of his proposed new towns would want to venture into the city. He said little about how to improve the metropolis other than that the building of satellite garden cities would lead to a decrease in density of the existing city, enabling it to be re-formed.

What makes Howard's manifesto unusual is that he devised not only a generic urban design type but also a strategy for getting specific designs built. To implement his ideas, Howard settled on limited dividend companies funded by public-spirited investors to build the garden cities. He founded the Garden City Association (which later became the Town and Country Planning Association) to promote his ideas.

In Germany, Bruno Taut, an architect and city planner, was synthesizing the ideas of Howard and some of those of Camillo Sitte in presenting his own concept of an ideal city in *The City Crown* (1919). He was an advocate for a "Garden City of apolitical socialism and peaceful collaboration" (Mindrup 2012, 4). His model city was considerably larger than Howard's, though presented in a similar circular diagram. Contemporaneous ideas about the organization of residential precincts are influential to this day.

Given an assumption about the distance that people are willing to walk and their preference for single-family homes, the size of the ideal neighborhood would have to be approximately 160 acres (65 hectares), according to Clarence Perry. Later, Clarence Stein (1882–1972) made explicit what was implicit in Perry's proposal, by suggesting that several connected neighborhoods could form the structure of a larger district or even a new town (Stein 1957). Perry made his proposal when the neighborhood public school was the center of community life in the United States. By then, the presence of the automobile in the lives of people was clear. While money was tight, households already had their own electricity supply, refrigerators, radios, and cars.

Wright's concept of what a city should be was based on the automobile as the prime unit of transportation. He presented his philosophy in a series of articles and in three books: *The Disappearing City* (1932), *When Democracy Builds* (1945), and *The Living City* (1958). The first two were written during the Great Depression and the third in the euphoric aftermath of World War Two, when great hopes for a new techno-utopian world reigned. By then, television had arrived.

His Broadacre City proposal was first presented in a *New York Times* article on March 20, 1932, as a rebuttal to Le Corbusier's visions for Paris that had been published in the paper earlier (see Chapter 8). He predicted that cities would become decentralized because of the car; their central business districts would thus become redundant. The idea of a walkable neighborhood, he believed, was meaningless in the motor age. Broadacre City was a view of the city as a sprawling suburbia of large open spaces and small holdings where householders would grow vegetables. Getting their hands dirty working the soil, Wright argued, would make them better citizens. This new city type would contain commercial, entertainment, and government centers. Howard's central metropolis would not be needed.

A controversial aspect of his vision of a city was its governance. Broadacre City would be no democracy. It would be led by unelected architects because architects are the "essential interpreters of America's humanity" (Wright 1958, 58). Wright thus rejected the views of the Progressive Party that he had supported earlier. In doing so, he also dismissed the existing city, the ways of life of its inhabitants, and its processes of governance. Like the contemporary rationalists, he thought them not worth retaining.

Generic Concepts and Illustrative Designs

For the urbanists, it was the life of the existing city that inspired. Geddes saw the city as an interwoven pattern of social behaviors and the built environment. Although he recognized the utility of the gridiron plan in creating ease of movement and orientation, he was against its being thrust onto cities that had different road networks. His was a generic procedural model of observation and diagnosis before prognosis.

Geddes opposed planning by legislation; he favored local people's being involved in changing their own worlds. This approach differs from the top-down design process where property developers, public or private, dictate how to regenerate precinct of cities and in so doing often destroying existing well-functioning communities in the name of progress. The urbanists never produced a generic design for architects to embrace. The garden city protagonists did, at least, for cities in temperate climates.

Howard's garden city was for 32,000 people—then the population of Salisbury—on a site of 6,000 acres (2,400 hectares). He proposed a town for healthy living and industry large enough but no larger than that required to afford a rich social life. He hoped that "land would be in public ownership, or held in trust for the community" (M. de Soissons 1988, 50). The town would be surrounded by a rural belt. Once its population had reached 32,000, another garden city would be built, ultimately forming, as noted, a 'necklace,' of such places around a metropolis (Howard 1902; L. Mumford 1965; Fishman 1977; Beevers 1988; Butcher 2010).

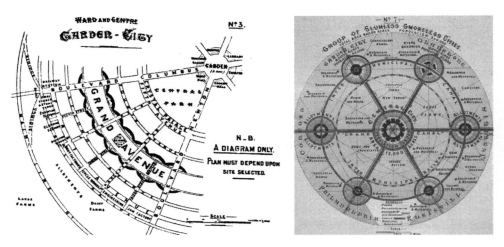

Figure 7.4 The garden city: The generic layout (left) and the necklace of garden cities in relationship to the metropolis (right)

Source (left): Howard (1902, 22)
Credit line (right): Howard (1898)
Source (right): Wikimedia Commons

The generic layout of Howard's model was not to be taken literally. It had to be adapted to the characteristics of the proposed town's site. His conceptual diagram consists of a concentric pattern with six 120-foot (37-meter) radial boulevards stretching from a central park to the periphery of the site. The slice between two boulevards forms a ward. The major institutions of the city are located around the park. A grand avenue circumscribes the center of the plan with housing areas on both sides of it. Public parks, schools, and shops are in the residential zones. Industry served by railroads are placed on the outside circle with the countryside beyond.

To accompany his advocacies, Howard devised a generic process whereby such towns could be implemented. He had hoped that they would be funded by working-class cooperatives so that the land would be held in common ownership. When this idea failed, he relied on having funding provided by limited dividend companies that raised their capital from wealthy investors. To attract industries, tax concessions were provided. Such processes succeeded in funding the first two garden cities: Letchworth (1903) and Welwyn (1920). Their ultimate profitability enabled the companies to pay dividends to their shareholders. Bruno Taut thought differently; he assumed that the government would sponsor projects and own the land. Inhabitants would be renters (Mindup 2012). His advocacy was for more urban a town than Howard had in mind.

The peripheral circle, in Taut's diagram for a new city, consists of a wall of trees. Two main streets run north–south in an arc and two run east–west in the same manner. The city center is in the space created where the two systems cross. Lesser roads run north–south following the arc form of the major roads. The houses are located on minor east–west roads, where they face south toward the sun. On one side of the city center is a church, administrative buildings, and a railroad station. Industrial areas are located on the rail line outside the perimeter of the city. On one side is a large park (Taut 1919). Taut did not deal directly with the nature of social communities. In this respect, the neighborhood unit model proposed by Clarence Perry has been influential.

Perry considered the neighborhood to be the building block for suburbia. Its size was based on a five-minute walk from its center to its periphery. The generic model of the neighborhood, as envisaged by Perry, is shown in Figure 7.6 (left). The community facilities are at its center within a quarter-mile (400-meter) radius of almost all the residential units. The most important of these nodal elements is a primary school, but other local institutions are also there. Shopping areas are at the periphery linking them across a road to the same elements in adjacent neighborhoods to form a retail cluster. The streets are in a hierarchy of widths according to the amount of traffic they had to accommodate. A safe journey by children on foot to school required the crossing of streets to be minimized.

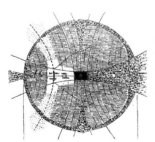

Figure 7.5 Bruno Taut's Crown City: The generic model (left) and the crown (right)
Source (left and right): Taut (1919, n.p.)

Early-Twentieth-Century Manifestoes

Clarence Stein built on this model but considered a half mile (800 meters) to be an acceptable walking distance (Stein 1949, 1966). His generic design is shown in Figure 7.6 (right). Another important difference from the neighborhood unit concept is that he thought that both local shops and the primary school should be at the center of a neighborhood. Three neighborhoods would be linked into a unit sufficiently large to support a high school, which would, along with commercial activities, be located at their intersection. Frank Lloyd Wright considered such a design to be irrelevant. Why walk when one can drive? His Broadacre City was based not only on his observations of US life but also on rationalist thinking.

Wright believed that settlements based on his Broadacre City model would eliminate the United States' social problems. The city that he proposed was 4 square miles (10 square kilometers) in size, multicentered, low-density, and full of sunlight and clean air. The streets he showed are channels for vehicular movement, not seams for community life. Given the city's automobile orientation, gasoline filling stations would be central elements in it. Land would be in public ownership, but each family would receive a 1-acre (0.4-hectare) plot of land from the federal land reserves on which they could grow vegetables. If they did not use their land in some productive manner, they would lose their right to it. There is a train station in Broadacre City and a few commercial and apartment buildings, but the supposed economic base of the city is not specified. Its population would only be 10,000 to 12,000 people—too small to support many common amenities. Wright's ideal is a nonurban city. His illustrations of it show helicopters in the sky.

Although no specific design emerged from Frank Lloyd Wright's ideas, much of modern US suburbia is reminiscent of the characteristics of Broadacre City. In contrast, many garden cities more or less following Howard's principles have been built in places around the world. Bruno

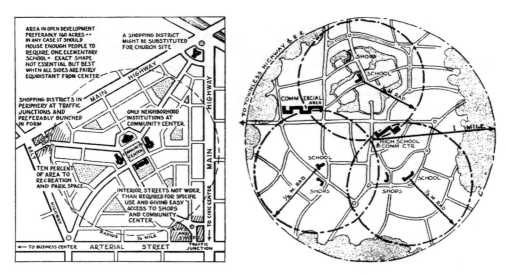

Figure 7.6 The Neighborhood Unit: Clarence Perry's generic model (left) and Clarence Stein's conceptual diagram, showing three neighborhoods forming a district (right)

Credit line (left): Perry (1929)

Source (left): Lang (2017, 93); courtesy of Taylor & Francis

Source (right): Gallion and Eisner (1993); courtesy of John Wiley & Sons

Modern Empiricism

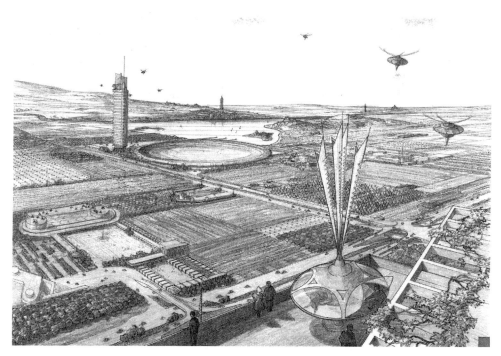

Figure 7.7 Broadacre City
Credit line: 2020 Frank Lloyd Wright Foundation, Scottsdale, AZ; all rights reserved

Taut was the actual designer of several large-scale developments that were based on his ideas but shaped by pragmatic necessities.

Specific Designs

The early garden cities set a precedent for those that followed by departing from the geometry of Ebenezer Howard's drawing. Letchworth Garden City (founded in 1903) was the first. Howard formed a limited dividend company, First Garden City Ltd., to implement it. An almost 4,000-acre (1,600-hectare) tract of land in the English county of Hertfordshire was purchased for the development. The competition held for its design was won by Raymond Unwin with Barry Parker (1867–1947). Welwyn Garden City (1920) took Howard's ideas a step farther than Letchworth did. It is a more fleshed-out scheme, so it is chosen here to illustrate the garden city ideals. Before it was initiated, however, Wekerle Estate, a town on the edge of Budapest, had already broken ground. It demonstrates the rapid impact of Howard's ideas outside Britain.

Of all the examples of the application of Clarence Perry's neighborhood unit, Radburn, New Jersey, in the United States is the most influential. It has become a generic model for suburban development. A scheme developed by Patrick Geddes in India for Belrampur, a slum, illustrates his constructive surgery approach to urban renewal. At the other end of the economic scale, Rockefeller Center in Manhattan, New York, is an exemplar of a large project that is innovative while respecting the character of its location.

Many urban designs created between the two world wars drew on several design ideas. Letchworth, for instance, has city beautiful overtones in its layout. Only two examples of hybrid designs, Hufeisensiedlung in Berlin and Tel Aviv in what was then Palestine, are described here, but they well illustrate the amalgamation of ideas. Both are products of the 1920s.

Exemplars of Empiricist Design

Wekerletelep, Budapest, Hungary (1908–); Welwyn Garden City, England, UK (1920–); Radburn, New Jersey, USA (1929); Rockefeller Center, New York, New York, USA (1928–34); and Belrampur, Madras (Now Chennai), India (1917)

Wekerletelep (Wekerle Estate) was named for Hungarian Prime Minister Sándor Wekerle (1848–1921). The government sponsored its development because private property developers were failing to provide sufficient salubrious living units in Budapest for the rapid-growing population of the city. The government stepped in. Wekerletelep was built as an independent commune, but in 1950, it was incorporated into the burgeoning city.

The development of Wekerletelep was initiated by József Fleischl and designed by Dezsö Zrumeczky (1883–1917) and Károly Kós (1883–1977). All three were leading Hungarian architects. As in Howard's generic scheme, the center of Wekerletelep is a park from which major avenues radiate. The park is a garden square rather than a circle. All the streets are lined with trees, and each garden allotment has four fruit trees giving the estate a garden-like atmosphere (Walker 2014).

The town was designed to accommodate low-level government employees, but a noticeable proportion of the early residents were local factory workers. Begun in 1908, building continued until the Great Depression put a halt to it. By then, 1,007 buildings providing for 4,412 households, four schools, and kindergartens, and police headquarters and barracks had been erected. The estate was administered by community associations and cooperatives. Its own gardening service looked after plantings in the public areas and helped individual households with their gardens. These organizations ceased to operate under Hungary's Communist regime (1949–89) but were revived with its fall. The buildings are in the Transylvanian style developed by Kós who, along with other prominent architects, designed the buildings around the square (Walker 2014).

Figure 7.8   Wekerletelep: The general layout (left) and a street scene (right)
Credit line (left): Adapted from various sources by the author
Credit line (right): Courtesy of Eva Beleznay

Modern Empiricism

Welwyn, also being a garden city, has many of the attributes of Wekerletelep, but it is a much larger development. Founded by Howard, Welwyn was located on redundant land and built by what became the Welwyn Development Corporation (Eserin 1995). The corporation continued operating it until 1966, when its responsibilities were taken over by the United Kingdom's Commission for New Towns. Ultimately, the control of the city's housing, shops, and parks came under the control of the local district council.

Louis de Soissons (1890–1962), an architect with an aristocratic background, was its master planner and the designer of several of its buildings. He followed the precedent set by Unwin and Parker at Letchworth and by Kós and others in Wekerle and rejected the pattern of Howard's generic design (M. de Soissons 1988). The architects involved in Welwyn's development wanted its design to be *their* design. The town consists of a center with a train station, tree-lined boulevards with grass verges, and houses set back from the street. Industries were located, as in Howard's model, on the periphery of the town. A wide, mile-long (1.6-kilometer-long) boulevard acts as the spine of the city. As at Letchworth and Wekerle, the architecture draws from the past. The center is neo-Georgian in character. Originally, there was only one store serving the needs of the city's population, but in 1968, the Commission for New Towns opened up retailing to competition. The station is now part of an enclosed shopping mall. Over time, new facilities, such as a major hospital, have been added to the city, but it has retained its garden city character.

Garden cities require considerable maintenance. To this day, Welwyn has its own environmental protection legislation, the *Scheme of Management for Welwyn Garden City*. The city now has a population of about 46,000 residents, which is substantially higher than Howard's ideal. It entered the motor age remarkably well. Radburn was designed for the motor age.

Figure 7.9 Welwyn garden city: An advertising poster (left), a residential area (above right), and the town's central spine (below right)

Source (left): Lang (1994, 219); courtesy of John Wiley & Sons

121

Early-Twentieth-Century Manifestoes

The neighborhood unit model of Clarence Perry offers one way of organizing the standard automobile-oriented suburban subdivision into something that is more than a pragmatic dormitory. Although never fully completed, Radburn is the exemplar of a development that both allows for driving and makes walking to local destinations easy. It was implemented by the City Housing Corporation, which was funded by Bing & Bing, who were major New York City real estate developers, on a site in New Jersey within easy commuting distance of Manhattan. The designers were Clarence Stein and Henry Wright (1878–1936), with the assistance of Kenneth Weinberger. Their objective was to design a railroad suburb as a community surrounded by a greenbelt. The design incorporated features that, as a package, have become widely known simply as the 'Radburn Plan.'

One of the features of the plan, the 'superblock,' is a generic design idea on which many suburbs, university campuses, and office parks built after World War Two have been based (see Chapter 9). A superblock has a pedestrianized core with vehicular circulation kept to the roads outside it. A seasonally evolving winding strip of landscape, designed by Marjorie Sewell Cautley (1891–1954), forms the central spine of the superblock in Radburn. The development has a predominantly segregated pedestrian path system with underpasses that allow pedestrians to avoid crossing the busier streets. The pathways converge, via the park, at Radburn's center, where there is a school, designed by Guilbert and Betelle, a swimming pool, and a library. Of these facilities, the swimming pool is the center of community life and the place where neighbors meet in the summer (Stein 1966). The external appearance of the houses is neo-colonial or neo-Tudor. The gardens behind them open onto paths that lead to the central park. From there, children can safely walk to the school.

Catering to vehicular movement was a central function of Radburn's design. The town has a hierarchy of roads, the lowest level being cul-de-sacs along which detached houses are located. The houses look away from the cul-de-sacs, facing gardens at the back; kitchens look onto the street. The cul-de-sacs inadvertently became playgrounds for children; the hard surfaces allowed for many of the children's games of the era, and their play could be supervised from the kitchens.

Radburn is governed by an association, empowered by a 1920s covenant. It is run by a self-perpetuating board of trustees chosen by sitting and former trustees. An elected member of the Citizen's Association serves only ex officio. The association administers Radburn's common properties and raises fees to cover the maintenance of communal facilities. To keep the community's aesthetic character intact, it controls the types and qualities of new developments. This arrangement has been upheld as legal despite challenges in the courts.

New York's Rockefeller Center was a contemporary but urban superblock. Rockefeller Center exemplifies the effort to get away from piecemeal building-by-building urban renewal in the heart of a city. Its design draws on what was perceived to be working in the city while enhancing the pedestrian's experience. The center is considerably more restrained than the imagery of the future city shown in Mujica's and Ferriss's drawings. It was developed by an advisory board supervised by a real estate agent, John R. Todd, and built on a central Manhattan site accumulated by John D. Rockefeller (1839–1937), a wealthy industrialist and property owner. The complex of buildings was designed by a consortium of architects under the direction of Raymond Hood (1881–1934), an architect known for his Art Deco designs. The scheme's unity is due to his control over the work of his collaborators.

The buildings are, like the pattern that gives New York its character, built to the property line to form a continuous street façade. They are shaped to enable all usable space

Modern Empiricism

Figure 7.10 Radburn: The city as built by 1928 (left), the conceptual diagram (above right), and a cul-de-sac (below right)
Source (left): Stein (1966, 43); courtesy of MIT Press
Source (above right): Gallion and Eisner (1993); courtesy of John Wiley & Sons
Source (below right): Lang (1994, 179); courtesy of John Wiley & Sons

to be within 30 feet (9 meters) of windows, to ensure that their interiors are illuminated by natural light. They are stepped back at the 100-foot (30.5-meter) height, as required by zoning laws, to allow sunlight to reach the street. The centerpiece of the pedestrianized interior of the block is a sunken plaza accessed from Fifth Avenue by a walkway with planter boxes at its center. The plaza accommodates a skating rink in winter and a restaurant in the summer. Parking for cars and a pedestrian network linking the buildings are underground (Balfour 1978; Lang 2005, 168–73). Rockefeller Center is one of New York's major nodes.

Patrick Geddes faced a different situation in his urban renewal work in Scotland and India. In renovating the Royal Mile area of Old Edinburgh, Geddes's design led to the demolition of the most decrepit houses, the turning of tenements into individual houses, and the re-forming of small closes into spacious courtyards open to sunlight. Inevitably such piece-by-piece 'conservative surgery' leads to the gentrification of areas because each action has a catalytic effect on the decisions that investors make on nearby buildings. A similar attitude to renewing existing areas of cities is displayed in his work in India (Tyrwhitt 1947; Munshi 2000).

During his times in India from 1914 to 1924, Geddes produced an extraordinary number of urban renewal proposals. In his designs, he preserved the existing fabric of places and the

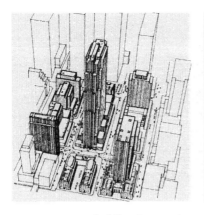 

Figure 7.11   Rockefeller Center: An overall image (left) and the sunken plaza in summer (right)
Credit line (left): Drawing by Thanong Poonterakul
Source (left): Lang (2005, 120); courtesy of Taylor & Francis
Credit line (right): Photograph by Alan Tan/Shutterstock.com

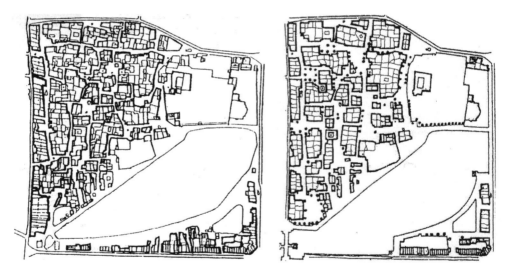

Figure 7.12   Belrampur: The quarter near the palace (left) and Geddes's proposal (right)
Source (left): Geddes (1917)
Credit line (right): Adapted from Geddes (1917) by the author

religious and other buildings of importance. His design goal was to promote civic pride and to make places for individuals to effectively carry out their daily activities. His efforts to deal with the cultural, religious, and economic condition of India, then a British colony, had a profound effect not only on his later work but also on the thinking of other planners. His attitude toward urban renewal is exemplified by his design for Belrampur, the small capital of a maharajah.

The precinct was a labyrinth of narrow streets, crowded houses, and dilapidated and fallen buildings. It was dirty and depressed. Geddes opposed having straight streets through the area and turning it into a generic Civil Lines–type neighborhood that disregarded the culture of the local people. He proposed retaining the dense mixed-use nature and intricate street pattern of the neighborhood and opening the *chowks* (small irregular squares) to more light. His design retained the shading effect of the surrounding buildings that is necessary in a tropical climate. He proposed the introduction of a boys' school and a girls' school and that a reticulated water supply and a sewerage system be provided. The proposal may appear to require much demolition and costly compensation payments, but this conclusion is inaccurate. The existing chowks, each with its temple and well, have been only slightly extended by clearing the adjacent fallen buildings. Geddes suggested that trees be planted to prevent encroachments on the extended easy-to-build-on empty sites.

Geddes's plan not only was more economical than demolition and reconstruction but retained the existing community networks necessary for the day-to-day survival of poverty-stricken people. The existing street pattern also provided a traffic-calming device, a lesson he heeded in the design of the lowest level in the street hierarchy in his master plan for Tel Aviv.

Hybrid Examples

Hufeisensiedlung, Britz, Berlin, Germany (1925) and Tel Aviv, Palestine, Now Israel (1925)

Hufeisensiedlung was one of the Berlin's interwar housing developments. *Hufeisen* is the German word for 'horseshoe.' It refers to the so-shaped 350-meter-long (382-yard-long) structure after which the whole project is named. The horseshoe pattern was not capricious but rather surrounds an old volcanic crater and Ice Age lake. The designers were Bruno Taut and Martin Wagner (1885–1957), an architect and political activist, and the landscape architects Lebere-cht Migge (1881–1935), author of the 1919 "Green Manifesto," a rationalist statement (see Chapter 8), and Ottokar Wagler (1881–1954). Migge's landscape concepts and Taut's Crown City diagram were merged into a specific design. As such, the design stands in contrast to both the perimeter block layout of central Berlin and the city's pragmatic suburbs. Hufeisen-siedlung was regarded as a political and organizational success, and as modernized, it remains a highly desirable residential neighborhood. It was designated a UNESCO World Heritage site in 2008.

The estate has 1,285 apartments in three-story buildings aligned with the streets and 679 row houses, each with a garden and a small terrace. The 'Hufeisen' consists of twenty-five housing units linked together around the pond. Taut saw color as an inexpensive way of creating variety and thus providing each building with a unique identity. Influenced by the colors used by the members of Blaue Reiter, an expressionist art group, the façades of the terraced houses are painted in dark red, yellow ochre, and, at the end of a terraced row, deep blue or white (Jager 2007). The color differentiation is reinforced by the variety of brick types used for fireplaces, entrances, and the base of walls. All the dwellings had a bathroom and kitchen and a separate bedroom. Few, however, had up-to-date heating or electric stoves. The apartments were let furnished because Taut believed that residents' own furnishings would debase his design. The development feels urban and rural at the same time. Tel Aviv is, in contrast, an urbanist urban design.

Figure 7.13 Hufeisensiedlung, Britz, Berlin
Credit line: Photograph by A. Savin
Source: WikiPhotoSpace; courtesy of the photographer

In architectural circles, Tel Aviv is best known for its buildings exemplifying Bauhaus ideals. They were designed by Jewish architects who fled Nazi Germany and settled in Palestine when it was a British mandate. Four thousand such buildings illustrate the adaptation of Bauhaus design principles to the conditions of the eastern Mediterranean to create a unique architecture. The buildings have undecorated surfaces; the windows are in ribbon strips; the roofs are flat, and each building has an outdoor living area. It is, however, the masterplan that is of interest here.

Tel Aviv's 1925 master plan was the work of Patrick Geddes. It underwent several changes, particularly in 1938, without losing its integrity. Geddes's contextual approach to urban design and his belief that the design of new precincts of cities should evolve out of local histories attracted Zionists such as Israel Zangwill (1864–1926), who admired Geddes's urban renewal work in Edinburgh. David Elder (1865–1936), another Zionist and a Fabian socialist, pressed for Geddes's employment in Palestine when the Zionist Commission was seeking an extension to the existing settlement of Tel Aviv. The commission wanted a link between the old and the new that would be in context historically but also modern and Hebrew (Welter 2012).

Geddes proposed a central feature, a square, to stitch the old and new towns together. His design had two major and three minor roads running north parallel to the Mediterranean Sea from the existing settlement. They formed important traffic arteries. Lesser crossroads ran west–east to allow sea breezes to penetrate the interior. Tertiary tree-lined boulevards were designed to provide pedestrian promenades. The fourth level of streets consisted of narrow, irregular lanes, somewhat like those in Belrampur, that were created to slow vehicular travel while providing access to the housing. Unlike Le Corbusier's contemporary prescriptions, the buildings are space makers lining the streets and have active ground floors like those of

Modern Empiricism

Figure 7.14 Tel Aviv: The 1925 plan (left) and a 2018 street view (right)
Source (left): Wikimedia Commons
Credit line (right): Courtesy of Christine Steinmetz

existing cities. The road pattern formed a type of superblock, but without the cul-de-sacs of the Radburn plan. Geddes's superblocks created city block–type garden villages. The institutional buildings in his plan were located together to act as a cultural symbol. The design has stood the test of time well.

Commentary: The Functions Addressed

The empiricists explicitly addressed some of the functions that the built environment can afford; much is implicit in their proposals. A unifying design goal among their disparate views was to uplift the sanitary conditions in which people lived, by providing better housing and greater access to sunlight and clean air. For the garden city advocates, providing people with easy access to parks and the countryside was of prime importance on both physiological and psychological health grounds. In temperate climates, this end also functioned as a sensual reminder of the changes of the seasons. For Frank Lloyd Wright, growing vegetables and other crops was a mark of good citizenship.

Almost universally, providing good educational facilities in a new settlement or in an urban renewal endeavor was seen as a means of providing everybody with opportunities to progress in life. It was a prime concern of Geddes's work in India. Providing for the informal educational learning opportunities that occur as part of everyday life may have been implicit in many schemes but was not explored in any of them. No mention was made of how designs might enrich the lives of people at different stages in the life cycle or of different socioeconomic levels.

Geddes, in dealing with urban renewal projects, strove to maintain existing community networks by not making major changes when renewing neighborhoods. In designing new towns or suburbs, most empiricists addressed the question of how a sense of community might be fostered. In the garden city and neighborhood designs, the function of the built environment

Early-Twentieth-Century Manifestoes

in providing opportunities for meeting this end was achieved, to the extent that it can be, by locating community facilities—particularly schools and, in some cases, shops—at their hearts. The assumption was that by providing opportunities for face-to-face interactions, a sense of local community could be established. Having a common aesthetic quality and an identifiable edge to a neighborhood by way of a greenbelt further enhanced the formation of a sense of community in places such as Radburn. The neighborhood associations were more important in achieving this end.

Implicit in many of the suburban designs is that they were going to be Peter Pan places. It was assumed that as the population aged, the elderly would move out and be replaced by younger adults with children. Residents, however, have mostly aged in place, raising the median age of people inhabiting a development. The demand for places in the local school thus drops. This result is almost inevitable in a new development unless great care is taken at the outset to include the dwelling types and facilities that attract a full range of age groups.

Taut sought a new architectural idiom in his designs, though one in scale with traditional views of good houses. More generally, the function of built forms to reinforce traditional group identities was met by reproducing architectural styles with which potential residents were famil-iar. Even though the design of individual buildings might be unique in the projects described in this chapter, they fall under a common design genre. Their visual unity thus reinforces the group identity of people who, as individuals, might hold different social opinions. Bruno Taut used color to individualize buildings, but the residents were not allowed to personalize either the exterior or the interior of their units, because such actions would detract from the designer's intentions. The legality of using covenants to maintain the architectural character of a develop-ment by suppressing any motivation for deviant individual self-expressions is well established. Few of the residents of the places described here were entrepreneurs seeking to express them-selves by having avant-garde dwelling designs.

Unusual among urban designers was the British garden city enthusiasts' explicit recogni-tion that property developments have to return a profit on the capital invested. In addition, tax concessions were organized to attract manufacturing industries that would provide jobs for residents. The downside of these arrangements was that, except for government-sponsored schemes, the rents were usually too high to attract low-income workers—one of the social objectives of many of the garden city proponents.

Observations

Although a wide range of empiricist approaches to urban design were employed in the first half of the twentieth century, the garden city model has attracted the most attention. It was applied to the design of new towns and suburbs in places as diverse as the colonial hill stations of the British in India and the French in Vietnam, the new town of Den-en chōfu (1918–) in Japan, Orechovka (1920) in the Czech Republic, and Käpylä (1920) in Finland. Tomáš Baťa's company towns associated with his shoe factories in Zlin in Czechoslovakia and in East Tilbury in England are related to Letchworth but are startlingly different in appearance. The 1932 East Tilbury, though a garden city in spirit, was designed by Czech architects; its buildings are strictly modernist, as promoted by CIAM on the continent (Burrows 2016).

Howard's ideas were the basis for the design of three US towns—Greenbelt in Wisconsin, Greenhills outside Cincinnati in Ohio, and Greenbelt in Maryland. They were built during the 1930s under the direction of Rexford Tugwell (1891–1979), a member of the Roosevelt New Deal government. Although regarded as successful, they were declared by the federal government to be unconstitutional ventures into the operation of the private property market. Canada and Australia have several garden city developments, but most of them were built after World War Two. More surprisingly, perhaps, because of the essential Englishness of the concept (Meacham 1999), is the extent to which the garden city principles were applied to new developments in Latin America and in Southern European countries, such as Italy. Den-en-chōfu might be even more unexpected (Watanabe 1980; Oshima 1996).

The Radburn Plan has been applied in many places, but frequently only the two-dimensional layout was emulated. Its three-dimensional, indeed four-dimensional, design principles were not heeded. The results disappoint. The conclusion drawn by planners and municipal officials has been that the Radburn Plan, as a generic idea, does not work when applied to specific instances. It appears that in these instances the principles of the Radburn design were simply not understood.

Geddes' principles of 'conservative surgery' in town planning, based on a study of a locale in its regional context, had a major influence on the ideas of critics such as Lewis Mumford, the sociologist Radhakarmal Mukerjee (1889–1963), vice-chancellor of the University of Lucknow, and architects such as Cebriá de Montoliu (1873–1923). De Montoliu introduced many of Geddes' concerns, particularly those linked to ecologically sensitive design, to architectural and city planning circles in Barcelona in Spain and New Mexico in the United States. Geddes's advocacies, however, were forgotten in the design of many urban renewal schemes throughout the world. It is pragmatically easier in thought and deed to demolish areas of cities and to start anew. Geddes's ideas need to be rediscovered.

Today the empiricist approach to urban design is often seen as something archaic. Its humanism and respect for context, however, remain important. The original radical, egalitarian advocacies of Howard have been lost; the concept of an affordable and collectively owned city for working people no longer persists. Interest in the garden city ideas nevertheless remains strong. What was not foreseen by the empiricists of the first half of the twentieth century was the impact of the world's significant population growth on the demand for large-scale urban developments. The rationalists were less frightened by large population numbers and set about providing for them. Their bold dreams and inventions excited many architects and the public, but their ideas had and have their limitations too.

Figure 7.15 Early garden cities: Den-en-chōfu, Japan, photographed in 1928 (left) and Greenbelt, Maryland, in the United States, photographed in 1938

Credit line (left): Collection of the author
Credit line (right): Photograph by Fairfield Aerial Survey

Key References

Boardman, Philip. 1978. *The Worlds of Patrick Geddes: Biologist, Town Planner, Re-Educator, Peace-warrior*. London: Routledge and Kegan Paul.

Fishman, Robert. 1977. *Urban Utopias in the Twentieth Century: Ebenezer Howard, Frank Lloyd Wright, Le Corbusier*. New York: Basic Books.

Howard, Ebenezer. 1902. *Garden Cities of Tomorrow*. London: Sonnenschein.

Miller, Mervyn. 1992. *Raymond Unwin, Garden Cities and Town Planning*. Leicester: Leicester University Press.

Stein, Clarence. 1966. *Toward New Towns for America*. Cambridge, MA: MIT Press.

8

The Rationalist Response

The rationalists, like the empiricists, considered the medieval city to be chaotic, dark, and dank. The industrial city was as bad or even worse. They abhorred the laissez-faire, pragmatic city and feared what it was becoming. Contemporary illustrations illuminate their pessimism. The German-born Dutch artist Paul Citroen (1896–1983), in his *Metropolis* series (1923), saw the future city as crammed full of streets and steeply angled buildings. Fritz Lang (1890–1976), in his 1927 film of the same name, portrays a city jammed full of skyscrapers with airplanes flying between buildings. Rationalist architects were concerned more broadly with the inefficiencies of places.

Le Corbusier noted,

> Man walks in a straight line because he has a goal and knows where he is going; he has made up his mind to reach some particular place and goes straight to it. The pack-donkey meanders along, meditates a little in his scatter-brained and distracted fashion, he zigzags in order to avoid the larger stones, or to ease the climb, or to gain a little shade; he takes the line of least resistance. But man governs his feelings by his reason.
>
> *Le Corbusier, cited in Guiton (1982, 93)*

In thinking about the nature of future cities, the Rationalists dismissed the ideas of Camillo Sitte and the ideas of the Empiricists. To do better meant sweeping away the old and starting again with bold new urban forms. It meant seizing on the new technological innovations of the age to imagine the city anew. In doing so they had many ancestors (Sharp 1978).

Antecedent Ideas

Colin Rowe (1920–99) pointed out that the rationalists' ideas of the early twentieth century have a strong link to Renaissance idealism, urban designs, and the geometries of Palladio (Rowe 1982). More immediately, the ideas of Reinhard Baumeister and Josef Stübben, who were trying to rationalize city planning, had an impact not only on Viennese design thinking but also on that of the Dutch, who in turn shaped the types of design produced by the Bauhaus intellectuals. Contemporary events in the art world were also influential.

Figure 8.1 Images of the future laissez-faire developed city: Paul Citroen's *Metropolis* (left) and a photograph of the set for Fritz Lang's film *Metropolis* (right)
Credit line (left): Courtesy of the Bauhaus Archiv, Mueum für Gestaltung
Credit line (right): Photograph by Horst von Harbou, Deustsche Kinematek

Cubism's break with the past had architects looking for new ways to progress architecture and urban design (Blau and Troy 2002). The impact was clearest on the De Stijl movement in the Netherlands, in the Bauhaus, and on the paintings and buildings of Le Corbusier. The integration of forms and multivalent spaces were concepts that Cubism and Le Corbusier shared. At the Bauhaus, architectural ideas were influenced by the avant-garde work of artists such as Wassily Kandinsky (1866–1944), Oskar Schlemmer (1888–1943), and Josef Albers (1888–1976). Contemporary social philosophers were also pushing the boundaries of thought.

The observations of Emile Zola (1840–1902) on political liberalism, the view of Henri de Saint-Simon that industrial workers needed to have fulfilling lives for a society to have an efficient economy, and Charles Fourier's socialist ideas all had an impact on French modernist architects. Aspects of Fourier's *phalanstères* were reinterpreted by Le Corbusier in his urban designs. He also drew on the ideas of Eugène Hénard (1849–1923), the French architect-planner as presented in his paper "The cities of the future" (Hénard 1911). Hénard was an advocate for high-rise housing, the efficient movement of traffic, and the use of the traffic circles to speed up the flow of vehicles. He also advocated for setting buildings back from streets to provide sunlight at ground level.

The rationalists could not help but be affected by the excitement of the technological developments occurring rapidly all around them (Banham 1960). Antonio Sant'Elia's thoughts were shaped by the machinery that powered the economic development of North America. The structural and construction aspects of the building types favored by the rationalists built on the pioneering work of structural engineers. Their use of concrete was based on the work of Anatole de Baudot (1834–1915). The construction techniques used in many of the housing projects characteristic of the work of Bauhaus and CIAM reflect the prefabrication approach used by Grosvenor Atterbury at Forest Hill Gardens in New York.

Perhaps most important of all was the moral and social background within which the architects grew up. The early designs of Le Corbusier, for example, reflect his rigid, frugal, Calvinistic heritage and his education when he was still Charles-Édouard Jeanneret at La Caix-de-Fonds

(Turner 1977; Brooks 1999; Flint 2014). He was sure about what people needed, how they should behave, and the values that they should have. Only relatively late in life did he develop an understanding of Roman Catholicism and a tolerance for its values.

Building on this frenzy of ideas, the rationalists' manifestoes of the first half of the twentieth century argued for a completely new world. They were forthright statements full of hope and compassion built on assumptions of what constituted good people and good environments for their lives.

Manifestoes and Paradigms

An extraordinary array of urban design manifestoes were produced by using rational logic. Several were written before those of the Bauhaus and CIAM that are most strongly associated with rationalist thought. They include the assertions of Otto Wagner (1841–1918), Tony Garnier (1869–1948), the futurists in Italy, Russian designers such as El Lissitzky (1890–1944), and members of the De Stijl movement in the Netherlands. They had in common a belief in the power of a radically new built environment to solve social problems and enhance human lives.

Otto Wagner, possibly the first modernist, presented his ideas on urban design in an essay, "The development of a great city" (Wagner 1912). They have a higher empirical content than the protestations of many of his successors. He opposed the traditional focus of city planners on traffic circulation and the enforcement of building codes. He worried about the destruction of Vienna's beautiful neoclassical buildings. He dismissed the picturesque and rejected the views of Camillo Sitte. If anything, he was for a modernized version of the contemporary City Beautiful movement.

City planning, Wagner believed, should begin with the design of a hierarchy of street types in relationship to topographic features and traffic requirements. Unlike Sitte, he argued for uninterrupted vistas on the main thoroughfares. Those streets should be flanked by fine stores and good restaurants and have open squares and monuments placed at intervals along them. A city, he wrote, should have an efficient public transport system and good affordable housing. What works well in a city's older precincts should be retained (Wagner 1912; Olsen 1986). These concerns laid the foundation for the urban design concerns of those who followed him. At about the same time, Tony Garnier (1869–1948) was producing radically different ideas for the future city.

Garnier conceived of his ideal industrial city while a student at the École des Beaux Arts during the first decade of the twentieth century. His treatise, *Une Cité Industrielle; Etude pour la Construction des Villes*, was published later, in 1917. He argued for a socialist city with urban design qualities to match its progressive social structure (Garnier 1917; Wieberson 1969). While Garnier was working on his ideas, the futurists were pursuing a different line of thought in Italy.

In 1914, the Nuove Tendenze movement produced its *Manifesto del Futurismo* on the *città nuova*. Believed to have been written by Antonio Sant'Elia (1878–1916), it rejected Italy's architectural traditions that, the futurists felt, were holding back the country's modernization (Marinetti 1982). Their vision was for a highly mechanized city with the aesthetic quality of bold industrial products. To support modern ways of life, the future city should consist of heroic, multilevel skyscrapers. The futurists' lack of political connections and economic power doomed their ideas. In addition, Gruppo 7, a set of young architects active from 1920 to 1940, believed that the futurists had gone too far in entirely rejecting the past. The Russian constructivists did not think so.

The Russian visions of what the future built environment of cities should be like were never realized, but their boldness continues to arouse interest. El Lissitzky's *Wolkenbügel* (1928)—sky

Figure 8.2 The constructivist city: *Hammer and Sickle*, 1933, by Iakov Chernikov (left), and a photomontage of El Lissitzky's earlier Wolkenbügel, 1924 (right)
Credit line (left): DIGITAL IMAGE 2020, The Museum of Modern Art/Scala, Florence
Source (right): Wikimedia Commons

hanger or cloud iron—was an attempt to amalgamate the basic functional requirements for a city and radical geometric forms. The photomontage on the right in Figure 8.2 gives a pedestrian's view of the spatial qualities of the city that the Russian rationalists were seeking: "Our idea for the future is to minimize the foundations that link to the earth" (Lissitzky, cited in Ades 1986, 103). He proposed a cluster of eight such horizontal skyscrapers for central Moscow. This idea defined the constructivist movement led by Moisei Ginzburg (1892–1946) in the 1920s and 1930s. The drawings of Yakov Chernikov (1889–1951) illustrate the intention well.

Ginzburg's *Style and Epoch: Issues in Modern Architecture* (1924) is regarded as *the* constructivists' manifesto. It was published a year after Le Corbusier's *Vers une Architecture* and illustrates the flow of ideas between Western Europe and the Soviet Union. Ginzburg advanced an architecture and urban design that applied modern technology to achieve Soviet collectivist purposes as displayed in the Derzhprom complex in Kharkiv (1926–28) and Narkomfin (1928–30) in Moscow (Figure 8.18 and Figure 8.17).

The rise of the Soviet Union led to questions of what constituted a Soviet city. Nikolay Alexandrovich Milyutin (1889–1942) presented his views in a book, *Sotsgorod: The Problem of Building Socialist Cities* (Milyutin 1930). What he sought was a workers' utopia—a modern, efficient, and aesthetically pleasing city. About twenty cities were built in what is now the Russian Federation following the general modernist model, but with an emphasis on communal facilities. Some were designed by internationally renowned foreign architects. Of them, Magnitogorsk and Orsk still play a role in the Russian economy; others were never completed or have, with the fall of the Soviet Union, been left to decay. Politically motivated, they were never economically viable. Meanwhile, Western Europe had seen the rise of the De Stijl movement (1917 to about 1930) in the Netherlands.

The group had an immediate effect on the evolution of the Bauhaus' and CIAM's thoughts, even though it produced few buildings and no urban designs. It sought a complete reformulation of European culture and the arts. *Manifest Proletkunst* (*Manifesto of Proletarian Art*), written in 1918 by Theo van Doesburg (1883–1931), prescribed three-dimensional design ideas that were influenced by the art of Piet Mondrian (1871–1944) and his compositions of vertical and horizontal lines in layers and planes. The Red and Blue Chair of Gerrit Rietveld (1888–1964) and his design of the Schröder house in Utrecht (1923) exhibit the patterns that were beginning to appear in the development of the International Style in architecture and urban design as furthered at the Bauhaus (Wingler 1969; Drost 2006).

The Rationalist Response

Figure 8.3 De Stijl architecture: The Schröder House, designed by Gerrit Rietveld
Credit line: Courtesy of Alexander Cuthbert

The Bauhaus was founded to be an educational institution in which all the productive arts were combined as advocated by the nineteenth-century Arts and Crafts movement. Walter Gropius (1883–1969), its first head, wrote the brief *Manifesto and Programme of the Weimar State Bauhaus*. His position was elaborated by Alfred Barr (1902–81), the first director of New York's Museum of Modern Art, in the preface to the book *Bauhaus 1919–1928* (Barr 1938). Students, the Bauhaus declared, should face the reality that their futures would be involved with mass production rather than with individual artisanship. Architects and, implicitly, urban designers should not look back in time for inspiration but should address the problems and concerns of the modern technological world (Bayer, Gropius, and Gropius 1938; Wingler 1969; E. Mumford 2000). They should exploit the new technologies that were changing the ways of life of modernizing people. Individualistic, profit-motivated urban design must be replaced by a coordinated public-interest-based approach (Wiedenhoeft 1985).

The Bauhaus' urban design position is best represented in the books of Ludwig Hilberseimer (1885–1967): *Building Large Cities* (1925), *Metropolis-Architecture* (1927), and *The New City: Principles for Planning* (1944). His advocacies were not entirely consistent. He argued for a decentralized city and for a mixed-use high-rise city. More importantly, he, the Bauhaus masters, Le Corbusier, and other leading modernist European architects formed CIAM in 1928.

Of the twenty-eight founding members of CIAM, the foremost were Le Corbusier, Hélène de Mandrot (1867–1948; a wealthy artist and owner of the Château, where the group first met), and Sigfried Giedion (1888–1986). Giedion, later the author of *Space Time and Architecture* (1944), which is regarded as *the* manifesto of modern architecture, was CIAM's first secretary-general. The elected executive body, CIRPAC (*Comité International pour la Résolution des Problèmes de l'Architecture Contemporaine*), produced a series of manifestoes. The first was drafted at the La Sarraz meeting in 1928 (see Figure 8.4). The best-known and most influential manifesto is, however, the 1933 *Charte d'Athènes* produced at the fourth congress but not published until 1943 (Le Corbusier 1943).

Early-Twentieth-Century Manifestoes

Key elements of CIAM's Serraz Declaration, 1928

On Architecture

It is only out of the present that our architectural works should be devised.

The intention which brings us together is that of attaining a harmony of elements by putting *architecture on its real plane, the economic and sociological plane*; therefore, architecture should be freed from the sterile influence of Academies of antiquated formulas.

. . .

To us, another point of view is that of economics in general, since it is one of the material bases of our society.

. . .

The most efficacious production is derived from rationalization and standardization. Rationalization and standardization directly affect labor methods, as much in modern architecture (its conception) as in the building industry (its achievement).

On Town Planning

Town planning is the organization of the functions of collective life; it applies just as well to rural places as urban agglomerations.

It cannot be conditioned by the pretensions of an established aestheticism; its essence is of a functional nature.

The functions it embraces are four in number: dwelling, work, recreation, and transportation (which connects the first three functions with one another).

The chaotic subdivision of land as a result of real estate speculation should be corrected.

Present technical means, which multiply ceaselessly, are the very key of town planning. They imply and propose a complete change in existing legislation; this change should be commensurate with technical progress.

Figure 8.4 CIAM's Serraz Declaration of Aims, 1928

Credit line: Compiled from several sources by the author

The *La Sarraz Declaration* was prepared by Hannes Meyer (1889–1954), a committed communist; Siegfried Giedion; Jean Lurçat (1892–1966), an artist noted for his tapestries; Jean Michel Frank (1885–1941), best known for his minimalist interior designs; and Le Corbusier. The manifesto started with two major statements. The first was that 'urbanism' is the organization of all the functions of collective life in both urban and rural agglomerations. The second was that the goal of urban design should be the achievement of functional order. The desire to create well-functioning built environments came to define the aspirations of CIAM.

The Charter of Athens was based on the observation that existing cities were so lacking in efficiency that they had to be demolished and rebuilt. No attention was paid to the much-loved characteristics of cities, including the features that the drafters of the charter enjoyed. Those qualities had to be sacrificed to get a well-functioning city. Like Frank Lloyd Wright, CIAM believed architects should oversee the design and administration of cities.

Le Corbusier had already presented his position on architecture and urban design in a number of major works: *Vers Une Architecture* (often translated as *Towards a New Architecture* 1923),

The Rationalist Response

Urbanisme (1925) on city planning, and *La Ville Radieuse* (*The Radiant City* 1935). He considered a socialist city of vertical buildings set in parkland as the ideal. In his early proposals, the housing was socioeconomically segregated, but later, no differentiation by status in the appearance or behavioral opportunities was presented in his generic designs.

CIAM's members were an elite group. Their urban designs proposals were based on an idealized model of people, imaginations of efficient ways of life, and the aesthetic tastes that should prevail. The *Charter of Athens*, ultimately authored by Le Corbusier, was primarily concerned with specifying the design principles for producing the 'functional city.' It stated the following (Sert and C.I.A.M 1944):

1. The natural environment of air, plant life, and sunlight are central to life, so they should be the basic considerations in any design.
2. A spatial layout and symmetrical spacing for urban forms were the solutions to modern society's social ills, congestion, general chaos, and blight.
3. Achieving harmony in the relationship between time and space, especially in dealing with mechanized transit, was the central organizing feature of a city.
4. It was necessary to strictly segregate land uses.
5. The population should be housed in widely spaced apartment and commercial blocks.

CIAM's solution was to do away with the street lined with buildings. When Le Corbusier visited New York in 1935, he was impressed by Manhattan's visual strength and the richness of life. He thought the city's large-scale gridiron Cartesian plan was a sound basis for the redesigned city, but he disliked Manhattan's "musky canyons" and the "appalling nightmares" of its streets (Le Corbusier and Jeanneret 1964). He enjoyed the boldness of the city's skyscrapers but thought that they should be larger, taller, and set back from the streets, with more open space among them. He sought a morphology for the city of the future dramatically different from that of the medieval or existing city.

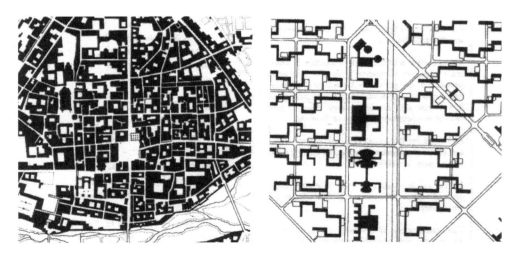

Figure 8.5 The morphology of cities: The medieval city, Parma (left), and the future city, Le Corbusier's proposal for Antwerp (right)

Credit line (left and right): Drawings by Wayne W. Copper; courtesy of the College of Architecture, Art and Planning, Cornell University

Early-Twentieth-Century Manifestoes

In the 1930s, Le Corbusier turned away from his machine-age design ideology. He looked to nature and vernacular architecture for guidance. His designs consisted of more-pliant forms as displayed in his urban renewal proposals for Algiers. His designs were still radically rationalist, and CIAM continued to promote rectilinear geometric forms in its urban designs.

CIAM's image of the city, Le Corbusier's writings and designs, and those of the Bauhaus intellectuals attracted international attention. In Sweden, the Stockholm Exhibition of Industry, Arts and Crafts of 1930 promoted functionalist design, but it was only after World War Two that modernist urban designs were produced not only in Sweden but also in other Scandinavian countries. In the United Kingdom, the MARS (Modern Architectural Research Society) was formed in 1933, after Sigfried Giedion sought a group that would represent the country at CIAM's events. Maxwell Fry (1899–1987) and F. R. S. Yorke (1906–62), both early British modernists, were its initial members. They were joined by members of Tecton, a group of radical architects founded in 1932; Ove Arup (1895–1988), a structural engineer; and John Betjeman (1906–84), a poet and contributor to *Architectural Review*. They produced a design for London that, if implemented, would have required the demolition of much of the metropolis. In the United States, Catherin Bauer Wursted (1905–1964) was an early advocate for modernist architecture and social consciousness among US architects. Her book *Modern Housing* (1934) ultimately led to the Housing Act of 1937 and the establishment of the United States Housing Authority. Landscape architects too were influenced by CIAM's imagery. Leberecht Migge (1881–1935) was the foremost of them.

Migge believed that a country's social and economic problems could be solved through landscape architecture. In his *Green Manifesto* (1919), he sought a functional, socialist, meaningful landscape architecture in which gardens embraced the latest technologies to supplement urban life (Haney 2007). His urban designs show an interpenetration of buildings and gardens in rational, straight lines (Migge 1919, 2013). He considered the English landscape architectural tradition to be an aesthetic affectation.

Some of the manifestoes produced by the early rationalists remained in verbal form, and it was up to the reader to imagine what they meant; others were translated into generic diagrams by their authors or their disciples. Those that were had an instantaneous, though small, impact on what was built before World War Two. After the war, it was a different story; their effect on the furthering of rationalist ideas and on what was implemented was vast (see Chapter 9).

Generic Concepts and Illustrative Designs

The rationalists' generic designs evolved over time, but the logic behind them remained constant. The ideas at the beginning of the century can best be explicated with Otto Wagner's *Grossstadt* (*Large City*) proposal of 1911 for how Vienna should be extended. He suggested that urban blocks be aggregated in a modular grid pattern to form new precincts. Squares and parks would be created by removing blocks from the overall grid. In his proposal, vegetation, particularly trees, was used architecturally to define open spaces. The buildings in his design line the street with continuous façades, which was something CIAM later rejected. They are no more than 23 meters (75 feet) tall; that height was the minimum width of a street. Only buildings such as museums and churches were foreground objects set in open space (Wagner 1912). Wagner's design may have been a harbinger of modernism, but it did not assume a new social order as its basis. More-radical designs did. Tony Garnier's *Cité Industrielle* was the first.

Une Cite Industrielle, a town for 35,000 inhabitants (about the same as Ebenezer Howard's proposal for garden cities), was first exhibited in 1904 but not published until a decade later (Garnier 1917). Garnier's proposal was based on an imagined utopian social system set in

138

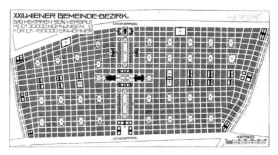 

Figure 8.6 Otto Wagner's generic ideas for urban form: The layout for an urban zone (left) and the cutting away of the urban fabric to form a major open space (right)
Source (left and right): Wagner (1912)

an environment of avant-garde architecture. There were no churches, jails, barracks, or law enforcement buildings in his city. Governed by socialist law and the inherent goodness of people, such facilities would not be needed. "As capitalism would be suppressed there would be no swindlers, robbers or murderers" in the city (Wieberson 1969, 102). This assumption echoed the beliefs underpinning some of the nineteenth-century model industrial villages, such as Bessbrook in Ireland.

The *Cite Industrielle* consists of civic, residential, leisure, health, and industrial activities in separate zones that were linked by vehicular and pedestrian routes. Garnier believed that mass education was a necessity for a society, so he included schools and vocational institutions in his scheme. The latter were located near the industries to which they were related, to provide workers easy access to them. The architectural qualities of the city featured many of the characteristics displayed later by Bauhaus architects. Garnier was not alone in producing illustrative designs of the future city before the onset of World War One.

Antonio Sant'Elia's drawings gave an image to the ideas that the Italian futurists presented in their 1914 manifesto (Sant'Elia 1973, originally 1914). His illustrations feature vast monolithic skyscrapers with terraces, bridges, and aerial walkways that incorporated the latest technologies

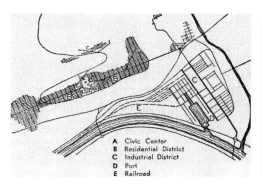 

Figure 8.7 The *Cité Industrielle*: The plan (left) and the proposed character of the industrial area (right)
Source (left): Gallion and Eisner (1993); courtesy of John Wiley & Sons
Source (right): Garnier (1917)

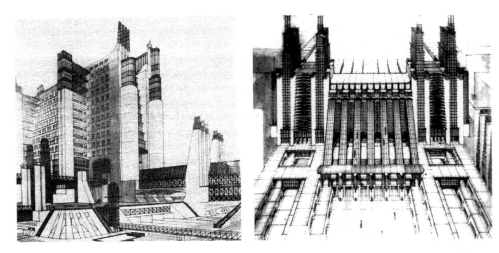

Figure 8.8 Sant'Elia's image of the future city: A high-rise development with multilevel transportation channels (left) and a transportation hub (right)

Source (left and right): Wikimedia Commons

as well as imagined future ones. The station he drew is a multipurpose structure with many platforms for trains and an airfield located behind it. (A future full of aircraft flying around cities was envisaged by architects as early as 1914). The futurists' cause was not helped by the Sant'Elia's death at the age of twenty-eight in one of the battles of Isonzo in 1916. Their concern for the efficiency of the infrastructural armature of cities nevertheless had an impact on CIAM and their imagery on several late-twentieth-century architects, such as John Portman (1924–2017).

Striving for movement-efficient built environments led to the consideration of the linear city as an ideal urban type (Gauthier 1995). Four generic ideas are described here. The first is the design by Arturo Soria y Mata (1844–1920) presented in 1882, the second is that of Edgar Chambliss (1870–1936), the third is the model of Nikolay Alexandrovich Milyutin (1889–1942), and the fourth is one by Le Corbusier.

Soria y Mata proposed that a city's infrastructure—gas lines, water pipes, rail lines, and roads—be arranged in parallel. Buildings would be plugged into the sides of this armature. It was partially implemented in the Ciudad Lineal in Madrid during the 1880s. Chambliss developed the concept of a linear city as an infinitely extendable single building in 1910. He envisaged Roadtown to be a skyscraper laid on its side with a railroad running under it. "The Roadtown is a scheme to organize production, transportation, and consumption in one systematic plan" (Chambliss 1910). The idea evoked little interest. Milyutin's concept was presented in his 1930 book, *Sotsgorod*. It is similar to that developed slightly earlier by Mikhail Okhitovich (1896–1937), who is better known for his dis-urbanism ideas. Okhitovich's linear city was bookended by industrial destinations limiting growth, whereas Milyutin's city is indefinitely extendable.

Milyutin, an economist, argued that the linear city was economically the most efficient in both capital and operating costs. In his model, the industrial zone of factories is located along a railroad. The housing zone was separated from it by a linear park. Milyutin envisaged employees' living opposite their places of employment so that they could walk to work and so eliminate or, at least, reduce the need for transportation facilities. Le Corbusier's design came much later, during World War Two. His plan has rail, road, and canal routes for bringing raw materials to factories and exporting fabricated products. It has an industrial zone followed by a green buffer bordered by a highway, across which lies the residential area with the countryside beyond. Where highways intersected in his model, he had 'radiocentric' cities accommodating intellectual and government pursuits (Guiton 1982). The linear city concept continues to attract interest, but no scheme has been built.

Of all the rationalist architects who produced generic designs for cities, those of Le Corbusier and Ludwig Hilberseimer have had the largest impact. Le Corbusier's generic designs were developed well before he presented his linear city model. His "City for Three Million" (*La Ville Contemporaine*) and the "Radiant City" (*La Ville Radieuse*) are well known and continue to be influential. Hilberseimer's ideas, through his work with CIAM, also affected much that was later built.

Le Corbusier's generic city designs consist of commercial and residential buildings as urban elements, the vertical and horizontal segregation of movement channels, and a free-flowing landscape all set within a gridiron plan. Each of the widely spaced, sixty-story office buildings in the central area of his city could accommodate 1,200 workers but occupied only 5% to 10% of the total land area (Le Corbusier and Jeanneret 1964). Each building would have an underground railway station. The distance the buildings are apart would be dictated by the requirements of the rail system. The open spaces in his scheme are heavily planted with trees and

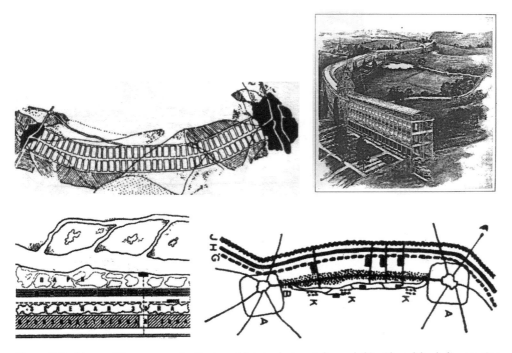

Figure 8.9 Linear City proposals: Soria y Mata's design (above left), Chambliss's linear city (above right), Milyutin's proposal (below left), and Le Corbusier's industrial city (below right)

Source (above left): Wikimedia Commons

Credit line (above right): Chambliss (1910)

Credit line (below left): Drawing adapted from several sources by the author

Source (below right): Gallion and Eisner (1993); courtesy of John Wiley & Sons

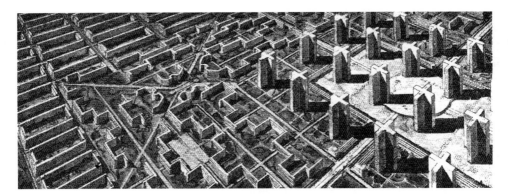

Figure 8.10 Le Corbusier's *La Ville Contemporaine*
Source: Le Corbusier (1960); FLC.ADAGP

other vegetation. Around the center are terraced housing and apartment blocks of maisonettes catering to families. The units in the apartment blocks have two-story balconies to provide light and air to their interiors.

The other residential areas of Le Corbusier's city consist of slab apartment buildings that are arranged parallel to or at right angles to each other. Open spaces are partially allocated to sporting facilities. Le Corbusier, unlike Wagner, considered the traditional street lined by sidewalks and buildings to be oppressive. He thought that they were dangerous for pedestrians in an age of motor traffic. No rational person, he believed, wanted such places. Streets in his design are straight channels of vehicular movement; pedestrians have their own independent circulation routes. He applied this model to his Plan Voisin for Paris (1925).

Hilberseimer had a commitment to the *Zeilenbauen* system—the ribbon development of buildings in straight rows—in opposition to the perimeter blocks of Berlin (E. Mumford 2000; Hake 2008). His High-rise City consists of a series of slab building on podiums arranged so that they align the street. It is a design type that he later regretted (Spaeth 1981). His Decentralized City model is very different. It owes a debt to linear city ideas. Like Frank Lloyd Wright's Broadacre City, its structure was based on automobiles and trucks as the prime means of transportation. It also recognized that the factories were becoming decentralized as part of a second industrial age, when manufacturing processes would be organized horizontally rather than vertically. Arranged along a linear transportation system, Decentralized City stands in sharp contrast to his High-rise City, in which uses were mixed vertically. In Decentralized City, the buildings are surrounded by vegetation, but it is an artificial construction of nature designed to reduce pollution levels and to give a visual order to the city (Hilberseimer 1944; Spaeth 1981; Velasquez and Barajas 2008).

The geometry on display in Hilberseimer's illustrative designs can also be seen in the integrated patterns of buildings and landscape in the generic designs of Leberecht Migge (Migge 1913). Plantings and trees are rationally arranged to enhance the spatial qualities of the artificial world. Migge regarded this approach as more honest than that of the equally artificial picturesque English landscape (Haney 2007).

Although these ideas for future cities are diverse, they have an underlying unity. They were founded on a belief that the new machine age required a new approach to urban designs. The new city was to be based on rational thinking about the best ways of carrying out rational activities rather than on what residents might like to do.

The Rationalist Response

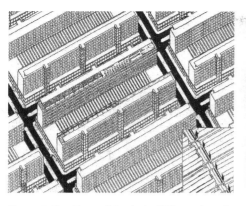

Figure 8.11 Two of Ludwig Hilberseimer's generic designs: High-rise City, 1929 (left), and Decentralized City, 1944 (right)
Credit line (left): Adapted from Hilberseimer (1927) by the author
Source (left): Lang (1994); courtesy of John Wiley & Sons
Source (right): Hilberseimer (1944); courtesy of the Ryerson and Burnham Archives, The Art Institute of Chicago

Figure 8.12 Leberecht Migge's generic model for the future city
Source: Migge (1919) and Haney (2010); courtesy of Taylor & Francis

Specific Designs

Architects designed many internationally renowned modernist buildings during the first decades of the twentieth century. The urban design projects implemented were meager in number but have proven to be influential. They included new towns, housing estates, and a scheme that is perhaps *the* exemplar of rationalist thinking of the time, the Illinois Institute of Technology (IIT) in Chicago. Many more proposed schemes remain unbuilt. They have been equally influential in shaping architects' thinking about the city.

The exemplars of rationalist urban thought of the first half of the twentieth century are diverse in character but show a consistent line of thinking. Le Corbusier's schemes for cities illustrate the development in his thoughts over time. They also show how he was influenced by the contemporary designs of others and how his work influenced their work. Of particular interest was the relationship of projects such as Narkomfin and Magnitogorsk in the Soviet Union to those in Western Europe and vice versa.

Some of the earliest urban design complexes were hybrid designs in which rationalist ideas mingled with earlier pragmatic or empiricist forms. Among them are Amsterdam South in the Netherlands (1914); Le Corbusier's Les Quartiers Modernes Frugès in Pessac in France (1924–34), which although an exemplar of his architecture of the period, is largely, a standard suburban subdivision; and Karl-Marx-Hof in Vienna, Austria (1927–30). Like the exemplars, they have been the basis of many future designs.

Exemplars of Rationalist Design

Le Corbusier's Plans for Paris, France (1924), Antwerp, Belgium (1933), and Algiers, Algeria (1931); Narkomfin, Moscow, Russia (1928–30); Derzhprom, Kharkiv, Ukraine (1926–28); Magnitogorsk, Chelyabinsk, Russia (1929–); the Housing Estates (1927–40); the MARS Plan for London, England, UK (1942); and the Illinois Institute of Technology, Chicago, Illinois, USA (1943–56)

One of the earliest of Le Corbusier's urban designs—the Plan Voisin for Paris—was sponsored by the luxury car manufacturer Gabriel Voisin (1880–1973). It was not a proposal prepared for a private property developer or public agency but rather an exploratory application of his *Ville Contemporaine* to a specific site. Implementing it would have required the demolition of a large tract of central Paris that was, admittedly, in decline. Only buildings of historical importance would be preserved.

The design consists of eighteen glass-façaded, cruciform, commercial towers and government buildings and residential apartments all set in a swathe of grass and trees. Planted mounds would be created from the soil dug for the buildings' foundations. Here and there, a building of historic note would be set as an object in the new parkland. The towers' roofs would be planted

 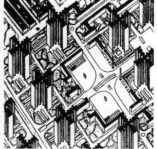

Figure 8.13 The Plan Voisin: A figure-ground image of its layout imposed on Haussmann's Paris (left) and a general view (right)

Source (left and right): Le Corbusier (1960): FLC.ADAGP

The Rationalist Response

with "spindelberries, thuyas, laurels and ivy" (Le Corbusier and Jeanneret 1964). Beneath each of them would be an underground station. The 400,000 clerks working in the precinct would be able to look out onto a verdant world. The design's objectives were to provide buildings and streets with sunshine and fresh air and to reduce air and sound pollution. Bold, straight streets without buildings lining them would allow the free flow of motorized vehicles. Adjacent to the office towers would be lower-rise governmental, cultural, and residential buildings. The design also had triple-tiered pedestrian circulation routes and an integrated network of highways, railroads, and subway systems. The web of lines is not described.

Le Corbusier believed that the scheme, if implemented, would be profitable for the government. It would result in a substantial increase in the price of land. Property taxes would thus soar, and the income yielded could be used for social purposes by the Parisian government (Le Corbusier 1960; Le Corbusier and Jeanneret 1964). He did not, however, suggest how demolition should proceed and how existing residents and businesses would be compensated or relocated.

Le Corbusier's 1930s design for Antwerp is more thoughtfully based on the performance characteristics of transportation modes than is his Plan Voisin. The integration of separate subway, bus, and road networks with pedestrian paths into a unified system is the armature for the design.

The phase in Le Corbusier's work when he became disenchanted with the rigid orthogonal machine-age aesthetic is represented by his 1930s plans for Algiers. The last of his schemes for the city represents his new approach to the form that urban designs should take. "Here" he said, "stands architecture . . . architecture is the masterly, correct, and magnificent play of shapes in the light" (Le Corbusier 1960, 88). His design consisted of a highway below which one- and two-story units formed a vertical garden city. A modern Roadtown, it, like all such proposals, remained unimplemented.

One area in which much self-conscious urban design was indeed constructed during the interwar years was in housing. The experimental German housing developments built during the period of the Weimar Republic (1918–30) were particularly important. They set the standard for much that followed. GEHAG (*Gemeinnützige Heimstätten-, Spar- und Bau-Aktiengesellschaft*) was a group established to construct housing estates. Weissenhofsiedlung in Stuttgart (1927),

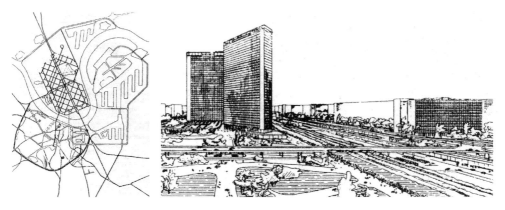

Figure 8.14 Le Corbusier's proposal for Antwerp: The plan (left) and a representative image of the design (right)

Source (left and right): Le Corbusier (1960): FLC.ADAGP

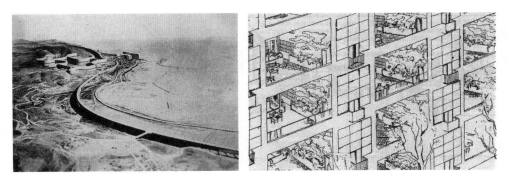

Figure 8.15 Le Corbusier's Plan Obus for Algiers: An image (left) and a detail of the 'wall' (right)
Source (left and right): Le Corbusier (1960): FLC.ADAGP

built for the Deutscher Werkbund exhibition of 1927, was its demonstration of what housing for workers should be (Pommer and Otto 1991).

Composed of twenty-one buildings, Weissenhofsiedlung was designed by seventeen major European modernists selected by Ludwig Mies van der Rohe (generally known as Mies; 1886–1969), who became the director of the Bauhaus in 1930. He oversaw the financing and construction of the project. The architects whom he chose included Le Corbusier, Walter Gropius, Ludwig Hilberseimer, Hans Poelzig (1869–1936), Max Taut (1883–1969), and Bruno Taut (Kirsch 1990; Pommer and Otto 1991). Many people visited the exhibition, and the architectural ideas presented in it had a major effect on a generation of architects. The scheme now has a UNESCO World Heritage listing.

Weissenhofsiedlung consisted of sixty dwelling units in detached houses and apartment blocks. The buildings have plain façades, flat roofs that form terraces, and windows in bands. All but the two designed by Bruno Taut were white. Taut noted, "We must recognize color as having absolutely the same rights as form" (cited in Kirsch 1990). The complex was created to demonstrate what workers' houses with open floor plans could be like and how they could be built. The units were, however, highly customized and unaffordable for workers. In addition, the specific prefabrication techniques employed could not be easily applied to mass housing. The Narkomfin complex in Moscow, initiated a year later, is an example of what the Russian constructivist movement could accomplish with less radical forms than those advocated by El Lissitzky (Vronskaya 2017).

Designed by Moisei Ginzburg and Ignaty Milinis (1899–1974), the housing complex was supposed to consist of four residential buildings set in an open park. Two were built. Each building was set on *pilotis* with a clear ground floor and connected to a block of collective facilities that served as a 'social condenser.' Consisting of kitchens, crèches, and laundries, their function was to liberate most of the women from the drudgery of housework. The units in the housing blocks were maisonettes—two stories in height with living space on one floor and bedrooms on the other—in much the same manner as in Le Corbusier's Unité d'habitation of the postwar years (Cathcart-Keays 2015).

Another complex that boldly demonstrates the hopes of the constructivists is Derzhprom, although El Lissitzky believed that it was not freed enough from the ground. The parliamentary complex built in Kharkiv when it was the capital of Soviet Ukraine (1919–34), Derzhprom is regarded as one of the major architectural achievements of the 1920s (Banham 1960). It consists of three main buildings with towers linked by overhead walkways. Wrapped around a

The Rationalist Response

Figure 8.16 Weissenhofsiedlung, Stuttgart: A 1927 postcard view
Credit line: Courtesy of Freunde der Weissenhofseidlung

Figure 8.17 Narkomfin, Moscow: A residential building (left) and communal block (right)
Credit line: Courtesy of Ginzberg Associates, Moscow

Figure 8.18 A pragmatic constructivist development: Derzhprom, Kharkiv
Credit line: Photograph by Capin Haidmac
Source: Wikimedia Commons

cul-de-sac, it is a monolithic concrete structure that has an open plan interior so that the setting sun can shine through the building. It is what would now be regarded as a brutalist building. Derzhprom was a total urban precinct design; Magnitogorsk was a total new town design.

Ernst May (1886–1970), a German architect, was hired by the Soviet authorities to design Magnitogorsk because of his egalitarian housing designs in German cities, but other hands were also involved. The development of the steel-making city was an element in the Soviet Union's political goal of becoming a modern industrial powerhouse rather than an agrarian society. As such, it was part of the decentralization objectives of the first Five-Year plan of Joseph Stalin (1878–1953), who governed the country as a dictator from the mid-1920s until his death.

The city is located on the northern edge of the Russian steppe, between the mountains and the Ural River in an iron ore mining region. May first designed a Milyutin-type linear city, but the site proved unsuitable for it. The development of a more conventional modernist city went ahead, and in only ten years, the population had reached 300,000 inhabitants. They were housed in superblocks of three- and four-story apartment buildings. The buildings are of brick, a more utilitarian and aesthetically pleasing material than the later concrete slab buildings built in the Soviet Union after World War Two. The steel plant, based on one in Gary, Indiana, and designed by Arthur McKee and Company, came into production in 1932 (Luhn 2016).

Magnitogorsk is a *Sotsgorod*, a socialist city providing the settings required to educate the predominantly rural workers into collectivist Soviet ways of life (Scott 1942). The city has public baths, laundries, cafeterias, nursery schools, cinemas, and worker's clubs with libraries, recreational facilities, and cinemas. An extensive streetcar system provides public transport. The

The Rationalist Response

Figure 8.19 Magnitogorsk
Credit line: Photographer Unknown/Shutterstock.com

design paid little heed to the harsh climate. The winds have had a dual impact on the city. The open spaces form channels for the freezing winter winds, and they spread pollution over much of the city and rapidly blacken any snow that falls (Luhn 2016). While some of the smokestacks have been removed, the level of carcinogenic material in the air is still high.

It is seldom acknowledged today in Russia that the town was built by forced labor. The construction workers lived in barbed-wire-ringed, shoddily constructed camps and toiled under harsh conditions. Industrial accidents were common, and many workers died in the effort to meet demanding deadlines (Scott 1942; Luhn 2016).

Perhaps the housing estates built between the two world wars represent the idea of functionalist design better than any other urban design project type or the Narkomfin. Dammerstocksiedlung (1929), an innovative German housing design, has been the most influential. It was a competition-winning scheme prepared by Walter Gropius, but its design was influenced by that of the second-placed entry of Otto Haesler (1880–1962). It also owes a debt to Hilberseimer's proposal for Friedrichstadt (1928), built along the lines of his generic *Zeilenbauen* model. Its site layout is an exemplar of Bauhaus thought and a major departure from the contemporary German urban norm of perimeter blocks. The rectangular buildings, designed by several architects following strict guidelines specifying the window types and smooth white rendered façades, were laid out in parallel rows facing south to catch the sunshine. Only 228 of the planned 750 housing units were ever built, because its implementation coincided with both the Great Depression and the coming to power of the National Socialists in Germany in 1933. The Nazis put an end to the rationalist explorations of what the city could be. Political attention in other countries, however, turned to renewing the deplorable areas of existing cities.

Although some of the crude nineteenth-century housing areas of European and North American cities have now been and are still being gentrified, in the 1930s, their rejuvenation seemed impossible. Slum clearance and urban renewal projects became part of the work of urban designers. In the United States, Lakeview Terrace in Cleveland, Ohio, was the first such urban renewal project authorized by the US federal government.

Figure 8.20 A rationalist housing scheme: Dammerstocksiedlung, Karlsruhe
Credit line: Photograph by Andreas Schwartkopf/Shutterstock.com

Lakeview Terrace, built on a 22-acre (9-hectare) sloping site in 1935, was fit into a hillside by a curving road. Many of the forty-four residential buildings were arranged in a fanlike pattern to provide a view of Lake Erie from as many of the apartments as possible. The complex had the first community center in a public housing project in the country. The structures, designed by Joseph L. Weinberg (1890–1947) and others, consisted of concrete roofs and floor slabs with steel casement windows arranged in horizontal bands. The windows, the iron railings, and the downturned hoods over the doorways were all common international style design elements. The scheme was also innovative in its incorporation of the artworks under the auspices of the Treasury Relief Art Project created in 1935 (Donnelly 2012). In other countries, much the same type of housing was being built but was drawing on different generic ideas.

Completed in 1938, Quarry Hill Flats in Leeds was the largest social housing complex in the United Kingdom. Designed in 1934 by Richard A. H. Livett (1898–1959) on a 29-acre (about 12-hectare) site, the estate consisted of six- to eight-story blocks containing 938 dwelling units. It cost over £500,000 in 1938 to build it. Like its European precedent, Karl-Marx-Hof, Quarry Hill Flats contained elevators, communal open spaces, and amenities such as a swimming pool, shops, and a day-care center. It had a Garchey waste disposal system. Refuse placed in a bin was compacted, flushed down a chute, and incinerated (Ravetz 1974). Social problems accompanied by neglecting maintenance led to the development's demolition in 1978. Many such projects have met the same fate. Yet other schemes continue to flourish, illustrating that cultural context and people's expectations are very much a determinant of the perceived quality of specific housing types. The nature of the buildings, the affordances of the spaces among them, and the quality of a project's maintenance have been significant factors in shaping a development's success in its inhabitants' eyes. Williamsburg Houses in New York shows it. It has survived better than most as an acceptable housing solution.

The Rationalist Response

Figure 8.21 A rationalist housing scheme: Quarry Hills Flats in 1955 with the Roundabout Petrol Station in the foreground, Leeds
Credit line: Leeds Libraries, www.leodis.net

Williamsburg Houses in New York is more typical than Lakeview Terrace of the form that public/social housing projects took in the United States. It also shows that the way the space between buildings is organized is as important as the buildings themselves. It was built between 1936 and 1938 under the direction of the US government's Housing Division of the Public Works Administration (PWA). One of the first public housing developments in New York City, it was strongly supported by the city's mayor, Fiorello La Guardia (1882–1947). The design team was headed by Richmond Shreve (1882–1947) of Shreve, Lamb & Harmon, architects of New York's Empire State Building. Its most influential member was, however, Swiss-born modernist William Lescaze (1869–1969), the architect of the PSFS (Philadelphia Saving Fund Society 1932) building, the first significant international style building erected in the United States.

The complex consists of 1,622 apartments in twenty four-story, fireproofed, predominantly H-shaped residential buildings, arrayed in a strong geometrical pattern. Its 20.2-acre (8.1-hectare) site necessitated the amalgamation of twelve standard city blocks to form four superblocks. The buildings are oriented east-west toward the sun at a 15-degree angle, and despite being individual objects set in lawns and trees, they are positioned to enclose open spaces and allow for courtyards, playgrounds, and ball courts to be located among them. A school and community building were included in the project.

Lescaze believed that an avant-garde scheme should include contemporary artworks. Five cubist and expressionist murals by artists such as Ilya Bolotowsky (1907–1981) were installed in the basement meeting rooms of the project. They were commissioned by the NYC Federal Arts Project under the direction of Burgoyne Diller (1906–1965), an artist who favored strong geometric forms in his paintings. Abstract sculptures were also part of the initial plans. A 70-million-dollar renovation was completed in 1999.

Figure 8.22 Williamsburg Houses, Brooklyn, New York: The plan (above) and a view (below))
Source (top): Gallion and Eisner (1993); courtesy of John Wiley & Sons
Credit line (bottom): Courtesy of Noel Corkery

The rationalist housing schemes of the interwar years changed the block structure of cities in a new manner. The MARS proposed a plan for London that, if implemented, would have been a much more radical transformation in a city's morphology. During World War Two, MARS proposed a dramatic scheme for the restructuring of postwar London. Although Soria y Mata's linear city model was partially the basis for the design, MARS's Town Planning Sub-committee picked up more specifically on the generic model of Nikolay Milyutin in its proposal. The group, chaired by Arthur Korn (1891–1978), a Jewish émigré architect from Germany, included Arthur Ling (1913–95), Maxwell Fry (1889–1987), and Felix Samuely (1902–59), a structural engineer. It proposed a socialist city exploiting the efficiency of rail transportation.

The heart of London would be left to evolve in its own manner, but the remainder of the metropolitan area would be radically transformed. The metropolis would be circumscribed by a mass transport rail line; railroad spurs would be linear spines extending across a belt of administrative and cultural centers to the circumferential rail line on the other side of the city. Along the spine would be the residential areas of apartment buildings. The housing would be uniform in character to obscure the socioeconomic differences of its residents (Sharp 1971; Gallion and Eisner 1978).

The scale of demolition required to implement the proposal would have put the work of Haussmann in Paris and the dreams of Le Corbusier to shame. Dennis Sharp (1933–2010), best known as an architectural historian, suggested that the design "was not a concrete scheme but a concept that would by its very nature produce interpretations" (Sharp 1971, 167). It was a model for guiding specific designs. That did not happen, but the design remains an exemplar of the rationalists' aspirations. The IIT may, however, be *the* exemplar of rationalist design, although Sabaudia designed by Lucio Piccinato (1899–1993) and built on the drained Pontine marshes of central Italy has its supporters for that accolade. Begun in 1938, it was one of the four new towns established during the dictatorship of Benito Mussolini (1883–1945; premier 1922–43).

The campus plan was a radical departure from traditional university campus designs. It was designed by Mies van der Rohe, who headed the School of Architecture at the university from 1938 to 1958. He was given a free rein to design IIT as a unified set of buildings each located as a separate object on the campus and not as a set of quadrangles. Instead, they form rows of buildings with a rectangular open space between them. The landscape was designed by Mies's academic colleague Alfred Caldwell (1903–98). The first buildings were erected in 1943, followed by a succession of others until 1957. In all, the campus has twenty works by Mies. Strictly geometrical with flat roofs, the buildings were constructed of well-detailed steel frames with curtain walls of brick and glass. The best known is the architectural school, S. R. Crown Hall. It is the type of campus design to which the new university city of Louvain-la-Neuve was reacting later in the century (see Figure 5.6). Its unity still impresses.

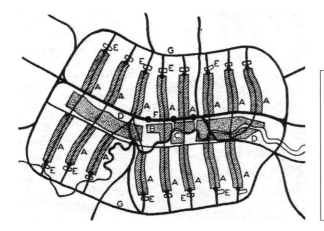

A	Residential units
B	Main shopping center
C	Administrative and cultural center
D	Heavy industry
E	Local industry
F	Main railway and passenger center
G	Belt rail line

Figure 8.23 The MARS conceptual plan for London concept
Source (left): Gallion and Eisner (1993); courtesy of John Wiley & Sons
Credit line (right): Derived from Gallion and Eisner (1993) by the author

Figure 8.24 The Illinois Institute of Technology, Chicago: A view (above) and Crown Hall (below)

Hybrid Examples

Amsterdam South, the Netherlands (1914); Les Quartiers Modernes Frugès, Pessac, France (1924); Le Quartier de Gratte-ciel, Villeurbanne, Lyon, France (1924–34); and Karl-Marx-Hof, Vienna, Austria (1927–30)

The first of these schemes was more a forerunner of twentieth-century rational modernism than an example of it (Giedion 1963, 703). Designed by Hendrik Petrus Berlage (1856–1934) in the second decade of the twentieth century, the Amsterdam South scheme retains many of the characteristics of pragmatic nineteenth-century urban housing developments, but with rationalist overtones. The plan even reflects aspects of city beautiful thinking with its strong axes.

In 1904, Berlage had produced a garden city–like design that the Amsterdam city council rejected. His 1914 design has a much more efficient layout. In his 1908 book, *Grundlagen und Entwicklung der Architektur*, Berlage insisted on the primacy of walls in shaping open spaces and the use of systematic proportional schemas in organizing them (Banham 1960, 140). The scheme exemplifies the application of his ideas. It consists of long blocks lined by buildings facing straight, narrow streets. These streets are intersected by several broad axes. Despite its modernist character, the design continued the tradition of buildings lining streets that Le Corbusier later opposed. Le Corbusier's design for Les Quartiers Modernes Frugès in Pessac outside Bordeaux was another that presaged what was to come.

Henry Frugès owner of a sugar refinery in Bordeaux bought a plot of land in Pessac and hired Le Corbusier, working with his cousin Pierre Jeanneret (1896–1967), to design housing for the workers of his refinery. Frugès gave them free rein to create a housing development that was economically and aesthetically minimalist. Their 1924 design is a small standard suburban development in its layout, but the architecture was different from contemporary models. The original goal was to have 135 houses, but only fifty units were built. They consist of six types of flat-roofed buildings: Ar*cade*, *Gratte-ciel* ('skyscraper,' although it was just three-stories high), *Isolée*, *Jumelie* (twin), *Quinconce*, and *Zig-zag*. All the houses had an entrance hall, a kitchen, a living room, and a bathroom with a shower on the ground floor and two or three rooms above. They were set back from the roadway with a garden patch in front of them. The whole design employed an identically sized module whose proportion was based on the golden rectangle (Lang 2017, 117–19).

The workers declined to move in. The complex was remote and not to their tastes. The houses were sold to private owners, who transformed their interiors and punched new windows into their exteriors, changing the external appearance of the buildings and the interior décor (Boudon 1972). The structural system allowed such alterations to be made easily. The original design intention was lost. In 1973, one owner restored an Arcade-type house and successfully applied to have it declared an historic monument. Other owners and new investors followed suit, restoring their houses sufficiently to turn the neighborhood into a prestigious precinct because of its association with Le Corbusier. Quartier de Gratte-ciel in Villeurbanne, Lyon, is another scheme whose design differs from the rationalist design principles being explicated contemporaneously by CIAM. Its axial plan also echoes city beautiful ideals.

The mayor of Villeurbanne, Dr. Lazare Goujon (1869–1960), a physician, was worried about the prevalence of illnesses among the workers of the new industries in the city. He also wished

Figure 8.25 Berlage's Amsterdam South design: The plan (left) and an aerial view (right)
Source (above): Wikimedia Commons
Credit line (below): Photograph by David de Kool; collection of the author

Figure 8.26 Les Quartiers Modernes Frugès, Pessac: The site plan (left) and the *Quinconces* (right)

Credit line (left): Lang (2017, 118); courtesy of Taylor & Francis

to raise their moral and artistic attitudes, so he sought not only salubrious housing but also a noteworthy civic center for Villeurbanne. The precinct was designed to comprise a Palais du Travail (Labor Institute) with a health clinic and recreational facilities, the Hotel de Ville (City Hall), a central square, and 1,500 housing units. Môrice Leroux (1896–1963), a largely self-taught architect, won the architectural competition for its design. He was not, however, entrusted with the design of the town hall. Robert Giroud (1890–1943), a 1922 winner of the prestigious Prix de Rome, won that commission (Mulazzani 2012).

The Avenue Henri Barbusse forms a bold axis for the quartier. It has the Hotel de Ville at one end and two 19-story residential towers at the other. The sidewalks on the avenue were generous in width and lined by trees. The units were up-to-date; they were provided with central heating obtained from a garbage-burning plant, and waste chutes delivered trash and garbage to the ground floor.

Like the workers for whom Les Quartiers Modernes Frugés was designed, those at the Quartier de Gratte-ciel were uncomfortable with its design. Potential residents considered the apartments to be "rabbit cages" at a "dizzying height" (Mulazzani 2012). The development came to life when people who sought to live there moved in. Many small flats were coupled into larger units for middle-income families, and the Avenue Barbusse was converted into an attractive pedestrian mall. In 1970, the Théâtre National Populaire was relocated from Paris to the Palais du Travail, adding prestige to the development. The Karl-Marx-Hof, an equally important design, begun a couple of years later in Vienna, also deviates from the pure rationalist model.

The Rotes Wien (Red Vienna) administration of Vienna, led by the Social Democrats, came to power after World War One in 1919. It initiated a comprehensive program of social reform that included the building of massive apartment blocks to provide housing for families left homeless by the war. These schemes had their own infrastructure, stores, services, and parks. The Karl-Marx-Hof is the most substantial of these *Gemeindebauten*. A 1-kilometer-long complex, it was built between 1927 and 1930 under the direction of Karl Ehn (1884–1959), a disciple of Otto Wagner. The building is seven stories in height and punctuated by arched portals. It consists of 1,382 apartments ranging in size from 30 to 60 square meters (322 to 644 square feet),

The Rationalist Response

Figure 8.27 Quartier de Gratte-ciel, Villeurbanne: The general layout (left), the Hotel de Ville (center), and the Avenue de Henri Barbusse today (right)
Credit line (left, center and right): Lang (2017, 132); courtesy of Taylor & Francis

laundromats, baths, kindergartens, a library, doctors' consulting rooms, and commercial space. Aspects of the design have antecedents in that of Die Wohenlage Ceciliengärten in Friedenau, Berlin, with its long façades, interior open spaces, and towers over arched entrances originally designed in 1912 by architect-planner Paul Wolf (1879–1957) but redesigned in 1920.

The complex was nicknamed the Ringstrasse des Proletariats to disparage the city's Ringstrasse, designed for the wealthy and to symbolize the glory of the Habsburg Empire. The Karl-Marx-Hof came to symbolize a socialist response to the rise of National Socialism in Germany, but its development arose from Vienna's needs for high-density inner-city housing.

Commentary: The Functions Addressed

The rationalists of the years between the world wars were a diverse group of people. Some had a conservative bias; others were daring and invented imaginary people and the designs to go along with them (Ellis and Cuff 1989). They were unified in their desire to be progressive through, though they might have denied it, the development of the symbolic aesthetic function of architecture to reflect its time: the First Machine Age (Banham 1960). The exemplars of rationalist thinking show that despite their general focus on 'functionalism,' the rationalists established a highly identifiable brand of architecture. The geometric qualities of cube forms and the fenestration and roof patterns were departures from vernacular patterns, the neoclassicalism of the city beautiful, and the predominantly regressive architecture of the empiricists.

At the city scale, the rationalists emphasized the efficient functioning of movement systems. Having an integrated, well-operating transportation system is an essential design goal to this day. In the *Ville Contemporaine*, smooth vehicular movement was particularly important, partly because the design's sponsor was an automobile company whose aspirations had to be met. Even so, the space required to park large numbers of cars was neglected, despite cars standing stationary for 90% of the time. In the linear city designs and in the *Sotsgorod*, well-functioning mass transport systems were the central concern in shaping urban designs.

Organizing the built environment to provide good sanitation and clean air was a paramount concern of all contemporary urban designers. Providing easy access to sunlight, air, and open

Figure 8.28 The Karl-Marx-Hof, Vienna: An aerial view (left) and the façade (right)
Credit line (left): Courtesy of Xavier Duran

spaces for lawns and trees was something the rationalists and empiricists had in common. But the way they did so differed radically. Le Corbusier's schemes also emphasized the desirability of opportunities for physical exercise, although everyday casual walking in carrying out daily activities was not something he contemplated, but walking for recreation was.

The rationalists paid a lot of attention to the design of houses and housing complexes because of the huge demand for accommodations after the havoc of World War One. While many of the individual buildings that they designed were for wealthy clients who shared their avant-garde aesthetic tastes, the focus of mass housing was on providing shelter for workers. Well-motivated though many architects were to meet users' needs, those needs were defined by what they considered they should be and not by the users themselves. Financing always placed a limitation on what could be accomplished, and ease of building was a major consideration.

One objective implicit in the designs was for the radically new building forms to change the tastes of the general population from the traditional to that of the avant-garde. The schemes provided little opportunity for residents to express themselves other than through the furnishings and furniture that they possessed. Bruno Taut did not even want them to do that. Doing so would destroy the aesthetic intent that fulfilled his own need for expression. The buildings at Les Quartiers Modernes Frugès were, however, different. They allowed easy changes to be made to their plans and fabric. They were much altered by their residents to meet their needs. The development lost much of its unified character, although it was unified in its decay. Now, as 'a work of art,' the project has been restored to Le Corbusier's design.

In the large-scale housing developments, communal facilities afforded the development of a sense of community. The need for mutual support among poor residents was probably a stronger factor in the development of any locally based social community. The buildings themselves functioned to obscure socioeconomic differences between people. If anything, the avant-garde aesthetics stigmatized the people who lived in the schemes by setting them apart from people living in standard market-driven, pragmatically designed houses.

Little thought was given to the functioning of the designs as a potentially educative environment where people, young and old, could learn from vicariously participating in the activities they were seeing around them as part of their everyday lives. The richness of life in traditional environments—their diversity of settings—was sanitized out of the developments designed (Smithson 1968; Huet 1985; Hughes 2006). Simplicity ruled over complexity. Thinking about the health of the natural world was yet to come. Landscapes were designed to serve aesthetic purposes and to raise the self-esteem of the residents of an area.

Observations

During the first half of the twentieth century, when so many major social, political, and technological changes were occurring in a remarkably short time, no wonder there was such a proliferation of ideas about what the future city should be like. The rationalists had a religious conviction that their ideas about how people should live and the environments that they should inhabit were morally and often, they claimed, 'scientifically' correct. They were responding to the same problems of contemporary urban life as the empiricists were, but the rationalists believed that no lessons could be learned from the past. They did not even consider worthwhile preserving those aspects of cities that they, themselves, enjoyed.

Concepts of what makes good streets varied in the pre–World War Two years. Le Corbusier's ideal opposed the ideas of Berlage. He could see only what was wrong with traditional streets (Le Corbusier and Jeanneret 1964). Other architects of the period saw streets as the seams of urban life, not solely as channels for the movement of motorized vehicles. Streets give the much-loved existing cities their individual character, as was rediscovered by the new urbanists later in the century.

The radical ideas of El Lissitzky of lifting the city off the ground was reflected in buildings on *pilitos*, but his more radical images of city precincts' consisting of Wolkenbügel towers has only been replicated in individual buildings. Examples are the 1974 Minavtodor building designed be Georgiy Chakhava (1923–2007) in Tbilisi, Georgia, and, in the twenty-first century, the Unilever Best Foods headquarters in the Netherlands, designed by JHK architects, and the Vanke Center in Shenzhen, designed by Steven Holl (b. 1947).

The linear city model continues to intrigue. Paul Rudolph (1918–97) proposed a Roadtown over the proposed Lower Manhattan Expressway in 1967. At a different scale, *The Plan for Melbourne* presented by Ruth Crow (1916–99) and Maurie Crow (1915–88) sponsored by the Communist Party of Australia consists of linear rapid transit corridors spreading out from the center of the city, with green wedges between them (Crow 1969, 1970, 1972). It was a modification of the MARS plan for London. The stations, in the Crows' design, would be in the center of traffic-free zones to encourage casual meetings among people.

The linearity of the Karl-Marx-Hof continued to attract attention. Individual 1920s and 1930s linear building and urban designs based on its design set further precedents for later projects. The Quarry Hills project in Leeds in the United Kingdom (Figure 8.21) was one of the first to be influenced by Karl-Marx-Hof. The Falowiec housing built in Gdansk in Poland in the late 1960s and the Byker Wall scheme built in Newcastle upon Tyne in England a decade later both owe a debt to it too. Neither, however, has the richness of offerings of its antecedents. They fall more in line with the mainstream of rationalist thinking, and their vastness goes out of and comes back into fashion.

The architectural and urban design ideas of the Bauhaus architects were much criticized by the political leadership during the 1933–45 Nazi era in Germany. Neighborhoods of single-family homes in regressive architectural styles were regarded as the ideal residential precinct type. German modernist design ideas were regarded in Germany as un-Germanic. Ironically, in Britain, CIAM's image of a good urban design, as represented in the Bata development at East Tilbury, was regarded as Germanic. Civic design in Germany under Adolf Hitler was dominated by the grandiose city beautiful proposal for Berlin prepared by Albert Speer. The result was the emigration of many modernist German architects, particularly those of Jewish background, to Western Europe, Palestine, and the Americas. Bruno Taut went to Turkey.

The ideas of rationalists as expressed in *The Charter of Athens*, and as promulgated in the wonderful drawings of Le Corbusier and the Bauhaus masters, became exemplars of good urban design and something for students to emulate at schools of architecture throughout Europe and many US and Asian institutions. The acceptance of rationalist concepts as *the* urban design paradigm began on a large scale in the immediate postwar years of the late 1940s. It was strongly promoted at the universities where architects fleeing Nazi Germany found a haven and an intellectual home. Contemporaneously, Le Corbusier's acolytes in South Africa, his Le Groupe Transvaal, were not so sure (Patricios 2000).

Key References

Banham, Reyner. 1960. *Theory and Design During the First Machine Age*. Cambridge, MA: MIT Press.

Ginzburg, Moisei. 1924. *STIL' I EPOKHA*. Moscow: GIZ. English translation by Anatole Senkevitch as *Style and Epoch*. Cambridge, MA: MIT Press, 1982.

Hermansen Cordua, Christian. 2010. *Manifestoes and Transformations in the Early Modernist City*. Farnham: Ashgate.

Le Corbusier. 1960. *My Work*. Introduction by Maurice Jardot. Translated from the French by James Palmer. London: Architectural Press.

Sert, José Luis and C.I.A.M. 1944. *Can Our Cities Survive? An ABC of Urban Problems, Their Analysis, Their Solutions*. Cambridge, MA: Harvard University Press.

Sharp, Dennis, ed. 1978. *The Rationalists: Theory and Design in the Modern Movement*. London: Architectural Press.

Wagner, Otto. 1912. "The Development of a Great City." *The Architectural Record* 31 (May): 485–500.

Wingler, Hans M. 1969. *The Bauhaus: Weimar Dessau Berlin Chicago*. Edited by Joseph Stein. Translated from the German by Wolfgang Jabs and Basil Gilbert. Cambridge, MA: MIT Press.

Part III

The Praça dos Três Poderes, Brasília

Post–World War Two Pragmatic Urban Design and the Rationalist and Empiricist Responses

During the second half of the twentieth century, many of the social, political, and technological achievements of the first half were consolidated. The period can be divided in many ways, but for the purposes of the discussion here, it is into two overlapping times. The first is widely known as the postwar years, despite many nations' continuing to be involved in conflicts. The second era stretches from the 1980s until about 2005. Thereafter, the development of information technology as a means of computation and communication began to significantly reshape many aspects of people's daily lives.

Urban design at both the city level and the project level started to bring together the knowledge and skills of architects, landscape architects, civil engineers, politicians, and economists in a manner that it had not done before. It was assisted in this development by the intellectual parting of ways of city planners and architects. City planners began to focus on social and economic policy approaches to urban development and architects on buildings as artworks based on individualistic aesthetic agendas. At the same time, critics believed that what was being provided by pragmatic urban developments and redevelopments could and should have been better designed.

The Postwar Years

The postwar years extended from the end of World War Two in 1945 to the final days of the 1970s. They were scarred by the Korean War (1950–53); the much longer Vietnam War, or,

Figure 1 World War Two destruction: Warsaw (left) and Hiroshima (right)
Credit line (left): World History Archive/Alamy Stock Photo
Credit line (right): Everett Historical/Shutterstock.com

as it is known in Vietnam, the American War (1957–75); and other conflicts in many other countries. Protest movements rocked Europe and the Americas. Civil war raged in China, resulting in the victory of the Communists under Chairman Mao Zedong (1893–1976). His Great Proletarian Cultural Revolution (1966–76) has had a lasting impact on China's urban designs. The revolution was a war on 'Four Olds': old customs, old culture, old habits, and old ideas. Large well-functioning traditional areas of Chinese cities were demolished to make way for "modernization" (Yu Hua 2018).

The European and East Asian economies were destroyed during the war, as was 70% of their industrial infrastructure. Although the figures are difficult to verify, in the Soviet Union alone, 1,710 cities, towns, and especially villages were at least partially destroyed. Substantial areas of Europe, Japan, the coastal cities of China, and the Pacific Islands were in ruins and needed to be rebuilt both economically and physically. Much of what had survived was antiquated. The Holocaust, the genocide of European Jews and others by Nazi Germany and its collaborators, has left a lasting wound on the psychology and politics of the world (Judt 2005; Woloch 2019).

Some countries took longer to recuperate from the effects of the war than others did. The United States' European Recovery program (the Marshall Plan), enabled West Germany to double its prewar industrial production by the end of the 1950s. The Monnet Plan (1946–50) led to the rapid revival of France's economy. The plan gave the country control over the coal and steel areas of Germany's Ruhr Valley and Saar. The Soviet Union also underwent a rapid increase in manufacturing output. By the 1980s, Japan had become one of the world's most powerful economies. Industrial production and the rebuilding of cities lagged in the United Kingdom.

The Soviet Union and the United States became the two international superpowers, economically and militarily. They created a bipolar world of Eastern and Western Blocs; some countries played one off against the other. The 'Cold War' between the blocs lasted until the revolutions in central and eastern Europe led to the collapse of the Soviet Union in 1991. Meanwhile, the end of World War Two saw the rapid decline of the British and French Empires, with the achievement of independence by formerly colonial countries. Among the most notable newly independent countries were India, which won independence from the United Kingdom; Indonesia, from the Netherlands; and the Philippines, from the United States. Many other nations in Asia and Africa followed.

The United Nations was formed by the victorious allies to replace the defunct League of Nations in overseeing international cooperation and diplomacy. In Europe, economic integration began in the 1950s, leading to the formation of the European Union by the century's end. Political struggles led to major shifts in attitudes and the legislation of new laws in many places. Agitation for equality for nonwhite people in the white-dominated societies of North America, Europe, and later South Africa changed the situation that stranded many people in poverty. Racism was seen more and more as abhorrent; sexism was increasingly challenged and by century's end women had the same legal rights as men in many parts of the world. Attitudes toward homosexuality only began to change toward the end of the century.

One technical innovation followed another but did not affect the general population's ways of life as dramatically as those inventions of the first half of the century. Many people watched the moon landing in 1969 on their television sets; it occurred under seven decades after the Wright brother's first flew an aircraft. The Jumbo Jet had already made international tourism available to many people for whom it had previously been a luxury. Advances were made in genetics, agricultural mechanization and production, atomic energy, and (from the mid-1970s) information technology. The technologies affecting daily life were incrementally improved in quality and became available to more people, shaping the lives of a growing population of middle-class people everywhere. The growth in wealth increased the demand for consumer goods, better housing, and better cities. The increase in the ownership of cars led to the demand for new highways and roads (Marling 1989).

The newly independent nations of Asia and Africa demanded considerable infrastructure investment to further their economic growth. They also required the building of capitol complexes to befit their newfound status. Much had to be accomplished in a hurry. Standard generic urban design solutions were applied on a large scale often out of the context in which they were developed and often in a whittled-down form by policymakers and architects who did not understand the functions that those solutions did and did not serve (Marmot 1982).

The years were characterized by the growth of the suburbs on the periphery of cities. Much urban design was suburban design. The designs were largely pragmatic solutions that met the minimum standards that the market demanded. In the United States, thanks to the benefits of the Serviceman's Readjustment Act of 1944 (the GI Bill) and the development of federally subsidized highways, working-class Americans could own homes in the suburbs. Continuing changes in manufacturing processes from a vertical to a horizontal organization saw the flight of industries from inner-city areas to large sites and lower tax havens in the suburbs and from highly unionized countries to those where regulations were less stringent and wages lower. The result was not only the legacy of abandoned sites in cities but a redistribution of political and financial power that had multiplier and side effects on concerns as diverse as the location of shopping centers, the provision of commercial services, race relations, and gender roles.

Government policies, such as the 1946 New Towns Act in the United Kingdom, and the decision to disperse industries as in the Soviet Union and India resulted in the building of many new towns as part of public policy. The Soviet Union had a strategy of building large new cities in its effort to politically dominate and control lands east of the major settlements of the nation. It is estimated that over a thousand cities, some with over a million inhabitants, were built in the nation during the postwar years. France, Germany, Italy, and the Scandinavian countries all built new towns as part of their development efforts. In other countries, many privately funded company towns were built (Crawford 1995). The morphology of cites was much changed by individuals and corporations seeking to maximize their own benefits, and government agencies sought to fill in the gaps. Pragmatic urban designs sufficed.

Pragmatic Urban Designs

Two broad categories of pragmatic urban designs characterized the postwar years. The first consists of those developments that were produced by private property developers striving to maximize their profits. In the second, public sector decision makers were the property developers. The first resulted in designs of capitalist expediency (Lai 1988). Property developers attended to what can be easily built and sold. Urban designs were created to minimally fulfill consumer demands within the tolerances of generic zoning laws and building codes that govern urban development. Public works were driven by the need to minimize expenditure and the desire not to draw too heavily on tax revenues. Both sets of designs tended to be responses to narrowly defined, frequently single-issue, concerns. They worked well enough but had their shortcomings.

Three generic solutions to three specific problems illustrate the pragmatic urban designs of the era. The first situation arose from the growth in number and use of cars and trucks that led to traffic congestion in towns and between towns. The second, allied to the first, was the difficulty in getting access to shopping and commercial destinations as populations swelled. Third,

Figure 2 Two pragmatic designs to facilitate vehicular movement in cities: Interstate 80–5, San Diego, California (left), and the High Five, Dallas, Texas (right)
Credit line (left): Courtesy of Joe Mabel, photographer
Credit line (right): Photograph by Spingun Films/Shutterstock.com

housing for both middle-income people and low-income people was in short supply, and thus whatever was available was in high demand.

From the 1950s to the 1980s, major divided highways were built around and into the hearts of many major cities around the world. Local streets were transformed from seams of neighborhood life into dividers to provide one-way traffic movement. The objective was to afford easy access for motorists from the city's outskirts and suburbs to their central business districts, to protect the financial interests of property owners. Pedestrians were largely neglected. The I-93 Central Artery in Boston in the United States built during the 1960s is an example. Few such highways penetrating cities were created in the country after the 1980s, but they continue to be built in cities, such as Beijing, Delhi, and Bangkok, that are dealing with a major growth in vehicular traffic. In the United States, suburban areas started to develop their own 'downtowns' as property developers seized on the opportunities provided by easier automobile access to locations on the urban periphery than the traditional Central Business Districts (CBDs) of cities (Marling 1989; Garreau 1992).

The I-93 project in Boston was conceived as early as 1930, but it took three decades to get it implemented. The objective was to reduce congestion on the tangled 'cow-path' streets of the center of the city. An elevated highway running north–south on the edge of the CBD was built to speed traffic through the city. It did not quite turn out that way. The new highway had tight turns and many exits that slowed traffic movement along it, creating extensive delays. It was simplified and later placed in a tunnel, the Big Dig, topped by parkland of dubious utility. Questions are now asked whether the effort was worth the trouble (Flint 2015). Unlike the Big Dig, the Inner Loop in Rochester, built between 1950 and 1965, was a depressed rather than an elevated highway. Its filling-in enabled roads previously cut off by the highway to be reconnected.

Several guidebooks on how to deal with the car were published in the decades immediately after the end of World War Two. The most influential was *Traffic in Towns* (Buchanan et al. 1963). Unlike most prescriptions that advocated for more highways, the book argued for a balanced approach to addressing traffic flow and pedestrian safety concerns by providing both for ease of automobile movements and enhancing public transport systems. Turning city centers into superblocks was one method of enhancing their quality for both drivers and pedestrians. The concept has become a generic solution for both cities and suburbs to follow. Pedestrianizing

Figure 3 The Central Artery/Tunnel project, Boston: The elevated highway in 1964 before the tunnel (left) and the Rose Fitzgerald Kennedy Greenway created over the tunneled artery (right)

Credit line (left): Collection of the author
Credit line (right): Photograph David L. Ryan/the *Boston Globe* via Getty Images

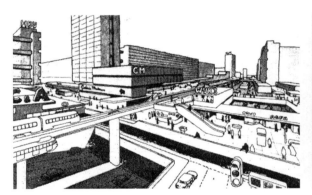 

Figure 4 The vertical segregation of transportation modes: The van den Broek and Bakema illustration (left) and the University of Illinois, Chicago campus (right)

Credit line (left): Collection of the author
Source (left): Lang and Moleski (2010, 133), courtesy of Taylor & Francis
Credit line (right): Courtesy of the University of Illinois, Chicago Archives Collection

selective streets was another. Such solutions have had mixed results. Little of what was contained in the book was, however, applied.

Another generic idea was proposed in many of the visions for future cities produced from the 1920s to the 1970s. It was the vertical segregation of the movement channels for vehicular and pedestrian traffic. An example is shown here. It was an illustrative design prepared by Van den Boek and Bakema, leading Dutch modernists, to show how the segregation could be carried out in Amsterdam. Separating pedestrians and other movement systems in vertical space has not always worked out well. Some elevated walkways have been demolished because pedestrians preferred using busier (and livelier) routes to reach their destinations. The elevated walkways at Charles Center in Baltimore are examples. Those at the University of Illinois campus in Chicago are others. They have now all been removed.

The University of Illinois at Chicago scheme was an award-winning total urban design created by Walter Nesch (1920–2008) of Skidmore Owings and Merrill. It was renowned for its pedestrian walkway built at the second-floor level to create a 'pedestrian expressway.' The walkway connected the buildings on the campus and went over adjacent streets to enable students and staff to avoid having to cross them at street level. At the center of the campus, where two paths crossed at rights angles, was a plaza located on the roofs of buildings (Discover UIC 2005). Pedestrians, however, preferred to hazard crossing streets at the ground-floor level because the walkways were unpleasantly cold in winter, boiling hot in summer, and almost always windy. They were demolished in the 1990s.

In a different context and with a different design, elevated walkways operate successfully. Begun in 1959, the Skyway System in Minneapolis continues to be extended piece by piece. The system was the idea of the president of a real estate company, Leslie Park. Architect Ed Barker was responsible for getting the project underway (Lang 2005). At the beginning of the twenty-first century, it consisted of 5 miles (8 kilometers) of pedestrian skyways and tunnels and sixty-two bridges between buildings. They joined sixty-five blocks in the center of the city, linking 2,000 retail stores, thirty-four restaurants, and numerous cafés. The pedestrian bridges have glass sides and meet the specifications of stringent prescriptive guidelines.

The skyway is well patronized in that it provides for a comfortable walk from structured parking on the edge of Minneapolis's Central Business District to almost anywhere in the precinct in summer and in the freezing winter. Successful though it is, the system has reduced the liveliness of streets; many ground-floor shops have closed. The street level tends to be the domain of the poor. In other places, subterranean pedestrian routes have had similar dual impacts.

Two commercial urban design types catering to the convenience of automobile drivers represent laissez-faire attitudes toward urban development. They are especially prevalent in the North American scene and in other automobile-oriented societies. The first is the commercial strip and the second what has been called, primarily in North America, the shopping mall. The former consists of a linear pattern of retail and/or commercial businesses arrayed in rows along a side, or both sides, of a roadway (usually a highway on the outskirts of a town). Access to parking is directly off the road in front of the driver's destination. The growth in number of

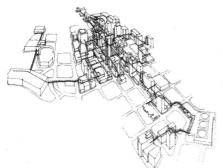 

Figure 5 The Minneapolis Skyway system: The network in 2004 (left) and Nicollet Mall transit way in the same year (right)

Credit line (left): Drawing by Yin Yin
Source (left): Lang (2005, 348); courtesy of Taylor & Francis
Source (right): Lang (2005, 348); courtesy of Taylor & Francis

Post–World War Two Pragmatic Urban Design

Figure 6 Two generic automobile-oriented development types: The commercial strip (left) and the shopping mall (right).
Credit line (right): Courtesy of Aerial Photographs of New Jersey

such strips between 1960 and 2000 was enormous. The shopping mall consists of one or more buildings with surface parking surrounding them. The interior of the built form is a spacious, roofed, temperature-controlled circulation space off which individual stores are located. Most are generic dumbbell designs with major stores at each end.

Convenient though they are for drivers, such commercial developments have been condemned because they consume excessive space, deplete natural resources, and have roads that are unfriendly for pedestrians, of whom there are few, and cyclists, of whom there are almost none. They are not localized into a geographic context, although they are clearly identified with the automobile era and, particularly, the United States. In a few cases, shopping malls were slotted into the hearts of cities, with structured parking nearby.

The suburban shopping mall has a cousin: the office campus. Commercial buildings are set as objects in a park-like setting with parking immediately adjacent to them. The generic idea has been applied to serve other instrumental functions such as those provided by suburban hospital complexes (now often called wellness centers). Such campuses are usually located in areas well removed from where their workers live and served poorly by public transport, so access by automobile is necessary.

The urban design types described here were highly profitable during the twentieth century and were built across North America and later in European and Asian countries. The story in the early twenty-first century is different because consumer tastes have evolved and easily available online shopping has led to a significant decline in the patronage of shopping malls, particularly in the United States. Between 2010 and 2014, there was a dramatic 50% reduction in visits (Lutz 2016). Some changes occurred in the housing market too.

Two generic solutions for housing developments were used to maximize profits and/or to limit costs. The first was based on the rationalist proposals from earlier in the century that consisted of lines of slab or point apartment blocks set as objects in open space. The second type consisted of single-family detached homes. The first is associated with the mass housing projects developed by the public sector to house people displaced by the destruction of large swaths of their cities in World War Two. Later, it was used to accommodate people migrating into cities from rural areas in Asia, South America, and, increasingly, Africa. Although the model of residential blocks set in open space was also used for private housing, the detached house in a yard was, almost entirely, used for private sector residential developments in the suburbs. There are many examples (see, e.g., Gans 1967 on the Levittowns). The exception was that in some countries, such as New Zealand and South Africa, it was also used for social housing developments.

Figure 7 Two pragmatic housing types in the United States: A single-family detached homes neighborhood for middle-income residents (left) and slab block housing, Pruitt–Igoe, East St. Louis, for the poor (right)

Credit line (left): Photograph by iofoto/Shutterstock.com
Credit line (right): US Geological Survey, Department of the Interior

Figure 8 The Soweto model: The basic 1950s housing type photographed in 1963 (left) and the model as applied in a post-apartheid South African government housing scheme, ca 2010 (right)

The number of housing projects built by local or central governments agencies or nongovernmental organizations and by private property developers across the world in the twentieth century is incalculable. Many were thoughtfully considered multifunctional designs; others were designed to meet minimal standards to provide shelter as cheaply as possible. The prewar standard rationalist model was easy to adapt to a site and to build. Most lack the spatial qualities of Williamsburg Houses, and their buildings are taller.

Soweto outside Johannesburg was planned as a racially segregated township for rural people who had to migrate to Johannesburg as workers to survive. It was begun in the late 1950s, after the establishment of apartheid as an official South African government policy. The high-rise form of housing was never adopted as a housing type for low-income African people during the apartheid era. The reasons were partly pragmatic, partly cultural, and partly ideological. First, it was easier to build small single-family detached houses using crude building techniques. Second, for rural migrants, the mass of housing on small lots was a shock but, at least, the taboo of having people living overhead was avoided. Third, by the early 1940s, many South African architects had lost their adoration for the Le Corbusian and Bauhaus mass housing models.

Now home to 1.3 million residents and covering 150 square kilometers (56 square miles) of what had been open veld, Soweto originally consisted of street after street of tiny single-family homes, some residents taking the option of accepting a site and building their own shack on it. Soweto was divided into subareas based on tribal and thus linguistic affiliations. The layout of these areas was based loosely on the neighborhood unit concept. As in mass-built suburbs around the world, Soweto has been transformed by its residents' adding onto their homes so that the original types are no longer recognizable. It remains the model for state-sponsored housing in post-apartheid South Africa.

Although all these designs have been presented as pragmatic solutions, each contains elements of contemporary self-consciously created urban design paradigms. In many other urban design projects of the second half of the twentieth century, the overlap of ideas is more obvious.

The Outline of the Discussion

The goal of this part of the book is to describe and explain the impact of the earlier twentieth-century urban design ideas of the rationalists and the empiricists on urban designs during the second half of the century. If in the first half of the twentieth century, rationalists were reacting to the urban design ideas of the empiricists, then in the second half, it was more the empiricists who were responding to what they perceived to be the deficiencies of rationalist designs. In responses to both pragmatic and rationalist concepts, the empiricists picked up on and developed the garden city ideas that come in and go out of fashion as the perception of the urban development problems shifts. The urbanists among the empiricists sought a 'New Urbanism.'

Chapter 9 reviews the rationalist design approaches and designs that had evolved and had an almost hegemonic control over urban designers' minds in academic institutions of the postwar years. Chapter 10 presents the empiricists' responses. In the 1970s, many architects and critics were unsatisfied with the tastes represented in the rationalists' and empiricists' ideas. Postmodernists sought to fill what they believed to be the deficiencies in the mainstream of both rationalist and empiricist urban design models. They sought a more visually lively world, but they thought little about the behavioral implications of their own design ideas when put into practice. Chapter 11 describes what postmodernists were trying to achieve.

Key References

Garreau, Joel. 1992. *Edge City: Life on the New Frontier*. New York: Anchor.

Judt, Tony. 2005. *Postwar: A History of Europe Since 1945*. London: Vintage.

Marling, Karan A. 1989. "America's Love Affair with the Automobile in the Television Era." *Design Quarterly* 146: 5–20.

Woloch, Isser. 2019. *The Postwar Moment: Progressive Forces in Britain, France and the United States After World War II*. New Haven: Yale University Press.

Yu Hua. 2018. "Revolutionary Roads." Translated from the Chinese by Allan H. Barr. *The Guardian Weekly* (September 21): 26–29.

9

The Post–World War Two Rationalists

After World War Two, rationalist architects convinced many national and municipal authorities and other clients that pragmatic and garden city approaches to urban design were backward-looking; the future needed to be addressed. In Europe, the need for reconstruction after the bombing campaigns of the Nazis and the Allies presented an opportunity to put prewar rationalist ideas into practice. The growth in urban populations added to the demand for new developments. For a while, CIAM's ideas had professional hegemony and dominated academia. Revolts within the organization's ranks, however, led to its demise in 1959. Several new ideas about urban design were advanced by their protagonists. The orthodox and the new, often-competing, strands of rationalist thought were manifested in the projects built (Richards 1962; Sharp 1978; Sherwood 1978).

The range of generic ideas and illustrative designs produced and of projects built from the 1940s to the 1990s was immense. Le Corbusier set the tone for them: "Modern life demands, and is waiting for, a new kind of plan both for the house and city" (cited in Conrads 170, 60). The variety of lines of thought was substantial. Le Corbusier and his colleagues continued to be professionally active until his death in 1965. Those architects who worked with him continued to work in his vein until they recognized the limitations of his ideas and developed their own approach to urban design (see Mallgrave and Contandriopoulos 2008). Competing ideas came from groups such as Team X, which broke away from CIAM, the more radical Metabolists in Japan and Archigram in England, and from the neo-rationalist La Tendenza architects in Italy. Although their ideas appear to have been newly inspired, many built on strands of antecedent paradigms.

Antecedent Ideas

The ideas that CIAM and Le Corbusier developed in the prewar years held sway in architectural circles from the immediate postwar period to the 1970s. His ideas were still much influenced by what he had seen in Moscow in the prewar years (Cohen 1992). The Bauhaus housing model also set a precedent for social housing projects across the world. Many urban design ideas flowed back and forth among contemporary architects. This cross-flow of ideas is demonstrated by the similarities in the handling of urban elements in the schemes of Team 10 and those of the

171

Metabolists. Kenzo Tange (1913–2005), a leading Japanese modernist and intellectual leader of the Metabolists, gave credit to the influence of Le Corbusier and to Dutch structuralism in the development of his proposals. Even though Louis I. Kahn (1901–74), a leading US modernist, said he was inspired by the planning of Carcassonne in France, his designs for his home city, Philadelphia, shows more strongly the influence of Buckminster Fuller (1895–1983), the US systems theorist and futurist.

Megastructure imagery was present in the design proposals of Antonio Sant'Elia in the second decade of the twentieth century. *The Metropolis of the Future* proposed by Hugh Ferris during the 1920s and Le Corbusier's scheme for Algiers (1933) set the stage for the postwar thought processes that resulted in the host of megastructure proposals. The Archigram group saw their work as the logical conclusion to the arguments of the Athens Charter (Dahinden 1972). Paul Rudolph's Roadtown was an update to Paul Chambliss's design.

The neo-rationalist La Tendenza movement in Italy was influenced by the Marxist concepts presented in *Architecture and Utopia: Design and Capitalist Development* (1976) by Manfredo Tafuri (1936–94), an architectural historian at the Università Iuav di Venezia. The university was the intellectual center for the group. The designs of Aldo Rossi (1931–97) and Giorgi Grassi (b. 1935) nevertheless owe a greater debt to neoclassical architecture, particularly to the ideas of Alberti, than to Tafuri and those of the rationalists from earlier in the century. The way their designs were inserted into cities was reflective, in spirit, of neoclassical and baroque urban designs.

The feminist ideas of Dolores Hayden and later by other women, such as Joan Rothschild, have origins in the writing of Mary Wollstonecraft. Hayden's line of thought echoes that of Moisei Ginzburg as displayed in the Narkomfin building in Moscow. That design was based on the desire to expand women's roles in society. The major changes in the role of women in the Americas and Europe can be traced back to the impact of World War One, when many were employed in industrial activities usually carried out by men, and the women's suffrage movement (founded in 1903). Hayden's own study of the utopian settlements of the nineteenth century made a significant contribution to the formulation of her ideas (Hayden 1976).

Some individual buildings gave architects ideas. The Narkomfin building in Moscow is also reflected in the design of the Unité d'habitation. Its initiation coincided with Le Corbusier's visit to the city in 1928 (J-L Cohen 1992). The standing of a building on *pilotis* and the two-story apartments were design features shared by the Narkomfin and the Unité. Both were designed to be one of a cluster of the same building type standing in a park. Le Corbusier's Unité did not have the gender-role-changing aspirations of Ginzburg's work.

The range and cross-fertilization of ideas was immense. They all owe a debt, in spirit at least, to the pioneering ideas of Garnier, CIAM, and the Bauhaus. Sigfried Giedion in *Space Time and Architecture: The Growth of a New Tradition* (1963, but first published in 1941) reaffirmed the earlier advocacies of CIAM

Manifestoes and Paradigms

Although modeled on Frank Lloyd Wright, Ayn Rand's Howard Roark, the heroic protagonist in her novel *The Fountainhead* (1943), was more akin to Le Corbusier in the context of urban design. Le Corbusier had, like Howard Roark, strong ideas boldly stated about cities, and he was certain of their external validity—their relationship to everyday life. At the end of World War Two, CIAM's urban design ideas still ruled.

CIAM held its first postwar conference at Bridgewater Arts Center in England in 1947. Others followed—in 1949 (Bergamo, Italy), 1951 (Hoddesdon, England), and 1953 (Aix-en-Provence, France)—but reactions to the mainstream of rationalist urban design thought had already set in.

CIAM was dissolved in 1956 at the Dubrovnik (Croatia) gathering and finally abandoned in 1959 at Otterlo in the Netherlands. By then, Giedion had his doubts. He was not alone.

Aldo van Eyck (1918–99) from the Netherlands produced a "statement against rationalism" at the Bridgewater meeting of CIAM (van Eyck 1954). At the 1956 congress, French architect Yona Friedman (1923–2020) presented his spatial city model. He argued for new cities to be built as space frames standing on stilts over the existing landscape, leaving enough space for sunlight to penetrate below. The elements would be easily changed to suit the needs of individual households, businesses, and industries (Friedman 1959). As part of a city, it would provide for urban agriculture sufficient to feed the population. His manifesto was largely forgotten until the late 1990s. The early CIAM manifestoes continued to have a profound effect on professional practice.

Their major impact began in the immediate postwar years, when many of Le Corbusier's ideas were being implemented and when José Luis Sert became dean of the Graduate School of Design at Harvard. Sert's urban design advocacies harkened back to his work with GATEPAC (Grupo de Artistas y Técnicos Españoles para el Progreso de l'Arquitectura Contemporañea), promoting architecture as a rationalist endeavor. A member of CIAM between 1947 and 1956, Sert brought to the United States a strong rationalist urban design ideology, as presented in his book *Can Our Cities Survive? An ABC of Urban Problems, Their Analysis, Their Solution* (Sert and C.I.A.M. 1944). His position was very much that of the 1928 CIAM Charter. In the postwar years, many US architects were socialized by émigrés from Europe to accept the tenets of that manifesto. As the United States was seen internationally as the place for advanced architectural education, many foreign students disseminated CIAM's ideas after their studies at US universities. In Latin America, architects such as Carlos Raúl Villanueva (1900–75)—a graduate of the École des Beaux Arts in Paris—in Venezuela and Oscar Niemeyer (1907–2012) in Brazil led the way, influenced by Le Corbusier.

Le Corbusier's postwar thinking was manifested in his plans for the capitol and city center complexes for Chandigarh and the Unité d'habitation in Marseille. He 'de-Anglo-Saxonized' the proposal for Chandigarh prepared by Albert Mayer (1897–1961) and Maciej (Matthew) Nowicki (1900–50) supported by Prem Nath Thapur (1903–69), a member of the pre-Independence Indian Civil Service, and P. L. Varma, Punjab state's chief engineer (L. Mumford 1954). In the Mayer–Nowicki plan, the streets followed the gentle contours of the site, but Le Corbusier rationalized it by straightening out the road network and the water courses. He rejected the Mayer–Nowicki capitol design that was based on Indian precedents. The rejection reflects his conviction in the rectitude of his own approach to urban design but other architects were not so sure.

Aldo van Eyck presented the manifesto of what has become known as the Dutch structuralist movement in a 1959 article, "Het verhaal van een andere gedachte." It was prepared for the Otterlo meeting of CIAM in 1959. Van Eyck harshly criticized the work of CIAM's Dutch members and called for a more humane, ethnographic, approach to urban design. His was a reaction to the lifelessness of urban designs in which the purity of geometry overrode many other considerations. Two streams of structuralist thought appeared in the Netherlands. One considered the city an organic system and its future development based on that analogy. The other was more focused on the nature of lively cities and residents' participation in decision-making. This view was best expressed in *Supports: An Alternative to Mass Housing*, by John Habraken (b. 1928) in 1972.

Other groups unhappy with CIAM's manifestoes also broke away from the association. Team 10 (or 'Team X') was one of them. The group met for the first time in Bagnols-sur-Cèze in 1960 and for the last time twenty-one years later in Lisbon, when only four architects attended. Its core members were Jaap Bakema (1914–81), Georges Candilis (1913–95), Giancarlo De

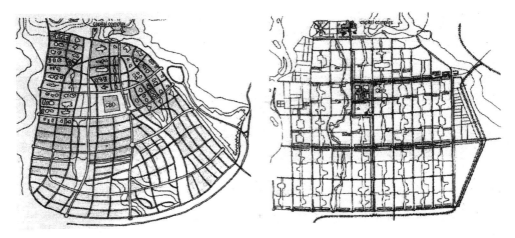

Figure 9.1 Chandigarh: The Mayer–Nowicki plan (left) and Le Corbusier's plan (right)
Credit line (left): L. Mumford (1954, 156)
Source (left): (Lang 2002, 62); courtesy of Permanent Black
Source (right): Lang (2002, 62); courtesy of Permanent Black; FLC.ADAGP

Carlo (1919–2005), Alison Smithson (1928–93), Peter Smithson (1923–2003), Shadrach Woods (1923–73), and Aldo van Eyck. The group was responsible for *The Doorn Manifesto* (1954) but presented its ideas more thoroughly in the *Team 10 Primer* (Smithson 1968). The manifesto lacks precision but suggests an anthropological approach to urban design and simultaneously not one that took precedence over architectural invention or creativity. Team 10's members were stronger in demolishing the ideas of CIAM than in producing a clear alternative model (Risselada and van der Heuvel 2005).

Team 10 advocated for a brutalist architectural aesthetic in which 'raw' concrete was left exposed and brickwork left rough. Brutalist housing complexes and places such as university campuses were built in an extraordinary array of countries. Its advocates considered it to be an honest art form; to its detractors, it was totalitarian. Much depended on the way it was used. Meanwhile, the *Charter of Machu Picchu* (1977), while giving lip service to the need for looking at cities anew, reaffirmed the rationalist ideas of the 1930s, but with some significant differences.

Convened by the Universidad Nacional Federico Villarreal in Lima, an international group of architects, historians, and educators met in 1977 to create a manifesto that was signed in Machu Picchu. Most of the ninety-five points in the *Charter of Athens* were reaffirmed, but the division of the city into residential, leisure, work, and movement components was rejected as too simplistic to meet a broad range of human needs: "Modernist designs have lost their vitality and significance." The charter stressed several points:

> Planning must . . . reflect the essential dynamic unity between the city and its surrounding regions and establish functional relationships between neighborhoods, districts, and other elements in the urban structure. . . . housing must no longer be regarded as a utilitarian commodity, but a powerful tool for fostering social development.

Designing well-functioning public transport systems, the charter stated, should take precedence over designing for automobile travel. Most importantly, perhaps, the charter rejected the notion that architecture was the visual play of pure volumes in Cartesian geometric space; it was instead the creation of spaces for activities and communication between people. Architecture should be "a process of creating spaces and environments capable of functioning under natural conditions. . . . it must be understood that technology is a means not an end" (Charter of Machu Picchu 1979).

Urban designs, according to the manifesto, should no longer consist of buildings in parkland but be a continuation of the urban texture of a locale. As the built environment is always evolving, urban designs should not be regarded as designing for permanent end states, but ones open to change. Historic precincts need to be conserved, restored, and/or reused. Urban designs thus must be indeterminate and result from a collaborative process involving professionals, users, and political leaders ("Four commentaries on the charter" 1979). Many of those thoughts could be presented anew today.

The charter presented several high-minded objectives, but its basic premises were based on assumptions about how people should behave and the values that they should have rather than being a statement on the needs and aspirations of the planned-for population. A contemporary manifesto, the *Habitat Bill of Rights* (1976), tried to address those issues. It was authored by several prominent international architects who had been closely identified with Le Corbusier's ideas: Nadar Ardalan (b. 1939), George Candilis of Team 10, Balkrishna V. Doshi (b. 1927), and Sert (Ardalan et al. 1976). The bill was presented at the Vancouver Human Rights Conference held in 1976.

Urban design, it was stated in the bill, should be "related to time and space and be based on considerations of human scale." It argued for a modern vernacular architecture as opposed to the more abstract qualities of modernist design. By 'human scale,' it meant that the built environment should provide opportunities for chance encounters and that it should thus be based on patterns of pedestrian movement and life. Designs should be climatically specific (Ardalan et al. 1976). The bill was an effort to bend rationalist thought toward embracing empiricist thinking. Some contemporaries were devising much bolder visions of the future city.

Among them was Louis Kahn, who presented his thoughts at the Otterlo CIAM congress. Kahn recognized streets as the locales of everyday life as well as vehicular movement channels. His thoughts were presented in a poetic language that captured the imagination: "The area framing expressways are like rivers. These rivers need harbors. The interim streets are like canals that need docks" (Ronner and Jhaveri 1987, 26; Arkarapasertkul 2016). Emphasizing streets as the armature of the city was central to his advocacies, but not to his urban designs. Kahn's early urban designs were Le Corbusian, but his design for Center City, Philadelphia, owes more to the megastructure ideas of Buckminster Fuller than to Le Corbusier. Other architects, excited by the potential use of new technologies, were producing megastructures and other dramatic new forms for cities (Dahinden 1972). Little of their proposals was ever implemented.

A megastructure consists of a city or, on a smaller scale, a precinct in a single structure. Many more exist in the realm of architectural science fiction than on the ground. The building of megastructures was promoted by individuals such as Paolo Soleri (1919–2013), Buckminster Fuller, and Yona Friedman and by the British group Archigram. In 1956, Friedman produced his *Ville Spatiale*—a city of stilts—that provided a framework that allowed individuals to create their own habitats (Friedman 1958, 1959). Of the megastructure proponents, Soleri most clearly articulated a vision of a new world. He promoted megastructures on the basis of his concept of arcology (architecture + ecology) in his book *The City in the Image of Man* (1969). Three principles form the basis of his arcology. The first is 'complexity.' Soleri believed that the behavior settings that constitute people's daily lives should be clustered together. The second principle, 'miniaturization,' refers to the efficient integration of resources by reducing the sizes of spaces and thus the time required to travel among them. The third principle he labeled 'duration,' which is the time consumed in carrying out the activities of life and the goal of "living outside time"—the capacity to renew oneself and one's surroundings (Soleri 1969). The Metabolists and Archigram differed from Soleri in their approach to megastructures.

The Metabolists were a group of Japanese architects formed after the annihilation of Hiroshima and Nagasaki. Takashi Asada (1921–90), Kisho Kurokawa (1934–2007), Kiyonori Kikutake (1928–2011), and writer-critic Noboru Kawazoe (1926–2015), led by Kenzo Tange, produced a series of visions of large, flexible, and expandable structures that were an analog of organic growth in plants. They presented their work at the 1959 CIAM congress and their manifesto in *Metabolism/1960: The Proposals for a New Urbanism* (Sha 1960). It is a highly philosophical statement based on Buddhist notions of impermanence and change and biological analogies. Short-lived as a group, the members soon followed their own paths.

Archigram was a contemporary. Archigram, formed in the 1960s, consisted of a clique of technology-enamored architects. Its important members were Peter Cook (b. 1936), Warren Chalk (1927–88), Ron Herron (1930–94), David Green (b. 1937), and Dennis Crompton (b. 1936). They observed that people in countries with advanced economies live in societies where products are discarded when no longer useful. They suggested that components of cities could be treated in the same way (Dahinden 1972; Sadler 2005). Their heroic hypothetical designs were promoted in *Architectural Design* and in its manifesto *Archigram 1*, a pamphlet printed in 1961. The group sought a high-tech, light-weight, modular, infrastructural approach to the design of cities. The simple pleasures of life were not given much thought. Little was implemented. La Tendenza architects, the Italian neo-rationalists, thought differently about cities and were more productive.

La Tendenza reacted to the loss of urbanity and complexity in the cities of Le Corbusier and the Bauhaus architects. They rejected the strict functionalism of the earlier rationalists in favor of a more empirical approach to urban design based on the reuse in imaginative new ways of traditional urban elements that give a city its character: "the street, arcade, the yard, the colonnade, the quarter, the avenue, the center, the nucleus, the crown, the radius, the knot" (Knox 2008, 96). An understanding of the functioning of such elements is, neo-rationalists argued, the basis for reordering the city. The goal of La Tendenza architects was to make an easy-to-walk-about-in new city that was a 'theater of memory.' They sought rules for the rational combining of urban elements of social and cultural importance as the basis for their designs. Their stance was presented in three books: Aldo Rossi's *Architecture and the City* (1966), Giorgio Grassi's *La Construzione Logica dell'architettura* (1967), and Vittorio Gregotti's *Il Territorio dell'architettura* (1966). Later, Rob Krier (b. 1938) in his book *Stadtraum* argued that the city should contain enclosed rather than amorphous spaces (R. Krier 1979).

La Tendenza's ideas were partially taken up by the neo-rationalists of the New York school of architecture. That group of architects, such as Peter Eisenman (b. 1932) and Michael Graves (1934–2015), was more interested in designing custom houses than in urban design. In 1970s Europe, Leon Krier (b. 1946) followed many of the ideas of La Tendenza, but his historicism is postmodern rather than rationalist in spirit. Suffice it to say that the neo-rationalists' were looking at the structure of cities in a different manner than those architects interested in exploiting modern technologies to create radically new urban forms (Broadbent 1990).

Later in the twentieth century, some rationalists born in the postwar years were thinking along different lines, based on their perceptions of changes taking place in society. One group consisted of feminists, and the second were the proponents of cohousing. The advocacies of Dolores Hayden represent the first group and those of Charles Durrett (b. 1955) and Kathryn McCamant (b. 1959) the second. In their proposals, they have in common the communalization of household activities and thus some of the facilities that usually occur separately in individual houses. The difference is that Hayden proposed a restructuring of society based on the aspirations of women, whereas Durrett and McCamant proposed a type of housing for those families seeking a communal way of life (Durett and McCamant 1988).

Hayden proposed a society in which men and women had equal rights and obligations, one in which both were breadwinners and responsible for household chores (Hayden 1981). To make such a society possible, she suggested that neighborhoods have communal dining halls, day-care centers, and public kitchens to enable women to fully participate in urban life. In cohousing, a group of likeminded people live in clusters of houses in which common facilities such as kitchens give them the option of cooking at home or in a communal setting. Other common facilities include childcare spaces and such items as a hobby room. The two concepts differ from the mainstream of rationalist thinking in that they were based on promoting what their advocates saw as positive developments occurring in segments of contemporary society.

The rationalists of the postwar years produced a wide array of different visions of the future city in their manifestoes. Some of this broad sweep of ideas was advanced through the production of generic designs that showed what urban designs should be doing. Others fell by the wayside.

Generic Concepts and Illustrative Designs

Several generic ideas are associated with the postwar rationalists of the era. One set led to numerous designs; the other set remained largely on the drawing board. The first included the prewar models of Le Corbusier and the Bauhaus, consisting of buildings set in park-like open space. Perhaps José Luis Sert's image of what the future Barcelona should be like is *the* illustrative image of the rationalists' postwar city. The second set consists of megastructure proposals. Arcosanti is the one genuine megastructure being built. No metabolist urban design has ever been built. Perhaps one will be one day.

The housing estates built on a massive scale in Europe, the Americas and Asia during the postwar years were based on a handful of rationalist models of slab and/or tower apartments blocks, set as objects in open space (Sherwood 1978). They were sometimes accompanied by community

Figure 9.2 The rationalist city: José Luis Sert and CIAM's proposal for Barcelona set against the nineteenth-century city of Ildefons Cerdà on the right

Source: Sert and C.I.A.M. (1944); courtesy of the Frances Loeb Fine Arts Library, GSD, Harvard University

centers and shops. Three types predominated. One consisted of slab buildings lined up in rows with parking for cars and/or park space in between them. In the second, the buildings formed loose perimeter blocks with large open spaces at their centers. These blocks differed from the perimeter blocks of cities such as Barcelona and Berlin, where the layouts were denser and the buildings created a sense of enclosure so that the interiors of the blocks could serve as outdoor rooms. The third type consisted of high-rise point blocks set in open space. Tower bocks (often three in number) surrounded by low-rise apartment blocks or town/row houses formed a variant of the type. This last model was used for housing high-income and low-income people alike, although for the latter, it was considerably sparser. Le Corbusier's Unité d'habitation was a fourth generic model.

Le Corbusier, in collaboration with painter Hadir Alfonso (1920–2013), offered the Unité as *the* solution to the postwar housing shortage in Europe (Richards 1962; Avin 1973; Jenkins 1993). It is a neighborhood for 1,000 to 1,200 people, along with the daily facilities they need, in a single building. Such vertical neighborhoods, Le Corbusier believed, should form the residential areas of future cities. The apartments are two stories in height with a balcony to provide fresh air and sunlight to their occupants. Access to an apartment is from a corridor reached via elevators stopping on every third floor. Two characteristics of the scheme had an impact on subsequent housing: the skip-stop elevator system and the freeing up of the ground floor, except for the entrance hall, to be an open space by setting the building on *pilotis*. Parking would be provided there in dedicated spaces, and the remainder of the ground floor would be available for recreation. Other rationalists were producing more-radical generic ideas for developing cities.

Much of Team 10's thinking can be seen in Alison Smithson and Peter Smithson's 1958 design for the Haupstadt Berlin competition (Garcia and Tartás Ruiz undated). Existing cities were clearly obsolete, but CIAM's image of demolishing the old city to establish a tabula rasa for the new, Team 10 believed, was both unrealistic and undesirable. The Smithsons' design proposal depicts a "matrix of elevated streets and sleekly modern towers superimposed over that city's historic core" (Ouroussoff 2006). The Smithsons' idea of layering is, however, better exemplified in Yona Friedman's many illustrative designs.

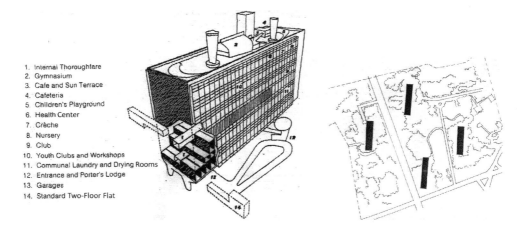

Figure 9.3 The Unité d'Habitation: The elements of the generic model as applied in Marseille (left) and the proposed site layout of a number of Unités (right)

Credit line (left): Richards (1962) and Lang (1994, 52); collection of the author; courtesy of John Wiley & Sons
Credit line (right): Drawing based on several sources by Thanong Poonteerakul

Friedman's spatial city consists of a homogenous space structure raised sitting on piles. The structure consists of three-dimensional layers, one on top of the others. The piles contain elevators and stairs. The lower level could have the community facilities. Only half of a layer would be occupied by structures built by individuals to suit themselves; the rest would allow sunlight to filter below. The whole structure could be placed over an existing city, unbuildable land, or a waterbody.

Megastructures represent a generic way of thinking about how modern technologies might be harnessed in the service of people on a large scale. Two proposals demonstrate this line of thought: Roadtown (1970), designed by Paul Rudolph (1918–97) and Ulrich Franzen (1921–2012), and Soleri's Hyperbuilding. Many other examples could serve just as well as illustrations of the generic idea (see Dahinden 1972). The work of the Metabolists and Archigram further demonstrates the variety of megastructure ideas

Figure 9.4 The layered city: One of Yona Friedman's drawings of his spatial city concept
Credit line: Courtesy of Le Fonds des Dotation Denise et Yona Friedman

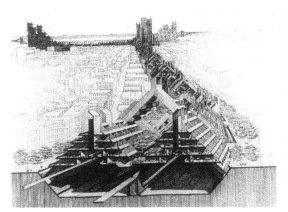 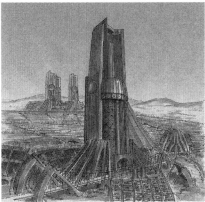

Figure 9.5 Megastructure ideas: Paul Rudolph's Roadtown, New York (left), and Paolo Soleri's Hyperbuilding as a precinct of a city (right)
Source (left): Lang (1994, 53); collection of the author; courtesy of John Wiley & Sons
Credit line (right): Illustration by Tomaki Tamura; courtesy of the Cosanti Foundation

Post–World War Two Pragmatic Urban Design

Metabolists' ideas of 'plugging in' and 'clipping on' were demonstrated in a host of conceptual designs. The best known is the 1960 Tokyo Bay scheme of Kenzo Tange. It was created to show how the evolution of the city could be made easier. It consisted of a set of efficient continuous, interlocking loops forming a megastructure of permanent and transient components.

Figure 9.6 Archigram and the Metabolists: "Walking City," designed by Ron Herron, plugged into Manhattan, 1964 (left), and the Tokyo Bay proposal of Kenzo Tange, 1960 (right)

Credit line (left): Collection of the author
Source (left): Dahinden (1972, 114) and Lang (1994, 53); courtesy of John Wiley & Sons.
Credit line (right): Collection of the author
Source (right): Dahinden (1972, 220)

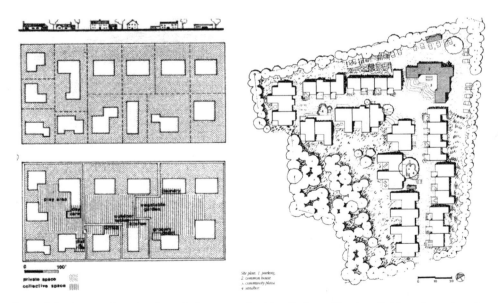

Figure 9.7 A generic suburban design reworked by Dolores Hayden (left) and a cohousing design for Trudesland, Denmark, by McCamant and Durrett, architects (right)

Credit line (left): 1980, Dolores Hayden
Source (left): Hayden (1980, S184); courtesy of Dolores Hayden and the University of Chicago Press
Credit line (right): Courtesy of McCamant and Durett, Architects

180

The pattern would enable drivers to turn off a fast highway to a slower street to arrive at a destination. Pedestrian and vehicular movement systems were separate. Archigram's walking city proposal plugged into Manhattan is illustrative of its aspirations. Later rationalist ideas were much more down-to-earth.

The ideas on how to provide for more-communal lives by Dolores Hayden and by Charles Durrett and Kathryn McCamant are examples. A proposal by each shows their authors' use of common facilities to relieve women of the sole responsibility for carrying out daily household tasks. Hayden illustrated what she had in mind for a future more communal way of life in a diagram showing how a standard suburban subdivision might be converted into one befitting new family organizations. Common land could be created among the dwellings and communal facilities built on it (Hayden 1980). She later refined these ideas (Hayden 1984). Durrett and McCamant designed several cohousing developments that illustrate their intentions (Durret and McCamant 1988).

By the 1970s, the more extreme advocacies of the rationalists were rebuffed by a distain of urban design dreams removed from the realities of everyday life. None of their ideas were whimsical, however. They all were carefully worked-out responses to a set of problems as they saw them. None were complete breaks from the past. They all had some empirical content. The specific designs illustrate this observation.

Specific Designs

Many urban design schemes based on rationalist thinking were proposed during the postwar years, and they continue to be to this day. None of the schemes for cities proposed by the Smithsons, Yona Friedman, the Metabolists, or Archigram were built. Although they have been unfeasible and would require a complete change in ways of life in all cultures to implement, they may be necessary one day. A quick survey of what the postwar rationalists had in mind for specific sites gives a feeling for the range of schemes from new cities to urban renewal projects that they envisaged. It will then be possible to place some exemplars of their work in context.

Several new capital cities were built following the rationalist paradigm. Chandigarh, a state capital, has already been introduced. Brasília in Brazil and Islamabad in Pakistan are early post-war examples of major national capitals. Belmopan (1967–), capital of Belize, is tiny in comparison. Abuja, the capital of Nigeria, and Putrajaya in Malaysia, a hybrid example, came later in the 1980s. The Pilot Plan for Brasília is offered as an exemplar of rationalist design in Figure 9.8; Islamabad, planned by Constantinos Apostolou Doxiadis (1913–75), could have been chosen in its stead, but it lacks Brasília's unity of design. Doxiadis established *Ekistics*, the science of human settlements, but whose central thesis was that settlements must be reorganized following systems thinking. Islamabad is an example of what he had in mind (Doxiadis 1965; Lovejoy 1966; Daechsel 2015).

Islamabad is divided into a 5-kilometer square grid of eight zones that almost picks up the grid of the adjacent city of Rawalpindi, a garrison town of the British Raj. Islamabad has a clear hierarchy of streets and segregated transportation modes and communities according to social status and land uses. There are separate areas for embassies, industries, education, and capitol and civic complexes. Various plans for a public square at the government quarter went unbuilt. The buildings there were designed by several internationally renowned modernists. Edward Durrell Stone (1902–78), a US architect, designed the Assembly Hall (Parliament House), the President's House, and Cabinet Secretariat. Arne Jacobson (1902–71) from Denmark designed ministerial buildings, as did Gio Ponti (1891–79), best known for the design of the Pirelli Tower in Milan. Kenzo Tange was the architect of the Supreme Court building. Each structure

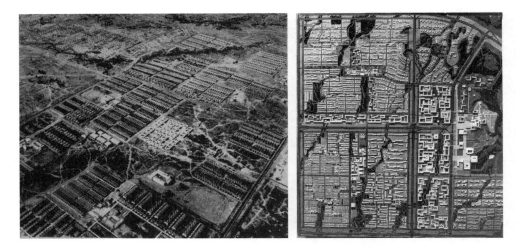

Figure 9.8 Islamabad: The city design (left) and a model of the central part of the city (right)
Credit line (left and right): Courtesy of the Doxiadis Archive, Constantinos and Emma Doxiadis Foundation

displays the brand of its creator, and no general guidelines were developed to ensure some unity in their composition. A substantial estate designed for President Ayub Khan (1907–74) by Louis Kahn in 1966 was never realized. Le Corbusier's work in Chandigarh has the unity that Islamabad lacks.

Two of Le Corbusier's designs of the period affirmed his international reputation: the city and, particularly, the capitol complex in Chandigarh and the Unité d'habitation in Marseille. The group of buildings of the capitol complex turns its back on streets to form a superblock with a vast square at its center. The Assembly Hall and the High Court are placed off-center at the ends of an east–west axis across the square. The Palace of the Governor was to terminate the north–south axis, which crosses the east–west axis, again off-center. Prime Minister Jawaharlal Nehru (1889–1964) regarded its placement as too ostentatious for a state governor, so it has never been built, but he thought the High Court and the Secretariat to be "magnificent" and "grand" (Prasad 1987, 18).

Le Corbusier's Unité d'habitation saw its application in several places over a period of twenty years. The Marseille Unité (1947–52) is the pure type and the first to be built. Standing on *pilotis*, it is 110 meters by 20 meters (360 feet by 65 feet) in plan. It contains 337 two-story residential units served by a skip-stop elevator system. As a vertical neighborhood, the building was designed to have a small hotel, shops on a central floor, and a communal nursey school and jogging track on the roof. Other Unités followed: Rezé-les-Nantes (1953–55), Berlin (1956–58), Meaux (1956–8), Briey en Forêt (1959–61), and Firminy (1965–67). They possessed few of the facilities included in the generic model. The Berlin Unité has only a post office as a communal service. The population of a Unité was simply not large enough to sustain more than a small shop.

The Unité at Marseille fitted the ways of life of the original population well; they chose to live there. A disproportionate number of them were engineers and architects, foreign born, and owners of second homes elsewhere (Avin 1973). They did not live local lives as did the lower-income groups who lived in other Unités. Over time, the Marseille Unité suffered from poor upkeep and became less hospitable (Hughes 2006). Although the Unité is a neighborhood in a building, it is not regarded as a megastructure, in a conventional sense. Other buildings are. Many were planned, but few were built (Dahinden 1972; Banham 1976).

The Post–World War Two Rationalists

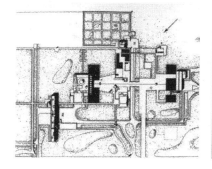 

Figure 9.9 The capitol complex, Chandigarh: The plan (left) and a view toward the High Court (right)
Source (left): Nilson (1973); FLC.ADAGP
Source (right): Lang and Marshall (2016, 210); courtesy of Taylor & Francis

Figure 9.10 The Unités d'habitation: Marseille in 1961 (left) and Berlin in 2012 (right)
Source (left): Lang and Marshall (2016, 210); courtesy of Taylor & Francis
Credit line (right): Photograph by A. Savin. WikiPhotoSpace; courtesy of the photographer

Proposals for the design of Battery Park City in New York varied, including versions of generic modernist designs in the 1960s and even a neo-traditional design in 1979 (Gordon 1997; Lang 2017, 154–59). Along the way was a 1969 megastructure proposal designed by Conklin and Rossant. It consisted of a partly enclosed lengthy interior mall containing shops, restaurants, parks, and recreational facilities topped with housing and commercial units. The financing for a development of its scale was impossible to find. The Bielefeld University design is as close to being a megastructure as one can get rapidly implemented, although it has characteristics of a suburban US shopping mall.

Figure 9.11 Megastructures: The Battery Park City, New York proposal
Credit line: Collection of the author
Source: Gordon (1977, 28)

A team of Klaus Köpke, Peter Kulka, Wolf Siepmann, and Katte Töpper, with Michael von Tardy, won the competition for the university's design. It consists of one building (380 meters long and 230 meters wide, or 1,247 by 754 feet) of 140,000 square meters (over 1.5 million square feet) in floor area. Located on the periphery of Bielefeld, it is a commuter college with surface parking around it in much the same manner as a shopping center. Like such centers, it has a glass-covered central mall, with anchors in the form of a swimming pool and an auditorium at its ends and small shops and cafés along its sides. The various faculties and schools are in rectangular blocks perpendicular to the axis of the mall. One aspiration of the design was to help integrate research and teaching efforts. Another was to provide comfortable shelter from Bielefeld's rainy weather. At the time of writing, the structure was being modernized.

Many mass housing developments are, arguably, exemplars of rationalist urban design concepts. The 23 de enero in Caracas is one of them. It was built at the behest of Venezuelan dictator Colonel Marcos Pérez Jiménez (1914–2001) and originally named La Unidad Residencial de 2 de diciembre, his election date. Carlos Raúl Villanueva, the country's leading architect, was its designer. Although his earlier housing schemes show an empiricist touch, in designing 23 de enero, he was captured by the international accolades that rationalists were receiving. The project, located on 90 hectares (220 acres), consists of 9,176 residential units in twenty-eight fifteen-story buildings, and forty-two smaller ones. It also includes commercial buildings, schools, other educational institutions, and recreational facilities. The buildings are located along terraces carved into the sloping site. (Lucente and Travante Mendes 2012.)

The Post–World War Two Rationalists

Figure 9.12 Mass Housing: The 23 de enero project, Caracas with squatter housing in the space between buildings (above) and a Khrushchyovka, Moscow (below)

Credit line (above): Collection of the author
Source (above): Caracas Chronicles (undated)
Credit line (below): Collection of the author

Squatters soon built ranchos along the terraces, filling in much of the open space between the buildings. Today 70% of the 84,000 population is living on the site illegally in single- and double-story dwellings. Despite this history, the development is now protected by the *Ley de Defensa y Protección del Patrimonio Cultural*. What, however, can be done to restore it to its original status?

Many housing projects based on the rationalist model have now been demolished; others are scheduled to be demolished as the general population's demands for the quality of the built environment rise. The most publicized of these demolished schemes is Pruitt–Igoe in East St. Louis (Newman 1972; Montgomery 1985; Lang 2005). In the second decade of the twenty-first century, in Moscow alone, 8,000 Khrushchyovkas, monotonous housing blocks built in the 1950s, are slated for demolition (Byrnes 2017). Others, as in Singapore, are being adapted to provide better facilities. At the same time, the continued acceptability of the generic rationalist housing designs can be seen in the late-twentieth-century housing developments of East Asian cities such as Shanghai and in the satellite towns around Seoul in Korea.

All these schemes illustrate aspects of postwar application of contemporary generic rationalist models. Some specific designs can, however, be considered to be exemplars of the strengths and limitations of the diverse strands of rationalist thought.

Exemplars of Rationalist Designs

Civic Center Proposals (1940s to 1970s); Punjab University, Chandigarh, India (1958–); the Pilot Plan, Brasília, Brazil (1956); Lafayette Park, Detroit, Michigan, USA (1960); La Grande Motte, Occitanie, France (1960s); the Work of Team 10 (1960s); Arcosanti, Scottsdale, Arizona, USA (Late 1960s but Continuing); and the Work of the Metabolists in Japan (1970s)

Le Corbusier's 1945 plan for the rebuilding of St-Dié after its wartime destruction was composed of eight Unités d'habitation and a civic center. The armature of the design was a seven-level hierarchical pattern of roads. The civic center consisted of a pedestrian square with an administrative building, a regional museum, a department store, movie theaters, and shops. The buildings were arranged asymmetrically to accentuate views of one from the other. The proposal, while praised as a milestone in the development of urban design ideas, was rejected by the local officials and residents of the city. They sought a more traditional layout. The Chimbote civic center (1946) scheme designed by Paul Lester Wiener (1895–1967) and José Luis Sert is similar in nature (Dede and Asto 2016). Chandigarh's capitol complex is a descendant. Louis Khan's later proposals for Abbas Abad in Iran (1974) has a different pattern but consists of buildings arrayed in an orthogonal order set in open space (Mohajeri 2015).

The generic spatial character of rationalist urban design proposals underpins the design of Panjab University by Le Corbusier's associate Jugal Kishore Choudhury (1918–98) and the Gandhi Bhavan (1959) by his cousin Pierre Jeanneret (1896–1967) (Bahga, Bahga, and Bahga 1993). The buildings are freestanding sculptures, but unlike Le Corbusier's designs, the campus composition has no clear unifying structure. The type of design has come to be known in India as 'Chandigarh architecture.' Important though Le Corbusier's Chandigarh is, the contemporary design for Brasília is often regarded as *the* exemplar of postwar modernism.

Brasília was planned by Lúcio Costa (1902–98), its key buildings designed by Oscar Niemeyer, Costa's former employee. The competition-winning Pilot Plan for the city features two great axes: the monumental to contain the government complex and the residential spine in the form of an arc following the drainage pattern of the site. The plan has four parts: the

The Post–World War Two Rationalists

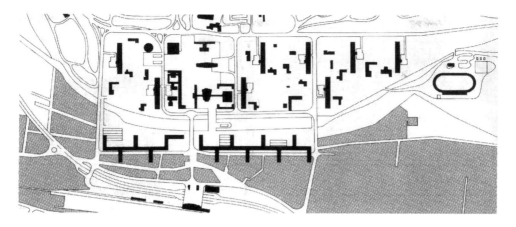

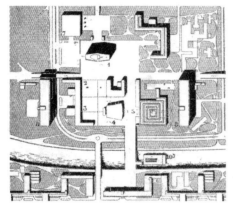

Figure 9.13 Civic center proposals: The St-Dié plan (above) with the civic center (below left) and Chimbote (below right)

Credit line (above): Drawing by Wayne W. Copper; courtesy of the College of Art, Architecture and Planning, Cornell University
Credit line (below left): FLCA.ADAGP
Credit line (below right): Courtesy of Frances Loeb Fine Arts Library, GSD Harvard University

government buildings set around but not framing the Praça dos Três Poderes, the residential superblocks with their community facilities, the city center, and the vehicular circulation pattern. The housing of the southern part of the Pilot Plan designed by Niemeyer owes much to the images of housing portrayed by Le Corbusier in the 1920s and 1930s. It is laid out in an orthogonal geometry, and the apartment buildings stand on *pilotis*. The southern *superquadras* unlike the 23 de enero scheme in Caracas, was designed for middle-class residents.

Each *superquadra* in Brasília was divided into four residential sub-*quadras* by a service strip for provisioning shops, a primary school, and other community facilities. The fronts of the shops were soon turned around to face the service corridor, making it a seam for shopping life. In the southern part of the Pilot Plan, the residential buildings designed by Oscar Niemeyer, like the Narkomfin in Moscow and the Unités, stand on *pilotis*. Unlike the Unités, the elevator system is standard. The open spaces between the buildings were planted with trees and lawns. The

Post–World War Two Pragmatic Urban Design

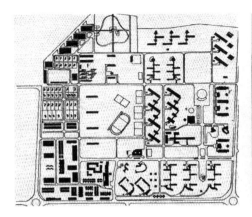

Figure 9.14   Panjab University: The plan (left) and Gandhi Bhavan designed by Pierre Jeanneret (right)
Source (left): Bahga, Bahga, and Bagha (1993); courtesy of Sarbjit Bahga
Source (right): Lang (2002, 78); courtesy of Permanent Black

Figure 9.15   Brasília: The Pilot Plan (above left), the capital complex (above right), the generic residential *superquadra* (below left), and a typical interior view (below right)
Credit line (above left): Various sources; collection of the author
Source (above right): Lang (2017, 38); courtesy of Taylor & Francis
Source (below right): Lang (2017, 107); courtesy of Taylor & Francis

local school in each *superquadra* originally provided education for children living in the housing, but as the residents aged in place and the population of children decreased, the schools became attended by the children of the household help working there. The housing matches the residents' requirements, behaviorally and aesthetically (Holston 1989; Evenson 1993). The northern residential segment of the Pilot Plan in Brasília has little of the design unity of its southern counterpart. It was developed in a more ad hoc, pragmatic manner.

Chandigarh and Brasília have in common the spatial qualities of individual buildings set in space and the distinctive architectural brand of their designers. The Praça dos Três Poderes and the capitol plaza in Chandigarh are large paved open areas, blistering hot on summer days. Grand settings for major spectacles, they are deserted most of the time. Chandigarh and the southern part of the Pilot Plan have aged well, although the substantial open spaces in Chandigarh are slowly being filled in by pragmatic developments to create a livelier, walkable world. As capital cities, Chandigarh and Brasília are well maintained.

The Pruitt–Igoe experience in St. Louis was different from that of the southern part of the Pilot Plan. Partially modeled on the Unité in Marseille to accommodate low-income people, Pruitt–Igoe had skip-stop elevators that halted on the fourth, seventh, and tenth floors. Access to the other floors was by staircases from spacious galleries on the stop floors. These galleries were designed to be playgrounds for children and gathering places for adults. The scheme received high praise in *Architectural Forum* for saving "not only people but also money" (Editorial 1951, 129). The journal's editors saw the complex as *the* paradigm for future social/public housing schemes in the United States. The reality proved to be different (Newman 1972; Montgomery 1985; Lang 2005). Many of the features praised by *Architectural Forum* were sources of frustration for the residents of the project. Its effort to resolve social problems through design was doomed.

Lafayette Park in Detroit has a different history. It is widely regarded as one of the most successful housing developments based on rationalists' ideas. The 78-acre (32-hectare) scheme was designed in 1955 by Mies van der Rohe, Ludwig Hilberseimer, and Alfred Caldwell. By then, Hilberseimer had repudiated the characteristics of his metropolis design (Spaeth 1981; Waldheim 2004). The scheme consists of one- and two-story townhouses, low- and high-rise apartment buildings that lie adjacent to a public park, local shops, and a club house with a

Figure 9.16 Lafayette Park, Detroit: The plan (left) and a ground-level view in winter (right)

Credit line (left): Edward A. Duckett Collection, Ryerson and Burnham Archives, The Art Institute of Chicago. Image file # 198602/.LafPl_final1

swimming pool. Its architectural qualities reflect the steel and glass precision associated with Mies's architecture for the IIT campus. The development's success is due to the social dynamics of the population's being in accord with the design. The tightness of its open spaces helps. It is a racially integrated, economically stable middle-class neighborhood of intact families. It drew younger, sophisticated residents to live in its towers. The buildings were no penny-pinching public housing designs. The towers had well-appointed, double-height, marble-clad lobbies; the apartments were spacious and well appointed. Another scheme of a different character, La Grande Motte, has also worked out well. It was designed as a resort for working-class French people (Schires 2017b).

La Grande Motte was a product of the *Mission Racine* when Charles de Gaulle (1890–1970) was President of France. The town was planned to rival the picturesque Mediterranean towns that attract wealthy vacationers. The design by Jean Balladur (1924–2002) and Pierre Pellet was inspired by the pyramid structures of Teotihuacán in Mexico, but not the complex's composition. Le Grande Motte consists of buildings set in open space stretching in a longitudinal form along the seafront. No building is more than a five-minute walk from a beach. The town has a fine marina, a conference center, and many 'intellectually accessible' sculptures, the work of Balladur and young artists. Parts of the city's center feature fill-in buildings to create a more traditional urban form. The regional Compagnie Nationale d'Aménagement designed the landscape with the salty spindrift site in mind when it chose plant material. As a resort, La Grande Motte is successful. It receives 2 million visitors a year, mostly in the summer months.

The members of Team 10 had difficulties in putting their more radical models into practice. When they managed to do so, they found out that the discrepancy between imagined and empirical realities can be substantial. Alison Smithson and Peter Smithson's brutalist design for

Figure 9.17 La Grande Motte: A bird's-eye view
Credit line (left): Photograph by MOPY/Getty Images

Robin Hood Gardens illustrates the struggle to match a design idea held in high esteem by architects for its innovativeness with a place for low-income residents to call home; the Free University of Berlin shows much the same thing, except in the world of academia.

Robin Hood Gardens, built in the early 1970s, was expected by Team 10 to be a generic model replacing the Unité d'habitation as a prototype for future social housing in Britain. The complex consisted of two long curving housing blocks, one of ten stories and the other of seven. A large quiet garden lay between them. The buildings had broad walkways in the sky conceived to be like the streets below. They, like the galleries at Pruitt–Igoe, were envisaged to become lively behavior settings. The development turned out to have "sad, lifeless places," and "the uniformity of the buildings' prefabricated concrete façades was more alienating than anything Le Corbusier had designed" (Ourossoff 2006). It never saw the personalization of the walkways that would have shown that tenants had taken possession of them. Peter Smithson blamed social stresses for the decline of the project. The poor maintenance of the complex did not help its residents to love it. A few nevertheless did, but in contrast to the architects' view of the building as an exemplar of fine architecture, 75% of its tenants favored its demolition, which took place in 2017. Other Team 10 members' experiences with the design of the Freie Universität aroused similar concerns.

In 1963, Candilis-Josic-Woods with Manfred Schiedhelm (1935–2011) won the competition to design a campus for the philological institute in Berlin. They proposed a single 35-hectare (87-acre) two/three-story modular grid building that owes a debt to Yona Friedman's spatial city explorations. It had internal streets, squares, courtyards, and multiple walkways reminiscent of an Arabic medina. The design goal was to have a flexible set of spaces that allowed easy communication between students and staff within and across disciplines. Classrooms, departments, and facilities were decentralized and distributed without any hierarchical organization. A red, yellow, green, blue, and purple color scheme was developed to help people find their way around the complex. The construction techniques were new too. French engineer Jean Prouvé (1901–84) developed a structural system of concrete-encased steel columns, I-section steel beams, and prefabricated reinforced concrete slabs. The Cor-ten steel façade modules were designed to be easily rearranged (Feld 1999).

Figure 9.18 The designs of Team 10 members: Robin Hood Gardens (left) with a walkway in the sky (right).

Credit line (left): Photograph by Claudio Divizia/Shutterstock.com
Credit line (right): Courtesy of Sandra Posada

Post–World War Two Pragmatic Urban Design

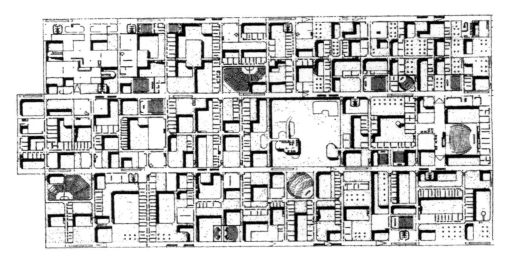

Figure 9.19 The designs of Team 10 members: The Freie Universität, Berlin proposal
Credit line: Courtesy of the Shadrack Woods Records, Avery Library, Columbia University

The designers' imagined way that a university should function differed from the way the staff worked. They were not predisposed to change. Structurally, the avant-garde façade deteriorated rapidly. In 1997, the layout was changed to improve the daily operation of the complex, but the basic physical design idea was retained. In 2004, further changes were made to the construction and operational functionality of the building. This search for a logical, rational design based on imagined ideal ways of life is also shown in the design of megastructures.

Arcosanti had its beginnings in 1956, when spouses Colly Soleri and Paolo Soleri bought 4,000 acres (1,690 hectares) of land to be the home of the nonprofit Cosanti Foundation that they founded to raise funds, conduct research, and establish an apprentice program for architects and students to build the complex. Construction began in 1970 with the building of earth-cast apses that soon became a feature of the design. Step-by-step, apse-by-apse, and room-by-room progress is inching along. As of 2015, forty-five years after the project was initiated, it was 10% built. The project is now directed by Jeff Stein, who hopes to turn the bits and pieces that have been constructed into a viable town much reduced in scale from the original intention (Tortello 2012). Few people live in Arcosanti, but 50,000 people visit it each year. The development has yet to show that a megastructure is a viable alternative to any present urban form. The same comment can be made about the proposals of the Metabolists in Japan (Dahinden 1972; Mansfield 1999).

The Metabolist proposals include a series of projects (Marine City, Tower City, Ocean City, Wall City) by Kiyonori Kikutake (1928–2011), Agricultural City and Helix City, and a proposal for Tokyo (1961) by Kisho Kurokawa (1934–2007). Few were created for specific sites. Bold new designs, the Metabolists believed, had to replace the current dysfunctional city. Kikutake's Marine City proposal consists, like the Archigram designs, of both permanent and disposable components. The design consists of a series of linked circles. Kikutake considered each to be a living cell. Like the trunk and branches of a tree, the fixed armature was organized in a hierarchical form and consisted of transportation routes and other services. The individual units for commercial, residential, and recreational uses could grow when needed and go when not.

The Post–World War Two Rationalists

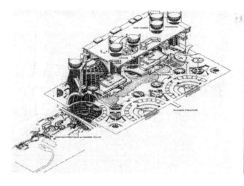

Figure 9.20 Arcosanti: The original design (left) and the progress on the its construction by 2015

Credit line (left): Drawing by Tomaki Tanmura; courtesy of the Cosanti Foundation
Credit line (right): Photograph by Ivan Pintar; courtesy of the Cosanti Foundation

Figure 9.21 A Metabolist proposal: Marine City
Credit line: Collection of the author

The most significant built example is the Nagakagin Capsule Tower (1972), designed by Kurokawa. Only a single building, it hardly features the changeable attributes of an environment for living that the Metabolists championed. The idea that individuals could shape or plug in their units into a framework was replaced by a total design in which everything was specified, down to the built-in furniture of the fixed capsules. Metabolist urban designs make one take notice and think, as do the hybrid examples of rationalist urban designs that were tempered by empirical realities and/or the desire of architects to further their own design brands.

193

Hybrid Examples

Universidad Nacional Autónoma de México, Mexico City, Mexico (1952–); Barbican Estate, London, England, UK (1959–82); La Défense, Haut-de-Seine, France (1958–); Empire State Plaza, Albany, New York, USA (1959); and the Work of the Tendenza Movement (1965–85)

Hybrid rationalist urban designs departed from the pure paradigm in a variety of ways. The Universidad Nacional Autónoma de México in Mexico City, now a UNESCO World Heritage site, while close to the mainstream of rationalist thought, illustrates one departure. The site has the spatial layout and the buildings exhibit the geometric forms that the rationalists extolled as ideal, but the expression of some buildings on campus differs.

In 1943, the Mexican government decided to consolidate the scattered buildings of the university on a site at San Angel outside Mexico City. Construction began in 1952. The campus was designed by Mario Pani (1911–93), Enrique del Moral (1905–87), Domingo Garcia Ramos (1911–87), and others to consist of a series of foreground buildings aligned in spacious grounds. The most notable buildings are the School of Architecture, the Fine Arts Museum, the School of Medicine, and the Central Library (1956) that was designed by Juan O'Gorman (1905–80). Very much influenced by Le Corbusier's *Vers Une Architecture*, O'Gorman had been designing functionalist buildings in Mexico since 1929. The closed stacks Central Library is indeed a functional building, but its four façades depart radically from the unornamented CIAM ideal. A vast mural composed of over 4 million colored stones adorns them. Each façade depicts an era in Mexico's history (Firestone 2017). The Barbican in London is another, but different, departure from the strictures of the rationalist paradigm.

The Barbican is a mixed-use high-density neighborhood built on a 62-acre (25-hectare) site on the northwestern edge of London that had been destroyed by bombing during World War Two.

Figure 9.22 Universidad Nacional Autónoma de México: A general view featuring the library
Source: Lang and Moleski (2010, 9); courtesy of Taylor & Francis

The Post–World War Two Rationalists

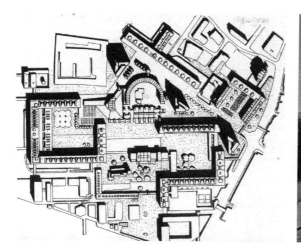

Figure 9.23 The Barbican: The plan (left) and an internal view of the estate (right)
Source (left): Lang (2005, 106); courtesy of Taylor & Francis

One of the goals of the City Corporation of London, the municipal authority, was to increase the resident population living in the city. It had dropped below 5,000 people; the daytime population was over 300,000. Another goal was to create an arts precinct that also provided residential accommodation, reduced traffic congestion, had substantial open space, and was monumental. The design went through several strictly rationalist iterations before a looser design by Le Corbusier devotees Chamberlain, Powell, and Bon was adopted and built (Lang 2005, 164–67).

The Barbican forms a superblock of brutalist buildings with a multilevel circulation system, tower and slab residential blocks, a theater (the Guildhall School for Music and Drama), restaurants, a school (the London School for Girls), a coroner's court and mortuary, two hotels, a fire station, and the Museum of London. It is set in lawns and water gardens. The scheme consists of 2,113 flats, maisonettes, and terrace houses, mostly in six-story blocks. The Barbican has been praised and derided. It does have a somewhat foreboding atmosphere and wayfinding for the visitor is not easy. Its detailed landscaping and attention to building finishes offsets have been commended. It is regarded as a great place to live but criticized for being subsidized housing for the middle class. The population of the city has doubled, but it had only 11,700 people in 2014. Its working day population is now about 400,000 despite the Canary Wharf development's being built as a second CBD for the metropolitan area. La Défense is Paris's new 'central' business district and Canary Wharf's predecessor.

La Défense is another superblock development on a cleared brownfield site. While outside Paris's *boulevard péiphérique* with its height controls, it is linked to the heart of the city by a view up the Avenue de La Grande Armée to the Arc de Triomphe. The conceptual design was influenced by Le Corbusier's image of what makes a city modern, but it possesses neither the distribution of buildings in space nor the geometrical purity of the rationalist ideal.

An EPAD (Établissement public pour l'aménagement de la région de La Défense) was established to buy the land, rehouse 25,000 people, and demolish 9,000 dwellings to create a cleared site. La Défense is a multi-layered development sitting on a 40-hectare (100-acre) pedestrian deck. The below-the-deck infrastructure acts as the armature to which the buildings above are

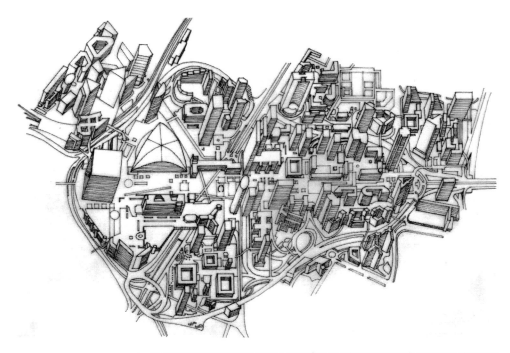

Figure 9.24 La Défense: The massing in 2000 (above) and a view from the Arche toward Place Charles de Gaulle (below)
Credit line (above): Drawing by Thanong Poonteerakul
Source (above): Lang (2005, 219); courtesy of Taylor & Francis

The Post–World War Two Rationalists

attached. The termination of the axis from l'Étoile is La Défense Arche, a competition-winning office tower designed by Danish architect Johan Otto von Spreckelsen (1929–87). Part of President François Mitterrand's *Grands Travaux*, the arche is thirty-five stories (100 meters) high and 328 feet (100 meters) wide and is slightly skewed to the axis. It is a major tourist attraction and gives La Défense an identity—a 'there' there (Lang 2017, 143–45).

The landscape of the D'Allee Centrale with its lines of plane trees linking the arche to the Seine was designed by Dan Kiley (1912–2004). The fountains and artworks along it give a Beaux Arts touch to the design. La Défense has undergone substantial redevelopment over the past twenty years to make it a more lively and pleasant place to be, mainly by providing a greater mix of uses and making it easier to find specific destinations. The Empire State Plaza in Albany, New York, also needs some attention, although as a total urban design based on a strong aesthetic idea, it would be difficult to change.

The plaza is a complex of ten buildings housing New York state's administration offices and cultural buildings. Designed by Wallace Harrison (1895–1981) of Harrison & Abramowitz, the architects favored by the then governor of the state, Nelson Rockefeller (1908–79), it has many of the features of a highly rationalist design but with some classical touches. The 98.5-acre (39-hectare) complex, like La Défense, sits on a platform. The buildings are reinforced concrete and/or steel-framed structures clad in stone and approximately rectangular in form. The egg-shaped Center for the Performing Arts is the exception. Reflecting pools stretch the length of the plaza. Its design has been both dismissed as outdated (even when it was built) and defended for its integrity as a bold, unified statement. Rockefeller saw it as "great art" worthy of the eminence of New York state (Lang and Marshall 2016). Like the squares at Chandigarh, Brasília, and La Défense, it is an inhospitable place for much of the year.

Figure 9.25 The Governor Nelson A. Rockefeller Empire State Plaza, Albany, New York
Credit line: Courtesy of Discover Albany

Three building complexes are used here to illustrate the thinking of La Tendenza architects. The quartiere Gallaratese (1960–80) with the Monte Amiata complex designed by Aldo Rossi and Carlo Aymonino (1926–2010) is, perhaps, *the* exemplar of La Tendenza's advocacies (Broadbent 1990). The cemetery of San Cataldo at Modena designed by Rossi is regarded as his finest work (Adjmi 1991). Park Kolonnaden at Potsdamer Platz in Berlin by Giorgio Grassi (b. 1935) shows the effort that some La Tendenza architects made to break away from considering urban design as the artistic organization of buildings in space to a concern for buildings as placemaking objects.

The Quartiere Gallaratese consists of residential blocks, social service buildings, and open space designed by several architects. The master plan was the work of Piero Bottoni (1903–73), who sought to link diverse components of the traditional city into a unique, unified artistic composition of platonic forms in space. The result has, however, little of the character of traditional cities. Access to sunshine and cross ventilation was an important criterion in the buildings' design. The one designed by Rossi is stark and white, echoing Le Corbusier's early designs. It contains three stories of apartments accessed from single loaded corridors. The galleries have square, blank window openings. The blocks are supported on heavy columns, creating undercrofts (Broadbent 1990). Bold though the scheme is, the geometrical forms sought by Rossi is clearer in the Cemetery at San Cataldo, a necropolis.

The cemetery, Aldo Rossi's allegorical invocation of the city, is a competition-winning entry by Rossi and his former student Gianni Braghieri (b. 1945) (Canniffe 2008). The scheme is an extension to an existing cemetery designed by Cesare Costa (1826–76) in the mid nineteenth century. The new design has an east–west axis linking it to that cemetery. Costa sought to represent the experience of death through a neoclassical design. Rossi's and Braghieri's goal was to create an air of timelessness.

The cemetery is a mixture of elements in space and space-making buildings. A courtyard surrounded by three-story-high ossuaries lies beyond the central axis. The walls are lined by niches, and the ground-floor windows are elongated but aligned with the square windows above them. At the northern end of this axis is a truncated cone that is a communal grave for the unclaimed corpses of people who die in hospitals, jails, and hospices. An amphitheater lies above it.

Figure 9.26 La Tendenza urban design: The Monte Amiata complex, Gallaratese, Milan (left), and a ground-level view (right)

Credit line (left): Collection of the author
Credit line (right): Courtesy of Karina Castro, photographer

The Post–World War Two Rationalists

At the southern end of the axis is a red cube, an ossuary built of brick with windows punched into it. One wall is solid; the other three have 1-meter square frameless windows without panes. Open to the sky, it has brightly colored metal balconies and stairs that provide access to burial niches. Rossi wanted it to be seen as an abandoned building. A second narrow spine raised on two-story septa—dividing walls—with a single-story ossuary above it lies immediately to the west of this group. The structure has pink walls and square windows with a pitched blue metal roof. The cemetery's design shows Rossi's concern for incorporating a representation of past types within the formal geometry of a rationalist schema (Broadbent 1990).

Park Kolonnaden is no necropolis. Grassi won the 1993 competition for the design of a group of buildings on a long narrow site located off Potsdamer Platz, but his firm designed only the central part of the string of buildings that are linked by a longitudinal arcade. The building at the head of the eleven-story complex facing Potsdamer Platz was designed by Schweger and Partners. It differs in form, materials, and fenestration pattern from the remainder of the complex. The central part of the complex, Grassi's work, shows the intention of the Tendenza movement to capture the form of the historic city. The buildings are H shaped in plan, their main façade facing directly onto the street. The rears of the buildings form courts. The one in the central building contains a pavilion intended to house restaurants.

The design with its geometrical, reductionist forms; the use of exposed brick; and square windows framed in green is typical of Grassi's work and reflects the broader aesthetic concern of La Tendenza architects. It also illustrates Grassi's use of buildings to make spaces and so departs from the strict basic rationalist model.

Figure 9.27 La Tendenza urban design: A necropolis; the Cemetery of San Cataldo, Modena
Credit line: Courtesy of Jacob Börner, photographer

Figure 9.28 La Tendenza urban design: Park Kolonnnaden, Berlin
Credit line: Photograph by Roman Babakin/Shutterstock.com

Commentary: The Functions Addressed

Universally the goal of the rationalist projects of the second half of the twentieth century was to create healthy environments by providing settings that were well ventilated, bathed in sunlight, and easily accessible to vegetated open spaces. The need to consider the health of the natural biological environment itself was not an expressed concern. The desire to maintain the countryside threatened by urban sprawl was, however, a motivating factor in some megastructure proposals. Another common desire in many of the megastructure schemes was to exploit the structural possibilities of new technologies, either existing or imagined, to create awe-inspiring designs. Most rationalist proposals, however, were based on existing structural and construction methods.

Dealing with issues of safety and security might have been implicit in the designs, but little attention was paid to concerns of natural 'eyes-on-the-street' surveillance and territorial controls as mechanisms to give the inhabitants of places a sense of security. The research on these concerns came in the 1970s, although Jane Jacobs in her book *The Death and Life of Great American Cities* had, a decade earlier, brought attention to the importance of natural surveillance in inhibiting antisocial behavior and contributing to the development of a sense of community at the neighborhood level (J. Jacobs 1961). Protecting pedestrians from clashes with vehicular traffic by segregating movement systems in vertical space is a feature in several rationalist design proposals, but the efficient movement of automobile traffic tended to dominate them still.

In many mass housing schemes, the layouts of buildings and the services provided at the precinct level were devoted to creating 'communities,' although the definition of community was never explicitly stated. Given our current understanding, little more can be expected of the layout of the built environment in promoting a sense of community than to provide common facilities and the affordances for people's paths to cross as part of everyday life (Hester 1975; Brower 1996; Lang and Moleski 2010). The search for geometric purity meant that the designs did not possess the richness of the affordances of many pragmatically developed parts of cites.

Almost nothing was said about how the generic designs proposed were climatically or culturally specific. More generally, little explicit attention was given to the motivations and needs of women, children, and frail people. Many of the housing schemes were bleak, boring places for children and adolescents and isolating locations for women. The assumption implicit in the

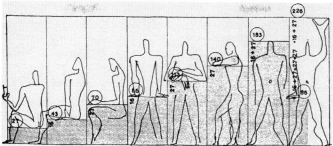

Figure 9.29 Models of man: The Vitruvian model as seen by Leonardo da Vinci, 1490 (left), and Le Corbusier's modular system, based on an idealized man, 1943–45 (right)
Source (left): Wikimedia Commons
Credit line (right): FLC.AGAGP

manifestoes, paradigms, and specific designs was that the whole population was 'healthy, strong, well-behaved, culturally homogeneous, and male,' as Le Corbusier portrayed in his modular man diagram and as Michelangelo and Vitruvius had done before him.

Issues of maintaining projects when in operation was widely neglected in the generic explorations and the specific designs of the rationalists. In the provision of social housing, the concern of governments was with reducing front-end capital costs; running costs were assumed to take care of themselves. Housing schemes such as Pruitt–Igoe in the United States, Robin Hood Gardens in England, and the Unités d'habitation in France were allowed to deteriorate, causing hardship to their residents. Ultimately, the residents ceased to care about the places in which they lived.

The designs described here are of great interest to the architectural cognoscenti as works of art. They can savor architects' generic ideas manifested logically in physical form. Le Corbusier and the architects of La Tendenza wished their designs to be regarded as innovative, aesthetic explorations. The ability of householders and businesses to express themselves by personalizing their environments in most of the projects described here was restricted to interiors; the exterior appearances were unified to display a common identity and the oeuvre of their designer.

Observations

The period between the end of World War Two and the 1970s was one of great optimism among architects. They believed, implicitly if not explicitly, that the correlation between a poor built environment and social ills meant that changing the built environment to meet their image of a good world would resolve social problems. It is easy to look back and dismiss such ideas as manifestations of individual egos striving for the limelight, but most generic ideas put forth by the rationalists were logically considered responses to the problems of cities as they perceived them. Many assumptions made by the members of CIAM about how cities function were simply incorrect.

Many of the generic designs of the rationalists that did not work well in application were incorrectly assumed to have universal applicability or were versions of generic ideas watered down by political and/or fiscal constraints. Some recent designs that seem to function well enough resemble unimplemented proposals of the early modernists. The Kranhäuser im Rheinhafen, Cologne, may owe a visual debt to El Lissitzky's Wolkenbügel but satisfy a different intellectual ideal. Hyper-modernist, they, like the light standards at Rotterdam's Schouwburgplein (Lang and Marshall 2017, 219–22), reflect the forms of shipyard cranes.

The Unité d'habitation was a model for many subsequent housing projects but applied in a meaner manner. Pruitt–Igoe did not possess the social amenities of the generic model on which it was based. The size of the buildings and apartments at Alton West designed by the London County Council architects was smaller and tighter (Marmot 1982). The three housing complexes—Haigh Heights, Canterbury, and Crosbie, known as 'the piggeries'—designed by Liverpool's city architects were even meaner. They and Pruitt–Igoe have been demolished. Alton West in Roehampton, London, considered by many British architects to be the exemplar of post–World War Two social housing, has fared better (Harwood 2003). Not so another highly regarded design: Robin Hood Gardens.

The design of many housing and commercial projects was well intentioned but based on paradigms inadequate for their purposes. The mass housing schemes show the limitations of architecture and urban form per se to shape social, or antisocial, behavior. The problem was that they provided too many of the latter and too few of the former. The Pruitt–Igoe type design with well-laid-out landscapes may have worked well as a housing type for upper-middle-income families who value privacy and anonymity and who have the finances and knowledge to make use of the region-wide resources of importance or interest to them. The necessity to design with a socially supportive as well as a physical design agenda is clear. This need was recognized in the 1930s but was forgotten, or disregarded, by the 1950s, when the political agenda focused on suppling large numbers of residential units rather than their quality. Much more attention should have been paid to the space between buildings—to the public realm of urban design schemes—and to the supporting facilities provided.

Some generic design solutions that came to prominence during postwar years continue to fascinate. The megastructure is one of them. New examples are presented to the public from time to time. Some early-twenty-first-century buildings in China and India are close to being megastructures. They strive to be urban precincts in single buildings.

Figure 9.30 The Kranhäuser im Rheinauhafen, Cologne
Credit line: Photograph by Fokke Baarssen/Shutterstock.com

Many rationalist urban design ideas that were impractical or that have failed to achieve their goals in practice but possess a bold architectural idea continue to be lauded for their innovative nature. By the early 1970s, Archigram's advocacies were rebuffed by the general bemusement that such urban design dreams caused. The group nevertheless received a gold medal from the Royal Institute of British Architects in 2002 for the exploratory nature of their work. Similarly, the 23 de enero scheme in Caracas is recognized for its 'indubitable' architectural value that has been obscured by its transformation by squatters. Its role and significance in the history of modern architecture and urbanism remain open to debate. Much the same can be said of the now largely forgotten Experimental Prototype Community of Tomorrow (EPCOT) dream of Walter Disney (1901–66), a US pioneer of animation.

EPCOT was the vision that Disney had of a utopian city. Proposed for 20,000 people on a site of 27,800 acres (11,025 hectares) of Florida marshland, it was to be a city to further the advanced technologies being developed at the time. The city's plan was laid out in a circle, with commercial and institutional buildings at its core. The residential neighborhoods, each with its community facilities, local shops, and recreational opportunities, were arrayed around its center. The overall layout is reminiscent of Ebenezer Howard's conceptual plan for a garden city but EPCOT's transport system, the spacing of its buildings, and their architecture were based on images of future technological possibilities. The vertically segregated transportation routes had automobile traffic moving on the ground level and pedestrians walking above. The Walter E. Disney Communications Oriented Monitoring and Management (WEDCOMM) system would allow for electronic banking and purchasing and the monitoring of the flow of people and goods.

With Disney's death, the project was shelved. The town of Celebration was built along new urbanist lines instead (see Chapter 10). Disney's dream was too utopian. Utopian thinking does, however, broaden designer's thoughts of what might be. EPCOT was designed in the 1960s to be a 'smart city' in twenty-first-century terms.

Key References

"Charter of Machu Picchu." 1979. *Journal of Architectural Research* 7 (2): 5–9.

Dahinden, Justis. 1972. *Urban Structures for the Future*. Translated from the German by Gerald Ohm. New York: Praeger.

Richards, J. M. 1962. *An Introduction to Modern Architecture*. Harmondsworth: Penguin.

Sharp, Dennis, ed. 1978. *The Rationalists: Theory and Design in the Modern Movement*. London: Architectural Press.

Sherwood, Roger. 1978. *Modern Housing Prototypes*. Cambridge, MA: Harvard University Press.

Spreiregen, Paul D., ed. 1971. *The Modern Metropolis: Its Origins, Growth, Characteristics, and Planning: Selected Essays of Hans Blumenfield*. Cambridge, MA: MIT Press.

Wingler, Hans M. 1969. *The Bauhaus: Weimar Dessau Berlin Chicago*. Edited by Joseph Stein. Translated from the German by Wolfgang Jabs and Basil Gilbert. Cambridge, MA: MIT Press.

10

The Post–World War Two Empiricists

The empiricists of the second half of the twentieth decried the rationalists' ideas. The perceptions of the limitations of the rationalist schemes led to a proliferation of new ideas that were based on empirical studies: some rigorous, much casual. The empiricists drew on a variety of precedents and adapted them to the new circumstances brought about by World War Two, its political consequences, the continued globalization of ideas, and technological changes. The garden city model continued to inspire one group of urban designers, but adaptations to its principles contributed to the rise of the New Urbanism and the rediscovery of the street as a basic unit of urban design. Other apparently new ideas such as those represented in the compact city model appeared on the scene to be considered as potential types for future cities.

Antecedent Ideas

Few of the design ideas presented in this chapter break new ground. They were a formalization of earlier propositions. The most general of the models for organizing the overall patterns of cites—the hierarchical urban composition model of a city center, villages with their centers, and neighborhoods with their centers—had been given shape before World War Two. It was the basis for structuring many new towns in the postwar years. The neighborhood unit for organizing the lowest level in the hierarchy, as proposed by Clarence Perry in the 1920s, continued to be influential.

Many empiricist designs of the second half of the century strove to create a sense of place through the re-creation of the pedestrian-scaled village while accommodating automobile usage. The most obvious antecedents were the garden suburb and the garden city as they were developed during the interwar years. They, in turn, were rooted in the implementation of Ebenezer Howard's generic plans at Letchworth and Welwyn and those of Frederick Law Olmsted and Calvert Vaux in places such as Riverside, Illinois.

The urbanists consciously or not, continued to reflect the ideas of Camillo Sitte. This debt is clear in the work of Gordon Cullen and the Townscape movement's advocacies (Cullen 1961). It is less obvious in *A Theory of Good City Form* (1981), by Kevin Lynch (1914–84), than in his and his colleagues' studies of the effect of patterns of built form on the sequential aesthetic experience of an observer moving through the built the environment (Appleyard, Lynch, and Myer 1965).

The rediscovery of the street as a basic unit of design characteristic of much empiricist thought can be traced back to John Nolen (1869–1937), a landscape architect and city planner. His book *New Towns for Old: Achievements in Civic Improvement in Some American Small Towns and Neighborhoods* (1927) focused on urban streets as the seam for life in a manner taken up by the new urbanists. The compact city idea was not new either. Many compact suburbs with the station at their cores, the railroad suburbs, were built during the interwar years (Stern and Massengale 1981). This pattern was also an antecedent of the generic transit-oriented development (TOD) development model.

The model for urban development based on the existing urban morphology of a city—the Transect Diagram of the new urbanists—has a somewhat different ancestry. It owes a debt to the ideas of Alexander von Humboldt (1769–1839), the Prussian polymath, scientist, and explorer. Humboldt argued that everything has its place in nature. He mapped the sequence of natural ecologies and how one type (e.g., wetlands) related to another (Humboldt 1847; Diedrich, Lee, and Braae 2018).

New urbanism has other ancestors. Pueblo Español de Montjuich, designed by Ramón Reventós (1892–1976) and Francesc Folguera (1894–1960) for the Barcelona Exposition of 1929, is a picturesque revivalist example (Broadbent 1990). Xavier Nogues (1873–1941) and Miguel Utrillo (1862–1934), a painter of many quaint village scenes, were also much involved. Pueblo Español consists of plazas and maze-like streets that provide the sequences of spatial experiences advocated by Camillo Sitte and later Gordon Cullen. The design draws on patterns present in the villages of the Iberian Peninsula. More generally, New Urbanism's intellectual foundations can be traced back and sideways to Camillo Sitte, Raymond Unwin, Colin Rowe, and the neo-rationalists of Italy. The description of urban form types by Rob Krier was another

Figure 10.1   Pueblo Español de Montjuich, Barcelona, 1929
Credit line: Photograph by Volkova Natalia/Shutterstock.com

inspiration (R. Krier 1979). Even earlier, a manifesto for a New Urbanism had been formulated by Ivan Chtcheglov (Chtchgelov 1953). It failed to attract much attention.

The superblock as a widely applied generic solution during the second half of the twentieth century was brought to the public eye earlier with the design of Radburn. The Radburn plan itself inspired many designs after World War Two. Often, however, it was the two-dimensional concept of Radburn and not the three-dimensional aspect of the design that was adopted in new designs. Often, too, it was applied outside its climatic, cultural, and socioeconomic context.

It was only late in the century that the health of the natural environment came to the fore-front of urban design concerns. Advocacies for dealing sensitively with it, however, have a long history. Ian McHarg's position as expressed in *Design with Nature* (1969) draws on the intellec-tual ideas of Patrick Geddes both directly through a study of his works and indirectly through the writings of Lewis Mumford. Geddes was a keen student of the natural ecology of the world and an advocate for the conservation of the natural environment. His ideas, in turn, can be traced back to George Marsh's *Man and Nature*, originally published in 1864 (Marsh 1967). The combination of these antecedent histories shaped the empiricist paradigms of the second half of the twentieth century.

Manifestoes and Paradigms

The empiricist urban design ideas of the first half of the twentieth century were set forth in a score of books and a handful of journal articles; the second half saw numerous publica-tions. Many of them, such as Albert Mayer's *The Urgent Future* (1967), called for more socially conscious designs and the decentralization of decision-making. They, however, added little to previous prescriptions, although Mayer's observation that "trend is not destiny" was a timely reminder to policymakers (Mayer 1967). Several books nevertheless took the conversation a step forward.

The first significant postwar advocacy for the garden city appeared in Clarence Stein's *Toward New Towns for America* (1966). It furthered his 1930s ideas of integrating buildings and landscape into unified schemes. He favored the neighborhood unit as promulgated by Clarence Perry as the basis for suburban designs. John Ormsbee Simonds (1913–2006), a US landscape architect, updated and enriched the same ideals in his *Garden Cities 21* (Simonds 1994). His proposal included free-form layouts for towns and neighborhoods to both protect the natural environ-mental and to ease traffic flows. He also advocated for paying attention to the multisensory qualities of experiencing the city—its sounds, odors, and tactile perceptions as identified by Steen Eiler Rasmussen (1898–1990) in *Experiencing Architecture* (1962). Peter Calthorpe's *The Next American Metropolis* (1993) advocated for new urbanist design principles, which brought the century to a close. Along the way, there were many digressions. The Townscape movement was one.

The movement was promoted by the British journal *Architectural Review* in the 1950s. Led by Nikolaus Pevsner (1902–83), an émigré architectural historian, and Gordon Cullen in Eng-land, the *Townscape Manifesto* was published during that decade. It was a reaction to the rational modernism approach to urban design but also built on it (Aitchison 2012). Cullen criticized the contemporary British new towns for their lack of vitality and, more generally, urbanity (Ellin 1996). The manifesto argued for variety, behaviorally and visually, in the built environment, for public spaces enclosed by buildings, streets lined by buildings and, more generally, the crea-tion of a rich set of places. Cullen's concern for the sequential experience of moving through cities shines through (Cullen 1961). In the United States, Jane Jacobs was expressing similar sentiments.

The most important observer/critic of urban designs during the period was Jane Jacobs. In *The Death and Life of Great American Cities* (1961), she criticized 1950s urban renewal programs in the United States (and, implicitly, elsewhere) that cleared large tracts of the city for redevelopment. She was against the bulldozing of socially well-functioning but dilapidated neighborhoods in the name of slum clearance and their replacement with high-rise apartment buildings set in park-like open space. Based on her experience of living in New York's Greenwich Village, Jacobs saw the elements of neighborhoods—sidewalks, buildings, squares, and parks—as ecological wholes that needed to be considered together when formulating urban design policies and specific designs. She was an advocate for high-density, low-rise, mixed-use developments.

To Jacobs, a good neighborhood should have buildings of mixed ages to give a sense of locale to a neighborhood. Although this end cannot be achieved in brand new neighborhoods, in renewing an existing city precinct, conservative surgery should be the approach used for urban renewal as advocated earlier by Patrick Geddes. She also believed that socioeconomic and age-diverse populations are necessary to create lively, educative environments—ones where individuals can learn vicariously from the activities taking place around them. She wanted zoning abolished and the free market to establish land uses (J. Jacobs 1961). Herbert Gans (b. 1927), a sociologist, drew similar conclusions about infilling rather than demolishing neighborhoods in his study of the consequences of city planning actions in the West End of Boston, as presented in his book *The Urban Villagers* (Gans 1962).

Some of these ideas were explored by Oscar Newman (1935–2004) in dealing with crime prevention. On the basis of empirical evidence, he defined what he called "defensible space" (Newman 1972). A defensible space is one that is controlled by the people living nearby. It has a hierarchy of open spaces from public to semi-public, semi-private, and private. It is one, as Jane Jacobs also noted, that affords easy natural surveillance of the street and other exterior spaces as part of daily life. A third principle is that buildings' appearances do not communicate that they are inhabited by vulnerable people. The visual distinctiveness of many housing schemes for low-income people does exactly that.

The first comprehensive empiricist urban design manifesto of the period was produced by Christopher Alexander and his colleagues. Building on his earlier work in *Notes on the Synthesis of Form* (1964), Alexander, with Sara Ishikawa and Murray Silverstein, published *A Pattern Language: Towns, Buildings, Construction* (1977). The language consists of a series of pattern statements from the regional to the building detail level structured as follows: 'to solve problem x, use pattern y, because z.' The z component explained the evidence for the link between the problem and the solution. It also explains the degree of confidence in the data used. Later, with another set of colleagues, Alexander produced *A New Theory of Urban Design* (1987; see Figure 10.2).

These books are based on the supposition that designing the affordances for a sense of community to develop is important. Places such as coffeeshops enable casual meetings to occur. The books also take the position that laypeople are knowledgeable about the built environment and its relationship to their everyday lives. They should thus be involved in making the decision affecting them. This argument is spelled out more forcefully in "Toward an Urban Design Manifesto," by Allan Jacobs (b. 1928) and Donald Appleyard (1928–82) at the University of California, Berkeley (Jacobs and Appleyard 1987).

The Berkeley manifesto notes that "the designer's prize is often the user's prison." Urban designers, the manifesto argues, should be addressing poor living conditions, the gigantism of projects, and the loss of control that people have over their own environments. Like Christopher Alexander, they believe that urban designers should be working directly with the people affected by a potential project.

> ### The planning/design rules presented in *A New Theory of Urban Design* by Alexander, Neis, Annimou and King
>
> **Growth should be**:
> Piecemeal: To "guarantee a mixed flow of small, medium and large projects—preferably in equal portion by cost."
>
> "Every building increment must help form a larger whole."
>
> **Visions**
> "Every project must first be experienced and then expressed as a vision which can be seen in the inner eye (literally)."
>
> **Positive Public Space**
> "Every building must create coherent and well-shaped public space next to it."
>
> **The Layout of Large Buildings**
> "The entrance, main circulation . . . main division . . . into parts . . . interior spaces . . . daylight, and . . . movement within the building, are all coherent and consistent with the position of the building in the street and neighborhood."
>
> **Construction**
> "The structure of every building must generate smaller wholes in the physical fabric . . . in its structural bays, columns, windows, building base, etc. . . . in its entire physical construction and appearance."
>
> **Formation of Centers**
> "Every whole must be a center in itself and must also produce a system of centers around it."

Figure 10.2   The precepts of a new theory of urban design

Credit line: Table based on Alexander et al. (1987), by the author

Perhaps the most important request emerging during the period was for the reconsideration of the central importance of streets in urban designs. Streets with buildings lining them on both sides should form a territory in themselves. Heavy traffic, it is recognized, turns streets into dividers. The claim over spaces in front of the residences of people living on them is limited on busy streets (Appleyard and Lintel 1981). Great streets make great cities, as Allan Jacobs proclaimed in *Great Streets* (A. Jacobs 1993). This concern for the life of the city is reflected in the advocacies of Manuel de Solà Morales (1939–2012), as in his *Ciudades, Esquinas = City, Corners* (2004) and *A Matter of Things* (with others, 2008). His thoughts parallel those of Christopher Alexander.

Streets are the places from which cities and neighborhoods are seen and evaluated. Gordon Cullen (1961), as already noted, brought attention to the importance of vistas opening from behind walls as one walks along streets. A visually unchanging townscape as one moves through it is boring. The same is true for automobile drivers and passengers, a concern addressed in *The View from the Road* (Appleyard, Lynch, and Myer 1965). Cullen's book *Townscape* (1961) led to the development of the Townscape school of urban design that was one antecedent of the new urbanists' ideas. The development of 'space syntax analysis' as presented in *The Social Logic of Space* took these ideas a step further. The method provides a powerful predictive device for understanding how people move through sequences of spaces (Hillier and Hanson 1984).

Two books explicitly advocating for the understanding of people's ways of life within specific cultures before creating design are Amos Rapoport's *Human Aspects of Urban Form* (1977) and Kevin Lynch's *Theory of Good Urban Form* (1981). Kevin Lynch, drawing on gestalt psychology and his empirical studies, had in *The Image of the City* already identified the elements of urban form that provide people with clear cognitive representations, or mental maps, of a city that aid finding their way around it (Lynch 1960). Both Lynch and Rapoport argue that urban designers need to heed what people of different cultural backgrounds, at various stages in their life cycles and of differing socioeconomic capabilities do and enjoy doing. Such statements were a plea for understanding the richness of human experiences and for understanding the unique identity of a city—its brand image—as Anselm Strauss identified in his *Images of the American City* (1961).

Dealing with the proliferation of vehicular traffic became an increasing urban design concern in the decades after World War Two as car ownership burgeoned. Of the several manifestoes and guidebooks on how to deal with the car, the most thoughtful and influential was Paul Buchanan and his colleagues' *Traffic in Towns* (1963). Victor Gruen's *The Heart of our Cities* followed a year later (Gruen 1964). It advocated for turning the core areas of cities into pedestrianized super-blocks. This concern for pedestrians' experiences increased as the twentieth century progressed.

Late in the century, the empiricist approach to urban design was developed into a clear new ideology by the new urbanists. Their ideas can be said to have begun with the switching of the advocacies of architects like Léon Krier (b. 1946) away from the urban design concepts of Le Corbusier toward more-traditional directions (Krier 1984; Broadbent 1990). The New Urbanism movement was spearheaded by Andrés Duany (b. 1949) and Elizbeth Plater-Zyberk (b. 1950) in the United States and had such prominent supporters as Charles, Prince of Wales (b. 1948), in the United Kingdom, who produced his own manifesto professing similar values (Bennett 2015). New urbanists' advocacies were first spelled out in the 1991 Ahwahnee principles (named after the hotel in the Yosemite National Park where the group first met). Two years later, the Congress for New Urbanism was founded to further the group's arguments.

The Congress' Ahwahnee principles (see Table 10.3) advocated for the pre-eminence of foot over automobile traffic, developing mixed-land-use neighborhoods with easy access to public transport, and using form-based rather than use-based zoning in new designs and in shaping existing precincts of cities (Parolek, Parolek, and Crawford 2006). The neighborhoods they advocated for would be 'walkable' and their architectural qualities based on regional models that respond to climatic and material supply exigencies. Such design principles can be applied to suburban design and the revitalization of distressed inner-city neighborhoods as part of a strategy to integrate changes into the built environment and economic, social, and community development programs (Bohl 2000). The application of their principles can also lead to the gentrification of neighborhoods, a process that has both advocates and detractors.

Peter Calthorpe (b. 1949), with Shelley Poticha, presented "a new vision of the American Metropolis and a new image of the American Dream" in *The Next American Metropolis* (Calthorpe 1993, 15). He, like Jane Jacobs, advocated for integrated and heterogeneous spatial communities that are mixed use in character, ecologically sound, and affordable and that exploit contemporary technologies. Precincts must have strong public domains, be 'human scaled,' and have a variety of building types. The book presents the principles for the design of circulation systems for automobiles and bicycles, the nature of commercial areas, squares, civic buildings, transit systems, and parking requirements (surface and structured). Calthorpe is an advocate for TOD.

A subset of empiricists' advocacies addressed the specific interests of people such as children and people with various disabilities. Environmental psychologists have been at the forefront of conducting this research. Important though the findings have been, they have seldom been fully applied in urban design. Little of the research findings has been translated into generic solutions to urban design problems in a manner that assists practitioners. In Berlin, the *Internationale Bau-ausstellung* (IBA) was more directly involved in showing the way, not through clear advocacies but through direct action.

Preamble

Existing patterns of urban and suburban development seriously impair our quality of life. The symptoms are more congestion and air pollution resulting from our increased dependence on automobiles, the loss of precious open space, the need for costly improvements to roads and public services, the inequitable distribution of economic resources, and the loss of a sense of community. By drawing upon the best from the past and the present, we can, first, infill existing communities and, second, plan new communities that will successfully serve the needs of those who live and work within them. Such planning should adhere to these fundamental principles:

Community Principles:
- All planning should be in the form of complete and integrated communities containing housing, shops, workplaces, schools, parks and civic facilities essential to the daily life of the residents.
- Community size should be designed so that housing, jobs, daily needs and other activities are within easy walking distance of each other.
- As many activities as possible should be located within easy walking distance of transit stops.
- A community should contain a diversity of housing types to enable citizens from a wide range of economic levels and age groups to live within its boundaries.
- Businesses within the community should provide a range of job types for the community's residents.
- The location and character of the community should be consistent with a larger transit network.
- The community should have a center focus that combines commercial, civic, cultural and recreational uses.
- The community should contain and ample supply of specialized open space in the form of squares, greens and parks whose frequent use is encouraged through placement and design.
- Public spaces should be designed to encourage the attention and presence of people at all hours of the day and night.
- Each community or cluster of communities should have a well-defined edge, such as agricultural greenbelts or wildlife corridors, permanently protected from development.
- Streets, pedestrian paths and bike paths should contribute to a system of fully connected and interesting routes to all destinations. Their design should encourage pedestrian and bicycle use by being small and spatially defined by buildings, trees and lighting, and by discouraging high-speed traffic.
- Wherever possible, the natural terrain, drainage, and vegetation of the community should be preserved with superior examples contained within parks or greenbelts.
- The community design should help conserve resources and minimize waste.

Figure 10.3 The Ahwahnee New Urbanism design principles

Source: Fulton (1997); courtesy of the Lincoln Institute of Land Policy

- Communities should provide for the efficient use of water through the use of natural drainage, drought tolerant landscaping and recycling.
- The street orientation, the placement of buildings and the use of shading should contribute to the energy efficiency of the community.

Regional Principles:
- The regional land-use planning structure should be integrated within a larger transportation network built around transit rather than freeways.
- Regions should be bounded by a provide a continuous system of greenbelt wildlife corridors to be determined by natural conditions.
- Regional institutions and services (government, stadiums, museums, etc,) should be located in the urban core.
- Materials and methods of construction should be specific to the region, exhibiting continuity of history and culture and compatibility with the climate to encourage the development of local character and community identity.

Implementation Strategy:
- The general plan should be updated to incorporate the above principles.
- Rather than allowing developer-initiated, piecemeal development, local governments should take charge of the planning process. General plans should designate where new growth, infill or redevelopment will be allowed to occur.
- Prior to any development, a specific plan should be prepared based on these planning principles. With the adoption of specific plans, complying projects could proceed with minimal delay.
- Plans should be developed through an open process and participants in the process should be provided visual models of all planning proposals.

Figure 10.3 (Continued)

Between 1975 and 1987, IBA, under the leadership of Josef Paul Kleihues (1933–2004) and Hardt-Waltherr Hämer (1922–2012), promoted urban design forms that were not aesthetically regressive but instead adapted the principles underlying well-functioning existing places (in their view) in new designs (Kleihues 1987; Cestnik and Cloyd 2008). In urban renewal, IBA strove to create mixed-use developments while retaining existing buildings to the greatest extent possible and integrating social planning and urban design. Careful attention was paid in their designs to the way plant materials were used, but that concern was addressed much more forcefully by others.

Strong advocacies for addressing the health of the biogenic environment before considering other factors in creating urban designs were presented by Ian McHarg in *Design with Nature* (1969), Michael Hough in *City Form and Natural Processes: Towards a New Urban Vernacular* (1984), and Anne Spirn in *The Granite Garden: Urban Nature and Human Design* (1989). The advocacies presented in the first two are easier to apply to designs on greenfield rather than brownfield sites. All three deal with the situation in temperate climatic zones. They were much influenced by Rachel Carson (1907–64).

Carson's *Silent Spring* (1962) brought the attention of politicians and planners not only to the health damaging effects of insecticides on animal life but more generally to the pollutants generated by wastes from industries and automobiles on the cyclical cleansing function of the biogenic environment. The acceleration of global warming as the result of the increased amount of greenhouse gases in the atmosphere and its impact on sea levels and, more generally, the change in both climate and weather patterns began to be a significant public concern in the 1980s, although few ameliorating actions ensued.

Advocates for greener cities suggest that many changes in attitudes are required to achieve climatically appropriate designs. In temperate climates, they argue, grass verges on roads and in parks should be left partly unmown, and paved areas of cities should be reduced in area to minimize the speed of water runoff into streams and rivers—to replenish water tables and to reduce heat-island effects (Spirn 1984). In addition, more trees should be planted along streets and in urban squares, not only to reduce heat-island effects and act as biological filters but also architecturally to define spaces, as argued by Henry Arnold in *Trees in Urban Design* (Arnold 1980). In hot, arid, and humid tropical conditions (Givoni 1998; T. Chandler 1976) and in arctic conditions (Pressman 2004; Jurrica and Valtman), the use of vegetation should reflect the necessities of the climate.

While much attention has been paid to designing individual buildings with the climate in mind, the concern for urban designing in a similar manner has lagged behind. Several advocacies for paying attention to the climate when designing the precincts of cities were voiced during the second half of the twentieth century (e.g., T. Chandler 1976; Givoni 1998). Much was written about tropical climes (e.g., Frey and Drea 1964; Koenigsberger et al. 1974) but less and yet equally importantly on designing in arctic areas (e.g., Pressman 2004; Mānty and Pressman 1988). In temperate climatic areas, cities should be compact. Existing wetlands and wildlife areas should be preserved, and greenbelts and green fingers linking the exterior to the interior of the site should be part of a city's form. In coastal cities, high buildings along waterfronts should be avoided to allow breezes to penetrate the interior of built-up areas. The urban texture should be aerodynamically rough by varying building heights and massing. Streets should be aligned to channel prevailing winds. Large open spaces should be close to built-up areas. *Cordon sanitaires* should be created between industrial and residential areas. Industries should not be placed in low-lying areas that have light winds and are subject to temperature inversions. Habitats need to be provided for flora and fauna. Indigenous rather than exotic plants should be used in them so that they can prosper.

The books advocating for climate-appropriate urban design, including Baruch Givoni's *Climate Considerations in Building and Urban Design* (1998), say little about creating a well-functioning natural world. Toward the end of the century, an effort was made by the landscape urbanists to take McHarg's and Hough's work a step forward by developing a coherent advocacy for a landscape-first approach to urban design (Waldheim 2006). Although poorly articulated, landscape urbanism is making major contributions to the twenty-first-century urban design debate. Consequently, it forms part of the discussion in Part IV of this book.

Two other approaches to urban design were part of the conversation during the latter part of the twentieth century. Religious canons played only a small part in the design upheavals of the postwar years, but advocates continue to espouse the empirical basis of astrological and magnetic forces on human health, both physical and mental. The Shilpa Shastras in India and the feng shui canons of China had their supporters as the basis for design. The former is best displayed, as noted in Chapter 1, in *The Spirit of Indian Architecture; Vendetic Wisdom of Architecture for Building Harmonic Spaces and Life* (Bubbar 2005). The writings on feng shui are more numerous.

Sites-and-service programs address the shelter needs of people who live in slums. Slums are crowded and have a poor water supply, inadequate drainage, and little sanitation. They are shoddily built of flammable materials, so when a fire starts, the whole physical and social community gets destroyed. The sites-and-service programs are a response to this situation. They provide a site along a road, with a toilet and a sewer connection with individual households erecting their own buildings. The concept was originally developed in India by Christopher Benninger (b. 1942) on the basis of his 1966 thesis at Harvard University that was supervised by Sert and guided externally by John F. C. Turner (b. 1927), who later wrote *Housing by People: Towards Autonomy in Building Environments* (1976). Sites-and-services programs have been implemented in Asia, Africa, and Latin America.

Many of the manifestoes of the second half of the twentieth century remained at a general level without their implications' being adequately revealed or explicated in generic or illustrative designs. In several generic designs, the set of beliefs on which they are based were never part of a formal manifesto. Their value base is implicit in them.

Generic Concepts and Illustrative Designs

Two overlapping sets of empiricist generic ideas dominated during the second half of the twentieth century. The first was based on garden city ideals and the second on more pro-urbanity positions. These positions are reflected in the various models described here. The discussion begins with a presentation of the major urban new town or citywide models. It then proceeds to a description of generic solutions for parts of the city and ends with a discussion of road networks and types. None is as detailed as one might expect from reading the manifestoes.

In the immediate postwar years, the Goodman brothers, Paul and Percival, proposed a socially radical garden city in *Communitas: Means of Livelihood and Ways of Life* (Goodman and Goodman 1947). The work was praised by Lewis Mumford for its re-formation of Howard's garden city concept (Mumford 1961). It has a high rationalist component in that it proposed a major change in the nature of social interactions away from individualism toward a more communitarian approach. In addition, the layout of individual buildings reflects Le Corbusier's ideas. Communitas was presented as a 'city of efficient consumption.' In its center is a precinct of markets, light industry, commercial offices, entertainment places, and transportation terminals. Around it are the city's cultural institutions, universities, museums, and zoological gardens. Residences, schools, and hospitals are in segments radiating from the center. Heavy industry, transportation terminals, and airports lie on the outskirts. The land beyond consists of forest preserves, vacation lands, and agricultural fields. Later, John Simonds updated Howard's garden city model (Simonds 1994).

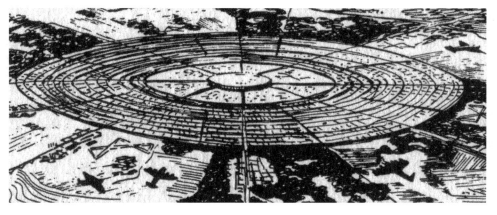

Figure 10.4   The City of Efficient Consumption: An image of the city in its regional setting
Source: Goodman and Goodman (1947, 133); collection of the author

Post–World War Two Pragmatic Urban Design

Simmonds assumed the existing ways of life in North America would continue. His model has a clear central business district at its core surrounded by a loop road and inner-city development. Outside this inner-city area is a ring transit system linking activity/commercial nodes. Transit ways lead from the edge of the city to its core via these nodes. A parkway encircles the inner city, with the suburbs lying outside it. A ring road circumscribing the whole allows traffic to go around it. The countryside lies beyond.

Emerging from these explorations and the work of Clarence Perry and Clarence Stein during the interwar years is the generic *urban composition model* that became widely accepted as the ideal structure for new towns in the postwar years. Cities, in the model, have a strong central core, and the surrounding areas are divided into districts that are in turn divided into neighborhoods. The districts and neighborhoods with distinctive names and surrounded by greenbelts would thus have a clear identity. Each would have a central node of shops and services where pedestrian and vehicular paths meet. The district centers provide more-comprehensive services than those in the neighborhoods. In this way, each would have the nodes and edges that Kevin Lynch found composed people's mental maps of cities (Lynch 1960). The organization forms the structure of the compact city model of mathematicians George Dantzig (1914–2005) and Thomas Saaty (1926–2017).

They sought an urban form that would be sustainable and efficient in the use of resources. Their city model is at a higher population density (i.e., 250 people/hectare, or 100 people/acre) than those existing in US cities. It is close to European norms but lower than those found in cities such as Mumbai and Cairo (Dantzig and Saaty 1973; see also Burton, Jenks, and Williams 1996). Their compact city is one of short distances between destinations. It has a central node of intense land use and thus land values. Most surrounding districts are of mixed uses, the services required for everyday life being close at hand. The need to use automobiles for transport would thus be reduced, leading to a reduction in the energy consumed and the level of pollutants in the air.

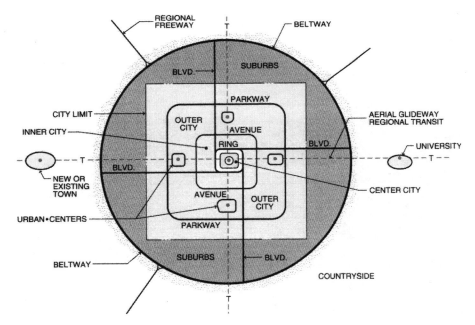

Figure 10.5 The garden city revisited: The generic model
Source: Simonds (1994, n.p.); courtesy of McGraw-Hill

The Post–World War Two Empiricists

The concept is loosely and less compactly reflected in the later *urban transect* model for the morphology of a region suggested by Andrés Duany and Elizabeth Plater-Zyberk. Their generic idea is shown in Figure 10.6 but would have to be adapted to specific cities. As presented, it is predominantly an Anglo-American model that is different from one that would be based on contemporary cities of Latin America or Asia. The diagram illustrates the character that each of the six zones has moving out from the city center (C5 and C6). The center is an intense, compact core, while T1 is a rural preserve. A new design, it was argued, should follow the characteristics of the zone in which it is to be located.

While much attention was paid to defining the nature of good neighborhoods by the empiricists, few provided a generic model for the central business districts of major cities. In the 1950s, Victor Gruen (1903–80) produced a model for CBDs that attracted considerable attention. Gruen suggested that CBDs be pedestrianized superblocks surrounded by ring roads with parking garages leading off them. Residents, workers, and shoppers would thus park their cars on the periphery of the CBD and walk to their destinations. Gruen proposed such a solution for Fort Worth that has become a generic idea referred to as the Fort Worth Plan (Gruen 1964). It had several precedents and descendants in the pedestrianized cores of many European cities. The nature of the residential neighborhood was simultaneously being more widely explored.

The earlier in the century idea of the neighborhood as an area in which a resident's daily needs are located within walking distance endured. Clarence Perry's scheme was updated by Duany Plater-Zyberk Associates, who recognized that shopping streets played an important role in neighborhood life. In its reorganized form, the unit has the shopping located along a street that acts as a seam for the community. The concept can be applied to new residential precincts or as a guide in upgrading existing urban neighborhoods. The pedestrian pocket is a similar idea.

The pedestrian pocket concept is another potential walkable suburb or small town that is an extension of Perry's formulation. The pocket is tied into a regional transit network via a station located in a mixed-use commercial and residential center (Kelbaugh 1987). Adjacent to the station is a square. The pedestrian pocket is a model for a more compact form of development than many suburbs, but it still has a substantial amount of open space. The design is pragmatically based on an acceptance of the values implicit in the US real estate market. Closely allied to the pedestrian pocket concept is the TOD precinct.

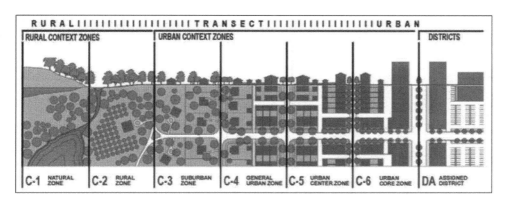

Figure 10.6 The transect classifying the built environment types from the rural preserve to the urban core

Source: Bohl and Plater-Zyberk (2008); courtesy iof DPZCoDesign

Post–World War Two Pragmatic Urban Design

Figure 10.7 The Fort Worth Plan: The CBD as a superblock (left) and an interior view (right)
Source (left): Gruen (1964); courtesy of Gruen Associates
Source (right): Gruen (1964); courtesy of Gruen Associates

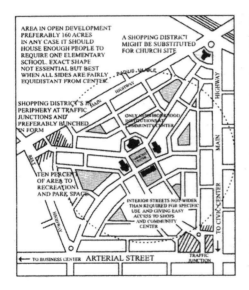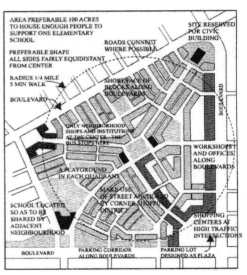

Figure 10.8 The neighborhood unit revisited: Perry's generic plan (left) and Duany Plater-Zyberk's update (right)
Credit line (left): Perry (1929)
Source (left): Lang (2017, 93); courtesy of Taylor & Francis
Credit line (right): Drawing adapted from various sources by Omar Sharif
Source (right): Lang (2017, 93); courtesy of Taylor and Francis

A TOD consists of a high-intensity precinct whose edges are within walking distance of a transit stop (Bernick and Cervero 1997). The stop could be a heavy-rail or a light-rail station or even a high-speed bus stop, as in Curitiba, Brazil. The high-density mixed-use core has lower-density areas spreading out from it, as shown in Figure 10.10. A TOD on a greenfield site

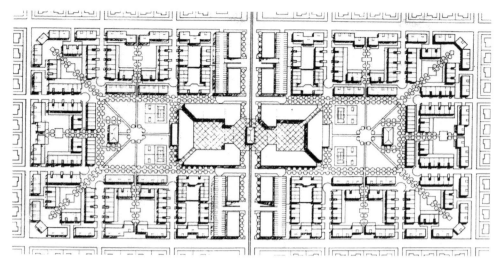

Figure 10.9 The pedestrian pocket: An illustrative design
Source: Calthorpe (1993, 45); courtesy of Princeton Architectural Press

would be designed with smaller-than-normal block sizes and with only minimal space provided for automobile use. As in the neighborhood unit schemes, the ideal walking distance to the transit stop is 400 meters (¼ mile), but generally a TOD is at the center of a walking radius of 800 meters (½ mile). A city would consist of TODs in a hierarchical fashion, as shown in Figure 10.10 (right). In tropical zones, it would have to be shorter and well shaded.

A detailed verbal image of the qualities of a good urban neighborhood was presented by Jane Jacobs. She, an advocate for redundancy and vibrancy as opposed to the order and efficiency of her rationalist contemporaries' design ideas, proposed a set of generic design principles for the design of urban areas in *The Death and Life of Great American Cities* (1961). She believed that cities should be lively places and 'fun.' She was much concerned with the nature of urban street blocks (J. Jacobs 1961).

A hallmark of the second half of the twentieth century was the rediscovery of the perimeter block as an organizing model for inner-city precincts. A variant is the Barcelona block of Cerda's Eixample with its chamfered corners that form diamond-shaped squares at the intersections of streets. The streets themselves become seams if they are not too wide or heavily trafficked, while the interior of the blocks can form courtyards or gardens.

Allied to the rediscovery of the urban block is the suggestion of how to relate the fabric of cities, as a backdrop, to foreground buildings such as religious edifices, museums, and civic institutions of importance. The proposition was put forward by Léon Krier in 1963 (L. Krier 1992). The idea is that important buildings should be placed at prominent sites (such as those terminating vistas) within the frame of a city's general fabric; they should be "set within the matrix of the city" (J. Jacobs 1961, 228). Jane Jacobs was opposed to the clustering of cultural facilities into single complexes such as New York's Lincoln Center.

The generic idea presented by Krier is based on the observation that if every building strives to be a spectacle, then none is. Specific buildings should be prominent objects acting as landmarks (see Figure 10.13). The model is easier to apply to greenfield developments, where the land uses and building forms can be dictated a priori, than in the existing city, where new value-added buildings

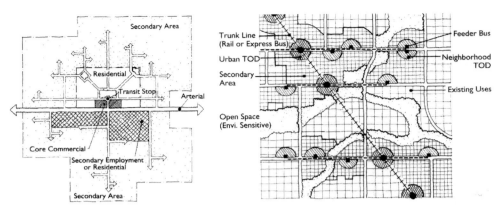

Figure 10.10 Transit-oriented development: The generic TOD model (left) and TODs as part of an urban area (right)
Source (left): Calthorpe (1993, 45); courtesy of Princeton Architectural Press
Source (right): Calthorpe (1993, 62); courtesy of Princeton Architectural Press

---

1. Urban blocks should have a mixture of facilities—land uses—to activate them
2. The blocks should be short with buildings directly facing them; stoops are a good idea
3. Building should be of various ages, styles, and states of maintenance
4. Neighborhoods should consist of high-density three- or four-story buildings
5. Buildings should afford the natural surveillance of public open spaces; people must be prepared to give up a level of privacy to attain security
6. Neighborhood parks need to be small, well located, and naturally surveilled.

In short, designers should make small plans and design for incremental change.

Figure 10.11 Jane Jacobs's generic neighborhood design principles

---

such as museums are built on whatever suitable site is available to build them. Krier's idea can nevertheless act as a guide to the placement of new buildings of importance in a city.

Streets form the armature on which all urban designs are strung. They are the place from which cities and suburbs are seen and appreciated. They come in well-documented forms from boulevards to alleys and in a variety of networks. The standard is the gridiron pattern. It probably has the greatest traffic-handling capacity (Steuteville 2018b). Several other patterns were used in the garden suburbs and cities from the beginning of the century through the postwar years and to today. The *cul-de-sac* has had its advocates and detractors; it has fallen out of favor because it regarded as old-fashioned. Property developers and urban designers come back to the *gridiron plan* as the armature for their projects—sometimes in short blocks, as advocated by Jane Jacobs, and sometimes long.

The conversion of some streets to pedestrian streets or malls, as they are often called, is a variant of the superblock model. The Lijnbaan, Rotterdam's major central shopping street, became the model for others to follow. Begun in 1949, it was completed in 1953. The area was destroyed by bombing during World War Two. Designed by van der Broek and Bakema, it remains one of Rotterdam's main shopping streets. These pedestrian streets work best if they

Figure 10.12 Perimeter blocks: The Barcelona example
Credit line: Photograph by Sanquan Deng/Shutterstock.com

follow a *dumbbell* design (i.e., one with destinations or drawcards at either end). A *woonerf*, in contrast, works best if it has no attraction at its ends—if it is not a route to major destinations. The *woonerf*, a 1970s Dutch idea, is a variant of the pedestrian street; it is shared space. Driving is restricted to walking speed, and drivers must be prepared to stop for a child running out in front of them. Such streets are called *home zones* in the United Kingdom. A US variant is the *complete street*. It has separate channels for the movement of bicycles, cars, and pedestrians.

The townscape advocates reminded urban designers that people experience the built environment as it is perceived when one moves thorough it. The movement's advocacy for the compact relationship between buildings and the nature of the sequential visual experience one attains is shown in the illustrative designs and analyses of Gordon Cullen, such as the one shown in Figure 10.14. The illustration also shows the type of tight-knit environment that influenced the movement.

Some of the generic proposals of the empiricists during the second half of the twentieth century were wholeheartedly put into practice, others partially, and yet others not. Some specific designs embraced a specific generic model, but many are based on a mixture of ideas. Much was pragmatically implemented.

Specific Designs

Columbia, Maryland (1962–), is a good representative of the many garden cities of the automobile era built around the world. It is an exemplar of the three-level urban composition model for organizing a new town. The plans of the first generation of British new towns, such as Stevenage (1946) and Crawley (1947), were based on the model. Valingby in Sweden (inaugurated

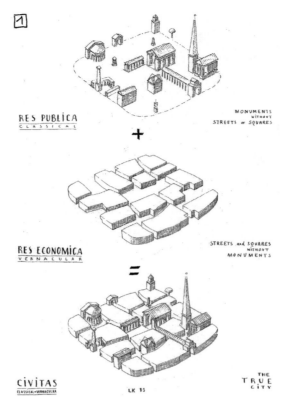

Figure 10.13 The integration of background and foreground buildings
Credit line: Courtesy of Léon Krier

in 1954) follows the same overall layout and has a pedestrianized town center associated with a rail connection to central Stockholm. The postwar suburban development of Canberra, Australia's capital, follows the same model. The new state capitals of the era in India, Bhubaneswar and Chandigarh, have a similar hierarchical structure (Nilsson 1973), as do the US new towns of Woodlands in Texas and Jonathan in Minnesota (Forsythe 2005).

Many new urbanist–type developments were built during the period. They range in location from Thimphu in Bhutan to Sydney's Breakfast Point in Australia. The overwhelming number were built in the United States. Well before the term 'New Urbanism' came into common usage, however, Port Grimaud on France's Mediterranean coast had been built. Better known are Seaside (1978) in the United States and Poundbury (1993) in England. "The idea of Seaside started with the notion of reviving the building tradition of Northwest Florida that had produced wood-framed cottages so well adapted to the climate that they enhanced the sensual pleasure of life by the sea" (Davis 1989, 92). Poundbury was inspired by the dislike that Charles, Prince of Wales, had for much contemporary pragmatic suburban development in the United Kingdom.

A predominantly vacation community, Seaside was designed by Duany Plater-Zyberk & Co. It set the tone for much that has followed. At the town's core is an octagonal square surrounded by shops, a library, and other community facilities. The center is within a five-minute walk from

The Post–World War Two Empiricists

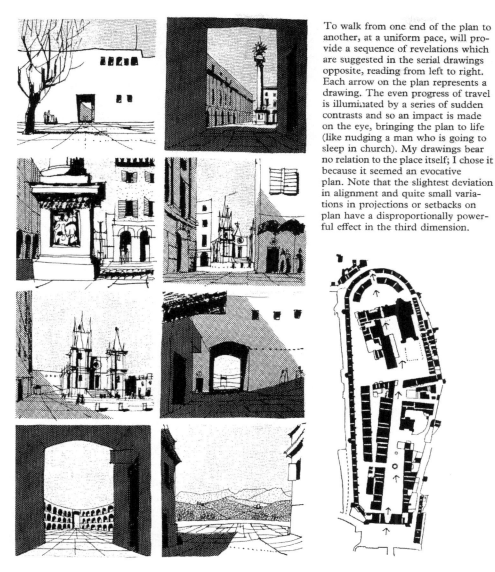

Figure 10.14 Gordon Cullen's analysis of the experience of moving through a sequence of spaces.
Source: Cullen (1961, 70) and Lang and Marshall (2016, 29); courtesy of Taylor & Francis

all residences, as is the beach (as at La Grande Motte). Housing and use types are scattered in the development, but a form-based code provided guidelines for the buildings' design. The objective was to provide enough flexibility to attain a diversity within an overall unified, aesthetic framework (Katz 1994). Poundbury, while similar in spirit, because it is in Dorset, England, drew on a different vernacular tradition.

Rector Place in New York's Battery Park City development is a highly urban new urbanist scheme and the one selected to describe next as an exemplar of a neo-traditional scheme.

Post–World War Two Pragmatic Urban Design

Figure 10.15 Regionalism and New Urbanism: Seaside, Florida (left), and Poundbury, Dorset (right)

Credit line (left): Photograph by Kristie Blokhim/Shutterstock.com

Village Homes is a good example of an early 'green' neighborhood; it also shows how difficult it is to sustain interests in a design idea once the people who drove it pass on. Arumbakkkam was one of the first sites-and-services designs. It too is an exemplar of the type but simultaneously illustrates how careful authorities must be in designing with maintenance in mind.

Exemplars of Empiricist Designs

Columbia, Maryland, USA (1962–2014); Port Grimaud, Var, France (1963–70–); Rector Place Battery Park City, New York, New York, USA (1979–2012); Village Homes, Davis, California, USA (1960–72); and Arumbakkam, Madras (Now Chennai), India (1973–80)

Designed under the direction of city planner Morton Hoppenfeld (1929–85), Columbia is composed of a city center surrounded by 'villages' that are subdivided into 'neighborhoods' (Hester 1975; Forsyth 2005; Mitchell and Stebenne 2007). Each village and each neighborhood has a set of facilities at its core. Despite the fact that a reviewing group, led by sociologist Herbert Gans, said that neighborhoods made little sense when people live metropolitan-wide lives, the property developer, James Rouse (1914–96), believed that neighborhoods foster a sense of community. He had the Easton, Maryland, of his childhood in mind.

The center of Columbia is a shopping mall, but commercial buildings have been built around it. They are surrounded by surface parking lots. Columbia has ten villages, each with its supermarket, shops, car service stations, recreational facilities, and, originally, teen centers. Each village has several neighborhoods within its boundaries. Each neighborhood has a primary school and local shops at its center in line with Clarence Perry's neighborhood unit idea. The village centers have undergone some dramatic changes since they were built, but they continue to thrive. The neighborhood centers struggle but survive. Once in their cars, residents find it easy to bypass their local shops in favor of the diversity of the village centers and their larger supermarkets.

In developing Columbia, Rouse had a social agenda in mind (Mitchell and Stebenne 2008). His aim was to create a diverse community. While racially and ethnically diverse, Columbia is largely an upper-middle-class city of well-educated people. It nevertheless represents the effort to create a

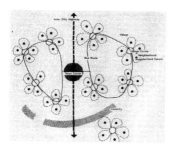 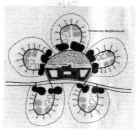 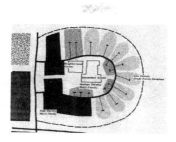

Figure 10.16 Columbia, Maryland: The conceptual diagram of the city layout (left), its villages (center), and its neighborhoods (right)
Source: Hester (1975, 8–10); courtesy of Randolph Hester and John Wiley & Sons

high-quality built environment that simultaneously achieves specific social goals in an automobile-oriented culture. Port Grimaud, a contemporary, is a typical new urbanist development.

The town was designed and built by François Spoerry (1912–99), an Alsatian property developer and architect. Located on what had been marshland on the Mediterranean coast, its character was based on the medieval towns of the adjacent Provence and Occitanie districts of France. Dredged sand was used to form irregular rings of land and water that are broken to allow access to the open sea for tidal flows and boats. The development is loosely a superblock with an interior that is largely pedestrianized, and much of the parking for cars is located outside the town, although many houses can also be reached by car. At the entrance to Port Grimaud is a town square. The buildings of the town consist of rows of houses, hotels, and shops in different patterns and colors. This looking back to the medieval past is what Port Grimaud has in common with Louvain-la-Neuve (see Chapter 5). Later, neo-traditional designs were related to more-recent precedents. Battery Park City is one.

Battery Park City's design went through several iterations during its gestation, beginning in the mid-1960s. Each reflected a contemporary paradigm and generic idea. Finally, in 1979, a new urbanist design by Alexander Cooper and Stanton Eckstut was accepted by the Battery Park City Authority responsible for coordinating the precinct's development (Gordon 1997). It was designed to be an integral part of Lower Manhattan, so its armature follows the area's street pattern. While its commercial core, designed by César Pelli, is international in character, the remainder of the development draws on New York's architectural heritage. Rector Place is a prime example (Barnett 1987).

The building design guidelines replicate the characteristics of the early-twentieth-century buildings in areas of Manhattan, such as Morningside Heights and Gramercy Park, that are admired by New Yorkers. The guidelines stipulated that buildings should have bases and cornices, specific window-to-wall ratios, be constructed of masonry, and have a string course at specific levels. Buildings had to be built to the street-front boundary with their entrances roughly in the center of the blocks not on the corners. The esplanade was designed by Hanna-Olin, a Philadelphia-based firm of landscape architects. Its hierarchy of levels has become a generic solution that more-recent waterfront designs have followed (Lang 2017, 154–59). While Battery Park City was designed with energy efficiency in mind, it is no exemplar of contemporary sustainable design efforts. Village Homes in Davis was.

Village Homes, designed by Michael and Judy Corbett, is widely regarded as an exemplar of the self-conscious effort to create what had been attained over time in unselfconsciously designed vernacular developments across the world—a sustainable environment. Planning for the development of the 70-acre (28-hectare) site began in the 1960s; by 1982, it consisted of 225 homes and twenty apartment units. The layout provided clear solar access to each house

Post–World War Two Pragmatic Urban Design

Figure 10.17 Port Grimaud: The market square (left) and part of the ring layout (right)

Figure 10.18 Battery Park City: A general view from Hoboken with One Liberty Place in the background (left) and Rector Place (right)

Source (right): Lang (2017, 157); courtesy of Taylor & Francis

to lower energy costs and enough space for residents to create an 'edible environment' of nuts, fruit, and vegetables (Corbett and Corbett 2012).

Street widths are narrow, reducing the extent of hard surfaces exposed to the heat of the sun during the summer months. Their curving nature symbolically relates to nature while the cul-de-sacs reduce traffic speeds and provide the possibility that they, along with shared values and endeavors, would foster a community spirit. The streets run east–west to maximize solar access to each house. Solar panels are used to provide energy for heating. The houses face common areas at the rear of the sites rather than the street at the front. The orientation enables homes to have passive solar designs that take year-round advantage of the sun's energy. Bioswales (grass-lined drainage channels) collect water that is used to irrigate the common areas and support the cultivation of crops.

Over time, aspects of the communal spirit characteristic of some newly founded developments has dissipated here. Newcomers buy houses as financial investments and are more interested in standard suburban neatness than in engaging in the hard work required to sustain an environmentally friendly way of life. Much of the original intention, nevertheless, remains intact. Arumbakkam, a sites-and-services development, is a response to a different problem, that of shelter for low-income families in an economically weaker country.

Planned by Christopher Benninger, the Tamil Nadu state government provided residents with a few basic requirements: potable water, a 1-meter-wide paved approach path, storm drainage, electric

The Post–World War Two Empiricists

Figure 10.19 Village Homes, Davis

Figure 10.20 Sites-and-services schemes: Self-built houses, Arumbakkam in 1979 (left) and 1985 (right)

Source (left): Lang (2017, 197); courtesy of Taylor & Francis

streetlights, and a toilet. Its site measures 730 meters (800 yards) by 425 meters (465 yards) and contains 2,034 served plots. Of them, 70% were reserved for the 'economically weaker class.' The site is divided into several subareas with plots varying in size from 40 square meters to 223 square meters.

Initially Arumbakkam had common toilet blocks which residents considered unacceptable. They were soon replaced with individual squat toilets that, unfortunately, for cost reasons had to be placed in the front of the houses, something also regarded as undesirable. Water was supplied to the large lots on an individual basis, but just one faucet per two smaller dwellings.

Arumbakkam met the basic requirement of shelter for low-income families. The population was, however, drawn from diverse castes, language groups, and occupations, so the precinct has little sense of being a community, and residents show little enthusiasm for participation in block associations. The men are happier with the district; they have fewer demands than do the women, who spend more time at home. Maintenance is a problem. Residents complain that broken pipes are not repaired and that the sewerage drains get blocked. The lanes and by-lanes are kept clean by residents, but the larger roads become the places for dumping refuse (Barker and Hyman 2002). The scheme met its goal at the time it was created and inspired many schemes around the world to be built following the same principles.

Hybrid Examples

Runcorn, Merseyside, England, UK (1965–); Ciudad Guasare Proposal, Zulia, Venezuela (1981); Superblocks, Pedestrian Malls, and Transit-Oriented Developments; and Auroville, Tamil Nadu, India (1965–)

Many urban designs, while essentially empiricist in nature, have rationalist and/or narrow pragmatic qualities. Three essentially garden city new towns—Runcorn, Ciudad Guasare, and Auroville—have rationalist overtones. Superblocks, pedestrian malls, and TODs have pragmatic underpinnings. Runcorn is a satellite town of Liverpool in the northwest of England. Ciudad Guasare is even more rationalist in character. It has a configuration not usually associated with the imagery of garden cities. Unlike Runcorn, it remains unbuilt. Auroville's design is based on a religious philosophy that its adherents believe is empirically related to the forces of the universe.

Runcorn was designed to house 90,000 people on a 7,250-acre (2,800-hectare) site. Designed by the Runcorn Development Corporation and Arthur Ling Associates, it closely follows the generic garden city principles. The town has a figure eight road plan that was deemed to be the most efficient for the high-speed movement of vehicles. Roads off it lead to the town center and to the residential precincts. The center, as in Columbia, is an internal shopping mall. The

Figure 10.21 Runcorn
Source: Lang (2005, 70); courtesy of Taylor & Francis

precincts are separated by the natural topography and greenways along the valleys. The whole town is surrounded by a greenbelt with fingers off it penetrating the residential areas (Runcorn Development Corporation 1967; Lang 2005, 69–73).

The hierarchical nature of the town's structure is that of many contemporary new towns. It is divided into 'communities' of about 8,000 people that are subdivided into neighborhoods of one hundred to two hundred inhabitants that, unlike Columbia, have no communal facilities. Each community has its own center, but the neighborhoods are too small to support one. The community centers are, nevertheless, within a five-minute walk of the residences, as are bus stops. The dwelling units are clustered around pedestrian cul-de-sacs that afford easy communications among neighbors. Children playing outdoors and in playlots tend to be the catalysts for adult interactions. Parking for cars is clustered into communal landscaped areas from which people walk to their units. The Ciudad Guasare new town proposal was very different in character.

Colombian architect Germán Samper Genecco (b. 1924), a participant at three CIAM congresses and an employee of Le Corbusier while working on his Chandigarh buildings, was the designer of the proposal, with Kevin Lynch and Christopher Alexander as consultants. The 179-hectare (442-acre) site lies in the potential Guasare coalfields region. The first phase of the town was designed to have 3,000 residential units for a population of about 15,000. It was to have a core area with a central square almost along the lines of the *Laws of the Indies*. Around it would be superblocks (*supermanzanas* in Figure 10.22), each block within it focused on a park-like center. It was hoped that the design would resurrect the neighborhood-based sense of community being lost in the new developments in Venezuelan cities. The Gujarat State Fertilizer Company (GSFC) township has a more typical garden city superblock layout.

The GSFC township was designed by Balkrishna V. Doshi. Built as part of India's decentralization policy (see Planning Commission, Government of India 1980), the layout is a departure from the standard pragmatically designed company towns built in India after its independence. The 56-hectare (140-acre) site has a single circumferential road. From it, cul-de-sacs lead to the interior of the block. The core of the township consists of shops, health facilities, other community facilities and a primary school. Its layout is a modified generic Radburn Plan. The residential units are located on the cul-de-sacs. Their nature depends on the place of their residents in the company's employment hierarchy. Pedestrian paths provide an easy walking distance between residences and the center. The factory is located on the periphery of the township, as in the nineteenth-century 'villages of vision.'

The GSFC township was a fiat development; in other cases where the superblock has been applied, it was formed out of an existing street pattern. Many mid-size European cities now have pedestrianized city centers. They differ from the GSFC township in that parking is kept on the periphery, either in surface lots or in parking structures. Utrecht in the Netherlands is an example.

Begun in 1965, a year after the first such effort was put in place in Copenhagen, it was initiated at the behest of the police, with business interests accepting their proposal. Some streets had already been pedestrianized, but these were amalgamated into a network. Cyclists must dismount and walk their bicycles while in the area. Further pedestrianizing the center was begun as an experiment, with streets being closed to traffic on Saturday and Wednesday afternoons, when children were out of school. The success led to permanent closures with the removal of curbs and the repaving of streets.

The use of experimental closures to evaluate design possibilities set a precedent that cities such as New York have subsequently employed. On a smaller scale, pedestrianized streets (or malls) form mini-superblocks. Service vehicles can enter only at certain hours of the day. The goal of pedestrian streets is to provide shoppers with a safe and pleasant, pollution-minimized environment. They have worked best when the pattern follows a 'dumbbell design' with major destinations at both ends or when they are in locations such as university towns and vacation destination where many people are without cars. In other places, they have been returned to vehicular traffic (Houston 1990).

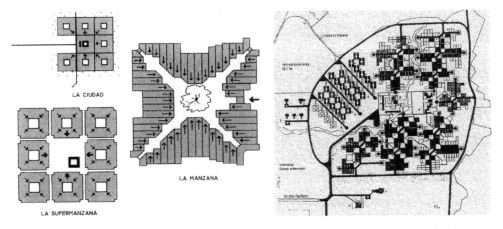

Figure 10.22 Superblocks: The Ciudad Guasare conceptual plan (left) and the GSFC township, Vadodara (right)

Credit line (left): Collection of the author
Source (right): Lang (2017, 110); courtesy of the Vastu Shilpa Foundation and Taylor & Francis

Figure 10.23 Pedestrianizing city centers, Utrecht: The station square (left) and a pedestrian-level view (right)

Credit line (left): Photograph by Fortgens Photography/Shutterstock.com
Credit line (right): Courtesy of Alexander Cuthbert

16th Street in Denver lies in the heart of the city. It has twice been extended. It is now 1.25 miles (2 kilometers) long and has Union Station at one end with the Colorado State Capitol at the other. It runs through several precincts, each with its own character and with amenities catering to a segment of the market. Designed by I. M. Pei (1917–2019) with Hanna-Olin as landscape architects, great attention was paid to the detailing of paving patterns and street furniture. Contributing to the street's success is the free MallRide bus service that plies it. With over three hundred shops and fifty restaurants, the mall is a popular destination. It attracts people which attracts buskers, who add to the street's life (Lang 2017, 65–66). Many such pedestrian streets have not been successes and have been returned to vehicular traffic (Houstoun 1990). Converted to pedestrian streets to benefit struggling businesses, they never became destinations. Avenue Henri Barbusse in Le Quartier de Gratte-Ciel in Villeurbanne has been a quiet success (Figure 8.27). It is a destination.

The Post–World War Two Empiricists

Figure 10.24 A pedestrian mall/transit way: 16th Street, Denver
Source: Lang (2017, 66); courtesy of Taylor & Francis

TODs often have pedestrian areas at their cores. Access to St Leonards station in Sydney is via a concrete platform built on the air rights over the train tracks. The project took long to implement as it ran into technical and financial difficulties. The platform has a reflecting pool and shops, mainly fast-food outlets and cafés, opening onto it. The core area of the complex comprises three commercial office buildings, two residential towers containing 782 apartments, a mini-supermarket, and several food and retail shops. The catalytic effect on property development in the area has been substantial. St Leonards may be an atypical example of a TOD. Most have been built in suburban areas as heavy- and light-rail systems have been extended out from the core of metropolitan areas.

Town layouts based on a cosmic order represent a different type of empiricist project. Only a few have been built in recent years. One under construction is Maharishi Vedic City in Jefferson County, Iowa. Its plan is related to the mandala form. Another that has a longer history is Auroville (City of Dawn). Its design is religion based, but it has French rationalist aspects to its design. Based on cosmological canons and with strong garden city precedents, it is the physical manifestation of the ways of life advocated by The Mother (Mirra Alfassa, 1878–1973) and the teachings of Sri Aurobindo (1872–1950) in what was then Pondicherry, a French colonial enclave in British India (The Mother 1990).

Auroville is a devotional community whose members are committed to meditation twice a day. People who wish to join the community must donate all their money to it. The funds are used to build them houses and working units as well as to support the construction and maintenance of communal buildings. The plan was created by Roger Anger (1923–2008), a French architect, based on The Mother's sketch of what its layout should be. The plan consists of four zones radiating out from a central zone in a spiral representing dynamic consciousness. At its heart is the Matrimandir, the symbolic focus of the community. The four zones are *Maheshwari*, representing wisdom; *Mahakali*, representing energy; *Mahalakshmi*, representing harmony; and *Mahasaraswati*, representing perfection. They accommodate residential, industrial, international, and cultural activities respectively. The buildings are located as objects in space, and the streets are primarily for vehicular traffic (Lang, Desai, and Desai 1997).

Post–World War Two Pragmatic Urban Design

Figure 10.25 St Leonards TOD, Sydney: The station (left) and the forum above the rail tracks (right)

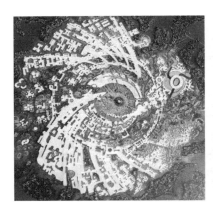

Figure 10.26 Auroville: The Galaxy Plan (left) and the Matrimandir (right)
Credit line (left): Courtesy of Auroville Outreach Media

Auroville was designed to be a city of 50,000 people when it was inaugurated, but fifty years later, in 2005, the population was only about 2,500, a quarter of whom were children. The residents are an international group of Indian, French, and German people. They form a well-educated middle-class society. The town was originally administered by the Aurobindo Society, but after the death of The Mother, rivalries within the Auroville community led to its being taken over by the government of India. It is now under the ownership of the Aurobindo Foundation and administered by a three-tier governing system: The Residents' Assembly, the Auroville International Advisory Council, and the Governing Board. Social problems, whose existence has been denied by the community, have led to remedial actions being taken.

Commentary: The Functions Addressed

A continuing underlying assumption in the empiricists' designs was that the patterns of the past provided the affordances for the fulfillment of the complete set of needs required by people.

The question is, what past? The strongest contrast in thinking of what are good worlds was between the garden city advocates and the urbanists. Each addressed the interests of specific groups of people: those who sought quiet, peaceful surroundings and those who enjoy living in diverse high-density urban environments.

Providing a salubrious environment for people's lives was more explicitly stated as a design objective by the garden city advocates than by the urbanists. It was assumed by both that water supplies and sewage and drainage systems would be part of developments. For the garden city proponents, the design mechanism to attain a healthy environment was for the natural world of waterways, grasses, shrubs, and trees to be closely integrated with residential areas. The assumption was that vegetation would help in providing clean air and that people would walk and exercise in the parks and playgrounds of a development. The use of nature was, however, as much to fill sensory and symbolic aesthetic needs as for providing healthy environments.

The urbanists paid less explicit attention to the requirements of automobile drivers than the pragmatists did, despite the motor age's being in full swing. In contrast, the ease of providing accessibility and high mobility to cars were major design criteria that had to be met in garden city designs such as Columbia and Runcorn. The concern for locating facilities and public transport stops within walking distance continued the concerns that designers thought important during the first part of the century.

Affording easy casual meetings between neighbors and thus developing a sense of belonging in a local community was an objective of most of the empiricist residential designs. An enduring goal was to create territorial communities of meaningful social interaction by shaping designs to simultaneously afford easy contacts among residents and provide the privacy they seek. Casual meetings may enhance the knowledge that people have of each other's existence but not much more unless they have other common interests (Suttles 1972). Neighbors automatically share some common concerns, but they are few. Children and the elderly were the true local people historically. Children may still be, but as the twentieth century progressed, those of middle-class parents began to lead more chauffeured metropolitan lives. In doing so, they lost a degree of independence (Parr 1969). Most elderly people still aged in place (as they still do) and continued to have parochial lives, but with the increasing health and financial resources, many led more metropolitan lives. For low-income people, parochial lives were still the norm.

The patterns of built forms that provide for the safety and sense of security of individuals in the city were identified by Jane Jacobs and more systematically by Oscar Newman in *Defensible Space Crime Prevention through Urban Design* (Newman 1972). Although their observations were not refuted, few urban designers purposefully incorporated patterns that enhance territorial control and natural surveillance into their designs. In contrast, artificial mechanisms such as security cameras became ubiquitous.

Two sets of cognitive needs were addressed in the research of the empiricists. The first dealt with wayfinding and the second with educative environments. Kevin Lynch's research on "the image of the city" provided the basis for navigating the built environment (Lynch 1960). The design principles derived from his studies are well known by designers and immediately applicable. Second and largely unselfconsciously, the empiricists designed for the human need for continued learning. The garden city proponents were particularly concerned with exposure to nature and the changing seasons as subtle mechanisms for informal intellectual development. Urbanists such as Jane Jacobs emphasized the importance of exposing people to diverse sets of other people: young and old, at different stages in their life cycles, and of different socioeconomic statuses and, ideally, ethnicities. Seeing others engaged in everyday activities, she believed, was an important part of daily life (J. Jacobs 1961). Neither group dealt explicitly with

Post–World War Two Pragmatic Urban Design

the concerns of the socioeconomic, ethnic, or racial diversity of the populations for whom they were designing.

The garden city advocates and the new urbanists, by their very nature, relied on images of familiar places as precedents in creating aesthetically pleasing environments. Sometimes the patterns were those of their childhood worlds, as in the case of the property developers of Seaside and Columbia. Aesthetically unified built environments were sought by both groups. The urbanists were, perhaps, more tolerant of disorder.

The patterns required for the natural ecological environment to function well were directly addressed only by the advocates for sustainable environments. In the short term, their advocacies and designs, such as that at Davis, had little impact on the projects being built, but they did sow the seeds for the level of concern that is with us today.

Observations

Looking back to the past for inspiration needs to be done with care. The world has changed. The Asiad Village in New Delhi dates from the late 1970s. Designed by Raj Rewal (b. 1934), a fine architect, for the 1982 Asian Games, it is a new urbanist–type design. The layout is based on the streets and chowks (small squares) of the traditional towns of Rajasthan that are much admired by architects for their picturesque streets and the utilitarian simplicity of their architectural forms. In the Asiad Village, the many terraces add a visual richness to the scheme. The site is a superblock because, given the narrow pre-automobile street forms of its precedent, vehicular traffic and parking had to be kept on the periphery.

The residents tend to use the back doors of their houses that open into the parking as their front doors rather than the traditional entrances from the chowks. The result is that the territorial order of the Rajasthani designs is lost. In addition, the climate of New Delhi differs from that of the Thar desert of Rajasthan. The use and meaning of the open spaces, including the flat roofs, is thus different from places in hot, arid zones. One of the lessons learned is that the utility of any generic design or precedent needs to be fully understood. Many of those generic designs described in this chapter are applicable only in specific contexts.

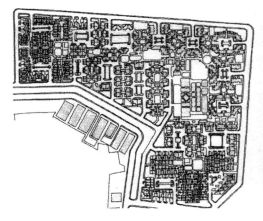 

Figure 10.27 Asiad Village, New Delhi: The plan (left) and a view from the parking area (right)
Source (left and right): Lang (2002, 130); courtesy of Permanent Black

The designs of the empiricists were inevitably not as boldly innovative as those of the rationalists, nor did they have the paucity of behavior settings of many rationalist designs. They may have afforded more in enriching people's lives, but rationalists continued to look at them with disdain. Postmodernism challenged the ideas and work of both streams of urban design thought.

Key References

Broadbent, Geoffrey. 1990. *Emerging Concepts in Urban Space Design.* London: Van Nostrand Reinhold International.

Calthorpe, Peter. 1993. *The Next American Metropolis: Ecology, Community, and the American Dream.* New York: Princeton Architectural Press.

Cullen, Gordon. 1961. *The Concise Townscape.* London: Architectural Press.

Jacobs, Jane. 1961. *The Death and Life of Great American Cities.* New York: Random House.

Simonds, John O. 1994. *Garden Cities 21: Creating a Liveable Urban Environment.* New York: McGraw-Hill.

Stein, Clarence. 1966. *Toward New Towns for America.* New York: Reinhold.

11

The Postmodernist and the Deconstructivist Response

Postmodern is a tricky term. In architecture, it can refer to anything that comes after the heyday of rationalist and empiricist modernisms (Ellin 1996). The position taken here is narrower. Postmodern urban designs were a response to the austerity of rationalist designs and the regressive aesthetics and artificial intricateness of the empiricists, who applied past patterns of built form in a literal manner to new designs.

One postmodern approach to urban design sought a return, in one way or another, to traditions and history in an abstract manner. A second was one of resistance that, while a critique of modernism, did not seek to draw ideas from the past (Jencks 2002). The first stream can be divided into two lines of thought: the 'classical revivalist' and the 'historical eclectic.' The second stream offered a totally different approach; it applied the concepts of literary deconstruction as an art form to architecture and urban design.

Antecedent Ideas

In the eighteenth and nineteenth centuries, colonial authorities attempted to localize their architecture by incorporating local elements into the design of buildings. These efforts were superseded by Art Deco districts in places as diverse as Asmara in Eretria, Napier in New Zealand, and Mumbai in India. Postmodern architecture was superficially similar to what the colonial authorities were striving to achieve when striving to indigenize their architecture but was different in spirit.

The application of the classical to urban design during the second half of the twentieth century is reminiscent of the city beautiful designs of seventy years earlier, but the roots of postmodernism went deeper. Postmodern neoclassical designs, somewhat contradictorily, often took on both a more romantic and a more bombastic flavor. They evoke the work of Albert Speer in his Welthaupstadt Germania of the late 1930s. They represent the idea of getting away from the search for an ideal city to one that is multivalent. The aesthetic quality of their designs has meaning for the public and is, simultaneously, a source of interest for the cognoscenti. Their debt to the earlier classical revival is clear.

Classical revival urban designs drew inspiration from the architecture of ancient Rome and ancient Greece via the Renaissance and the École des Beaux Arts. More immediately, the

The Postmodernist and Deconstructivist Response

Figure 11.1 Listers Hārads Tinghus 1920, Sölversborg, designed by Gunnar Asplund
Credit line: Photograph by Arnand Contet
Source: Wikimedia Commons

classical tradition in postmodern urban design relates back to what architects were seeking in the design of individual buildings in Scandinavia at the beginning of the twentieth century, as reflected in the work of Kay Fisker (1893–1965) in Denmark, Gunnar Asplund (1885–1940) in Sweden, and the early work of Alvar Aalto (1898–1976) in Finland. In the United States, architects such as McKim, Mead & White inspired the postmodernists. The design of Portmeirion, built between 1925 and 1975, could well have served as a precedent for the more eclectic postmodern urban designs.

Portmeirion, as an anti-rationalist protest, presages the more flamboyant character of much postmodern urban design. A total urban design, it was developed, devised, and built by Sir Clough Williams Ellis (1883–1978) on his own land in North Wales. The buildings are a collection of historical building types very much influenced by Mediterranean traditions and flights of fancy. Sir Clough recognized how little the Le Corbusian vision of the city afforded in meeting the aspirations of the public. Portmeirion is a carefully worked-out "deliberately irresponsible . . . desire to reclaim for architecture the freedom of invention and the possibility of pleasurable fantasy" but "a joke" whose economic success staggered Lewis Mumford (L. Mumford 1962, 91–93). It is a collage of bits and pieces aligned with popular tastes. Postwar Las Vegas may be the US equivalent, as Robert Venturi (1925–2016) and his colleagues recognized in *Learning from Las Vegas: The Forgotten Symbolism of Architectural Form* (Venturi, Brown, and Izenour 1977). Deconstruction, in contrast, was and remains a highly intellectualized urban design paradigm. The literary analysis of Jacques Derrida (1930–2004), the Algerian-born French philosopher, was the inspiration.

Derrida cooperated with Peter Eisenman and Bernard Tschumi (b. 1944) on their designs for Parc de La Villette (Wocke 2014). It seems, however, that the antecedent idea for the design is 'analytical cubism' in theories of art—the use of cubist forms in an artistic manner that exploits technological innovations. Architectural forms became deformed, distorted, and

Figure 11.2 The eclectic architecture of Portmeirion
Credit line: Photograph by Heather Raulerson/Shutterstock.com

dislocated when viewed from different sides, as in the abstract expressionism of the Russian futurists. Tschumi's desire for complexity is what relates his work to the views that Venturi articulated in *Complexity and Contradiction in Modern Architecture*.

Manifestoes and Paradigms

Contemporary approaches to urban design were much challenged during the politically and intellectually turbulent decades of the 1960s and the 1970s. The response to the ahistorical nature of rationalist modernism was certainly spurred by Venturi's 1966 book and his book with Denise Scott Brown (b. 1931) and Steven Izenour (1940–2002), *Learning from Las Vegas: The Forgotten Symbolism of Architectural Form*, first published in 1972. *Collage City* (1979), by Colin Rowe and Fred Koetter (1938–2017), was equally important in considering the nature of urban design. Deconstruction theory in urban design was influenced by the publication of Derrida's *Of Grammatology* in 1967.

Venturi, a Quaker, challenged orthodox modernism for the internationalism of its plain, freestanding buildings located in parkland settings. When studying in Rome in the mid-1950s, he had admired the way that streets and plazas were lined by space-making buildings in much the same way that Jane Jacobs found the streetscape a positive aspect of New York's Greenwich Village. Venturi found the purity of modernist designs boring.

> "Less is more" bemoans complexity. . . . [Architects] can exclude important considerations only at the risk of separating architecture from the experience of life and the needs of society. . . . "Less is a bore."
>
> *(Venturi 1966, 25)*

He was for a "messy vitality" in both buildings and urban streetscapes. He argued that complexity in the patterns of the built environment makes places interesting. Contemporaneously, Colin Rowe was looking critically at modernist urban design, but in a different way.

Rowe, believing that modernism had had a destructive effect on cities, was for a contextualism in design in which the new harmonized with the old (Rowe 1982). He, with Fred Koetter,

The Postmodernist and Deconstructivist Response

also recognized that society was becoming increasingly fragmented and that the qualities of Disney World were closer to what people enjoy than the built environment that architects were designing. They believed that the idea of having generic models of ideal environments on which designers can draw is flawed unless accompanied by well-designed programs/briefs that thoroughly deal with the complexity of issues (Rowe 1982).

Rowe and Koetter sought a greater understanding of how to apply historical precedents in urban design. They argued for the inversion of objects to create figurative voids, the collision of set pieces, and the use of nostalgia-evoking patterns as the basis for composing urban design schemes. "A collage approach," they argued, "is at present the only way of dealing with the ultimate problems of either or both utopia and tradition" (Rowe and Koetter 1978). They gave Portmeirion as an illustration of a collage of bits and pieces, a bricolage. Despite their observations, no radical approach to urban design grew directly out of their arguments. Instead, it was a type of classical revivalism that caught the attention of several architects as the way forward.

Two significant approaches to the use of the classical in urban design emerged from these discussions. In the first, the designs are immutably classical, while in the second, they were informed but not overwhelmed by strict canonical rules. The first approach was strongly advocated by Andreas Papadakis (1938–2008), the critic Charles Jencks (b. 1939), and Léon Krier. Proponents of classical architecture and urban design argued that the classical represents timeless values. Its application creates dateless compositions rather than short-lived fashionable designs. Classical urban designs find their intellectual strength not in their originality but in their application of traditional forms in a well-crafted and detailed manner. Of the group, Krier produced the strongest manifesto in his charter for *The Reconstruction of the European* City (L. Krier 1984).

Krier observed that the preindustrial city had weathered change better than the rationalists' functional city when its economic raison d'être disappears. Jane Jacobs made the same observation in *The Economy of Cities: How to Study Public Life* (1969). The preindustrial city was more functional than the 'functional city' (Delevoy, Vidler, and Krier 1978). It was more adaptable. Krier was also highly critical of the division of cities into single-use areas. He argued for a city of mixed-use, walkable precincts, 33 hectares (81 acres) in size that would be home to 10,000 to 15,000 people. The city center should, he stated, be crossable in a ten-minute walk, and its streets and squares should be like those of traditional European cities (Broadbent 1990, 196–97). Other urban designers advocated for a more eclectic approach to architecture and urban design.

A type of historical revival eclecticism was advocated by Robert Venturi, although he and his partner, Denise Scott Brown (b. 1931), vehemently denied any association with it in application. Venturi advocated for using abstractions of historical elements in new designs. An approach to urban design by other architects resulted from various interpretations of the message presented by Venturi, Scott Brown, and Izenour in *Learning from Las Vegas*. Rather than condemning the strip developments lining the approaches to US cities, the book argued that much could be learned from their exuberance and signage. The criticism of the sterility of modernism's architectural forms led to idiosyncratic, singular buildings such as Portland Town Hall, designed by Michel Graves (1931–2015), No. 1 Poultry Street in London with its bands of pink stone designed by James Stirling (1926–1992), and Hundertwasserhaus in Vienna, the work of artist Friedensreich Hundertwasser (1928–2000) with architect Joseph Krawina (1928–2018).

An urban design drawing on the tastes of mass culture began to appear on the scene in the 1980s (Larson 1993). Its open-space pattern was classical, and the buildings were full of oversized columns, vaults, and bright colors. It is often dismissed as kitsch (a German word for cheap, tacky objects) or as 'non-judgmental kitsch.' The term is applied to garish and overly sentimental artworks that appeal to the popular tastes of a consumer society (Elias 1935; see also Gans 1975). The term is often used pejoratively, but not here.

237

Figure 11.3 Postmodern architecture: The Municipal Services Building, Portland, Oregon (left), and Hundertwasserhaus, Vienna (1983–85)

Credit line (left): Photograph by EQRoy/Shutterstock.com
Credit line (right): Photograph by Habrus Liudmila/Shutterstock.com

Kitsch architecture and urban design consist of a hybrid of historical items not applied as originally employed but rather in an overblown, heterogeneous manner. Its architectural qualities rather than its plan lead to an urban design's being regarded as kitsch. Some designs are regarded as kitsch because they are an unacademic mix of bits and pieces. Portmeirion is an example. In contrast to these lines of urban design, deconstruction is highly intellectual.

Deconstruction has been more influential as an approach to architecture than to urban design. Although they do not necessarily agree with being categorized in this manner, it is characteristic of the geometric juxtapositions in the architecture of people such as Zaha Hadid (1950–2016) and Frank Gehry (b. 1929). Fragmented times require fragmented designs. The garishness of much of modern Tokyo, for instance, is thus fully legitimate. Urban designs should not have an artificial order. This position is most clearly articulated by Bernard Tschumi in *Architecture and Disjunction* (1994). An urban design should thus consist of dislocated elements brought together. Ironically, the new such complexes have an inherent order in the absence of harmony, continuity, and symmetry that needs to be recognized.

Generic Concepts and Illustrative Designs

Few generic, but several illustrative, designs were produced to demonstrate the principles of postmodern urban design. One generic architectural concept that captured the attention of designers was the distinction between 'ducks' and 'decorated sheds.' Venturi and his colleagues introduced the terms in *Learning from Las Vegas* to distinguish between two building types. Ducks are structures "Where the architectural systems of space, structure, and program are submerged and distorted by an overall symbolic form," whereas decorated sheds are ones "where systems of space and structure are directly at the service of program, and ornament is applied independently" (Venturi, Scott Brown, and Izenour 1977, 18).

Atlantis, an illustrative design, reflects the decorated shed approach. It also shows the advocacies of the classical revivalists among postmodernists. Designed by Léon Krier between 1986 and 1992, the project was commissioned by Hans-Jürgen Müller, an art gallery owner who wished to preserve European culture in a globalizing world. Atlantis was presented as an "international place of encounter and research for the arts, science, politics, and business" (Broadbent 1990, 336).

The Postmodernist and Deconstructivist Response

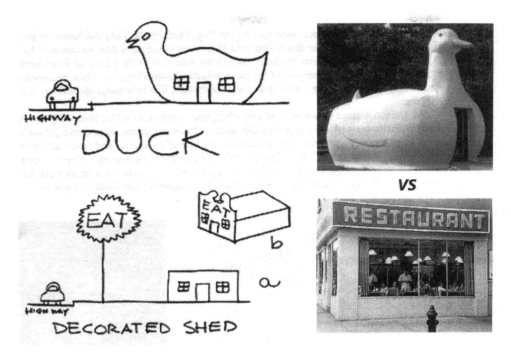

Figure 11.4 Ducks and decorated sheds
Credit line: Courtesy of Venturi, Scott Brown and Associates, Inc., and of MIT Press

Located on a steeply sloped hypothetical island, the design in plan and architecture hearkens back to ancient Greek models.

Atlantis's plan consists of narrow streets lined with plain-faced background buildings such as residences. A corniche promenade lies at the bottom of the slope, and the design contains an agora and an acropolis. The agora has a twenty-four-columned stoa with cafés and shops and an art museum. If Atlantis represents classical postmodern urban design, then Portmeirion, the bits and pieces of Las Vegas, and Disneyland (1955) reflect a more eclectic historical approach to urban design. All three are based on a mixture of historical referents that are easy to dismiss as kitsch. Portmeirion and Disneyland are pedestrian worlds; Las Vegas is an automobile-oriented city of strip development and decorated shed building set in space. They, alike, drew on a range of historical precedents to create a fantastical collection of structures and, in Las Vegas, billboards.

Two generic ideas are, correctly or not, associated with the term 'deconstruction' in urban design. The first involves a way of working, and the second involves the juxtaposition of geometrical forms in the creation of architectural and urban patterns. The first requires the identification and design of the individual systems of a proposed design, maximizing their functionality, and then layering them one on top of the other before adjusting them so they that can function effectively as a whole. The goal is to achieve a controlled entanglement. Unity is obtained through diversity and complexity. Such designs are, it was argued, more appropriate for fragmented societies than were designs representing a nostalgia for an imagined well-ordered and unified past. The second approach focused on possibilities of different geometries set next to each other to satisfy their creators' need for self-expression. The function of forms as artistic works overrides their efficiency in serving instrumental purposes.

Post–World War Two Pragmatic Urban Design

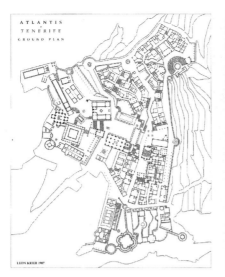

Figure 11.5 Atlantis: The plan (left) and a representational view, a painting by Hans-Jürgen Müller and Milan Kunc (right)
Credit line (left): Courtesy of Léon Krier
Credit line (right): Helga Müller; courtesy of Helga Müller and Leon Krier

Figure 11.6 Venturi, Scott Brown, and Izenour's Las Vegas: A composite photograph
Credit line: Courtesy of Venturi, Scott Brown and Associates, Inc., and of MIT Press

Specific Designs

City beautiful urban designs were built throughout the twentieth century. Professional practices, large and small, continued to produce classical buildings—commercial offices, museums, concert halls, and residences—for a variety of clients covering the spectrum of political attitudes. John Blatteau in Philadelphia and Allan Greenberg (b. 1938) in New Haven practice in the United

States; Adam Architecture/Urbanism is a firm based in the United Kingdom that works internationally. John Simson Architects is another UK practice inspired by the neoclassical idiom, particularly the Georgian. Although these practices produced classical buildings, the firm most closely associated with classical postmodernism is the Taller de Arquitectura of Ricardo Bofill (b. 1939) founded in Barcelona in 1963. Les Arcades du Lac is an example of the firm's work.

It is a social housing complex in Saint Quentin-en-Yvelines, a town forming part of the 1960s Villes Nouvelles policy of the French government. The complex of residential units is arranged in four squares that have spacious internal courtyards, four wings facing the water, and a peninsular of buildings jutting into it. Located not far from Versailles, it is regarded by some as a 'Versailles for low-income people.'

Aspects of the design owe a debt to the architecture of Claude Nicolas Ledoux (Jencks 1988). The design was further inspired by the Pont d'Avignon and the Château de Chenonceau, spanning the River Cher in France, and the Aqueduct of Segovia in Spain (Guillot-Harrold 1993). While the buildings form streets and squares, the whole scheme is an isolated precinct set in open space. The Belvedere Saint Christophe in the new town of Cergy-Pontoise is another social housing development by the Taller that follows the same philosophy (Bofill and André 1989). Completed in 1985, the building is in the form of a colonnade.

At about the same time, a design for Paternoster Square in London to replace a poorly functioning rationalist building complex of the immediate postwar years represents a purer classical postmodernism. Several designs were proposed for the project before any classical options were produced (Toy 1992). Modernist in nature, neither architectural critics nor the public held those earlier efforts in high esteem. A classical scheme was produced in response. It was a complete and unified design based on an architectural language comprehensible to the public. The architectural cognoscenti disparaged it. The architect was John Simpson (b. 1954), who then redid it with Thomas Beeby (b. 1941) and Terry Farrell (b. 1938), both known for postmodern tendencies in their architecture. The design, although not implemented, received an American Institute of Architects Honor award. The scheme that was finally built was a more pragmatic neo-modernist one. It functions well as a quasi-public space, but the architectural cognoscenti wanted an avant-garde scheme (Lang 2005, 248–53).

ADAM Urbanism contemporaneously created designs in a similar idiom. Fortescue Fields is a restrained revivalist postmodern development. Built on a 1.8-hectare (about 4.5-acre) brownfield site that had housed a chicken processing factory, it is an extension to the village of Norton St. Philip in Somerset, England. The complex is a mixed-use development of fifty-seven

Figure 11.7 The designs of Ricardo Bofill Taller de Arquitectura: Les Arcades du Lac, Saint Quentin-en-Yvelines (left), and Belvedere Saint Christophe, Cergy-Pontoise (right)

Credit line (left): Courtesy of Ricardo Bofill Taller de Arquitectura
Credit line (right): Courtesy of Ricardo Bofill Taller de Arquitectura

Figure 11.8 Postmodern classicism: Paternoster Square, London, the John Simson proposal (left), and Fortescue Fields, Norton St. Philip (right)

Credit line (left): Courtesy of John Simpson Architects
Credit line (right): Courtesy of Adam Architects

Figure 11.9 Tegel Harbor housing, Berlin, Phase 1: An aerial view (left) and the architectural character (right))

Credit line (left): Collection of the author

residential units, sheltered accommodation, and shops. Classical in spirit, it also draws on regional precedents in a new urbanist manner.

Some urban design projects followed a more eclectic historical approach than Fortescue Fields did. The Wohnbebauung am Tegler Hafen in Berlin was designed by Charles Moore (1925–1993), from the firm Moore Ruble Yudell, located in Santa Monica, California. It was the winning entry in a competition where most submissions were postmodern schemes. The jurors selected it because it retained the scale and texture of Tegel. It was no flamboyant postmodern scheme. Its historicism was closer to that suggested by Venturi and Scott Brown.

Illustrative though these schemes are, several others can be regarded as exemplars of the above lines of thinking, but only one implemented project can be regarded as an urban design based on deconstruction philosophy. It is Parc de La Villette, designed by Bernard Tschumi. Federation Square in Melbourne, Australia, is an example of a total urban design whose architecture is regarded as deconstructivist because of its juxtaposition of geometries, but it is not a manifestation of Derrida's philosophical position.

The Postmodernist and Deconstructivist Response

Exemplars of Postmodern and an Exemplar of Deconstructivist Urban Design

Quartier Antigone, Montpelier, France (1979–); Place de Toscane, Marne-la-Valée, France (2006–); Plaza d'Italia, New Orleans, Louisiana, USA (1975–78); and Parc de la Villette, Paris, France (1982–83)

Quartier Antigone in Montpellier is arguably *the* exemplar of the work of Ricardo Bofill Taller de Arquitectura. The precinct (named for the tragic central character of the play by Sophocles) was built on the grounds of a former barracks and an industrial precinct. It lies between Montpellier's old city center and the river Lez. In 1977, the municipal government led by Mayor Georges Frêche (1938–2010) initiated the planning of the precinct. Completed, it consists of grand neoclassical structures that have large pediments, entablatures, and pilasters. On the other side of the river is the Hôtel de la Région Languedoc-Roussillon, also designed by Bofill (Bofill and André 1989). The combination makes a bold, architecturally unified kilometer-long scheme along a bold axis. Its grandeur is recognized in its nickname: the 'Champs-Élysées of Montpellier.'

The buildings enclose classical plazas with formally laid-out landscapes. The composition makes a thematically unified precinct of boulevards, plazas, parks, fountains, housing (primarily for low-income residents), shops, schools, and sports, cultural, and governmental facilities. In the center of the Place de Thessalie is a fountain, *Fontaine de Thessalie Antigone*, designed by J. M. Bourry and P. Gounard. The result is a monolithic design (Cruells 1992; Lang and Marshall 2016). The idea of low-income people's living in housing behind a palatial façade as in Les Arcades du Lac and Belvedere Saint Christophe is regarded as peculiarly French.

The Place de Toscane is part of the Val d'Europe downtown district of Marne-la-Vallée in France (see also Figure 14.11). It was designed by Pier Carlo Bontempi (b. 1954), an architect based in Collecchio, Parma, Italy. Opened in 2006, the design is in a modernized version of

Figure 11.10 Quartier Antigone, Montpellier: Aerial (left) and ground level (right) views
Credit line (left): Collection of the author
Credit line (right): Photograph by trabantos/Shutterstock.com

243

Post–World War Two Pragmatic Urban Design

Figure 11.11   Place de Toscane, Val d' Europe, Marne-la-Vallée
Credit line: Photograph by R. C. Smit
Source: Wikimedia Commons

Figure 11.12   Piazza d'Italia, New Orleans
Credit line: Photograph by O. Tomasini/Getty Images

classical architecture. Its dimensions are based on the Roman Forum in Lucca. The scheme illustrates the continued interest in classical architecture and how well received it is by many people today. Classical elements used in a more abstract manner, as in the Piazza d'Italia in New Orleans, can be also well received provided that the abstractions are not obscure.

The Piazza was designed by Charles Moore and his Urban Innovations Group, along with local firm Perez Associates. Its design is different from the classicism of the Paternoster Square proposal. The piazza was designed to symbolize the contribution of Italian Americans to the development of New Orleans. Its central feature is a fountain organized as a relief map of Italy stepping up toward the Alps at its center. It is surrounded by a hemi-cycle colonnade and contains a clocktower, a campanile, and a Roman temple façade in an abstracted form. The composition reflects the exuberant design language of Charles Moore and is a memorial as much to his architectural legacy as to the Italian pioneers of New Orleans. Moore's face appears on two of the square's medallions (Lang and Marshall 2016). The work of Ricardo Bofill, in contrast to the Plaza d'Italia, is less light-hearted. His design for the Quartier Antigone drew almost entirely on classical design elements; his design for Les Arcades du Lac was more diverse.

While several postmodern urban designs imbued with historical referents can be identified, no urban design can be said to fully represent deconstructivist design theory. The Parc de la Villette is the closest. In 1982, the Establishment Public du Parc de la Villette (EPPV) held an international design competition for the redevelopment of a 55-hectare (136-acre) site of semi-abandoned industrial buildings in Paris. A team headed by Bernard Tschumi and Colin Fournier (b. 1944) won it. The program included a museum of science and industry, a *Cité* of music, a major hall for exhibitions, a popular music concert hall, and a park. It required two existing structures on the site to be reused. Unlike Central Park in New York, which excludes the city, Parc de la Villette brings the city into the park (Blundell Jones 2012; Wocke 2014).

An intellectual goal of the design was for it to have no inherent referents. The design consists of three independent patterns superimposed on each other (see Figure 11.13 top right). Each has its own internal logic. The superimposition reflects Tschumi's desire for the layering of individual systems and the conflicts that might ensue. The first of the three systems is made up of a series of follies at the intersections of a 120-meter (390-foot) grid. Their structural envelopes are covered by bright-red-enameled framework and/or steel sheets. The follies are 10.78-meter (36-foot) cubes "divided three dimensionally into 12-foot cubes forming 'cases.'" These cases "can be decomposed into fragments . . . or extended through the addition of other elements" (Tschumi 1987). The second system consists of a set of lines that form paths of pedestrian movement. One consists of cross axes of covered galleries and another a meandering 'cinematic' promenade that offers a sequence of vistas for the pedestrian walking along it. The third system is composed of the surfaces of the park. In addition, alleys of trees link the major activity sites of the design (Tschumi 1987; Lang 2017, 75–77).

The follies were intended to have no instrumental function, although some now house an activity; one is a television studio. They are unusual garden decorations. Visitors interpret what they see as they wish. The Parc has been dismissed by some critics as inhuman, but it is much admired by the cognoscenti and is popular with locals. Over 10 million visitors, young and old, use its various facilities each year, whatever they may think of the design.

Post–World War Two Pragmatic Urban Design

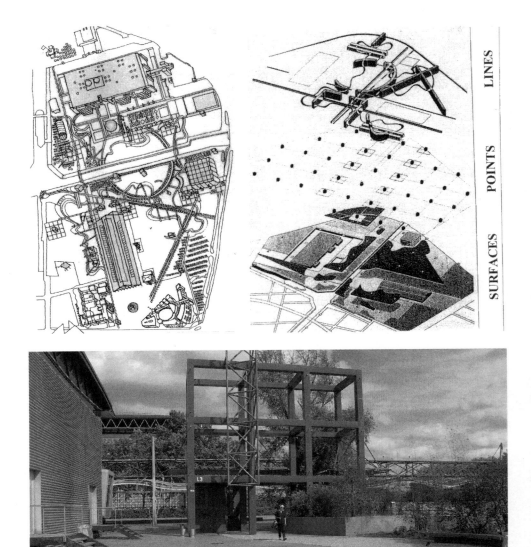

Figure 11.13 Parc de la Villette, Paris: The design (above left), the three patterns (above right), and one of the sequence of follies (below)

Credit line (above left): Drawing by Yin Yin
Source (above left): Lang (2017, 76); courtesy of Taylor & Francis
Credit line (above right): Bernard Tschumi Architects
Source (above right): Lang (2017, 76); courtesy of Taylor & Francis
Source (below): Lang (2017, 76); courtesy of Taylor & Francis

The Postmodernist and Deconstructivist Response

Hybrid Examples

M. S. Ramaiah Medical College, Bengaluru, Karnataka, India (1979); Tsukuba Civic Center, Tsukuba, Japan (1980–3); Richmond Riverside, London, England, UK (1984–); and Federation Square, Melbourne, Australia (1996–2002)

Neoclassical urban designs are not unique to Europe and the Americas. The M. S. Ramaiah Medical College campus in Bengaluru was founded in 1979. Its buildings are located along one side of a central roadway; gardens lie on the other side. The interiors of the buildings meet the requirements of modern education, but their exteriors draw on several Indian and European architectural traditions. Hindu and Buddhist elements mingle with classical pediments. The hospital itself is a neo-modernist structure.

The college is easy to dismiss as kitsch because of its lack of intellectual purity. As an urban design, it has no central idea comparable to the city beautiful schemes. It is, however, decoratively rich, and the symbolism is bold and easy for locals to understand. Missing are referents that might appeal to the cognoscenti. The Tsukuba Civic Center, in contrast, is a mixture of referents and inspirations that bemuse the cognoscenti. There is certainly much in both designs for them to ponder.

Figure 11.14 M. S. Ramaiah College of Medicine, Bengaluru
Source: Lang, Desai, and Desai (1997, 265); courtesy of CEPT University Press

The Tsukuba Civic Center, designed by Isozaki, Aoki, and Associates, consists of a collage of elements whose patterns are drawn from several sources. Arata Isozaki (b. 1931), in his effort to symbolize the state of a nation with scientific aspirations, inverted the meanings of historical European building forms. The sunken plaza is the same size as Michelangelo's Piazza del Campidoglio built in Rome in the 1540s, and its floor pattern is a replica of that in the square. A major difference between the two places is that one goes down from a rectangular terrace into the plaza at the Civic Center, whereas one goes up to the Campidoglio via the Cordonata—a spacious stairway/sloping road—designed by Giacomo della Porta (1532–1602) in 1581. The Campidoglio is a space enclosed on three sides by buildings but that at the Tsukuba Center is more amorphous. In addition, one part of the Tsukuba design is wrinkled as if gnawed. Water flows into a fountain void as a commentary on the reputed "lack of a heart to Japanese life" (Broadbent 1990, 290–92).

The buildings that surround the plaza incorporate references to the paintings of noted artists such as Giulio Romano (1499–1506) and architects Ledoux and Wagner but also to those of Isozaki's contemporaries, Aldo Rossi (1931–1997), Léon Krier (b. 1946), and Hans Hollein (1934–2014). Their works are used in an abstracted form. The buildings are fabricated of an equally diverse set of materials: aluminum, glass block, ceramic tile, granite, and artificial stone. Other designs are much more literal and immediate in the meanings they convey. The Richmond Waterfront is one. Its design by Quinlan Terry is little admired by the cognoscenti. Terry is, however, a strongly religious architect with a puritan streak that makes him impervious to criticism (Watkin 1996).

The project has been an economic success. It has, however, been much criticized by both those who are supporters of avant-garde design and those who are pure, canonical classicists.

Figure 11.15 Tsukuba Civic Center
Credit line: Collection of the author

The Postmodernist and Deconstructivist Response

Figure 11.16 The Richmond Waterfront seen from Richmond Bridge; Hotham House is at the center

Source: Lang and Moleski (2010, 201); courtesy of Taylor & Francis

The former say that the design is out of step with the contemporary zeitgeist, and the latter say that it is a mishmash of bits and pieces. It has ended up being rather like the traditional piece-by-piece developments of an English High Street and has proven to be more appropriate to the English climate than many modernist designs are.

Federation Square, an air rights development over railroad tracks leading out of Melbourne's Flinders Street Station, is regarded as being deconstructivist, but many of its qualities are derived from the traditions that make a square a central place. The square faces the busy station across a street, with the Yarra River on one side of it and heritage-listed buildings such as St. Paul's Cathedral on the other. The competition for the design of the square was won by a joint entry from Lab Architectural Studio of London and the local firm Bates Smart, with Karres + Brand as landscape architects. It was designed to commemorate the centenary of the unification of the Australian colonies into a single nation and to architecturally rival Sydney's Opera House (Lang and Marshall 2016).

Located on a 3.8-hectare (9-acre) site, the design consists of two squares. A small one faces the cathedral and the other the station. A covered atrium makes a third such space. The major square is enclosed on three sides by a mixture of institutional and commercial uses. It also contains a large screen on which sporting and other events are displayed. The buildings enclosing the square are irregular and covered with a pattern of triangular tiles composed of five smaller triangular ones. The tiles are composed of solid zinc and sandstone, while

Figure 11.17   Federation Square, Melbourne
Credit line: Photograph by Nils Versemann/Shutterstock.com

the glazing over the atrium is green in color. Each building has a unique geometry, but the overall fractal nature of the buildings' surfaces gives the complex an architectural unity. The surface of the square is a slightly undulating blue stone work of art, "Nearamnew," by Paul Carter. Few people pay attention to it, but it provides the surface for a variety of formal and communal activities.

The winner of many design awards, the deconstructivist nature of the fractal geometries is much admired by the cognoscenti, although the public generally and persistently regards the buildings as ugly. What the square does clearly illustrate is that the quality of the open space and what happens on the ground floors of the enclosing building is what is important rather than their architectural qualities. Federation Square is much loved in a city that otherwise would be devoid of such a heart.

Commentary: The Functions Addressed

Postmodern urban designs are predominantly decorated sheds. They serve a basic instrumental function almost independently of the meanings that the façades of their buildings communicate. The focus of attention in their designs was explicitly on the function of designs as nonverbal communicators of meanings. It is the one common concern of the diverse projects presented in this chapter, even though the revivalists and Tschumi had different objectives and met them in different ways.

The classicist and the historical revivalist postmodern schemes, by all reports, are satisficing designs; they serve their instrumental functions well enough. Les Arcades du Lac functions well as basic social housing; the buildings of the Richmond Waterfront function well in meeting the requirements of modern, up-to-date, indeed avant-garde, commercial companies. The

The Postmodernist and Deconstructivist Response

regressive exterior appearance of the R. M. Ramaiah Institute does not inhibit its function as a modern educational institution.

On sunny afternoons and evenings during the summer, the west-facing sloping lawns of the Richmond waterfront, intentionally or not, function well as places for people to relax on the grass or seated on the benches. There is, however, little overt concern for the way the classicist and the historical revivalist postmodern layouts might foster opportunities to form a sense of community. To the extent people have chosen to live or work in a development, their aesthetic tastes form at least one common bond among them. The urban designs do include the facilities that provide chances for people to get together casually.

The historical precedents on which postmodern urban designs of the twentieth century drew, if literal rather than abstract, located a new development in its cultural context. In multicultural societies, the referents may be meaningful only to subsets of the population. Much in postmodernism is only meaningful to the cognoscenti. Few visitors to the Tsukuba Civic Center will recognize the referents in its architecture. It, like many postmodern urban designs, possesses a sense of liveliness and fun. They do not have to be taken too seriously, although many of the cognoscenti do. Deconstruction is different.

A significant function of the Parc de la Villette was to re-establish Paris rather than New York as the world's leading art center. It had to be something intellectually new to engage the attention of the art community. The role of President François Mitterrand (1916–96; in office 1981–95) in achieving that end served to reinforce his reputation as a patron of the arts. Tschumi's design was created to have no coherent associations, but it does have meanings for visitors based on their experiences (Blundell Jones 2012). Visitors (other than architects) are drawn to the Parc de la Villette not because of the intellectual idea behind its design but for the instrumental functions its components serve; its architecture is largely irrelevant. The same comment can be made about Federation Square. The venues located at both places make them destinations. In addition, the grassed surfaces at the Parc de la Villette function well as places for impromptu football games, and the sequence of experiences moving through the complex holds the attention of pedestrians. It, like most parks, is a bleak place on a rainy winter day.

Many projects are designed to function as catalysts spurring development around them. Certainly, upgrading run-down sites with new buildings, as in Richmond, can lead to the rebuilding of surrounding areas, although in Richmond's case, the core of the suburb was already working well. The hope that Plaza d'Italia would lead to investments in adjacent areas of New Orleans was not fulfilled. Indeed, the square itself deteriorated to the point where it became an unattractive place to be. It has now been renovated. If a latent demand for development exists, a well-designed project can serve as a catalyst enhancing adjacent development opportunities. It did not in contemporary New Orleans.

Observations

Of the designs described in this chapter, only the Parc de la Villette is held in high esteem by the architectural cognoscenti. Its innovative intellectual aesthetic basis gives them much food for thought. The other projects are of interest but are either too derivative or considered too kitsch for the avant-garde to appreciate. This observation illustrates the general gap between the values of many designers and those of the public: "Most people don't want what architects want" (Michelson 1968). Historicist postmodern urban design attempted to close the gap between taste cultures. Districts of such a character continue to be built. The Brandevoort district of Belmond in the Netherlands designed by Paul van Beek, Rob Krier, Christoph Kohl and Maerten Ouwens is a work of the early twenty-first century.

Figure 11.18 Brandevoort, Helmond, 1997–2017
Credit line: Photograph by Hans Blok/Shutterstock.com

It seems a substantial intellectual leap from the neo-traditional work of Léon Krier at Poundbury to the work of Quinlan Terry at the Richmond waterfront, but the gap is not all that great. There is little 'neo' about the latter; it is simply traditional. The use of historical precedents that are known, or are believed, to have worked in the past is at the heart of much postmodern urban design. The question is, in a changing world, how can the past be best learned from?

Venturi advocated for applying past forms to new buildings in an abstract manner (Venturi 1966). Careful studies show that only the very erudite can understand the referent of most abstracted patterns unless it is explained to them. Most people regard postmodernism simply as modernism (Groat 1982). The same observation applies to urban design schemes. The abstractions of Italian referents in the Piazza a d'Italia are literal enough to be recognized by the public and abstract enough to be appreciated by the cognoscenti. If designers want a design to have a broad appeal, it is important to first use, or invent, a symbol system that enhances the everyday experiences of diverse people. Once that has been done, architects can get their own 'jollies' and appeal to the cognoscenti. That is the lesson that postmodernist urban designs offer us.

Key References

Ellin, Nan. 1996. *Postmodern Urbanism*. Revised edition. New York: Princeton Architectural Press.
Jencks, Charles. 2002. *The New Paradigm in Architecture: The Language of Post-Modernism*. New Haven: Yale University Press.
Krier, Léon. 1984. "Reconstruction of the European City." *Architectural Design* 54 (November–December): 16–22.
Larson, Magali S. 1993. *Behind the Postmodern Façade: Architectural Change in Late Twentieth Century America*. Berkeley and Los Angeles: University of California Press.
Rowe, Colin and Fred Koetter. 1979. *Collage City*. Cambridge, MA: MIT Press.
Tschumi, Bernard. 1994. *Architecture and Disjunction*. Cambridge, MA: MIT Press.
Venturi, Robert, Denise Scott Brown, and Steven Izenour. 1977. *Learning from Las Vegas: The Forgotten Symbolism of Architectural Form*. Revised edition. Cambridge, MA: MIT Press.

Part IV

Marina Bay Sands development, Singapore

Urban Design in an Age of Corporate Financial Capital

By 1990, World War Two was an ancient memory. Armed conflicts continued in Eastern Europe, West Asia, Central Africa, and parts of Latin America. Despite disputes and economic upheavals, the period since 1990, especially after about 2005, has been characterized by the rapid spread of new communications technologies. The mobile/cell phone and the Internet represent major technological advances. Internet shopping promises to revolutionize the retail industry and the nature of shopping streets. Robotization is changing the nature of the workplace. Cities around the world are now striving to be 'smart,' aided by increasingly sophisticated monitoring systems. At the same time, the finiteness of Earth's resources and a concern about the warming of the planet raise questions about the nature of urban development taking place in a more laissez-faire world than before 1990. Much of the social concern and optimism that characterized the postwar years has dissipated.

The collapse of world communism at the beginning of the 1990s has been followed by a general swing toward conservative politics in much of the world as the limitations of socialist approaches to governance became clear. In China, the Tiananmen Square massacre in Beijing in June 1989 (the June Fourth Incident) squashed pro-democracy agitations. Far-right parties have obtained increasing support in Europe, and traditionally socialist countries have moved to the right politically.

The late twentieth century saw China become a global economic and, increasingly, military power. The country's growth in a relatively short time can be traced back to its emergence as an independent state upon the defeat of Japan by the allied forces in World War Two and the end of the civil war won by the Communists. The country was rocked by the Cultural Revolution that began in 1966 under Mao Zedong (1883–1976) and ended with his death. The revolution led to China's rejecting all that was in the past, good and bad, and setting the stage for a rationalist future. The failure of communist economics to drive the country forward led to the changes in policies under Deng Xiaoping (1904–97) that started China on the path to a burgeoning economy.

The growth in urban populations worldwide has been extraordinary. In China alone, a billion people will be leading urban lives by 2030. Many of them will be upwardly mobile, social-status-conscious, middle-class people. They will be seeking to live in a style comparable to their counterparts in the historically wealthy countries of the world. The amount of urban development that has already taken place has been accompanied by some unpleasant side effects: traffic congestion and extremely high levels of atmospheric, water, and sonic pollution.

Metropolitan areas everywhere are increasing in population and spatial spread. In highly populated regions such as the East Coast of the United States and in China, some cities are merging to form ever-enlarging poly-nucleated cosmopolises. The distribution of wealth in cities is also undergoing change. Middle-class people are being displaced from the attractive centers of cities by the wealthy, and conveniently located neighborhoods formerly inhabited by the poor are, for better or worse, being gentrified. Their inhabitants have to fend for themselves. Much has been sparked by neoliberal thinking.

Neoliberalism

The term 'neoliberalism' has had several meanings since it was introduced to economic theory in 1938 (Harvey 2005). Today it refers to the resurrection of nineteenth-century free market fundamentalism and laissez-faire urban development. Adam Smith, in *The Wealth of Nations*, argued that people's selfish urge to serve their own interests is the basis for the growth of the collective wealth of populations. This view is the basis for uncontrolled capitalist thinking. What emerged is a new elite supporting the capitalist creed (Harari 2011, 348–51; O'Toole 2007; Schumacher 2013). Its current manifestation has been in government policies of economic liberalization and deregulation.

Attitudes toward city planning and urban design began to be, at least partially, associated with the economic policies of Ronald Regan (1911–2004), president of the United States from 1981 to 1989, and the 'Thatcherism' associated with Regan's contemporary, Margaret Thatcher (1925–2013), prime minister of the United Kingdom from 1979 to 1990. Regan and Thatcher were admirers of Friedrich Hayek (1899–1992), a defender of classical liberalism, Michael Polanyi (1891–1976), an advocate for individual rather than government initiatives, and Milton Friedman (1912–2006), an advocate for privatization and deregulation. The general perception, in Friedrich Hayek's terms, is that control leads ultimately to totalitarianism (Hayek 1948).

The situation in some countries is somewhat different. China's decision to open to the Western world, for example, has created an order that is a combination of a private enterprise market economy and a one-party dictatorial political system. The accompanying economic boom has led to a profusion of urban design projects in the country.

Neoliberalism and Urban Design

The way our contemporary cities are evolving is a realization of Rowe's and Koetter's *Collage City* (Rowe and Koetter 1979). Each new building competes with its neighbor for attention. Any sense of decorum tends to be lost. Many investors in the property market seek a 'radical free market urbanism' with minimal controls over what can be built and where it can be built (Sklair 2005). The market is regarded as the best arbiter of the opportunities and problems that need to be addressed and the design decisions that need to be made. Whatever sells rapidly is regarded

Figure 1 Global urban designs: Lujiazui, Pudong, Shanghai (left), and the GIFT, Ahmedabad proposal (right)

Credit line (right): Collection of the author

as good. The increased movement of financial capital internationally has led to a new era of globalization. A relatively few large architectural firms dominate the international competition for urban design services (Olds 2001; Marshall 2003). They represent the power elite of the design professions. Each firm has its own recognizable genre of work, its own style, and applies it haphazardly across the globe. Specific design models are seen as prestigious products that can be bought. Local conditions get forgotten in the search for the dramatic. Similar designs were produced for the warm temperate and moist climate of Shanghai and for the hot, semi-arid monsoon climate of Ahmedabad in India. The Gujarat International Finance Tech City (GIFT) proposal is the work of a Shanghai architectural firm.

China has imported design services from across the world and has been exporting its expertise in rapidly building large urban design schemes to the countries of Latin America, Asia, and Africa. These schemes are designed in China on the basis of Chinese models. They are built by Chinese hands and use Chinese materials. Particularly poignant are the ghost towns created in countries such as Angola and Libya. The recipients of the largesse are left with unnecessary, uninhabited major projects and financial and moral debts.

Across the world, the private sector's role in property development has been enhanced, while government responsibility for public interest concerns such as housing subsidy programs and the design of the public realm have been reduced. The private sector has taken over leadership in the provision and maintenance of many traditionally publicly owned urban spaces, such as squares. The choice that individual urban designers and firms face is either to ride the economic tide of our times or to attempt to swim against it, which can be self-destructive.

On the surface, the argument in urban design circles may seem to boil down to two opposing views of the future. The neoliberal approach is reflected in hyper-modernist projects and

Figure 2 Competing design paradigms: A hyper-modernist proposal (left) and a neo-traditional proposal (right) for the new business district of Dammam, Saudi Arabia (2009)

Source (left): Lang (2017, 131); courtesy of Taylor & Francis
Source (right): Lang (2017, 131); courtesy of DPZCoDesign and Taylor & Francis

the continued application of easy-to-build generic rationalist modernist designs of individual buildings set in open space with the buildings, designed by using computer-aided tools. They are more geometrically elaborate than modernist tastes would allow. The other approach is a reaction to the excesses of hyper-modernist design. It is the continued use of the new urbanist paradigm. These two views are exemplified in opposing designs for a new business district to be located on the outskirts of Dammam in Saudi Arabia. They represent the clash between aesthetic abstraction and lived-in realities. The situation is, however, more complex than this comparison allows.

The idealism combined with the desire for profitably that characterized the social and philanthropic movement of the nineteenth century has largely disappeared. Current political attitudes in urban development are rewarding to those who wish to release their own creative imaginations on society. Architects such as the late Zaha Hadid and Patrik Schumacher (b. 1965), her business partner, Rem Koolhaas and Office for Metropolitan Architecture (OMA), its offshoot, the Buro of Ole Scheeren (b. 1971), the Greg Lynn (b. 1964) FORM Office, Alejandro Zaera-Polo (b. 1963), and Farshid Moussavi (b. 1965) have made hay while the neoliberal economic sun shines. Their work is heralded as a new era of playful built environments (Willis 2017), but its critics believe that their designs, while capturing the imaginations of the cognoscenti and municipal officials, are already appearing to be dated (Hatherley 2017).

Project Types

Urban designers continue to design new towns (including national capitals) and the precincts of cities as well as individual projects. Much of their work continues to involve suburban development. At the same time, brownfield sites proliferate as districts of industrial cities become obsolete and abandoned. The second half of the twentieth century saw docklands, rail lines and yards, industrial areas, and military bases become redundant due of technological and political changes.

Suburbs have spread farther and farther away from the traditional hearts of cities and been developed into 'edge cities' with their own central business districts (Garreau 1992). Vast housing estates continue to be built. Suburban office parks have been joined by 'wellness centers' of health-related facilities. World fairs and Olympic Games sites and villages present recurring opportunities to explore new ideas and to consider how the sites might be redeveloped once the event is over.

Most dramatic of the new urban design schemes are the fiat cities being built from scratch around the world. It has been estimated that there are well over two hundred of them, many for populations of over a million people. They include New Kabul in Afghanistan, New Baghdad in Iraq, and Duqm in Oman. Egypt and Indonesia plan to build new capital cities. Kazakhstan has acquired one. They all serve dual functions. The first is to house new basic industries and expanding urban populations, along with the infrastructure required to support their activities. The second is to rebrand the countries in which they are located. The goal is for them to be seen as up-to-date technologically and international in spirit. They tend to be modernist and hyper-modernist developments, especially in those countries whose present fiscal situation is built on oil income.

In the postwar years, many traditional central business districts and ribbon-shopping streets in North America went into decline as the use of the car for transport became ubiquitous. Some are now being rejuvenated by significant urban design projects. In several countries, the fear of crime has led to the building of gated residential neighborhoods; wars and fear for life in

In an Age of Corporate Financial Capital

war-torn countries have resulted in the creation of vast refugee camps—mini-cities. Cohousing developments became a new type of residential accommodation. As we go farther into the twenty-first century, some of these trends continue; others are being reversed.

Many traditional central business districts are recovering; new commercial districts comparable to traditional ones are being built in many metropolitan areas. Many shopping streets are dying; others are being redesigned to make them attractive places to be. Large shopping malls on the outskirts of cities in the United States are in financial trouble. In the economically developed world, few new universities are being built in the twenty-first century. Many new ones were built in the postwar years. Airports are becoming major business hubs; aerotropolises are a new mixed-use urban design product type located at or near airports (Kasarda and Lindsay 2012).

One of the challenges facing the world but particularly rapidly expanding countries, such as China, India, Nigeria, and Brazil, is to design high-density built environments that are rich in behavior settings at a time when the image of looking up-to-date is regarded as more important in a competitive world than providing the range of settings that enhance the quality of everyday life. Many projects being built are simply pragmatic solutions based on narrowly defined programs. They are being designed unguided by any central idea other than to be built rapidly and to be profitable. They have to appeal well enough to the public.

Urban Development and Pragmatic Urban Design

In a neoliberal political world, projects driven by market demands are seen to maximize public benefits. Contemporaneously, public sector developers strive to maximize the amount of development they can implement while minimizing cost. The nature of their public realms in both

Figure 3 Central Doha, Qatar
Credit line: Photograph by Kirill Neiezmaklov/Shutterstock.com

cases is the product of adhering to the minimal standards prescribed by generic zoning policies and building bylaws. The individual-building-by-individual-building development of the core of cities has produced several eye-catching complexes of buildings when seen from afar. The resulting pedestrian environment is often ill-considered.

One consequence of the continued urban growth is the farther sprawling of cities into, often valuable, agricultural land around them where it is relatively inexpensive to build. While such expansions are viewed as largely a twentieth-century phenomenon, two centuries ago, it was also a change in the morphology of urban areas that was viewed with alarm. The development of the automobile and the ease and convenience that it provides hastened the development of far-flung low-density suburbs. Such growth continues. The megastructure proposals were one response. The high-rise metropolis was another. In the Epilogue, I argue that the compact city concept is the most promising guiding model for the future, but the ideas of the rationalists attract urban designers more.

The twentieth-century housing schemes of the rationalists were based on the premise that access to sunlight and air are the crucial variables to consider in any urban design project but especially in the design of housing precincts. Access to air and sunlight are, indeed, fundamental human requirements but responding only to them often overrides many other concerns, particularly in those countries where getting large numbers of residential units built quickly is urgent.

The 1930s rationalist housing and urban development models that have largely been abandoned as the basis for new designs in Europe and the Americas are still widely adopted as *the* pragmatic solution to housing the rapidly growing urban populations in Asia and Africa. Many housing developments in China and Korea consist of long rows of residential towers aligned east–west to face south into the sun and sometimes to meet feng shui requirements. The model is being applied across the region in all climatic zones. Access to sunlight in winter months to the lower stories of the buildings gets completely lost, especially in the projects located at the higher latitudes. It is also being applied by Chinese government developers in different climatic and cultural settings in Latin America, Africa, and other parts of Asia. They may seem to be alienating places, but their residents often desire anonymity and privacy. One way of breaking down this seemingly endless pattern in China is by creating a *xiaoqu*, which is both a physical design and a social model. More frequently, however, designs simply follow the standard paradigm. It is easier.

Large urban design schemes get pragmatically adjusted based on the shortcomings that arise. Sometimes these adjustments are significant. The Canary Wharf component of the London Docklands development started out as a single-use commercial development—a second business

Figure 4 Pragmatic early-twenty-first-century urban developments: The generic modernist city—Tianjin (left) and Rajarhat, Kolkata (right)

Credit line: Photograph by Keep Watch/Shutterstock.com

In an Age of Corporate Financial Capital

Figure 5 Docklands, London: Canary Wharf
Source: Lang (2017, 147); courtesy of Taylor & Francis

district for London. As its dullness became clear, other uses were added during the first decade of the twenty-first century to enliven the place and to cater better to office workers. The individual office buildings are generic types; One Canada Square is like the earlier World Finance Center (now Brookfield Place) at Battery Park City and not dissimilar to the Iberdrola Tower in Bilbao. Cézar Pelli was the architect of all three.

What have urban designers learned from past experiences? The redevelopment of abandoned docklands in one city sparked the redevelopment in others without learning much from earlier experiences. What did the designers of the Docklands in Melbourne learn from the London experience? The Promenade Plantée in Paris led to High Line Park in New York, which, being the better known, has been the catalyst for the transformation of other abandoned rail lines in cities. Few are as interesting.

The Outline of the Discussion

Urban design thinking today relies heavily on the ideas generated during the early twentieth century as they were taken forward after World War Two. This part of the book describes the paradigms that coexist today. Each chapter focuses on an approach that is a response to a set of observations about cities and urban life and/or the designing process. The approaches are not necessarily mutually exclusive, but reconciling the attitudes shaping them is difficult.

This discussion begins with two chapters on the urban designs that neoliberal ideas and advanced computer-based algorithms have enabled. The first reviews the continued application of earlier rationalist urban design models as they have evolved into neo- and hyper-modernism and the second the utility of parametric approaches to urban design. Some of our contemporary urban design paradigms suggest directions opposed to these approaches. They follow the values that informed urban design during much of last century. Neo-traditional tendencies under the guise of the New Urbanism and smart growth ideals continue to be a reaction to hyper-modernist designs. Meanwhile, the 'design with nature' and landscape urbanism advocates have continued to promote what they regard as fundamentally important with proposals for ecologically

In an Age of Corporate Financial Capital

sound, sustainable cities. Their concerns must be heeded by future urban designers. Two chapters are devoted to describing the paradigms that the two groups promote. While seemingly opposed in advocacies, they can be reconciled.

The final chapter in this discussion of urban design in an age of neoliberal economics is devoted to the topic of smart (or cyber) cities. While not strictly an urban design paradigm, 'smartness' might well shape urban design projects of the future, although it is not obvious in what way. The chapter describes the visions that municipal authorities have in striving to harness technological advances in information and communications to enhance the functioning of built environments. The goal is to improve the quality of life of the inhabitants of a city, although it is unclear what the imagined quality of life being sought is. One of the objectives is certainly to make life easier and more comfortable.

Key References

Harvey, David. 2005. *A Brief History of Neoliberalism*. Oxford: Oxford University Press.
Hayek, Friedrich. 1944. *The Road to Serfdom*. Chicago: University of Chicago Press.
Olds, Kris. 2001. *Globalization and Urban Change: Capital, Culture, and the Pacific Rim Mega- Projects*. Oxford: Oxford University Press.
O'Toole, Randall. 2007. "Preserving the American Dream by Cost, Not Coercion." In *Planetizen Contemporary Debates in Urban Planning*, edited by Abhijeet Chavan, Christian Peralta, and Christopher Steins, 34–38. Washington, DC: Island Press.
Schumacher, Patrik. 2013. "Free-Market Urbanism—Urbanism Beyond Planning." In *Masterplanning the Adaptive City—Computational Urbanism in the Twenty-First Century*, edited by Tom Verebes. London and New York: Routledge.

12

Modernist, Neo-modernist, and Hyper-modernist Urban Design

Postmodern ideas still prevail in parts of the world. The appearance of privately developed estates of individual houses localizes them because the forms and decoration match the tastes of potential local purchasers. In China, the wealthy are beginning to throw off the legacy of the 1966–76 Cultural Revolution and pick up on traditional elements in their houses (Holland 2016). The modernist paradigm nevertheless remains widely employed, self-consciously or unselfconsciously, as a model for current urban design projects. Neo-modernists, finding such work boring, strive to create visually richer built environments without incorporating historical elements in their designs as the postmodernists did. Architects then asked, Why not play with the forms of buildings and urban designs that are made possible by structural and computational advances? Hyper-modernist designs have been the result. It has yielded attention-grabbing "postmodernism hyperspace" (Jameson 1991; Virilio 2000; see also Fraker 2007). They additionally observed that we live in an era of rapid transportation between countries, instantaneous email communication and mobile phones. So why should we worry about the locality of any proposed new building or urban design?

The neoliberal era is manifested in designers' striving for geometric uniqueness and boldness in the structure and appearance of their work in competition with that of others. Forms as objects are celebrated not for their fitness in accommodating their instrumental functions or for their relationship to their context but rather for the cleverness of their forms. The results are much admired for their vivacity (Willis 2017), but some observers have their misgivings (Fraser and Kim 2015; Hatherley 2017; Curl 2018). Hyper-modernist design has been and continues to be a response not only to new technical possibilities but also to the greater individualism and the competitive nature of the times. These remarks do not mean that all property developers and their architects are unconcerned about human experiences of the built environment as part of their everyday lives but rather that those concerns often get overridden in the search for novelty.

Antecedent Ideas

The modernist urban designs of the first decades of the twenty-first century, as exemplified in East Asia, but largely abandoned in Western Europe and the Americas, clearly harken back to the rationalist advocacies and schemes of the interwar years. Their bold character continues to

In an Age of Corporate Financial Capital

beckon, although the garden city model in all its permutations remains the basis for many urban designs, as will be shown in a Chapter 14.

In many recent urban designs, it is the plan that is modernist, whereas the buildings are livelier, drawing on late-twentieth-century neo-modernist or the emerging hyper-modernist ideas. Their appearance is thus more geometrically diverse than the rigidity of orthogonal modernist designs. Many recent developments are in a superblock form, an idea that can be traced back to Radburn and Victor Gruen's Fort Worth plan. In China, the gated *xiaoqu* is a development of colonial Japanese neighborhood ideas that were implemented in the 1930s.

Hyper-modernist buildings and urban designs have their roots in our contemporary ways of life. While hyper-modernism is a continuation of the rationalist spirit, it represents an inversion of the thinking of Le Corbusier, Walter Gropius, and CIAM. What the hyper-modernists do have in common with those architects is a self-referential view of the world. Hyper-modernist architecture takes designs such as the TWA Flight Center building (1962; now the foyer of a hotel) designed by Eero Saarinen (1910–61) at New York's John F. Kennedy International Airport, and the Sydney Opera House (opened 1973), designed by Jørn Utzon (1918–2008), a step farther. Both of those buildings incurred opportunity costs in terms of the instrumental functions that they were supposed to serve, but their sculptural qualities make them instantly recognizable symbols. In hyper-modernist designs, the concern for the eye-striking quality of the exterior is paramount. Urban designs consist of clusters of such eye-catching buildings each standing as an object in its own space.

Hyper-modernism and hip-hop—a defiant form of urbanism—have formal antecedents in Russian constructivism, but they also take inspiration from Le Corbusier in a different way. The scale of intervention that he planned for his designs and the impact that urban planner Robert Moses (1888–1981) had on New York were precedents for the size of several current urban designs. The parkways, housing projects, playgrounds, and urban designs implemented under Moses's direction were acts of will on a scale that Le Corbusier never succeeded in carrying out. In that sense, the attitude reflected in Baron Haussmann's design for Paris is an antecedent to the intrusive attitude underlying hyper-modernist urban designs.

Manifestoes and Paradigms

The modernists, the neo-modernists, and, in particular, the hyper-modernists argue for cities designed to meet the spirit of our times. What is meant by the 'spirit of our times' is not clearly defined but involves growth in personal entrepreneurship and the speed of interpersonal communications rather than the stability of most of the world's population's daily lives. Many urban designers, particularly in East Asia, pragmatically follow rationalist models of urban design because they are easy to copy and implement. Although no manifesto presses for the continuation of the modernists' spirit, the advocacy for urban environments designed along CIAM lines is implicit in designs.

Neo-modernist urban designs show a greater consideration for buildings as space enclosing elements than in the schemes of the modernists and hyper-modernists. The buildings, while retaining the geometrical restraint promoted by CIAM, have a greater visual richness and often the boldness of color advocated by Bruno Taut. The hyper-modernists find the forms of both modernist and neo-modernist urban designs to be uninspired; they are advocates for geometrically varied urban designs. The world is perceived to be changing so rapidly that designing to meet the instrumental functions of a building beyond a satisficing level is futile. The form is what counts, and activities can be shoehorned in well enough. A good city should thus, implicitly, consist of varied individual buildings standing as objects in space. Unity is achieved by the

264

sheer diversity of building forms. An awe-inspiring skyline when seen from afar is attained, but the ground level where life in public takes place can end up being gloomy.

Architect Daniel Libeskind (b. 1946) captures the essence of much current architectural thinking when commenting on the evolution of the urban design qualities of the World Trade Center site in New York:

> [The site design is] the reverse of the Potsdamer Platz in Berlin, which is just a bunch of architects following exactly what was on paper. . . . [The World Trade Center site design shows] the art of making a master plan rather than an 18th century plan that is obediently followed. We're not living in Haussmann's Paris. We have a pluralistic society.
>
> *(cited in Lubell 2004, 47)*

Diversity, it is argued, is part of this world. It is what should be sought in an urban design.

Hyper-modernist buildings are often referred to as 'modernism on steroids.' They impress. They are architecturally clever and appear to be, and sometimes are, structurally innovative. They amaze the beholder and are seen to be 'futuristic.' This amazement is further enhanced when they are clustered into an urban design composition. Little is said about them as places to be and inhabit.

Libeskind's view was echoed by Thom Mayne (b. 1944), a US architect. It reflects the world he inhabits:

> The precinct, district, township, neighborhood—the idea of this—is dead. Kids no longer play stick ball in the streets. [Cities need] a radical heterogeneity or pluralism. Everything everywhere is now a must.
>
> *(cited in Green 2016)*

Despite Mayne's observations, a journey through New York or his own Los Angeles or any major city in the world reveals that neighborhoods are strong and precincts unique. They may not be as self-contained as before—even the poor live more metropolitan ways of life than in the past—but they continue to exist. The rationalist position today is that we should all be living metropolitan lives. At the same time, in China, for example, there are calls for reforming modernist residential areas of cities into something akin to neighborhood units (Kan, Forsyth, and Rowe 2017). More-radical positions on urban design that reject such ideas are now attracting attention if not action. Hip-hop urbanism is one.

Young urban Black Americans and Latino Americans in the postindustrial cities of the United States began hip-hop as a music and dance form in the 1970s. Hip-hop or ruffneck urbanism's manifesto for change was presented by Kara Walker (b. 1969), an artist. She wrote, "The following is a manifesto, in search of a movement. . . . In it, I am proposing a theory of architecture based around a ruffneck, antisocial, hip-hop, rudeboy ethos" (Walker 2014, 9). It is inspired by rapper MC Lyte's 1993 hit song *Ruffneck*. It sees itself as a "thuggish" response to softness and compromise, not through total urban designs but rather through a series of 'assaults' on the urban scene. What it has in common with mainstream hyper-modernism is its concern for urban design as an act of individualistic display rather than a medium for better affording people's ways of everyday life in a pleasurable manner. It advocates for urban design as an expression (along with theater, music, and dance) that represents a minority cultural presence in the US city. Hip-hop's structure gives a unique creative framework for spatial relationships, which, rather like graffiti, lays a territorial claim over parts of the city (Walker 2014). Reflecting the individualistic attitudes of our times, hip-hop urbanism little respects existing urban forms

(Cooke 2017; Jeffries 2014). It has yet to see its manifestation in built form, although a few schemes built following another paradigm seem to fit the bill.

Critics such as Tom Dyckhoff and Chris Abel and organizations such as the Council on Tall Buildings and Urban Habitat celebrate the rebelliousness of such works and the spectacular brashness of hyper-modernist architecture where "form is the function" (Abel 2010; Dyckhoff 2017). Such urban designs may not be the norm today, but neither are they deviant from much that is occurring.

Generic Concepts and Illustrative Designs

The rationalist modern generic models of urban designs remain those of the twentieth century. No generic or illustrative designs have been produced for neo-modernist urban design. Specific designs of different natures, such as Longnan Gardens, a housing development in China, and Tjuvholmen, a mixed-use precinct on a former shipyard sited in Norway, enable the generic qualities of neo-modernist designs to be identified. Their layouts are tighter and depart from the strict orthogonal geometry of modernist designs, and the buildings are less austere.

No single diagram illustrates hyper-modernist urban design aspirations. Dubai sets the pace for the world as a model to follow in order to be seen as up-to-date in a world where cities compete to be noticed. The goal is to attract international commercial companies and property developers to build in them. Dubai is the envy of many of the power elite around the world. It is also a place where architects like to work because they can create built forms that they are unable to create at home because they need to meet the requirements of zoning regulations, building codes, and, often, hostile local opposition to unusual building forms (Willis 2017).

The hyper-modernist city consists of a haphazard collection of individualistic buildings. Each celebrates its own geometrical qualities, although the internal design of buildings may follow generic types. They accommodate gardens, balconies, and communal open spaces that catch some sunlight. Streets are seen much as Le Corbusier presented them in the 'City for 3 Million' and the 'Radiant City'—as places for the movement of vehicles not as the seam joining the activities on their sides into a unit. Not much is said about the pedestrian experience or that of people with disabilities or, more broadly, about the diverse needs of different people. Streets remain dividers, 'edges' in Kevin Lynch's terms (Lynch 1960). Urban districts are bounded by them creating islands of individual property developments.

Figure 12.1   The hyper-modernist city: Dubai, United Arab Emirates
Credit line: Photograph by Renate Sedmakova/Shutterstock.com

Modernist, Neo-Modernist, and Hyper-Modernist Design

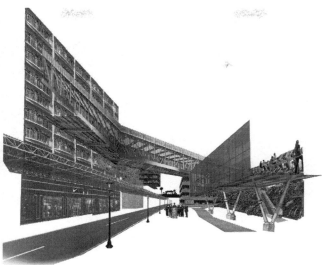

Figure 12.2 Hip-hop urbanism: One of Filip Dujardin's "Untitled" from his series *Fictions*, 2007 (left), and "Collage" from "Ivy City," an exploratory example of hip-hop urbanism (right)

Credit line (left): Filip Dujardin; courtesy of Filip Dujardin
Credit line (right): Kyle Simmons; courtesy of Kyle Simmons
Source (right): Cooke (2017)

Hip-hop urbanism takes a revolutionary stance toward public health, safety, and human welfare. Design qualities are perhaps exemplified by the imaginary architectural structures of Filip Dujardin (b. 1971) as presented in his *Fiction* series (Vollmer 2012). His surreal images, like hip-hop dance, are of buildings that defy the laws of gravity and of physics. If put into practice on a large scale, hip-hop urbanism would result in a collage of building designs of individuals' artistic expressions. The way it bridges the gap between the ideas of designers and the qualities of the environment sought by people who are going about their everyday lives is unclear.

Specific Designs

Much building has taken place in cities around the world during the thirty years from 1990 to when this book was written. Urban design projects have been built on sites of abandoned ports and shipyards, on air rights over railyards, on obsolete industrial sites, and on cleared residential areas, including slums and low-density areas ripe for intense development. Many new towns are being built; others are being planned. Urban renewal projects can be seen in almost every city, even in those in decline. Suburbs sprawl.

Many current developments simply follow the rationalist model of buildings as rows in open space. Other modernist development such as New Cairo, while basically modernist, have new urbanist overtones in the way buildings meet the streets, as in the well-functioning areas of Cairo. Several recent neo-modernist projects have also striven to get away from the strictures of the pure rationalist model. Longnan Garden Housing Estate in Xuhui District, China, is an example. Designed by Atelier GOM and completed in 2017, it represents the effort to recreate, in abstract form, the 'fortress besieged' nature of the courtyards of traditional Chinese houses

Figure 12.3 A modernist urban design with strong pragmatic overtones: A now superseded proposal for New Cairo

Credit line: Skidmore, Owings & Merrill (Europe) LLP
Source: Lang (2017, 22); courtesy of Skldmore, Owings & Merrill and Taylor & Francis

Figure 12.4 Neo-modernist designs: Longnan Garden Housing Estate, Xuhui District (left), and WagnisART, Munich (right)

Credit line (left): Chen Hao; courtesy of Atelier GOM
Credit line (right): Photograph by Claudia Nesser; collection of the author

(Atelier GOM 2017). The configuration of the scheme has buildings facing different directions, but all receive good sunlight. The open spaces form courtyards; the buildings of the complex provide a sense of enclosure. Similar comments can be made about the WagnisART development (2005) in Munich, Germany, and Tjuvholmen in Oslo, Norway.

WagnisART is a neo-modernist, total urban design. Consciously or not, its layout follows the principles that Oscar Newman identified as necessary for a well-functioning urban design (Newman 1972). The design was created by Bogevischs Buero and SHAH Schneider Hable Architekten (Nesser 2017). The cooperative group that now lives there had a substantial say in the evolution of the multiple-award-winning design. The spaces are much tighter, have a variety of configurations, and are composed of a mixture of hard and soft surfaces. The character of such schemes is much more varied than the pure modernist model advocated. In neo-modernist

Modernist, Neo-Modernist, and Hyper-Modernist Design

urban designs, the buildings are more conventionally functionalist but visually livelier. The open spaces form the hearts of a design; they are not leftover spaces.

Hyper-modernist examples, with their spatial layouts and radical shapes, increasingly abound and attract attention. Sometimes it is simply that the spaces are overwhelmingly large in the search for a prestigious environment, as in Beijing's historic Tiananmen Square or the recent Sukhbaatar Square layout in Ulaanbaatar. At other times, the spaces between buildings and the buildings themselves are often contorted and depart radically from the box-like forms of the Bauhaus and the Calvinist rigidity of Le Corbusier's early designs. They are governed by their investors' desire to be architecturally fashionable and at the cutting edge of new ideas. Civic leaders around the world want to showcase their city's avant-garde nature. The bourgeoisie too have wanted their

Figure 12.5 Hyper-modernist urban designs: The mile-tall Sky Mile Tower proposed for 2045 in Tokyo Bay (left), Zhuhai Opera House complex (right), and Karle Town Centre, Bengaluru (bellow)

Credit line (above left): Courtesy of Kohn Pedersen Fox, architects
Credit line (above right): Photograph by Sleeping Panda/Shutterstock.com
Credit line (bottom): Courtesy of UNStudio

269

In an Age of Corporate Financial Capital

cities to be in the international limelight. While the authorities in Dubai may have led the way, cities such as Shanghai have followed and others such as New York are striving to catch up.

Perhaps better examples of hyper-modernist urban designs are some of the new towns being built around the world. Bahria Town outside Karachi is a satellite new town for 1 million people. Neom in Saudi Arabia is to be a sprawling city larger than New York in area. Forest City in southern Malaysia is a city being built with Chinese financing to be a 'New Shenzhen.' Khorgos is rising on the Silk Road at the China-Kazakhstan border (Wainwright 2019b) and Eko Atlantic City in Lagos State, Nigeria. All of them are hyper-modernist statements drawing on bits and pieces of garden city and rationalist ideas. That observation also holds for smaller urban developments on both greenfield and brownfield sites.

In Singapore, the Marina Bay Sands district with its casino-hotel and ArtScience Museum is a 1990s example of a hyper-modernist design of individual buildings tied together by an elaborate walkway. The surfboard top linking three towers that have a shopping mall at their base is an image of up-to-dateness. The ten-fingered-lotus-inspired museum is an independent sculpture. While the overall scheme is well executed, many hyper-modernist urban designs around are less well coordinated. The precinct is the city-state's most recent flagship design.

Exemplars of Modernist, Neo-modernist, and Hyper-modernist Urban Design

The One, Hangzhou, Zhejiang, China (2016); Wohnpark Neue Danau, Vienna, Austria (1993–98); Hudson Yards, New York, New York, USA (2010–24); the Central Business District, Beijing, China (2000–); and Nur-Sultan, Kazakhstan (1997–)

The schemes selected, somewhat arbitrarily, as exemplars of current modernist, neo-modernist, and hyper-modernist thought are presented in paradigmatic order, not chronological order. The discussion begins with a modernist housing development in Hangzhou in Zheijang. It then describes two neo-modernist schemes—one bordering on hyper-modernism—before considering two thoroughly hyper-modernist designs.

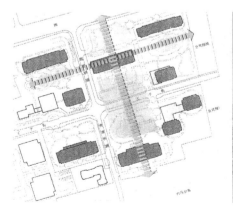

Figure 12.6 An early-twenty-first-century modernist urban design: The One, Hangzhou, Zhejiang (2016): The plan (left) and an image of the design (right)

Credit line (left and right): © Yao Li; courtesy of GAD Architects

The One, Hangzhou, is located at the edge of the city's center on an abandoned dock site. The design goal was to have a unified peaceful scheme consisting of several of slab apartment blocks set in gardens. Its plan is symmetrical, with its buildings aligned east–west, facing the south. Cross axes link the complex into its surroundings. More thought has gone into the landscaping of the open space than in many such schemes. Its designers, GAD Architects, says that an effort was made to blend its cultural context and a modern character (GAD Architects 2017). The size, geometry, and spatial relationship of the buildings make for a strong visual impact. Many residential urban design schemes follow a similar model. Others are more neo–modernist in character. Wohnpark Neue Danau is one of them.

Wohnpark Neue Danau may be seen as just another descendent of 1960s–type rationalist housing complexes, but it is more than that. Built over a substantial freeway, it sits as an independent island of housing separated from the Danube by two promenades with a steep grassy slope between them. Stairways allow access to the waterfront. Commissioned by the city government of Vienna and designed by the modernist Australian firm of Harry Seidler & Associates, it follows the concern for well-designed social housing in the city that dates back to Red Vienna and the building of such schemes as the Karl-Marx-Hof.

Each housing block, white in color, is generic modernist in form, but the design is more than a pragmatic response to the need to provide shelter for its inhabitants. Setting the building in diagonals across the site serves two purposes: structurally, it helps distribute loads over the freeway below, and it provides views, if dull, of the Danube from all the apartments. The layout also provides a partial view of corridors for the strictly modernist, pre-existing housing blocks inland of the site. The housing is complemented by a triangular office-cum-residential tower 100 meters (330 feet) in height at the northern end of the site. The tower faces a tree-lined square with a fountain. On one side are shops, and on the other side is a cinema (Förster 2002).

In all, there are 850 apartments, mostly two bedrooms in size, but some are smaller; the rooftop terraces house three-bedroom flats. The buildings are lower in height as they approach the Danube. The detailing of the landscaping between the diagonals sets the complex apart from much social housing. The outdoor spaces, however, showed few signs of usage in 2017, while several buildings were displaying some deterioration. The Hudson Yards in New York is a more ostentatious neo–modernist development than Wohnpark Neue Danau. Some may regard it as hyper–modern.

"Hudson Yards will not only change the way New York City looks but how the world looks at New York City" (Bravo 2016). The project is a 26–acre (11-hectare) hyper–commercial air rights development over the Westside Railyards between Hudson River Park and midtown Manhattan. The property developer is a combination of The Related Companies, Oxford Properties, and Collingwood Inc.; the urban designers were Kohn Pedersen Fox Associates. The developers of the individual components of the complex read like a who's who of the New York real estate establishment. The infrastructure for the development was funded partly by the City of New York, the State of New York, and the Metropolitan Transportation Authority (MTA) and partly by private interests. The financing has been aided by the district's being made a tax-increment zone in which growth in the property taxes collected from the precinct are used to further its development and maintenance (Gluttman 2013). The leading tenants are companies with global interests and markets.

With foresight, the railyard was built in the 1980s with the possibility of its air rights being exploited. Space was left for columns to be built between the sets of rail tracks. The MTA extended a subway line and created a station at 34th Street and 11th Avenue to facilitate accessibility to the site and ensure its financial success. High Line Park, another asset to the development, approaches from the south, and its termination has become part of the complex.

In an Age of Corporate Financial Capital

Figure 12.7 Neo-modernism: Wohnpark Neue Danau, Vienna—an aerial view (left) and a ground-level image (right)

Credit line (left): Courtesy of Eric Sierens

Hudson Yards is the largest urban design project in North America and will cost at least US$25 billion by the time it is completed in the 2020s. When built out, it will consist of sixteen skyscrapers, over one hundred retail shops, restaurants, a hotel, over 5,000 residential units, planted open areas, and a public school. The buildings are individualistic and thus diverse but with some similarities. They come in glass-sheathed exteriors, with a variety of tapers, angular geometries, and generous atriums. As a group, they are said to form a 'dynamic' composition. A 6-acre (2-hectare) public square, designed by Nelson Byrd Woltz and Heatherwick Studios, will be the centerpiece of the development. It contains Vessel, a folly with eighty viewing platforms, the creation of Thomas Hetherwick (b. 1970). It is a tourist attraction capable of holding 1,000 people at a time. On the square's south is a canopy of trees. While much applauded, critics regard Hudson Yards as "a private fantasy of angular glass towers stuffed with offices and expensive apartments, rising above a seven-storey shopping mall on an endless gray carpet, sprinkled with small tufts of 'park'" (Wainwright 2019b). Other projects are strictly hyper-modern.

The Beijing Central Business, the city's center for finance and for media and business services, occupies about 4 square kilometers (close to 1,000 acres) of the Chaoyang district of the city. It consists of a mixture of standard modernist commercial buildings—maybe three hundred in all—and generic hotels, coated in different, sometimes postmodern, skins and a few hyper-modernist buildings. Stylistically international, they could be located anywhere in the world. The most notable hyper-modernist building that features as the foreground element to a background of modernist structures is the CCTV tower, designed by Rem Koolhaas and Ole Scheeren of the Rotterdam-based OMA. More such vanity buildings may come to central Beijing, although the 2009 Development Plan suggested that the city's planners think that Beijing has enough of them.

The CCTV tower was the winning entry in an international design competition (See Figure 12.9). It is a 234-meter (768-foot), forty-four-story building that is immediately recognizable. Its horizontal and vertical sections create an irregular grid with an open center. Its complex structural design was provided by Arup Associates. In 2013, the tower won the best skyscraper award from the Council of Tall Buildings and Urban Habitat. It has certainly given central Beijing an identity

Modernist, Neo-Modernist, and Hyper-Modernist Design

 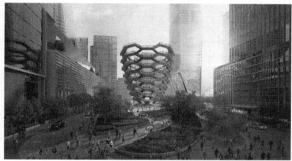

Figure 12.8 A neo-modernist/hyper-modernist urban design: Hudson Yards seen from mid-Hudson (above) and from above the railyards (below left) and a rendering of the interior square with Vessel (below right)

Credit line (above): Photograph by Gagliardi Photography/Shutterstock.com
Credit line (below left): Photograph by Todamo/Shutterstock.com
Credit line (below right): Courtesy of Forbes Massie Studio

and a landmark. The building is nevertheless contentious. In true modernist fashion, it stands as an object in space. In true hyper-modernist fashion, it has a contorted geometry. It is regarded by some architectural critics as the precedent for commercial building for the twenty-first century and an exemplar of what future cities will/should become (Willis 2017). Locals think it looks like a pair of pants. Taking hyper-modernism a gigantic step farther in scale is Nur-Sultan (Astana until March 2019) on the banks of the Ishim River in Kazakhstan.

Nur-Sultan was planned by Japanese modernist Kisho Kurokawa a member of the Metabolists. It is a heroic composition of independent components designed by world-famous architects. The whole project was initiated and directed by Kazakhstan's eccentric, powerful, and long-serving dictator, President Nursultan Nazarbayev (b. 1941), and now named after him. Nazarbayev was the country's leader from 1989 and its first president upon its gaining independence from the Soviet Union in 1991. The city is the first new capital city of the twenty-first century and, possibly, a portent of the future design paradigm for new towns that free-spending

Figure 12.9 A hyper-modernist design: Beijing CBD with the CCTV tower
Credit line: Photograph by Phillipe Rault; courtesy of OMA

politicians, municipal leaders, and urban designers will embrace. The city consists of a collage of various urban design projects, individualistic buildings, grand open spaces, and monuments (Wainwright 2017). Overall, the desire for a signature design, or set of grand designs of unique character, seems to have overridden designing for the continental climate of the northern steppe of Kazakhstan (winters as low as -40°C and summers as high as 35°C).

While Nurzhol Boulevard—a dumbbell design with major features at each end—is a major axial gesture, the city is based on a loose gridiron plan with specific sectors for government and other activities. The spatial layout with its large open spaces—parks and squares—is designed for its spectacular qualities rather than for its livability. Unlike the visual unity of the southern portion of Brasília's Pilot Plan, the architecture of Nur-Sultan is varied in nature. The European architectural cognoscenti regard the city's design as discordant and has dismissed the presidential palace as a Disneyland version of Washington's White House (Fraser and Kim 2016). Much is certainly grandiose. The Khan Shatyr Shopping Centre, designed by Norman Foster, for instance, is the world's largest marquee. It houses not only shops but also a temperature-controlled beach with sand imported from Maldives.

The city's Abu Dhabi Plaza is relatively restrained in character. Like the Khan Shatyr Shopping Centre, also designed by Foster + Partners, it forms one of the city's precincts. It is a mixed-use development with an antecedent in Abu Dhabi's Central Market Plaza. It consists of a podium of retail and leisure facilities at the base of several office buildings, residential towers, and a cluster of hotels. The design has year-round temperate winter gardens that serve as public open spaces and as a mechanism that allows light to penetrate the complex. Like Montreal's Golden Mile, it is possible to move through the whole precinct in climate-controlled comfort. Unlike much of Nur-Sultan, the towers are conventional modernist designs.

Modernist, Neo-Modernist, and Hyper-Modernist Design

Figure 12.10 A hyper-modernist new town: A view of central Nur-Sultan from the president's palace looking down Nurzhol Boulevard

Credit line: Photograph by pp1/Shutterstock.com

The design is, apparently, rich in occult masonic symbolism. The occultism may be a mark of the respect for religious freedom in Kazakhstan. Although upon the demise of the Soviet Union, Nazarbayev embraced Islam, the city, in addition to mosques, has churches and synagogues. It also has a fine university that employs many foreign academics. The city, at present, is a mixture of Soviet-era architectural designs and aspirations to be *the* up-to-date city of the globalized world. It certainly seeks to be another, but grander, Dubai, and its current planners are striving to make it so.

Hybrid Examples

EuropaCity, Berlin, Germany (2008–25); The Interlace, Singapore (2007–15); Huangshan Mountain Village, Anhui, China (2017); and Namba Parks, Osaka, Japan (2003)

The schemes identified earlier as exemplars of hyper-modernist urban design are a mixture of independent ideas. Some urban designs are self-consciously an integration of different paradigms. EuropaCity is fundamentally a modernist design with neo-modernist characteristics. Singapore's The Interlace consist of modernist components combined into a design of structural dexterity. Huangshan Mountain Village and Namba Parks are modernist schemes with both hyper-modernist and green characteristics.

EuropaCity is a district under construction on a 40-hectare (almost 100-acre) site that has clearly defined edges. On its south is the River Spree, and to the north, it is bordered by Perleberger Brücke, while the Spandau Ship Canal lies on its east and rail lines on its west. It is directly linked to Berlin's main railroad station. The character for the development was established in 2008, when a competition was held for its design, but its history goes back to an earlier

275

competition for the southern portion of the site won by Oswald Mathias Ungers (1926–2007) in 1994. The development proposal was approved by the Berlin Senate, the city's government, in 2009 and is being implemented primarily by a private company, CA Immo. The company has sold individual development sites to other private developers. They, as is increasingly happening in this neoliberal age, are paying for the infrastructure elements that form the public realm: streets, waterside promenades, and a central square with a fountain.

When completed, the project will consist of 2,000 residential units and 400,000 square meters (4.3 million square feet) of offices, retail stores, and restaurants. Buildings are built to the property line, as in the historic areas of Berlin. The site is divided in a modernist manner into parts, each with a predominant land use. The design is centered on a boulevard and consists largely of neo-modernist background buildings, although the 69-meter-high (226-foot-high) Total Tower marks one entrance to the site. A cube, Kunstcubus, an arts museum, will be a foreground building sitting in an open space.

The Interlace was designed by Ole Scheeren (b. 1971) when he was still with OMA in Rotterdam. The complex's form is a major departure from the earlier modernist, postmodernist, and neo-traditional housing developments in Singapore. It is an example of a total urban design—urban design as large-scale architecture. It sits as an independent element surrounded mainly by a green landscaped area between it and the adjacent roads; parklands lie beyond.

The complex consists of thirty-one six-story, modernist stacked 'bricks' laid in a honeycomb pattern of twos, threes, and fours to create three twenty-four-story peaks and eight large hexagonal courtyards. The Interlace has the qualities that those advocating a hip-hop approach to urban design seek. It contains 1,040 residential units, ranging from studio apartments to rooftop penthouses. While it includes swimming pools and other recreational facilities rather than being a village, it remains a housing scheme for high-income residents. The Queensway Shopping Centre is a five-minute drive away.

Green areas, wise or not, are prestigious throughout the world. At The Interlace, they thread through the courtyards and vertical gardens. They, along with the adjacent parks, are advertised as key features of the 'lifestyle' offered by The Interlace. The spaces for communal activities do not seem to have been as successful as in Bedok Court (1985), another village with The Interlace's social aspirations (see Lang and Moleski 2010, 181–82). The open spaces

Figure 12.11 A neo-modernist precinct design: EuropaCity, Berlin:
Credit line: Courtesy of ASTOC Architects

Modernist, Neo-Modernist, and Hyper-Modernist Design

Figure 12.12 A hyper-modernist urban design akin to hip-hop's aspirations: The Interlace, Singapore

Credit line: Courtesy of Iwan Baan

do, however, allow for light to penetrate the development and for the cross ventilation of apartments.

Innovative though the scheme may be, others before it had similar qualities. Montreal's Habitat designed by Moshe Safdie in 1967 consists of individual brick-like apartment used as building blocks piled into a residential structure. The Jeanne-Hachette Centre, a housing complex in Ivry-sur-Seine, Paris, designed by Jean Renaudie (1925–1981) and Renée Gailhoustet (b. 1929) in the early 1970s, could also easily be seen as a precedent. In contrast to The Interlace, it is an urban project that is very much part of its context.

Another project that is described as a village but does not seem to be one except in name is Huangshan Mountain Village. Like Le Corbusier's ideal, it consists of buildings in a park. Its and Namba Park's development integrate sustainability concepts with hyper-modernist attitudes. The scheme was designed for Greenland Hong Kong Holdings Limited by a team led by Ma Yansong of MAD Architects with Broadacre Source Landscape responsible for the site design. The project consists of ten apartment buildings set as separate objects in its surroundings. Each building has a unique outline, but, in common, the floorplates decrease in size toward the buildings' tops, giving them peak-like profiles. The apartments have copious wavy-profiled balconies (MAD Architects 2017; Mairs 2017). Each building is approached by a road that gives automobile access to it. For pedestrians, a meandering pathway following the contours of the site links the buildings.

The scheme is hyper-modernist without the bombastic geometrical forms of much of such architecture. The luxurious accommodation and sweeping balconies that provide views over the surrounding countryside and lake were designed to make visitors feel spiritually at one with the natural world. Whether it does depends on their predispositions, but the affordance for such an experience is there.

Namba Parks, on the site of the former Osaka Stadium, was designed by Jon Jerde (1940–2015), a Los Angeles architect. Spanning several city blocks, it is a multilevel complex consisting of a thirty-story office building, residential units, a 120-tenant shopping mall with international restaurants and a rooftop garden, and spaces for small personal vegetable gardens for residents. An amphitheater provides a setting for live entertainment.

The rooftop park starts at street level and rises eight levels across the site. It was designed to integrate nature into a high-density urban environment. The garden contains tree groves,

In an Age of Corporate Financial Capital

Figure 12.13 Two restrained hyper-modernist urban designs: Huangshan Mountain Village (left) and Namba Parks, Osaka

Credit line (left): Photograph by Shu He; courtesy of MAD architects
Credit line (right): Photograph by 663 Highland
Source (right): Wikimedia Commons

lawns, and outcrops of rocks. A canyon loops through the complex. The curving forms are a departure from the mainstream of modernist urban design and have the flamboyance of many hyper-modernist designs but in a controlled manner. The scheme won an Urban Land Institute's award for excellence in 2009. Being a total urban design driven by one organization, it has a highly unified character.

Commentary: The Functions Addressed

Modernist designs function well enough in meeting the basic needs for shelter and security of the people who inhabit them for work or as residents. No special attention in their designs is paid to enriching the lives of specific groups of people such as children and frail people. The schemes function well in providing high levels of comfort to their inhabitants, although required heating and cooling levels are achieved almost universally through artificial mechanisms, in almost all climatic zones. The desire to have a high image quality often outweighs the thoughtful use of materials that are environmentally sensible and often outweighs climatically sensible orientations. The comfort level provided in the outdoor spaces is left to chance. In many cases, they appear to be designed as objects to look at rather than as places to inhabit.

Many aspiring cities are trying to reinvent themselves through the acquisition of dramatic buildings and urban design schemes. They seek to compete with those who are already established and who have a patina of history that enriches them and that cannot be created de novo. The focus of attention in creating many hyper-modernist designs is thus on the innovative forms that they present to the world. Being part of a geographic or cultural locality is a seldom-addressed issue. The goal is to establish a new brand image so that a city can attain a prestigious location in the pecking order of cities in an increasingly globalized and competitive world. Ideally, they are places that locals and tourists want to visit—for them to be destinations. They thus include places and objects that attract attention. They must photograph well.

Modernist, Neo-Modernist, and Hyper-Modernist Design

The claims of designers of many recent hyper-modernist urban designs that their designs are environmentally sustainable needs to be queried. They may have been built of materials with low embodied energy and designed to minimize energy consumption in their operation and maintenance, but the data are seldom presented to substantiate claims. They do not seem to be particularly sustainable in another way. Buildings and urban designs remain hard architecture. Changing them to meet new instrumental functions is expensive in time, energy consumption, and cost.

One of the prime functions of an architectural design is to establish a professional practice's secure place in the marketplace for services. One way an architectural firm achieves this end (and many international firms have clearly done so) is through their designs' having a recognizable geometric consistency. The geometry of an individual scheme must be a unique variant of the generic type or approach that the firm can apply to wherever the site is. In doing so, it attains a clear identity in the marketplace.

Observations

In democratic societies, urban designs are now led primarily by private property developers promoting their own interests rather than by municipal governments striving to meet what they perceive to be public interest ends. As noted, neoliberals argue that this approach is the only way of guaranteeing that public interest goals can indeed be met and that the marketplace is best equipped to identify what they are. The result is that a new urban morphology is emerging consisting of sets of individual clusters of buildings sited as inward-facing islands adjacent to each other.

In the immediate future, many urban designs in cities striving for recognition are likely to be more heroic and more radically different from those we are becoming habituated to seeing. Schemes are turning out to be more and more elaborate, and the sculptural qualities of the individual buildings that constitute them are having more and more deviations from the norm; in doing so, they create a new norm. Is the Rublyovo-Arkangelskoye smart city proposed for the outskirts of Moscow the new norm? An exaggerated image is sought by many international corporate clients and municipal authorities to place themselves at the forefront of contemporary thinking. Will the result be as shown in the Zaha Hadid Partners' design for Rublyovo-Arkangelskoye? Will these types of designs soon be seen as boring? If so, what next? Back to the simplicity of modernist designs? Those designs were, after all, a response to the visual richness and often-gaudy architecture of the Victorian era.

Twentieth-century rationalist modern architecture resulted, and in the twenty-first century continues to result, in some fine individual buildings, but the thought processes underpinning their designs seem to lead to disappointing urban design achievements if they are evaluated on a multifunctional scale. Has hyper-modernist urban design been any different? It is easy to dismiss it as a hallmark of neoliberal materialism and cynical attitudes toward the environmental and the social problems that face societies, but it is a carefully considered response to the basic human need to be held in high esteem. A disproportionate number of hyper-modernist urban designs schemes are found in the cities of Asia and Africa. European cities have a brand image, and most are thriving on the images of themselves that they have found to be successful in the past. Even there, however, having hyper-modernist designs is an attractive proposition.

Although the phenomenon should not be exaggerated, many people have become de-territorialized. Their behaviors and values are global in nature. Certainly, the large architectural practices operate globally. What is lost is indeed a sense of locality. Even the behavior settings in cities around the world are becoming similar, and this actuality is reflected in urban

Figure 12.14 The future hyper-modernist city? The proposal for the smart city Rublyovo-Arkangelskoye, near Moscow

Credit line: Rendering Flying-Architecture; courtesy of Flying-Architecture

designs. Luckily, for the foreseeable future, the people, or mix of people, that inhabit them are unique to each locality and give a sense of where a place is.

Key References

Fraker, Harrison. 2007. "Where Is the Urban Design Discourse?" *Places* 19 (3): 61.
Jameson, Fredric. 1991. *Postmodernism, or, the Logic of Late Capitalism*. Durham, NC: Duke University Press.
Jeffries, Michael P. 2014. "Hip-Hop Urbanism Old and New." *International Journal of Urban and Regional Research* 38 (2): 706–15.
Virilio, Paul. 2000. *From Modernism to Hyper-Modernism and Beyond*. Edited by John Armitage. London and Thousand Oaks: Sage.
Willis, William. 2017. "Playfulness on the Rise." *The Australian Financial Review* (December 22–26): 28–29.

13

Hyper-modernism, Parametricism, and Urban Design

Parametricism is a new global style for architecture and urbanism (Schumacher 2008). Architects and urbanists, it is argued, must adapt to the demands of the existing neoliberal sociopolitical environment and not the idiosyncratic needs of specific populations unless it is financially beneficial to do so. They must address the design variables of importance to the market economy. Parametric design as a method is one response, but it is not inherently aligned with any view of the sociopolitical economy of cities.

Parametric design refers to the manipulation of parameters, or variables, that are linked in a relationship by mathematical equations. Scripts are computer languages that can be edited by the user. They rely on correlations and differentiations as mechanisms to create/synthesize compositions based on the value assigned to each variable. The variables are much like those that Jane Jacobs identified as the generators of urban form: streets, blocks, and buildings (J. Jacobs 1961). In parametric design, the individual variables can be exogenously edited/manipulated and the consequential impact on an overall design/pattern immediately discerned. The ramifications of a change made on one variable on the whole design are thus understood (Jabi 2016). For instance, by changing the height of a building, the computer-based algorithms will calculate the impact on the system's other components (e.g., traffic flows or shadowing effects). Parametric design's efficacy depends on the variables included and the validity of the relationships accepted to exist among them. The questions are as follows: What are the variables of concern, and what approaches to problem-solving does parametric design draw on? And what is the basis for this line of thinking?

Antecedent Ideas

Although the application of land-use and transportation simulation models in city planning go back to the 1970s, the immediate antecedents of parametric design have a short history. Only since the 1990s have major graphic advances occurred in digital animation. Parametric design is an advance attributed to progress in LAB systems and more-powerful microchips. Several architects have been experimenting with algorithms that enable them to manipulate patterns of form. The idea of rapidly synthesizing urban and/or building patterns meeting different objectives is the essence of their efforts. They can simulate how built forms change because of altering the values in a set of parameters.

The major intellectual antecedent to parametric design is the concept of pattern. Used later by Tschumi in the Parc de la Villette, it was explicitly used earlier by Christopher Alexander and his colleagues in the 1960s and 1970s in their pattern language (Alexander, Ishikawa, and Silverstein 1977). Alexander's observation was that in a particular context, individual recurrent behavior settings (although he did not use the term) are the building blocks of a design (Alexander 1964). The relationships that exist among them are governed by rules. Parametric design manipulates only the patterns of physical form. The behaviors that they afford are assumed. Discursive grammars provide a method of describing physical settings and provide the specifications for defining how patterns are combined (Beirão, Nourian, and Mashhoodi 2014). The results come in a flow of surfaces across the site of concern in a manner much like in the membrane designs of Frei Otto (1925–2015).

Patrik Schumacher (b. 1961), managing director of Zaha Hadid Architects and a major proponent of parametric design, gives major credit for his ideas to Frei Otto. Otto argued that 'occupying' and 'connectivity' (in other words, 'places' and 'links') are the fundamental elements of any urban design. The two elements form the basis of parametric design. Otto's experiments with light-weight materials and tensile structures through form-finding models were important to Schumacher. Otto used physical models to explore his ideas. Changing one element in one of his models resulted in a ripple effect of changes throughout the whole structure. His design, with Günter Behnisch (1992–2010), for the Munich Olympic stadium (1972) is a direct ancestor of the parametric designs of today. Even earlier, Antonio Gaudi i Cornet (1852–1926) used physical models in working out the structural integrity of the shapes that he proposed for his buildings in Barcelona.

Gaudi, in his design for the Church of Colònia Güell and the Basilica I Temple Expiatori de la Sagrada Familia, used models consisting of weighted-down strings to formulate his geometrically unusual vaulted ceilings and arches. He could adjust the position of the weights and/or strings' lengths to change the shape of one arch to see the impact it had on the structure and form of the others. In parametric design today, computer-based algorithms do the calculations and show the results.

Parametricism has other antecedents. The research and the calculations of Ralph Lewis Knowles (b. 1928) into environmental conditions, building orientation, and solar envelope zoning prefigure

 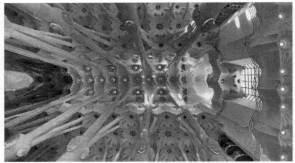

Figure 13.1 Antecedents of parametric design forms: The 1972 Olympic Games Stadium and allied facilities, Munich (left), and the ceiling of the Basilica i Temple Expiatori de la Sagrada Familia, Barcelona (right)

Credit line (left): Photograph by Tiia Monto
Source (left): Wikimedia Commons
Credit line (right): Photograph by dnaveh/Shutterstock.com

the parametric tools that architects use today (see Knowles 1999). He used equations whereby changing the shape of a building would predict the amount of sunlight it would receive on its façades and/or reach the street throughout the year at a specific latitude. The concept of solar envelopes has its own antecedents stretching back to the colonies of ancient Greece.

Manifestoes and Paradigms

Parametric urban design is promoted by architects desiring to be unfettered in creating exuberant urban forms with novel precinct configurations and building shapes. They seek pliant building envelopes and geometries that, within only minor constraints, may be shaped internally as desired by future occupants.

In a series of publications, Patrik Schumacher argues for the utility of parametricism as a technique for urban designing (Schumacher 2008, 2010, 2012, 2013, 2016). His own political position is clear: He seeks strong limitations on what authorities can prescribe and proscribe in total and all-of-a-piece urban designs. He argues for the abandonment of all land-use master plans, housing standards, social housing programs and projects in the belief that private enterprise can deal with the conflicts between the different aspirations of people better than government agencies. In addition, he believes that the public environment of streets, squares, and other open spaces in cities should be privatized (Frearson 2016). His views, while not independent of his advocacy for parametric design methods, should not reflect on the methods themselves. Schumacher argues that the application of parametric design approaches will produce outcomes that represent a new style to replace rationalist modernism as the way to deal with the twenty-first-century concerns of the marketplace. Advocates for parametric urban design claim that it deals effectively with the multivariate complexities of cities.

The objective in applying parametric processes to urban design is to create patterns that have no prescribed cubes, pyramids, or spheres and no other geometrical forms but rather are fluid in shape. A design that, as Schumacher notes, "interarticulates, morphs, decentralizes, deforms, iterates, uses spines, nurbs, generative components, scripts rather than models is what is needed" (Schumacher 2016). Parametric techniques, it is claimed, allow the order in complex urban patterns to be analyzed and the correlations between patterns that serve different purposes to be understood. The context of a development is largely irrelevant, a position that echoes Le Corbusier's, Hegemann's, and other architects' desires to create a universally applicable architectural and urban design type. It also reflects a lack of concern for the qualities of cities that enrich everyday life, although these matters can be dealt with once an overall design has been parametrically generated.

Generic Concepts and Illustrative Designs

Using traditional methods, a designer synthesizes a design by amalgamating a set of generic patterns into a whole, resolving conflicts among them along the way. In parametric design, a project evolves from the individual design patterns programmed into scripts that deal with the interrelationships among them. The software manipulates the characteristics of each site, within the overall design, as circumstances change, based on the values of the parameters entered by the designers and the interrelationships among them. The input variables include generic street types and patterns, building types, and generic public spaces. The qualities of the design depend on the quality of the individual patterns that are part of the of the modeling process.

The first step in creating a parametric design is to identify the variables of concern and the desired connections between them. Examples are gridiron or radial street patterns, neighborhood

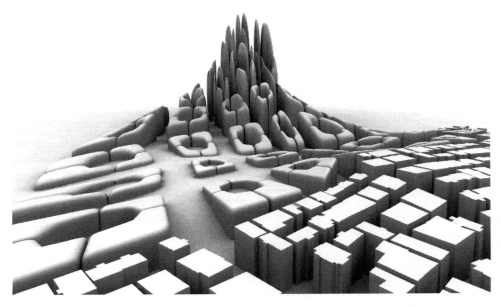

Figure 13.2 An illustrative design by Patrik Schumacher showing density gradients
Credit line: Courtesy of Zaha Hadid Architects

population sizes, standard walking distances, and so on. The second step is to define the key features, such as attraction points, that are to be manipulated. The relationship of one cell to the next is then defined. Using the basic elements of urban form, parametric urban design, instead of producing conceptual designs such as those described in the earlier and later chapters of this book, produces schemes of ordered complexity, with a smooth transition from one proposed development density level in one part of a design to another. In this way, parametric procedures generate profiles for districts such as that shown in Figure 13.2. Following neoliberal economic attitudes, minimalist massing and envelop requirements acting as design guidelines are allocated by the algorithms to each site within the proposed scheme. Reflecting Jane Jacobs's views and form-based zoning codes, they do not specify building uses. Market demands and what can be fit into a building configuration determine its use.

The intention is much the same as the generative planning and design process proposed by Christopher Alexander in his book *Notes on the Synthesis of Form* (Alexander 1964). Urban designers today have the computer-based algorithms that can synthesize a set of, sometimes-contradictory, patterns into a design, by using techniques that Alexander did not have at his disposal. A script generates different building forms. Designers have the attributes of each site available for them to manipulate as circumstances change. Conceptually, it is an ideal urban design tool.

Specific Designs

Most specific urban designs generated via parametric methods are hyper-modernist building projects. Some rely on computer-aided design (CAD) techniques rather than a full array of parametric methods. The Absolute Towers development in Mississauga, Ontario, Canada; 8150 Sunset Boulevard in Los Angeles, California, USA; and the Center for Fulfillment and

Hyper-modernism and Parametricism

Figure 13.3 Two designs using advanced computer-based algorithms: Absolute Towers, Mississauga (left), and the Union Station precinct proposal, Los Angeles (right)
Credit line (left): Courtesy of Sarbjit Bahga
Source (right): LA Metro (2014, 14); courtesy of Gruen Associates and Grimshaw Architects

Knowledge in Detroit, Michigan, USA, are examples. The first has been built, and the second is likely to be implemented, but the third is not. The design for Union Station precinct in Los Angeles (2014) is a bold urban design proposal. Groundlab's proposal for Longgang Center, Shenzhen, China, and the Thames Gateway master plan are others of an increasing number of proposals based on advanced CAD and/or parametric methods.

Several designs of Zaha Hadid Architects are being implemented under the direction of Patrik Schumacher. Two master-planned precincts of the firm's work are introduced here. Kartal Pendik in Istanbul is only now underway, and it is presented here as an exemplar of the application of parametric methods. The other that is largely implemented. One North District in Singapore, which is described in some detail here, has turned out to be a hybrid of approaches to urban design. It illustrates the types of departures from the computer-generated image of the plan that take place when it comes to implementing a scheme. Other similar schemes have been prepared by the firm for mixed-use districts for several cities, including Bilbao and Beijing. The hybrid schemes are more architectural in character.

Exemplars of Parametric Urban Design

Kartal Pendik, Istanbul, Turkey (2006–), and Longgang City Center, Shenzhen, China (2008)

Kartal Pendik is an exemplar of the use of parametric design in the creation of the profile for an urban precinct. Its design is a 2006 competition-winning mixed-use development prepared for the Istanbul municipal government. The site is an abandoned industrial estate on the Asian side of the Bosphorus. The development is to be a major civic subcenter located about 25 kilometers (15 miles) from the center of the European side of Istanbul. It will contain residential and commercial areas and cultural facilities such as museums and concert halls (Çalişkan 2017).

The master plan establishes a net-like framework, or armature, that ties into the infrastructure of its surroundings to form a soft grid under a single continuous and seamless surface of high- and

285

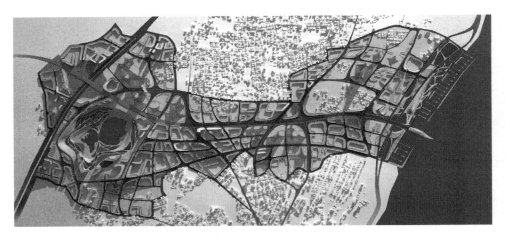

Figure 13.4 Kartal Pendik master plan
Credit line: Courtesy of Zahah Hadid Architects

low-density areas and open spaces (Arcspace 2012; Çalişkan 2017). In some places, the net rises to form tall buildings that are located, in a modernist manner, as objects in open space. In other places, the net lowers to form parks. A scripting language generates different types of building forms, some set in space and others in Berlin-like perimeter blocks. The algorithm generates easy transitions between various density areas, defined by the intensity of activities taking place in them and/or buildings per unit area. By manipulating the variables, changes can be made that alter the densities of areas. No doubt further changes will be made as the implementation of the plan gets underway. The same approach was used in preparing the Longgang city center proposal.

Longgang Centre in Shenzhen, a regeneration development for 350,000 people in the Pearl River Delta, was a competition-winning scheme produced in 2008 by Groundlab, a firm based in London, in collaboration with Arup ILG. The design goal was to integrate existing villages, landscapes, and built forms into a unified ecological corridor, with the river as an integral part of the design rather than being a backwater and sewer.

The intellectual basis for the design was Ian McHarg's method of superimposing layers of ecological factors, environmental benchmarks, and development targets on each other. These variables were combined with density and building types in a series of equations. The design resulted from a three-dimensional modeling process specifying a set of relationships. The modeling enabled "the generation of options with a relatively minor effort" and the development of a set of controls to ensure the design objectives are met (Groundlab 2008).

Hybrid Designs

One North District, Singapore (2001–16); the 8150 Sunset Boulevard Proposal, Los Angeles, California, USA (2015); and the Center for Fulfillment, Knowledge, and Innovation, Detroit, Michigan, USA (2016)

One North is a 200-hectare (500-acre) business park devised to be a global talent hub. It is part of Singapore's goal to rebrand itself as a city-state with an innovative knowledge-based economy. The district was developed to be a place where locals and expatriates work together in making significant advances in fields such as infocomm technology (ICT) and biomedical science and

Hyper-modernism and Parametricism

Figure 13.5 Longgang City Center, Shenzhen
Credit line: Collection of the author

the products that they generate. The brief specified a residential population of 138,000, and the accompanying educational, recreation, and research facilities required to make One North an attractive place to conduct research and to live. The Singapore government hoped that One North's avant-garde design would attract creative researchers.

The master plan by Zaha Hadid with Patrik Schumacher was for the district to have

> . . . an urban architecture that truly embraces the spatial repertoire and morphology of natural landscape formations—One North takes shape, creates its own skyline in Singapore applying for the very first time the concept of artificial landscape formation to an entire urban quarter.
>
> *(Zaha Hadid Architects 2017)*

The master plan is a three-dimensional diagram "mandating an ebb and flow in heights [of buildings] that does not run with, but offers a counterpoint to the natural landscape" (Betsky 2016). The undulating lines presented in the master plan reflect the outline of Singapore's hills. Observers may be subconsciously aware of the similarity, but they are more likely to take note of the park that runs through the center of the precinct and what it affords them for recreation or as an aesthetic experience.

To implement One North, the district was divided into subareas that are being developed by individual property developers, and their architects, according to their own plans. Each

In an Age of Corporate Financial Capital

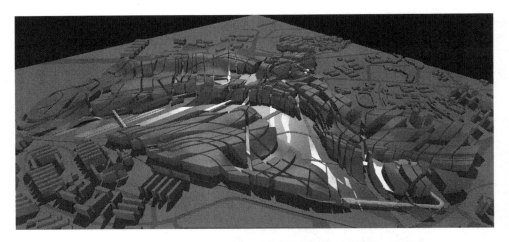

Figure 13.6 One North District, Singapore: The Zhah Hadid Architects' master plan (above) and the precinct as being built (below)

Credit line (above): Courtesy of Zaha Hadid Architects
Credit line (below): Courtesy of JTC Corporation, Singapore

subarea is an all-of-a-piece urban design with its own guidelines. The ICT and Nepal districts, for instance, were designed by Chris Moller Architecture + Urbanism. The guidelines the firm developed for the individual buildings within the district follow the pattern outlined in the master plan. Few of the constructed buildings, however, follow the intended profile. It is difficult to see a reflection of the master plan's goals in their designs. In practice, the building forms were constrained by numerous programmatic requirements and the capital available to build them. The implicit original intention that behavior settings be shoehorned into given buildings fell by the wayside. The character of the still-uncompleted project stems largely from its central park and from the adaptive reuse of colonial relics in the district as residences and clubs. They give a sense of historical continuity to the site (Betsky 2016).

One North today contains a few high-profile buildings. Some follow the principles and forms explicated in its master plan; some do not. The design intention for One North was clearly different to that for the Marina Bay development in Singapore. That hyper-modernist district, containing the Marina Bay Sands Hotel with its surfboard top, has created a distinct updated image for Singapore. It and One North, in common, are all-of-a-piece urban designs. One North District illustrates what can happen when a conceptual design based on a strong geometric idea gets implemented by several hands. The 8150 Sunset Boulevard scheme and the Center for Fulfillment, Knowledge, and Innovation design are, in contrast, total urban designs, the work of a single group.

The proposal of property developers, Townscape Partners, for 8150 Sunset Boulevard, a 2.50-acre (1-hectare) site at the eastern end of Sunset Strip in Los Angeles was prepared by Pritzker prize–winning architect Frank Gehry. Gehry, whose genre consists of sculpturally exciting architectural forms, has long explored the use of CAD tools to assist him in generating the sculptural forms for which his practice in known. In many ways, their use approximates parametric methods, but they allow the designer greater control over the design generated. The design approach is more akin to Gaudi's work than to that of Patrik Schumacher. It does, however, rely on computer-based form–generating algorithms for computations.

The five-building complex includes two residential towers, terraced gardens, an open-air plaza, and a shopping center. It was presented to the public as an 'iconic and powerful' design. The proposal was approved by the Los Angeles City Council in 2016 after its height and density were reduced. Although the project is an object to be admired, it, unlike many heroic and hyper-modernist designs, has a framed internal space (see J. Chandler 2016 for an image of the design). It also seeks to be energy–efficient, attaining a silver or even higher Leadership in Energy and Environmental Design (LEED) designation upon completion.

The property developers state that the scheme will be a socially responsible mixed-use composition of buildings and open space. The housing comprises 229 units, thirty–eight of which are to be rented at below market rates to low–income residents. The retail outlets at the base of the complex will spill onto the landscaped courts. It ends up being a conventional scheme with an eye-catching architectural geometry that differs from of its surroundings. The design for the Center for Fulfillment, Knowledge, and Innovation, by GREG LYNN FORM, is more dramatic.

Parametric technology, using Microsoft HoLoLens software, not only enabled the architects to see the overall design as a hologram set in its urban context but also allowed them to tweak aspects of the design and understand the consequences. The design was first presented to the public at the Venice Architectural Biennale in 2016 (WA Content 2016). Reusing the long-abandoned site of the Detroit Packard Plant for the manufacture of automobiles, the proposal is for a 2.7-kilometer-long (1.7-mile-long) 'logistic super-highway' linking twenty-five existing elevator shafts on the site to form a mixed-use industrial park. The complex, as proposed, contains large transportation tubes and elements/places in various soft sculptural forms. It also has plug-in elements that can, as per Archigram's ideas, be moved around the site as necessary.

The layout of the design seeks to maximize the ease of movement of people, products, and ideas, relying on the use of robotics in manufacturing and autonomous movement systems. It was proposed as "an interconnected network of products, people and ideas" (WA Content 2016). While this scheme is exploratory in nature, it is an indicator of what the new computer-based algorithms may offer urban designers. The design is also an artistic display of somewhat whimsical forms. The character of the final design, if implemented, will depend on the quality of the values used within the parameters of the composition.

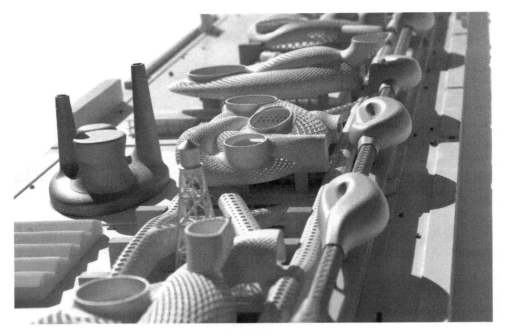

Figure 13.7 The Center for Fulfillment, Knowledge, and Innovation proposal
Credit line: Courtesy of Greg Lynn, GREG LYNN FORM

Commentary: The Functions Addressed

In both One North and the unimplemented schemes outlined earlier, it is difficult to understand the range of opportunities and problems being addressed and the full range of functions that the implied behavior settings are supposed to fulfill. In the all-of-a-piece urban design schemes, the desire is to constrain as little as possible how the individual components get carried out by competing individuals. The implemented scheme would reflect the homogeneity or diversity of ideas behind its components. All the designs clearly have an aesthetic function. The desire is to attain an eye-catching, innovative design that deviates from standard types. Other functions that might be included in the scheme depend on the parameters that are part of the form-generating algorithms. The multiplier and side effects of changing one variable of a design on the whole is a focus of attention, but a potential design's impact on its surroundings is not always considered.

Parametric designs designate primarily surface configurations across the cells of a scheme. The urban designer's detailed concern is to ensure that the links among the cells in the pattern of the district work efficiently and are pleasant places to be. Although it does not have to be so, within a neoliberal economic intellectual framework, the instrumental function of each cell, or site, is left to the discretion of a site's purchasers. In making decisions, they would ideally be able to maximize their own benefits unfettered by controls other than the building envelope. They and their architects would then decide on how the needs of a building's users/inhabitants are to be met. The concern for the quality of the public realm gets lost.

To cynics, the major function of the urban designs of parametricism is to meet the needs of architects and other designers for self-aggrandizement to obtain public recognition and additional, high-profile, financially rewarding commissions. The real questions are as follows: What should the functions be that the patterns of the built environment need to afford well? And do the present parametric algorithms consider the important functions such as the ability of individuals to personalize their environments? (Mattern 2017). Or, less demandingly, do the designs meet the fundamental needs of their various users and the public's interests? The designs described earlier say little about the qualities of the public realm of open spaces contained in them.

Neoliberal ideas in the property development world have led to an approach to architecture and urban design such as design-and-build and various cost-cutting measures, as exemplified by value engineering. Such measures whittle away at the range of building forms possible resulting in "cost-cutting vulgarization," according to one critic (Hatherley 2017). To create multifunctional designs, parametric algorithms need to deal with such concerns. The danger is that functions difficult to describe mathematically are ignored.

Observations

Patrik Schumacher's 2008 claim that parametricism is "crystalizing into a solid new hegemonic paradigm" for urban design supports the processes that result in the hyper-modernist schemes proliferating around the world. The contemporary new urbanist designs described later in the book deal with exactly the complexity that Schumacher says, but does not demonstrate, that parametric approaches do. Parametric designs replace land-use plans to form a new type of master plan. As presently advocated, they leave all the detailed decisions that result in high-quality multifunctional environments to the marketplace to decide. They are likely to be made on financially pragmatic grounds. In practice, parametric designs with neoliberal economic intentions have not been carried out in their extreme form, because the generic controls of urban governance over the property market remain in place.

The excitement generated by new tools of computational design, such as scripting and parametric modeling, may lead to their being applied simply because they are technologically progressive (see the essays in Poole and Shvartzberg 2016). Detailed human- and environment-based program/brief development as the precursor to designing specific schemes gets displaced. Parametric design shifts the role of the urban designer from one of creator to one of controller (Çalişkan 2017).

The variables considered in a design are those easy to include in parametric equations, not necessarily those that need to be. Landscape urbanists would challenge the key variables included in most present parametric designs, although in the Longgang design, ecological factors were very much included in the parameters manipulated by the algorithms used. The proponents of parametricism argue that dealing with key variables such as density, the height of buildings, and network geometries is what is important. The correlations between patterns of architectural forms that serve different purposes meet this requirement, and thus, parametricism, they state, is the paradigm best suited for urban design practice for the world today. As with modernism, the forms of its designs assume a that efficiency in movement is the major criterion that urban designers need to consider.

The concept underlying parametric design promises much. The idea of having a system where a designer can manipulate one variable and then immediately discern the impact that the change has on the whole system is attractive. Parametric design simply must deal with more variables than it presently does if it is to be more than a generalized aesthetic tool for creating exotic building and precinct shapes.

In an Age of Corporate Financial Capital

Key References

Çalışkan, Olgu. 2017. "Parametric Design in Urbanism: A Critical Reflection." *Planning Practice & Research* 32 (4): 417–43.

Mattern, Shannon. 2017. "A City Is Not a Computer." *Places* (February). https://doi.org/10.22269/170207 accessed February 24, 2017.

Poole, Matthew and Manuel Shvartzberg. 2016. *The Politics of Parametricism: Digital Technologies in Architecture*. London: Bloomsbury Academic.

Schumacher, Patrik, ed. 2016. *Parametricism 2.0: Rethinking Architecture for the 21st Century. Architectural Design*. Hoboken, NJ: John Wiley.

14

The Empiricist Responses

Geometrically innovative and eye-catching, hyper-modernist designs receive considerable publicity. Empiricist designs, although strongly promoted by their advocates, receive little such exposure in architectural journals, and empiricist lines of thought are seldom explored in schools of architecture (Solomon 2017). The designs do not have the novel appearances that architects and architectural students relish. Many clients seek such designs too and accept any inconveniences to be up-to-date. In the search for novelty, many quality-of-life and environmental concerns get lost. Do empiricist lines of thought serve the public and designers any better? On what observations do they draw?

Antecedent Ideas

The late-twentieth-century reflections on modernist urban designs by Colin Rowe and by Vincent Scully had an impact on new urbanist thinking by attempting to reconcile the traditional with the pragmatic and the formal (Solomon 2017; Steuteville 2018a). The antecedent ideas of empiricist design ideas today are primarily those developed in the nineteenth and early twentieth centuries. Suburban developments such as Riverside, Illinois; Forest Hills, New York; and the neighborhood unit of Clarence Perry still inspire. Letchworth and Welwyn, the first garden cities, the UK new towns of the postwar years, and many other such designs built around the world are a testament to the persistence of Howard's advocacies. Achieving his social goals has, however, proven to be elusive.

The current urban design principles proposed by the new urbanists/smart growth advocates learn directly from the design and social outcomes of the developments of the late twentieth century such as Seaside and Kentlands in the United States and Poundbury in the United Kingdom. Going back in history, the layout of Savannah, Georgia, directed by James Oglethorpe (1696–1785), founder of the colony of Georgia, is being re-examined. Its design was based on many of the principles now advocated by smart growth proponents in the United States. Its network of wards, each with a central civic square, has survived well despite the many social, economic, and political changes that have occurred since the city was laid out in 1773. Its design has proven to be resilient.

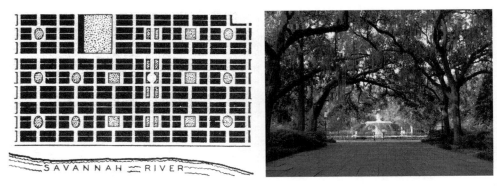

Figure 14.1 Savannah, Georgia: The Oglethorpe plan (left) and the center of one ward, Forsyth Square (right)

Credit line (left): Collection of the author
Credit line (right): Photograph by Sean Pavin/Shutterstock.com

Several specific urban designs of the late twentieth century also shape current thinking. Their patterns are something that can be emulated even though the claims for how well they work, on what dimensions, and for whom have not necessarily been verified. Hammarby Sjöstad (1990–2017) in Stockholm (see Chapter 15), with its concern for the quality of both the biogenic environment and the built form, is emerging as a model for current urban designs. It is based on considerable forward thinking about both new infrastructure technologies and environmental concerns. Much development continues to learn from pragmatic urban designs, like the Levittowns, that work well enough and that their residents enjoy.

Few researchers who are studying people and their use and appreciation of various patterns of the built environment believe that their findings have had a significant impact on design thinking. Scholars believe that their findings simply get in the habitual way that planners and architects think and what they want to design. This view is not entirely accurate. Studies such as that by Kevin Lynch (1960) on cognitive images of the urban environment and the more general observations and pattern language of Christopher Alexander and his colleagues (Alexander, Ishikawa, and Silverstein 1977) do shape design thinking. Similarly, many of the new urbanist design principles at the neighborhood level owe a debt to the research during the late twentieth century on the nature of communities. Nevertheless, unsubstantiated claims about the impact of the built environment on social behavior and community formation continue to be made by property developers and design professionals. It helps in marketing services and projects.

Manifestoes and Paradigms

The garden city, the neo-traditional new towns and suburbs, and smart growth principles continue to overlap with contemporary design paradigms. Advocates for garden cities continue to promote the principles that were cherished by early-twentieth-century urban design pioneers. They argue for the collective ownership of land, the long-term stewardship of the natural environment, and the capture for the benefit of society of the land value increases that new developments accrue. A manifesto prepared by Philip Ross, a former mayor of Letchworth, and Yves Cabannes of the University College London on what their underlying values should be reflects

The Empiricist Responses

many of the aspirations of Ebenezer Howard (Ross and Cabannes 2014). It says little about the qualities that a design should possess.

The neo-traditional urban designs being implemented around the world fly less boldly in the face of many neoliberal ideals than such a manifesto professes. While properties are individually owned, the form of buildings is heavily controlled—the opposite of what the practitioners of parametric design advocate. Design controls limit the changes that owners can make to the exteriors of their buildings. The marketing success of new urbanist design ideas is a surprise in countries such as the United States, where people take pride in their individual freedoms.

The neo-traditional position continues to be that if some aspects of urban form work well in application, continue to use those patterns as the basis for new designs (Talen 1999). In urban renewal projects, this means that the traditional block form and building–street relationship is preserved or reused. New urbanists extend this position to the architecture of buildings because of the way premodernist vernacular forms respond well enough to climatic conditions, without having to rely heavily on artificial mechanisms.

What is it that so many people find so attractive about new urbanist designs? Much is suggested in the design principles promoted by the Smart Growth Network formed in 1996. The network consists of property developers and other interest groups who address issues such as historical preservation, the provision of housing for low-income people, and the promotion of public health measures. The network advocates for a set of urban design strategies. It argues, in common with prominent architects such as Richard Rogers (b. 1933), for first building on redundant brownfield rather than greenfield sites.

Smart growth advocacies are a response to the perception that single-use precincts can be monotonous and require the excessive use of the automobile for the simplest of journeys. Their design principles represent an effort to abate the negative effects of urban sprawl, the concomitant consumption of agricultural land, the destruction of the habitats of wild animals, and the

---

THE NEW GARDEN CITY MANIFESTO FOR TWENTY-FIRST-CENTURY GARDEN CITIES

The fundamental propositions are as follows:

- Residents are citizens.
- The city owns itself.
- The garden city is energy-efficient and carbon-neutral.
- Access to land for living and working is available to all.
- Fair trade principles are practiced.
- Prosperity is shared.
- All citizens are equal; all citizens are different.
- Fair representation and direct democracy.
- Garden cities are produced through participatory planning and design methods.
- A city of rights builds and defends the right to the city.
- Knowledge is held in common, shared, and enhanced.
- Wealth and harmony are measured by happiness.

Figure 14.2 The new garden city movement principles

Credit line: Derived from Ross and Cabannes (2014) by the author

long commute by automobile to work for many people. The smart growth advocates also state that new buildings should be appropriate to their region in the way they respond to climate, material resource, and local building practices rather than copying currently fashionable building styles.

They argue that open spaces, parkland, and critical animal habitats should be preserved. A variety of transportation options—walking, bicycling, public transport, and the automobile—should be available for people to move comfortably around the city. The advocates seek less reliance on the use of cars in order, first, to reduce noxious emissions and, second, to promote public health by making it easy and interesting to walk to local destinations. To achieve these ends, urban and suburban precincts should have a mix of shops, offices, apartments, and homes that cater to people at different stages in their life cycles, socioeconomic statuses, and cultural backgrounds (Duany, Speck, and Lydon 2010). To enhance the well-being of the natural environment, the policy is to lessen the amount and rate of rainwater runoff by reducing the quantity of impervious surfaces. The intention is to improve the water quality in rivers and prevent the scouring of their banks. This lofty range of goals is more radically promoted by advocates for sustainable development, as discussed in the next chapter.

The position of various groups of empiricists is perhaps best summarized in the placemaking manifesto of the Boston Society of Architects (Lanzi, Tullis, and Schultz 2017). In it, the society states that new designs should enhance the quality of life of a place's inhabitants by creating a sense of place that gives a local community an identity. The aim is to counter the deterritorialization of people. The society argues for the collaboration and communication among individuals of different backgrounds, interests, and talents in making design decisions. It argues that designers must be aware of well-functioning traditions while embracing the opportunities provided by new communications technologies.

Neoliberal market mechanisms act against achieving many of these ends. Pragmatism often prevails. The manifestoes remain lofty statements of what should be achieved, but not on how ends should be met.

Generic Concepts and Illustrative Designs

Empiricists presented more-generic ideas than conceptual diagrams representing their views. The generic design patterns for new towns are largely the same as those of the twentieth century. A major difference is that the new settlement layouts now have a two-level hierarchy of centers, not three, as in Columbia in Maryland and the postwar new towns in Europe, or in cities such as Canberra in Australia and Bhubaneswar in India. The current new town designs have a single center surrounded by a set of districts/villages that reduce in density the farther out they are from the center.

The design directives of the *Smart Growth Manual* (Duany, Speck, and Lydon 2010) that operationalize the positions presented in the manifestoes are summarized in Figure 14.3. Given these directives, it is possible to develop a statement of a generic district design.

The generic district layout of a new town or suburb has a public open space at its center and a clear boundary—a node and an edge, in Kevin Lynch's terms (Lynch 1960). The central open space is a place for formal and communal activities, a link between destinations, a display, and a work of civic art. A tenet of New Urbanism and smart growth is that cities should be walkable. 'Walkable' has been defined as the distance between origins and destinations should be no more than 800 meters and ideally 400 meters, a ten-minute walk. This understanding implies that the generic design consists of a range of mixed uses in buildings of different types and

The Empiricist Responses

> ### GENERIC SMART GROWTH DESIGN PRINCIPLES
>
> Urban designs should have a mix of land uses. They should also do the following:
>
> - Take advantage of compact building design.
> - Create a range of housing opportunities and choices.
> - Create walkable neighborhoods.
> - Foster distinctive, attractive communities with a strong sense of place.
> - Preserve open space, farmland, natural beauty, and critical environmental areas.
> - Strengthen and direct development toward existing communities.
> - Provide a variety of transportation choices.
> - Make development decisions predictable, fair, and cost-effective.
> - Encourage community and stakeholder collaboration on development decisions.

Figure 14.3   A summary of smart growth design principles

Credit line: Derived from NewUrbanism.org (undated) by the author, with the acknowledgment of the Smart Growth Association

densities (NewUrbanism.org undated). In addition, the territorial habitats and corridors the of movement of wild animals are preserved, and open-space recreation facilities exist for people of all ages and capabilities. An interconnected hierarchy of street types, from boulevards to alleys, handles traffic flows at different densities and speeds. Not only the streets but also the pedestrian and bicycle networks are easy to use and safe to negotiate.

The territorial hierarchy of the spaces between buildings that function well in cities is that hinted at by Jane Jacobs (1961) and made explicit by Oscar Newman (1972). The hierarchy begins with private spaces over which people have the complete control. *Semi-private* spaces are those that are privately owned and that outsiders can enter only with permission. Often, they can be seen into but not entered. *Semi-public* spaces are those that are in public ownership but assumed to be under the control of people holding adjacent properties or those to which the public has right of entry but are privately owned. Genuine *public* spaces are those publicly owned and those that people have the full right to enter them. This right might be curtailed at specific times of day or season. In some countries, the distinctions may be subtler.

Some thoughts emerging in China have general applicability (see Figure 14.4). In response to the tedium of many pragmatic urban designs in the country, authorities there have produced a set of ten generic guidelines for the design and redesign of residential areas. Because they are general, they are open to considerable interpretation. One of the major features of the guidelines is that it opposes the development of gated communities. The utility of some of these principles can be challenged. In many American and European cities, for instance, the two-way streets that were transformed into one-way ones have now been converted back into the two-way movement of traffic in order to slow traffic and thus enhance neighborhood life.

The generic empiricist ideas for urban renewal projects in the heart of cities promoted by new urbanists continue to be based on the block layout of their host cities. They maintain the building–street relationship of those cities. In other words, they retain the 'texture' of existing places. The buildings themselves, however, can follow a variety of architectural paradigms. Many smart growth designs have occurred on the periphery of cities and favor automobile usage in their designs. These developments nevertheless stand in sharp contrast to the hyper-modernist designs being built in much of the world.

> ## GUIDELINES FOR NEW NEIGHBORHOODS
>
> Designs should do the following:
>
> - Reinforce the planning and construction of a refined urban block structure. Clearly distinguish areas of newly constructed urban blocks in a hierarchical manner, developing open, convenient, appropriately scaled urban blocks.
> - Establish an urban road layout comprising 'narrow roads and a dense network of streets' and construct an urban road system that combines expressways, arterial roads, collector and distributor roads, and local streets.
> - Expand the urban block structure in new residential neighborhoods. In principle, do not build enclosed residential neighborhoods.
> - Gradually open existing residential neighborhoods and work unit compounds. Transform internal streets into public ones, resolving street layout problems and promoting efficient land use.
> - Open up various types of 'dead-end roads,' forming a complete street network, improving overall road connectivity.
> - Scientifically and systematically install traffic safety and management facilities, enhancing roadway safety.
> - By 2020, increase the average road network density to 8 km/2 km^2 in urban built-up areas. Roads should constitute up to 15% of the land-use area.
> - Actively adopt one-way streets to organize traffic.
> - Construct bicycle lanes and pedestrian networks, to promote green mobility.
> - Appropriately allocate parking facilities, encourage public–private (social) partnerships, and relax market barriers, to gradually alleviate the parking problems.

Figure 14.4   Generic design guidelines for new urban designs in China

Credit line: Adapted from Kan, Forsyth, and Rowe (2017) by the author, with the permission of Taylor & Francis

Specific Designs

Empiricist projects range across all product types and are being built for a variety of reasons. The new towns being built along garden city lines are primarily speculative private sector developments. In the United Kingdom, "They are using the language of garden cities to build public confidence in [their] development," notes Kate Henderson, the chief executive officer of the Town and Country Planning Association. "But using 'garden cities' as a buzzword is not enough" (Booth 2016). Pragmatically based, the towns are nevertheless far removed from the modernist version.

An exploratory alternative design for Corviale, a visionary scheme outside Rome, is an example of a recent response to a modernist design. Corviale is an *Instituto Autonomo per le Case Popolari*–sponsored housing project built on the outskirts of the city during the 1970s, at time when Pruitt–Igoe in East St. Louis was being demolished. It is a neighborhood of 8,000 people with retail shops, schools, recreation facilities, and a church. The key element is a narrow eleven-story slab building almost a kilometer long that is a legacy of linear city and megastructure ideas. A long five-story residential block is placed diagonally to the slab (Carini et al. 1979). The complex has not had a happy history, because it has been haunted by narcotics trade, sex work, and other anti-social or criminal activities. Its dreary corridors may not cause stigmatized activities, but they afford them well.

The Empiricist Responses

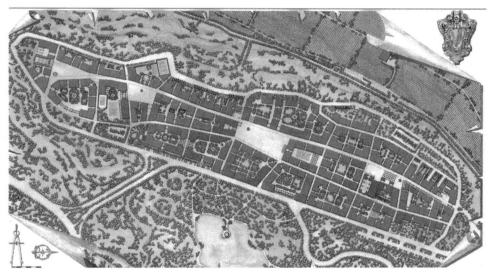

Figure 14.5 The Corviale proposal: The existing building (top left and right) and a new urbanist proposal by Ettore Maria Mazzola (bottom)
Credit line (above left): Courtesy of Neela Shukla
Credit line (above right): Courtesy of Neela Shukla
Credit line (below): Courtesy of Ettore Maria Mazzola

Whether a new urbanist response would help to alleviate its social problems is doubtful, but it would provide a richer environment and allow for the self-expression of its inhabitants in a manner that Corviale does not. Designs by Ettore Maria Mazzola (b. 1965), Gabriele Tagliaventi (b. 1960), and others demonstrated the variety of new urbanist designs possible for its site. The Mazzola design consists of three- to five-story buildings tightly knit together by pedestrian and vehicular connections and supported by a network of urban spaces that include a central square. The design draws on the typical Italian rowhouse patterns of houses built to the property line to form streets. As in traditional Italian towns, neither the streets nor the square are lined with trees. The number of trees planted in the other open spaces is a deviation from past traditions. The suggestion was to move some resident from Corviale into new buildings and then to repeat the process until the entire Corviale was replaced within its present site boundaries. The proponents of the scheme believe that the redevelopment of Corviale would pay for itself.

The original Corviale design and the new urbanist designs illustrate the clash of views on what is important in urban design. Several mass housing projects in Italy are regarded as exemplars of the failures of the rationalist school of urban design in the twentieth century and, simultaneously, as exemplars of innovative Italian architecture. Corviale is one of them (Salingaros 2010).

Exemplars of the Empiricist Responses

Celebration, Florida, USA (1990–2020); Rouse Hill Town Centre, Hills District, New South Wales, Australia (2000–07); and Legacy Town Center, Plano, Texas, USA (1998–2010)

Many new towns built in recent years are satellite developments around major metropolises, as Ebenezer Howard advocated for. They tend to house considerably more people than the number he considered ideal. Celebration is an exception. The town, while having garden city characteristics, is a new urbanist scheme. Its total population is planned to be close to the 32,000 that Howard suggested. The Disney Company decided to build Celebration to serve its theme and office parks near Orlando in Florida when it became clear that an exit would be built on the I-4 highway, giving easy access to a suitable site. The design being implemented is a collaborative effort of the firm of Robert A. M. Stern (b. 1939) and Jaquelyn Robertson (1933–2020) of Cooper, Robertson & Partners, with EDAW of San Francisco as the landscape architects. The group, with Raymond Gindroz, formulated *The Celebration Pattern Book* that contains the guidelines to which individual properties must adhere (Urban Design Associates 1997). The guidelines are based on the principles that had shaped the development of cities, such as Savannah and Charleston, in the southern United States, as well as the earlier new urbanist developments like Seaside and Kentlands. The *Charter of New Urbanism* was the guide.

Celebration's plan features a curved grid layout that considers the wetland nature of the site. The town center lies adjacent to a lake that forms part of the town's drainage system. It has the mixed-use characteristics of a US small town's main street. The buildings consist of apartments above shops, commercial offices, banks, a cinema adjacent to a late-night bar, and individually owned restaurants. Community facilities located in the center include a church, a school, and a branch of Stetson University. The residential area of Celebration is divided into several villages that are not further subdivided. Outside the center, the layout and housing are reminiscent of Riverside, Illinois. The gross density is about ten to fifteen people per acre (thirty to forty people per hectare).

The phasing of developments such as Celebration is often problematic. The town's center was built before there was a critical mass of residents in the town. Some of the first retail shops thus failed financially. In 2010, Celebration had about 7,400 residents, of whom 90% were non-Hispanic white people. Although both the Florida law and the goal of the new urbanists is to provide affordable housing for low-income people, the Disney Corporation made payments to Florida's housings agency in lieu of building such housing. The agency prefers this outcome because it can then build houses in clusters that it can easily administer.

The application of *The Pattern Book* has resulted in a unity of Celebration's design quality. Several foreground buildings were, however, designed by architectural luminaries. César Pelli

Figure 14.6 Celebration: An aerial view (above), a residential street (below left), and downtown (below right)
Credit line (above): Photograph by Felix Mizioznikov/Shutterstock.com
Source (below left): Lang (2017, 137); courtesy of Taylor & Francis

designed the Cinema, Charles Moore the Preview Center, Venturi and Scott Brown the Sun Trust Bank, Philip Johnson the Welcome Center, and Michael Graves the Post Office. Their works stand out from a background of neo-traditional designs in much the way envisaged by Léon Krier (see Figure 10.13).

Celebration received a New Community of the Year Award from the Urban Land Institute for its design. It has also been much criticized by those who feel that it lacks 'authenticity' (A. Ross 1999; Frantz and Collins 2000). As an environment to live in, it is much sought after, as the escalation in its property values testifies. Its success means that it is difficult for schoolteachers and service workers to find affordable accommodation there. Different precedents shaped Rouse Hill Town Centre, a new urbanist scheme, in suburban Sydney. The design of the eThekwini center in South Africa, described later in this chapter, is also a reminder that there are many traditions that shape human settlements.

The spatial character of Rouse Hill Town Centre is derived from traditional major Australian city centers. Its architecture is more suburban modern than neo-traditional. The Legacy Town

Center in Plano, Texas, is a comparable North American example. These two, overtly or not, follow several smart growth principles. The developments have the traditional CBD street-to-building patterns so that their designs are different from the standard suburban shopping mall.

Privately owned by its developer, Lendlease, the conceptual design/plan for Rouse Hill Town Centre was the work of Civitas Urban Design and Planning, Inc. Its components are the work of almost a hundred other designers. They followed a set of guidelines to ensure that a degree of design unity was achieved. The layout consists of four generic 'big-box' stores at its corners that are linked by pedestrian ways lined with shops, creating four sets of 'dumbbell' designs. These routes have kinks in them that provide a sequence of short vistas to pedestrians rather than the straight, wide, unimpeded pedestrian ways that are generally favored by shopping center developers. Adjustable fabric awnings line the paths and the west-facing shop windows. They add to the center's neo-traditional flavor (Harding 2008). Two cross streets, Main Street and Civic Way, divide the site into quadrants, each with its own character. Four- to six-story apartment buildings line the streets, enabling the open spaces to be naturally surveilled. Some parking spaces for cars are on the street, but the majority are in a single subterranean garage extending under the whole site. At the heart of the complex is a square with the Vinegar Hill Memorial Library opening onto it. The square, like many such places, has ground fountains in which children can play on a summer day (Lang 2017, 159–60).

The center has 220 retailers, 104 apartment units, ten restaurants, a cinema, a medical center, and a library. The housing has proven to be popular, especially with empty nesters. At the eastern end of the center is the Rouse Hill Station of the North West rail link to central Sydney. The passive solar design is used to control the interior temperature of the buildings. Energy costs are reputedly 40% lower than in comparable suburban developments. A similar claim is made for the Legacy Town Center in Plano.

Legacy Town Center is located on a potential transit link to the heart of Dallas. Like Rouse Hill, it lies on a major highway, the Dallas North Tollway. Designed on a 150-acre (61-hectare) site—by Duany Plater-Zyberk & Co., in collaboration with RTKL and Post Properties—the mixed-use center houses several corporate headquarters, commercial enterprises, lodgings, and housing. At its heart is a 3-acre (1.2-hectare) lake. The center employs 50,000 people (DPZ 2016).

Figure 14.7 A new urbanist suburban shopping center: The Town Square and the Vinegar Hill Library (left) and apartments over shops along Main Street (right) in Rouse Hill Town Centre

Source (left and right): Lang (2017, 160); courtesy of Taylor & Francis

The Empiricist Responses

Figure 14.8 A new urbanist city center: Legacy Town Center, Plano
Credit line: Courtesy of Gensler

The development also possesses a four-hundred-room convention hotel and 2,400 units of housing. A traditional and so-named Main Street has shops, restaurants, and entertainment facilities along it. The parking is located on the streets and in structures placed within the courtyard apartment perimeter blocks. Parking in this manner made possible a pleasant, walkable streetscape with broad, tree-lined sidewalks that provide opportunities for outdoor dining. A buffer of vegetation separates pedestrian and vehicular movements, as done so effectively in Singapore.

Hybrid Examples

Ebbsfleet, Kent, England, UK (2012–); HafenCity, Hamburg, Germany (2008–30); Val d'Europe, Marne-la-Vallée, France (2000–16); and eThekwini, KwaZulu-Natal, South Africa (2017)

Ebbsfleet is the most prominent of several new 'garden city' towns in the United Kingdom. It is being developed by a government-created authority, the Ebbsfleet Development Corporation, but is being built by several private property companies. Start-up costs are being subsidized to the tune of £300 million from public coffers. Individual property developers are demanding that the plan be adapted to what they want to build to meet their profit goals. Some building not in accordance with the plan has already taken place.

The houses, constructed of brick with traditional gable roofs, resemble UK council houses of the 1960s. Presumably, the property developers believe that the style meets the tastes of potential purchasers. The mixed-use character of the neighborhoods is a hallmark of neo-traditional designs that replicate, in an up-to-date manner, the complexities and liveliness of traditional cities. The spatial layout differs. It is closer to that of traditional suburbs (Price 2016).

HafenCity is an urban renewal project on an old port site that has had to deal pragmatically with potential flooding problems. In doing so, the traditional link between land and water of a

Figure 14.9 Ebbsfleet: An early, now largely abandoned, image of the future new town
Source: Ebbsfleet Valley Masterplan (2008)

port gets lost. The complex nevertheless retains the configuration of its life as a working harbor. It consists of ten mixed-use precincts located on the 220-hectare (540-acre) Grasbrook island on the Elbe River. It is one of the many ports around the world that were made redundant by the increase in size of container-carrying ships. The scheme is marketed as "a sustainable city for the twenty-first century" (Bullivant 2012). Its redevelopment follows the conservative surgery approach to urban design suggested by Patrick Geddes.

HafenCity was designed to be a fine place to work, live, and relax for its residents and workers and to be attractive to tourists. It will ultimately house 12,000 residents in refurbished and new buildings and provide commercial space for 40,000 workers. Located on a metro line, the precinct is home to educational institutions ranging from elementary schools to a university. At the time of writing, sixty-four individual projects had been completed and sixty-nine others were underway. Design guidelines ensure a diversity of settings while creating a unified sense of place. The pragmatic need to protect the site from flooding means that new roads must be 7.6 meters (25 feet) above normal high tide level, and existing buildings have to be waterproofed to this level. Except for some foreground buildings, the massing of the new buildings is that of the old warehouses on the wharfs. The unique building is a new concert hall sitting atop a prominently located old warehouse.

If HafenCity is neo-traditional drawing on north German traditions on a brownfield site, Val d'Europa is a predominantly neo-traditional greenfield development drawing on French architectural and urban design traditions of the nineteenth century. It has postmodern characteristics (see Figure 11.11), but it fundamentally owes a debt to the work of Baron Haussmann in Paris. The relationship of buildings to the street, their height, the window–solid wall ratio, roof treatment, and continuous ground-floor arcades are traditionally nineteenth-century French in form. Its adherence to traditions differentiates it from much of what is regarded as postmodern work. The project is also an example of the globalization of property development interests.

The developer was Value Retail, based in London, along with Euro Disney Associés, a private US company based in France. Not only are architects whose genre is modernist or hyper-modernist working internationally, but so are those whose work follows the neo-traditional paradigm. The difference is that the modernists and hyper-modernists take their generic design

The Empiricist Responses

Figure 14.10   An urban renewal scheme: HafenCity, Hamburg
Source: Lang (2017, cover); courtesy of HafenCity, Hamburg GMmb/Fotofrizz and Taylor & Francis

Figure 14.11   Val d'Europe, Marne-la-Vallée
Credit line: Collection of the author

types with them, whereas the neo-traditionalists consider local precedents. The architects were Cooper, Robertson & Partners of New York.

The center occupies 150 hectares (371 acres) in the heart of the new town of Marne-la-Vallée, which was created as a catalyst to encourage growth in the area and as a service town for Euro Disney. The town is expected to have a residential population of 40,000 people; another 60,000 will work there. The center was opened in 2006 and in 2018 had 160 shops, a food court (Les Terrasses), an aquarium, and 100,000 square meters of office space.

Many town centers are being developed at a totally different scale and in different socioeconomic and cultural settings. What they have in common with those just described is that they draw on local precedents. eThekwini, a hypothetical scheme in South Africa, is one. It also raises questions of how best to reconcile designing for a pleasant environment when people's expectations are shaped by images of a good modern world that they see presented in the mass media.

305

In an Age of Corporate Financial Capital

Figure 14.12 The proposed village center of Umbumbulu, eThekwini municipality, South Africa
Credit line: Courtesy of the School of Architecture and Interior Design, Andrews University
Source: Illustration by Pearl Choo/faculty advisors (Andrew von Maur and Troy Homenchuk)

The proposed center of the 30-hectare (80-acre) village is based loosely on the traditional Zulu kraal surrounded by huts. The design was developed by an architectural team from Andrews University in Michigan, USA, who organized a charrette involving architects, students from the university, local authorities, a nonprofit organization, and villagers. The center would be the heart of the community. Instead of being surrounded by traditional huts, it is loosely enclosed by modern communal facilities, vendor stalls, and seating (Steuteville 2017). Many locals see the design as condescending and not modern. While it may be behaviorally congruent, it is not mentally attuned with their aspirations, despite its design's emerging from a community charrette.

Commentary: The Functions Addressed

In economically advanced countries, at least, the way the layout of built environment serves as shelter and a healthy backdrop to life is accepted as a basic function that any new development must afford well. Heavy reliance is still put on artificial mechanisms to ensure that expected levels of comfort are met. Developments such as Rouse Hill Centre show that the knowledge is now at our disposal to create urban designs that are relatively frugal in their consumption of energy. The parking all being underground rather than in surrounding surface lots contributes to the quality of the development.

Smart growth advocates, like the modernists, want cities to be designed so that movement around them is easy. They seek development patterns that allow a city's inhabitants and visitors to have a variety of transportation options available to them. The goal is to decrease people's dependency on cars as the prime means of transportation, particularly at the local level. More attention is thus being given in empiricist designs to enhancing the experience of pedestrians. How best to do so and how to simultaneously provide a safe environment are still major issues in designing the streets and other open spaces of any design.

Crime and antisocial behaviors remain concerns in many cities around the world. Crime is a social problem, and the empirical reality is that the ability of patterns of built form to reduce negative behaviors is limited. Built forms can function to provide natural surveillance of the outdoor environment of cities as many urban designers understand, but it is seldom a stated goal of any of the advocacies presented in this chapter. Dealing with terrorist activities has created an industry for defensive devices. Bollards, in various forms, to prevent access by explosives-laden trucks are increasingly ubiquitous retrofitted elements of the public realm in urban areas, although that is not obvious from the projects discussed here.

Few of the architectural cognoscenti can countenance the aesthetics of New Urbanism. The buildings in new urbanist schemes can, however, be any style, provided that they are designed for local conditions. The 'regressive aesthetics,' using the term in the sense of looking backward and not pejoratively, of most new urbanist schemes nevertheless seems to function well in providing settings in which many people feel comfortable and that reinforce their images of who they are or who they aspire to be. The opportunities to individualize schemes by changing exterior appearances, even color, is, however, often proscribed so that the unified character of a development is maintained. The sustainability of new urbanist schemes has been challenged because of the controlled nature of their designs. Meeting changing circumstances becomes difficult without infringing on original intentions (Durack 2005). That happened at the Le Corbusier designed housing in Pessac.

Empiricist designs generally, but not universally, display some effort on the part of their designers to function well while respecting the processes of the natural environment. That desire, as explicated in the next chapter, is at least partly an aesthetic concern in order to increase the marketability of projects. The land values in schemes that meet middle-class tastes often makes the housing unaffordable to people working in social welfare agencies, education, and medical services. The desire of the garden city advocates of the beginning of the twentieth century to provide equitable housing has now been largely lost despite the hopes expressed in the manifesto of the New Garden City movement.

Observations

Christopher Alexander and his colleagues were careful to explain the design problems they considered important, the patterns of built form that they suggested to resolve them, and the context in which the patterns were observed to be valid. They provided the evidence supporting their argument, to the extent it was available in the 1970s (Alexander, Ishikawa, and Silverstein 1977). That is not always the case with new urbanist designs. As with any other set of generic design solutions, the patterns advocated by the various factions of empiricists can easily be adopted in contexts other than the geographical and socioeconomic context in which they were produced. The patterns are regarded as good per se. Images of garden cities published in the literature or available on the Internet are seductive but need to be adapted to the soil and climatic conditions and to the cultural context at hand. It is, however, often only the image that is replicated, not the substance of the generic design ideas. It is easier.

Neo-traditionalism implies that the patterns of built form applied in new urban design projects draw on the forming principles underlying the traditional architectural and urban patterns of their locale. Those patterns were shaped by the ways of life developed within the economic,

In an Age of Corporate Financial Capital

climatic, geographical, and resource context of a place at some point in its history. The danger is that it is the Anglo-Saxon model, rather than what works in the local context, that gets copied. This inappropriate copying has occurred in places as diverse as Venezuela and Indonesia. The Corviale proposal wisely draws on the Italian urban heritage. The work of Mohammad Hassan Forouzanfar takes a retrofuturistic approach to traditions in his work in Iran. He uses traditional forms in new guises (Stouhi 2019).

The Corviale proposal was never implemented, so the design was not tested as an environment for the lives of the project's inhabitants. What the scheme does illustrate, however, is the often-yawning discrepancy between the criteria used by avant-garde rationalist members of the architectural profession in evaluating schemes and those used by the people inhabiting them. For many architects, architectural critics, and the cognoscenti, the internal logic of the innovative 'architectural idea' behind a design specifies its quality. If the idea departs from the norm, it is regarded as 'creative'; its utility in making places for life is of lesser importance. The architectural idea, to the cognoscenti, needs to be compared only to other architectural ideas.

Neo-traditional concepts in the guise of the new urbanist urban design ideas have much merit, but the nostalgic architecture, although clearly appealing to many architects and members of the public, seems to stand in the way of the progressive thought needed to deal with a changing world. How do new urbanists deal with change? Will buildings become redundant and need to be changed?

Figure 14.13 Retrofuturism: The designs of Mohammad Hassan Forouzanfar in Iran
Credit line: Mohammed Hasan Forouzanfar

Key References

Duany, Andres, Jeff Speck, and Mike Lydon. 2010. *The Smart Growth Manual.* New York: McGraw-Hill.

Ross, Andrew. 1999. *The Celebration Chronicles: Life, Liberty and the Pursuit of Property Values in Disney's New Town.* New York: Ballantine Books.

Ross, Philip and Yves Cabannes. 2014. *21st Century Garden Cities of Tomorrow: A Manifesto.* Letchworth Garden City: The New Garden City Movement.

Talen, Emily. 1999. *Charter of the New Urbanism: Congress for the New Urbanism.* Second edition. New York: McGraw-Hill.

15

Sustainable Urbanism and Urban Design

Most twentieth-century urban design paradigms considered the world of animals other than humans, insects, and plants to be something to manipulate to enhance the health and aesthetic requirements of people. The concern with the health of the natural environment only began to seriously manifest in the 1960s as the fragility of Earth became increasingly obvious. It is, however, only since 2010, with the recognition of the impact of changes in the world's climates on the functioning of its natural ecology, that it came to the forefront of issues that urban designers must address (Calthorpe 2009; Cuthbert 2011). Extreme weather events have created havoc in widely disparate places. Continuing to build on sites prone to damage and rebuilding in the same place after their destruction by natural forces is a precarious choice.

The goal becomes one of designing for sustainability. A sustainable city is a resilient city. It is one in which the natural world functions well and future generations can enjoy a healthy, low-energy-consuming, self-replenishing environment in which all desired species should be able to survive in harmony.

Antecedent Ideas

Prescriptions for self-consciously designing with the climate and local ecosystems in mind have a long history. The Indian Vaastu Shastras and the Shilpa Shastras specify layouts for a variety of human settlements that are based, at least partially, on climate considerations. The same observation can be made of the sixteenth-century *Laws of the Indies* issued by the Spanish crown to decree the layout of settlements in its colonies. The design principles bore both social and climatic conditions in mind.

More importantly, the way vernacular settlements respond to climatic conditions by using limited local material resources has been illuminating, although there are many examples of cultural needs overriding climatic considerations (Rapoport 1969). Shibam in Yemen could easily be the model for the designs of Masdar and Ras Al Khaimah Eco-City.

The intellectual basis for current manifestoes' arguing for designing sustainable cities can be traced back directly to the work of Patrick Geddes (1915), the warnings of Rachel Carson (1965), the advocacies of Ian McHarg (1969), and such developments as Davis in California.

310

Sustainable Urbanism and Urban Design

Figure 15.1 The vernacular built environment: Shibam Hadramawt, Yemen—a hot, arid climate settlement
Credit line: Photograph by Javarman/Shutterstock.com

More-radical architectural ideas, such as Yona Friedman's 1956 Ville Spatiale, a layered megastructure that could be placed over existing farmlands, have been less influential, but their thesis may be resurrected in the future to meet the demands of ever-increasing populations. A manifesto on designing sustainable environments, *A Declaration of Concern*, was presented in 1966 by Campbell Miller, Grady Clay, Ian McHarg, Charles Hammond, George Patton, and John Simonds.

> A sense of crisis has brought us together. What is merely offensive or disturbing today threatens life itself tomorrow. We are concerned over misuse of the environment and development which has lost all contact with the basic processes of nature.
>
> . . .
>
> There is no one-shot cure, nor single purpose panacea, but the need for collaborative solutions. A key to solving the environmental crisis comes from the field of landscape architecture, a profession dealing with the interdependence of environmental processes.
>
> *(C. Miller et al. 1966)*

The concept of a sustainable city was picked up and promoted in the 1970s by the Club of Rome, a group concerned about the future of humanity.

Charles Waldheim, a leading advocate for a landscape urbanism, sees current thought more directly related to three conjectural urban design proposals (Waldheim 2010). They are Frank Lloyd Wright's Broadacre City (1934–35; see Figure 7.7), which influenced Ludwig Hilberseimer's "New Regional Pattern" (1945–49; see Figure 8.11b), which in turn influenced Agronica (1993–94) and later "Territory for the New Economy" (1999), both proposed by Andrea Branzi (b. 1938) (Branzi et al. 1995). The three have in common the belief that the city should be dissolved into an exurban world. The consequences in terms of population numbers and human lives and aspirations have yet to be fully considered.

A city exemplifying twentieth-century thinking is Curitiba in Brazil. During the 1960s, when cities elsewhere were building ring roads and superhighways, architect-planner Jaime

Figure 15.2 Agronica—an antecedent of present Agrarian Urbanism
Credit line: Courtesy of Andrea Branzi

Lerner (b. 1937) suggested that a balanced approach to enhancing people's movement around the city would alleviate many environmental problems. A fine, fast, reliable public transportation system, he believed, encourages people to reduce the number of journeys they make in cars. Curitiba also promoted many social goals, such as providing a high level of education and addressing problems of youth unemployment (del Rio 1992; Hawken, Lovins, and Lovins 1999). Such endeavors led to a series of statements on sustainable design, each of which has its own core concerns.

Manifestoes and Paradigms

The argument made in all the statements on designing 'with nature in mind' is that at all scales, an ecologically based urban design is required in an increasingly urbanizing world (Koh 2013a). Three streams of thought lead the way. The first focuses on reducing the energy consumed by Earth's inhabitants as part of their everyday lives. The second is a bolder approach. Its proponents insist that the well-functioning of the natural world must be the first consideration in the creation of any urban design proposal. They advocate for greening the open spaces of the city in temperate climates and/or radically restructuring urban areas, on the basis of the need to provide for urban agriculture. The third concern, picking up on twentieth-century advocacies, is simply for designing with the climate in mind. It is inevitably an integral part of the first two approaches. Many recent statements on what is meant by a 'sustainable city' and 'sustainable urban designs' draw on these three approaches. Implicit in them all is that the biodiversity of Earth must be enhanced to avoid the potential extinction of many of the planet's species, including humans.

The means proposed to reduce energy consumption are harnessing renewable sources: solar and wind power and, in specific circumstances, water power. Proponents argue for environmentally friendly buildings with low levels of embodied energy and meager energy consumption in operation. They demand better public transportation systems and bicycle lanes to reduce the public's reliance on private cars for transport and in doing so the reliance on fossil fuels. They seek an integrated and generous set of public parks and green corridors to reduce heat-island effects and to allow for the movement of wildlife. Comprehensive recycling and composting systems are also something deemed important (Farr 2008; Charlesworth and Adams 2011).

A manifesto that took Ian McHarg's 1969 advocacy for designing with nature a step forward was presented by Michael Hough in *Cities and Natural Processes; A Basis for Sustainability* (2004). Hough argued that the whole idea of a duality between people and nature should disappear; the two are parts of the same co-adaptational system. Hough advocated for linking neighborhoods with greenways, providing habitat areas, and making urban farming part of an urban way of life. Others have been making similar arguments at a metropolitan scale (e.g., Tjallingii 1996; Thompson and Steiner 1997; Steiner, Thompson, and Carbonell 2016) and for urban design (Barnett and Beasley 2015; Waldheim 2016). From such positions, the advocacies of landscape urbanism emerged.

Several tenets form the basis of the arguments of landscape urbanists (Corner 2003; Shane 2003; Waldheim 2006; Lehmann 2010; Thompson 2012; Koh 2013b; Gintoff 2016). The most general, echoing Hough, is that country and city are part of the same ecosystem. A second tenet is simply that the patterns of the natural world should replace the generic view that the open spaces network of streets, squares, and parks form the armature of a design. A third might be that a green urban infrastructure is necessary to deal with climate change (Gill et al. 2007). The last generalization needs to be tempered. It applies only to specific climatic zones. The arid world falls outside them. Some regions would be better 'browned.'

The landscape is seen as "machinic": The functioning of its components need to be considered together, not as separate parts (Mostavi and Naijie 2003; Murphy 2005). Landscape urbanists focus on how things work, not how they look. They reject New Urbanism's basic position that walkability is the basis for creating sustainable cities. They dismiss the square surrounded by buildings and the *rue corridor* of streets lined by buildings as ideal urban types. The sprawl of cities per se does not worry them (Mehaffy 2010). They say little about people's social lives and social issues.

Agrarian urbanists support the type of city in which the inhabitants are involved in growing food. Agrarian urbanism differs from both urban agriculture (cities that are retrofitted to grow food as spaces become or are made available) and agricultural urbanism (where an intentional community, such as an Israeli kibbutz, is built in association with a farm and farmland) (de la Salle and Holland 2010). An agrarian urbanist city is one laid out with the purposeful growing of food in mind. It is not simply leftover or abandoned land that is allocated to agricultural pursuits. Broadacre City was clearly one precedent for this line of thought. Incorporating the production of food sources into an urban master plan, agrarian urbanists argue, will result in economic and environmental efficiencies. Many costs will be reduced, even eliminated, including those associated with waste disposal, the use of artificial fertilizers, and the amount of transportation involved in bringing products to market (Duany, Speck, and Lydon 2010).

All these advocacies must be considered with specific climates in mind. Despite the apparent lack of professional attention to creating climate-appropriate urban designs, much research has been completed on the subject (as noted in Chapter 10) and is being brought up-to-date (Eliasson 2000; Oke et al. 2017). More recently, dealing with climate change has become a key concern of the twenty-first century.

Overwhelming scientific evidence suggests that global temperatures and consequently sea levels are rising as glaciers recede and polar ice caps melt. Concomitantly, the frequency and severity of extreme weather events with their damaging winds and storm surges are increasing. Advocates for dealing with climate change argue for, first, mitigating the effects of human activities on emitting greenhouse gases and, second, adapting cities to deal with changing circumstances (Hamin and Gurran 2008; Cuthbert 2011).

Mitigation involves switching to low-carbon forms of energy generation. In temperate and tropical climates, urban forests need to be planted to reduce heat-island effects. Flood water management requires replacing channeling and piping with natural infiltration mechanisms and the use of bioswales. Levees can channel flood waters away from built-up areas. Land-use policies can be implemented to prohibit building on flood-prone areas and places likely to be affected by the rise in sea levels, ferocious winds, storm surges, and tidal effects. Retrofitting cities is no easy task.

Advocates for planning and designing sustainable cities reject the idea of end-state comprehensive plans and think instead of initial strategic acts that create diverse opportunities for subsequent decisions (Durack 2005). The task of urban design is thus to create potentials, or affordances, for new patterns of behavior and to retain those that society considers beneficial. This position allows for designing for spontaneous situations and for genuine citizen participation in the design of the built environment that affects them. Advocates also argue for an open-ended planning review process. These views apply particularly to the public policy aspects of precinct and new town design rather than to smaller-scale total and all-of-a-piece urban designs. The idea of an open-ended, stage-by-stage urban design process nevertheless presents a challenge to all designers.

Generic Concepts and Illustrative Designs

Few of the ideas presented in the manifestoes have been translated into generic solutions that illustrate what their authors have in mind. They remain verbal prescriptions. For agrarian urbanism, Andres Duany and his colleagues, however, argue that at each level of development portrayed in the transect model (Figure 10.6) there are appropriate levels of food production, as shown in Figure 15.3. Every dwelling is expected to contribute to the production of food, "either by labor or by wages"; instead of standard gardens, the land would be dedicated to agriculture through subsidies organized by an owner's association (Duany et al. 2012).

The research on designing with the climate in mind has yielded a series of generic ideas and illustrative designs. Baruch Givoni argues that in warm and hot climates, streets should be oriented to cooling breezes; they should be designed to provide shelter in cold climes. In Mediterranean and hot, arid climates, courtyards help create venturi effects, pulling air through buildings and in doing so providing them with natural ventilation. The use of water in channels and fountains has a cooling effect in hot, arid areas but increases sultriness in the humid zones of the world (Givoni 1998). Cities in Australia have already begun to experience unprecedented fluctuations in humidity levels.

Figure 15.3 Illustrative images of agrarian urbanism in a suburban zone (left) and a rural zone (right)

Source (left and right): de la Salle and Holland (2010), courtesy of DPZCoDesign

Sustainable Urbanism and Urban Design

In the subarctic, the icy world needs to be embraced, not shunned. High-density urban designs are needed to reduce space-heating requirements. Mixed land uses reduce the need for commuting; complementary functions should thus be located close together. Special attention should be paid to how topographic features shape wind conditions and access to sunlight. Wider streets should be located perpendicular to prevailing winds with continuous lines of buildings along them to reduce wind speeds. Some shopping streets can be enclosed with glazing to enhance human comfort levels (Pressman 1988, 2004).

Increasingly, studies provide updated examples of designs that are climatically appropriate (e.g., Oke and his colleagues 2017). Climatic-appropriate designs often differ considerably from standard, pragmatic ones. Implementing such proposals must, it is argued, consider cultural sensitivities. Despite all such prescriptions, vested interests in maintaining, or increasing, land values and other economic contingencies often override the need to design with climate in mind. Short-term necessities displace concerns for enriching the quality of life of a city's inhabitants and long-term savings. But dealing with climate change in particular is a long-term proposition.

While only bits and pieces of the prescriptions in the manifestoes have been put into practice, several specific designs, described later as exemplars of what has been achieved, have become generic types that other urban designers seek to emulate. Hammarby Sjöstad has already set a precedent for designs in cold temperate climates. Norman Foster regards Masdar as a generic solution not only in setting a precedent for urban design in the hot, arid zones of the world but also as a way of thinking about sustainable urban designs.

Specific Designs

A brief review of several schemes designed with one or other measure of sustainability in mind, before looking at exemplars of sustainable designs, provides a basic understanding of what is being sought today. The review begins with a look at general efforts to create sustainable designs and then considers the advocacies of landscape urbanists. While Hammarby Sjöstad may be the exemplar of current thought, the Quartier Vauban in Freiburg im Breisgau, Germany, is a recently implemented experimental urban design whose sustainable credentials are held in high esteem.

Completed in 2014, Quartier Vauban was built on a 40-hectare (100-acre) site that was previously the barracks of Forçes Françaises en Allemagne. The Freiburg city administration had both social and environmental objectives in mind when it developed the site. The social objective was to have a fully-fledged heterogenous community, and the environmental one was for it to be energy-efficient. Different accommodations and services sought to fulfill the first goal. To meet the second, buildings were fitted with solar panels and insulated walls and roofs. The quartier also has a local heating and power plant run on wood, a renewable fuel source. Trench troughs handle rainwater, and a biotope area along a stream bed and substantial green areas help breezes to flow through the neighborhood. In 2010, it had a young and well-educated population of about 5,500 people living in 2,472 households (Lang 2017, 194–76). Quartier Vauban lies in a moderate continental climate zone; the 2017 proposal for Alai in the Latin America tropics has the same objectives in a different world.

Alai is planned for the Mexican Rivera, a commercial and tourist region in Quintana Roo on Mexico's Caribbean coast. The heavily forested site is part of a fragile ecosystem; any intrusion can easily have negative side effects. This scheme for a residential area near Cancun has been designed by Zaha Hadid Architects not only to mitigate damage but also to remedy the effects of present incursions. The buildings occupy only 7% of the site, thus allowing for the retention of existing vegetation and reserving for reforestation the area cleared by the site's previous owner. The buildings and their connecting pedestrian system are elevated on piles so that

315

Figure 15.4 An energy-efficient design: Quartier Vauban, Freiburg im Breisgau
Credit line: Freiburg Wirtschaft Touristik und GMHb & CoKG

Figure 15.5 A new ecodevelopment: Alai on the Mexican Riviera
Credit line: Courtesy of Zaha Hadid Architects

pedestrians will not walk on the ground and so that wildlife can wander unimpeded through the development. The platforms are perforated to allow sunlight to stream through them. The coastal wetlands will be replanted to increase the site's biodiversity, and the existing mangrove swamps will be protected. The architecture is said to reflect local traditions, but it still bears the hallmark of the architectural firm's avant-garde designs.

Promenade Plantée (or Coulée Verte René-Dumont; 1980–93 and 1999–2015), a 4.7-kilometer (2.9-mile) linear park in Paris, is a partially elevated structure that illustrates the landscape urbanists' ambitions. Once the Vincennes railway viaduct, Promenade Plantée was designed by landscape architect Jacques Vergely (b. 1941) and architect Philippe Mathieux. The park is planted with cherry trees and maple trees and possesses rose trellises, bamboo corridors, and much lavender. Accessible by staircases, much of it is three stories above ground level. In its northwestern section is the Viaduc des Arts, consisting of art galleries and workshops in the arches of the viaduct. Promenade Plantée serves its surrounding neighborhoods well, but it is barely known to Parisians; it is not a tourist destination (Lang 2017).

The project foretold similar developments. Minneapolis has its Midtown Greenway, primarily a bicycle route. In Chicago, the almost 3-mile (5-kilometer) Bloomingdale Trail runs through several city neighborhoods. High Line Park in New York (as described later in this chapter) is the project that has captured the most attention. The 500-meter-long (about 550-yard-long) Goods Line in Sydney opened in 2015, and the proposed 24-kilometer-long Kertepi Tanah Melayu Railway project in Singapore is in the planning stage. The Huangpu East Bank Urban Forest in Shanghai is another type of landscape urbanist design.

The 2017 proposal forms part of the effort to create a more sustainable city by reducing energy consumption and improving air quality (Li 2008). The woodland, stretching for 21 kilometers (13 miles) on what was declining industrial land, exemplifies the advocacies of landscape urbanists. It will increase the parkland area of Shanghai by 25%. A promenade, studded with follies to aid wayfinding, will pass in and out of the trees along the riverfront, providing views of Shanghai across the river. An allied goal is to enhance the image of the rather dreary environment of modernist and hyper-modernist Pudong.

These projects show the range of efforts to deal with some aspects of sustainability. The data on how well they function or are predicted to function are, however, limited. The exemplars nevertheless set the standard for others to follow.

Figure 15.6 A landscape urbanism scheme: Promenade Plantée, Paris
Source (left and right): Lang (2017, 79); courtesy of Taylor & Francis

In an Age of Corporate Financial Capital

Figure 15.7   The Huangpu East Bank Urban Forest, Shanghai
Credit line: Courtesy of HASSELL

Exemplars of Sustainable Urban Design

Hammarby Sjöstad, Stockholm, Sweden (1990–2017); Alternative 20, Los Angeles River Restoration, California, USA (2014–); Masdar, Abu Dhabi, UAE (2007); Eco-City, Ras Al Khaimah, UAE (2007); Forest City, Cancun, Mexico, Proposal (2019); Downsview Park, Toronto, Ontario, Canada (2000–); and the Disaster Mitigation Proposal for New York City, New York, USA (2012–)

Hammarby Sjöstad is described as a neighborhood for 'ecofriendly living.' Los Angeles River Restoration exemplifies the aspiration of the landscape urbanists. Masdar and Ras Al Khaimah in the Emirates were designed to be climatically appropriate, carbon-neutral, sustainable cities. The development strategy created for Downsview Park is regarded by some urban designers as the procedural model for future urban design. New York City's response to climate change and more immediately to the 2012 Hurricane Sandy is being closely watched by officials in other low-lying cities.

Hammarby Sjöstad is a 200-hectare (494-acre) urban regeneration project built on an abandoned industrial harbor site (Foletta 2011; Iverot and Brandt 2011; Lang 2017). It was designed under the direction of Stockholm's city planner, Jan Inghe-Hagström (1944–2005), to be an environmentally friendly precinct. While the density of the precinct creates a sense of urbanity, linear green fingers leading into the site provide a habitat for wildlife. Each residential building has a green area/square of 25 to 35 square meters (270 to 376 square feet) within 300 meters (330 yards) of it.

Several easy-to-operate, closed-loop infrastructure networks provide the armature of the scheme. A vacuum waste suction system delivers burnable and compostable household wastes to central points for collection. The waste is transported to substations and used to generate heat and cogenerate electricity. Storm water harvesting and filtering mechanisms are part of the infrastructure. The buildings have solar panels and cells that generate 50% of the electricity consumed by the precinct during the summer. An educational center, Glashus Ett (Glasshouse

Sustainable Urbanism and Urban Design

One), provides newcomers with information on how to use these devices. Few efforts to create sustainable environments are as comprehensive. Landscape urbanists would have argued for the site to have been turned back into a forest. They also advocate for turning derelict storm water channels, rail lines, and elevated highways into parks.

While the restoration of the Los Angeles River has long been discussed, master plans date only from 2007. A proposal by Frank Gehry for 36,000 housing units in the river's surroundings was fought by those forces seeking the river's rehabilitation. Alternative 20 prepared by the Army Corps of Engineers proposes to restore riparian and freshwater marshlands and to create new ones while maintaining the river channel as a flood-mitigating device. The project was optimistically budgeted for US$1 billion to restore 11 miles (about 18 kilometers) of the river, to acquire properties adjacent to its channel, to prepare for the restoration of a historic ecosystem, to connect habitats for wildlife, and to link up with the ecological zones of the surrounding mountains. The overall goal is to improve the biodiversity of the region.

Figure 15.8 Hammarby Sjöstad, Stockholm
Credit line: Swedish Armed Services photograph by Johan Frederiksen
Source: Wikimedia Commons

Figure 15.9 Alternative 20 for the regeneration of the Los Angeles River: Images of the existing (left) and the proposed remediation (right)
Credit line (left): Courtesy of Victoria Di Palma
Source (right): US Army Corps of Engineers (2007)

In an Age of Corporate Financial Capital

In these projects, the focus was not on creating climate-appropriate designs per se but rather on the functioning of the natural environment. Masdar, the work of Norman Foster Associates, and the Ras Al Khaimah Eco-City, designed by Rem Koolhaas of the Office for Metropolitan Architecture, are two projects designed in 2007 to be energy-efficient in an arid climate where greenery, while much desired aesthetically and also a symbol of wealth, can impede progress in achieving a settlement that is ecologically sound. The two designs have much in common. They follow, consciously or not, the design principles laid out by Baruch Givoni in *Climate Considerations in Building and Urban Design* (1998).

Masdar is to be a substantial settlement on a 600-hectare (15,000-acre) site. The master plan was designed to be flexible, with the initial buildings and urban elements leaving open a variety of options for the future. It is thus more a strategic proposal than are most urban design master plans. The design is for a low-rise, high-density city designed to be carbon-neutral and to generate no waste beyond its borders. It consists of several precincts that are linked by linear parks. Its plan was designed to encourage walking so that no point is more than 200 meters (220 yards) on foot from a transit link. (This distance is half that regarded as walking distance in temperate climates.) That closeness, combined with shaded pedestrian ways, was designed to make walking comfortable. On the periphery of the town are to be solar and wind farms. Learning from Yemen, irrigated agriculture holdings lie outside the development. Implementing the scheme has proven to be difficult, and many sustainability goals are being heavily compromised. Market forces and the aspirations of architects designing individual buildings may prevent Masdar or Ras

Figure 15.10 An urban design for a hot, arid region: Masdar
Credit line: Courtesy of Norman Foster Associates

Sustainable Urbanism and Urban Design

Al-Khaimeh from turning out to be carbon-neutral. Much remains to be built and inhabited (Goldenberg 2016).

Ras Al Khaimah Eco-City, like Masdar, is intended to be a sustainable community powered by solar energy generators. Being built on a 120-hectare (about 300-acre) site, it follows traditional patterns of vernacular arid climate settlements. The streets are narrow and the buildings sited to provide as much shade over streets and open spaces as possible. Like Masdar, Ras el-Khaimah is both a specific design and an exemplar of a way of thinking about all designs today. It is not easy to apply the principles shaping these two designs to existing cities except in a piecemeal manner as urban design opportunities arise.

In a completely different climatic zone, a recent proposal may be an exemplar of landscape urbanism's idea of a new town. Designed for Grupo Karim, Forest City in Cancun, Mexico, is proposed, like Alai, to be appropriate for its tropical climate. It is also presented as an exemplar of a smart city that will attract companies that innovate technologies and those committed to creating a sustainable world. The proposal is for the city to house 150,000 people on a 557-hectare (1,376-acre) site, of which 400 hectares (almost 1,000 acres) is open green space. The urban designer is the Milan-based company of Stefano Boeri (b. 1956), with agronomist and designer Laura Gatti as the landscape architect. Both are well known for their forested buildings. Their aim is to have a development that absorbs 116,00 tons of carbon dioxide and stores 5,000 tons each year.

The city is designed to be self-sustaining in the production of food and energy. It is also planned to be innovative in its use of water. Water is to be stored and, if necessary, desalinated, on the periphery of the scheme and distributed via navigable waterways throughout the settlement and the adjacent agricultural areas. The layout is designed to be resilient to flooding. Like Port Grimaud, most of the automobile parking will lie outside the city; a semi-autonomous mobility system is envisaged to take people to their destinations. Like the Masdar and Ras el-Khaimah developments, its final form will no doubt be battered by exigencies of the neoliberal marketplace and the whims of the architects designing individual buildings. Dealing with the impacts of climate change faces similar problems.

A variety of efforts have been implemented. In Venice, flood barriers of the MOSE project at the Lido, Malamocco, and Chioggia and, in London, the Thames Barrier protect the two cities from flooding from extra-high tides and storm surges. Tokyo has built super levees to protect low-lying lands, and in the Netherlands, new building sites have been created well above flood levels, as in Rotterdam's new outer harbor developments. To retain water and disperse it slowly as in a sponge, wetlands have been created on the edge of residential developments in Hong Kong.

The impact of Hurricane Sandy on the Eastern Seaboard of the United States in 2012 showed that it is not only small island nations such as those of Kiribati in the Pacific Ocean and Maldives in the Indian Ocean that can be destroyed by storm surges. Cities around the world are reluctantly responding with plans to both mitigate and adapt to the potential impacts of climate change. Since the 2000s, New York City's administration has been concerned about the impacts not only of hurricanes but also of nor'easters (winter storms) creating storm surges into the low-lying areas of the city's boroughs. The risks had been pointed out by Ian McHarg in the late 1960s. Maps had been drawn showing the impact of a one-in-a-one-hundred-year and a one-in-a-five-hundred-year flood on the city. A report prepared by Dutch consultants for New York City looked at flood zoning, flood insurance policies, and building codes that could be designed to shape the way the city's water fronts are developed (Aerts and Botzen 2011).

Sandy caused damage estimated to be US$75 billion on the East Coast of the United States. In New York City, it flooded streets, destroyed some neighborhoods on Long Island, and caused widespread power outages. The consequences added a sense of urgency to the city's planning to mitigate the effect of future disasters. Before Hurricane Sandy, the *Vision 2020: New York*

In an Age of Corporate Financial Capital

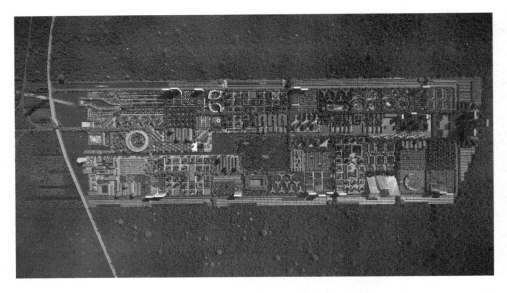

Figure 15.11 Forest City, Cancun, Mexico: The plan (above) and an image (below)
Credit line: Courtesy of Stefano Boeri Architetti
Credit line: Courtesy of Stefano Boeri Architetti

Comprehensive Waterfront Plan (2011) had established policies for the protection of 500 miles (800 kilometers) of the city's waterfront.

The city's policies follow the US mayors' agreement on what should be done in the face of climate change. In addition, the city organized a design competition to generate innovative ideas

US MAYORS' CLIMATE PROTECTION AGREEMENT

Sample actions and measures

Government measures

Short term

- Plant shade trees in and around local government parking lots and facilities.

Long term

- Co-locate facilities to reduce travel time and maximize building use.
- Utilize brownfield sites where possible.

Community Measures

Short term

- Maintain healthy forests and street trees.
- Promote tree planting to increase shading and to absorb carbon dioxide.

Long term

- Preserve open space.
- Promote high-density and infill development through zoning practice.
- Institute growth boundaries, ordinances, or programs to limit suburban sprawl.
- Give incentives and bonuses for development in existing downtown areas and areas near public transit.
- Encourage brownfield development.
- Discourage sprawl through impact, facility, mitigation, and permit types.

Figure 15.12 US mayors' proposed climate change mitigating actions
Source: United States Conference of Mayors (2005)

that are "flexible, easily phased, and able to integrate with existing projects in progress" (Aerts and Botzen 2011). The winning design of BIG (Bjarke Ingels Group) envisioned a 10-mile (16-kilometer) system that would protect lower Manhattan from storm water surges while providing the public with passive and active recreational opportunities.

The design includes the Battery Berm that makes an elevated path with a series of upland knolls, providing the possibility for people to farm or to relax in a garden setting. Much of it will be planted with diverse salt-tolerant trees, shrubs, and perennials, selected for their resilience. In other areas, walls are ready to flip down to hold floodwaters back.

Whether the scheme, or anything similar, is implemented remains to be seen. Without some sort of protection, New York City, like many other cities around the world, will remain vulnerable to considerable damage. Some predictions of the effects of climate change are dire.

Although the trend should not be exaggerated, municipal authorities have been moving from creating end-state master plans to thinking of starting the property development process with a strategic step that will act as a catalyst for further development. Options as to what future developments will take place are left open. At each stage, decisions are made not because the choice is the best available but because it meets specified criteria and constrains future decisions the least. While the implementation of the Masdar proposal follows such a process, probably the

Figure 15.13 BIG's proposal for Manhattan: The levee snaking its way around Battery Park (left) and an illustration of what it may be like (right)

Credit line (left): Courtesy of BIG
Credit line (right): Courtesy of BIG

most direct expression of this philosophy is the plan by Rem Koolhaas and Bruce Mau (b. 1959) for Downsview Park in suburban Toronto.

Downsview Park is located on a 231-hectare (572-acre) former air force base closed by the Canadian government in 1994. Koolhaas and Mau's entry, Tree City, won the competition for the development of the site with a strategy, not a design, arguing that

> the process of landscape planning and development itself, necessarily an open-ended set of complex processes developed over time, was more significant to the urban outcome than was a detailed physical design that would be rendered redundant by subsequent social, economic and cultural developments.
>
> *(Waldheim 2001, 82)*

The proposal consisted of a framework for structuring the site, but with allowances for future developments to be implemented in a series of steps, depending on the opportunities that arise. The framework consisted of guidelines that allowed for flexibility, depending on how the initial plant growth developed and on future economic and political circumstances (Czerniak 2002). The question that has arisen due to the lack of progress in creating the park is, "How loose a strategy will work?" (Martin del Guayo 2011). Without a specific image of an end state, who will fund a project? Such visions remain important in getting the attention of politicians and the public. In 2004, the design was taken over by a team that produced a more conventional end-state master plan. Little had been implemented by 2017.

Hybrid Examples

Punggol 21-plus, Singapore (2007–); Meixi Lake Eco-City, proposal, Zhengdong New District, China (2009–); Liuzhou Forest City, China (2016–20); The Springs, Shanghai, China (2018–20); and High Line Park, New York, New York, USA (1999–2018)

Many ecofriendly new designs have to cater to large populations on small sites. They draw on different urban design paradigms, and in fulfilling one function, they trade off fulfilling others.

Sustainable Urbanism and Urban Design

Punggol 21-plus, Meixi Lake Eco-City, and Liuzhou Forest City are developments on greenfield sites, and The Springs is an urban renewal scheme with ecological sensitivities. High Line Park is a landscape architectural project of the type advocated by the landscape urbanists.

Punggol 21 was designed in 1988 to be a model for Singapore's twenty-first-century developments. The economic crisis of the late 1990s brought its implementation to a halt. Punggol 21-plus took its place in 2007. It shows urban designers' increasing awareness of the need to design with nature in mind even if it is an artificially constructed ecology. The development has taken place within the guidelines set by Singapore's Inter-Ministerial Committee's *Sustainable Singapore Blueprint* (2009). The goal is to turn Singapore into an ecologically sustainable garden. It has other purposes too.

Two rivers on the edge of the site were dammed to form a freshwater reservoir. (The reservoir was a pragmatic response to Singapore's reliance on Malaysia for its supply of fresh water.) A 4.2-kilometer-long (2.6-mile-long), 20–30-meter-wide (65–100-foot-wide), artificial waterway now runs through the estate, linking the rivers. It is used recreationally for kayaking and canoeing. Public gardens and parks along it have jogging and cycling tracks. Rooftops have gardens. Streets are lined with trees. Upon completion, Punggol 21-plus will have 96,000 residential units. An almost 9-kilometer-long (5.5-mile-long) promenade will run on its northern seafront. An integrated waterfront commercial and residential development with a community club, regional library, and hawker center has been planned at the town center. As well as enhancing the sustainability of its new towns, Singapore has introduced minimum-energy and water-efficiency standards for most household appliances. The Centre for Livable Cities shares information on what makes an environment sustainable. Other high-density developments with intentions like those of Punggol 21-plus are being built around the world as examples for others to follow. China's Meixi Lake Eco-City is one.

Meixi Lake Eco-City is being funded by China's Ministry of Housing and Urban-Rural Development to be a model of an environmentally sensitive built environment. Designed by

Figure 15.14 Punggol 21-plus: The 4.2-kilometer My Waterway
Credit line: Photograph by happycreator/Shutterstock.com

In an Age of Corporate Financial Capital

New York's Kohn Pedersen Fox Associates, it is planned to have a population of 180,000 people on a 650-hectare (3,670-acre) site. At its center is a 40-hectare (100-acre) artificial lake. The CBD is a mixed-use area with parklands. Roads and canals radiate from the center to form an efficient, low-polluting transportation system. Eight neighborhood clusters have standard pragmatic layouts, although they do provide for pedestrian and cycle routes. The design incorporates gray water recovery and water runoff filtration systems to reduce the impact on the nearby Xiang River. "Meixi Lake establishes a paradigm of living in balance with nature," according to the architectural firm's website (2018). The performance of the town will depend on the quality of empirical information on which the design relies. The same can be said of Liuzhou Forest City.

Liuzhou Forest City is a new town of 30,000 people located in the mountainous area of Guangxi. It was designed, like the Forest City in Cancun, by Stefano Boeri. The town will have hotels, a hospital, and two schools in addition to its residential units. Built on a site of 175 hectares (432 acres), it will be linked to Liuzhou proper by a high-speed rail line. The development has been designed to be energy self-sufficient. Power will come from geothermal sources and from rooftop solar panels. The number of plants and trees is vast. The goal of Alai in Mexico is to restore the natural vegetation while making a new development. Here it is to use an artificial landscape to increase the biodiversity of an area. The planting is designed to handle carbon dioxide emissions and reduce temperature levels in the summer. The same end is sought in some urban renewal projects.

Danish firm Henning Larsen's design of The Springs, a mixed-use complex of buildings in Shanghai, was inspired by *shan shui*, a traditional form of Chinese landscape art as much as concepts of sustainability. The goal reflects the craggy, terraced mountains and green valleys of the rural areas of the country. Lushly planted, it houses offices, residential apartments, and retail shops. Its sustainability credentials rely on the way the sunshine and breezes penetrate the open space of the complex and the way it affords the easy movement of pedestrians. Its designers refer to it as an oasis in the city (Myall 2018).

Figure 15.15 Meixi Lake Eco-City
Source: Lang (2017, 141); courtesy of Kohn Pedersen Fox, architects, and of Taylor & Francis

Sustainable Urbanism and Urban Design

Figure 15.16 A new eco-city: Liuzhou Forest City with the high-speed rail line in the foreground
Credit line: Courtesy of Stefano Boeri Architetti

Figure 15.17 The Springs, Shanghai: A bird's-eye view (left) and the proposed courtyard (right)
Credit line (left): Courtesy of Henning Larsen Architects
Credit line (right): Courtesy of Henning Larsen Architects

In many urban designs, compromises have to be made between designing with the ecology of the natural world in mind and having an architectural expression that is new and thought provoking. New York's High Line Park strives to do both.

The High Line, an elevated freight railroad, was built in 1934 to enhance public safety at the ground level. After the last train ran down it in 1980, the structure was left to decay. A photographic essay in the *New Yorker* by Joel Sternfeld depicting the beauty of the self-seeded tracks led to the idea of making the High Line a linear park (Gopnik 2001). In 1999, the Friends of the High Line, a nonprofit organization, was formed to attain that dream.

A 2003 design ideas competition was won by James Corner Field Operations and Diller Scofidio+Renfro, along with Piet Oudolf. The team took an "agri-tecture" approach to the design, integrating plantings and hard materials to accommodate jogging, walking, sitting, and lying down. Using the self-seeded grasses and shrubs as a basis for those selected for the project ensured that the scheme's vegetation would be appropriate to the local microclimate. Access points to the park are located at easy walking distances from each other; several are linked to mass transport options at the street level. One entrance is by ramp, making it easy for people in wheelchairs to access the park; in other locations along it, access is by elevators as well as stairs. The furniture was designed for its expected use, its up-to-date aesthetic design quality, its

Figure 15.18 The High Line (left) and High Line Park, New York, in 2016 (right)
Source (left): Lang (2017); courtesy of Taylor & Francis
Source (right): Lang (2017); courtesy of Taylor & Francis

symbolic associations with the Line's past surroundings, and its sustainability. The final segment tying the park into the Hudson Yards development was completed in 2018.

High Line Park, as a plug-in urban design, has proven to be a catalyst for expensive, high-density urban redevelopment nearby that has increased New York City's property tax base. Simultaneously, the gentrification of the area and the number of tourists who visit the High Line have resulted in many businesses that previously catered to the local population failing financially. The adjacent population seems, however, to have accommodated itself to the influx of visitors. In 2012, there were 4.4 million of them.

Commentary: The Functions Addressed

The manifestoes advocating for designing with nature in mind have focused on creating ecologically sustainable built environments from humans' perspectives as much as from the natural world's. Implicit, if not explicit, in them is that a well-functioning biodiverse world is the issue requiring immediate attention in designing for the future. It, after all, addresses the most basic of motivations: humanity's need for survival. The advocacies are seldom fully heeded in practice. Pragmatic economic functions almost inevitably rule.

An assumption behind several of the urban designs described here is that they will require continued community participation in maintaining them. To the extent that the new designs require the mutual support of residents and their involvement in making the decisions that affect their day-to-day lives, a sense of a social and territorial community might be engendered (Gans 1968; Hester 1975; Brower 1996). Ecologically sustainable designs may also reinforce residents' sense of self-worth. The designs may reinforce people's self-image of being progressive.

Little is said in any of the manifestoes about how the ways of life of people will be affected by the ideas they present other than that people will be engaged in agricultural pursuits in the agrarian urban designs. All of us will nevertheless simply have to adapt to the changes in the urban morphology and the nature of urban designs brought about by the environmental and social policies that are required to create a sustainable world if humans and other species, animate and inanimate, are to survive and to survive well. Those projects that have been brought to fruition show that for a subset of the population, at least, adaptations to existing ways of life have been straightforward and that the designs function well in meeting basic sustainability goals. In some cases, the catalytic effect has been substantial, though not necessarily in promoting the sustainability of adjacent areas.

None of the ideas presented here pays specific attention to the requirements of people with low incomes. Most of the projects have been substantially more expensive to implement than predicted. The ballooning cost of High Line Park is an example, though it is mitigated by the increased tax income to the City of New York generated by property developments in adjacent neighborhoods. The increased revenue has enabled the city to initiate social and physical design programs elsewhere in the city.

Observations

Given the worldwide concern for the future of our planet, every urban design project underway will have addressed or self-consciously avoided addressing issues of sustainability. Often, only lip service is being paid to the subject, but in other cases, particularly those being built on fragile sites, considerable effort is being made to mitigate negative environmental effects and indeed to improve the functioning of existing natural systems. The scientific base for making decisions—the evidence for what works and what does not work—is being advanced rapidly. Some concerns have been easier to consider in new designs than have others.

Urban designers are increasingly aware of the necessity to reduce the heat-island effects of hard surfaces in cities everywhere and the damaging effects of hard-surface rainwater runoffs such as the scouring of riverbeds. Water recycling systems are in place in many projects. As the twenty-first century progresses, the concern for dealing with climate change will seriously impact urban development and reshape the morphology of cities.

The principles on which the designs presented in this chapter are based will no doubt lead to generic environmental patterns that mitigate the ecological problems arising from urban development. What is important is that the evidence underlying the patterns is understood as Norman Foster has said about Masdar. The way of looking at the world and the design process is what is important to heed, not the design patterns per se. Urban designers nevertheless continue to rely on precedents and antecedent ideas in their professional practices.

If Promenade Plantée was a precedent for High Line Park, the success of High Line Park has led to other cities' looking at their decaying infrastructure elements and wondering whether they can do the same thing. De Hofbogen in Rotterdam and Seoul's Skygarden are different examples. De Hofbogen, formerly an electrified rail line, is being turned into Rotterdam's version of the High Line. The project has been broadened to take in adjacent areas as part of an effort to create a sustainable Rotterdam. Seoul's Skygarden builds on the success of the city's Cheonggyecheon, the replacement in 2005 of an elevated highway with a park along a stream. Skygarden is an example of hard-surface landscape architecture and a type of landscape urbanism, but not really the type that landscape urbanists promote. They really want forests.

During the twenty-first century, people will have to make adaptations to the ways they invest in property and conduct their everyday lives if a sustainable world is to be achieved. Some current images of what these behavior patterns are and what the consequent design paradigm being proposed seem to be stretching the imagination. The idea of an agrarian urbanist world is unlikely to have widespread appeal unless some unimaginable cataclysmic event occurs. Despite all the warnings about the impact of severe climate events on cities, it was not until Hurricane Sandy hit the East Coast of the United States that large segments of the US public sat up and thought about the need to address the probability of an increased number of such occurrences confronting them. Many still do not believe that there is such a need. The residents of island nations in the Pacific and Indian Oceans see the evidence around them every day. Their concerns have been remote from the minds of the mass of the world's population. The situation is now changing. In the future, urban designers will have to think more like physical and social scientists than artists in dealing with the impact of their designs on the biodiversity of the world.

Key References

Branzi, Andrea, D. Donegan, A. Petrillo, and C. Raimondo. 1995. "Symbiotic Metropolis Agronica." In *The Solid Side: The Search for Consistency in a Changing World: Projects and Proposals*, 101–20. Naarden: V + K Publishing.

Charlesworth, Esther and Rob Adams, eds. 2011. *The Ecoedge—Urgent Design Challenges in Building Sustainable Cities*. London and New York: Routledge.

Corner, James. 2003. "Landscape Urbanism." In *Landscape Urbanism: A Manual for the Machinic Landscape*, edited by Mohsen Mostafavi and Ciro Najle, 58–63. London: AA Print Studio.

Cuthbert, Alexander R. 2011. "Sustainable Theory: Sustainable Form—the Future of Urban Design." In *Sustainable Urbanism and Beyond: Rethinking Cities for the Future*, edited by Tigran Haas, 180–83. New York: Rizzoli.

Koh, Jusuck. 2013b. "Articulating Landscape Urbanism: Ten Defining Characteristics." In *Landscape Urbanism and Its Discontents: Dissimulating the Sustainable City*, edited by Andrés Duany and Emily Talen, 245–62. Gabriola Island, BC: New Society Publishers.

Murphy, Michael D. 2005. *Landscape Architecture Theory: An Evolving Body of Thought*. Long Grove, IL: Waveland Press.

Waldheim, Charles. 2016. *Landscape as Urbanism: A General Theory*. New York: Princeton University Press.

16

Smart Cities and Urban Design

A smart city is one that integrates information and communication systems to manage a city's assets. The assets include its information systems, schools, libraries, transportation networks, hospitals, power plants, water supply networks, waste management, law enforcement, and other community services and elements such as lamp posts and trees. "Not since the laying of water mains, sewage pipes, subway tracks, telephone lines, and electrical cables . . . have we installed such a vast and versatile new infrastructure for controlling the physical city" (Townsend 2013, xii).

The image of a smart city is one where daily life is sped up and made easier by using self-parking cars, using drones for ferrying goods, having supplies delivered in immediate response to emergencies, having street lights replaced as soon as they fail, and removing traffic snarls. Everything is monitored by sensors linked to intelligent computer systems via advanced algorithms. Alternatively, a smart city is one in which people are well educated, creative, entrepreneurial, and happy. It retains such people and attracts new ones to migrate to it.

Cities have always functioned as centers of communication, and their morphologies have been altered as communication, particularly transportation, technology has changed. It is now argued that the integration of all information technologies will improve cities' delivery of services and meet their residents' needs by allowing city officials to monitor what is happening in them. Collectively this accumulation of information is known as 'big data.' Big data is then processed and analyzed to make a city operate efficiently.

It now appears that the greatest impact of the use of big data on urban designs concerns will be through the management of transportation modes. Instantaneous traffic flow analysis will coordinate traffic lights to speed up traffic movements and prevent congestion. Autonomous vehicles are still in the experimental stage. If/when they come into operation, they will operate as public taxis. In addition, the use of drones to gather data on how well street patterns function and, more actively, to deliver goods will affect traffic on the ground. Drones could change the way goods are brought from dispersed warehouses to their purchasers. Cities are likely to see the redistribution of activities and an increase in the importance of the quality of the public realm as they vie to be good places for business and everyday life.

The application of big data is changing the global economy. Self-healing power grids, air-quality sensors, new waste disposal systems, and solar-powered trash compactors are already in use in some places. The movement and activities of people in the public realm are already monitored through public surveillance cameras. The objective in the design of smart cities and smart neighborhoods is to coordinate all the monitoring systems. In sum, a smart city is one in which economic, social, ecological, political, and cultural phenomena are monitored and policies made to optimize functions in all their dimensions (Goldsmith and Crawford 2014).

Antecedent Ideas

Most of the early-twentieth-century predictions of the effect of new technologies on urban forms have been wide of the mark, as shown in Howard Mansfield's *Cosmopolis: Yesterday's Cities of the Future* (1990). Science fiction writers have produced many thought-provoking ideas, but no direct antecedents for smart cities exist. It is tempting to think of cities as circuit boards, much as Le Corbusier saw a house as a machine for living and human ecologists of the Chicago school saw cities as organic systems (e.g., Hawley 1950). "A city is not a computer," warns Shannon Mattern (2017).

Technological advances have been shaping ways of life and thus the morphologies of cities in a piece-by-piece manner over the past 150 years. This history has shown that the overall forms of cities has been remarkably resilient. We have learned that the twentieth century's overwhelming focus on the needs of automobile drivers was shortsighted. The quality and vitality of life and the sense of local precinct-based communities were much damaged by the way new highways intruded into the city.

The lesson is that the wholehearted focus in planning on the needs for the efficient operation of communications technology and monitoring systems must be tempered by greater consideration for the qualities of the public domain of cities. Many municipal governments are aware of this reality, but because the advocates for smart cities have quantitative data to support their positions, the qualitative nature and more-human-centered characteristics of the built environment can easily be forgotten.

Manifestoes and Paradigms

The proponents of smart cities argue that communities, business clusters, urban agglomerations, and metropolitan regions must integrate their information systems to be economically competitive in a neoliberal world. Information technology and energy management companies assume this position, and it is accepted by municipal and national governments. Their view is that cities will become better places in which to live by taking advantage of the efficiencies engendered by new technologies. They also believe that a broad range of high-quality behavior settings in a city is required to attract creative people with the entrepreneurial skills necessary to enhance a city's economy (Florida 2002).

Carlo Ratti and Matthew Claudel's *The City of Tomorrow: Sensors, Networks, Hackers and the Future of Urban Life* (2016) shares part of its title with Le Corbusier's *The City of Tomorrow*. It is a manifesto for smart cities. The authors believe that applying big data to the management of cities is the only way to make them sustainable—that is, adaptable to changing circumstances. The individual information and control systems of a city's infrastructure need to be integrated and automated. Advocates generally state that the systems should offer members of the public, whatever their education, skills, or income level, the means for providing input to the systems that monitor the quality of a city's natural ecosystems, built environment, and services (Angelakis et al. 2017; Han and Hawken 2018).

The efficiency and reliability of the city's modes of transport, mass and individual, are important in enhancing personal mobility. Autonomous vehicles are likely to be on the road within the next generation. Their developers say that they will eliminate accidents and traffic congestion if regulations monitoring their behavior are in place. How autonomous automobiles are called, used, parked/stored, and recalled will be important if safe, efficient, nonpolluting transport is to be achieved. Information technology systems, it is claimed, will handle high-demand periods and minimize waiting times for vehicles.

A set of broad design directives (see Figure 16.1) cautions city planners against allowing the exciting potential applications of new information technologies and big data to dictate the

---

In creating smarter cities, the following should be taken into account:

- Urban life should be considered before urban place; consider urban place before technology.
- Any design should consider sustainability, scalability, and resilience over an extended time frame.
- Flexibility in thinking about urban futures should be considered over an extended time frame.
- New or renovated buildings should be built to contain sufficient space for current and anticipated future needs for technology infrastructure, such as broadband cables, and of materials and structures that do not impede wireless networks. Spaces for the support of fixed cabling and other infrastructures should be easily accessible to facilitate future changes in use.
- New or renovated buildings should be constructed to be as functionally flexible as possible, especially in respect to their access, infrastructure, and the configuration of interior space—to facilitate future changes in use.
- Any development should ensure that wired and wireless connectivity is available throughout it, to the highest standards of current bandwidth, and with the capacity to expand to any foreseeable growth in that standard.
- Any new development should demonstrate that all reasonable steps have been taken to ensure that information from its technology systems can be made openly available without additional expenditure. Whether or not information is actually available will depend on commercial and legal agreements, but it should not be additionally subject to unreasonable expenditure. And where there is no compelling commercial, legal, or privacy reason to keep data closed, it should be made open.
- The information systems of any new development should conform to the best available current standards for interoperability between IT systems in general and for interoperability in the built environment, physical infrastructures, and smarter cities specifically.
- New developments should demonstrate that they have considered the commercial viability of providing the digital civic infrastructure services recommended by credible research sources.
- Any data concerning a new development that could be used to reduce energy consumption within that development, or in related areas of a city, should be made open.
- Property development proposals should indicate how they will attract business and residential tenants through providing up-to-date sustainable infrastructures for heat and

---

Figure 16.1   Design directives for smarter cities

Source: Robinson (ca 2014), https://theurbantechnologist.com/smarter-city-design-principles/; courtesy of Rick Robinson

In an Age of Corporate Financial Capital

> power such as combined heat and power (CHP) smart metering, local energy grids, and solar energy.
> - Consultations on plans for new developments should fully exploit the capabilities of social media, virtual worlds, and other technologies to ensure that communities affected by them are given the widest, most immersive opportunity possible to contribute to their design.
> - Management companies, local authorities, and developers should have a genuinely engaging presence in social media so that they are informally approachable.
> - Local authorities should support awareness and enablement programs for social media and related technologies, particularly grassroots initiatives within local communities.
> - Urban development and regeneration programs should support the formation, activity, and success of local food initiatives by cooperating with local community and business support programs to support the infrastructures that they need to succeed and grow.
> - Residential accommodation should incorporate space for environmental monitoring, interactive portals, and connectivity, to enable remote support, telehealth systems, and homeworking.
> - New developments should demonstrate through the use of the latest urban modeling techniques that they will increase connectivity—particularly by walking and cycling—between important value-creating districts and economic priority zones that are adjacent or near them.
> - Developments should offer the opportunity of serendipitous interaction and innovation between stakeholders from different occupations.
> - Developments should provide, or should be adaptable to provide, facilities to enable the location and success of future ways of working including remote and mobile working, 'pop-up' establishments, and collaborative working spaces.
> - Planning usage and other policies governing the use of urban space and structures should facilitate innovation and changes of use, including temporary changes in use.
> - Any information system in a city development should provide a clear policy for the use of personal information. Any use of that information should have the consent of the individual that it concerns.
> - A transport plan supporting new developments should demonstrate that it has provided for not only traditional transport demand but also that which might be created by online business models and other social technologies.
> - New developments should demonstrate that their design takes account of the latest, best, and emerging practices and patterns from smarter cities, smart urbanism, digital urbanism, and placemaking.

Figure 16.1   (Continued)

nature of cities (R. Robinson ca 2014). A social plan based on ideals, evidence, and cultural trends must precede the design of new schemes and the upgrading of the layout of cities and their precincts. Based on present experiences in retrofitting cities, the design of monitoring systems by using big data can be accommodated in urban designs of any configuration. The same observations may not hold in the future.

Such a list is based on our present understandings and aspirations. The case for strategic approaches to urban designing is strengthened by the need to leave open opportunities to respond to new technological developments as design decisions are made one after the other.

Generic Concepts and Illustrative Designs

No generic or illustrative urban design shows what the layout of a smart city should be or what it should look like. The idea of a smart city is not static; there is no specific end to be reached. New opportunities and challenges that need to be addressed will constantly arise. We have instead a generic four-step procedural model suggested by Sam Musa, a cyber security professor (Musa 2016). The first is to define the community of interest, the stakeholders. The second is to figure why to even bother. What is the integration of systems striving to achieve? The third is to create a smart city policy. And the fourth is to engage citizens in drawing conclusions before implementing it. Implementation will an ongoing piece-by-piece process. A further step—monitoring the outcomes—should be added. As new information technologies and algorithms become available, the monitoring systems will need to be upgraded. As transportation technologies change, so will the procedures for operating them. The designing process for the creation of smart cities, like any designing activity, will be an iterative one with the constant conjecturing and evaluation of possibilities.

The community of concern at the precinct scale may be a locally based one or one of special interests. Identifying people who form the community and their concerns is more difficult. What are the needs of people at different stages in their life cycles, from different socioeconomic statuses, and who have different interests and views? What activities, what behavior settings, are important to community life? An example of the diversity of concerns is Safetypin. It is an app to help people navigate public spaces in major cities without fear of harassment. It not only provides women, strangers, and children but also men with navigational information but it also informs them of places that are dangerous (Viswanath and Basu 2017). The generic question is, What policies are needed to further applications such as this one?

Any generic model for establishing the policies for smart cities must start with what we are trying to achieve. Smart city advocates are clear about establishing efficiencies in the operation of the information systems that affect the city. What else is the goal? The dream is to create cities where embedded sensors, ubiquitous cameras, and computer-based operating systems with links are brought together to create high levels of efficiency and connectivity and thus, it is argued, provide social benefits. Such places would be e-topias.

Specific Designs

No city or any precinct within it can fully claim to be smart. Many of each of them are being designed to be so. The companies seeking to provide the services for 'intelligent' cities include such giants as Cisco, IBM, and Microsoft. William Henry (Bill) Gates III (b. 1955), principal founder of Microsoft Corporation, has bought a 25,000-acre (10,000-hectare) site in Arizona for a smart new town. A US$10 billion high-density smart city of 250,000 people in Portugal is still a dream.

It is premature to talk about any development being smart. The construction of Songdo City in Korea is well underway, but while it is being consciously designed to be a smart city, its character is based on several precedents; it is a hybrid example. Retrofitting cities to make them smart is more widespread than designing fiat towns. The most unified networks are emerging in the cities of Asia and Middle Eastern countries, where Cisco, Siemens, and IBM are working with property developers to build smart projects.

At present, bits and pieces of smart systems exist in cities widely scattered around the globe. Among the leaders is Amsterdam, which has set up an interconnected platform through wireless instruments, with the goal of enhancing the city's spontaneous decision-making abilities. Tel Aviv has established a platform that provides a connection between its municipal government and residents that alerts the residents to road closures and provides them with reminders of events. Residents, in turn, can inform the municipality of the current state of factors that affect their lives. Smart Dublin is an initiative in that city. In the United Kingdom, Manchester and the 1970s new town of Milton Keynes have embarked on a series of initiatives to turn themselves into smart cities. Singapore plans to become a smart city/nation. Under the administration of Narendra Modi (b. 1950), India's Ministry of Urban Development initiated its smart cities program in 2015. It has identified small pockets of ninety-nine cities for intensive development as smart precincts. If successful, they will act as generic solutions that guide officials in 'smartening' other precincts (Nair 2017). The program will be partially funded by US$4.5 billion in cut-rate loans from Japan. In return, 30% by value of project contracts must go to Japanese firms (Goyal 2017). The list of cities striving to be smart can go on and on. Madrid is a somewhat-arbitrary choice as an example, but the city is striving to become smart both technologically and in the skills and entrepreneurial characteristics of its population.

Exemplars of Smart Designs

Karle Town Centre, Bengaluru, Karnataka, India (2019–), and Madrid, Spain (2011–)

Karle Town Centre illustrates what is accepted as a smart city urban design today. It shares much in common with other such proposals (e.g., that for Union Point outside Boston) of the second decade of the twenty-first century. Designed by UNStudio based in Amsterdam and in collaboration with the Indian information technology firm Karle Infra, the goal is to create a green development and a smart development. It is located in Bengaluru (still widely known as Bangalore), India's information technology hub, at a latitude that ameliorates its tropical situation, and the goal of the forms of its buildings and their white paint is to reduce energy consumption and heat-island effects. Being green is as much a marketing device establishing a brand image for the development as a desire to reduce harmful environmental impacts. The goal is to attract creative people and their families as well as creative organizations to settle in the precinct.

The project will have sensors located throughout the development to collect big data. They will be used to monitor traffic flows, external ambient conditions of the environment, and, more generally, the life of the community. Much of the development will be in the form of a superblock, with vehicular traffic kept on the outside. The surrounding streets will have strategically located drop-off points. The architecture tends toward the hyper-modernist (see also Figure 12.5), where individual buildings are located as elements in space. Intended to be a total urban design, the scheme will have unity in appearance not characteristic of much hyper-modernist urban design. How the scheme will evolve as it gets implemented and inhabited by the diverse sociocultural population of Bengaluru remains to be seen.

More progress seems to be being made in making existing cities smart than in building new ones. Madrid is arguably Spain's smart city, although many observers would claim that title for Barcelona. Madrid is a lively capital, rich in restaurants, theaters, art galleries, and museums. It is being fitted out to make it a smart city in terms of both its technological systems and its citizenry. The city uses the MiNT Inteligente/Smarter Madrid system, along with IBM's Intelligence and National Security Alliance (INSA), to improve the quality and efficiency of the services that it provides. The objective is to furnish the city's people with the means to speedily interact and communicate with the city's municipal offices. The technology takes advantage of big data and analytics to improve the way those who provide municipal services can respond to demands made of them.

Smart Cities and Urban Design

Figure 16.2 Karle Town Centre: The conceptual design
Credit line: Courtesy of UNStudio

Madrid has an annual consumption of 15 million cubic meters of water and produces 1 million tonnes of household waste. In the city, 1.7 million vehicles pass through its streets each weekday; it has more than 5 million assets, including 252,000 lamp posts and 287,000 trees. The providers of maintenance services for roads, lighting, trees, and green spaces and the clearing and management of garbage and waste will be managed and compensated according to the quality of the amenities and/or services that they offer (Global Site Plans 2014). Over three hundred key performance indicators will be monitored through 1,500 daily inspections. By using smartphones, tablets, other mobile devices, and social media, Madrileños—the people of Madrid—can report problems to their local municipal office and receive an immediate response. City officials can track an event or the impact of an incident and keep respondents informed about what is occurring until it has been resolved.

The platform integrates information supplied by people, along with data provided by sensors and cameras. It analyzes data provided by inspectors and service providers and data on the management of human resources, task planning, and geographic information systems. In this way, Madrid makes use of real-time updates from different processes, services, organizations, and providers involved in environmental management, allowing municipal officials to respond to its citizen's needs more quickly and efficiently than before. Do all these systems when functioning effectively make Madrid a smart city? In terms of the application of information technology, it is on its way to becoming one; in terms of the city's people, it may already be one.

If one thinks of a smart city as a sociopolitical and cultural entity in which lively citizens are aware of the processes of city government, Madrid is a smart city on the basis of its gross domestic product per capita and the size of its 'creative class,' in Richard Florida's terms (Florida 2002). It has a substantial, well-educated, and entrepreneurial population. Accessibility across the city and to the outside world is relatively easy by public transport. The percentage of households

337

In an Age of Corporate Financial Capital

with Internet access and the number of headquarters of major commercial organizations that it possesses are high. On other key variables, such as controlling pollution, it is smart in comparison to other European cities (Mella-Marquez, López-López, and Mella-Lopez 2014). It also has a high level of social cohesion.

A Hybrid Example

Songdo International Business District, Korea (2003–)

Korea has been a leader in developing big data. Seoul already has high-speed Wi-Fi on its streets. Electronic panels at stations provide the timings of incoming buses so that passengers arriving by train can easily make transport connections. The Samsung corporation is linking household devices to mobile phones. Songdo International Business District (IBD) takes these advances a full step forward. Its development is the center of attention as the world's first significant fiat smart city (Williamson 2013).

IBD is being built on a 600-hectare (1482-acre) greenfield site. Marshland until 2000, the site required 500 million tons of sand landfill to prepare it for development. The tidal flats were home to a wide variety of water birds and acted as a resting spot for migratory waders. They have been largely displaced. Lying adjacent to Seoul's Incheon International Airport, IBD is an example of an aerotropolis (Kasarda and Lindsay 2011). Gale International is the developer, with Posco and Morgan Stanley Real Estate as minority shareholders. The master plan for a city of 200,000 is the work of Kohn Pedersen Fox Associates. It has a spacious design with broad streets and sidewalks and a 40-hectare (101-acre) central park that has an island for rabbits and deer. Approximately 40% of the IBD site is parkland, a habitat for indigenous birds that are absent in the more polluted atmosphere of Seoul.

IBD has sensors to monitor ambient temperatures, energy use, and traffic flows. Sensors tell waiting bus passengers where on their route buses are. Recharging electric car stations are

Figure 16.3 Songdo City
Credit line: Photograph by DreamArchitects/Shutterstock.com

available throughout the city. Water recycling systems avoid using drinking water to flush toilets. Household wastes are pumped directly, via a network of underground tunnels, to waste-processing centers, where they are sorted, recycled, or incinerated to create energy. A telepresence system is being pioneered by Cisco. Seven employees are all that is required run the whole system.

The city attracts people seeking to get away from dense Seoul. Its residential blocks provide them with both privacy and a safe financial investment. For others, it is a boring place lacking the liveliness and richness of the behavior settings of existing Korean cities. Songdo's promotion material states,

> Songdo IBD boasts the wide boulevards of Paris, a 100-acre Central Park reminiscent of New York City, a system of pocket parks similar to those in Savannah, a modern canal system inspired by Venice and convention center architecture redolent of the famed Sydney Opera House.
>
> *(Trivett 2011)*

It is not the type of environment that attracts many of the creative class of US and European cities, nor are many commercial organizations located there, despite its advanced smart city characteristics. Growth is slow by Asian standards. Songdo remains a city in the making.

Commentary: The Functions Addressed

A smart city, given its primary definition, is one in that operates with technically advanced information technologies to bridge the communications gap between people and the processes that manage the places in which they live and that they visit. The function being addressed is the operation of the city's services. The goal is to enhance their efficiencies and also to manage the costs of service provisions. Wi-Fi capabilities now exist on the streets of many cities. In the future, infrastructure nodes may exchange messages with autonomous vehicles and drone delivery systems. The broad function of the systems is, however, to increase the quality of people's lives by making urban services operate efficiently. It is also to make cities places where creative people want to live.

Smart cities should function to give people an enhanced sense of safety and security. CCTV cameras already provide video surveillance not only of traffic movements but also of the activities on a city's sidewalks, squares, and other public areas as well as the interior spaces of buildings, such as bank lobbies, hotel corridors, and subterranean parking lots. They intrude on privacy more than does the natural surveillance of the public realm from windows and lobbies of apartment and other buildings. Surveillance systems may act as a deterrent but do not seem to substantially reduce antisocial behavior. They do, at least, make it easier to apprehend perpetrators of crime.

The way the technologies incorporated in smart cities affects the formation of territorially based communities is open to conjecture. They will probably enhance communities of common interest and a sense of belonging to the global modern world. Advocates see that one of the functions of smart cities is to give places corporate marketing advantages in a competitive economic world and thus the economic security of its business interests. A parallel goal is for cities to function to increase their citizens' pride in living in an up-to-date locale. Pride in a city is not easily quantifiable. Being technologically smart alone will not attract businesses, as the Songdo city experience shows. The quality of the public realm and the behavior settings it contains remain crucial.

Observations

Municipal officials report that they feel a greater pressure to improve services than to reduce costs (Pattani 2016). The efficiency of a high-quality, speedy service provided by integrated information networks promises to make life easier, with fewer irritations for the residents and workers of a city as well as visitors to it. The efficiency should make it possible for them to immediately access the data that they need to move around in it and to make day-to-day decisions, provided that the data work. Data failures can cause havoc.

Predicting the way that technological changes will shape the future is rife with difficulties. Futurists, demographers, and planners have had an appalling record in forecasting the future more than a generation ahead. One certainty is that the full implications of smart city requirements, for the layout of cities and their precincts, need to be understood well in terms of people's everyday activities. Most current efforts to create smart cities state that plans are being made to support the development of productive, accessible, livable places that attract talented people. Livable is seldom defined except in surprisingly modernist terms of efficiency. Important though it is, we have learned that this notion is not the most significant criterion in making cities desirable destinations for either commercial enterprises or residents. 'Livable' needs to be more broadly defined (Greenfield 2013).

Existing cities have fixed patterns of streets, buildings, squares, and other open spaces. Their hearts contain essentially the same patterns of built form that have accommodated changes in transportation technology over the millennia, but with hyper-modernist urban designs, new spatial patterns not known for their efficiencies are appearing in many societies that are aspiring to be seen as modern. What has changed is the distribution of activities and the overall morphology of cities with the growth of suburbs. First it was the railroad suburbs clustered around stations and then the urban sprawl that the freedom of movement by automobiles allows. Now Internet retailing is changing the modes of how people move and the nature of retail shopping streets in many parts of the world. More people work from home. What should the distribution of activities in a city be? The economic consequences of smart city infrastructure on property development decisions will determine much pragmatically.

Key References

Angelakis, Vangelis, Elias Tragos, Henrich Pöhls, Adam Kapovits, and Alessandro Bassi, eds. 2017. *Designing, Developing, and Facilitating Smart Cities: Urban Design to IoT Solutions*. Cham: Springer.

Goldsmith, Stephen and Susan Crawford. 2014. *The Responsive City: Engaging Communities Through Data Smart Governance*. San Francisco, CA: Jossey-Bass.

Greenfield, Adam. 2013. *Against the Smart City (The City Is Here for You to Use Book 1)*. London: Verso.

Ratti, Carlo and Matthew Claudel. 2016. *The City of Tomorrow: Sensors, Networks, Hackers and the Future of Urban Life*. New Haven and London: Yale University Press.

Robinson, Rick. ca 2014. "Smart City Principles." *The Urban Technologist*. https://theurbantechnologist.com/smarter-city-design-principles/ accessed March 12, 2018.

Epilogue

Vienna in 2017

Looking Back to Look Forward

It is easy to dismiss critiques of the urban design paradigms and the designs themselves as a 'sniping from the sidelines' by those observers and academics not having to make design commitments. Architects and other professionals tend to ignore findings on what functions well in their designs and what does not. For them, little other than research on technical matters addresses the pragmatic day-to-day design problems that they face. Property developers and the power elite make the major decisions about what to build and where to build it; designers follow. Designers, however, have the power to shape discussions about future property development through their expertise and ability to give images to visions of potential designs.

Legislation promoted by activists has helped make the pragmatically developed city a more ecologically sound and healthier place for people's lives (Glaeser 2011). Most urban design schemes indeed work well enough; they are satisficing solutions. If they meet the requirements of the marketplace to make a profit, the opportunity costs that a design may have incurred, especially in foregoing long-term social and environmental benefits, are deemed to fall outside the scope of designers' concerns. People are adaptable and make the most of the environment in which they live, work, and recreate. Besides, it is argued, it is really the cultural and social world that they inhabit that affects the quality of their lives.

Despite all the conflicts, political upheavals, and natural disasters that have occurred during the period covered in this book, the world is a better place than before for humans, on almost any dimension of measurement. Although subjective feelings of well-being and views of the future may differ, the built environment provides a better setting for life for much of the world's population (Rothman 2018). Many urban design projects have turned out to be good places to live and/or work while providing something for the architectural cognoscenti to ponder. Many problems nevertheless remain: Much of Earth is highly polluted, social divisions seem even wider than in the past, and diverse groups of people are displaced by war or prolonged droughts. Parts of world, urban and rural, are overcrowded. The functioning of the natural environment, on which all the species that inhabit Earth depend, continues to be degraded. Many species are in a more precarious position than humans are. Some have adapted to changing conditions (Schilthuizen 2018), but others face extinction.

The Pragmatic Future

After five decades of incremental changes in the technologies that led unselfconsciously to changes in the morphologies of cities, the world seems to be on the cusp of major changes in the ways of life of many segments of the world's population (Brynjolfson and Mcafee (2014). What will these changes be? History suggests that one can with any confidence look no further ahead than only one generation. The city in twenty-five years will be very much like that of today. There will simply be more of it. Technological changes in the way we transport ourselves, our goods, and information will no doubt be intruding on present patterns of life.

Cities will be changed pragmatically, piece by piece, as their economic fortunes rise and fall and as property developers perceive investment opportunities. Many architects are drawing images of what they would like the city to look like. Most of such images are highly creative and

Figure 1 The pragmatically developed city in 2045?
Credit line: Image by Peter Linforth
Source: Wikimedia Commons

full of high-tech skyscrapers in hyper-modernist forms. Other images are projections of trends. Hugh Ferriss and Francisco Mujica showed in their imaginations of what the late twentieth century would be like the limitations of doing so (see Chapter 7). Simultaneously, numerous highly self-conscious total and all-of-a-piece urban designs will be built during the next twenty-five years, if for no other reason than to accommodate the world's growing and increasingly urban population. Many new towns are currently being designed. Urban renewal plans upgrading segments of cities proliferate. Can we do better than to simple allow the market to dictate what is to be built, where and how? What strategies should we adopt to make settlements better places for all species? What can we learn from the urban design approaches described in this book?

The Outline of the Discussion

This epilogue consists of two chapters. The first reviews the observations made by critics of the major urban design paradigms of the past sesquicentenary. It begins with a consideration of the general criticism of how designers think and then proceeds to discuss the observations that critics have made about specific design paradigms. Each paradigm still offers us much, but each also has its limitations. Is it possible to have a more comprehensive view of the task of urban designers when decisions must be made under severe time constraints?

An empirical, theory-based problem-solving approach to design seems to be the best way forward. Designers, however, are disinclined to work that way (Francescato 1994). They will continue to work by adapting contemporary generic design ideas to the situation at hand. The best guiding urban design model for the future is the compact city. It is claimed, in the last chapter of this book, that working toward it is the best way forward. But is it?

Key References

Brynjolfson, Eric and Andrew Mcafee. 2014. *The Second Machine Age: Work, Progress, and Prosperity in a Time of Brilliant Technologies*. New York: W. W. Norton & Company.

Francescato, Giulio. 1994. "Type and the Possibility of an Architectural Scholarship." In *Ordering Space: Types in Architecture and Design*, edited by Karen A. Franck and Lynda H. Schneekloth, 253–70. New York: Van Nostrand Reinhold.

Glaeser, Edward. 2011. *Triumph of the City: How Urban Spaces Make Us Human*. London: Palgrave Macmillan.

Rothman, Joshua. 2018. "The Big Question." *The New Yorker* (July 23): 26–33. www.newyorker.com/magazine/2018/07/23/are-things-getting-better-or-worse accessed June 7, 2019.

Schilthuizen, Menno. 2018. *Darwin Comes to Town: How the Urban Jungle Drives Evolution*. London: Picador.

17

A Critique of Twentieth- and Early-Twenty-First-Century Urban Design

"Those who cannot remember the past are condemned to repeat it" (Santayana 1905, 284). If the field of urban design is to make progress, it is important to know what of past ideas works well and what does not in various individual's eyes. No urban design is perfect. Many schemes fulfill specific instrumental functions well. Some are also intellectually interesting to the architectural cognoscenti because they differ from the norm. That said, the criticism that has been leveled at the design paradigms and specific designs described in this book should not be dismissed without serious consideration.

Many of the observations of critics apply to all urban design thinking, but some address specific design paradigms (Garvin 1996; Cuthbert 2007). The goal of this chapter is to summarize the points made in the commentaries and observations made in this book to provide an intellectual basis for the argument made in the final chapter.

General Commentaries

The achievements and limitations of the ideas of both the empiricists and the rationalists were clear by the 1960s. The most general criticism is that in focusing on eliminating urban problems, what works—the behavior settings that give people of different stripes pleasure—was neglected. The result has been that they are not included in new designs. It also meant that large rundown swaths of cites were demolished without recognizing their positive qualities (Jacobs 1961; Gans 1962). The design professions have little heeded the observations made about their efforts, so much so that it was possible to repeat commentaries from the 1970s (e.g., Brolin 1976 and Blake 1977) thirty years later as if they were original (e.g., Hughes 2006).

Three significant observations made in the 1970s still apply in the early twenty-first century to all the urban design paradigms presented in this book. The first is that urban designers have assumed too simplistic a model of the human being as the basis for their work. The criticism is that too little thought has been given to the way the evolving roles of men and women (Hayden 1984; Rothschild 1999) and children (Parr 1969; Pollowy 1977; Ward 1990; Kyttä et al. 2018) affect the range of behavior settings required of a design. That settings must be accessible to all people is the position advocated by universal design proponents (Steinfeld and Maisel 2012). The second is that the model of 'function' that designers rely on fails to explicitly recognize

345

the importance of the symbolic aesthetic nature of built forms as one of their basic functions (Fitch 1980; Scott Brown 2004; Lang and Moleski 2010). The third is that designers and critics from the days of the City Beautiful movement to the modernists to Jane Jacobs assumed too deterministic a belief in the impact of the built environment on human social behavior (Broady 1966; Gans 1968; Lang 1980; Dostoğlu 1986). The qualities of the built environment contribute substantially to feelings of well-being and the richness of life, but cultural attitudes and the politics of everyday life, rather than the form of the city, are the major determinants of social behavior. The patterns of the built environment provide the 'affordances' for life (Gibson 1979). They have a greater impact on the lives of the less competent, physically or psychologically, than on those of the more competent (Lawton and Nahemow 1973; Golembewski 2014). If the built form of a city does not afford a behavior, then it does work deterministically by precluding it. Urban designers have been better at catering to people who use wheelchairs (and people wheeling baby carriages) and, in very specific locations, blind people than for other human characteristics that make navigation in cities difficult.

Many urban designs have been based on designers' self-referent images of the ways of life and values of people for whom they are designing and/or how they should behave (Gans 1962; Michelson 1968; Rapoport 1977). Property developers and architects seeking other than pragmatic designs often seem to have been trapped by their childhood worlds. Frank Lloyd Wright sought to recreate the world of his childhood in Spring Valley, Wisconsin. James Rouse wanted Columbia to be like Easton, Maryland, where he grew up, and Robert Davies wished Seaside to reflect the places of his childhood vacations (Davis 1989). Le Corbusier took years to modify the impact of his Calvinist upbringing on his design ideas (Turner 1977; Brooks 1999). Because most urban designers have been male, the images of good design are based on an idealized model of the ways of life of healthy, young, vigorous adult males (Hayden 1984; Rothschild 1999). More generally, designing with multiculturalism in mind has been neglected (Sandercock 1998). Our own experiences are certainly important; we can learn much from them, but using them as a basis for designing for others needs to be done with prudence.

The aphorism 'form follows function' associated with the modernists is a fine guide for urban design provided that the meanings of 'form' and 'function' are clearly understood. Form refers to patterns of the built and natural environments and the way their characteristics are related to each other, their material qualities, and the way they are illuminated, naturally and artificially. The environment and the activities that take place within it are experienced via all our senses, but little attention has been paid to that reality (Rasmussen 1962). The focus in design has been on the visual world as modeled in drawings. The surfaces of the patterns have haptic qualities when touched; sounds reverberate or are screened by them. They shape the flow of odors, and some emit odors themselves.

As noted in the Prologue, one of the criticisms that urban design projects received during the twentieth century was that they were not functional enough. That observation is still valid. Too few of the potential functions of the built environment are considered in establishing the programs on which designs are based. In addition, many fine designs require considerable maintenance to keep them functioning well. Often, too little thought has been given to how patterns of built form and the materials of which they are made work over time. Property owners, public or private, and the designers of projects have been more concerned with the immediate impact of their proposals than with what they might be like after a decade or two of low maintenance or neglect. Brise-soleils are dust catchers as much as shade providers. Weeds soon grow up through pavers, and monsoon rains wreak havoc on unprotected walls and overflow drainage channels. Filled-in waterways lead to flooding, often catastrophic.

A Critique of Urban Design

Until recently, the lives of nonhuman animals have fallen outside the domain of concern of policymakers and thus urban design paradigms. The potential place of wild animals, desirable and undesirable, in cities has been overlooked. Shrinking habitats have made animals such as foxes, bears, and monkeys urban dwellers in many places (Donovan 2015; Barkham 2017). Feral or domestic, they acclimatize to the necessities of urban life and are shaped by it (Schilthuizen 2018). The only wild birds in some polluted cities are pigeons; songbirds sing in cages. Migratory animals and birds are often disoriented by urbanization, and their resting places are lost as suburban development takes over their habitats. More recently, it has been pointed out that the needs of household pets, specifically dogs and cats, have been considered, as if they do not exist (Carou and Aird 2017). Clashes between dog owners and other users of beaches and parks are not uncommon. The list can go on and on. Most urban designers consider all these issues to fall outside their responsibilities. They are public policy matters. More immediately important is the way we apply generic solutions in urban design practice.

Many generic designs have been used as the basis for specific designs in other than the cultural and geographic environments in which they were developed. Many have been assumed to be universally relevant (Rapoport 1977; Wolfe 1981). Some are, but others are not. Many planning jurisdictions have observed, for instance, that 'the Radburn plan hasn't work when we applied it.' A closer examination has shown that the Radburn design was applied out of the cultural context in which it was developed and/or that it was only the two-dimensional, not the three-dimensional, aspects of the design that was used as the basis for a design (Judd and Samuels 2005).

While some generic ideas (e.g., congestion charging) have been developed in Asia (Lim 2007), most of the urban design paradigms and generic solutions at an architect's or landscape architect's disposal were developed in Europe or North America. The globalization of design education and professional practice has led to their being applied unchanged in climates ranging from cool temperate to tropical and from monsoon areas to deserts and in cultures that have different ways of life and aesthetic tastes. On top of that, where they were appropriate, the funds available to implement them were insufficient to do the generic ideas justice (Marmot 1982).

The City Beautiful

The City Beautiful movement, although a reform movement, promoted an urban design of grandeur. Some highly admired, much-loved civic spaces based on its principles were built during the twentieth century. While the claims for the paradigm's utility were neither new nor unique, the advocates for city beautiful concepts argued that urban beautification improves the moral and social character of a citizen. When applied, they do help to ameliorate some social ills and increase the pride that residents have in their cities, but they fail to deal with the social complexities of urban life (J. Jacobs 1961).

The City Beautiful offered hope for upgrading cities at a time when there were many calls for reform. Ironically, where implemented, it was necessary, purposefully of not, to displace the poor, something that urban renewal projects accomplished with some frequency throughout the twentieth century and still do. The Benjamin Franklin Parkway in Philadelphia, Pennsylvania, USA, cuts across the city's grid street pattern from City Hall to the Museum of Art. Its construction involved the destruction or partial destruction of a dozen low-income, predominantly ethnically Irish neighborhoods (Brownlee 1988). The Avenue of the Victory of Socialism (1997–89) in Romania, built under the dictatorship of President Nicolae Ceauşescu, purposefully displaced 40,000 people whom he wished to remove from the center of Bucharest

347

(Cavalcanti 1997). Many people will think the results worth the social upheavals that such projects created. What would Paris be without Haussmann's boulevards?

City Beautiful concepts exemplify the power of bold utopian ideas to run roughshod over urban patterns and the historical reasons for their being the way they are. Although one goal was to create a salubrious environment, the city beautiful principles were also criticized for their focus on the visual aesthetic character of cities. Its proponents downplayed the inefficiency for the vehicular traffic of the axial patterns of the built form that they supported. Comments similar to those made about the City Beautiful can be made about modernist endeavors.

The Modernists

Modernist urban designs have received both praise and criticism. Rationalists and empiricists have disparaged each other's ideas. Liverpool University's civic design program's educators did not hold back in their criticism of many rationalist urban design ideas, despite feeling that they were being left behind by the boldness of the projects advocated by CIAM's members (Adshead 1930). The disagreements between Frank Lloyd Wright and Le Corbusier, neither known for modesty, were played out in the pages of the *New York Times* in 1932. The two seemed more intent on disparaging each other's ideas than on focusing on the affordances and limitations of their design proposals.

The population density for Le Corbusier's Plan Voisin was 1,000 people per hectare, which Frank Lloyd Wright considered to be 980 too many. He also thought Le Corbusier's ideas to be childish because they involved tearing down the existing city to obtain more green space only to build it up again. The Plan Voisin was, to Wright, simply a "set of feudal towers set a little farther apart" (cited in Schires 2017a, para. 4). Skyscrapers were unnecessary, he believed, except for landlords to receive rental income. Despite this view, Wright designed Crystal City for Washington, DC, in the 1940s (Duran 2017) and a mile-high skyscraper, The Illinois, two decades later in 1956. It was to be a 580-story megastructure housing 100,000 people and providing 14,000 parking spots for cars and a hundred for helicopters.

Perhaps the harshest criticism of the modernist's ideas came from architects about their own work. Maxwell Fry and Albert Mayer are among the early post–World War Two modernists who criticized their earlier advocacies (Fry 1961; Mayer 1967). Ludwig Hilberseimer's comment on his 1924 *Metropolis* is illustrative: "It was not a metropolis but a necropolis. Its streetscape of concrete and asphalt would have been a most inhumane environment" (Spaeth 1981, 48). Peter Blake's *Form Follows Fiasco: Why Modern Architecture Hasn't Worked* (1977) is a repudiation of many of the thoughts that he presented earlier in *God's Own Junkyard: The Planned Deterioration of America's Landscape* (1964). Jane Jacobs's *Death and Life of Great American Cities* was inspired by the disappointed she felt when the proposals that she praised while writing for *Forum* turned out to be poor lived-in places (Laurence 2011). We can learn much from reflecting on our own experiences, provided that we are willing to reflect on them (Schön 1983).

Some criticisms of the modernists' ideas apply to the thinking of both rationalists and empiricists. The major one is that neither considered the richness of life in existing cities and the broad range of experiences that a city can afford. The rationalists abandoned the past; the empiricists never fully analyzed the environments they admired. Rem Koolhaas suggested that much can be learned from observing the development of Manhattan, the diversity of its precincts, the utility of the grid layout, and the opportunities it provides for building heterogeneous structures (Koolhaas 1978). How it feeds into his own work is not obvious.

Purifying the city can reduce its offerings. Manuel de Solà-Morales i Rubió (1939–2012) argued that the richness of cities comes from the unselfconscious, piece-by-piece decisions that are made by people over time. That quality cannot be created de novo, but a wealth of opportunities can be afforded through new carefully constructed and detailed designs. Heroic architecture has its place, but trying to make the city a heroic work of art can destroy its richness. Apart from key buildings, the designers of a city should be anonymous. Koolhaas and de Solà Morales, along with Jane Jacobs and many others, agree that the quality of streets and street life with its conflicts and congestions is what make a city a city (J. Jacobs 1961; A. Jacobs 1993; de Solà Morales 2004; de Solà Morales et al. 2008).

The observations about rationalist designs are uniform across the spectrum of the individual advocacies and so are treated here as a single entity. Some of the comments have nevertheless been aimed specifically and inevitably at the work of CIAM and Le Corbusier, the intellectual giant among twentieth-century rationalists. The observations about the designs of the empiricists vary considerably depending on the type of urban design advocated.

Rationalist Urban Design

The rationalists came in for praise and criticism from the time that their first manifestoes were promulgated. Their progressive thinking and lack of concern for the pragmatic meant that many of their ideas remain on the drawing board. When built, many of their schemes failed to capture the hearts of those who inhabited them. *The Charter of Athens* did not deal with the city as a dwelling place (Huet 1984), and its advocacies were overgeneralized (Irazábal 2001). The exception has been in the custom designs of individual houses where there was a close relationship between architect and client (see Soth 1983 on Le Corbusier's clients and Eaton 1969 on the clients of Frank Lloyd Wright). The major departure from this observation is the Farnsworth House in Plano, Illinois, designed by Mies van der Rohe. Regarded as an 'iconic' masterpiece of minimalist architecture and now a museum, it was never inhabited by Dr. Edith Farnsworth; it was not a place to which she could retreat and enjoy her hobbies. The building was a work of art to be admired, not lived in. The family of Frederick (Woodie) Garber (1877–1960) hated living in the glass Miesian house that he designed for them (Garber 2017). Many of the modernist houses were simply uncomfortable; Le Corbusier's Villa Savoye was "cold and damp" (Sbriglo 1999, 145).

The rationalists' boldness of thought resulted in the invention of a new urban design language that excited the cognoscenti. The rationalists shattered past design paradigms. They recognized that the world was being changed by technological developments and believed that the patterns of existing cities were inadequate to deal with this change. They came to grips with the requirements of automobile drivers and the necessity to have a hierarchy of roads catering to vehicular traffic moving at different speeds. Cities may already have had such a hierarchy, but the rationalists codified it. The short blocks of the pedestrian-friendly city gave way to long blocks with as few intersections as possible that might impede traffic flow. Streets became the separators of blocks, not the seams for everyday life. Their function as the location of human interactions became lost. A functional city became one of free-flowing traffic with buildings set in parkland. The timeless qualities of urban life were forgotten.

Rationalists argued that their designs allowed for a maximum liberty of action, but their critics say it meant a liberty to not do much and a liberty to avoid responsibility (J. Jacobs 1961; Irving 1993; Hughes 2006). Tony Garnier took the deterministic view of the impact of a rational environment on human behavior to the extreme in arguing that having a good built environment would result in well-behaved people. Neither police force nor law courts formed part of his *Cité Industrielle*. Making this kind of assumption about the impact of the affordances of the built environment on the behavior of a city's inhabitants needs to be avoided. People's satisfaction with the places that they inhabit is based on their ability to choose the environments in which they wish to live (see Cooper 2007 on Leon Festinger's 1957 dissonance theory).

The Unité d'habitation in Marseille was originally popular with its inhabitants; they chose to live there because of what it offered toward their ways of life. The closing down of the shops in the building because their service areas were too small did not affect them much; they lived metropolitan, not parochial, lives. Many had second homes elsewhere (Avin 1973). Unités in other places were inhabited by people who had no choice. Thankful though they were for shelter, they did not perceive the Unités as good places in which to live. The one in Marseille deteriorated in quality, and its population changed such that by the 1990s it was in poor shape (Hughes 2006).

Perhaps the most telling criticism of rationalist design has been that CIAM promoted a self-serving and unrealistic view of architects' competencies. Architects' knowledge of cities and how they function was more limited than they believed and less than they believed they needed to know. To CIAM's members, architects were a special caste of (usually) men who possessed a special expertise that could resolve the problems of the world by designing 'objectively.' Architects may be a special caste of people, but their work, as all designs are, is value laden and biased by the way they examine their surroundings and the evidence on which they draw. Indeed, the rationalists eschewed knowledge of how cities function in favor of their own carefully thought-out logic of what should be done to make them efficient. Several of CIAM's tenets are therefore questionable. Although contemporary empiricists tended to believe the same thing, possibly the most frequent and the one to which the current empiricists respond the most vigorously has been the proposition that the segregation of land uses in a city enhances people's quality of life. In some cases, it does, but this line of thinking became embodied in many zoning ordinances that are now, in the early decades of the twenty-first century, being reconsidered (Talen 2012).

The diversity of people and local cultural and climatic contexts was something that urban designers of the rationalist school failed to consider until late in the twentieth century. The aftermath of World War Two demanded rapidly produced urban designs, particularly mass housing schemes, on a large scale. The rationalists' provided authorities with a set of generic design ideas that could be rapidly deployed. It was pragmatically easy. The buildings could be mass-produced. Yet, Team 10 architects Michel Écohard and George Candilis, in their work in ABAT-Afrique, showed a much more empiricist attitude than they had in many of their earlier designs (Eleb 2000). Attitudes toward applied decorative elements were nevertheless authoritarian.

Adolf Loos (1870–1933), an early theorist of the Modern movement, advocated in his essay *Ornament and Crime* (1908) for plain façades for buildings. He opposed the decorative nature of the fin de siècle and *Vienna Secession* buildings. Le Corbusier's Calvinism is evident in his eschewing any added decoration in his designs. His mass housing types and their lack of decoration that might give a sense of locale culminated in Le Corbusier's aspiration: "I would create a single building for all nations and all climates" (Le Corbusier originally 1930; 1990, 110). He was an advocate for a global architecture. Werner Hegemann made a telling comment on why Le Corbusier's generic urban designs were so intoxicating. They attracted attention, he believed, "not because they are desirable, healthy, reasonable . . . but because they are theatrical . . . unreasonable and generally harmful and . . . [are] part of the moneymaking activity of the metropolis" (Oeschlin 1993, 287). Yet Hegemann too sought a universal urbanism that would benefit humanity (Collins 2005).

The rationalists paid little consideration to the needs of specific populations. Children's needs were relegated to the provision of playgrounds and schools (Parr 1969; Ward 1990). Nothing was said about their ability to negotiate the city independently and the behavior settings that

A Critique of Urban Design

could provide them with both fun and educational experiences as part of everyday life. Similarly, little was said about the requirements of other people at different stages in their life cycles.

Residents adapted to the affordances of the new, sunny, well-ventilated habitats provided for them. The accommodation was better than that in the slums, even if the neighborhoods did not have the intricate patterns that easily afford the development of the social networks that made life in the slums, at least, interesting and survivable. The designs were often over-manicured, not messy enough (Buchanan 2013). Perhaps the most telling of all criticisms is Aldo van Eyck's comment on the design of the Dutch rationalists. He observed,

> Instead of the inconvenience of filth and confusion we have the boredom of hygiene. The material slum has gone—but what has replaced it? Just mile upon mile of unorganized nowhere, and nobody feeling he is somewhere.
>
> *(Smithson 1968)*

Alison Smithson and Peter Smithson's design for Robin Hood Gardens fared little better even though it is regarded by several major UK architects as an architectural masterpiece, as Italian architects regard Corviale and many of the cognoscenti the Farnsworth House. The three examples reinforce the point that attempts to change people's behavior through design will not succeed unless they are predisposed to change.

The overall judgment of the rationalists' ideas was that they threw the baby out with the bath water. They focused on ridding the city of what they perceived to be its problems and chaotic nature (Hall 1988, 4). Consequently, the positive aspects of urban life did not form part of the generic solutions they were formulating for cities. This view is reflected in Robert Hughes's overly harsh comment on Le Corbusier's *Cite Contemporaine*:

> the car would abolish the human street, and possibly the human foot. Some people would have airplanes too. The one thing no one would have is a place to bump into each other, walk the dog, strut, one of the hundred random things that people do . . . being random was loathed by Le Corbusier . . . its inhabitants surrender their freedom of movement to the omnipresent architect.
>
> *(Hughes 2006)*

Many urban designs today continue to be derivations of the purist modernist paradigm.

Critics outside East Asia look with awe and puzzlement at the modernist urban design schemes, particularly the vast high-rise housing developments that are being built on a massive scale in China and Korea. The east–west aligned rows of multistory slab buildings facing south are so close together that it is difficult to believe that sunlight reaches the ground floor of many apartments during the winter months. The latitude in which a scheme is located seems to make no impact on how a generic design is employed. After the experience in the United States and Europe where many such projects have been demolished to make way for lower-rise, street-related buildings at the same population density, the new East Asian projects seem to have major opportunity costs associated with them. They nevertheless continue to be built.

The designs, often walled and gated superblocks, are isolated from their surroundings and pay no attention to traditions (Miao 2003; Kan, Forsyth, and Rowe 2017). The services they supply are insufficient relative to their size. The model of life on which they are based is a limited one. Many of the surrounding sidewalks are deserted. Their inhabitants, however, seem pleased with their living conditions. The units meet their expectations, and the complexes' socially isolating nature affords much-prized privacy. Residents desire a way of life that fits their newfound social status and the architecture that displays it. The urbane qualities of messier, more-disorderly environments are not something they desire.

Neo-modernist urban designs are more empirical than the purist modernist schemes. In many, using the 'street' to act as a 'seam' for local life has been rediscovered. The buildings depart from the modernist norm; they are visually richer, and each has its own identity. The more sculptural buildings tend to stand alone as individual displays. Hyper-modernist urban designs have yet to discover the street, but they take the sculptural qualities of buildings to the extreme.

The urban designs consisting of hyper-modernist buildings are visually dramatic; they push the boundaries of geometric and structural inventiveness. They certainty provide excitement, if momentary, as works of art (Buchanan 2015). Spectacular buildings have a place in the city, but it is not the way to create precincts for the enjoyment of people as they go about their daily lives. Few hyper-modernist urban designs seem to be overly concerned with the nature of the public realm, except to allow enough space for each building to be observed and admired as an individual object.

One of the questions that must be addressed in any urban design project is, Who develops the goals and objectives of a proposed scheme? A second questions is, Where should the information providing the basis for a design come from? The designing process envisaged by the rationalists was strictly a top-down one; the users of the built environment had no expertise to offer architects. To Walter Gropius, the masses were "too intellectually undeveloped to offer any assistance" (Ley 1989, 5). This view is now regarded as shortsighted: After all, who would know more about the ways of life of those for whom one is designing than the people themselves? Yet they are neither very good at explicating their views nor knowledgeable about possibilities from which they might choose.

Empiricist Urban Design

Empiricists are often regarded as a backward-looking coterie. Many appeared not to like the liveliness of cities. Jane Jacobs, an empiricist thinker, accused people such as Ebenezer Howard and Clarence Stein of being decentralists who neglected the positive qualities of existing urban environments (J. Jacobs 1961). Jacobs came under criticism because her model world was essentially *her* world. She did succeed in bringing attention to the urban qualities of Greenwich Village in New York that she and many residents but few city planners and architects of the 1960s admitted to admiring. She, however, failed to explicitly recognize that those qualities did not form everybody's idea of a good place to live and raise a family.

Another observation was that, as a group, the empiricists failed to embrace modern technology and its potentials. They believed in technological progress but failed to consider what it meant for the design of cities and the precincts within them. In Ebenezer Howard's defense, he was writing before car use became widespread and so did not consider the potential impact of automobile traffic when he drew up the garden city; Clarence Stein in his design for Radburn certainly did (Stein 1949, 1966).

A broader criticism was that the post-Sitte empiricists encouraged urban sprawl and the loss of agricultural land. They failed to deal with the evolving nature of the city and the opportunities provided by the brownfield sites within it. Sitte's ideas were dismissed as being romantic. Specific empiricist design models also came under criticism.

The Garden City

The garden city model had and still has its supporters and detractors. Among the twentieth-century champions were critics such as Lewis Mumford. He wrote that "people who regard city and garden as antithetical terms need to look anew at lived areas of major cities" (L. Mumford 1965). The harshest criticism of the garden city idea was that it took the inherent beauty of two environments—the city and the countryside—and replaced it with a monotonous, though greener, setting for life. Le Corbusier dismissed the garden city as a combination of the worst of the countryside and the worst of the city (Fishman 1977).

Howard's contributions to urban design thought and subsequent designs are many. He identified the basic components of a community as part of a holistic approach to city planning and urban design. His idea of a greenbelt-bounded city was directly responsible for several postwar policies to constrict the sprawling city (Butcher 2010). His proposal for locating industries in satellite towns on cheap farmland was a concept that brought together urban planning and socioeconomic reform. His greatest legacy is, perhaps, the importance of providing the affordances for the development of a sense of community in new towns. He, nevertheless, like others, overestimated the power of local facilities to create a sense of community. A sense of community has to grow from the grassroots; only formal organizations can be dictated from above (Suttles 1972).

While a garden city was to be a self-contained unit, Howard recognized that people would want to travel from a garden city to the central city and from one garden city to another. The location of the station on the periphery of the city in the generic city model limited access to the system. Clarence Stein, who regarded Radburn as a dormitory settlement, and the pedestrian pocket advocates deal with commuting more directly. Stein thought the station should be located where three neighborhoods intersect. Advocates of the pedestrian pocket model for suburban designs include a station at the center of a pocket (Kelbaugh 1987). TODs today are similar in concept. The automobile nevertheless remains the central transportation mode in these suburban models, as it does in life.

Residents who have chosen to live in garden cities enjoy living in them and take pride in their surroundings (Eserin 1995; Rook 2013). Renowned UK architect Richard Rodgers (b. 1933), however, believes that building new towns along garden city lines in the United Kingdom, at least, is ridiculous given the large number of brownfield sites of former industrial and abandoned residential areas that exist in cities today. These sites already have the infrastructure for new developments and have easy access to the whole metropolitan area via existing modes of transportation whose capacity and quality of service can be boosted. He worries that garden city–type developments are strictly middle-class environments in which the residents rely heavily on automobile use (Stott 2017). Much the same comment had been made about Radburn (Birch 1980). What garden city enthusiasts did not foresee was the massive increase in the world's urban population. The same observation can be made about Frank Lloyd Wright's Broadacre City.

A Note on Broadacre City

Broadacre City is based on the correct assumption that most people love their cars. Driving is a rewarding experience that drivers engage in day after day. The love of the automobile and Frank Lloyd Wright's stated dislike of 'steel and stone' urban areas fueled his vision of an ultra-low–density city. He believed that 'nature' was 'Nature' and the built environment should be in 'Nature' even if it was highly manicured (Wright 1932, 1935, 1945).

Broadacre City, like the ideas of Le Corbusier, assumed a universal model of a family and a universally accepted good way of life. Wright also assumed that a spontaneous pedestrian life was neither desired nor desirable. His proposal also belittled the idea of creating territorial communities. Space was provided for formal gatherings, such as fairs in Broadacre City, but it was assumed that all other gatherings of people would be independently prearranged. The residents would have maximum autonomy and be highly self-reliant. The irony is that a strong public authority would be required to administer any such city.

The population density that Wright envisaged for his city was five hundred people per square mile (three hundred people per square kilometer), which is considerably lower than current US suburban densities of between 2,000 and 3,000 people per square mile. Given the growing population of the United States, let alone other countries, such densities are implausible. A city of 1 million would require 2,000 square miles (5,180 square kilometers) of land. Consider what a city of 10,000,000 would require. Wright's proposal, like those of Le Corbusier and Howard, made us sit up and think about ways of life and the patterns of built form required to sustain them.

New Urbanism and Smart Growth

If new urbanists have been critical of rationalist designs, rationalists have been dismissive of the new urbanist paradigm. In academia, the designs have been derided as outmoded, and they have been ignored in much of the architectural press (Solomon 2017). New urbanist designs have nevertheless been widely implemented and are much liked as places in which to live. The architectural cognoscenti prefer to see a more up-to-date aesthetic. Critics, such as Randall O'Toole (b. 1952), who favor free market and libertarian ideologies, prefer pragmatic, market-driven approaches to urban development. Standard, spacious suburban areas and the extensive use of automobiles is what people like (O'Toole 2007). Joel Kotkin (b. 1952), a geographer, points out that most Americans, at least, want to live in a suburban home set among trees (Kotkin 2017). Pragmatic suburban designs with these features sell well, and that is the criterion by which success, so the libertarians state, should be measured. New urbanist developments sell well too. Despite that, the architectural cognoscenti find places such as Celebration aesthetically stultifying. The buildings, they believe, are trapped by the precedents on which they draw and thus lack authenticity and architectural integrity.

The libertarians argue that the new urbanist developments and smart growth principles are draconian in their guidelines and design controls (Inam 2011). They believe that the whole idea of New Urbanism and the form-based design codes stifle individual rights. Ironically, they point out that new urbanist developments, because they are in high demand, turn out to have property values that exclude the very people, such as schoolteachers and paramedics, who are needed to operate them.

One of the criticisms of new urbanist ideas is that they encourage urban sprawl. Many new urbanist projects have indeed been on the urban fringe, but the others have been remarkably well-accepted inner-city developments on brownfield sites (Mehaffy 2010). Their designs draw on urban models.

Some observers believe that new urbanist designs are not sustainable in their present controlled form. To be sustainable, a settlement, whatever its size, must be adaptable to change (Durack 2001). Ruth Durack recognizes the point that civil libertarians make about meeting market demands but sees New Urbanism in a different light. New urbanist schemes are not easy to change without destroying the idea on which they are based. The degree to which this lack of flexibility matters is open to debate.

The hyper-modernists regard new urbanist developments to be irrelevant in today's times. People live metropolitan lives, and the local community concept makes no sense. Yet an observation of any city shows that local areas do matter. They may only be neighborhoods of limited liability—neighbors have few mutual obligations—but those obligations remain important

A Critique of Urban Design

(see Lang and Moleski 2010). The opinion that hyper-modernists share with the architectural cognoscenti is that the architecture of most new urbanist developments is neither eye-catching nor forward-looking.

Postmodernism

Postmodernism, whether it is a style or a frame of mind, had one crucial effect on urban design. Its acceptance in intellectual circles allowed many architects to loosen the bonds of the strict rectangular geometry of the rationalist model. It rekindled an awareness of the past even though it has often been brushed aside as kitsch, catering to popular commercial consumer tastes (Kjellman-Chapin 2010). Postmodern designs have been dismissed as the result of a twenty-year flirtation with historicism. It is, however, more than that and is now being reappraised (Farrell and Furman 2017). It has returned to popularity because its designs are more interesting and fun than the dreariness of much-earlier rationalist urban design. People are also beginning to tire of the new, 'clever,' geometrically distorted hyper-modernist buildings that dot cities (Ray 2017). How widespread this distain is remains to be seen.

A telling criticism of postmodernism is that it focused on the appearance of buildings and open spaces and not on the social opportunities that designs should provide. In that sense, it was narrowly functional. Postmodern architects set out to be progressive, but that spirit was not evident in the projects they designed. Deconstruction, also a reaction to rationalist modernism, was something different.

Deconstruction

Deconstruction's concepts influenced only a minority of architects, landscape architects, and urban designers. There is little to show in the way of completed urban design schemes. Parc de la Villette was given earlier as an exemplar of the approach to urban design; the project is also claimed by landscape urbanists as an exemplar of their thinking.

One of the criticisms of deconstruction is that architects and urban designers should not be borrowing techniques and ideas from other disciplines. They should be drawing on the field's own history. That history, however, shows that the design fields have long been borrowing concepts from other disciplines. The idea of creating urban design proposals by superimposing layers of partial designs on the basis of single concerns, such as service areas for groceries or distribution of pocket parks or road networks, one on top of the other and adjusting/synthesizing them to make a multifaceted design, is appealing. It reflects Ian McHarg's analytical layering approach to deciding what areas of land can be built on and what needs to be left in order to maintain a well-functioning natural ecological system (McHarg 1969).

The results achieved by using deconstructive methods approach the complexities of multi-nuclear cities that have evolved unselfconsciously, over time following several underlying functional and economic orders. The question is, What are the important variables that constitute the layers? For the design of Parc de La Villette, Tschumi used three layers for structuring the design. How many does one use in applying his method to other types of urban design projects? What should they be? Can parametric equations accurately describe the relationships among layers?

Parametric Urban Design

Applying parametric methods to create an urban design is a seductive idea. Using them is becoming straightforward because the software needed is now readily available. Current

355

designing approaches involve iterative conjectures about what should be done and about evaluating what is produced. Parametric design automates that process. The idea that a designer can change a value of one variable in a computer-based model and be shown how the whole design is altered is attractive. How well does parametric design really work? Questions arise about the algorithms that form its basis.

What are the variables taken into consideration? How are they related? How do the algorithms embrace qualitative variables such as the history of a locale that contribute so much to design quality? Are such considerations simply outside the interest of those city planners and architects who are promoting parametric design? Is the concern simply one of creating novel overall geometric shapes for a design? Recent developments promise to include a broader range of variables than parametric design presently does (Speranza 2016).

Parametric design has produced novel architectural and urban forms on the computer screen. But does it result in cost-effective, pleasant streets to walk along and buildings in which to work or live? The experience in implementing the One North Plan in Singapore is instructive. The original visually exciting, curving profile generated by the parametric design has given way pragmatically to a series of all-of-a-piece urban designs projects under the loose umbrella of the original master plan. The overall form that has been built has only a slight resemblance to that plan. It ends up being a scheme based on a generic neo-modernist urban design that is relatively frugal in its consumption of energy.

Sustainable Designs, Landscape Urbanism, and Agrarian Urbanism

The need for urban designs to minimize their carbon footprint and respect the natural ecology of their sites is not a passing fad. Many claims have been made by the proponents of various approaches to create sustainable built worlds. Evaluating them is difficult because few data are available on how well projects meet specific ends. The greening goal of landscape urbanists seems to be an aesthetic end as much as one to achieve an ecologically sound built environment for the everyday lives of diverse sets of people. Not much is said about its social aims.

As a design paradigm, landscape urbanism has been held back by its difficult-to-decipher academic rhetoric and the failure of its proponents to produce any clear generic models, procedural or substantive, of their positions. The best-known schemes have been plug-in urban designs such as High Line Park in New York. Its many visitors have found it to be an interesting and pleasant place, and intended or not, it has served as a catalyst for high-income development around it.

Landscape urbanists, like new urbanists, address the question of urban sprawl, but they are not antagonistic to it. They regard it as inevitable and not a problem to solve. In this way, they support the position of civil libertarians that sprawl is what individual householders want so it should be regarded as an acceptable aspect of the changing morphology of metropolitan areas. Sprawl, however, results from the choices that people make from the pragmatic, market-driven possibilities available to them.

Cities' sprawling into the countryside stems from decisions made by governments, from the national level down to the municipal one, in establishing the incentives and regulations that govern where and how property investment decisions are made. These processes can be reformed; sprawl is not inevitable.

The strongest objection to landscape urbanists' thinking is that they, like the modernists, have fallen into the deterministic trap: "the magical belief that the form of soft (that is vegetated) open space by itself can generate good-quality urban form" (Mehaffy 2011). People's ways of

A Critique of Urban Design

life get lost in the shuffle. The full range of functions of the built environment for a full range of people is forgotten. Landscape urbanists now seek a broader approach to ecological design based on the cultural peculiarities of a place, much as advocated by Anne Spirn in *The Granite Garden: Urban Nature and Human Design* (1985).

Smart Cities

The history of urban planning and design is replete with situations where the enthusiasm for technological solutions overwhelms quality-of-life concerns when designers plan their urban designs (Leimenstoll 2017; Riggs, LaJeunesse, and Boswell 2017. The potential problem in developing smart cities is that the physical environment is adapted to making the control systems easier to operate, rather than the systems' being adapted to create high-quality environments for the lives of people and other species. Smart cities may provide efficient and safe environments for their inhabitants, but their protagonists say little about the qualities of smart cities as places to live or about the nature of future urban design projects (Angelakis et al. 2017). Songdo is hardly an example for the world to emulate. Existing cites such as New York, London, and Tokyo, in all their messiness, are more likely to become genuine smart cities, both technologically and as creative places, than any *new* smart town. At present, the development of smart cities is a top-down process led by the major global information technology companies seeking to maximize their own interests. A bottom-up approach to the design of the systems is also needed.

The development of technological advances such as autonomous vehicles and smart garbage disposal systems will be a blessing for residents of cities. The challenge will be to retain 'what works well' in cities in the face of the demand for technical innovation. The worry is that the chase for efficiency disregards the cultural characteristics of specific locations. Observers of the 2015 India government's Smart Cities Mission worry that the way efficiency, an admirable goal, is attained will destroy the informality and diversity of the cities and precincts where the program is being be rolled out: "How, for instance, will it deal with the slums of the country's cities at a time when the rural poor continue to migrate to them in their hundreds of thousands?" (Langar 2017). What will happen to the sacred cattle and pye-dogs that are ubiquitous in Indian cities?

Commentary: The Functions Addressed

Each urban design paradigm focuses on a set of design concerns that overlap but differ from those of the others. Proponents of each paradigm claim that their approach is the only way forward and should have hegemony in a competitive world. Landscape urbanists, for instance, believe that their concerns are the essential ones to addresses in cities. The functioning of the natural ecological environment and/or the artificially reconstructed natural environment is indeed an issue of paramount concern for the survival of people and other animate species. Other concerns, however, require equal attention in urban design.

The empiricist approaches to urban design, as exemplified in the garden city and in new urbanist and smart growth ideals, are conservative in nature. They, like much pragmatic design, are based on the sought-after settings for family life in a tranquil setting. The empiricists' advocacies say little about the lives of people who are not part of traditional nuclear families in an era when people such as students, single people, and couples without children are the largest population cohort in several countries.

Current paradigms seem to assume the position that designing to attain territorially based communities at the local level is largely irrelevant in an age of modern communications. The agrarian urbanists, however, believe that shared participation in urban farming endeavors will

357

enhance a sense of community at the local level. Countering such expectations are the changes in the way people conduct their lives. The elderly, parents with young children, and children themselves no longer necessarily lead parochial lives. Children in societies with advanced economies, it is said, no longer play informally in local open spaces. This view is culturally and, often, socioeconomically biased.

In some states of the United States, it is illegal for children to walk to school or be a playground unaccompanied by an adult (Sorrel 2016), but in many countries, children can still roam if their parents allow it. Not much attention is paid in any of the current urban design paradigms to how the design of cities can help children (or frail elderly people) to act independently. The concept of walkable neighborhoods based on ease of pedestrian access to services and the purchase of daily necessities is still part of the garden city and new urbanist agendas. Creating street layouts that make walking easier and, as importantly, pleasant and interesting, is a goal that they, and landscape urbanists, have in common (Speck 2013).

The ultimate impact of developments in information, communications, and transportation technologies may have on the morphology and functioning of cities for different segments of the population is unclear. Smart cities promise much in making the operation of traffic management more efficient, and more broadly, they will enable their residents and visitors to be better informed about how their city operates. Autonomous vehicles are likely to have a significant effect on the operation of cities, because they should, all being well, decrease the capacity required of many existing streets, enabling the leftover space to be allocated to the use of pedestrians and/or for other uses. The amount of space required for parked cars may also be substantially reduced as the amount of time cars stand idle lessens (Snyder 2018).

No current approach to urban design addresses the full set of functions that the built environment can serve; no approach can fulfill the needs of the full range of people, other species, and the ecological world at the same time. The question is, Can we create a paradigm and a set of generic solutions that are more inclusive?

Observations

Twentieth-century design paradigms were often presented to the world with a religious zeal. Proponents of each strove to sell their approach to potential clients and other designers because it was, they argued, the best way forward. Both rationalists and empiricists of the twentieth century were fervent in their faith that they had the correct intellectual basis for urban designing. They needed to recognize which functions of built form they were addressing and which ones they were neglecting. The evidence for what works and what does not work is substantial even if incomplete.

Organizations such as the Environmental Design Research Association (EDRA) and the International Association of People-Environment Studies (IPAS) were founded in the late 1960s and 1970s to further the work that architectural psychologists had begun. The research provides the information and theoretical basis for making design decisions, but its effect on the work of urban designers has been minimal. The design paradigm that researchers assume is not one that designers are willing to adopt (Francescato 1994). The researchers assumed a functionally rich, program-based problem-solving approach to design, whereas designers use a generic types-based approach. Consequently, all the evaluations/analyses of projects and the knowledge of what works and does not work had little effect on the way that twentieth-century architects and other designers thought about their work. Where does urban design go from here?

At the beginning of this century, in the *New Athens Charter*, the European Council of Town Planners presented a widely shared view of what existing cities should strive for in the future.

> Cities should do the following:
>
> - retain their cultural richness and diversity, resulting from their long histories, linking the past through the present to the future
> - become connected in a multitude of meaningful and functional networks
> - remain creatively competitive while striving for complementarity and cooperation
> - contribute decisively to the well-being of their inhabitants and users
> - integrate the human-made and natural elements of the environment
>
> The vision includes a framework for implementation consisting of the main issues and challenges that affect cities at the beginning of the third millennium and the commitment required by spatial planners in realizing that vision.

Figure 17.1   A summary of the basic precepts for cities in the *New Athens Charter*

Credit line: Derived from European Council of Town Planners (2003) by the author

The Athens Charter of 1933 promoted a functional, orderly city; the *New Athens Charter* of 2003 seeks a sustainable, connected utopia. The vision of future urban designs for cities is outlined in Figure 17.1.

What can we learn from these different precepts for urban designs and urban designing? The answer is the subject of the final chapter of this book.

Key References

Brolin, Brent C. 1976. *The Failure of Modern Architecture*. New York: Van Nostrand Reinhold.

Conn, Steven. 2014. *Americans Against the City: Urbanism in Twentieth Century*. New York: Oxford University Press.

Cuthbert, Alexander R. 2007. "Urban Design: Requiem for an Era: Review and Critique of the Last 50 Years." *Urban Design International* 12 (4): 177–223.

de Solà Morales i Rubió, Manuel. 2004. *Ciudades, Esquinas = City, Corners*. Barcelona: Forum.

Jacobs, Jane. 1961. *The Death and Life of Great American Cities*. New York: Random House. www.buurtwijs. nl/sites/default/files/buurtwijs/bestanden/jane_jacobs_the_death_and_life_of_great_american.pdf accessed June 5, 2019.

Kotkin, Joel. 2017. *The Human City: Urbanism for the Rest of Us*. Chicago: Agate.

18

The Way Forward

Toward Compact Cities

Stephen Hawking (1942–2018), the UK theoretical physicist, believed that Earth will come to a fiery end between 1,000 and 10,000 years from now. He strongly advocated for searching for another planet suitable for colonization (Savva 2018). It is intriguing to look that far ahead, but for the purposes here, a generation ahead is all that is reasonable. Cities and their suburbs in twenty-five years will not be that different from now. Or will they?

Smart cities, autonomous vehicles, and a more generally automated, robotic world will lead to changes in ways of life and thus the qualities of the built environment expected by diverse populations. Predicting those expectations with precision is impossible but pragmatically going forward on the path of financial least resistance is foolhardy. Scholars across the world have been diligently studying cities and the qualities of urban, suburban, and rural life in considerable depth during the past six decades. A plethora of thoughtful studies on our contemporary concerns and the nature of good cities has been published (e.g., Brown, Dixon, and Gillham 2014; Rose 2016). Much can be learned from them. What becomes clear is that some image of a good city is needed to guide us. It needs to be adaptable for use in specific cultural zones and climatic zones. It is also clear that a detailed program, or brief, is needed as a basis for any urban design (Rowe 1982).

Whereas

All cities, as noted in the Prologue, have a design, a morphology that evolves piece by piece with some of the pieces—major infrastructure projects and urban designs—being larger than others, such as individual buildings, street furniture, and flower boxes. Many self-consciously designed new towns, suburbs, and urban renewal projects are being built molded by the finances available, property developers' ideas, their designers' knowledge, and the design paradigm that they follow. Each paradigm knowingly addresses some functions that the built environment can serve and inadvertently others, some positively but others negatively. Some design parameters will be able to be defined with precision, others not. In addition, any new design, whether on a brownfield site or on a greenfield site, must accept existing conditions as a point of departure.

The four types of urban design projects that characterize current professional practice will continue to shape the field, new town design, and significant parts of cities well into the future. In summary, they are *total* urban design, *all-of-a-piece* urban design, *plug-in* urban design, and *piece-by-piece* urban design. They are all purposeful interventions into the ongoing processes of urban development made on behalf of some client, public or private, or some combination of the two. All designs will inevitably have an impact on the social environment, but societal problems such as homelessness, crime levels, and unemployment are public policy concerns that must be dealt with at the supra-urban level. Urban designers will confront them, nevertheless.

Societal Issues Confronting Urban Designers

During the next twenty-five years, any set of objectives for good urban designs needs to recognize the demographic, social, and cultural realities of a neoliberal economic world and the potential technological changes taking places within it. Current trends are unlikely to change dramatically during the coming generation. Some of the issues, such as the often-competing rights of property owners and of society at large, have a direct impact on urban design advocacies. Others have indirect consequences.

Individual Rights of Property Developers

Much future urban design work will be in capitalist or quasi-capitalist societies. Striving to produce sound schemes almost inevitably intrudes on the rights of property developers to create projects solely in their individual interests rather than for long-term, broad social benefits. Such a limited approach to urban development is, however, shortsighted at best and highly detrimental to large segments of society at worst. Property developers, public and private, need to respond to a broad range of human needs rather than seek to create pragmatic, easy-to-implement designs that are based entirely on maximizing profits.

Michael Porter and Mark Kramer recently observed that a large market exists for a 'shared-value' approach to urban design that property developers can seize on to make profits. They and their designers need to find development strategies that address business opportunities while they deal with social concerns. It is possible to do well financially by doing good work (Porter and Kramer 2011). Simultaneously, governments need to establish regulations that enable a shared-value approach to urban development. The implication is that urban designers need to be more aware of the problems and issues confronting society. They should bring the attention of property developers to the need to deal with a set of concerns beyond meeting the requirement of the instrumental functions of the projects that they initiate. This task is not easy, because the problems facing designers are complex.

Dealing With Complexity

In developing the program for any project, designers are confronted with a multiplicity of concerns raised by a variety of people. The problems that they face have been colorfully described as "wicked" (Rittel and Webber 1984). They are better considered as meta-problems (Cartwright 1973). They cannot be unequivocally resolved, because they deal with situations where many often-difficult-to-define variables are at play, and the values assigned to them are open to question. The whole design process is an argumentative one in which the people involved define issues of concern in their own terms (Bazjanic 1974). Development and architectural programs are devised without fully knowing what needs to be known. The power of designers comes either from their knowledge and skills or from their political adroitness in convincing

361

others that they have the expertise necessary to create worthwhile, multifunctional designs. Knowledge and skills are preferable.

The tendency is for those involved in creating a design to act as if problems that they face are simple. Simple, in this context, does not mean easy but rather that designers redefine problems in the terms of a generic solution that they see as a close fit to the situation that they are addressing and/or one that coincides with their body of work. In this way, only partial solutions to the array of concerns get addressed. The interest of specific groups of people and the side effects of potential designs get neglected. If we recognize and face the complexity of situations without oversimplifying them, we can do better. The difficulty is that even seemingly clearly understood concerns are difficult to define with precision. Take sustainable environments for example.

Sustainable Environments

The necessity of creating a well-functioning biogenic environment may be the most important concern for the long-term survival of *Homo sapiens*. The changes taking place in the morphology of cities raise many questions concerning designing not only in fragile environments such as in marshlands or on brownfield sites but on any site.

Many issues relating to the natural environment fall outside the realm of abilities of urban designers to address when they are considering which requirements to focus on when designing specific projects. They are global in scale and need to be addressed at the international policy level by collaborating nations. At an urban design scale, the requirement is to design well for both human habitation and the welfare of the biogenic environment. City plans and urban designs almost automatically affect all of the following:

1. land forms
2. the hydrology of a site
3. the way that winds move over, across, and through building complexes, precincts, and cities
4. the level of pollutants and wastes generated
5. the habitat of insects, birds, and animals
6. the way hard surfaces—roads, roofs, surface parking lots, and city squares—create heat islands and after rainfalls transmit pollutants into waterways
7. the biodiversity of a site

The goal is to create a biologically self-correcting system of built and open spaces. On green-field sites, healthy landscapes can be created as part of an urban design project. They will inevitably differ from the original state of the land. Remediating brownfield sites is more difficult. All these considerations should nevertheless be given a higher priority than they are given at present. Designing with the climate in mind is a step forward.

Tailoring new built environments to the qualities of specific climates can eliminate or, at least, reduce the impact of damaging weather events and also minimize the amount of energy consumed in maintaining human comfort levels. The mechanisms required to achieve climate-appropriate designs involve the spacing of buildings and the use, or not, of vegetation and water as temperature-modifying elements (Chandler 1976; Arnold 1988; Givoni 1998; Emmanuel 2005; Oke et al. 2017). A major concern now is with the changing climate of planet Earth (Gill et al. 2007; Hamin and Gurran 2008; Calthorpe 2010; Kellett 2016).

Urban designs in many locations will need to respond to the effects of global warming and the concomitant rise in sea levels. Weather patterns are becoming more extreme, so buildings and the spaces between them need to become more robust. In addition, more concern will need

The Way Forward

to be paid to the wind-channeling attributes of streets and other urban open spaces. Three-dimensional urban profiles and the effects that they have on the turbulence of air movement will need to be considered in creating the skylines of new developments. These concerns will, however, not be seriously addressed by either property developers or design professionals until public policies are enacted that dictate where building can take place and the configuration of individual structures.

Policymakers need to be concerned with mitigating the effects of climate change and from this concern establish programs retrofitting those parts of cities in danger of being flooded by rising sea levels or storm surges. The retrofitting will almost certainly involve a range of plug-in urban designs: the building of berms and other flood-control measures. More generally, in many parts of the world, designing for sustainability must deal with the demands of expanding populations.

Population Growth and Demographic Changes

Most metropolitan areas around the world are swelling in population numbers. Migrants continue to pour into cities from rural areas in countries as diverse as Angola, India, and China. Refugees increase the populations of the countries in Europe, and emigrants leave poorer and/or politically unstable countries in search of better lives. The question is, How best should cities house this growing and, often, culturally diverse population?

The solution in many countries, as shown in the earlier chapters of this book, has been to pragmatically apply generic designs derived from the rationalists' design paradigm to the provision of housing on a massive scale. This approach has been largely abandoned in the countries of Europe and North America. Metropolitan areas in those countries are undergoing a densification of residential units in their centers and the continued growth of suburbs on their peripheries. Many suburban areas have core areas approximating those of the traditional central business districts of cities (Garreau 1992).

The solution is multipronged: continuing the development of low-rise, high-density, but mixed-use residential neighborhoods on urban brownfield sites, clustering housing in inner-city neighborhoods, and decentralizing employment opportunities. New town and suburban developments must be attractive to a broad segment of the population by having efficient infrastructure components and strong supportive services: schools, healthcare facilities, and other social facilities. High-density developments need to have the number and variety of potential entertainment and recreational behavior settings that are commensurate with population numbers. The public domain of streets and open spaces should be culturally specific but adaptable. The architecture needs to be easy to personalize without compromising the overall design qualities of an area. In the past, immigrant groups have personalized the neighborhoods that they have inherited over time and will no doubt strive to do so in the future.

While many countries have populations with a low median age; countries with highly developed economies are seeing an increase in the proportion of the population of people who are over sixty-five years old. This increase should lead to a growing concern for designing barrier-free environments and the provision of supportive services for frail people whose orbit remains close to home. A portion of the elderly population will be suffering from dementia. Designing neighborhoods to be easy for them to navigate would make the urban world a pleasant place for all (Mitchell, Burton, and Rahman 2004). Designing with children's independent behavior in mind would achieve the same end.

Culturally appropriate ways of dealing with the dead and how bodies are treated and disposed of has major land-use implications for cities. The design of necropolises is not something

363

Looking Back to Look Forward

that urban designers often contemplate. The swelling of the world's population and the filling of existing burial grounds may mean that some societies/religions will need to rethink the way that they deal with their dead. This concern raises the question of multiculturalism more generally.

MULTICULTURALISM

Cities in countries that are perceived to be prosperous and safe attract immigrants. Often, new arrivals bring with them patterns of behavior and values that are substantially different from those of the countries in which they have found a haven. They seek psychological security in enclaves of people like themselves, thus forming ethnic precincts. Over time, individuals and/or their children have adapted to function well in the settings of the broader, often-unwelcoming society while retaining something of their own heritage.

Historically, migrants have had much in common with their new cultural environments, but nowadays, they can have radically different and difficult-to-reconcile attitudes to life and relationships among people. How best should their interests and those of the broader society be considered? Although this is an important societal and political concern, such issues of homogeneity and heterogeneity impinge on the creation of programs/briefs for urban design projects (Lang 2016). Small homogenous enclaves within a heterogeneous set, with their members using common central facilities, may well be the way to design large mixed-use, predominantly residential developments.

DESIGNING FOR DECLINING CITIES

Most urban designs are built in expanding economies. Designing for contraction presents different problems. A significant number of cities and many small towns and villages are in decline; the industries that formed their economic base have left or are leaving. Their inhabitants, particularly the young, follow, seeking opportunities elsewhere. These places include the 'rust belt' cities of North America, Europe, and Asia (Dewar and Thomas 2012; Ryan 2012). The landscape urbanist approach is to turn abandoned land in cities into parkland, and new urbanist approaches have been used in revitalizing surviving neighborhoods. Villages in many rural areas also become deserted as farmlands go out of production. They return to something approximating their prior conditions, depending on whatever vegetation takes root there.

Income and Resource Disparities

Not only is the proportion of elderly people in economically developed countries increasing, but an hour-glass-shaped distribution of the population by income is being predicted for the future (Florida 2017; Savoia 2017). The bulges at the top and the bottom represent the number of the rich and poor and the narrow neck the middle class. Without public policy interventions, the change could lead to an ever-increasing disparity in the quality of the built environment of the wealthy and those living in poverty. Life in the behavior-setting rich central neighborhoods of cities of the wealthier countries of the world has become very expensive. Poverty-stricken inner-city neighborhoods, brimming with social problems, are likely to be gentrified because their locations provide access to the benefits of the dense inner parts of cities that many higher-income people find attractive. The poor thus get displaced, and the middle-class gets squeezed out in the bidding war for existing desirable living environments.

Responding on the scale necessary to reduce this imbalance is a political problem that few societies wish to address wholeheartedly. The public sector needs to reassert a leadership role in setting the program for urban development policies in general and urban design projects in particular. It needs to take a proactive role. A double-pronged approach to dealing with the situation is required. In the first place, affordable housing, particularly for service workers, is needed. Second, the rental market needs to be prompted, through legislation, to make the vast number of empty units in cities such as London and New York available to the middle class. Slum clearance must be accompanied by rent control and subsidized housing. Equal attention must be paid to the maintenance of the public component of the built environment and the services provided in poor neighborhoods and in wealthy ones. Urban designers, except in the design of publicly sponsored new towns and social housing estates, have not been engaged in designing for/with poor people. Designing to improve the quality of life of people living in slums in wealthy countries has proven to be an intractable problem. Demolition and rebuilding in the way that we have done almost everywhere have frequently been soul destroying. In poorer countries, the problems are even more severe.

A slum, in the context of the economically developing world, is an unauthorized settlement of poorly constructed structures on land to which residents have no legal right of tenure. It is unsanitary and short on basic amenities. The behavior settings that exist have more than the desirable number of people required for them to work effectively. In other words, they are overcrowded. Despite such squalid, unhygienic living conditions, the social networks of mutual assistance may be strong. The infrastructure of such areas needs to be improved piece by piece through a coordinated strategy of sequentially making small-scale adjustments, as Geddes suggested for Belrampur in the 1920s (Geddes 1917; Tyrwhitt 1947). The results will not be visually dramatic but will work well in incrementally improving the lives of people living in slums. Access to outside employment opportunities through efficient and inexpensive transportation modes is crucial.

Competing Functions/Goals

All urban design deals with creating places and links that serve many purposes. A clash often exists between the function of developments as expressive statements of their creator(s) and their function as supportive settings for life. Residents want places to be enjoyable *and* affordable; property developers and financing organizations want a development to be as profitable as possible. The distribution of power to make decisions varies depending on a person's or a group's financial resources and/or political connections. How comprehensive can any urban design be?

The design goal in any situation should be to attain a Pareto improvement—one that may favor one group's interests but does not make others worse off. For instance, designing neighborhoods that are rich in behavior settings that meet the needs of children, elderly people, and those individuals and families who enjoy using parochial facilities does not place limitations on those who lead metropolitan ways of life. The latter can ignore local possibilities.

A Changing World

If people living in 1960 were suddenly placed in a city fifty years later, in 2010, they would be mildly confused, whereas a person picked up in 1910 and placed in a city in 1960 would have been totally bewildered. Changes in cities and design practice between 1970 and the early 2000s were piecemeal and incremental, not radical. The world now seems to be on the cusp of some major city-changing technological developments. What are the implications for urban design?

It is impossible to predict all the technological changes that are likely to affect urban design in the future. One can look at current trends and extrapolate on the basis of them, but that may not yield valid predictions. Autonomous vehicles, when/if they become the norm as a mode of

Looking Back to Look Forward

transport, are likely to lead to a significant reduction in the amount of space required for parking and for street widths (Snyder 2018). New developments will be designed on the basis of the performance characteristics of such vehicles. Drones may be widely used to deliver small-scale goods to individual households and businesses. If so, they will require buildings to have places that will have unique addresses that can be recognized by drones. In addition, they will need places where it is safe to leave packages. Will this change occur, or is this imagined future as fanciful as the early-twentieth-century images of cities full of personal aircraft flitting down air corridors above streets?

Urban designers need to start thinking in terms of the strategies required to attain specific urban qualities, rather than achieving specific ends through hard and fast master plans. 'Strategy' here refers to planning/designing a sequence of actions directed at attaining a goal in a logical, step-by-step manner. The outcomes at each step can be evaluated before deciding on the next course of action. Such a process could take place at a breakneck pace, but it could stretch out over years, depending on the nature of a project and the political and economic context in which it is being developed.

Thinking about the design and implementation process in this way implies a breadth-first approach to urban designing, where the first step taken is the one that leaves a variety of future options open rather than the one that immediately seems best. The creative process is one of conjecturing, producing ideas, testing them in the abstract, and implementing one. If it meets specific criteria well enough, then another step forward is taken (Simon 1956). This observation has implications for the way we go about developing the programs and design characteristics of all types of urban design projects. Many total urban designs will, however, be developed as the result of depth-first approaches, where the target is to get a design produced as quickly as possible and then, if time is available, repeat the process in the hope of creating a better one.

Fiscal Responsibilities

One of the functions of all urban designs, other than those that are purely philanthropic gestures, is to turn a profit on the money invested by property developers and financial agencies. For municipal governments, new urban designs enhance tax revenues. Much of the questioning about urban design proposals is over their financial feasibility and the identification of potential sources of finance for the capital costs of designing and building a project and for the operating cost of running and maintaining it. The second is often neglected in bringing a project into existence. The world is replete with urban designs, buildings, and landscapes that are poorly maintained. Indeed, many of the perceived failures of projects in terms of the social well-being of their users are attributed to poor maintenance rather than design flaws.

Many designers believe that being concerned with fiscal issues falls outside the domain of their responsibility. For them, the fiscal success of a project and the plaudits that it receives in the architectural press are nevertheless important in obtaining further commissions. Urban designers thus need to be fully aware of the costs of the proposals they create and promote. This position does not mean that idealistic designs cannot be sought, but the ability to design well-crafted projects, within budgetary limitations, is a necessary skill for designers. Where does this discussion leave us? We need a clear goal toward which to strive.

The Goal

Having an idealized goal is important in guiding one's thoughts and actions. The goal in life for structural engineer Robert Le Nicolais (1897–1977) was to design a beam of infinite span and zero weight (Motro 2007). Unattainable, it remains a worthwhile guiding light. Urban design efforts should be guided by an image of what constitutes a good city, and each project should be shaped in the direction of that image. What, however, makes a good city given the societal issues under discussion?

A Good City

Everybody has some representation, however vague, of what constitutes a good city, a good small town, or a good neighborhood in their heads. It will be an image of the built environment of streets and buildings; its social offerings are implicit in the depiction (Strauss 1961). The images are largely subconscious, based on personal experiences and the influence of what is portrayed in movies, books, advertising, and on television. The images of good places that property developers and urban designers have may be more concrete, but they are still largely subconscious.

The neoliberal attitude is that there is no idealized design to guide design actions; good cities result from the free flow of investment capital and property developers' creating pragmatic projects that meet the set of concerns important to them. This view leaves many issues of design quality unaddressed. The position here is thus that urban designers should have a clear image of a good world that can guide development to meet a broad range of objectives that enhance people's experiences. What should this image be?

The image presented here is founded on the research, to the extent it exists, on what functions well in specific circumstances. It is based on scholarly observations, systematic and casual, of what people do and the choices that they make rather than what they say; it is thus based on striving to attain behaviorally congruent designs in terms of activities and aesthetic values rather than ones congruent with mental images. Some of these requirements are conservative; others are more progressive. They will evolve, so there is no single ideal end-state image but rather a set of characteristics that should guide urban designers in their work. Some of these characteristics are mutually supportive, but others are contradictory. Such contradictions are inevitable in urban design, as noted by Hans Blumenfeld (1892–1988), one of the major urban planners of the twentieth century (Spreiregen 1971).

Recognizing these realities, a good city should do the following:

- It should respect the natural ecological potential of a site. For greenfield sites, the implication is that the natural ecological systems are designed first to ensure that they function well despite the changes due to take place on them. For brownfield sites, it means that the natural processes that exist need to be preserved and latent/dormant ones restored to function well. This directive recognizes that economic forces can intervene. Whatever the project is, if it creates greater ecological problems than it solves, then it will be a step backward rather than forward. If the environment suffers, the burden will fall on us all.
- It should be designed with people in mind and have the range of behavior settings that meets both their known and their latent aspirations given the resources available. Many settings can be designed with certainty, but much about the future is uncertain. The implication is that designers must be prepared to argue for options by using evidence and the schemes proposed be designed with change in mind.
- It should allow people to feel physically and psychologically comfortable. The implication is that the city must have a structure at a citywide and precinct level that enables habitués and tourists to develop a clear cognitive image of it. It should have districts with nodes of distinctive character, with landmarks and clear paths (Lynch 1960). Clear edges may not be necessary, but they help (Pocock and Hudson 1978).

- It should bring to the forefront its natural features—rivers, water fronts, topography—to enrich its visual character and provide opportunities for active and passive recreation. The implication is that these features are part of the public domain and not privately controlled. They should be open to everyone except where it is necessary to protect the natural habitat of animals and other animate or inanimate species.
- It should be where birds, butterflies, and desired animals and other species thrive. The implication is that the city possesses an abundance of indigenous vegetation. It also implies that the habitat of such species is protected when a city expands. Corridors of movement for animals need to be retained or created.
- It should fit its climatic setting. The spacing of buildings, widths of its streets, and vegetation are based on the nature of the climate, even though global and local economic considerations and desired architectural imagery may dictate otherwise. In temperate climates, it is one in which the four seasons are recognized. In winter cities, it is one that celebrates the cold while recognizing the human need for comfort. In desert cities, it is one that provides shade during the day as one goes about one's business and exploits the cooling effect of water. Much can be learned from vernacular settlements, although we demand much higher levels of comfort nowadays.
- It should have streets full of light and air. The implication is that the heights of buildings lining streets in temperate zones is restricted to avoid the negative effects of the shadows they cast. Great attention must be paid to the quality of the public realm within its geographical setting. The character of the shade and sunlight provided must be climate-specific.
- It should be where movement around the city is comfortable and straightforward. People must have several transportation options so that the city is easily navigable. It must possess an efficient public transportation network. Children by the age of ten, frail elderly people, and people with disabilities, should be able to move independently and safely around the city and the precincts within it. Smart cities are conceptually good, but the implication is that a city and the precincts within it are first designed with the pedestrian in mind. That is, it must be easy to walk to local destinations. The implication is that it is as compact as climatically sensible.
- It should have short blocks akin to those in Portland, Oregon (264 feet, or 80 meters, on a side, making an area of 1.6 acres, or 0.64 hectares). They serve the dual purpose of making many ways for negotiating a city on foot and being large enough to be commercially developable.
- It should be barrier-free. It affords access to all places of public use for people who use wheelchairs as their basic mode of transportation.
- It should have a heart, and its precincts and any urban developments within them should also have hearts. The implication is that the location and design of nodes is central to city and precinct design. The key precinct is the central one. The implication is that it must have a density of mixed activities with a strong central node and an open space, such as a square where meetings can be held. It must have the range of attractions that appeal to different segments of a society.
- It should have precincts that have their own architectural and social characters that give them an identity and thus a clear, if not unique, sense of place. The implication is that a precinct has behavior settings that distinguish it from others and a physical character, a texture, that distinguishes it from others.
- It should have precincts consisting of background buildings with a few of civic importance that are set in the foreground as displays. These foreground buildings can be sculptural works of fine art but must meet the criteria in this list.

The Way Forward

- It should be where the architecture is climatically specific and has the least possible amount of embodied energy in its construction and is energy-efficient in its operation. The implication is that the architects of individual buildings must resolve basic programmatic requirements first, before seeking their own 'jollies'—expressing their artistic attitudes.
- It should be where all segments of society can find a home that can be used as a base for having access to the whole city and its resources. The implication is that new towns and residential neighborhoods must have a mix of dwelling unit types and services for the households of each segment of society. In existing cities where precincts of minority populations—on any dimension of identification—reside, urban renewal must be accompanied by rent control, subsidized housing programs, and other services that market forces do not provide.
- It should be where the residents and workers tolerate, if not celebrate, individual differences. The implication is that the public domain must provide the affordances for people to, at least, see each other as part of everyday life and thus not one that creates barriers among them. The further implication is that the layout of the city must be permeable, and paths of movement must intersect at clear nodes. The nodes, in addition to their qualities noted earlier, must have a mix of attractions that appeal to people of different economic levels and cultural tastes. Some major parks should be designed with opportunities for cross-cultural integration in mind, as in Paris's Parc de la Villette.
- It should have clear distinctions between public, semi-public, semi-private, and private open spaces (Jacobs 1961; Newman 1972) and opportunities for naturally surveilling outdoor public and semi-public areas.
- It should have a layout of predominantly residential precincts that follows the basic precepts of the neighborhood unit idea, with the heart consisting a shopping street with a public square enclosed by communal amenities. This directive needs to be taken with caution. Changing shopping habits and the convenience of Internet purchasing are changing patterns of neighborhood life. Local shopping streets and both coffeeshops and restaurants can still thrive.
- It should possess open spaces for relaxation and recreation for all segments of society, on the basis of their level of competence. These spaces must meet cultural and climatic considerations. Cultures are constantly evolving, some more rapidly than others, and the use of open spaces shifts over time. The implication is that open spaces, whatever their type, be considered as a nested set of behavior settings in which the milieu is synchronous with a broad set of behaviors. The danger is that spaces are made too large. Perhaps designers should follow Christopher Alexander's dictum that one should design such spaces to fit the activities they are supposed to house and then the size should be halved to get the best fit (Alexander, Ishikawa, and Silverstein 1977)!
- It should have control over access to public spaces that are privately owned. It should remain in public hands, and the rights of admission not be controlled by private interests.
- It should be where efficiency is a goal but the utility of inefficiencies is recognized. Not everything has to have its own high-speed channel of movement. Paths should cross. The implication is also that there must be time for people to stand and stare: "A poor life this, if full of care we have no time to stand or stare" (Davies 1911, 15). This statement implies that there is something worth staring at. An active environment is one. Vistas are another.
- It should have places carefully designed for formal events such as concerts, parades, and political gatherings and have spaces that afford the development of communal activities, where habitués and visitors can arrange to meet and linger. Spaces for relaxation are important too.

- It should be where streets are the seams, not the dividers, for life. The implication is that both sides of a street should house similar activities and be of the same height and architectural quality. The implication is also that there should be a hierarchy of streets at both the city scale and the precinct scale. The elements in this hierarchy should extend from heavily trafficked streets designed for ease of vehicular movement to streets narrow enough to see objects in shop windows across them and to laneways that can serve as pedestrian shortcuts.
- It should enable residents to deal with the rituals of life and death according to the cultural patterns of the segments of its population. The latter directive may be difficult to attain in the face of rising population numbers and will most likely lead to cremation as the necessary, if not the desired, mode of committal.
- It should be robust. It should maintain its positive qualities as changes take place with it.

The conclusions are that cities need to become more compact and that urban design projects need to be as compact as is compatible within their climatic context. Compact cities will not solve all the problems facing urban designs. They may, for instance, result in traffic congestions, despite high transit usage (Neuman 2005). The compact city is nevertheless the model that functions best on a multiplicity of dimensions.

Compacting Cities as a Design Goal

Cities with an overall compact form enable energy resources and infrastructure elements to be used efficiently (Dantzig and Saaty 1973; de Roo and Miller 2001; Burgess and Jencks 2004; Bay 2017). They make it easier to provide facilities that cater to a wide range of needs of people among the population. Daily necessities can be organized within walking distance. High population densities can be attained in relatively low-rise—four- or five-story—environments. The advantage in doing so is that good light and air can be attained at the street level. Population densities in compact cities are necessarily higher, and the range of behavior settings required to cater to such densities needs great programmatic attention to avoid overcrowding. Many individuals become isolated when behavior settings become overpopulated (Altman 1975; Lang and Moleski 2010).

On the urban scale, public policy initiatives need to be introduced that over time work toward creating compact urban environments. This observation recognizes that many people do not like to use public transportation and will continue to seek spacious environments where they use cars that allow for great autonomy. Compact cities need to be designed to be more attractive to them. At the urban design project level, whether dealing with new suburbs or urban renewal efforts within cities, compactness is the ideal to strive toward. Many European cities are already compact in nature. Consider Paris, Vienna—frequently regarded as the world's most livable city—and Barcelona, for instance. Berlin is striving to become more compact. Outside Europe, cities such as Melbourne in Australia, Portland in the United States (which, as already noted, has a compact block pattern), Toyama in Japan, and Vancouver in Canada have policies aimed at making them more compact.

The design strategy in Toyama consists of three major components: revitalizing the transportation system, redeveloping the city center, and developing catalysts to attract people and corporations to locate near stops on the transit system (Takami and Hatayama 2008; Mori 2015). The catalyst can take many forms. In Chattanooga, Tennessee, in the United States, investment in developing good schools has been used to attract people to live and work in the city center (Lang 2005, 2017). Certainly, transit orient development (TOD) is to be encouraged through public policy incentives. Seeking compactness is a suitable objective for the immediate future,

The Way Forward

but ongoing evidence-based development programs must form the basis for individual designs. Program and paradigm must go hand in hand (Rowe 1983).

Therefore

To make progress, urban design, as a professional field, must adopt a neo-functional approach to design, one that is based on an understanding of the existing and potential affordances of the built environment. Understanding the existing behavior settings requires a strong knowledge base of how cities work for different people and critical observations of present conditions. Creating the future requires imagining possibilities. If urban designers are to do more than simply meet the financial needs of the power elite of cities in their proposals, they must be willing to bring the attention of the property developers, their financiers, the politicians, and potential user populations with whom they are working to the range of design possibilities and opportunities and/or problems that they may create. The political power of designers in their professional capacity should not be exaggerated, but neither should it be dismissed.

Urban designers need to be extraverts. First, they must be conscious of the environment around them and be able to observe it evaluatively. They must also be extraverts in seeking knowledge about how cities function for different segments of the population. Second, they must be willing to act by making proposals for improving a city at the policy and design levels as socioeconomic and technological circumstances change. Few people, it seems, are extraverts on both dimensions (Ackoff 1978), but urban designers, both as parts of organizations and as individuals, need to be so if their work is to serve society well. Many architects seem to be introverted in examining the world around them and seeking knowledge but extraverted in their willingness to act.

Design goals are always political in nature. The mechanisms/patterns that meet those goals can be based on evidence. A deep-seated knowledge of case studies and of the architectural psychology research literature can provide a solid evidence base for many urban design decisions. This evidence is, however, descriptive and explanatory of only present conditions. It is also incomplete. Designers are creating a future not a past, so they will often need to stick their necks out when they make decisions. Using the incompleteness of evidence as an argument for eschewing it is not, however, the best way to go forward, even if it is pragmatically easier.

An Agenda for the Next Generation of Urban Designs

In urban designers' professional capacity as the designers of projects, their ability to deal with social opportunities and problems is limited. Often, the general program for a new development is worked out before they are brought onboard. Usually, however, designers are involved in establishing what the concerns being addressed are, even though they are seldom the ultimate arbiters of how they are defined. The role and obligations of urban designers will vary by the type of project in which they are engaged. What follows is an attempt to outline the different roles from the most general to the specific by type of urban design.

Piece-by-Piece Urban Design

Piece-by-piece urban design is closely allied with city planning but is more focused in its intentions and its scope of application. It is concerned with the character of specific precincts, whether they be slums, areas of wealth, or ones that have specific qualities worth retaining or changing. The polices formulated by central governments and local authorities need to be

371

aimed at making the city more compact in the behavior settings it offers and thus the patterns of the built environments required to house them.

Cities have always been shaped socially and physically by the invisible web of public policy regulations, such as zoning ordinances and building bylaws that control what can be built where, but they can also provide incentives that guide development in a particular direction (Lai 1988; Talen 2012; Carmona 2017). Piece-by-piece urban design re-forms these policies and invents new ones to attain specific social and built environment qualities (Barnett 1974; Punter 2007; Lang 2017, 209–22). The design ends sought are in some pressure group's interests or what is deemed by some participant in the problem-defining process to be in the public's interest. It can and should be both.

Urban designer groups, in taking the initiative to identify and develop urban design schemes, need to be able to see opportunities for enhancing the affordances of the built environment. In doing so, they need to both identify what works well and have the imagination to identify potential changes in the localities they are considering. The ability to develop strategies for getting the support for an idea is also important. Being able to argue for a project, based on evidence, gives an urban designer some power in discussions about options for the future of a place.

As designers of policies for changing an area of a city or maintaining the status quo and as deal makers rather than project architects, urban designers need to be aware of the generic legal techniques used to control urban development as well as the incentives that can be used to shape development in specific directions. Incentives have often involved enabling property developers to build larger/taller buildings than current zoning ordinances allow. This technique needs to be used with caution because tall buildings can overshadow public areas at the ground level. Tax-increment zoning and the transfer of development rights may offer more in many circumstances.

Plug-In Urban Design

Plug-in urban designs are likely to become increasingly important as cities strive to deal with burgeoning populations. Every urban intervention—laying a new railway track, creating a new road or building, placing a sculpture, planting a tree—is, in a loose sense, plug-in urban design because it has an effect, positive or negative, on its surroundings, but the design concern is with major infrastructure projects. Infrastructure decisions must go hand in hand with land-use and institutional location planning processes that enhance the walkability of a city's precincts. Such decisions must also deal with their impact on the natural world.

The catalytic effect of plug-in urban designs has been employed to successfully attain social and economic benefits and a high-quality built environment rich in behavior settings. The Metrocable system in Medellín is an example of an element that has had a major positive effect on the lives of low-income barrio residents on the steep hill slopes of the city. Resulting from a public policy decision, it has given them access to mainstream employment opportunities in the valley below. Coupled with social service elements, such as libraries and police posts plugged into the stops of the aerial system, it has had an immediate impact on the areas around the stops (Lang 2017, 194–95). With other infrastructure elements, the effect has been negative. Some new urban highways have neither enhanced traffic flows nor the quality of the neighborhoods through which they have been built.

Urban designers can play three roles in creating plug-in designs. The first is as advocates for infrastructure elements being built, the second is as analyzers and predictors of the implications of proposed schemes, and the third is as the designers of projects. The implication is that an understanding of the potential catalytic effects of new infrastructure schemes needs to be part of their knowledge base, or they must know where to find that knowledge.

As the advocates for a project, urban designers are obliged to have, or develop, the ability to rally support for an idea. Robert Hugman (1902–80), in his perception that the San Antonio River could be changed from a flood-control scheme and sewer into the environment that River Walk (Paseo del Rio) in the city is today, decided to first get groups such as the San Antonio Real Estate Board, the city's Advertising Club, and the Daughters of the America Revolution to lobby municipal authorities to implement the scheme rather than attempting to do so alone. These groups had considerable political resources on which they could draw as members of the city's power elite (Lang 2005, 350–53).

All-of-a-Piece Urban Design

All-of-a-piece urban design is the core activity of the field. It involves the development of a conceptual design for a locality on behalf of a private or public property developer. The design is divided into parcels each with design guidelines for its development. These guidelines add to or alter the generic zoning and other controls that apply to a site. The objective is usually to attain a unified urban design with a diversity of buildings.

Twentieth- and early-twenty-first-century all-of-a-piece urban designs have varied considerably in product type, as the chapters of this book have shown (see also Lang 2017, 130–84). Among them have been new towns, central business districts, residential neighborhoods, university campuses, historic precincts, and waterfront designs. When economic conditions are positive, these designs have been implemented in a rush, but they have sometimes taken decades to get accomplished and have undergone changes in both the program and the design paradigms applied. Battery Park City in New York is an example. Begun in the 1960s, it was not built out until 2012. It continues to undergo change. Designs for its site began with rationalist modernist proposals and ended up with an implemented, largely neo-traditional, design. Along the way were pragmatic designs and a proposal for a megastructure (Gordon 1997; Lang 2017, 154–59).

Successful all-of-a-piece urban designs have been guided by some authority, public or private, that has the power to make decisions and ensure that the guidelines established by the urban design team are followed. Such authorities are subject to considerable political pressure because governments are voted into and out of power and by the impact of the economic ups and downs of the real estate market. Such fluctuations as designs evolve may well be the norm in our current century.

The roles of urban designers in the argumentative process of making design decisions are as follows:

1. to be involved in shaping, or reshaping, the design program
2. to produce a conceptual design
3. to establish design guidelines that retain the unity (whether through similarity or diversity) of a scheme while it undergoes change
4. to be involved in the selection of subdevelopers and their architects
5. to participate in the phasing, or sequencing, of development
6. to perhaps design the building and/or landscape components of the project

Throughout this process, designers need to be cognizant of, and be advocates for, the characteristics of the project that will help create a good city as defined earlier.

Urban designs proposals, as already noted, need to be presented in the form of a strategy because they often take considerable time to implement and because social, political, and economic circumstances may well have changed since the conceptual design was first established.

The first step in the process of implementation is thus particularly important. It needs to be part of a strategy that foresees possible divergent lines of design as the development of the site proceeds. The strategy needs to be concerned with the qualities of the public realm as much as the economic concerns of property developers. The position taken here is that it is in the public interest for developments to serve a diversity of users' interests.

Major debates arise in determining how far an urban design team should go in controlling the design of a proposal's individual components. Property developers and architects would prefer no controls over them unless those controls enhance the profitability of developers' proposals. Many of the best-loved parts of cities in the world with extraordinarily high property values have a remarkable unity in appearance, but some critics believe that this level of uniformity leads to the stifling of innovative designs. Patrik Schumacher of Zaha Hadid Architects calls for the abandonment of all controls and for free market mechanisms to dictate what should be built (Frearson 2018). Codirectors of the firm oppose his position.

Virginia Postrel (b. 1960), a US political author, believes that the aesthetic appearance of the individual buildings and, more generally, precincts of cities are of utmost importance in a competitive neoliberal world. She points out that in urban design, "if you get the lots right, and the blocks right and the setbacks right, somebody can design a crummy building and the ensemble is still fine" (Postrel 2003, 58). I added elsewhere that you also need to "get the nature of ground floors of buildings and the quality of the public realm right" (Lang 2017, 180). This statement implies that the quality of daylight on the street and sidewalks is fine in terms of illuminating the world and allowing vegetation to thrive. The same position applies to total urban designs.

Total Urban Design

Many urban designs ranging in size from new towns of a million or more people to small precincts are the work of one organization, from the creation of the building program to the overseeing of the implementation of a design (Lang 2017, 105–29). The development team has, or can raise, the capital investment required to proceed on its own.

Urban designers are more likely to be deeply involved in the early stages of a property development when they are part of the overall team, in comparison to where they are brought onboard only once the property developer has devised the basic idea for a scheme. Their early involvement often occurs when the design team is an in-house division of the property development organization. It does not, however, mean that the in-house discussions are less political and heated than those for other types of urban design. The role of the urban designer remains the same as that for all-of-a-piece urban design. It is to ensure design quality and the meeting of the diverse needs of diverse people while being constrained by the resources available.

Conclusion

The goal of any urban design effort should be to create a good place, one that satisfies not only the demands of the power elite and property developers but also the needs of the diverse population of a city. This task is not easy: Most urban designs target specific groups of people and ignore the concerns of other people and the ecological world. Doing so simplifies creating the program for a development and makes synthesizing a design easier, but that is not an ideal procedural paradigm.

The urban design process is one in which the designer should be both an educator, raising questions about what the character of a scheme should be, and a delineator. Design decisions are always made under uncertainty, and designers must be willing to make them and to argue that property developers should go along with their proposals. To argue well, having an understanding of the way cities function and how urban morphologies evolve at the hands of many actors, as well as an empirical understanding of what works and does not work, is an essential part of an urban designer's knowledge base. Learning from the functioning of past design paradigms, generic concepts, and the performance of specific designs forms part of that base.

Key References

Bay, Joo H. P. 2017. *Growing Compact: Urban Form, Density, and Sustainability*. New York: Routledge.

Dantzig, George B. and Thomas L. Saaty. 1973. *Compact City: A Plan for a Livable Urban Environment*. San Francisco: W. H. Freeman.

Florida, Richard. 2017. *The New Urban Crisis: How Our Cities Are Increasing Inequality, Deepening Segregation, and Failing the Middle Class—and What Can Be Done About It*. New York: Basic Books.

Lynch, Kevin. 1960. *The Image of the City*. Cambridge, MA: MIT Press.

Rowe, Colin. 1983. "Program vs Paradigm." *Cornell Journal of Architecture* 2: 8–19.

Bibliography and References

Abel, Chris. 2010. "The Vertical Garden City: Towards a New Urban Topology." *Journal of Tall Buildings and Urban Habitat* 11. www.planetizen.com/node/50957 accessed June 20, 2017.

Acharya, Prasanna K. 1933. *Architecture of Manasara with a Synopsis by Praso*. London: Oxford University Press.

Ackoff, Russell L. 1978. *The Art of Problem Solving—Accompanied by Ackoff's Fables*. New York: Wiley.

Adjmi, Morris, ed. 1991. *Aldo Rossi Architecture, 1981–1991*. New York: Princeton University Press.

Adshead, S. D. 1909. "An Introduction to the Study of Civic Design." *Town Planning Review* 1 (3): 1.

Adshead, S. D. 1930. "Camillo Sitte and Le Corbusier." *Town Planning Review* 14 (2): 85–94.

Aerts, Jeroen C. J. H. and W. J. Wouter Botzen. 2011. "Flood-Resilient Waterfront Development in New York City: Bridging Flood Insurance, Building Codes, and Flood Zoning." *Annals of the New York Academy of Science* 1227. www.ivm.vu.nl/en/Images/ANYAS_Aerts_Botzen_2011_tcm234-342234.pdf accessed May 27, 2017.

Aitchison, Mathew. 2012. "Townscape: scope, Scale, Extent." *The Journal of Architecture* 17 (5): 621–42.

Alberti, Leon Battista. 1452. *On the Art of Building Cities in Ten Books*. Translated from *De Re Aedificatoria* by Joseph Rykwert, Neil Leach, and Robert Travenor. Cambridge, MA: MIT Press, 1988.

Alexander, Christopher. 1964. *Notes on the Synthesis of Form*. Cambridge, MA: Harvard University Press. https://monoskop.org/images/f/ff/Alexander_Christopher_Notes_on_the_Synthesis_of_Form.pdf accessed June 8, 2019.

Alexander, Christopher, Sara Ishikawa, and Murray Silverstein. 1977. *A Pattern Language: Towns, Buildings, Construction*. New York: Oxford University Press.

Alexander, Christopher, Hajo Neis, Artemis Anniniou, and Ingrid King. 1987. *A New Theory of Urban Design*. New York: Oxford University Press.

Allen, Robert C. 2017. *The Industrial Revolution: A Very Short Introduction*. Oxford: Oxford University Press.

AlSayyad, Nezar. 1991. *Cities and Caliphs: On the Genesis of Arab Muslim Urbanism*. Westport, CT: Greenwood Press.

Altman, Irwin. 1975. *Environment and Social Behavior; Privacy, Personal Space, Territory, Crowding*. Monterey, CA: Brooks, Cole.

Angelakis, Vangelis, Elias Tragos, Henrich Pöhls, Adam Kapovits, and Alessandro Bassi, eds. 2017. *Designing, Developing, and Facilitating Smart Cities: Urban Design to LoT Solutions*. Cham: Springer.

Appleyard, Donald and Mark Lintell. 1981. "The Environmental Quality of Streets: The Residents' Viewpoint." *Journal of the American Institute of Planners* 38 (March): 84–101.

Appleyard, Donald, Kevin Lynch, and John R. Myer. 1965. *The View from the Road*. Cambridge, MA: MIT Press.

Arcspace. 2012. "Kartal-Pendik Masterplan." https://arcspace.com/feature/kartal-pendik-masterplan/ accessed January 8, 2018.

Ardalan, Nader, George Candilis, Balkrishna V. Doshi, Moshi Safdie, and José Luis Sert. 1976. *Habitat Bill of Rights*. Tehran: Hamdami Foundation.

Argan, Giulio C. 1970. *The Renaissance City (Planning and Cities)*. New York: George Braziller.

Arkaraprasertkul, Non. 2016. "The Social Poetics of Urban Design: Rethinking Urban Design Through Louis Kahn's Vision for Central Philadelphia. 1939–1962." *Journal of Urban Design* 21 (6): 731–45.

Arndt, Ingo. 2014. *Animal Architecture*. New York: Harry N. Abrams.

Arnold, Henry F. 1988. *Trees in Urban Design*. New York: Van Nostrand Reinhold.

Bibliography and References

Atelier GOM. 2017. "Longnan Garden Social Housing Estate/Atelier GOM." *ArchDaily* (June 30). www.archdaily.com/874649/longnan-garden-social-housing-estate-atelier-gom?utm_medium= email&utm_source=ArchDaily%20List accessed July 2, 2017.

Avin, Uri. 1973. "Le Corbusier's Unité D'habitation: Slab for All Seasons." Unpublished master's thesis, University of Cape Town.

Aziz, Iram. undated. "Islamic Principles for Planning Cities." www.slideshare.net/iramaziz/islamic-princi ples-for-cities accessed March 15, 2018.

Bacon, Edmund. 1967a. "The City as an Act of Will." *Architectural Record* 141 (1): 113–28.

Bacon, Edmund. 1967b. *Design of Cities*. Revised edition. New York: Viking.

Bahga, Sarbjit, Surinder Bahga, and Yashinder Bahga. 1993. *Modern Architecture in India*. New Delhi: Galgotia Press.

Balfour, Alan. 1978. *Rockefeller Center: Architecture as Theater*. New York: McGraw Hill.

Banerjee, Jacqueline. undated. "Salt's Mill by Lockwood and Mawson." *The Victorian Web*. www.victorian web.org/art/architecture/lockwood/3.html accessed October 21, 2016.

Banham, Reyner. 1960. *Theory and Design During the First Machine Age*. Cambridge, MA: MIT Press. https://monoskop.org/images/6/65/Banham_Reyner_Theory_and_Design_in_the_First_Machine_ Age_2nd_ed.pdf accessed May 7, 2017.

Banham, Reyner. 1976. *Megastructure: Urban Futures of the Recent Past*. London: Thames and Hudson.

Barker, A. and B. Hyman. 2002. "Assessing Residential Health in Low Income Sites and Services Housing Schemes, Madras, India." In *Urban Health in the Third World*, edited by Rais Akhtar, 27–64. New Delhi: S. B. Nangia and A. P. H. Publishing Corporation.

Barker, Roger G. 1968. *Ecological Psychology: Concepts and Methods for Studying the Environment of Human Behavior*. Stanford, CA: Stanford University Press.

Barkham, Patrick. 2017. "Urban Beasts: How Wild Animals Have Moved to Cities." *The Guardian* (May 20). www.theguardian.com/environment/2017/may/20/urban-beasts-how-wild-animals-have-moved-into-cities accessed August 1, 2018.

Barnett, Henrietta. 1905. "A Garden Suburb at Hampstead." *Contemporary Review* 87 (February): 231–37.

Barnett, Jonathan. 1974. *Urban Design as Public Policy: Practical Methods for Improving Cities*. New York: Architectural Record Books.

Barnett, Jonathan. 1986. *The Elusive City: Five Centuries of Design, Ambition, and Miscalculation*. New York: Harper and Row.

Barnett, Jonathan. 1987. "In the Public Interest: Design Guidelines." *Architectural Record* 175 (8): 114–25.

Barnett, Jonathan. 2016. *City Design: Modernist, Traditional, Green and System Perspectives*. Second edition. New York: Routledge.

Barnett, Jonathan and Larry Beasley. 2015. *Ecodesign for Cities and Suburbs*. Washington, DC: Island Press.

Barr, Alfred H. 1938. "Preface." In *Bauhaus 1919–1928*, edited by Herbert Bayer, Walter Gropius, and Ise Gropius. New York: Museum of Modern Art. www.moma.org/documents/moma_catalogue_ 2735_300190238.pdf accessed June 3, 2019.

Baumeister, Reinhard. 1876. *Stadterweiterungen in Technischer, Baupolizeilicher und Wirtschaftlicher Beziehung*. Berlin: Ernst & Korn.

Bay, Joo H. P. 2017. *Growing Compact: Urban Form, Density, and Sustainability*. New York: Routledge.

Bayer, Herbert, Walter Gropius, and Ise Gropius, eds. 1938. *Bauhaus 1919–1928*. New York: Museum of Modern Art. https://monoskop.org/images/8/80/Bayer_Herbert_Gropius_Walter_Gropius_Ise_eds_ Bauhaus_1919-1928.pdf accessed May 25, 2017.

Bazjanic, Vladimir. 1974. "Architecture Design Theory: Models of the Design Process." In *Basic Questions of Design Theory*, edited by W. R. Spillers, 3–20. New York: American Elsevier.

Beevers, Robert. 1988. *The Garden City Utopia: A Critical Biography of Ebenezer Howard*. London: Palgrave Macmillan.

Beirão, José N., Pirouz Nourian, and Bardia Mashhoodi. 2014. "Parametric Urban Design: An Interactive System for Shaping Neighborhoods." *eCAAD* 29: 225–34. http://papers.cumincad.org/data/works/ att/ecaade2011_050.content.pdf accessed February 25, 2017.

Bellamy, Edward. 1888. *Looking Backward 2000–1887*. Boston: Houghton-Mifflin, 1898.

Benevolo, Leonardo. 1971. *The Origins of Modern Town Planning*. Translated from the Italian by Judith Landry. Cambridge, MA: MIT Press.

Benevolo, Leonardo. 1980. *The History of the City*. Translated from the Italian by Geoffrey Culverwell. Cambridge, MA: MIT Press.

Bibliography and References

Bennett, Will. 2015. "Prince Charles's Manifesto." *LinkedIn*. www.linkedin.com/pulse/prince-charless-urban-design-manifesto-will-bennett/ accessed November 4, 2018.

Berlepsch-Valendás, Hans E. von. 1910. *Die Garten-Stadt München-Perlach*. München: E. Reinhardt. http://perlach.hachinger-bach.de/downloads/GartenstadtPerlach_1910.pdf accessed June 3, 2019.

Berlyne, Daniel. 1974. *Studies in the New Experimental Aesthetics: Steps Toward an Objective Psychology of Aesthetic Appreciation*. Washington, DC: Hemisphere.

Bernet, Claus. 2004. "The 'Hobrecht Plan' 1862 and Berlin's Urban Structures." *Urban History* 31 (3): 400–19.

Bernick, Michael and Robert Cervero. 1996. *Transit Villages in the 21st Century*. New York: McGraw Hill.

Betsky, Aaron. 2016. "Zaha Hadid's Undulating Master Plan in Singapore." *Architect*. www.architectmagazine.com/design/urbanism-planning/master-planning-in-singapore_o accessed February 22, 2017.

Birch, Eugenie L. 1980. "Radburn and the American Planning Movement." *Journal of the American Planning Association* 46 (4): 424–31. https://repository.upenn.edu/cgi/viewcontent.cgi?article=1030&context=cplan_papers accessed June 3, 2019.

Blake, Peter. 1964. *God's Own Junkyard: The Planned Deterioration of America's Landscape*. New York: Holt, Rinehart & Winston.

Blake, Peter. 1977. *Form Follows Fiasco: Why Modern Architecture Hasn't Worked*. Boston: Atlantic-Little, Brown.

Blau, Eve and Nancy J. Troy, eds. 2002. *Architecture and Cubism*. Cambridge, MA: MIT Press.

Blundell Jones, Peter. 2012. "Parc de la Villette in Paris, France by Bernard Tschumi." *Architectural Review* (June 7). www.architectural-review.com/buildings/in-the-parc-de-la-villette-rules-can-be-invented-or-perverted/8630513.article accessed April 12, 2017.

Boardman, Philip. 1978. *The Worlds of Patrick Geddes: Biologist, Town Planner, Re-Educator, Peace- Warrior*. London: Routledge and Kegan Paul.

Bodenschatz, Harald. 2013. *Berlin Urban Design: A Brief History of a European City*. Second edition. Berlin: DOM.

Bofill, Ricardo and Jean-Louis André. 1989. *Espaces d'une Vie*. Paris: Éditions Odile Jacob.

Boguslaw, Robert. 1965. *The New Utopians: A Study of System Design and Social Change*. Englewood Cliffs, NJ: Prentice Hall.

Bohl, Charles C. 2000. "New Urbanism and the City: Potential Applications and Implications for Distressed Inner-City Neighborhoods." *Housing Policy Debates* 11 (4): 761–801.

Bohl, Charles C. and Jean-François Lejeune, eds. 2008. *Sitte, Hegemann and the Metropolis: Civic Art and International Exchanges*. London and New York: Routledge.

Bohl, Charles C. and Elizabeth Plater Zyberk. 2008. "Building Community Across the Rural-to-Urban Transect [the Transect]." *Places* 18 (1). https://placesjournal.org/assets/legacy/pdfs/building-community-across-the-rural-to-urban-transect.pdf accessed May 5, 2019.

Booth, Robert. 2016. "Vision of Ebbsfleet Garden City for 65,000 Struggles to Take Root." *The Guardian* (January 4). www.theguardian.com/artanddesign/2016/jan/04/ebbsfleet-garden-city-richard-rogers-critics accessed May 12, 2017.

Boudon, Philippe. 1972. *Lived-in Architecture: Le Corbusier's Pessac Revisited*. Cambridge, MA: MIT Press.

Branzi, Andrea, D. Donegan, A. Petrillo, and C. Raimondo. 1995. "Symbiotic Metropolis Agronica." In *The Solid Side: The Search for Consistency in a Changing World: Projects and Proposals*, 101–20. Naarden: V + K Publishing. Available as Agronica: Modello di urbanizzazione debolo. www.youtube.com/watch?v=VhfjHhhxSZc accessed December 30, 2018.

Bravo, Carolina. 2016. "Hudson Yards: Massive Real Estate Development to Alter New York Skyline." www.linkedin.com/pulse/hudson-yards-massive-real-estate-development-alter-new-carolina-bravo accessed February 21, 2017.

Bray, David. 2005. *Social Space and Governance in Urban China: The Danwei System from Origins to Reform*. Stanford, CA: Stanford University Press.

Broadbent, Geoffrey. 1990. *Emerging Concepts in Urban Space Design*. London: Van Nostrand Reinhold International.

Broady, Maurice. 1966. "Social Theory in Architectural Design." *Architectural Association Quarterly* 81 (887): Whole Issue.

Brolin, Brent C. 1976. *The Failure of Modern Architecture*. New York: Van Nostrand Reinhold.

Brooks, H. Allen. 1999. *Le Corbusier's Formative Years: Charles-Edouard Jeanneret at la Chaux-de-Fonds*. Chicago: University of Chicago Press.

Brower, Sidney N. 1996. *Good Neighborhoods: A Study of In-Town and Suburban Residential Environments*. Westport, CT: Praeger.

Bibliography and References

Brown, Lance J., David Dixon, and Oliver Gillham. 2014. *Urban Design for an Urban Century: Shaping More Livable, Equitable, and Resilient Cities*. Second edition. Hoboken, NJ: John Wiley.

Brown, Robert M. 1988. *Spirituality and Liberation: Overcoming the Great Fallacy*. Louisville, KY: The Westminster Press.

Brownlee, David B. 1989. *Building the City Beautiful: The Benjamin Franklin Parkway and the Philadelphia Museum of Art*. Philadelphia, PA: University of Pennsylvania Press and Philadelphia Museum of Art.

Brynjolfson, Eric and Andrew Mcafee. 2014. *The Second Machine Age: Work, Progress, and Prosperity in a Time of Brilliant Technologies*. New York: W. W. Norton & Company.

Bubbar, D. K. 2005. *The Spirit of Indian Architecture, Vedantic Wisdom for Building Harmonious Spaces and Life*. New Delhi: Rupa.

Buchanan, Colin, Geoffrey Crowther, William Holford, Oleg Kerensky, Herbert Pollard, T. Dan Smith, and Henry W. Wells. 1963. *Traffic in Towns*. London: HMSO.

Buchanan, Peter. 2013. "The Big Rethink Part II: Urban Design." *The Architectural Review* (March 6). www.architectural-review.com/rethink/campaigns/the-big-rethink/the-big-rethink-part-11-urban-design/8643367.article accessed September 2, 2013.

Buchanan, Peter. 2015. "Empty gestures: Starchitecture's Swan Song." *The Architectural Review* (February 27). www.architectural-review.com/rethink/viewpoints/empty-gestures-starchitectures-swan-song/8679010.article accessed March 12, 2018.

Buckingham, James Silk. 1849. *National Evils and Practical Remedies*. London: Peter Jackson.

Bullivant, Lucy. 2012. "Hafen City." In *Masterplanning Futures*, 45–56. London and New York: Routledge.

Buls, Charles. 1899. "L'esthétique des Villes." *Municipal Affairs* 3 (December): 732–41. Translated from the author's *L'esthétique des Villes*. Bruxelles: Bruyland-Christophe, 1893. http://urbanplanning.library.cornell.edu/DOCS/buls.htm accessed November 1, 2016.

Burgess, Rod and Mike Jenks, eds. 2004. *Compact Cities: Sustainable Urban Forms for Developing Countries*. London: Spon Press. http://istoecidade.weebly.com/uploads/3/0/2/0/3020261/compact_cities.pdf accessed August 7, 2018.

Burnham, Daniel H. and Edward H. Bennett. 1909. *Plan of Chicago Prepared Under the Auspice of the Commercial Club During the Years MCMVI, MCMVII and MCMVIII*. Edited by Charles Moore. Chicago: The Commercial Club. Reprinted New York: De Capo Press, 1970.

Burrows, Tim. 2016. "The Town That Bata Built; A Modernist Marvel on the Marshes of Essex." *The Guardian* (September 8). www.theguardian.com/artanddesign/2016/sep/08/essex-architecture-weekend-east-tilbury-bata-shoe-factory accessed October 12, 2018.

Burton, Elizabeth, Mike Jenks, and Katie Williams, eds. 1996. *The Compact City: A Sustainable Urban Form?* London: E & FN Spon.

Butcher, Luke. 2010. "Ebenezer Howard: Garden Cities of Tomorrow." *Architecture + Urbanism* (October 30). http://architectureandurbanism.blogspot.com.au/2010/10/ebenezer-howard-garden-cities-of-to.html accessed June 6, 2017.

Byrnes, Mark. 2017. "The Disappearing Mass Housing of the Soviet Union." *CityLab* (March 8). www.citylab.com/equity/2017/03/the-disappearing-mass-housing-of-the-soviet-union/518868/ accessed March 29, 2017.

Çalışkan, Olgu. 2017. "Parametric Design in Urbanism: A Critical Reflection." *Planning Practice & Research* 32 (4): 417–43.

Calthorpe, Peter. 2010. *Urbanism in an Age of Climate Change*. Washington, DC: Island Press.

Calthorpe, Peter and Shelley Poticha. 1993. *The Next American Metropolis: Ecology, Community, and the American Dream*. New York: Princeton Architectural Press.

Canniffe, Eamonn. 2008. *The Politics of the Piazza: The History and Meaning of the Urban Square*. Aldershot: Ashgate.

Carey, Brycchan, Markham Ellis, and Sara Salih, eds. 2004. *Discourses of Slavery and Abolition: Britain and its Colonies, 1760–1838*. Gordonsville, VA: Palgrave Macmillan.

Carini, Alessandra, et al. 1979. *Housing in Europa, Seconda Parte, 1960–1979*. Bologna: Luigi Parma.

Carmona, Matthew. 2017. "The Formal and Informal Tools of Design Governance." *Journal of Urban Design* 22 (1): 1–36, http://discovery.ucl.ac.uk/1529308/1/Carmona_Formal_informal_tools.pdf accessed June 3, 2019.

Carou, Barbara and Brie Aird. 2017. "Has the Public Realm Gone to the Dogs? The Challenges of Incorporating Dog Ownership into Planning." *Planning Exchange* (June 1). https://ontarioplanners.ca/blog/planning-exchange/june-2017/has-the-public-realm-gone-to-the-dogs-the-challenges-of-incorporating-dog-ownership-into-planning accessed June 9, 2017.

Bibliography and References

Carson, Rachel. 1962. *Silent Spring*. Boston: Houghton Mifflin. http://library.uniteddiversity.coop/More_Books_and_Reports/Silent_Spring-Rachel_Carson-1962.pdf accessed June 3, 2019.

Carthian, Jean Paul. 1979. "The Ecole des Beaux Arts: Modes and Manners." *Journal of Art Education* 33 (2): 7–17.

Cartwright, Timothy J. 1973. "Problems, Solutions, and Strategies: A Contribution to the Theory and Practice of Planning." *Journal of the American Institute of Planners* 39 (May): 179–87.

Cataneo, Pietro. 1554. *Quatro Primi Libri di Architectura*. Venetia: Paolo Manuzio.

Cathcart-Keays, Athlyn. 2015. "Moscow's Narkomfin Building: Soviet Blueprint for Collective Living." *The Guardian* (May 5). www.theguardian.com/cities/2015/may/05/moscow-narkomfin-soviet-collective-living-history-cities-50-buildings accessed August 5, 2018.

Cavalcanti, Maria de Betânia Uchôa. 1997. "Urban Reconstruction and Autocratic Regimes: Ceausescu's Bucharest in Its Historic Core." *Planning Perspectives* 12: 71–109.

Cestnik, Jenny and Justin Cloyd. 2008. "International Building Exhibition, Berlin: The Inner City as a Place to Live." www.jcestnik.com/pdf/BerlinIBA.pdf accessed April 14, 2018.

Chambliss, Edgar. 1910. *Roadtown*. New York: Roadtown Press. Republished 2017 by Triste Books. https://archive.org/stream/roadtown00chamgoog/roadtown00chamgoog_djvu.txt accessed June 15, 2018.

Chandler, Jenna. 2016. "Frank Gehry's Sunset Strip Project Is Approved—'I Will Do My Best to Make You Proud.'" http://la.curbed.com/2016/7/29/12315196/frank-gehry-sunset-strip-project-approved accessed February 26, 2017.

Chandler, T. J. 1976. *Urban Climatology and its Relevance to Urban Design*. Geneva: World Meteorological Organization. https://library.wmo.int/pmb_ged/wmo_438.pdf accessed June 3, 2019.

Charlesworth, Esther and Rob Adams, eds. 2011. *The Ecoedge—Urgent Design Challenges in Building Sustainable Cities*. London and New York: Routledge.

"Charter of Machu Picchu." 1979. *Journal of Architectural Research* 7 (2): 5–9.

Chernikov, Iakov. 1933. *Arkhitekturnye fanatasii. 101 Kompozitsiia v Krashakh. 101 Arkhitekturnaia Miniatiura (Fantasie Architettoniche: 101 Composizioini a Colori, 101 Minature Architoniche)*. New York: Museum of Modern Art (MOMA).

Chtcheglov, Ivan. 1953. "Formulary for a New Urbanism, as Reported by Mark Byrnes, 2012: The Manifesto for a New Urbanism That Came Before New Urbanism." *The Atlantic CityLab* (March 30). www.citylab.com/equity/2012/03/manifesto-new-urbanism-new-urbanism/1580/ accessed February 27, 2017.

City of Melbourne. 2010. "A More Compact City." In *Melbourne 2030*. Melbourne: Victorian Government Department of Sustainability and Environment. www.planning.vic.gov.au/__data/assets/pdf_file/0021/100668/Direction-1-A-More-Compact-City.pdf accessed August 11, 2018.

Cohen, Jean-Louis. 1992. *Le Corbusier and the Mystique of the USSR: Theories and Projects for Moscow 1928–1936*. Translated from *Le Corbusier et la mystique de l'URSS* by Kenneth Hylton. Princeton, NJ: Princeton University Press.

Collins, Christiane C. 2005. *Werner Hegemann and the Search for a Universal Urbanism*. New York: W. W. Norton & Company.

Collins, George R. 1959. "Linear Planning Throughout the World." *Journal of the Society of Architectural Historians* 18 (3): 35.

Collins, George R. and Christiane Crasemann Collins. 1965. *Camillo Sitte and the Birth of Modern City Planning*. New York: Random House.

Congress for New Urbanism. undated. "The Charter of the New Urbanism." www.cnu.org/who-we-are/charter-new-urbanism accessed February 27, 2017.

Conn, Steven. 2014. *Americans Against the City: Urbanism in Twentieth Century*. New York: Oxford University Press.

Conrads, Ulrich, ed. 1970. *Programs and Manifestoes on 20th Century Architecture*. Translated from the German by Michael Bullock. Cambridge, MA: MIT Press.

Cooke, Sekou. 2017. "Envisioning a Hip-Hop Urbanism in Washington, DC." *ArchDaily* (June 30). www.archdaily.com/874826/envisioning-a-hip-hop-urbanism-in-washington-dc?utm_medium=email&utm_source=ArchDaily%20List accessed July 1, 2017.

Cooper, Joel. 2007. *Cognitive Dissonance: 50 Years of a Classical Theory*. Newbury Park, CA: Sage.

Corbett, Michael and Judy Corbett. 2012. *Designing Sustainable Communities: Learning from Village Homes*. Washington, DC: Island Press.

Corner, James. 2003. "Landscape Urbanism." In *Landscape Urbanism: A Manual for the Machinic Landscape*, edited by Mohsen Mostafavi and Ciro Najle, 58–63. London: AA Print Studio.

Crawford, Margaret. 1995. *Building the Workingman's Paradise: The Design of American Company Towns*. London and New York: Verso.

Crane, David. 1960. "The City Symbolic." *Journal of the American Institute of City Planners* 26 (4): 285–86.

Crow, Ruth and Maurie Crowe. 1969, 1970, 1972. *Plan for Melbourne*, 3 vol. Melbourne: Victorian State Committee of the Communist Party of Australia.

Cruells, Bartomeu. 1992. *Ricardo Bofill. Taller de Arquitectura: Obras y Proyectos, Works and Projects*. Barcelona: Gustavo Gili.

Cullen, Gordon. 1961. *The Concise Townscape*. London: Architectural Press.

Curl, James S. 2018. *Making Dystopia: The Strange Rise and Survival of Architectural Barbarism*. Oxford: Oxford University Press.

Cuthbert, Alexander R. 2006. "Pragmatics." In *The Form of Cities: Political Economy and Urban Design*, 235–57. Oxford: Blackwell.

Cuthbert, Alexander R. 2007. "Urban Design: Requiem for an Era: Review and Critique of the Last 50 Years." *Urban Design International* 12 (4): 177–223.

Cuthbert, Alexander R. 2011. "Sustainable Theory: Sustainable Form—the Future of Urban Design." In *Sustainable Urbanism and Beyond: Rethinking Cities for the Future*, edited by Tigran Haas, 180–83. New York: Rizzoli.

Czerniak, Julia, ed. 2002. *Downsview Park Toronto*. Munich: Prestel.

Daechsel, Markus. 2015. *Islamabad and the Politics of International Development in Pakistan*. Cambridge: Cambridge University Press.

Dahinden, Justus. 1972. *Urban Structures for the Future*. Translated from the German by Gerald Onn. New York: Praeger.

Dantzig, George B. and Thomas L. Saaty. 1973. *Compact City: A Plan for a Livable Urban Environment*. San Francisco: W. H. Freeman.

Darley, Gillian. 1978. *Villages of Vision: A Study of Strange Utopias*. St. Albans: Granada.

Davies, W. H. 1911. "Leisure." In *Songs of Joy and Others*, 15. London: A. C. Fifield.

Davis, Robert. 1989. "Seaside, Florida, USA." *GA Houses* 27: 90–123.

Dede, Aldo F. and Ricard Asto. 2016. "El plan regulador de Weiner y Sert." *Habitar*. https://habitar-arq.blogspot.com.au/2016/06/chimbote-entre-la-utopia-y-la_8.html accessed November 13, 2017.

Dejtiar, Fabian. 2017. "César Pelli: 'Los arquitectos tenemos que ser parte de la sociedad, sino quedamos afuera.'" *ArchDaily* (July 13). www.plataformaarquitectura.cl/cl/872584/cesar-pelli-los-arquitectos-tenemos-que-ser-parte-de-la-sociedad-sino-quedamos-afuera accessed July 14, 2017.

de la Salle, Janine and Mark Holland, eds. 2010. *Agricultural Urbanism: Handbook for Building Sustainable Food & Agricultural Systems in 21st Century Cities*. Winnipeg: Green Frigate Books.

Delevoy, Robert L., Anthony Vidler, and Léon Krier. 1978. *Rational Architecture: The Reconstruction of the European City—Architecture Rationnelle: La Reconstruction de la Ville. Europeene*. Bruxelles: Archives d'Architecture Moderne.

Delhi Town Planning Committee. 1913. *Final Report of the Delhi Town Planning Committee on the Town Planning of the New Imperial Capital*. New Delhi: Superintendent Government Printing.

del Rio, Vicente. 1992. "Urban Design and Conflicting City Images of Brazil: Rio de Janeiro and Curitiba." *Cities* 9 (4): 270–79.

de Roo, Gert and Donald Miller, eds. 2001. *Compact Cities and Sustainable Urban Development: A Cultural Assessment of Policies and Plans from an International Perspective*. Farnham: Ashgate.

Derrida, Jacques. 1967. *Of Grammatology*. Translated from the French *De La Grammatologie* by Gayatri Chakravorty Spivak. Paris: Les Éditions de Minuit. https://is.muni.cz/el/1421/jaro2016/DU2794/um/Grammatology.pdf accessed June 4, 2019.

Desai, Madhavi, Miki Desai, and Jon Lang. 2012. *The Bungalow in Twentieth Century India: The Cultural Expression of Changing Ways of Life and Aspirations in the Domestic Architecture of Colonial and Post-Colonial Society*. Farnham: Ashgate.

de Soissons, Maurice. 1988. *Welwyn Garden City: A Town Designed for Healthy Living*. Cambridge: Publications for Companies.

de Solà Morales i Rubió, Manuel. 2004. *Ciudades, Esquinas = City, Corners*. Barcelona: Forum.

de Solà Morales i Rubió, Manuel, Kenneth Frampton, and Hans Ibelings. 2008. *De Solà Morales: A Matter of Things*. Translated by Peter Mason and Debbie Smirthwaite. Rotterdam: NAi Publishers.

Bibliography and References

Dewar, Margaret and June M. Thomas, eds. 2012. *The City After Abandonment*. Philadelphia, PA: University of Pennsylvania Press.

Dickens, Charles. 1854. *Hard Times*. London: Bradbury & Evans.

Dickens, Charles. 1859. *A Tale of Two Cities*. London: Chapman and Hall.

Diedrich, Lisa, Gini Lee, and Ellen Braae. 2018. "The Transect as a Method for Mapping and Narrating Water Landscapes: Humboldt's Open Works and Transareal Travelling." *NANO: New American Notes Online* 6. www.nanocrit.com/issues/issue6/transect-method-mapping-narrating-water-landscapes-humboldts-open-works-transareal-travelling accessed July 9, 2018.

Discover UIC. 2008. "Historic Netsch Campus at UIC." http://uicarchives.library.uic.edu/historic-netsch-campus/ accessed June 17, 2017.

DoE [Department of Environment]. 1997. *General Policy and Principles*. London: The Authors.

Donnelly, Jennifer. 2012. "Myth, Modernity and Mass Housing: The Development of Public Housing in Depression-Era Cleveland." *Traditional Dwellings and Settlements Review* 25 (1): 55–67. http://iaste.berkeley.edu/iaste/wp-content/uploads/2012/09/2014/05/Donnelly-25.1.pdf accessed October 16, 2018.

Donovan, Tristan. 2015. *Feral Cities: Adventures with Animals in the Urban Jungle*. Chicago: Chicago Review Press.

Doré, Gustave and Blanchard Jerrold. 1868. *London: A Pilgrimage*. London: Grant and Co. https://archive.org/details/in.ernet.dli.2015.12905/page/n4 accessed June 4, 2019.

Dostoğlu, Neslihan. 1986. "Architectural Deterministic Thinking in the Development of Urban Utopias." Unpublished doctoral dissertation, University of Pennsylvania Press, Philadelphia, PA.

Doxiadis, Constantinos. 1965. "Islamabad: The Creation of a New Capital." *Town Planning Review* 36 (1): 1–28. www.doxiadis.org/Downloads/islamabad_the_capital_of_pakistan.pdf accessed 20 May 2018.

DPZ. 2016. "Legacy Town Center." www.dpz.com/Projects/9808 accessed May 17, 2017.

Drexler, Arthur, ed. 1977. *The Architecture of the École des Beaux-Art*. New York: Museum of Modern Art.

Drost, Magdalena. 2006. *The Bauhaus: 1919–1933: Reform and Avant Garde*. Cologne: Taschen.

Duany, Andres and Duany Plater-Zyberk. 2012. *Garden Cities: Theory & Practice of Agrarian Urbanism*. Miami: Duany Plater-Zyberk & Company.

Duany, Andres, Jeff Speck, and Mike Lydon. 2010. *The Smart Growth Manual*. New York: McGraw Hill.

Durack, Ruth. 2001. "Village Vices: The Contradiction of New Urbanism and Sustainability." *Places* (November). https://placesjournal.org/article/village-vices-the-contradiction-of-new-urbanism-and-sustainability/?gclid=CO3i1t7U19ICFYGZvAodsUYAeQ accessed March 15, 2017.

Duran, Rodrigo. 2017. "Crystal City: Frank Lloyd Wright's Long-Lost D.C. Masterpiece." *Curbed*. (October 5). https://dc.curbed.com/2017/10/5/16416038/crystal-city-frank-lloyd-wright-roy-thurman accessed January 10, 2019.

Durrett, Charles and Kathryn McCamant. 1988. *Cohousing: A Contemporary Approach to Housing Ourselves*. Berkeley, CA: Habitat Press.

Dyckhoff, Tom. 2017. *The Age of the Spectacular: Adventures in Architecture and the 21st Century*. New York: Random House.

Eaton, Leonard K. 1969. *Two Chicago Architects and their Clients: Frank Lloyd Wright and Howard Van Doren Shaw*. Cambridge, MA: MIT Press.

Ebbsfleet Valley Masterplan. 2008. https://ebbsfleetcvalley.co.uk accessed November 5, 2019.

Editorial. 1951. "Slum Surgery in St. Louis: A New Apartment Type." *Architectural Forum* (April): 128–36.

Eleb, Monique. 2000. "An Alternative to Functionalist Universalism: Écohard, Candilis, and ABAT-Afrique." In *Anxious Modernisms: Experimentation in Postwar Architectural Culture*, edited by Sarah Williams Goldhagen and Réjean Legault, 55–73. Cambridge, MA: MIT Press.

Elias, Norbert. 1935. "The Kitsch Style and the Age of Kitsch." In *The Norbert Elias Reader*, edited by Johan Goudsblom and Stephen Mennell, 27–29. Oxford: Blackwell, 1996.

Eliasson, Ingegärd. 2000. "The Use of Climate Knowledge in Urban Planning." *Landscape and Urban Planning* 48 (1–2): 31–44. www.seedengr.com/The%20use%20of%20climate%20knowledge%20in%20urban%20planning.pdf accessed May 26, 2017.

Ellin, Nan. 1996. *Postmodern Urbanism*. Revised edition. New York: Princeton Architectural Press.

Ellis, Russell and Dana Cuff, eds. 1989. *Architects' People*. New York: Oxford University Press.

Emmanuel, M. Rohinton. 2005. *An Urban Approach to Climate Sensitive Design: Strategies for the Tropics*. London: Spon Press.

Engels, Friederich. 1845. *The Condition of the Working Class in England*. Panther edition, 1969. www.marxists.org/archive/marx/works/download/pdf/condition-working-class-england.pdf accessed May 31, 2017.

Eserin, Angela. 1995. *Welwyn Garden City*. Stroud: The History Press.

European Council of Town Planners. 2003. *The New Charter of Athens 2003: The European Council of Town Planners' Vision for Cities in the 21st Century*. Firenze: Alinea Editrice. https://architexturez.net/doc/az-cf-172768 accessed August 7, 2018.

Evenson, Norma. 1973. *Two Brazilian Capitals: Architecture and Urbanism in Rio de Janeiro and Brasília*. New Haven: Yale University Press.

Farr, Douglas. 2008. *Sustainable Urbanism: Urban Design with Nature*. Hoboken, NJ: John Wiley. See also: http://citeseerx.ist.psu.edu/viewdoc/download?doi=10.1.1.456.3151&rep=rep1&type=pdf accessed June 4, 2019.

Farrell, Terry and Adam N. Furman. 2017. *Revisiting Postmodernism*. London: RIBA Publications.

Feld, Gabriel. 1999. *Free University, Berlin: Candilis, Josic, Woods, Schiedhelm*. London: Architectural Association Publications.

Ferris, Hugh. 1929. *The Metropolis of Tomorrow*. New York: Ives Washburn. https://archive.org/details/mettomo00ferr accessed April 28, 2017.

Festinger, Leon. 1957. *A Theory of Cognitive Dissonance*. Evanston, IL: Row, Petersen & Co.

Firestone, Rebecca. 2017. "Mexico's UNAM Campus: Revolution Pasts and Present." *The Architects' Take* (September 11). https://thearchitectstake.com/editorials/mexicos-unam-campus-revolution-past-and-present/ accessed July 5, 2018.

Fishman, Robert. 1977. *Urban Utopias in the Twentieth Century: Ebenezer Howard, Frank Lloyd Wright, Le Corbusier*. New York: Basic Books.

Fishman, Robert. 1987. *Bourgeois Utopias: The Rise and Fall of Suburbia*. New York: Basic Books.

Fitch, James M. 1980. "A Funny Thing Happened . . ." *American Institute of Architects Journal* 69 (1): 66–68.

Fletcher, Bannister. 1954. *A History of Architecture on the Comparative Method*. Sixteenth edition. London: Batsford.

Flint, Anthony. 2014. *Modern Man: The Life of Le Corbusier, Architect of Tomorrow*. Boston, MA: New Harvest; New York and Houghton Mifflin Harcourt.

Flint, Anthony. 2015. "10 Years Later; Did the Big Dig Deliver?" the *Boston Globe* (December 29). www.bostonglobe.com/magazine/2015/12/29/years-later-did-big-dig-deliver/tSb8PIMS4QJUEtsMpA7SpI/story.html accessed July 9, 2017.

Flores García, Marisol. 2001. *Tourist Guide to Urban Colonia Hipódromo*. Mexico City: Universidad Iberoamericana.

Florida, Richard. 2002. *The Rise of the Creative Class: And How It Is Transforming Work, Leisure and Everyday Life*. New York: Basic Books.

Florida, Richard. 2017. *The New Urban Crisis: How Our Cities Are Increasing Inequality, Deepening Segregation, and Failing the Middle Class—and What Can Be Done About It*. New York: Basic Books.

Foletta, Nicole. 2011. "Hammarby Sjöstad, Stockholm, Sweden." In *Europe's Vibrant Low Carbon Communities*, edited by Nicole Foletta and Simon Field, 30–46. New York: Institute for Transportation and Development Policy. www.itdp.org/wp-content/uploads/2014/07/16.-LowCarbonCommunities-Screen.pdf accessed June 4, 2019.

Förster, Wolfgang. 2002. *Harry Seidler: Wohnpark Neue Donau Wien/New Danube Housing Vienna*. Munich: Prestel.

Forsyth, Ann. 2005. *The Planned Communities of Irvine, Columbia, and the Woodlands*. Berkeley and Los Angeles: University of California Press.

Fourier, Charles. 1996. *The Theory of the Four Movements*. Edited by Gareth Stedman Jones and Ian Patterson. Translated from the French by Ian Patterson. Cambridge: Cambridge University Press, originally 1808. https://libcom.org/files/Fourier%20-%20The%20Theory%20of%20the%20Four%20Movements.pdf accessed June 4, 2019.

Fraker, Harrison. 2007. "Where Is the Urban Design Discourse?" *Places* 19 (3): 61. https://placesjournal.org/assets/legacy/pdfs/where-is-the-urban-design-discourse.pdf accessed July 3, 2010.

Francescato, Giulio. 1994. "Type and the Possibility of an Architectural Scholarship." In *Ordering Space: Types in Architecture and Design*, edited by Karen A. Franck and Lynda H. Schneekloth, 253–70. New York: Van Nostrand Reinhold.

Francis, David R. 1905. *The Universal Exposition of 1904*. St. Louis: Louisiana Purchase Exposition Company.

Frantz, Douglas and Catherine Collins. 2000. *Celebration, USA: Living in Disney's Brave New Town*. New York: Henry Holt.

Fraser, Giles and Marina Kim. 2015. "Welcome to Astana, Kazakhstan: One of the Strangest Capital Cities on Earth." *The Guardian* (July 21). www.theguardian.com/cities/2015/jul/28/astana-kazakhstan-strangest-capital-cities-on-earth accessed February 21, 2017.

Bibliography and References

Frearson, Amy. 2016 "Patrik Schumacher Calls for Social Housing and Public Space to Be Scrapped." *Dezeen* (November 18). www.dezeen.com/2016/11/18/patrik-schumacher-social-housing-public-space-scrapped-london-world-architecture-festival-2016/ accessed February 25, 2019.

Freeman, Robert. 2014. *The Interwar Years.* London Kendall Lane.

Freestone, Robert. 2007. *Designing Australia's Cities: Culture, Commerce and The City Beautiful.* Kensington, NSW: UNSW Press.

Friedman, David. 1988. *Florentine New Towns: Urban Design in the Middle Ages.* Cambridge, MA: MIT Press.

Friedman, Yona. 1958. *Prodomo.* English edition. Barcelona: Aktar Publishing, 2006. https://issuu.com/actar/docs/prodomo accessed September 6, 2019.

Friedman, Yona. 1959. *Agglomeration Spatiales Disponibilite pour la Vie Urbaine et pour l'Agriculture une Agglomeration de la Grandeur de Paris pourrait loger et Nourier 7 millions d'Habitants.* Paris: Collection Centre Pompidou.

Fritsch, Theodor. 1896. *Die Stadt der Zukunft: Mit Einer Farbigen Tafel und 14 Text-Abbildungen.* Leipzig: Fritsch. Published in English by Books on Demand.

Fry, Maxwell. 1961. "Problems of Chandigarh Architecture." *Marg* 25 (1): 20–21, 25.

Fry, Maxwell and Jane Drew. 1964. *Tropical Architecture in the Dry and Humid Zones.* London: Batsford.

Fulton, William. 1996. *The New Urbanism: Hope or Hype for American Communities.* Cambridge, MA: Lincoln Institute of Land Policy. www.lincolninst.edu/sites/default/files/pubfiles/the-new-urbanism-full.pdf accessed February 27, 2017.

GAD Architecture. 2017. "The One/GAD." *ArchiECHO* (November 6). www.archiecho.com/item/35325_the-one-gad accessed December 30, 2017.

Galinou, Mireille. 2010. *Cottages and Villas: The Birth of the Garden Suburb.* New Haven: Yale University Press.

Gallion, Arthur B. and Simon Eisner. 1975. *The Urban Pattern: City Planning and Design.* Third edition. New York: D. Van Nostrand Company.

Gallion, Arthur B. and Simon Eisner. 1993. *The Urban Pattern: City Planning and Design.* Sixth edition. Hoboken, NJ: John Wiley.

Gans, Herbert J. 1962. *The Urban Villagers: Group and Class in the Life of Italian-Americans.* New York: The Free Press.

Gans, Herbert J. 1967. *The Levittowners: Ways of Life and Politics in a New Suburban Community.* New York: Pantheon.

Gans, Herbert. 1968. "Urban Vitality and the Fallacy of Physical Determinism." In *People and Plans: Essays on Urban Problems and Solutions,* 25–33. edited by Herbert Gans. New York: Basic Books.

Gans, Herbert. 1975. *Popular Culture and High Culture: An Analysis and Evaluation of Taste.* New York: Basic Books.

Garber, Elizabeth W. 2017. *Implosion: Memoir of an Architect's Daughter.* Berkeley, CA: She Writes Press.

Garcia, Rafael G. and Cristina Tartás Ruiz. undated. "Infrastructure as Public Space Modelers: The Case of the Hauptstadt Berlin in the Proposals of Hans Sharoun and Alison & Peter Smithson." http://eurau12.arq.up.pt/sites/default/files/357.pdf accessed July 10, 2018.

Garnier, Tony. 1917. *Une Cité Industrielle: The Cité Industrielle.* Paris: Massin, 1930. Reprint edited by Riccardo Marianni. Translated from the French by Andrew Ellis. New York: Rizzoli, 1990.

Garreau, Joel. 1992. *Edge City: Life on the New Frontier.* New York: Anchor.

Garvey, James and Jeremy Stangroom. 2012. *The Story of Philosophy: A History of Western Thought.* London: Quercus.

Garvin, Alexander. 1996. *The American City: What Works, What Doesn't.* New York: McGraw Hill.

Gauthier, Gilles. 1995. "Linear City: Environmental & Social Solution." http://linearcity.photographex.com/index.html#Origins accessed October 28, 2018.

Geddes, Patrick. 1904. *City Development: A Study of Parks, Gardens, and Culture-Institutes.* Edinburgh: Geddes and Company; Bournville: St George Press, https://archive.org/details/citydevelopment00geddgoog accessed September 21, 2017.

Geddes, Patrick. 1915. *Cities in Evolution: An Introduction to the Town Planning Movement and to the Study of Civics.* London: Williams and Norgate. https://archive.org/stream/citiesinevolutio00gedduoft/citiesinevolutio00gedduoft_djvu.txt accessed September 22, 2017.

Geddes, Patrick. 1917. "Town Planning in Behrampur." A Report to the Hon'ble the Maharaja Bahadur, Lucknow.

George, Henry. 1879. *Progress and Poverty: An Inquiry into the Cause of Industrial Depression and of Increase of Want with the Increase of Wealth: The Remedy.* New York: Appleton. 1935 edition, published in

New York by the Robert Schalkenbach Foundation. https://mises.org/sites/default/files/Progress%20 and%20Poverty_3.pdf accessed June 4, 2019.

Gerolympos, Alexandra K. 1995. *The Redesign of Thessaloniki After the Fire of 1917*. Thessaloniki: University Studio Press.

Gibson, James J. 1979. *The Ecological Approach to Visual Perception*. Boston: Houghton Mifflin.

Giedion, Sigfried. 1963. *Space, Time and Architecture: The Growth of a New Tradition*. Cambridge, MA: Harvard University Press, originally 1941.

Gill, S. E., J. F. Handley, A. R. Ennos, and S. Pauleit. 2007. "Adapting Cities for Climate Change: The Role of Green Infrastructure." *Built Environment* 33 (1): 115–33.

Gintoff, Vladimir. 2016. "12 Projects That Explain Landscape Urbanism and How It Is Changing the Face of Cities." *Archdaily* (April 6). www.archdaily.com/784842/12-projects-that-show-how-landscape-urbanism-is-changing-the-face-of-cities accessed May 25, 2017.

Ginzburg, Moisei. 1924. *STIL' I EPOKHA*. Moscow: GIZ. English translation by Anatole Senkevitch as *Style and Epoch*. Cambridge, MA: MIT Press, 1982. https://monoskop.org/images/e/eb/Ginzburg_Moisei_Style_and_Epoch.pdf accessed June 4, 2019.

Givoni, Baruch. 1998. *Climate Considerations in Building and Urban Design*. Hoboken, NJ: John Wiley.

Glaeser, Edward. 2011. *Triumph of the City: How Urban Spaces Make Us Human*. London: Palgrave Macmillan.

"Global Site Plans—The Grid@theglobalgrid. 2014: Madrid, Spain Launches IBM Smarter Cities." www.smartcitiesdive.com/ex/sustainablecitiescollective/madrid-spain-launches-ibm-smarter-cities-project/316481/project accessed June 24, 2017.

Gluttman, Avraham. 2013. "Story of Hudson Yards: New York's Long Awaited Development Finally a Reality." www.slideshare.net/rayglattman/avraham-glattmanstory-of-the-hudson-yards accessed February 21, 2017.

Goldenberg, Suzanne. 2016. "Masdar's Zero-Carbon Dream Could Become World's First Green Ghost Town." *The Guardian* (February 17). www.theguardian.com/environment/2016/feb/16/masdars-zero-carbon-dream-could-become-worlds-first-green-ghost-town accessed January 3, 2019.

Goldsmith, Stephen and Susan Crawford. 2014. *The Responsive City: Engaging Communities Through Data Smart Governance*. San Francisco, CA: Jossey-Bass.

Golembewski, Jan. 2014. "Building a Better World: Can Architecture Shape Behavior?" *The Conversation* (January 7). https://theconversation.com/building-a-better-world-can-architecture-shape-behaviour-21541 accessed August 1, 2018.

Goodman, Paul and Percival Goodman. 1947. *Communitas: Means of Livelihood and Ways of Life*. New York: Vintage Books.

Gopnik, Adam. 2001. "A Walk on the High Line." *The New Yorker* (May 21): 44–47.

Gordon, David L. A. 1997. *Battery Park City: Politics and Planning on the New York Waterfront*. London: Routledge and Gordon & Breach.

Goyal, Malini. 2017. "Why Japan Is Pouring Lakhs of Crores in Cut-Rate Loans to Build Infrastructure Across India." *The Economic Times* (September 17). https://economictimes.indiatimes.com/news/economy/infrastructure/why-japan-is-pouring-lakhs-of-crores-in-cut-rate-loans-to-build-infrastructure-across-india/articleshow/60712934.cms accessed July 22, 2018.

Green, Jared. 2016. "Which Way to Baltimore's Future?" https://dirt.asla.org/2016/03/31/which-way-to-a-better-future-for-baltimore/ accessed February 21, 2017.

Greenfield, Adam. 2013. *Against the Smart City (The City Is Here for You to Use Book 1)*. London: Verso.

Greeves, T. Affleck. 1975. *Bedford Park: The First Garden Suburb*. London: Anne Bingley.

Groat, Linda. 1982. "Meaning in Post-Modern Architecture: An Examination Using the Multiple Sorting Task." *Journal of Environmental Psychology* 2 (1): 3–22.

Gropius, Walter. 1962. *The Scope of Total Architecture*. New York: Collier.

Groundlab. 2008. "Deep Ground, Masterplan for Longgang City, Shenzhen, China." http://grounlab.org accessed July 17, 2018.

Gruen, Victor. 1964. *The Heart of Our Cities. The Urban Crisis: Diagnosis and Cure*. New York: Simon and Schuster.

Gruson, Luc. 2008. "Claude Nicholas Ledoux, Visionary Architecture and Social Utopia." International Conference of Territorial Intelligence, Besançon. https://hal.archives-ouvertes.fr/hal-00767259/document accessed June 3, 2018.

Guillot-Herrald, Julie. 1993. "Les Arcades du Lac. L'esprit des lieux." *Miroir* (6–7): 21.

Bibliography and References

Guiton, Jacques. 1982. "On Urban Planning." In *Le Corbusier on Architecture and Urban Planning*, translated from the French and edited by Margaret Guiton, 93–112. New York: George Braziller.

Habrakan. N. J. 1972. *Supports: An Alternative to Mass Housing*. Translated from the Dutch by R Falkenburg. London: Architectural Press.

Hake, Sabine. 2008. *Topographies of Class: Modern Architecture and Mass Society in Weimer Berlin*. Ann Arbor, MI: University of Michigan Press.

Hakim, Besim S. 1986. *Arabic-Islamic Cities: Building and Planning Principles*. London: KPI.

Hakim, Besim S. 2003. "Built Environment and Law." In *Understanding Islamic Architecture*, edited by Attilio Petruccioli and Khalil K. Pirani, 176–79. New York: Routledge.

Hall, Edward T. 1966. *The Hidden Dimension*. New York: Anchor Books.

Hall, Peter. 1998. *Cities of Tomorrow: An Intellectual History of Urban Planning and Design in the Twentieth Century*. Oxford: Basil Blackwell.

Hallas-Murula, Karin. 2005. *Suurlinn Tallinn: Eliel Saarineni "Suur-Tallinna" projekt, 1913 = Suurkaupunki Tallinna: Eliel Saarisen Suur-Tallinna-suunnitelma, 1913 = Greater Tallinn: Eliel Saarinen's Greater-Tallinn*. Tallinn: Finish Embassy in Tallinn and Museum of Estonian Architecture.

Hamilton, C. Mark. 1995. *Nineteenth Century Mormon Architecture and City Planning*. Oxford: Oxford University Press.

Hamin, Elisabeth M. and Nicole Gurran. 2008. "Urban Form and Climate Change: Balancing Adaptation and Mitigation in the US and Australia." *Habitat International* 33: 238–45. http://citeseerx.ist.psu.edu/viewdoc/download?doi=10.1.1.469.289&rep=rep1&type=pdf accessed May 27, 2017.

Han, Hoon and Scott Hawken. 2018. "Introduction: Innovation and Identity in Next-Generation Smart Cities." *City, Culture, and Society* (March). http://doi.org/10.1016/j.ccs.2017.12.0003 accessed January 6, 2018.

Haney, David H. 2007. "Leberecht Migge's 'Green Manifesto': Envisioning a Revolution of Gardens." *Landscape Journal* 26 (2): 201–18.

Haney, David H. 2010. *When Modern Was Green: The Life and Work of Landscape Architect Leberecht Migge*. New York: Routledge.

Harari, Yuval N. 2011. *Sapiens: A Brief History of Humankind*. New York: Vintage Books.

Harding, Laura. 2008. "Rouse Hill Town Centre." *ArchitectureAU* (July 1). http://architectureau.com/articles/rouse-hill-town-centre-1/ accessed July 15, 2015.

Harvey, David. 2005. *A Brief History of Neoliberalism*. Oxford: Oxford University Press.

Harwood, Elain. 2003. *England: A Guide to Post-War Listed Buildings*. London: Batsford.

Hatherley, Owen. 2017. "Relics of an Era Now in Ruins." *The Guardian Weekly* (February 3): 19.

Hawken, Paul, Amory B. Lovins, and L. Hunter Lovins. 1999. "Weaving the Web of Solutions: The Curitiba Example." In *Natural Capitalism: Creating the Next Industrial Revolution*, 288–308. London: Earthscan.

Hawley, Amos. 1950. *Human Ecology: A Theory of Community Structure*. New York: Ronald Press.

Hayden, Dolores. 1976. *Seven American Utopias: The Architecture of Communitarian Socialism*. Cambridge, MA: MIT Press.

Hayden, Dolores. 1980. "What Would a Non-Sexist City Look Like? Speculations on Housing, Urban Design, and Human Work." *Signs: Journal of Women in Culture and Society* 5 (3): S170–86.

Hayden, Dolores. 1981. *The Grand Domestic Revolution: A History of Feminist Design for American Homes*. Cambridge, MA: MIT Press. https://monoskop.org/images/a/a7/Hayden_Dolores_The_Grand_Domestic_Revolution_A_History_of_Feminist_Designs_for_American_Homes_Neighborhoods_and_Cities_1981.pdf accessed June 5, 2019.

Hayden, Dolores. 1984. *Redesigning the American Dream: The Future of Housing, Work, and Family Life*. New York: W. W. Norton & Company.

Hayek, Friedrich. 1944. *The Road to Serfdom*. Chicago: University of Chicago Press. Condensed version. https://mises.org/sites/default/files/Road%20to%20serfdom.pdf accessed January 10, 2018.

Hayek, Friedrich. 1948. *Individualism and the Economic Order*. Chicago: University of Chicago Press.

Hayes, K. Michael, ed. 1998. *Architectural Theory Since 1968*. Cambridge, MA: MIT Press.

He, Congrong. 2007. "Architecture of Xia, Shang, Zhou Dynasties and Spring and Autumn Period." *CORE OCW*. https://web.archive.org/web/20081110104828/http://202.205.161.91/CORE/architecture/the-history-of-ancient-chinese-architecture/chater-2-architecture-of-xia-shang-zhou-dynasties-and-spring-and-autumn-period/ accessed November 20, 2016.

Heft, Harry. 2001. *Ecological Psychology in Context: James Gibson, Roger Barker and the Legacy of William James's Radical Empiricism*. Mahwah, NJ: Lawrence Erlbaum Associates.

Bibliography and References

Hegemann, Werner and Elbert Peets. 1922. *The American Vitruvius: An Architects' Handbook of Civic Art*. New York: The Architectural Book Publishing Co.

Hénard, Eugène. 1911. "The Cities of the Future." In *Transactions*, 345–67. London: Royal Institute of British Architects. http://urbanplanning.library.cornell.edu/DOCS/henard.htm accessed June 25, 2018.

Hermansen Cordua, Christian. 2010. *Manifestoes and Transformations in the Early Modernist City*. Farnham: Ashgate.

Herrington, Susan. 2016. *Landscape Theory in Design*. New York: Routledge.

Hester, Randolph T. Jr. 1975. *Neighborhood Space*. Stroudsburg, PA: Dowden, Hutchinson, and Ross.

Hilberseimer, Ludwig. 1925. *Building of Large Cities*. Hanover: Aposs.

Hilberseimer, Ludwig. 1927. *Grossstadarchitekur: Metropolis-Architecture*. Stuttgart: Julius Hoffman.

Hilberseimer, Ludwig. 1944. *The New City; Principles of Planning*. Chicago: Paul Theobald. https://archive.org/details/newcityprinciple00hilbrich/ accessed December 30, 2018.

Hill, Miss Octavia. 1875. *Homes of the London Poor*. New York: State Charities Aid Association. https://en.wikisource.org/wiki/Homes_of_the_London_Poor accessed June 3, 2018.

Hillier, Bill and Julienne Hanson. 1984. *The Social Logic of Space*. Cambridge: Cambridge University Press.

Holland, Oscar. 2016. "Why China's Super Wealthy Shun Western Looking Suburbs." *CNN Style* (November 21). https://edition.cnn.com/style/article/luxury-china-homes-most-expensive/index.html accessed July 16, 2018.

Holston, James. 1989. *The Modernist City: An Anthropological Critique of Brasília*. Chicago: University of Chicago Press.

Hough, Michael. 1984. *City Form and Natural Processes: Towards a New Urban Vernacular*. London: Croom Helm.

Hough, Michael. 2004. *Cities and Natural Processes: A Basis for Sustainability*. Second edition. New York: Routledge.

Houstoun, Lawrence O. Jr. 1990. "From Street to Mall and Back Again." *Planning* 56 (6): 4–10.

Howard, Ebenezer. 1898. *Tomorrow: A Peaceful Path to Real Reform*. London: Swan Sonneschein.

Howard, Ebenezer. 1902. *Garden Cities of Tomorrow*. London: Sonnenschein.

Huet, Bernard. 1984. "The City as Dwelling Space: Alternatives to the Charter of Athens." *Lotus International* 41: 6–16.

Hughes, Robert. 2006. "Paradise Now." *The Guardian*, Australian edition (March 20). www.theguardian.com/artanddesign/2006/mar/20/architecture.modernism1 accessed December 14, 2017.

Humboldt, Alexander von. 1847. *Kosmos, Entwurf einer physischen Weltbescreibung*. Frankfurt: Eichborn.

Huxtable, Ada L. 2004. *Frank Lloyd Wright: A Life*. New York: Viking.

Inam, Aseem. 2011. "Smart Growth: A Critical Review of the State of the Art." In *Companion to Urban Design*, edited by Tridib Banerjee and Anastasia Loukaitou-Sideris, 632–43. London: Routledge. www.academia.edu/1901734/Smart_Growth_A_Critical_Review_of_the_State_of_the_Art accessed May 13, 2017.

Irazábal, Clara. 2001. "Da Carta de Atenas à carta do Novo Urbanismo: Qual seu significado para América Latina." *Arquitextos* 2 (Deciembre). www.vitruvius.com.br/revistas/read/arquitextos/02.019/821 accessed November 12, 2017.

Irving, Alexander. 1993. "The Modern/Postmodern Divide and Urban Planning." *University of Toronto Quarterly* 62 (4): 474–87.

Irving, Robert G. 1981. *Indian Summer: Lutyens, Baker and Imperial Delhi*. New Haven: Yale University Press.

Iverot, Sofie and Nils Brandt. 2011. "The Development of a Sustainable Urban District in Hammarby Sjöstad, Stockholm, Sweden?" *Environment, Development and Sustainability* 13 (6): 1043–64.

Izumi, Kiyo. 1968. "Some Psycho-Social Considerations of Environmental Design." Mimeographed.

Jabi, Wassim. 2013. *Parametric Design for Architecture*. London: Laurence King.

Jackson, Richard H. 1992. "City Planning." In *Encyclopedia of Mormonism: The History, Scripture, Doctrine and Procedure of the Church of Jesus Christ of the Latter-day Saints*, edited by Daniel H. Ludlow. New York: Palgrave Macmillan. https://eom.byu.edu/index.php/City_Planning accessed July 20, 2017.

Jacobs, Allan. 1993. *Great Streets*. Cambridge, MA: MIT Press.

Jacobs, Allan and Donald Appleyard. 1987. "Toward an Urban Design Manifesto." *Journal of the American Planning Association* 53 (1): 112–20. https://pdfs.semanticscholar.org/293a/15cd8ad1e63d3676e577dca120872a80e771.pdf accessed June 4 2018.

Jacobs, Jane. 1961. *The Death and Life of Great American Cities*. New York: Random House. www.buurtwijs.nl/sites/default/files/buurtwijs/bestanden/jane_jacobs_the_death_and_life_of_great_american.pdf accessed June 5, 2019.

Bibliography and References

Jacobs, Jane. 1969. *The Economy of Cities: How to Study Public Life*. New York: Vintage Books.

Jager, Markus. 2007. *Housing Estates in the Berlin Modern Style*. Edited by Jörg Haspel and Annemarie Jaeggi. Berlin: Deutscher Kunsverlag.

Jameson, Fredric. 1991. *Postmodernism, or, the Logic of Late Capitalism*. Durham, NC: Duke University Press.

Jay, Di. 2006. "Planning." Walter Burley Griffin Society. www.griffinsociety.org/Lives_and_Works/urban_planning.html accessed November 29, 2016.

Jeffries, Michael P. 2014. "Hip-Hop Urbanism Old and New." *International Journal of Urban and Regional Research* 38 (2): 706–15.

Jencks, Charles. 1988. *Architecture Today*. Revised edition. New York: Harry N. Abrams.

Jencks, Charles. 2002. *The New Paradigm in Architecture: The Language of Post-Modernism*. New Haven: Yale University Press.

Jencks, Charles and Karl Kropf, eds. 2006. *Theories and Manifestoes of Contemporary Architecture*. Second edition. London: Academy Editions.

Jenkins, David. 1993. *Unité d'Habitation, Marseille, France 1945–52*. London: Phaidon.

Jerram, Leif. 2007. "From Page to Policy: Camillo Sitte and Planning Practice in Munich." *Manchester Papers in Economic and Social History* 57 (September). www.worldcat.org/title/from-page-to-policy-camillo-sitte-and-planning-practice-in-munich/oclc/182662770 accessed October 27, 2016.

Judd, Bruce and Robert Samuels. 2005. "The Effectiveness of Strategies for Crime Reduction in Areas of Public Housing Concentration." 2nd State of Australian Cities Conference, Griffith University, November 30–December 2.

Judt, Tony. 2005. *Postwar: A History of Europe Since 1945*. London: Vintage.

Jung, Carl. 1968. *Man and His Symbols*. New York: Dell.

Jurica, David and Brad Valtman, eds. 2013. *Coldscapes: Design Ideas for Winter Cities*. Cleveland, OH: Cleveland Urban Design Collaborative.

Kan, Har Ye, Ann Forsyth, and Peter Rowe. 2017. "Redesigning China's Superblock Neighbourhoods: Policies, Opportunities and Challenges." *Journal of Urban Design* 22 (6): 757–77.

Kasarda, John D. and Greg Lindsay. 2011. *Aerotropolis: The Way We'll Live Next*. New York: Farrar, Straus, and Giroux.

Katz, Peter. 1994. *The New Urbanism: Toward an Architecture of Community*. New York: McGraw-Hill.

Kelbaugh, Doug, ed. 1987. *The Pedestrian Pocket Handbook: A New Suburban Design Strategy*. Princeton, NJ: Princeton Architectural Press.

Kellett, Jon. 2016. "Australian Cities and Climate Change." *Built Environment* 42 (1): 145–57.

Khazanova, V. 1970. "Vkhutemas-Vkhutein." *Architectural Design* (February): 80–81.

Kirsch, Karen. 1990. *The Weissenhofsiedlung: Experimental Housing Built for the Deutscher Werkbund, Stuttgart 1927*. New York: Rizzoli.

Kjellman-Chapin, Monica. 2010. "The Politics of Kitsch." *Rethinking Marxism* 22 (1): 27–41.

Klaus, Susan L. 2004. *A Modern Arcadia: Frederick Law Olmsted Jr. and the Plan for Forest Hills Gardens*. Amherst and Boston: University of Massachusetts Press.

Kleihues, Josef Paul. 1987. *Internationale Bauausstellung Berlin 1987: Projektübersicht*. Berlin: IBA.

Knox, Paul L. 2008. *Metroburbia USA*. New Brunswick, NJ: Rutgers University Press.

Knowles, Ralph. 1999. "The Solar Envelope." http://www-bcf.usc.edu/~rknowles/sol_env/sol_env.html accessed February 26, 2017.

Koenigsberger, Otto H., T. G. Ingersoll, Alan Mayhew, and S. V. Szokolay. 1974. *Manual of Tropical Housing and Building: Climatic Design*. London: Longman. Reissued 2011, Himayatnagar: Universities Press.

Koh, Jusuck. 2013a. *On a Landscape Approach to Design: An Eco-Poetic Interpretation of Landscape*. Wageningen: Landscape Architecture Group of Wageningen University.

Koh, Jusuck. 2013b. "Articulating Landscape Urbanism: Ten Defining Characteristics." In *Landscape Urbanism and Its Discontents: Dissimulating the Sustainable City*, edited by Andrés Duany and Emily Talen, 245–62. Gabriola Island, BC: New Society Publishers.

Kohler, Sue and Pamela Scott. 2006. *Designing the Nation's Capital: The 1901 Plan for Washington, D.C.* Washington, DC: U.S. Commission of Fine Arts.

Koolhaas, Rem. 1978. *Delirious New York: A Retrospective Manifesto*. New York: Monacelli Press. https://monoskop.org/images/8/81/Koolhaas_Rem_Delirious_New_York_A_Retroactive_Manifesto_fr_Manhattan.pdf accessed December 24, 2017.

Kostof, Spiro. 1985. *A History of Architecture: Settings and Rituals*. Second edition. New York: Oxford University Press.

388

Bibliography and References

Kostof, Spiro. 1993. *The City Shaped: Urban Patterns and Meanings Through History*. Boston: Bulfinch Press.

Kotkin, Joel. 2017. *The Human City: Urbanism for the Rest of Us*. Chicago: Agate.

Krier, Léon. 1984. "Reconstruction of the European City." *Architectural Design* 54 (November–December): 16–22.

Krier, Léon. 1985. *Albert Speer: Architecture 1932–1942*. Bruxelles: Archives d'Architecture.

Krier, Léon. 1992. *Léon Krier: Architecture & Urban Design, 1967–1992*. Edited by Richard Economakis. London: Academy Editions.

Krier, Rob. 1979. *Urban Space*. Translated from the German, *Stadtraum in Theorie und Praxis*, by Christine Czechowski and George Black. New York: Rizzoli.

Kyttä, Marketta, Melody Oliver, Erika Ahmadi, Ichiro Omiya, and Tina Laatikainen. 2018. "Children as Urbanites: Mapping the Affordances and Behavior Settings of Urban Environments for Finnish and Japanese Children." *Children's Geographies* 3. www.tandfonline.com/doi/full/10.1080/14733285.2018. 1453923 accessed May 31, 2018.

LaConte, Pierre. 2009. *La Recherche de la Qualité Environnementale et Urbaine, Le Cas de Louvain-la-Neuve. Belgique*. Lyon: Éditions du Certu.

Lagopoulos, Alexandros Ph. 2005. "Monumental Urban Space and National Identity: The Early Twentieth Century Plan for Thessaloniki." *Journal of Historical Geography* 31: 61–77. www.urbanlab.org/articles/Lagopoulos%20Thesalonik%20monum%20nat%20id.pdf accessed January 10, 2019.

Lai, Richard Tseng-yu. 1988. *Law in Urban Design and Planning: The Invisible Web*. New York: Van Nostrand Reinhold.

Laimer, Christoph. 2014. "Smart cities: Zurück in die zukunft." *dérive—Zeitschrift für Stadtforschung* 56. https://derive.at/texte/smart-cities-zuruck-in-die-zukunft/ accessed May 13, 2018.

Lang, Jane. 1956. *The Rebuilding of St. Paul's After the Great Fire of London*. London: Oxford University Press.

Lang, Jon. 1980. "The Built Environment and Social Behavior, Architectural Determinism Re-Examined." In *Culture and the Social Vision VIA 4*, edited by Mark A. Hewitt, Benjamin Kracauer, John Massengale, and Michael McDonough, 140–53. Philadelphia, PA: GSFA, University of Pennsylvania Press and Cambridge, MA: MIT Press.

Lang, Jon. 1994. *Urban Design: The American Experience*. New York: Van Nostrand Reinhold.

Lang, Jon. 2005. *Urban Design: A Typology of Procedures and Products Illustrated with Over 50 Case Studies*. Oxford: Architectural Press.

Lang, Jon. 2016. "Urban Designing in Heterogeneous Cities: Issues and Response." *Journal of Urban Design and Planning* 21 (5): 561–63. Published online. http://dx.doi.org/10.1680/jourdp.15.000032.

Lang, Jon. 2017. *Urban Design: A Typology of Procedures and Products Illustrated with Over 50 Case Studies*. Second edition. New York: Routledge.

Lang, Jon, Madhavi Desai, and Miki Desai. 1997. *Architecture and Independence: The Search for Identity—India 1880–1980*. New Delhi: Oxford University Press.

Lang, Jon and Nancy Marshall. 2016. *Urban Squares as Places Links and Displays*. New York: Routledge.

Lang, Jon and Walter Moleski. 2010. *Functionalism Revisited: Architectural Theory and Practice and the Behavioral Sciences*. Farnham: Ashgate.

Langar, Suneet Z. 2017. "Is India's Plan to Build 100 Smart Cities Inherently Flawed?" *ArchDaily* (June 29). www.archdaily.com/874576/is-indias-plan-to-build-100-smart-cities-inherently-flawed?utm_medium=email&utm_source=ArchDaily%20List accessed June 30, 2017.

Lanzi, Christina, Robert Tullis, and Anne-Catrin Schultz. 2017. *Place-Making Manifesto*. Boston: Boston Society of Architects. https://urbannext.net/urbancultureinstitute/placemaking-manifesto-issued-november-2017/ accessed May 8, 2018.

Larson, Magali S. 1993. *Behind the Postmodern Façade: Architectural Change in Late Twentieth Century America*. Berkeley and Los Angeles: University of California Press. https://publishing.cdlib.org/ucpressebooks/view?docId=ft7c60084k;chunk.id=0;doc.view=print accessed December 3, 2019.

Laurence, Peter L. 2011. "The Unknown Jane Jacobs: Geographer, Propogandist, City Planning Idealist." In *Reconsidering Jane Jacobs*, edited by Max Page and Timothy Mennel, 15–36. Washington, DC: Planners Press.

Lavrov, Leonid and Feodor Petrov. 2016. "The Phenomenon of Saint Petersburg Variant of the Regular City." *Architecture and Engineering* 1 (1): 31–39. https://cyberleninka.ru/article/n/the-phenomenon-of-the-saint-petersburg-variant-of-the-regular-city accessed June 16, 2018.

Lawson, Bryan. 1990. *How Designers Think: The Design Process Demystified*. Second edition. Oxford: Butterworth Architecture.

Bibliography and References

Lawton, M. Powell and Lucille Nahemow. 1973. "Ecology and the Aging Process." In *Psychology of Adult Development and Aging*, edited by C. Eisoderofer and M. P. Lawton, 619–714. Washington, DC: American Psychological Association.

Leach, Neil. 2009. "Architecture or Revolution?" https://neilleach.files.wordpress.com/2009/09/architecture-or-revolution.pdf accessed April 4, 2018.

Leach, Peter and Nikolaus Pevsner. 2009. *Yorkshire and West Riding: Leeds, Bradford and the North*. New Haven and London: Yale University Press.

Le Corbusier. 1923. *Towards a New Architecture*. Translated from the French *Vers une Architecture* by Frederick Etchells. New York: Praeger, 1960.

Le Corbusier. 1925. *Urbanisme. Collection de 'l'Esprit Nouveau.'* Paris: Les Éditions G. Crès & Cie.

Le Corbusier. 1943. *The Athens Charter*. Translated from the French *Charte d'Athènes*, by Anthony Eardley. New York: Grossman, 1973. https://modernistarchitecture.wordpress.com/2010/11/03/ciam%E2%80%99s-%E2%80%9Cthe-athens-charter%E2%80%9D-1933/ accessed June 5, 2019.

Le Corbusier. 1960. *My Work*. Introduction by Maurice Jardot. Translated from the French by James Palmer. London: Architectural Press.

Le Corbusier. 1967. *The Radiant City: Elements of a Doctrine of Urbanism to Be Used as the Basis of Our Machine Age Civilization*. Translated from the French, *La Ville Radieuse*, 1933 by Pamela Knight, Eleanor Levieux, and Derek Coltman. New York: Orion.

Le Corbusier. 1990. *Precisions: On the Present State of Architecture and City Planning*. Translated from the 1930 French edition by Edith Schreiber Aujame. Cambridge, MA: MIT Press.

Le Corbusier and Pierre Jeanneret. 1964. "Plan Voisin, Paris, France 1925: The Street." In *Ouevre Complete, Vol. 1, 1910–1929*. Zurich: Les Editions d'Architecture. www.fondationlecorbusier.fr/corbuweb/morpheus.aspx?sysId=13&IrisObjectId=6159&sysLanguage=en-en&itemPos=2&itemCount=2&sysParentName=Home&sysParentId=65 accessed May 3, 2018.

Lehmann, Steffan. 2010. *The Principles of Green Urbanism: Transforming the City for Sustainability*. London: Earthscan.

Leimenstoll, William. 2017. "An Unprecedented Mobility Revolution? We've Been There Before." *Eno Transportation Weekly* (June 5). www.enotrans.org/article/unprecedented-mobility-revolution-weve/ accessed July 6, 2017.

Ley, David. 1989. "Modernism, Post-Modernism and the Struggle for Place." In *The Power of Place: Bringing Together Geographical and Sociological Imaginations*, edited by John A. Agnew and James S. Duncan, 44–65. Boston: Unwin Hyman.

Li, Junxiang, Yujie Wang, and Yong-Chang Song. 2008. "Landscape Corridors in Shanghai and Their Importance in Urban Forest Planning." In *Ecology, Planning and Management of Urban Forests: International Perspectives*, edited by Margaret M. Carreiro, Yong-Chang Song, and Jianguo Wu, 219–39. New York: Springer.

Lim, William S. W. 2007. *Asian Alterity: With Special Reference to Architecture and Urbanism Through the Lens of Cultural Studies*. Singapore: World Scientific Publishing.

Linnabery, Ann M. 2016. "Niagara Discoveries: Echota, a Utopian Community." *Lockport Union-Sun & Journal* (May 21). www.lockportjournal.com/news/lifestyles/niagara-discoveries-echota-a-utopian-community/article_79e04e1d-2c2f-50aa-ad6e-485a017dc847.html accessed December 20, 2016.

Llewelyn-Davies. 2000. *Urban Design Compendium*. London: English Partnerships and Housing Corporation. www.newham.gov.uk/Documents/Environment%20and%20planning/UrbanDesignCompendium.pdf accessed June 6, 2019.

Longworth, Guy. 2015. "Rationalism and Empiricism." http://www2.warwick.ac.uk/fac/soc/philosophy/people/longworth/keyideasrationalismempiricism.pdf accessed August 10, 2017.

Loos, Adolf. 1910. *Ornament und Verbrechen, Sämtliche Schriften in zwei Bänden—Erster Band*. Wien: Herold, 1962.

Los Angeles Metro. 2014. *Union Station Master Plan*. Los Angeles, CA: Los Angles Metro. https://media.metro.net/projects_studies/union_station/images/20141023rbmitem19.pdf accessed May 22, 2018.

Lovejoy, Derek. 1966. "The Design of Islamabad—New Capital of Pakistan." *Journal of the Royal Society of Arts* 114 (5123): 923–41.

Lu, Dufang, ed. 2011. *Third World Modernism: Architecture, Development and Identity*. London: Routledge.

Lubell, Sam. 2004. "Libeskind's World Trade Center Guidelines Raise Doubts." *Architectural Record* 192 (6): 47.

Lucente, Roberta and Patricia S. Travante Mendes. 2012. "The *23 de enero* Public Housing in Caracas: Rethinking the Relationship Between the Formal and Informal City." *EURAU' 12*. https://

housingchallenges.files.wordpress.com/2018/09/lucente-mendes-2012-the-23-de-enero-public-housing-in-caracas.pdf accessed March 30, 2017.

Luhn, Alec. 2016. "Story of Cities #20: The Secret History of Magnitogorsk, Russia's Steel City." *The Guardian*. Australian edition (April 12). www.theguardian.com/cities/2016/apr/12/story-of-cities-20-the-secret-history-of-magnitogorsk-russias-steel-city accessed April 25, 2017.

Lutz, Ashley. 2016. "American Malls Are Dying Faster Than You Think—and It's About to Get Even Worse." *Business Insider Australia* (September 1). www.businessinsider.com.au/are-malls-really-dying-2016-8 accessed November 18, 2017.

Lynch, Kevin. 1960. *The Image of the City*. Cambridge, MA: MIT Press. www.miguelangelmartinez.net/IMG/pdf/1960_Kevin_Lynch_The_Image_of_The_City_book.pdf accessed June 18, 2017.

Lynch, Kevin. 1981. *A Theory of Good Urban Form*. Cambridge, MA: MIT Press.

M@. 2017. "How St John's Wood Almost Got a Huge Circus." *Londonist* (January 11). http://londonist.com/london/history/britishcircus accessed May 10, 2017.

Madeddu, Manuela and Xiaoqing Zhang. 2017. "Harmonious Spaces: The Influence of Feng Shui on Urban Form and Design." *Journal of Urban Design* 22 (6): 709–25.

Maertens, Hermann. 1877. *Der Optische Maßstab oder die Theorie und Praxis des ästhetischen Sehens in den bildenden Künsten: auf Grund der Lehre der Physiologischen Optik für Architekten, Maler, Bildhauer, Musterzeichner, Modelleure, Stukkateure, Möbelfabrikanten, Landschaftsgärtner und Kunstfreunde*. Bonn: Cohen.

Mairet, Philip. 1957. *Pioneer of Sociology: The Life and Letters of Patrick Geddes*. London: Lund Humphries.

Mairs, Jessica. 2017. "MAD's Huangshan Mountain Village Mimics the Topography of a Rocky Chinese Landscape." *Dezeen* (November 14). www.dezeen.com/2017/11/14/mad-huangshan-mountain-village-housing-towers-eastern-china-taiping-lake/ accessed December 30, 2017.

Mallgrave, Harry F. and Christina Contandriopoulos, eds. 2008. *Architectural Theory: Volume II, An Anthology from 1871 to 2005*. Oxford: Blackwell.

Manchester, William. 2003. *The Arms of Krupp: 1587–1968: The Rise and Fall of the Industrial Dynasty That Armed Germany at War*. Boston, MA: Back Bay, Little, Brown, originally 1968.

Mansfield, Howard. 1990. *Cosmopolis: Yesterday's Cities of the Future*. New Brunswick, NJ: Rutgers University Center for Urban Policy Research.

Mänty, Jorma and Norman Pressman. 1988. *Cities Designed for Winter*. Helsinki: Building Book.

Marinetti, F. T. 1909. "The Founding and Manifesto of Futurism." www.unknown.nu/futurism/manifesto.html accessed September 25, 2017.

Marling, Karan A. 1989. "America's Love Affair with the Automobile in the Television Era." *Design Quarterly* 146: 5–20.

Marmot, Alexi F. 1982. "The Legacy of Le Corbusier and High-Rise Housing." *Built Environment* 7 (2): 82–95.

Marozzi, Justin. 2016. "The Birth of Baghdad." *The Guardian* (March 16). www.theguardian.com/cities/2016/mar/16/story-cities-day-3-baghdad-iraq-world-civilisation accessed June 23, 2018.

Marsh, George O. 1864. *Man and Nature*. Republished and edited by David Lowenthal. Cambridge, MA: Harvard University Press, 1967.

Marshall, Richard. 2003. *Emerging Urbanity: Global Urban Design Projects in the Asia Pacific Rim*. London: Spon.

Martin del Guayo, Patricia. 2011. "Downsview Park Toronto: Frameworks as Design." *Ecosistema Urbano* (June 21). http://ecosistemaurbano.org/english/downsview-park-toronto-frameworks-as-design/ accessed March 6, 2018.

Marx, Karl and Friedrich Engels. 1848. *The Manifesto of the Communist Party*. London: Workers' Education Association. www.marxists.org/archive/marx/works/download/pdf/Manifesto.pdf accessed March 11, 2019.

Maslow, Abraham. 1987. *Motivation and Personality*. Revised by Robert Frager, James Fadiman, Cynthia Reynolds, and Ruth Cox. Third edition. New York: Harper and Sons.

Mattern, Shannon. 2017. "A City Is Not a Computer." *Places* (February). https://doi.org/10.22269/170207 accessed February 24, 2017.

Mawman, J. 1805. *Excursion to the Highlands of Scotland and English Lakes*. London: The Author. https://archive.org/details/excursiontohighl00mawm/page/n8 accessed May 30, 2019.

Mayer, Albert. 1967. *The Urgent Future, People, Housing, City, Region*. New York: McGraw-Hill.

McHarg, Ian. 1969. *Design with Nature*. New York: Natural History Press.

Meacham, Richard. 1999. *Regaining Paradise: Englishness and the Early Garden City Movement*. New Haven: Yale University Press.

Bibliography and References

Mehaffy, Michael. 2010. "The Landscape Urbanism: Sprawl in a Pretty Green Dress?" *Planetizen* (October 4). www.planetizen.com/node/46262 accessed March 14, 2018.

Mehaffy, Michael. 2011. "How Landscape Architecture Can Save the World." *Planetizen* (April 18). www.planetizen.com/node/48993 accessed May 24, 2016.

Mella-Marquez, Jose M., Asunción López-López, and Victor Mella-Lopez. 2014. "European Smart Cities: The Case of Madrid." *Regional Studies Association*. https://3ftfah3bhjub3knerv1hneul-wpengine.netdna-ssl.com/wp-content/uploads/2018/07/POWERPOINT_SC_FORTALEZA.pdf accessed June 24, 2017.

Melosi, Martin V. 2000. *The Sanitary City: Urban Infrastructure in America from Colonial Times to the Present.* Baltimore, MD: Johns Hopkins University Press.

Meyer, Michael. 2015. "Welcome to the Most Japanese City in China." *Foreign Policy* (September 2). http://foreignpolicy.com/2015/09/02/welcome-to-the-most-japanese-city-in-china-manchuria-changchun/ accessed September 4, 2017.

Miao, Pu. 2003. "Deserted Streets in a Jammed Town: The Gated Community in Chinese Cities and Its Solution." *Journal of Urban Design* 8 (1): 45–66.

Michelson, William. 1968. "Most People Don't Want What Architects Want." *Transactions* 5 (8): 37–43.

Migge, Leberecht. 1913. "Die Gartenkultur des 20. Jahrhunderts." https://digi.ub.uni-heidelberg.de/diglit/migge1913 accessed May 12, 2019.

Migge, Leberecht. 2013. *Garden Culture of the Twentieth Century.* Edited and translated from the German, *Die Gartenkultur des XX. Jahrhunderts*, published in 1919 by David H. Haney. Cambridge, MA: Harvard University Press.

Miller, Campbell, Grady Clay, Ian L. McHarg, Charles R. Hammond, George E. Patton, and John O. Simonds. 1966. "A Declaration of Concern." Landscape Architecture Foundation. www.lafoundation.org/who-we-are/values/declaration-of-concern accessed July 5, 2019.

Miller, Mervyn. 1992. *Raymond Unwin, Garden Cities and Town Planning.* Leicester: Leicester University Press.

Miller, Mervyn and A. Stuart Gray. 1992. *Hampstead Garden Suburb. Arts and Crafts Utopia.* Chichester: Phillimore.

Millon, René. 1973. *The Teotihuacán Map.* Austin, TX: University of Texas Press.

Mills, C. Wright. 1956, 2000. *The Power Elite.* Afterword by Alan Wolfe. New York: Oxford University Press.

Milyutin, Nikolay. 1930. *Sotsgorod: The Problem of Building Socialist Cities.* Translated from the Russian by Anatole Senkevitch. Cambridge, MA: MIT Press, 1974. https://modernistarchitecture.wordpress.com/2010/11/01/nikolai-miliutin%E2%80%99s-sotsgorod-the-problem-of-building-socialist-cities-1930/ accessed October 12, 2018.

Mindrup, Matthew. 2012. "Introduction: Advancing the Reverie of Utopia." In *The City Crown by Bruno Taut*. Translated from the German *Die Stadtkrone*, published in Berlin by Mann in 1917 by Matthew Mindrup and Ulrike Altenmüller-Lewis, 1–30. London and New York: Routledge.

Mitchell, Joseph R. and David Stebenne. 2007. *New City upon a Hill: A History of Columbia, Maryland.* Charleston, SC: The History Press.

Mitchell, Lynne, Elizabeth Burton, and Shibu Rahman. 2004. "Dementia Friendly Cities: Designing Intelligible Neighbourhoods for Life." *Journal of Urban Design* 9 (1): 89–101.

Mohajeri, Shima. 2015. "Louis Kahn's Silent Space of Critique in Tehran, 1973–74." *Journal of the Society of Architectural Historians* 74 (4): 385–504.

Montgomery, Roger. 1985. "Pruitt–Igoe: Policy Failure or Social Symptom." In *The Metropolitan Midwest: Policy Problems and Prospects for the Future*, edited by Barry Checkoway and Carl V. Patton, 229–43. Urbana and Chicago, IL: University of Illinois Press.

Moore, Charles. 1921. *Daniel H. Burnham, Architect, Planner of Cities, Volume 2.* Boston: Houghton Mifflin.

Moore, Rosamie. 2016. "Piazza del Popolo." In *Rome in the Footsteps of an XVIIIth Century Traveller.* www.romeartlover.it/Vasi21.htm accessed May 7, 2017.

Moorhouse, Roger. 2010. *Berlin at War: Life and Death in Hitler's Capital, 1939–1945.* London: Bodley Head.

Moravánszky, Ákos. 2012. "The Optical Construction of Urban Space: Hermann Maertens, Camillo Sitte and the Theories of 'Aesthetic Perception.'" *Journal of Architecture* 17 (5): 655–66.

Mori, Masashi. 2015. "Toyama's Compact City Strategy: Revitalizing Public Transportation." www.iges.or.jp/files/research/pmo/PDF/20160515/1_1_en.pdf accessed August 11, 2018.

Morris, William. 2012. *The Collective Works of William Morris with Introductions by His Daughter May Morris, Vol. 13, Signs of Changes: Lectures on Socialism.* Cambridge: Cambridge University Press.

Mostavi, Moshen and Ciro Naijie. 2004. *Landscape Urbanism: Manual for the Machinic Landscape*. London: AA Publications.

The Mother. 1990. *Search for the Soul in Everyday Living*. Wilmot, WI: Loftus Light Publishing.

Motro, René. 2007. "Robert le Ricolais 1894–1977 'Father of Spatial Structures.'" *International Journal of Spatial Structures* 22 (4): 233.

Mujica, Francisco. 1920. *100-Story City in Neo-American Style*. Paris and New York: Archaeological and Architectural Press.

Mujica, Francisco. 1929. *History of the Skyscraper*. Paris and New York: Archaeological and Architectural Press. Reprinted by DaCapo Press in 1977.

Mulazzani, Marco. 2012. "I 'gratte-ciel' de Villeurbanne: Nascita di una città." *Casabella* 820: 74–87.

Mumford, Eric P. 2000. *The CIAM Discourse on Urbanism, 1925–1960*. Cambridge, MA: MIT Press.

Mumford, Eric P. 2009. *Defining Urban Design: CIAM Architects and the Formulation of a Discipline*. New Haven: Yale University Press.

Mumford, Lewis. 1938. *The Culture of Cities*. New York: Harcourt, Brace, Jovanovich. Republished Westport, CT: Greenwood Press, 1981.

Mumford, Lewis. 1954. "Nowicki's Work in India." *Architectural Record* 116 (3): 153–59.

Mumford, Lewis. 1961. *The City in History, Its Origins, Its Transformations, and Its Prospects*. London: Secker & Warburg.

Mumford, Lewis. 1962. "From Crochet Castle to Arthur's Seat." In *The Highway and the City*, 89–94. New York: Harcourt, Brace & World.

Mumford, Lewis. 1965. "Revaluations I: Howard's Garden City." *The New York Review of Books* (April 8). www.nybooks.com/articles/1965/04/08/revaluations-i-howards-garden-city/ accessed December 15, 2017.

Munshi, Indra. 2000. "Patrick Geddes: Sociologist, Environmentalist, and Town Planner." *Economic and Political Weekly* 35 (6): 485–91.

Murphy, Michael D. 2005. *Landscape Architecture Theory: An Evolving Body of Thought*. Long Grove, IL: Waveland Press.

Musa, Sam. 2016. "Smart City Roadmap." www.academia.edu/21181336/Smart_City_Roadmap accessed June 22, 2017.

Myall, Nick. 2018. "Creating an Urban Oasis." *World Architectural News* (September 13). www.worldarchitecturenews.com/article/1518699/creating-urban-oasis accessed January 3, 2019.

Nair, Shalini. 2017. "Smart City Project: We Start Small so That It Can Be Replicated Says Govt." *The Indian Express* (June 14). http://indianexpress.com/article/india/smart-city-project-we-start-small-so-that-it-can-be-replicated-says-govt-4702919/ accessed March 10, 2018.

Nesser, Claudia. 2017. "WagnisART—Cooperative Housing in Munich." *Guiding Architects* (June 15). www.guiding-architects.net/wagnisart-cooperative-housing-munich/ accessed January 28, 2018.

Neuman, Michael. 2005. "The Compact City Fallacy." *Journal of Planning Education and Research* 25 (1): 11–26. https://pdfs.semanticscholar.org/c11d/e325aa55a05c502522c4a373dbc312721bca.pdf accessed June 1, 2019.

Newman, Oscar. 1972. *Defensible Space: Crime Prevention Through Urban Design*. New York: Palgrave Macmillan.

Niemi, Marjaana. 2016. "Bridge to a Better Future: Town Planning in Helsinki, Tallinn and Dublin in the 1910s." *Helsinki Quarterly* 2. www.kvartti.fi/en/articles/bridge-better-future-town-planning-helsinki-tallinn-and-dublin-1910s accessed May 11, 2017.

Nilsson, Sten Åke. 1973. *The Capital Cities of India, Pakistan and Bangladesh*. London: Curzon Press.

Oeschlin, Werner. 1993. "Between Germany and America: Werner Hegemann's Approach to Urban Planning." In *Berlin/New York Like and Unlike, Essays on Architecture and Art from 1870 to the Present*, edited by Josef Paul Kleihues and Christina Rathgeber, 281–95. New York: Rizzoli.

Oke, Timothy R., Gerald Mills, Andreas Christen, and James A. Voogt. 2017. "Climate Sensitive Design." In *Urban Climates*, 408–52. Cambridge: Cambridge University Press. www.aerisfuturo.pl/wp-content/uploads/2018/09/Urban_Climates-1.pdf accessed June 6, 2019.

Olds, Kris. 2001. *Globalization and Urban Change: Capital, Culture, and the Pacific Rim Mega- Projects*. Oxford: Oxford University Press.

Olmsted, Frederick L. 1852. *Walks and Talks of an American Farmer in England*. New York: George Putnam.

Olsen, Donald J. 1986. *The City as a Work of Art: London, Paris, Vienna*. New Haven and London: Yale University Press.

Oshima, Ken T. 1996. "Denenchōfu: Building the Garden City in Japan." *Journal of the Society of Architectural Historians* 55 (2): 140–51.

Bibliography and References

Ostler, Craig J. 2011. "Salt Lake City: City stake of Zion." In *Salt Lake City: The Place God Prepared*, edited by Scott C. Esplin and Kenneth L. Alford, 339–52. Provo, UT: Religious Studies Center, Brigham Young University. https://rsc.byu.edu/archived/salt-lake-city/17-salt-lake-city-city-stake-zion accessed August 21, 2017.

Osterhammel, Jürgen. 2014. *The Transformation of the World: A Global History*. Translated from the German by Patrick Camiller. New York: Princeton University Press.

O'Toole, Randall. 2007. "Preserving the American Dream by Cost, Not Coercion." In *Planetizen Contemporary Debates in Urban Planning*, edited by Abhijeet Chavan, Christian Peralta, and Christopher Steins, 34–38. Washington, DC: Island Press.

Ouroussoff, Nicolai. 2006. "New Ideas for Building in the Face of Modernism." *Architectural Review* (September 27). www.nytimes.com/2006/09/27/arts/design/27ten.html accessed March 29, 2017.

Owen, Robert. 1813. *New View of Society: Essays on the Formation of the Human Character*. London: Cadell and Davies.

Parin, Claire. 2004. "The Recognition of Local Specificities in Cross-Cultural Design." *Urban Design International* 9 (4): 197–207.

Parker, Barry and Raymond Unwin. 1901. *The Art of Building a Home*. Second edition. London, New York and Bombay: Longmans, Green & Co. www.hgstrust.org/documents/the-art-of-building-a-home.pdf accessed April 16, 2017.

Parolek, Daniel C., Karen Parolek, and Paul C. Crawford. 2006. *Form-Based Codes: A Guide for Planners, Urban Designers, Municipalities, and Developers*. Hoboken, NJ: John Wiley.

Parr, Albert E. 1969. "Lessons from an Urban Childhood." *American Montessori Society Journal*, 7 (4). Reprint.

Patricios, Nicholas. 2000. "International Style Diaspora: Le Corbusier's Le Groupe Transvaal." *Proceedings of the International Conference Building & Living: The New Architecture of the City. Bologna, Italy*. http://works.bepress.com/nicholas_patricios/14/ accessed June 5, 2019.

Pattani, Aneri. 2016. "Building the City of the Future—at a $41 Trillion Price Tag." *CNBC* (October 28). www.cnbc.com/2016/10/25/spending-on-smart-cities-around-the-world-could-reach-41-trillion.html accessed June 24, 2017.

Payre, Renaud. 1998. "Review by Marcel Smets of Charles Buls's Les Principes de l'Art Urbain." *H-Net Reviews in the Humanities and Social Sciences* (January). www.h-net.org/reviews/showpdf.php?id=1643 accessed November 1, 2016.

Pearlman, Jill. 2007. *Inventing American Modernism: Joseph Hudnut, Walter Gropius and the Bauhaus*. Charlottesville and London: University of Virginia Press.

Pearson, Caspar. 2011. *Humanism and the Urban World: Leon Battista Alberti and the Renaissance City*. University Park, PA: Penn State University Press.

Perry, Clarence. 1929. "The Neighborhood Unit: A Scheme Arrangement for the Family Life Community." In *Regional Survey of New York and Environs, Vol. VII, Neighborhood and Community Planning*. New York: Routledge, Thoemmes Press. Reprinted 1998.

Peterson, Jon A. 1976. "The City Beautiful Movement: Forgotten Origins and Lost Meanings." *Journal of Urban History* 2 (4): 415–34.

Phibbs, John. 2017. *Place-Making: The Art of Capability Brown*. Swindon: Historic England Publishing.

Pinkney, David H. 1958. *Napoleon III and the Rebuilding of Paris*. Princeton, NJ: Princeton University Press.

Planning Commission, Government of India. 1980. *Report on Industrial Dispersion*. New Delhi: Planning Commission. http://planningcommission.nic.in/reports/publications/pub_inddis.pdf accessed June 1, 2017.

Pocock, Douglas C. D. and Raymond Hudson. 1978. *Images of the Urban Environment*. London: Palgrave Macmillan.

Pollowy, Anne-Marie. 1977. *The Urban Nest*. Stroudsburg: Dowden, Hutchinson and Ross.

Pommer, Richard and Christian F. Otto. 1991. *Weissenhof 1927 and the Modern Movement in Architecture*. Chicago and London: University of Chicago Press.

Poole, Matthew and Manuel Shvartzberg, 2016. *The Politics of Parametricism: Digital Technologies in Architecture*. London: Bloomsbury Academic.

Porter, Michael E. and Mark Kramer. 2011. "Creating Shared Value: How to Reinvent Capitalism—and Unleash Innovation and Growth." *Harvard Business Review* 89 (1–2): 62–77.

Postrel, Virginia. 2003. *The Substance of Style: How the Rise of Aesthetic Style Is Remaking Commerce, Culture, and Consciousness*. New York: HarperCollins.

Prasad, Sunand. 1987. "Le Corbusier in India." *Architecture + Design* 3 (6): 14–27.

Bibliography and References

Pressman, Norman. 1988. *Northern Cityscape*. Houghton, MI: Winter Cities Institute.

Pressman, Norman. 2004. *Shaping Cities for Winter*. Houghton, MI: Winter Cities Institute.

Price,,Chris. 2016. "Ebbsfleet Garden City Masterplan and Images Revealed." *KentOnline* (September 30). www.kentonline.co.uk/kent-business/county-news/first-images-ebbsfleet-garden-city-103322/ accessed May 12, 2017.

Punter, John. 2007. "Developing Urban Design as Public Policy: Best Practice Principles for Design Review and Development Management." *Journal of Urban Design* 12 (2): 167–202.

Rand, Ayn. 1943. *The Fountainhead*. Indianapolis, IN: Bobbs Merrill.

Rapoport, Amos. 1969. *House Form and Culture*. Englewood Cliffs, NJ: Prentice Hall.

Rapoport, Amos. 1977. *Human Aspects of Urban Form: Towards a Man-Environment Approach to Urban Form and Design*. New York: Pergamon Press.

Rapoport, Amos. 1990. *History and Precedent in Environmental Design*. New York and London: Plenum Press.

Rasmussen, Steen E. 1962. *Experiencing Architecture*. Cambridge, MA: MIT Press.

Ratti, Carlo and Matthew Claudel. 2016. *The City of Tomorrow: Sensors, Networks, Hackers and the Future of Urban Life*. New Haven and London: Yale University Press.

Ravetz, Alison. 1974. *Model Estate: Planned Housing at Quarry Hill, Leeds*. London: Croom Helm.

Ray, Debika. 2017. "Why Postmodern's New-Found Popularity Is All About Looking Forward Not Back." *ArchDaily* (December 15). www.archdaily.com/885422/why-postmodernisms-new-found-popularity-is-all-about-looking-forward-not-back?utm_medium=email&utm_source=ArchDaily%20 List&kth=1,285,646 accessed December 15, 2017.

Reddy, Gouru T. 1994. *The Secret World of Vaasthu*. Translated from the Telugu by Radullparti C. Sekhar. Proddatur: Prajahita. https://archive.org/stream/SecretWorldOfVastuThirupatiReddy/Secret%20 World%20of%20Vastu%20Thirupati%20Reddy_djvu.txt accessed June 7, 2019.

Reed, Henry H. 2005. *The United States Capitol: Its Architecture and Decoration*. New York: W. W. Norton & Company.

Regional Plan Association. 1929. *The Regional Plan of New York and Its Environs*. New York: The Regional Plan Association.

Reps, John W. 1991. *Washington on View: The Nation's Capital Since 1790*. Chapel Hill: University of North Carolina Press.

Reps, John W. 1997. *Canberra 1912: Plans and Planners of the Australian Capital Competition*. Carlton South, VIC: Melbourne University Press.

Richards, J. M. 1962. *An Introduction to Modern Architecture*. Harmondsworth: Penguin.

Riggs, William, Seth LaJeunesse, and Michael Boswell. 2017. "Autonomous Vehicles: Turn On, Tune In, Drop Out?" *Planetizen* (July 6). www.planetizen.com/node/93598?utm_source=newswire&utm_medium=email&utm_campaign=news-07062017 accessed July 7, 2017.

Riis, Jacob A. 1890. *How the Other Half Lives: Studies Among the Tenements of New York*. New York: Charles Scribner's Sons. https://archive.org/details/howotherhalfliv00riisgoog accessed May 9, 2017.

Risselada, Max and Dirk van den Heuvel, eds. 2005. *Team 10, 1953–8 in Search of a Utopia of the Present*. Rotterdam: NAi Publishers.

Rittel, Horst and Melvin Webber. 1984. "Planning Problems Are Wicked Problems." In *Developments in Design Methodology*, edited by Nigel Cross, 135–44. New York: John Wiley. http://blogs.lt.vt.edu/design/files/2013/11/Rittel.pdf accessed June 7, 2019.

Roberts, J. M. 1999. *Twentieth Century: The History of the World 1901–2000*. New York: Penguin.

Robinson, Charles M. 1899. "Improvements in City Life: Aesthetic Progress." *Atlantic Monthly* 83 (June): 171–85. http://urbanplanning.library.cornell.edu/DOCS/robin_01.htm accessed May 11, 2017.

Robinson, Charles M. 1901. *The Improvement of Towns and Cities: Or, the Practical Basic of Civic Aesthetics*. New York: G. P. Putnam's Sons.

Robinson, Charles M. 1903. *Modern Civic Art: Or, the City Made Beautiful*. New York and London: G. P. Putnam's Sons. https://archive.org/details/moderncivicartor000938mbp accessed November 25, 2016.

Robinson, Rick. ca 2014. "Smart City Principles." *The Urban Technologist*. https://theurbantechnologist. com/smarter-city-design-principles/ accessed March 12, 2018.

Rodriguez, Roberto. 2005. "The Foundational Process of Cities in Spanish America: The Law of Indies as a Planning Tool in Early Colonial Towns in Venezuela." *Focus* 2 (1): 46–57. https://pdfs.semantic scholar.org/49cf/6eedf6e584c142796ed10aa09a8368968a2b.pdf accessed June 7, 2019.

Ronner, Heinz and Sharad Jhaveri. 1987. *Louis I. Kahn: Complete Works 1935–1974*. Basel: Birkhäuser.

Rook, Tony. 2013. *Welwyn & Welwyn Garden City Through Time*. Chalford: Amberley.

Bibliography and References

Rose, Jonathan. 2016. *The Well-Tempered City: What Modern Science, Ancient Civilizations and Human Nature Teach Us About the Future of Urban Life*. New York: HarperCollins.

Rosenau, Helen. 1959. *The Ideal City and Its Architectural Evolution*. London: Routledge and Kegan Paul.

Ross, Andrew. 1999. *The Celebration Chronicles: Life, Liberty and the Pursuit of Property Values in Disney's New Town*. New York: Ballantine Books.

Ross, Philip and Yves Cabannes. 2014. *21st Century Garden Cities of Tomorrow: A Manifesto*. Letchworth Garden City: The New Garden City Movement.

Rossi, Aldo. 1982. *The Architecture of the City*. Translated from the Italian by Diane Ghirardo and Joan Ockman and revised by Aldo Rossi and Peter Eisenman. Cambridge, MA: MIT Press, originally 1966.

Roth, Leland M. 1979. "Three Industrial Towns Designed by McKim, Mead & White." *Journal of the Society of Architectural Historians* 38 (4): 317–47.

Rothman, Joshua. 2018. "The Big Question." *The New Yorker* (July 23): 26–33. www.newyorker.com/magazine/2018/07/23/are-things-getting-better-or-worse accessed June 7, 2019.

Rothschild, Joan, ed. 1999. *Design and Feminism: Re-Visioning Spaces, Places and Everyday Things*. Piscataway, NJ: Rutgers University Press.

Rowe, Colin. 1976. *The Mathematics of the Ideal Villa and other Essays*. Cambridge, MA: MIT Press. https://monoskop.org/images/9/96/Rowe_Colin_1947_1976_The_Mathematics_of_the_Ideal_Villa.pdf accessed June 7, 2019.

Rowe, Colin. 1982. "Program vs Paradigm." *Cornell Journal of Architecture* 2: 8–19.

Rowe, Colin and Fred Koetter. 1979. *Collage City*. Cambridge, MA: MIT Press.

Runcorn Development Corporation. 1967. *Runcorn New Town*. Runcorn: The Authors.

Ruskin, John. 1865. *Sesame and Lilies: Two Lectures Delivered at Manchester, 1864*. London: Smith, Elder & Co. https://archive.org/details/liliestwolsesame00ruskrich/page/n25 accessed April 16, 2017.

Ryan, Brent D. 2012. *Design after Decline: How America Rebuilds Shrinking Cities*. Philadelphia, PA: University of Pennsylvania Press.

Sachdev, Vibhuti and Giles Tillotson. 2002. *Building Jaipur: The Making of an Indian City*. London Reaktion Books.

Sadler, Simon. 2005. *Archigram: Architecture Without Architecture*. Cambridge, MA: MIT Press.

Salingaros, Nikos. 2010. "Tear Down the Corivale! New Urbanism Comes to Rome." *Planetizen* (May 24). www.planetizen.com/node/44338 accessed May 18, 2017.

Salomon, Dieter. 2010. "A Model Sustainable Urban Development Project: The Quartier Vauban in Freiburg." In *Large Scale Projects in German Cities: Urban Development 1990–2010*, edited by Federal Ministry of Transport, Building and Urban Affairs, Englebert Lütke Daldrup, and Peter Zlonicky, 154–59. Berlin: Jovis.

Sandercock, Leonie. 1998. *Towards Cosmopolis: Planning for Multicultural Cities*. Chichester and New York: John Wiley.

Santayana, George. 1905. *The Life of Reason: Reason in Common Sense*. New York: Charles Scribner's Sons.

Sant'Elia, Antonio. 1973. "Manifesto of Futurists Architecture, 1914." In *Futurist Manifestos*, edited by Umbro Apollonio, translated from the Italian by Robert Brain et al., 160–72. New York: Viking.

Saoud, Rabah. 2010. "Introduction to the Islamic City." *Muslim Heritage*. www.muslimheritage.com/article/introduction-islamic-city accessed April 17, 2017.

Savoia, Antonio. 2017. "Global Inequality Is on the Rise—but at Vastly Different Rates Across the World." *The Conversation* (December 14). https://theconversation.com/global-inequality-is-on-the-rise-but-at-vastly-different-rates-across-the-world-88976 accessed August 12, 2018.

Savva, Anna. 2018. "Five Ways Stephen Hawking Predicted the Way the World Will End." *Mirror* (March 14). www.mirror.co.uk/science/stephen-hawking-predicted-end-world-11766792 accessed March 18, 2018.

Sbriglio, Jacques. 1999. *Le Corbusier: La Villa Savoye, the Villa Savoye*. Paris: Fondation Le Corbusier; Basel and Boston: Birkhäuser.

Scamozzi, Vincenzo. 1615. *L'idea dell'Architecttura Universale*. Vinezia: Girolano Abrizze. https://archive.org/details/dellideadellaarc00scam/page/n6/mode/2up accessed February 10, 2020.

Schilthuizen, Menno. 2018. *Darwin Comes to Town: How the Urban Jungle Drives Evolution*. London: Quercus.

Schires, Megan. 2017a. "When Frank Lloyd Wright and Le Corbusier Had a Public Argument in 'The New York Times.'" *ArchDaily* (May 26). www.archdaily.com/871380/when-frank-lloyd-wright-and-le-corbusier-had-a-public-argument-in-the-new-york-times?utm_medium=email&utm_source=ArchDaily%20List accessed May 27, 2017.

Bibliography and References

Schires, Megan. 2017b. "When Architecture and Tourism Meet; La Grande Motte's Pyramids by the Sea." *ArchDaily* (July 21). www.archdaily.com/876270/when-architecture-and-tourism-meet-la-grande-mottes-pyramids-by-the-seaside accessed July 29, 2017.

Schlossberg, Herbert. 2000. *The Silent Revolution and the Making of Victorian England.* Columbus, OH: Ohio State University Press.

Schoggen, Phil. 1989. *Behavior Settings: A Revision and Extension of Roger G. Barker's Ecological Psychology.* Stanford, CA: Stanford University Press.

Schön, Donald. 1983. *The Reflective Practitioner: How Professionals Think in Action.* New York: Basic Books.

Schumacher, Patrik. 2008. "Parametricism as Style—Parametricist Manifesto." Presented and discussed at the Dark Side Club, 11th Architecture Biennale, Venice. www.patrikschumacher.com/Texts/Parametricism%20as%20Style.htm accessed February 24, 2017.

Schumacher, Patrik. 2010. *The Autopoiesis of Architecture, Vol. I: A New Framework for Architecture.* Chichester: Wiley.

Schumacher, Patrik. 2012. *The Autopoiesis of Architecture, Vol. II: A New Agenda for Architecture.* Chichester: Wiley.

Schumacher, Patrik. 2013. "Free-Market Urbanism—Urbanism Beyond Planning." In *Masterplanning the Adaptive City—Computational Urbanism in the Twenty-First Century*, edited by Tom Verebes. London and New York: Routledge. www.patrikschumacher.com/Texts/Free%20Market%20Urbanism%20-%20Urbanism%20beyond%20Planning.html accessed June 2, 2019.

Schumacher, Patrik, ed. 2016. *Parametricism 2.0: Rethinking Architecture for the 21st Century. Architectural Design.* Hoboken, NJ: John Wiley.

Scott, John. 1942. *Behind the Urals: An American Worker in Russia's City of Steel.* Edited by Stephen Kotkin. Bloomington and Indianapolis: Indiana University Press, 1989.

Scott Brown, Denise. 2004. "The Redefinition of Function." In *Architecture as Signs and Systems for a Mannerist Time*, edited by Robert Venturi and Denise Scott Brown, 142–74. Cambridge, MA: MIT Press.

Scranton, Laird. 2014. *China's Cosmological Prehistory: The Sophisticated Science Encoded in Civilization's Earliest Symbols.* Rochester, VT: Inner Traditions.

Secrest, Meryle. 1998. *Frank Lloyd Wright: A Biography.* New York: Alfred A. Knopf.

Seidel, Andrew, John Gibson, Wolfgang F. E. Preiser, and David M. Pellish. 1979. "Four Commentaries on the Charter." *Journal of Architectural Research* 7 (2): 10–12.

Sen, Amartya. 2000. "East and West: The Reach of Reason." *The New York Review of Books* (July 20): 33–38.

Senkevitch, Anatole. 1974. "Trends in Soviet Architectural Thought 1917–1937." Unpublished doctoral dissertation, Cornell University Graduate School, Ithaca, NY.

Sert, José Luis and C.I.A.M. 1944. *Can Our Cities Survive? An ABC of Urban Problems, Their Analysis, Their Solutions.* Cambridge, MA: Harvard University Press.

Sha, Bitjutu S. 1960. *Metabolism 1960: The Proposals for a New Urbanism.* Tokyo: Bitjutu Syuppan Sha.

Shane, Grahame. 1975. "Contextualism." *Architectural Design* 46 (11): 676–70.

Shane, Grahame. 2003. "The Emergence of 'Landscape Urbanism': Reflections on 'Stalking Detroit.'" *Harvard Design Magazine* 19: 1–7. http://archtech.arch.ntua.gr/forum/harvard-design-magazine/19_onlandscape.pdf accessed March 23, 2018.

Sharp, Dennis. 1971. "Concept and Interpretation: The Aims and Principles of the MARS Plan for London." In *The MARS Plan for London*, edited by Arthur Korn, Maxwell Fry, and Dennis Sharp. *Perspecta* 13–14: 163–73.

Sharp, Dennis, ed. 1978. *The Rationalists: Theory and Design in the Modern Movement.* London: Architectural Press.

Sherwood, Roger. 1978. *Modern Housing Prototypes.* Cambridge, MA: Harvard University Press. https://archive.org/details/ModernHousingPrototypes accessed March 23, 2017.

Simon, Herbert A. 1956. "Rational Choice and the Structure of the Environment." *Psychological Review* 63 (2): 129–38. https://pdfs.semanticscholar.org/23a9/4ce42fe0d50f5c993f34d4c9602f8aeac507.pdf accessed June 30, 2018.

Simonds, John O. 1994. *Garden Cities 21: Creating a Liveable Urban Environment.* New York: McGraw-Hill.

Sitte, Camillo. 1889. *Der Städtebau nach Seinen Künstlerischen Grundsätzen.* Translated from the German by George R. Collins and Christiane Crasemann Collins as *City Planning According to Its Artistic Principles.* London: Phaidon Press, 1965. http://urbanplanning.library.cornell.edu/DOCS/sitte.htm accessed March 24, 2018.

Bibliography and References

Sklair, Leslie. 2005. "The Transnational Capitalist Class and Contemporary Architecture in Globalizing Cities." *International Journal of Urban and Regional Research* 29 (3): 485–500.

Smets, Marcel. 1995. *Charles Buls: Les Principes de l'art Urbain*. Bruxelles: Editions Mardaga.

Smith, Adam. 1776. *An Inquiry into the Nature and Causes of the Wealth of Nations*. London: W. Strahan and T. Cadell. https://books.google.com.au/books?id=C5dNAAAAcAAJ&pg=PP7&redir_esc=y#v=onepage&q&f=true accessed May 31, 2017.

Smith, Joseph. 1833. "An Explanation of the Plat of the City of Zion, Sent to the Brethren in Zion, the 25th of June, 1833." In *History of the Church of Jesus Christ of the Latter-Day Saints*. Salt Lake City: Deseret Book, Co., 1961. http://urbanplanning.library.cornell.edu/DOCS/smith.htm accessed August 18, 2017.

Smith, Michael E. 2011. "Cosmograms, Sociograms, and Cities Built as Images." *Wide Urban World* (April 4). http://wideurbanworld.blogspot.com.au/2011/04/cosmograms-sociograms-and-cities-built.html accessed November 19, 2016.

Smithson, Alison. 1968. *Team 10 Primer*. Cambridge, MA: MIT Press.

Snyder, Ryan. 2018. "Street Design Implications of Autonomous Vehicles." *Public Square* (March 12). www.cnu.org/publicsquare/2018/03/12/street-design-implications-autonomous-vehicles accessed March 17, 2018.

Solomon, Daniel. 2017. "The Thirty Years' War: New Urbanism and the Academy." *Public Square* (September 27). www.cnu.org/publicsquare/2017/09/27/thirty-years-war-new-urbanism-and-academy accessed November 28, 2017.

Soleri, Paolo. 1969. *Arcology: The City in the Image of Man*. Cambridge, MA: MIT Press.

Soria y Puig, Arturo, ed. 1999. *Cerdà: The Five Bases of the General Theory of Urbanization*. Milan: Electa.

Sorrel, Charlie. 2016. "Federal Law Now Says Kids Can Walk to School Alone." *Fast Company*. www.fastcompany.com/3055107/federal-law-now-says-kids-can-walk-to-school-alone accessed April 19, 2018.

Soth, Lauren. 1983. "Le Corbusier's Clients and Their Parisian Houses of the 1920s." *Art History* 6 (2): 188–98.

Spaeth, David A. 1981. *Ludwig Karl Hilberseimer: An Annotated Bibliography and Chronology*. New York: Garland.

Speck, Jeff. 2013. *Walkable City: How Downtown Can Save America, One Step at a Time*. Berkeley, CA: Northpoint Press.

Speranza, Philip. 2016. "Using Parametric Methods to Understand Place in Urban Design Courses." *Journal of Urban Design* 21 (5): 661–89.

Spirn, Anne. 1984. *The Granite Garden: Urban Nature and Human Design*. New York: Basic Books.

Spreiregen, Paul D., ed. 1971. *The Modern Metropolis: Its Origins, Growth, Characteristics, and Planning: Selected Essays of Hans Blumenfield*. Cambridge, MA: MIT Press.

Stein, Clarence. 1949. "Toward New Towns for America." *Town Planning Review* 20 (3): 203–82.

Stein, Clarence. 1966. *Toward New Towns for America*. Cambridge, MA: MIT Press, originally 1957.

Steiner, Frederick R., George F. Thompson, and Armando Carbonell, eds. 2016. *The Ecological Imperative in Urban Design and Planning*. Washington, DC: Lincoln Institute of Land Policy. www.lincolninst.edu/sites/default/files/pubfiles/nature_and_cities_w16ll.pdf accessed June 2, 2019.

Steinfeld, Edward and Jordana Maisel. 2012. *Universal Design: Creating Inclusive Environments*. Hoboken, NJ: John Wiley and Sons.

Steinhardt, Nancy S. 1990. *Chinese Imperial City Planning*. Honolulu: University of Hawaii Press.

Stelter, Gilbert A. 2000. "Rethinking the Significance of the City Beautiful Idea." In *Urban Planning in a Changing World: The Twentieth Century Experience*, edited by Robert Freestone, 98–117. New York: Taylor & Francis.

Stern, Robert A. M., David Fishman, and Jacob Tilove. 2013. *Paradise Planned: The Garden Suburb and the Modern City*. New York: Monacelli Press.

Stern, Robert A. M. and John Massengale. 1981. "The Anglo-American Suburb." In *Architectural Design Profile*. London: Architectural Design.

Steuteville, Robert. 2017. "New Urban Design for an African Village." *Public Square* (July 5). www.cnu.org/publicsquare/2017/07/05/new-urban-design-african-village accessed July 8, 2017.

Steuteville, Robert. 2018a. "Vincent Scully: 'Spiritual Father of New Urbanism.'" *Public Square* (January 11). www.cnu.org/publicsquare/2018/01/11/vincent-scully-%E2%80%98spiritual-father-new-urbanism%E2%80%99 accessed January 13, 2018.

Steuteville, Robert. 2018b. "The Copious Capacity of Street Grids." *Public Square* (June 18). www.cnu.org/publicsquare/2018/06/28/copious-capacity-street-grids accessed July 9, 2018.

Stott, Rory. 2014. "Richard Rogers Speaks Out Against Garden City Proposals." *ArchDaily* (September 10). www.archdaily.com/546802/richard-rogers-speaks-out-against-garden-cities-proposals accessed July 25, 2017.

Stouhi, Dima. 2019. "Retrofuturism Gives Traditional Iranian Architecture a Modern Twist." www. archdaily.com/921725/retrofuturism-gives-traditional-iranian-architecture-a-modern-twist?utm_medium=email&utm_source=ArchDaily%20List&kth=1,285,646 accessed July 27, 2019.

Strauss, Anselm. 1961. *Images of the American City.* New York: The Free Press.

Streissguth, Tom. 2016. *World War 1: Aftermath.* Minneapolis, MN: ABDO Publishing.

Stübben, Hermann J. 1907. *Der Städtebau.* Revised edition. Darmstadt: Geheimer Baurat. https://archive. org/details/bub_gb_iONLAAAAMAAJ. Translated from the German by Adalbert Albrecht as *City Building*, published by Julia Koschinsky and Emily Talen. https://s3.amazonaws.com/stubben/Stubben_Part3.pdf accessed September 14, 2017.

Suttles, Gerald. 1972. *The Social Construction of Communities.* Chicago: University of Chicago Press.

Swaffield, Simon, ed. 2002. *Theory in Landscape Architecture: A Reader.* Philadelphia, PA: University of Pennsylvania Press.

Tafuri, Manfredo. 1976. *Architecture and Utopia: Design and Capitalist Development.* Translated from the Italian by Barbara Luigia La Penta. Cambridge. MA: MIT Press.

Takami, Kiyoshi and Kiichiro Hatoyama. 2008. "Sustainable Regeneration of a Car-Dependent City: The Case of Toyama Toward a Compact City." In *Sustainable City Regions*, edited by T. Kidokoro, N. Harata, L. P. Subanu, J. Jessen, A. Motte, and E. P. Seltzer, 183–202. Tokyo: Springer.

Talen, Emily. 1999. *Charter of the New Urbanism: Congress for the New Urbanism.* Second edition. New York: McGraw-Hill.

Talen, Emily. 2012. *City Rules: How Urban Regulations Affect Urban Form.* Washington, DC: Island Press.

Taut, Bruno. 1919. "The City Crown." Translated from the German *Die Stadtkrone* by Ulrike Altenmüller and Matthew Mindrup. *Journal of Architectural Education* 63 (1): 121–34. http://socks-studio. com/2013/09/28/bruno-taut-the-city-crown-1919/ accessed April 7, 2018.

Taylor, Frederick W. 1911. *The Principles of Scientific Management.* New York and London: Harper and Brothers. https://archive.org/details/principlesofscie00taylrich/page/n5 accessed June 8, 2019.

Thiel, Philip. 1964. "The Tourist and the Habitué: Two Polar Modes of Environmental Experience, with Some Notes on an Experience Cube." Mimeographed.

Thompson, George F. and Frederick Steiner, eds. 1997. *Ecological Design and Planning.* Hoboken, NJ: John Wiley.

Thompson, Ian H. 2012. "Ten Tenets and Six Questions for Landscape Urbanism." *Landscape Research* 37 (1): 7–26.

Tjallingii, Sybrand P. 1996. *Ecological Conditions, Strategies and Structures in Environmental Planning.* Wageningen: DLO Institute for Forestry and Nature Research.

Tortello, Michael. 2012. "An Early Eco-City Faces the Future." *The New York Times* (February 15). www. nytimes.com/2012/02/16/garden/an-early-eco-city-faces-the-future.html? accessed November 20, 2015.

Townsend, Anthony M. 2013. *Smart Cities: Big Data, Civic Hackers and the Quest for a New Utopia.* New York: W. W. Norton & Company.

Toy, Maggie, ed. 1992. *Architectural Design: Paternoster Square and the New Classical Tradition.* London: Architectural Design.

Trivett, Vincent. 2011. "Korea Is Building the City of the Future on an Artificial Island." *Business Insider Australia* (June 24). www.businessinsider.com.au/korea-is-building-the-city-of-the-future-from-scratch-2011-6#songdos-50-million-square-feet-of-office-space-includes-the-68-story-northeast-asia-trade-tower-this-is-a-photo-of-the-partially-constructed-city-1 accessed March 12, 2018.

Tschumi, Bernard. 1987. *Cinégram Folie: Le Parc de la Villette.* Princeton, NJ: Princeton Architectural Press.

Tschumi, Bernard. 1994. *Architecture and Disjunction.* Cambridge, MA: MIT Press.

Turner, John F. C. 1976. *Housing by People: Towards Autonomy in Building Environments.* London: Marion Boyars. http://library.uniteddiversity.coop/Ecological_Building/Housing_By_People-Towards_Autonomy_in_Building_Environments.pdf accessed June 8, 2019.

Turner, Paul V. 1977. *The Education of Le Corbusier.* New York: Garland.

Turner, Paul V. 1984. *Campus: An American Planning Tradition.* Cambridge, MA: MIT Press.

Turrisi, Patricia A., ed. 1997. *Pragmatism as a Principle and Method of Right Thinking: The 1903 Harvard 'Lectures on Pragmatism.'* Albany, NY: State University of New York Press.

Tyrwhitt, Jacqueline. 1947. *Patrick Geddes in India.* London: Lund Humphries. https://archive.org/stream/ PatrickGeddesIndia/Patrick%20Geddes_djvu.txt accessed April 21, 2017.

United States Conference of Mayors. 2005. "Climate Mitigation and Adaptation in American Cities." Energy, Environment, Mayors Climate Protection Center, Reports.

Bibliography and References

Unwin, Raymond. 1909. *Town Planning in Practice: An Introduction to the Art of Designing Cities and Suburbs.* London: T. Fisher Unwin. https://archive.org/details/townplanninginp00unwigoog accessed September 14, 2017.

Unwin, Raymond and Barry Parker. 1901. *The Art of Building a Home: A Collection of Lectures and Illustrations.* London: Longmans, Green & Co.

Urban Design Associates. 1997. *The Celebration Pattern Book.* Los Angeles: The Disney Company.

Urbano, Judith. 2016. "The Cerdà Plan for the Expansion of Barcelona: A Model for Modern City Planning." *Focus* 12 (1): Article 9. http://digitalcommons.calpoly.edu/cgi/viewcontent.cgi?article=1323&context=focus accessed September 2, 2017.

US Army Corps of Engineers. 2017. "The Los Angeles River Revitalization Master Plan." http://boe.lacity.org/lariverrmp/ accessed July 27, 2018.

van Eyck, Aldo. 1954. "Statement Against Rationalism." In *A Decade of Modern Architecture*, edited by Sigfried Giedion, 43–44. Zurich: Ginsberg.

van Schaik, Leon. 1985. "Rationalism and Contextualism." *Architecture SA* (May–June): 52–56.

Velasquez, Marisol V. and Diego Barajas. 2008. "Ludwig Hilberseimer: Radical Urbanism." *Architecturaltheory.txt.* (April 28). www.a-u-r-a.eu/upload/research_radicalurbanism_100dpi_2.pdf accessed November 9, 2017.

Venturi, Robert. 1966. *Complexity and Contradiction in Modern Architecture.* New York: The Museum of Modern Art.

Venturi, Robert, Denise Scott Brown, and Steven Izenour. 1977. *Learning from Las Vegas: The Forgotten Symbolism of Architectural Form.* Revised edition. Cambridge, MA: MIT Press.

Virilio, Paul. 2000. *From Modernism to Hypermodernism and Beyond.* Edited by John Armitage. London and Thousand Oaks: Sage.

Viswanath, Kalpana and Ashish Basu. 2015. "SafetiPin: An Innovative Mobile App to Collect Data on Women's Safety in Indian Cities." *Gender and Development* 23 (1). www.tandfonline.com/doi/abs/10.1080/13552074.2015.1013669 accessed November 3, 2017.

Vollmer, Andi. 2012. "Photographs of Impossible Architecture." *Feature Shoot.* www.featureshoot.com/2012/01/photographs-of-impossible-architecture-by-filip-dujardin/ accessed May 5, 2017.

von Frisch, Karl and Otto von Frisch. 1974. *Animal Architecture.* Translated from the German by Lisbeth Gombrich. New York: Harcourt Brace Jovanovich.

von Hoffman, Alexander. 1998. "The Origins of American Housing Reform." Joint Center for Housing Studies, Harvard University. www.innovations.harvard.edu/sites/default/files/von_hoffman_w98-2.pdf accessed May 10, 2017.

Vronskaya, Alla. 2017. "Making Sense of Narkomfin." *The Architectural Review* (October 2). www.architectural-review.com/essays/making-sense-of-narkomfin/10023939.article accessed October 16, 2018.

WA Content. 2016. "Greg Lynn Transforms Detroit Car Factory with Microsoft HiLoLens at Venice Biennale." *United States Architectural News* 16 (June 4). http://worldarchitecture.org/articles-links/cemch/greg_lynn_transforms_detroit_car_factory_with_microsoft_hololens_at_venice_biennale.html accessed February 26, 2017.

Wagner, Otto. 1912. "The Development of a Great City." *The Architectural Record* 31 (May): 485–500. http://urbanplanning.library.cornell.edu/DOCS/wagner.htm accessed November 25, 2016.

Wainwright, Oliver. 2017. "'Norman Said the President Wants a Pyramid': How Starchitects Built Astana." *The Guardian* (October 17). www.theguardian.com/cities/2017/oct/17/norman-foster-president-pyramid-architects-built-astana accessed April 5, 2019.

Wainwright, Oliver. 2019a. "Horror on the Hudson: New York's $25bn Architectural Fiasco." *The Guardian* (April 12). www.theguardian.com/artanddesign/2019/apr/09/hudson-yards-new-york-25bn-architectural-fiasco accessed April 12, 2019.

Wainwright, Oliver. 2019b. "'The Next Era of Human Progress': What Lies Behind the Global New Cities Epidemic." *The Guardian* (July 8). www.theguardian.com/cities/2019/jul/08/the-next-era-of-human-progress-what-lies-behind-the-global-new-cities-epidemic accessed July 15, 2019.

Waldheim, Charles. 2001. "Park = City? The Downsview Park Design Competition." *Landscape Architecture Magazine* 91 (3): 82–85, 98–100.

Waldheim, Charles, ed. 2006. *The Landscape Urbanism Reader.* New York: Princeton Architectural Press.

Waldheim, Charles. 2010. "Notes Towards a History of Agrarian Urbanism." *Places* (November). https://placesjournal.org/article/history-of-agrarian-urbanism/ accessed May 27, 2017.

Waldheim, Charles. 2016. *Landscape as Urbanism: A General Theory.* New York: Princeton University Press.

Bibliography and References

Waldheim, Charles. 2004. *Lafayette Park Detroit; Hilberseimer/Mies van der Rohe*. Munich: Prestel Publishing and Cambridge, MA: Harvard Graduate School of Design.

Walker, Jennifer. 2014. "The Wekerle Estate: Budapest's hidden Garden City." *The Huffington Post* (March 26). www.huffingtonpost.com/jennifer-walker/the-wekerle-estate-budape_b_4660505.html accessed April 20, 2017.

Walker, Kara, ed. 2014. *Ruffneck Constructivists*. Brooklyn, NY: Dancing Foxes Press.

Walter, U. 2014. "Die Gartenstadt Perlach." http://perlach.hachinger-bach.de/downloads/Gartenstadt Perlach_1910.pdf accessed January 6, 2019.

Wantanabe, Shun-ichi J. 1980. "Garden City Japanese Style: The Case of Den- en Teshi Company, 1918–28." In *Shaping an Urban World*, edited by Gordon E. Cherry, 129–43. New York: Palgrave Macmillan.

Ward, Colin. 1990. *The Child in the City*. Revised edition. London: Bedford Square.

Waterford County Museum. 2010. "Portlaw: A Nineteenth Century Industrial Village." www.waterford museum.ie/exhibit/web/Display/article/321/1/Portlaw_A_Nineteenth_Century_Industrial_Village_ Introduction.html accessed May 18, 2016.

Watkin, David. 1996. "A New Order for Office Buildings." *City Journal* (Spring). www.city-journal.org/html/new-order-office-buildings-11733.html accessed April 11, 2017.

Weirick, James. 1998. "Spirituality and Symbolism in the Work of the Griffins." In *Beyond Architecture: Marion Mahony and Walter Burley Griffin—America, Australia, India*, edited by Anne Watson, 56–58. Sydney: Powerhouse Publishing.

Weirick, James. 2006. *Canberra*. Sydney: The Walter Burley Griffin Society. www.griffinsociety.org/lives_ and_works/a_canberra.html accessed November 28, 2016.

Weller, Richard and Billy Fleming. 2016. "Has Landscape Architecture Failed? Reflections on LAF's 50th Anniversary." *LAF News* (March 21). https://lafoundation.org/news-events/blog/2016/03/21/has-landscape-architecture-failed accessed March 14, 2018.

Welter, Volker M. 2012. "The Master Plan for Tel Aviv by Patrick Geddes." In *Tel Aviv, the First Century: Visions, Designs, Actualities*, edited by Maoz Azaryahu and S. Ilan Troen, 299–330. Bloomington and Indianapolis, IN: Indiana University Press.

Wheatley, Paul. 1971. *The Pivot of Four Quarters: A Preliminary Enquiry into the Origins and Character of the Ancient Chinese City*. New York: Aldine.

White, Morton G. and Lucia White, eds. 1962. *The Intellectual Versus the City: From Thomas Jefferson to Frank Lloyd Wright*. Cambridge, MA: Harvard University Press and MIT Press.

WHO [World Health Organization]. 2007. *Global Age-Friendly Cities: A Guide*. Geneva: WHO. www.who.int/ageing/publications/Global_age_friendly_cities_Guide_English.pdf accessed June 8, 2019.

Whyte, William H. 1980. *The Social Life of Small Urban Spaces*. Washington, DC: The Conservation Foundation.

Wieberson, Dora. 1960. "Utopian Aspects of Tony Garnier's Cité Industrielle." *Journal of Architectural Historians* 19 (1): 16–23.

Wieberson, Dora. 1969. *Tony Garnier: The Cité Industrielle*. New York: George Braziller.

Wiedenhoeft, Ronald. 1985. *Berlin's Housing Revolution: German Reform in the 1920s*. Ann Arbor, MI: UMI Research Press.

Williamson, Lucy. 2013. "Tomorrow's Cities: Just How Smart Is Songdo?" *BBC News Seoul*. (September 2). www.bbc.com/news/technology-23757738 accessed June 25, 2017.

Willis, William. 2017. "Playfulness on the Rise." *The Australian Financial Review* (December 22–26): 28–29.

Wilson, William H. 1989. *The City Beautiful Movement*. Baltimore and London: Johns Hopkins University Press.

Wingler, Hans M. 1969. *The Bauhaus: Weimar Dessau Berlin Chicago*. Translated from the German by Wolfgang Jabs and Basil Gilbert, edited by Joseph Stein. Cambridge, MA: MIT Press.

Wocke, Brendon. 2014. "Derrida at Villette: An Aesthetic of Space." *University of Toronto Quarterly* 83 (3): 739–55.

Wolfe, Tom. 1981. *From Bauhaus to Our House*. New York: Farrar Straus Giroux.

Wollstonecraft, Mary. 1796. *A Vindication of the Rights of Women with Strictures on Political and Moral Subjects*. Third edition. London: J. Johnson. https://books.google.com.au/books/about/A_Vindica tion_of_the_Rights_of_Woman.html?id=qhcFAAAAQAAJ&printsec=frontcover&source=kp_read_ button&redir_esc=y#v=onepage&q&f=false accessed May 31, 2017.

Woloch, Isser. 2019. *The Postwar Moment: Progressive Forces in Britain, France and the United States After World War II*. New Haven: Yale University Press.

Bibliography and References

Wright, Frank L. 1932. *The Disappearing City*. New York: William Farquhar Payson. www.siteations.com/courses/edgeops2014/readings/wk9/wright_disappearing.pdf accessed May 3, 2018.

Wright, Frank L. 1935. "Broadacre City: A New Community Plan." *Architectural Record*. http://courses.washington.edu/gmforum/Readings/Wright.pdf accessed March 2, 2018.

Wright, Frank L. 1945. *When Democracy Builds*. Chicago: University of Chicago Press. https://archive.org/details/in.ernet.dli.2015.205607/page/n2 accessed June 11, 2019.

Wright, Frank L. 1958. *The Living City*. New York: Horizon Press.

Wright, Frank L. 1969. *Skyscraper Regulation, 1926*. Scottsdale, AZ: The Frank Lloyd Wright Foundation.

Wursted, Catherine Bauer. 1934. *Modern Housing*. Boston: Houghton Mifflin.

Yu Hua. 2018. "Revolutionary Roads." Translated from the Chinese by Allan H. Barr. *The Guardian Weekly* (September 21): 26–29.

Yu Zhuoyun. 1984. *Palaces of the Forbidden City*. New York: Viking.

Zaha Hadid Architects. 2017. "One North Masterplan." www.zaha-hadid.com/masterplans/one-north-masterplan/ accessed February 22, 2017.

Zivkovic, Lilia. 2009. *Forest Hills Gardens*. New York: FastPencil.

Credits

I, the author, hold the copyright for all the images in this book except for those listed next. As noted in the Preface, items whose copyright holders were impossible to trace are identified as being part of the collection of the author. I will be glad to correct errors of omission or commission that appear in this list of acknowledgments of the sources of the illustrations.

Cover	Source: Lang (2017, 8); courtesy of Taylor & Francis
Frontispiece	Source: Lang (2017, 153); courtesy of HafenCity Hamburg GmBH/fotofrizz and Taylor & Francis

Prologue

Figure 1 left	Collection of the author. Source: Lang and Marshall (2017, 3); courtesy of Taylor & Francis
Figure 1 right	Redrawn from various sources by the author
Figure 2	United Nations photograph by Mark Garten
Figure 3	Johnny Miller/Millefoto
Figure 4	Source: Wikimedia Commons
Figure 5	Photograph by Geert Koolen/Shutterstock.com

Part One

Introductory image	Photograph by Balkorstat/Shutterstock.com
Figure 1 left	Collection of the author
Figure 1 right	Photograph by Jacob Riis. Source: Riis (1890)
Figure 2 left	Library of Congress, Geography and Map Division
Figure 2 right	Collection of the Ewing Galloway Agency, Syracuse University

Chapter 1

Figure 1.1 left	Source: Lang, Desai and Desai (1997); courtesy of CEPT University Press
Figure 1.1 right	Gurdjieff at en.wikipedia
Figure 1.2 left	Collection of the author
Figure 1.2 right	Source: Wheatley (1971); courtesy of Edinburgh University Press
Figure 1.3 left and right	Source: Lang, Desai and Desai (1997, 29); courtesy of CEPT University Press.
Figure 1.4 left	Drawing based on several sources by the author

403

Credits

Figure 1.4 right	Photograph by M. Khebra/Shutterstock.com
Figure 1.5 left	Source: Madeddu and Zhang (2017, 719); courtesy of Taylor & Francis
Figure 1.5 right	Source: Lynch (1981, 76); courtesy of Julian Smith and MIT Press
Figure 1.6	Photograph by Christian Andries/Shutterstock.com
Figure 1.7	Photograph by Serge Ruddick/Shutterstock.com
Figure 1.8	Source: Jean Scott/Look at Science/Science Photo Library
Figure 1.9 left	Source: Lang, Desai and Desai (1997, 48); courtesy of CEPT University Press
Figure 1.9 right	Courtesy of Airpano
Figure 1.10 left	Collection of the author
Figure 1.10 right	Adapted from an 1870 drawing by Augustus Koch
Figure 1.11 left	Drawing based on several sources by the author

Chapter 2

Figure 2.1	Source: Fletcher (1954, 143); Courtesy of Pavilion Books
Figure 2.2 left	Source: Hegemann and Peets (1922, 175)
Figure 2.2 right	Source: Lang (2017, 132); courtesy of Taylor & Francis
Figure 2.3	Collection of the Urbino National Gallery. Source: Wikimedia Commons
Figure 2.4 left	Collection of the author. Original source: Cataneo (1554)
Figure 2.4 right	Collection of the author. Original source: Scamozzi (1615)
Figure 2.5 left	Source: Wikimedia Commons
Figure 2.6	Photograph by pio3/Shutterstock.com,
Figure 2.7	Source: Biom/Getty Images
Figure 2.8 left	Courtesy of Pedro Ferreira/Bruno Soares Arquitectos
Figure 2.8 right	Photograph by TTstudio/Shutterstock.com
Figure 2.9	Courtesy of Airpano
Figure 2.10 left	Source: Wikimedia Commons
Figure 2.10 right	Photograph by Daniel Jedzura/Shutterstock.com
Figure 2.11 left	Source: Wikimedia Commons
Figure 2.11 right	Photograph by Wolfgang M.; source: Wikimedia Commons
Figure 2.12 left	Photograph by Manselli/Getty Images
Figure 2.14	Source: Wikimedia Commons
Figure 2.15	Drawing by psynovec/Shutterstock.com
Figure 2.16 left	Source: Bodenschatz (2012, 35); courtesy of DOM Publishers
Figure 2.16 right	Photograph by Claudio Divizia/Shutterstock.com
Figure 2.17 left	Map by Shinkyō. Source: Wikimedia Commons
Figure 2.17 right	Source: Wikimedia Commons

Chapter 3

Figure 3.1 left	Source: Wikimedia Commons
Figure 3.1 right	Source: Wikimedia Commons
Figure 3.2 left	Source: Gallion and Eisner (1993), courtesy of John Wiley & Sons
Figure 3.2 right	Source: Gallion and Eisner (1993), courtesy of John Wiley & Sons
Figure 3.3	Drawing by Charles Fourier. Source: Wikimedia Commons
Figure 3.4 left and right	Courtesy of Archives départementales de Seine-et-Marne
Figure 3.5	Courtesy of *The Victorian Web*

Figure 3.6 left — Collection if the author
Figure 3.6 right — Photographer unknown. Source: Wikimedia Commons
Figure 3.7 — Courtesy of the Familistère at Guise
Figure 3.8 — Courtesy of the Niagara County Historical Society

Chapter 4

Figure 4.1 — Photograph by Caron Balkin/Shutterstock.com
Figure 4.2 left — Source: Wikimedia Commons
Figure 4.2 right — Source: Wikimedia Commons
Figure 4.4 left — Collection of the author
Figure 4.6 left and right — Source: Berlepsch-Valendás (1910, 4 and 6)
Figure 4.7 left — Photograph by Mikladin/Shutterstock.com
Figure 4.7 right — Courtesy of Miki Desai
Figure 4.8 — Photographer unknown. Source: Wikimedia Commons
Figure 4.9 left and right — Source: Lang (1994, 97); courtesy of John Wiley & Sons

Chapter 5

Figure 5.1 — Photograph by JaySi/Shutterstock.com
Figure 5.2 — Source: Hegemann and Peets(1922, 43)
Figure 5.3 — Adapted from Hegemann and Peets (1922, 17) by the author
Figure 5.4 — Source: Hegemann and Peets (1922, 21)
Figure 5.5 — Photograph by Raphael Saulus. Source: Wikimedia Commons
Figure 5.6 left and right — Source: Lang (2017, 135); courtesy of Taylor & Francis

Part Two

Introductory image — Source: Lang (2017, 118); courtesy of Taylor & Francis
Figure 1 — Official photograph. United Kingdom Government
Figure 2 above left — Adapted from various sources by the author
Figure 2 above right — American Studio. Source: Wikimedia Commons
Figure 2 below — Adapted from various sources by the author

Chapter 6

Figure 6.1 — Photograph by Cynthia Liang/Shutterstock.com
Figure 6.2 — Photograph by C. D. Arnold. Source: Wikimedia Commons
Figure 6.3 — Source: Gallion and Eisner (1993); courtesy of John Wiley and Sons
Figure 6.4 left — Courtesy of the Estonian Museum of Architecture
Figure 6.4 right — Source: Wikimedia Commons
Figure 6.5 — Source: Wikimedia Commons
Figure 6.6 — Source: Wikimedia Commons
Figure 6.7 — Courtesy of The Art Institute of Chicago/Art Resources NY
Figure 6.8 — Courtesy of the Alexander Architectural Archives, University of Texas, Austin
Figure 6.9 — Collection of the author
Figure 6.10 left and right — Courtesy of the National Archives of Australia

Credits

Figure 6.11 left	Adapted from various sources by the author
Figure 6.11 right	Photograph by R. K. Dayal. Source: Lang, Desai and Desai (1997, frontispiece); courtesy of CEPT University Press
Figure 6.12 left	Source: Wikimedia Commons
Figure 6.12 right	Source: Wikimedia Commons
Figure 6.13	Photograph by Piotr Tomaszewski-Gullion. Source: Wikimedia Commons
Figure 6.14	Adapted from Cavalcanti (1979) by Chao Wang. Source: Lang (2017, 126); courtesy of Taylor & Francis

Chapter 7

Figure 7.1 left	Source: Howard (1902, 129)
Figure 7.1 right	Photograph by Alexey Fedorenko/Shutterstock.com
Figure 7.2 left	Source: Mujica (1929, Plate CXXIV)
Figure 7.2 right	Source: Ferriss (1929, 63)
Figure 7.3 above	Copyright 2020 Frank Lloyd Wright Foundation, Scottsdale AZ; all rights reserved
Figure 7.3 below	Copyright 2020 Frank Lloyd Wright Foundation, Scottsdale AZ; all rights reserved
Figure 7.4 left	Source: Howard (1902, 22)
Figure 7.4 right	Howard (1898). Source: Wikimedia Commons
Figure 7.5 left and right	Source: Taut (1919, n.p.)
Figure 7.6 left	Perry (1929). Source: Lang (2017, 93); courtesy of Taylor & Francis
Figure 7.6 right	Source: Gallion and Eisner (1993); courtesy of John Wiley & Sons
Figure 7.7	Copyright 2020 Frank Lloyd Wright Foundation, Scottsdale, AZ; all rights reserved
Figure 7.8 left	Adapted from various sources by the author
Figure 7.8 right	Courtesy of Eva Beleznay
Figure 7.9 left	Source: Lang (1994, 219); courtesy of John Wiley & Sons
Figure 7.10 left	Source: Stein (1966, 43); courtesy of MIT Press
Figure 7.10 above right	Source: Gallion and Eisner (1993), courtesy of John Wiley & Sons
Figure 7.10 below right	Source: Lang (1994, 179); courtesy of John Wiley & Sons
Figure 7.11 left	Drawing by Thanong Poonteerakul. Source Lang (2005, 120); courtesy of Taylor & Francis
Figure 7.11 right	Photograph by Alan Tan/Shutterstock.com
Figure 7.12 left	Source: Geddes (1917)
Figure 7.12 right	Adapted from Geddes (1917) by the author
Figure 7.13	Photograph by A. Savin, WikiPhotoSpace; courtesy of the photographer
Figure 7.14 left	Source: Wikimedia Commons
Figure 7.14 right	Courtesy of Christine Steinmetz
Figure 7.15 left	Collection of the author
Figure 7.15 right	Photograph by Fairchild Aerial Survey

Chapter 8

Figure 8.1 left	Courtesy of the Bauhaus Archiv, Museum für Gestaltung
Figure 8.1 right	Photograph by Horst von Harbou; courtesy of Deutsche Kinemathek

Figure 8.2 left	DIGITAL IMAGE 2020, The Museum of Modern Art/Scala, Florence
Figure 8.2 right	Source: Wikimedia Commons
Figure 8.3	Courtesy of Alexander Cuthbert
Figure 8.4	Compiled from several sources by the author
Figure 8.5 left and right	Drawings by Wayne W. Copper; courtesy of the College of Architecture, Art and Planning, Cornell University
Figure 8.6 left and right	Source: Wagner (1912)
Figure 8.7 left	Source: Gallion and Eisner (1993); courtesy of John Wiley & Sons
Figure 8.7 right	Source: Garnier (1917)
Figure 8.8 left	Source: Wikimedia Commons
Figure 8.8 right	Source: Wikimedia Commons
Figure 8.9 above left	Source: Wikimedia Commons
Figure 8.9 above right	Source: Chambliss (1910)
Figure 8.9 below left	Drawing adapted from several sources by the author
Figure 8.9 below right	Source: Gallion and Eisner (1993); courtesy of John Wiley & Sons
Figure 8.10	Source: Le Corbusier (1960); FLC.ADAGP
Figure 8.11 left	Adapted from Hilberseimer (1927) by the author. Source: Lang (1994). Courtesy of John Wiley & Sons
Figure 8.11 right	Source: Hilberseimer (1944); courtesy of the Ryerson and Burnham Archives, The Art Institute of Chicago
Figure 8.12	Source: Migge (1919) and Haney (2010); courtesy of Taylor & Francis
Figure 8.13 left	Source: Le Corbusier (1960); FLC.ADAGP
Figure 8.13 right	Source: Le Corbusier (1960); FLC.ADAGP
Figure 8.14 left	Source: Le Corbusier (1960); FLC.ADAGP
Figure 8.14 right	Source: Le Corbusier (1960); FLC.ADAGP
Figure 8.15 left	Source: Le Corbusier (1960); FLC.ADAGP
Figure 8.15 right	Source: Le Corbusier (1960); FLC.ADAGP
Figure 8,16	Courtesy of Freunde der Weissenhofsiedlung
Figure 8.17	Courtesy of Ginzburg Associates, Moscow
Figure 8.18	Photograph by Cepin Haidmac. Source Wikimedia Commons
Figure 8.19	Photographer unknown/Shutterstock.com
Figure 8.20	Photograph by Andreas Schwartkopf. Source: Wikimedia Commons
Figure 8.21	Leeds Libraries, WWW.leodis.net
Figure 8.22 top	Source: Gallion and Eisner (1993); courtesy of John Wiley & Sons
Figure 8.22 bottom	Photograph courtesy of Noel Corkery
Figure 8.23 left	Source: Gallion and Eisner (1993); courtesy of John Wiley & Sons
Figure 8.23 right	Derived from Gallion and Eisner (1993) by the author
Figure 8.25 above	Source: Wikipedia Commons
Figure 8.25 below	Photograph by David de Kool; collection of the author
Figure 8.26 left	Source: Lang (2017, 118); courtesy of Taylor & Francis
Figure 8.27 left	Source: Lang (2017, 132); courtesy of Taylor & Francis
Figure 8.27 center	Source: Lang (2017, 132); courtesy of Taylor & Francis
Figure 8.27 right	Source: Lang (2017, 132); courtesy of Taylor & Francis
Figure 8.28 left	Courtesy of Xavier Duran

Credits

Part Three

Figure 1 left	World History Archive/Alamy Stock Photo
Figure 1 right	Source: Everett Historical/Shutterstock.com
Figure 2 left	Courtesy of Joe Mabel, photographer
Figure 2 right	Photograph by Spingun Films/Shutterstock.com
Figure 3 left	Collection of the author
Figure 3 right	Photograph by David L. Ryan/the *Boston Globe* via Getty Images
Figure 4 left	Collection of the author. Source: Lang and Moleski (2010, 133), courtesy of Taylor & Francis
Figure 4 right	Courtesy of the University of Illinois, Chicago, Archives Collection
Figure 5 left	Drawing by Yin Yin. Source: Lang (2005, 348); courtesy of Taylor & Francis
Figure 5 right	Source: Lang (2005, 348); courtesy of Taylor & Francis
Figure 6 right	Courtesy of Aerial Photographs of New Jersey
Figure 7 left	Photograph by iofoto/Shutterstock.com
Figure 7 right	US Geological Survey, Department of the Interior

Chapter 9

Figure 9.1 left	L. Mumford (1954, 156). Source: (Lang 2002, 62); courtesy of Permanent Black
Figure 9.1 right	Source: Lang (2010, 62); courtesy of Permanent Black. FLC.ADAGP
Figure 9.2	Source: Sert and CIAM (1944); courtesy of Frances Loeb Fine Arts Library, GSD, Harvard University
Figure 9.3 left	Source: Richards (1962) and Lang (1994, 52). Collection of the author; courtesy of John Wiley & Sons
Figure 9.3 right	Drawing based on several sources ny Thanong Poonteerakul
Figure 9.4	Courtesy of le Fonds des Dotation Denise et Yona Friedman
Figure 9.5 left	Source: Lang (1994, 53). Collection of the author; courtesy of John Wiley & Sons
Figure 9.5 right	Illustration by Tomaki Tamura; courtesy of the Cosanti to Foundation
Figure 9.6 left	Collection of the author. Source: Dahinden (1972, 114) and Lang (1994, 53), courtesy of John Wiley & Sons.
Figure 9.6 right	Collection of the author. Source Dahinden (1972, 220)
Figure 9.7 left	1980, Dolores Hayden. Source: Hayden (1980, S185); courtesy of Dolores Hayden and the University of Chicago Press
Figure 9.7 right	Courtesy of McCamant and Durrett, Architects
Figure 9.8 left and right	Courtesy of the Doxiadis Archive, Constantinos and Emma Doxiadis Foundation
Figure 9.9 left	Source: Nilsson (1978). FLC.ADAGP
Figure 9.9 right	Source: Lang and Marshall (2016, 210); courtesy of Taylor & Francis
Figure 9.10 left	Source: Lang and Moleski (2010, 179); courtesy of Taylor & Francis
Figure 9.10 right	Photograph by A. Savin, WikiPhotSpace; courtesy of the photographer
Figure 9.11	Collection of the author. Source: Gordon (1977, 28)
Figure 9.12 above	Collection of the author. Source: *Caracas Chronicles* (undated)

Figure 9.12 below	Collection of the author
Figure 9.13 above	Drawing by Wayne W. Copper; courtesy of the College of Architecture, art and Planning, Cornell University
Figure 9.13 below left	FLC.ADAGP
Figure 9.13 below right	Courtesy of the Frances Loeb Fine Arts Library, GSD, Harvard University
Figure 9.14 left	Source: Bahga, Bahga, and Bahga (1993), courtesy of Sarbjit Bahga
Figure 9.14 right	Source: Lang (2002, 78); courtesy of Permanent Black
Figure 9.15 above left	Various sources; collection of the author
Figure 9.15 above right	Source: Lang (2017, 107); courtesy of Taylor & Francis
Figure 9.15 below right	Source: Lang (2017, 107); courtesy of Taylor & Francis
Figure 9.16 left	Edward A. Duckett Collection, Ryerson and Burnham Archives, The Art Institute of Chicago. Image file # 198602/.LafPl_final1
Figure 9.17 left	Photograph by MOPY/Getty Images
Figure 9.18 left	Photograph by Claudio Divizia/Shutterstock.com
Figure 9.18 right	Courtesy of Sandra Lousada
Figure 9.19	Courtesy of the Shadrack Woods Records, Avery Library, Columbia University
Figure 9.20 left	Drawing by Tomaki Tanmura; courtesy of the Cosanti Foundation
Figure 9.20 right	Photograph by Ivan Pintar. Courtesy of the Cosanti Foundation
Figure 9.21	Collection of the author
Figure 9.22	Source: Lang and Moleski (2010, 9), courtesy of Taylor & Francis
Figure 9.23 left	Source: Lang (2005, 165), courtesy of Taylor & Francis
Figure 9.24 above	Drawing by Thanong Poonteerakul. Source: Lang (2005, 219); courtesy of Taylor & Francis
Figure 9.25	Courtesy of Discover Albany
Figure 9.26 left	Collection of the author
Figure 9.26 right	Courtesy of Karina Castro, photographer
Figure 9.27	Courtesy of Jakob Börner, photographer
Figure 9.28	Photograph by Roman Babakin/Shutterstock.com
Figure 9.29 left	Source: Wikipedia Commons
Figure 9.29 right	FLC.ADAGP
Figure 9.30	Photograph by Fokke Baarssen/Shuttetrstock.com

Chapter 10

Figure 10.1	Photograph by Volkova Natalia/Shutterstock.com
Figure 10.2	Table based on Alexander et al. (1987) by the author
Figure 10.3	Source: Fulton (1997); courtesy of the Lincoln Institute of Land Policy
Figure 10.4	Source: Goodman and Goodman (1947, 133); collection of the author
Figure 10.5	Source: Simonds (1994, not paginated); courtesy of McGraw-Hill
Figure 10.6	Source: Bohl with Plater-Zyberk (2008); courtesy of DPZ CoDesign
Figure 10.7 left and right	Source: Gruen (1964); courtesy of Gruen Associates
Figure 10.8 left	Perry (1929). Source: Lang (2017, 93); courtesy of Taylor & Francis

Credits

Figure 10.8 right	Drawing adapted from various sources by Omar Sharif. Source: Lang (2017, 93); courtesy of Taylor & Francis
Figure 10.9	Source Calthorpe (1993, 45), courtesy of Princeton Architectural Press
Figure 10.10 left	Source Calthorpe (1993, 45), courtesy of Princeton Architectural Press
Figure 10.10 right	Source Calthorpe (1993, 62), courtesy of Princeton Architectural Press
Figure 10.12	Photograph by Sangquan Deng/Shutterstock.com
Figure 10.13	Courtesy of Léon Krier
Figure 10.14	Source: Cullen (1961,17) and Lang and Marshall (2016, 29); courtesy of Taylor & Francis
Figure 10.15 left	Photograph by Kristie Blokhim/Shutterstock.com
Figure 10.16	Source: Hester (1975, 8–10); courtesy of Randolph Hester and John Wiley & Sons
Figure 10.18 right	Source: Lang (2017, 157); courtesy of Taylor & Francis
Figure 10.20 left	Source: Lang (2017, 197); courtesy of Taylor & Francis
Figure 10.21	Source: Lang (2005, 70); courtesy of Taylor & Francis
Figure 10.22 left	Collection of the author
Figure 10.22 right	Source: Lang (2017, 110); courtesy of the Vastu Shilpa Foundation and Taylor & Francis
Figure 10.23 left	Photograph by Fortgens Photography/Shutterstock.com
Figure 10.23 right	Courtesy of Alexander Cuthbert
Figure 10.24	Source: Lang (2017, 66); courtesy of Taylor & Francis
Figure 10.26 left	Courtesy of Auroville Outreach Media
Figure 10.27 left and right	Source: Lang (2002, 130); Courtesy of Permanent Black

Chapter 11

Figure 11.1	Photograph by Arnand Contet. Source: Wikimedia Commons
Figure 11.2	Photograph by Heather Raulerson/Shutterstock.com
Figure 11.3 left	Photograph by EQRoy/Shutterstock.com
Figure 11.3 right	Photograph by Habrus Liudmila/Shuttterstock.com
Figure 11.4	Courtesy of Venturi, Scott Brown and Associates, Inc., and of MIT Press
Figure 11.5 left	Courtesy of Léon Krier
Figure 11.5 right	Helga Müller; courtesy of Helga Müller and Léon Krier
Figure 11.6	Courtesy of Venturi, Scott Brown and Associates, Inc., and of MIT Press
Figure 11.7 left and right	Courtesy of Ricardo Bofill Taller de Arquitectura
Figure 11.8 left	Courtesy of John Simpson Architects
Figure 11.8 right	Courtesy of Adam Architects
Figure 11.9 left	Collection of the author
Figure 11.10 left	Collection of the author
Figure 11.10 right	Photograph by trabantos/Shutterstock.com
Figure 11.11	Photograph by R. C. Smit. Source: Wikimedia Commons
Figure 11.12	Photograph by O. Tomasini/Getty Images

Credits

Figure 11.13 above left	Drawing by Yin Yin. Source Lang (2017, 76); courtesy of Taylor & Francis
Figure 11.13 above right	Bernard Tschumi Architects. Source Lang (2017, 76); courtesy of Taylor & Francis
Figure 11.13 below	Source Lang (2017, 76); courtesy of Taylor & Francis
Figure 11.14	Source: Lang, Desai and Desai (1997, 265); courtesy of CEPT University Press
Figure 11.15	Collection of the author
Figure 11.16	Source: Lang and Moleski (2010, 201); courtesy of Taylor & Francis
Figure 11.17	Photograph by Nils Versemann/Shutterstock.com
Figure 11.18	Photograph by Frans Blok/Shutterstock.com

Part Four

Figure 1 right	Collection of the author
Figure 2 left	Source: Lang (2017, 131); courtesy of Taylor & Francis
Figure 2 right	Source: Lang (2017, 131); courtesy of DPZ CoDesign and Taylor & Francis
Figure 3	Photograph by Kirill Neiezmaklov/Shutterstock.com
Figure 4	Photograph by Keep Watch/Shutterstock.com
Figure 5	Source: Lang (2017, 147); courtesy of Taylor & Francis

Chapter 12

Figure 12.1	Photograph by Renate Sedmakova/Shutterstock.com
Figure 12. 2 left	Filip Dujardin; courtesy of Filip Dujardin
Figure 12.2 right	Source: Cooke (2017); Kyle Simmons; courtesy of Kyle Simmons
Figure 12.3	Skidmore, Owings & Merrill (Europe) LLP. Source: Lang (2017, 22); courtesy of Skidmore, Owings & Merrill and Taylor & Francis
Figure 12.4 left	Chen Hao; courtesy of Atelier GOM
Figure 12.4 right	Photograph by Claudia Nesser; collection of the author
Figure 12.5 above left	Courtesy of Kohn Pedersen Fox, architects
Figure 12.5 above right	Photograph by Sleeping Panda/Shutterstock.com
Figure 12.5 bottom	Courtesy of UNStudio
Figure 12.6 left	Courtesy of GAD Architects
Figure 12.6 right	© Yao Li; courtesy of GAD Architects
Figure 12.7 left	Courtesy of Eric Sierens
Figure 12.8 above	Photograph by Gagliardi Photography/Shutterstock.com
Figure 12.8 below left	Photograph by Todamo/Shutterstock.com
Figure 12.8 below right	Courtesy of Forbes Massie Studio
Figure 12.9	Photograph by Philippe Rault; courtesy of OMA
Figure 12.10	Photograph by ppi/Shutterstock.com
Figure 12.11	Courtesy of ASTOC Architects
Figure 12.12	Photograph by Iwan Baan
Figure 12.13 left	Photograph by Shu He; courtesy of MAD Architects
Figure 12.13 right	Photograph by 663Highland. Source: Wikimedia Commons
Figure 12.14	Rendering Flying-Architecture; courtesy of Flying-Architecture

Credits

Chapter 13

Figure 13.1 left	Photograph by Tiia Monto. Source: Wikimedia Commons
Figure 13.1 right	Photograph by dnaveh/Shutterstock.com
Figure 13.2	Courtesy of Zaha Hadid Architects
Figure 13.3 left	Courtesy of Sarabjit Bahga
Figure 13.3 right	Source: LA Metro (2014, 34); courtesy of Gruen Associates and Grimshaw Architects
Figure 13.4	Courtesy of Zaha Hadid Architects
Figure 13.5	Collection of the author
Figure 13.6 above	Courtesy of Zaha Hadid Architects
Figure 13.6 below	Courtesy of JTC Corporation, Singapore
Figure 13.7	Courtesy of Greg Lynn, GREG LYNN FORM

Chapter 14

Figure 14.1 left	Collection of the author
Figure 14.1 right	Photograph by Sean Pavan/Shutterstock.com
Figure 14.2	Derived from Ross and Cabannes (2014) by the author
Figure 14.3	Derived from NewUrbanism.org (undated) by the author with the acknowledgment of the Smart Growth Association
Figure 14,4	Adapted from Kan, Forysth and Rowe (2017) by the author with the permission of Taylor & Francis
Figure 14.5 above left	Photograph by Neela Shukla
Figure 14.5 above right	Photograph by Neela Shukla
Figure 14.5 below	Courtesy of Ettore Maria Mazzola
Figure 14.6 above	Photograph by Felix Mizioznikov/Shutterstock.com
Figure 14.6 below left	Source: Lang (2017, 137); courtesy of Taylor & Francis
Figure 14.7 left and right	Source: Lang (2017, 160); courtesy of Taylor & Francis
Figure 14.8	Courtesy of Gensler
Figure 14.9	Source: Ebbsfleet Valley Masterplan (2008)
Figure 14.10	Source: Lang (2017, cover); courtesy of HafenCity Hamburg GMmb/Fotofrizz and Taylor & Francis
Figure 14.11	Collection of the author
Figure 14.12	Courtesy of the School of Architecture and Interior Design, Andrews University. Illustration by Pearl Choo/Faculty Advisors: Andrew von Maur and Troy Homenchuk
Figure 14.13	Mohammad Hassan Forouzanfar

Chapter 15

Figure 15.1	Photograph by Javarman/Shutterstock.com
Figure 15.2	Courtesy of Andrea Branzi
Figure 15.3 left and right	Source: de la Salle and Holland (2010); courtesy of DPZ CoDesign
Figure 15.4	Freiburg Wirtschaft Touristik und GmbH & CoKG
Figure 15.5	Courtesy of Zaha Hadid Architects
Figure 15.6 left and right	Source: Lang (2017, 79); courtesy of Taylor & Francis

Figure 15.7	Courtesy of HASSELL
Figure 15.8	Swedish Armed Services photograph by Johan Frederiksen. Source: Wikimedia Commons
Figure 15.9 left	Courtesy of Victoria Di Palma
Figure 15.9 right	Source: US Army Corps of Engineers (2007)
Figure 15.10	Courtesy of Norman Foster Associates
Figure 15.11	Courtesy of Stefano Boeri Architetti
Figure 15.12	Source: United States Conference of Mayors (2005)
Figure 15.13 left and right	Courtesy of BIG
Figure 15.14	Photograph by happycreator/Shutterstock.com
Figure 15.15	Source: Lang (2017, 141); courtesy of Kohn Pedersen Fox, architects, and of Taylor & Francis
Figure 15.16	Courtesy of Stefano Boeri Architetti
Figure 15.17 left and right	Courtesy of Henning Larsen Architects
Figure 15.18 left and right	Source: Lang (2017, 79); courtesy of Taylor & Francis

Chapter 16

Figure 16.1	Source: Robinson (ca 2014), https://theurbantechnologist.com/smarter-city-design-principles/. Courtesy of Rick Robinson
Figure 16.2	Courtesy of UNStudio
Figure 16.3	Photograph by DreamArchitects/Shutterstock.com

Epilogue

| Figure 1 | Image by Peter Linforth. Source: Wikimedia Commons |

Chapter 17

| Figure 17.1 | Derived from European Council of Town Planners (2003) by the author |

Index

Note: Page numbers in *italics* indicate figures on the corresponding page.

abandoned rail lines reused 317, *317*, 327–8, *328*
Adelaide, Australia: plan 52, *111*, 112
Adshead, Stanley 6
aerotropolises 257; *see also* Songdo, Korea
agenda for future urban design 371–5
agrarian urbanism 312, *312*, 313, 357; basic propositions 313–14, *314*; limitations of 356–7; *see also* Broadacre City
Albany, New York, USA: Empire State Plaza 197, *197*
Alberti, Leon Batista 39, 41, 51, 78, 172
Alexander, Christopher 207, 282, 284, 294, 307, 369; *A New Theory of Urban Design* with others 207–8; *A Pattern Language* with others 207
Algiers, Algeria: Le Corbusier's proposals 145–6, *146*
Ahmedabad, India: GIFT proposal *256*
Amsterdam, Netherlands: Amsterdam South proposal 155, *155*, 159; as a smart city 335
Angkor Wat, Cambodia 29
animals/wildlife in cities 4, 17, 297, 347; animal architecture 3
Antwerp, Belgium: Le Corbusier's proposal *137*, 145, *145*, 145
Arc-et-Senans, France: The Salt Works 54–5, *55*
Archigram group 171, 203; *Archigram I* 176; members 176; projects *180*
Arcosanti, Arizona, USA 35, 177, 192, *193*
Arnold, Henry: *Trees in Urban Design* 212
Art Deco designs 234
Arts and Crafts movement 71, 135
Atlantis proposal 239, *240*
Atterbury, Grosvenor 73, 132
Atwood, Charles B. 97
Augsburg, Germany: The Fuggerei 54
Auroville, India 35, 229–30, *229*
autonomous vehicles 331, 333, 339, 357, 360, 364

Baghdad: Abbasid Baghdad 30, 32, *32*, 37, 55; walls 52
Baltimore, Maryland, USA: Charles Center 166

Bangkok, Thailand 165
Barcelona 49, 336; block type *219*; church 282; CIAM proposal for 177, *177*; Còlonia Güell 59; *Eixample* 19, 50, *50*, 52, 177, 217, *219*; Pueblo Español de Montjuicj 205, *205*; Sagrada Familia 282; walls 18, 52
Barnett, Jonathan xiv
Bauhaus 12, 92, 131, 133, 134, 135, 160, 170; influence of 171, 172, 177; *Manifesto and Programme of the Weimar State Bauhaus* 135
Baumeister, Reinhard 11, 77, 78, 85, 93, 131; *Stadterweiterungen* 13, 77–8, 92
Bazalgette, Joseph 51
behaviour settings 4, 79, 112, 258, 279, 282, 288, 290, 332, 335, 339, 345, 350, 363, 364, 370; definition 3
Beijing, China 165; Central Business District 272–3, *274*; Forbidden City 29, 30–2, *31*; Tiān'anmen Square 254, 269
Bellamy, Edward: *Looking Backward: 2000–1887* 111
Belmont, The Netherlands: Brandevoort 251–2, *252*
Bengaluru, India: Karle Town Centre 269, *327*, 336–7; M. S. Ramaiah College 247, *247*, 251
Bennett Edward H. 99, 101
Benninger, Christopher 213, 224–5
Bentham, Jeremy 9
Berlage, Hendrik Petrus 154; Amsterdam South design 155, *155*, 159; *Grundlagen und Entwuckling der Architektur* 155
Berlin, Germany: Europa City 275–6, *276*; Freie Universität 191–2, *192*; Gartenstadt Falkenberg 69; Gartenstadt Staaken 69; Hobrecht's plan 50–1, *51*; Hufeisensiedlung 120, 125, *126*; Kurfürstendamm 53; Park Kolonnaden 199, *200*; Potsdamer Platz 265; Reinisches Viertel 69; Speer's design 102–3, *104*, 160, 234; Tegel Harbor housing 242, *242*; Wohenlage Ceciliengarten in Friednau 157
Berlyne, Daniel 85

Index

Bessbrook, Ireland 58, 139
Bills of Rights 16
Birmingham, England: Bournville 59, 112
block forms 178, 217, 295; Barcelona block *219*;
Berlin Block 50, *51*, 125, 286; block sizes 51,
349, 368; *see also* superblocks
Blumenfeld Hans 367
Boeri, Stefano 321, 326; his design 321, *322*
Bofill, Ricardo *see* Taller de Arquitectura Bofill
Boston, USA: Route I-93 165, *166*
Boston Architectural Society: *Place-Making
Manifesto* 296
Branzi, Andrea 310, 311; *Agronica* 311, *312*
Brasília, Brazil *161*, 181, 186, 197; Pilot Plan
186–9, *188*
Broadacre City 93, 110, 115, 118, *119*, 311, 313;
limitations of 353–4
Brown, Lancelot (Capability) 13; his designs 66
Brussels, Belgium 18, 80; Grand Place 80
Bubbar, Darshan 24, 36; *The Spirit of Indian
Architecture* 24, 212
Buchanan, Colin: *Traffic in Towns* with others
165, 209
Bucharest, Romania 107; Boulevard of the
Victory of Socialism 53, 108–9, *109*, 347
Buckingham, James Silk 56, 57, 111; Temperance
Community *57*
Budapest, Hungary 18, 99; Andrássy út 53;
Wekerletelep 119, 120–1, *121*
Buenos Aires, Argentina 40; Avenida 9 de Julio
53, 99
Buls, Charles 77, 79, 85; *L'esthétique des Villes* 79,
80–1
Burnham, Daniel 97, 99, 107; *The Plan of Chicago*
with Edward Bennett 101

Cairo, Egypt 77, 214; New Cairo proposal
267, *268*
Calthorpe, Peter 206; *The Next American Metropolis*
206, 209
Canberra, Australia 99; Griffin plan 103–4, *105*
capital cities, new 18, 257; Abuja xii, 181;
Belmopan 181; Bhubaneswar 220; Brasília
181, 186–9, *188*; Chandigarh 182, *183*, 197;
Gaborone xii; Islamabad 181–2, *182*; Lilongwe
xii; Nur-Sultan 273–5, *275*; Putrajaya 181
Caracas, Venezuela: 23 de enero housing 184,
185, 187, 203
Carcassonne, France *78*, 172
Çatalhöyük, Turkey 16
Cataneo, Pietro di Giacomo 40; ideal city plan *41*
Celebration, Florida, USA 203, 300–1, *301*, 354
Central Business Districts 257; Beijing 272,
274; Fort Worth plan 215, *216*, 264; London
Docklands 259, *260*
Cerda, Idelfons i Sunyer 19, 40, 50, 177, 217;
Teoria de la Construcción de las Ciudades 40

Cergy-Pontoise, France: Belvedere Saint
Christophe 241
Chandigarh, India 173, 181, 189, 197; capitol
complex 182, *183*, 186; City Centre 186; plans
173, *174*; Punjab University 186–7, *188*
Changchun, China 53, *53*
Charter of Machu Pichu 174–5
Chateau de Vaux-le-Vicomte, France 95–6, *96*
Chennai, India: Arumbakkam 222, 224, *225*;
Belrampur, Geddes' proposal 123–5, *124*,
126, 365
Chernikov, Iakov 134; Hammer and Sickle *134*
Chicago, Illinois, USA 19, *20*; Bloomingdale Trail
317; *The Chicago Plan 98*; dead horses in 90;
Illinois Institute of Technology 143, 153–4,
154; University of Illinois campus 166, *166*,
190; World's Columbian Exposition *96*, 97, 101
Chimbote, Peru: Civic Center proposal 186, *187*
China: Cultural Revolution 25, 163, 254, 263;
imperial cities 25; as a world power 254
Chinese cosmological texts 25; *Book of Rites*
25, 30
Chinese projects abroad 256–7, 259, 269
Christian philosophies: New Jerusalem 26
Chtcheglov Ivan: *Formulary for a New
Urbanism* 206
CIAM *see* Congres Internationaux d'Architecture
Moderne
Citadelle de Vauban de Neuf-Brisach, France 45
cities as collages 3, 236, 255
cities as sets of behavior settings and displays 3;
see also behaviour settings
City Beautiful movement 53, 92, 95–109, 240,
346; limitations of 347–8
Ciudad Gusare proposal, Venezuela 226, 227, *228*
civic centers: Brasília *161*, *188*; Chandigarh
capitol complex 182, *183*, 186; Chimbote 186,
187; St-Dié *187*
Cleveland, Ohio: Lakeview Terrace 149–50, 151
climate/climate appropriate design 4, 6, 212,
274, 312, 314–15, 362–3; climate change
4, 211–12, 254, 313, 315, 321, 329, 363;
disaster mitigation design 321–4, *324*;
looking ahead 368
Code Civile des Français/Napoleonic Code 10, 16
Co-Housing movement 57, 176, *180*, 181, 258
Cologne, Germany: Kranhäuser im Rheinhafen
201, *202*
colonization, impact of 17, 21
Columbia, Maryland, USA 219, 222–3, *223*,
226–7, 231
compact cities 205, 214, 343, 370–1; *Compact
City* 214
Congrês Internationaux d'Architecture Moderne
(CIAM) 78, 92, 93, 128, 133, 134, 155, 171,
172, 264, 348, 349, 350; *Charter d'Athene/
Athens Charter* 135, 136, 137, 160, 174, 349,

415

Index

358–9; congresses 171, 172–3; members 135, 137; Serraz *Declaration* 136
conservative surgery 110, 123, 129, 207
constructivism/constructivist city 134, *134*
Copenhagen, Denmark 227
Corbett, Harvey W. 112
cosmology/ritual structures 23–36; Chinese city design *27*; specific designs 29–33, 229–30, *230*
Costa, Lúcio 186
Council on Tall Buildings and Urban Habitat 266, 272
Cret, Paul 102
cubism/cubist art 132
Cullen, Gordon 86, 205, 206, 219; *Townscape Manifesto* 204, 206, *221*
Curitiba, Brazil 311–12

Dammam, Saudi Arabia: competing design paradigms 257, *256*
Dantzig, George B.: *Compact City* with Thomas L. Saaty 214
Darwin, Charles 16
Davis, California, USA: Village Homes 222, 223–6, *225*, 310
Declaration of Concern of Campbell Miller and others 311
deconstruction in urban design 239; limitations of 355; projects 245–6, *246*, 249–50
defensible space 13, 207, 231, 268, 297, 369
Delft, The Netherlands: Agnetapark 58
Delhi, New Delhi, India 103; Asiad Village 232, *232*; capitol complex 103, 105–6, *106*; Civil Lines 69, 72–3, *72*, 75, 125; garden suburbs 75; Old Delhi (Shahjahanabad) 72, *72*, 77
Den-en-chöfu, Japan 128, *129*
Denver, Colorado, USA: 6th Street Mall 228, *229*; capitol complex 99
Depression, Great 89, 111, 115, 120, 149
Derrida, Jacques 235; *Of Grammatology* 236
design, self-conscious and unselfconscious 2, *9*, 24, 86
De Stijl movement 132, 134; *Manifest Proletkunst* 134; Schröder House 134, *135*
determinism/deterministic thinking 43, 56, 58, 118, 133, 139, 201, 202, 294, 346, 353, 356
Detroit, Michigan, USA: Center for Fulfillment, Knowledge and Innovation 284, 289–90, *290*; Layfette Park *189*, 189–90
Dickens, Charles 16
Disraeli, Benjamin 56, 59
Doha, Qatar *258*
Doré, Gustave 19
Doshi, Balkrishna V. 36, 175, 227
Doxiades, Constantinos 181
Duany Plater-Zyberk & Co., Duany, Andres and Elizabeth Plater-Zyberk 209, 215, 220, 302,

316, 317; *Smart Growth Manuel* 296; *see also* New Urbanism
Dubai, UAE 266, *266*, 275; Al Bastakiya (Al Fahidi Historic District) 30, *34*, 34–5
Dublin, Ireland: the city beautiful design 99; as a smart city 336
ducks and decorated sheds 238–9, *239*, 250
Dujardin, Filip 267; his work *267*
Dutch Structuralists 173

East Tilbury, England 128, 160
Ebbsfleet, England 303–4, *304*
Echota, New York, USA 62–3, *63*
École Supérieure des Beaux-Arts 6, 13, 37, 42, 95; influence of 37, 101, 102, 112, 173
Edinburgh, Scotland: Geddes' designs 123
El Lissitzky 133, 146, 159, 201; his Wolkenbügel proposal 133–4, *134*, 201
empiricism 12–13; empiricist urban design 110–30, 204–33
Engels, Friedrich 17, 20, 54, 60
English Common Law 12
English landscape architecture 138
Environmental Design Research Association (EDRA) 13
environments, anthrophelic versus anthropozemic 5–6
EPCOT proposal, Florida 203
Essen, Germany: Kronnenberg 61, *61*; Margarethenhöhe 61, 69, 71–3, *73*
European Council of Town Planners: *The New Athens Charter* 358–9
Eyck, Aldo van 173, 351; *Het Verhaal van een andere Gedachte* 173

feminist views 52, 57–8, 172, 177
feng shui 25, 26, 28, 36, 212, 259
Ferriss, Hugh 112, 122; *Metropolis* 112, *113*
flood control 311, 321–4
Forest City, Cancun, Mexico 321, *322*, 326
Fortescue Fields, England 241, *242*
Fort Worth plan 215, *216*, 264
Fourier, Charles 11, 57, 132; *Théorie des Quatre Mouvements* 11; *see also* phalanstére
Freiburg, Germany: Quartier Vauban 315, *316*
Friedman, Yona 173, 175, 178–9, 191, 311; *Ville Spatiale* 173, 175, *179*
Fritsch, Thomas 113; *Die Stadt der Zukunft* 113
Fry, Maxwell 138, 152, 348
Fuller, Buckminster 175
function/functionalism 3–7, 346; advanced 5; basic 4–5; and urban design 5–6
Futurist, Italian *see* Sant'Elia

Gans, Herbert 207, 222
garden cities/garden city movement 13, 57, 76, 117–23, 171, 213, 232, 264, 307; conceptual

Index

diagrams 116–17, *116*; international applications 128; limitations of the paradigm 352–3

garden city movement, new 293, 307; *The New Garden City* 294–5, 307

gardens: Chinese 66, *67*; classical 95–6, *96*; *see also* Budapest, Hungary; Columbia, Maryland, USA; Letchworth Garden City, England; Welwyn Garden City, England

garden suburbs 65–76, 204; British 69–71; Chinese 75; German 69, 73; Latin American 75; North American 69–70, 73–4; *see also* Delhi, New Delhi, India, Civil Lines

Garnier, Tony 21, 133, 172; *Une Cité Industrielle* 133, 138–9, *139*, 349

Gaudi i Cornet, Antonio 50, 59, 282

Geddes, Patrick 110, 113, 116, 119, 127, 185, 310, 365; *City Development* 113; his work in Edinburgh 123, 126; in India 123–5, *124*, 365; influence of 129, 206; and Tel Aviv 125, 126–7, *127*

Gehry, Frank 238, 289, 319

generic solutions, the nature of 8

gentrification 123, 209, 254

George, Henry 111; *Progress and Poverty* 111

Giedion, Siegfried 135, 136; *Space Time and Architecture* 172

Ginzburg, Moisei 92, 133, 146; *Style and Epoch* 134

Givoni, Baruch 212, 314, 320; *Climate Considerations in Architecture and Urban Design* 212, 314

Göbekli Tepe, Turkey 23, 24

Godin, Jean-Baptiste André 58, 61; *see also* Guise, France

Goodman, Paul and Percival 213; *Communitas* 213, *213*

Gothenburg, Sweden: Bagaregården 83, *84*

Grassi, Giorgio 198, 199; *La Construzione Logica dell'architectura* 176

Greenbelt towns, USA 128; Greenbelt, Maryland 128, *129*

green design, greening cities 223; projects 223–6, *224*

Gregotti, Victorio 176; *Il Territorio dell'architettura* 176

Griffin, Walter Burley and Marion Mahony Griffin 97, 104

Gropius, Walter 6–7, 135, 146, 149, 264; attitude towards the public 352

Gruen, Victor 209, 215, 216; *The Heart of our Cities* 209, 216

guidelines, building design 38, *39*, 149, 302, 373; Battery Park City 223; criticism of 354; Val d'Europa 304

Guise, France: *Le Familistère* 58, 61–2, *62*

Habitat Bill of Rights of Nadar Ardalan and others 175

Habraken, John 173; *Supports: An Alternative to Mass Housing* 173

Hadid, Zaha *see* Zaha Hadid Architects

Hall, Peter xiv

Hamburg, Germany: HafenCity viii, 303, 304–5, *305*

Hammarby Sjöstad *see* Stockholm, Sweden

Hangzhou, China: The One *270*, 270–1

Hanna-Olin 223, 228

Hanoi, Vietnam 53, 106

Harmony, Indiana and in Pennsylvania, USA 55

Harvard University, Graduate School of Design 6–7, 12, 173

Haussmann, Baron Georges-Eugène 18, 19, 42, 44, 51, 86, 153, 264; *see also* Paris

Hayden, Dolores 58, 172, 177, 180–1; design proposal *180*

Hébrard, Ernést 106; *see also* Thessaloniki

Hegemann, Werner xiv, 6, 85, 283, 350; *The American Vitruvius* with Elbert Peets xiv, 85

Helmholtz, Hermann von 11, 78, 79, 86

Helmond, Netherlands: Brandevoort 251, *252*

Hénard, Eugene: *The Cities of the Future* 132

Hershey, Pennsylvania, USA 59

Hilberseimer, Ludwig 135, 141, 142, 149, 189, 348; *The New City* 135; other manifestoes 142, *143*, 311

highways 165, 168; impact of 165, 168; removal of 165, 167

Hill, Octavia 56

hip-hop urbanism 264, 265, 267, *267*, 276; *Ruffneck Constructivists* 265

Hiroshima, Japan *162*

Hobrecht, James 50, 52

Hood, Raymond 122

Hough, Michael 211, 212, 313; *City Form and Natural Processes* 211, 313

housing, housing estates/schemes 19, 149–51, 177; Amsterdam South 155, *155*, 159; Arumbakkam, Chennai 225, *225*; Barbican Estate, London 194–5, *195*; Bedford Park, London 69; Brandevoort, Helmond *252*; Byker Wall, Newcastle-upon-Tyne 159; Corviale, Rome 298–300, *299*, 308; Dammerstocksiedlung, Karlsruhe 149, *150*; Falowiec, Gdansk 159; Fuggerei, Augsburg 54; Garden City, Long Island, New York 113; Hampstead Garden Suburb 69, 70–1, *71*, 75; Huangshan Mountain Village, Anhui 277–8, *278*; Hufeisensiedlung, Berlin 125–6, *126*; Interlace, Singapore 276, *277*; Karl-Marx Hof, Vienna 144, 150, 156, *158*; Lakeview Terrace, Cleveland 149–50, 151; Lafayette Park, Detroit *189*, 189–90; Levittown, USA 168; Longnan Garden Housing, Xuhui District 267, *268*; Monte Amiata, Milan 198, *198*; Norkomfin, Moscow 144, 146, *147*, 149; Pruitt Igoe, St Louis *169*, 186, 189, 201, 202; Quarry Hills, Leeds 150, *151*; Quartiers Modernes

Fruges, Pessac *87*, 144, 155, *156*, 158, 307; Robin Hood Gardens, London 191, *191*, 351; St John's Woods, London 66, *67*; Soweto, Johannesburg 169–70, *169*; Tegel Harbor housing, Berlin 242, *242*; The One, Hangzhou 270, 270–1; Unité d'habitation, Marseille 173, *178*, *183*; Weissenhofsiedlung, Stuttgart 145–6, *147*; Werkerletep Estate, Budapest 120–1; *121*; Williamsburg Houses, New York 150–1, *152*; Wohenlage Ceciliengärten, Berlin 157; Wohnpark Neue Danau, Vienna 271, *272*

Howard, Ebenezer 13, 21, 110, 111, 119, 203, 204, 293, 295, 300, 352, 353; *Garden Cities for Tomorrow* 114; his background 111

Hsinking, Manchukuo *see* Changchun, China

Huangshan Mountain Village, China 275, 277, *278*

Hudnut, Joseph 6

humans, models of 111, 137, 200, *201*, 345, 353

Humboldt, Alexander von 205

hypermodern design 256–7, 263, 267–8; definition 263; examples 269–70, *270*, 273–4, *275*, *276*, 336–7, *337*; limitations of 352

Industrial Revolution and its impacts 17, 46, 51, 54, 110

Indus Valley civilization 16, 56

International Association for People-Environmental Studies 13

Internationale Bauausstellung (IBA) 210, 211

Islam: Islamic city, historic generic model 27–8, *28*; *see also* Dubai, Al Bastakiya

Islamabad, Pakistan 181–2, *182*

Islamic philosophers/scholars 13; *see also* Sharia Law

Istanbul: Kartal Pendik proposal 285–6, *286*

Jacobs, Allan 206; *Great Streets* 207, 208; *Toward an Urban Design Manifesto*, with Donald Appleyard 207

Jacobs, Jane 200, 207, 209, 217, 231, 281, 284, 297, 348; *The Death and Life of Great American Cities* 200, 206, 207, 217; limitations of her views 352; neighborhood design principles 218

Jaipur, India 30, 32–3, *33*, 36; Vidyadhar Nagar proposal 36

James Corner Field Operations 327

Jeanneret, Pierre 155, 186

Jung, Karl 5

Kahn, Louis I. 172, 175, 182, 186; City Center, Philadelphia design 175

Käpylä, Finland 128

Karlsruhe, Germany 49; Bundesverfassungsgericht 43, *43*; Dammerstocksiedlung 149, *150*

Kharkiv, Ukraine: Derzhprom 134, 146–7, *148*

kitsch/kitsch design 237–8, 247, 251, 355

Kohn Pedersen Fox Associates 271, 326, 338

Kolkata, India: Rajarhat *259*

Koolhaas, Rem 272, 348, 349

Krakow, Poland: Nowa Huta 107, *108*

Krier, Léon 176, 208, 217, 237, 238, 252, 301; Atlantis proposal 239, *240*; *The Reconstruction of the European City* 237

Krier, Rob 176, 205, 251; *Stadtraum* 176

Krupp family 59, 60–1; Krupp villages *see* Essen, Germany

Kyoto, Japan 29

Ladovsky, Nikolai 92

La Grande-Motte, France 190–1, *190*

laissez-faire development *see* pragmatism

landscape urbanism 212, 313, 319, 329, 357; principles 313; projects *317*, 317–18, 322–3, 327–8, *328*

Las Vegas, Nevada, USA 239, *240*; *see also* Venturi, Robert

La Tendenza 171, 176, 201; manifestoes 176; members 198; projects 198–200

Laws of the Indies 11, 227, 310

Le Corbusier 13, 21, 63, 86, 131, 136, 140, 155, 160, 177, 186, 195, 198, 201, 227, 235, 264, 277, 283, 332, 348; *The City of Tomorrow* 332; on the garden city 353; his Calvinism 132–3, 269, 346, 350; *La Ville Contemporaine* 141, *142*; *La Ville Radieuse* 137; on New York City 137; *Vers une Architecture* 136, 194

Ledoux, Claude-Nicholas 11, 54, 241, 248; *L'Architecture considérée sous rapport de l'art* 11

L'Enfant, Pierre Charles 48–9; *see also* Washington, DC, USA

Letchworth Garden City, England 117, 119, 128, 204, 293

Liebeskind, Daniel: on urban design 265

linear city ideas 140–1, *141*, 148, 157, 159

Lisbon, Portugal: Baixa Pombalina 44, *44*

Liuzhou Forest City, China 326, *327*

Liverpool, University of: civic design program 6, 348

Locke, John 13

London, England 18, 54, 65; Barbican Estate 194–5, *195*; Bedford Park 69; Belgravia *67*; Clapham 65; Docklands development 195, 260, *260*; Great Fire 41; 'great stink' 46 ; Hampstead Garden Suburb 69, 70–1, *71*, 75, 201; MARS plan 152–3, *153*; Paternoster Square 241, *242*, 245; Regency London 18; Richmond Riverside 248–9, *249*, 250, 251; Robin Hood Gardens 191, *191*, 202; slums 18, 54; squares 18; St John's Wood 66, *67*; Thames Barrier 311; Wren's plan 41, *42*, 108

Los Angeles, California, USA: 8150 Sunset Boulevard proposal 289; Los Angeles River proposal 319, *319*; Union Station precinct proposal *285*

Index

Louvain-la-Neuve, Belgium 83–4, *84*, 153, 223
Luther, Martin 16
Lutyens, Sir Edwin 75, 105
Lynch, Kevin 13, 209, 214, 231, 266, 294; *Theory of Good City Form* 204, 209

Madras, India *see* Chennai, India
Madrid, Spain: Ciudad Lineal 140, *141*; as a smart city 336–8
Madurai, India *29*, 30
Maertens, Hermann 13, 77–81, 85; *Optische Maaßstab* 79
Magnitogorsk, Russia 107, 134, 144, 148–9, *149*
Maharishi Vedic City, Iowa, USA 35, 229
Mandala 24, *25*, 36; Chinese city forms *25*; Vastu-Purusha Mandala 26; *see also* Jaipur, India
Marne-la-Vallée, France: Place de Toscane 243, *244*; Val d'Europa 304–5, *305*
MARS group *see* Modern Architecture Research Society
Marseille, France: Unité d'habitation 173, *178*, *183*
Marx, Karl 17, 56; *Manifesto of the Communist Party* with Friedrich Engels 17, 56
Masdar, UAE 315, 318, 320, *320*, 329
Maslow, Abraham 4; model of human motivations and functionalism 3–6
May, Ernst 74, 148
Mayer, Albert 173, 206; *The Urgent Future* 206
Mayne, Thom 265
McCamant and Durett Architects 176; *see also* Co-Housing movement
McHarg, Ian 206, 212, 286, 310, 313, 319, 311, 355; *Design with Nature* 206, 211
Mckim, Mead and White 59, 62, 235
medieval towns 39, 51, 77, 83, 86, 131, 223; *see also* Carcassonne, France
megastructures 172, 177, 179–80, 183–4, 200, 202, 259; definition 175; examples *179*, 179–80, *180*, *184*, 348
Meixi Lake proposal, China 325–6, *326*
Melbourne, Australia: the Crows' plan for 159; Docklands 260; Federation Square 242, 249–50, *250*, 251
Metabolists 171, 180, 192–3; members 176, 273; *Metabolism/1960* 176; projects *180*, 192–3, *193*
Mexico City: Garden suburbs 75; Universidad Nacional Autónoma 194, *194*
Mies van der Rohe, Ludwig 146, 153, 349
Migge, Leberecht 125; *Green Manifesto* 125, 138, *143*
Milan, Italy: Monte Amita, Gallaratese 198, *198*
Miletus, Asia Minor 10, *10*
mills: dark satanic 19, *20*
Milton Abbas, Dorset, England 65–6, *66*
Milyutin, Nikolai 134, 140; *Sotsgorod* 134, 140, *141*

Minneapolis, USA: Midtown Greenway 317; Skyway system 167, *167*
Mississauga, Canada: Absolute Towers 284, *284*
Modena, Italy: Cemetery of San Cataldo 198–9, *199*
Modern Architecture Research Society (MARS): members 152; plan for London 152–3, *153*, 159
Montpellier, France: Quartier Antigone *243*, 243–4, 245
Moore, Charles, Moore, Ruble Yudell 242; designs 242, *242*, *244*, 245, 301
Montreal Canada: Golden Mile 274; Habitat 277
Mormon design philosophy 26; City of Zion 26, 28–9, 57; Salt Lake City 33, *34*
morphology of cities 2, *2*, 5, 56, 90, 137, *137*, 152, 164, 259, 279, 331, 332, 340, 342, 358, 360
Morris, William 39, 54
Moscow, Russia 171; constructivist proposals 133–4, *134*; Khrushchyouvkas *185*, 186; Narkomfin 134, 144, 146, *147*, 149, 172, 187; Rublyovo-Arkangelskoye 279, *280*; schools of design 11, 92
Moses, Robert 264
Mujica, Francisco 112–13; his image of the future city *113*
Mumford, Lewis: observations of 7, 58, 68, 213, 235, 352
Munich, Germany: Olympic stadium 282, *282*; WagnisART scheme 268, *268*
Munikkiniemi-Haaga, Finland *99*
Muthesius, Hermann 68

Napoleonic Code *see Code Civile des Français*/Napoleonic Code
neighborhoods/neighborhood design 60, 204, 222; for Chinese cities 298; Jane Jacobs' neighborhood design guidelines 218; *see also* neighborhood unit
neighborhood unit: Chinese *xiaoqu* 259, 264; concept 28, 117–18, *118*, 204, 206, 222, 293; new urbanist model 216, *216*
neoliberalism/neo-liberal thinking 255; and urban design 255–7
neo-modernism 263, 271–3; definition 263, 264; projects *272*, *273*, *275*, *276*, 277
New Athens Charter 358–9
New Delhi *see* Delhi, New Delhi, India
New Earswick, England 59
New Lanark, Scotland 11, *11*, 63
Newman, Oscar 268, 297; *Defensible Space* 3, 207, 231
New Orleans, USA: Plaza d'Italia *244*, 245, 251, 252
new towns 19, 219–20, 257, 298; projects 222–3, *223*, 226, *226*, 300–2, *302*, 303–4,

304, 325–6, *326*, 338–9, *339*; as public policy 164, 241; *see also* Auroville; capital cities, new; Columbia, Maryland, USA; Forest City; Magnitogorsk, Russia; Runcorn, England
New Urbanism 204, 205, 209, 220, 232; *Ahwahnee New Urban Principles* 209–11; *Charter of New Urbanism* 300; limitations of 354–5; neighborhood unit 216, *216*; projects 220, *222*, 223–5, *224*, *225*; Transect model 215, *215*
New York, New York, USA 138, 270; Battery Park City 183, 184, 221, 223, *224*; Broadway in the 1920s *91*; Central Park 245; Flood Mitigation proposal 321–4, *324*; Forest Hills Gardens 69, 73–4, *74*, 75, 112, 132, 293; Garden City 113; Gramercy Park 223; Greenwich Village 207, 236, 352; High Line Park 260, 271, 317, 325, 327–8, *328*, 329, 356; Hudson Yards 271–2, *273*; Le Corbusier's reaction to 138; Morningside Heights 223; Rockefeller Center 122–3, *124*; TWA Flight Center 264; Williamsburg Houses 150–1, *152*, 169; World Trade Center site 265; Wright's Skyscraper City proposal 112–13, *114*; zoning code of 1916 112
Niemeyer, Oscar 186, 187
Noisiel-sur-Seine, France 58, *59*
Nolan John: *New Towns for Old* 205
Nolli, Giambattista, Nolli plan 2, *2*
Nôtre, André le 95
Nur-Sultan, Kazakhstan 273–5, *275*

Olmsted, Frederick Law 59, 66, 70, 95, 111, 204
Olmsted, Frederick Law, Jr. 73, 100
Orechovka, Czech Republic 128
Osaka, Japan: Namba Parks 275, 277–8, *278*
Oslo, Norway: Tjuvholmen 266, 268
Otto, Frei 282
Owen, Robert 11, 55, 56, 60, 111, 115; model towns 55, *55*, *57*; *A New View of Society* 11; *see also* New Lanark, Scotland

Palladio, Andrea 40
Palmanova, Italy 43, *43*
parametricism/parametric design 281–92; limitations of 355–6; projects *284*, 284–92, *285*, *286*, *287*, *288*, *289*
Paris, France: Arc de Triomphe 44, 47, *47*; Avenue de Champs-Élysées 44, 47, 99; Avenue de la Grande Armée *15*; Jeanne-Hachette Centre 277; La Défense 195–7, *196*; Napoléon III and Haussmann's Paris 15, 18, 19, *47*, 50, 51, 52, 62, 99, 10, 107, 108, 264, 348; Palais de Luxembourg 43; Parc de La Villette 235, 242, 245–6, *246*, 251, 282, 355, 369; Place de la Trinité 81, *82*; Place de l'Opera *47*; Place des Voges 43; Plan Voisin 144, *144*, 145, 348; Promenade Plantée 260, 317, *317*, 329; Rue

de Rivoli 38, *39*, 47; slums 46; stench of the medieval city 46
Parker, Barry 119
Parma, Italy *137*
pedestrian pocket 215, *217*, 353
Pei, I. M. 228
Perlach, Gardenstadt, Germany 69, *71*, 71–2
Pelli, Cézar 223, 260, 300
Perry, Clarence 76, 112, 117, 119, 204, 206, 222, 214, 215, 293; *see also* neighborhood unit
Pessac, France: Les Quartiers Modernes de Frugès 87, 144, 155, *156*, 158, 307
phalanstère 57, *58*
Philadelphia, Pennsylvania, USA 52; Benjamin Franklin Parkway 99, 347; PSFS building 151
philosophies: Eastern and Western 14
Plano, Texas, USA: Legacy Town Center 301, 302–3, *303*
Plater-Zyberk, Elizabeth *see* Duany Plater-Zyberk & Co., Duany, Andres and Elizabeth Plater-Zyberk
Port Grimaud, France 220, 223, *224*, 321
Portlaw, Ireland 58
Portmeirion, Wales 235, *236*, 237, 238, 239
Port Sunlight, Merseyside, England 58, 112
postmodernism/postmodern urban design 234–52; architecture 237–8, *238*; limitations of 355
Poundbury, Dorset, England 220, *222*, 252, 293
pragmatism 9–10; images 131, *132*, *258*, 259, 342–3, *343*; pragmatic urban designs 9, 19–20, *20*, 90–1, *91*, 164–70, 171, 258–61
pre-Colombian urban design 24; *see also* Teotihuacán
Pullman, Illinois 59
Pyongyang, North Korea 53, 107

Quakers/designs by Quakers 58, 59
Quintana Roo, Mexico: Alai 315–17, *316*

Radburn, New Jersey 121, 122, 206, 352, 353; international application 129, 206, 218; Radburn plan *123*, 125, 206
Rapoport, Amos 35, 209; his manifesto 209
Rapp, George/Rappites 55
Ras Al Khaimah, UAE 321
Ratti, Carlo: *The City of Tomorrow* with Matthew Claudel 332
rationalism/rationalists 10–13; rationalist urban designs 131–60, 171–203; *see also* La Tendenza
rationalist urban designs 131–60
religious canons and prescriptions
Renaissance 24, 37, 39, 77, 131; ideal city plans 41, 41–3, *43*; *La Citta Ideale* 40, *40*; treatises on architecture 40
Retrofuturism 308, *308*
Rietveld, Gerrit 134; Schröder house 133, *134*

Index

Riis, Jacob 19; *How the Other Half Lives* 19, *18*
Riverside, Illinois 59, 66, 69–70, *70*, 75, 293, 300
Robinson, Charles M. 6, 97; *Modern Civic Art* 97
Robinson, Rick: *Design Directives for Smarter Cities* 333–4
Rochester, New York: Inner Loop 165
Rohe, Ludwig Mies van der *see* Mies van der Rohe, Ludwig
Rome: Corviale 298–300, *299*, 308, 351; Forum Romanum 37, *38*; Nolli map of 2, *2*; Piazza del Campidoglio *81*, 248; Piazza del Popolo 46, *46*, 97; Piazza San Pietro (St Peter's Square) 46, *81*; Pope Sixtus V's Rome 38, 47, 95; Via della Conciliazione 108
Root, John Wellborn 97
Ross, Philip: *The New Garden City* with Yves Cabannes 295, 307
Rossi, Aldo 176, 198; *Architecture and the City* 176, 198–9
Rossi, Carlo di Giovanni 45, 95; *see also* St Petersburg, Russia
Rotterdam, Netherlands: De Hofbogen 329; Lijnbaan 218; Outer Harbor developments 321; Schouwburgplein 202
Rowe, Colin 131, 205, 236–7, 293; *Collage City* with Fred Koetter 236, 255
Rowntree, England 59, 112
Runcorn, England *226*, 226–7, 231
Ruskin, John 111

Saarinen, Eliel 99; his designs *99*
Sabaudia, Italy 153
Safdie, Moshe 277
St-Dié, France: plan and civic centre 187, *187*
St Louis, Missouri, USA: Louisiana Purchase Exposition 101, *102*; Pruitt-Igoe *169*, 186, 189, 201, 202
St Petersburg, Russia: classical *44*, 45, 95
Saint-Simon, Claude-Henri de 56
Salisbury, England *111*
Saltaire, Yorkshire, England 58, 59–60, *60*
Salt Lake City, Utah, USA 30, 33, *34*
San Francisco, California, USA: City Beautiful plan 99
Sant'Elia, Antonio 133, 139–40; *Manifesto del Futurismo* 133, 139–40, *140*
Savannah, Georgia, USA 300; Ogelthorpe's design 293, *294*
Scamozzi, Vicenzo 40; ideal city plan *41*
Schopenhauer, Arthur 78
Schumacher, Patrik 282, 283, 285, 291; his designs *285* (*see also* Zaha Hadid Architects); his manifestoes 283
Scott Brown, Denise *see* Venturi, Robert
Seaside, Florida 220, *222*, 293, 346
Seoul, Korea 186; Cheonggyechon 329; Skygarden 329

sequential experience 21, 80, 81, 85, 86, 205, 206, 209, 219, *221*; at Parc de la Villette 251
Sert, José Luis 7, 173, 175, 177, 186, 213; *Can Our Cities Survive* with CIAM 173
Settlement House Movement 56
sewerage and drainage systems 51, 97
Sforzina, Poland 37, 42
Shakers, The 55
Shanghai, China 186, 270; Bund in 1936 *91*; Huangpu East Bank Forest 317, *318*; Lujiazui, Pudong *255*; The Springs 326, *327*
Sharia Law 23, 25, 34
Shaw, John 67
Shaw, Richard Norman 69
Shenzhen, China: Longgang Center 286, 287, 291; Vanke Center 159
Shibam, Yemen *311*
Shilpa Shastras 24, 33, 212, 310; generic urban forms *27*, 33
Silent Spring, Rachel Carson 211, 310
Simonds, John O. 206, 213–14; *Garden Cities 21* 206, 214, *214*, 311
Singapore 88, 186, 303; Bedok Court 276; interlace 275, 276–7, *277*; Kertepi Tanah Melayu Railway 317; Marina Bay development *253*, 289; One North 286–8, *288*, 356; Punggol 21 plus 325, *325*; *Sustainable Singapore Blueprint* 325
sites and services housing 212–13; Arumbakkam, Chennai 225, *225*
Sitte, Camillo 13, 77, 79, 82, 83, 85, 110, 115, 131, 133, 205; *Der Städtbau* 79, 80–1, 83; Le Corbusier's response 86
Skidmore, Owings and Merrill 167
slavery/slave trade 17
slums and slum life 18, *18*, 54, 212, 365; in developing countries 365; slum clearance 19, 149, 267, 351, 365; *see also* sites and services housing
smart cities 203, 331–44, 360; definition 331; design directives 333–4; in India 336, 357; limitations of 357; procedural design model for 335
smart growth, Smart Growth Network 295–7; *see also* New Urbanism
Smith, Adam 17; *The Wealth of Nations* 16, 17, 255
Smith, Joseph 26
Smithson, Alison, and Peter Smithson 174, 178, 181, 190, 191
Social and Philanthropic Movement 54–64
Soissons, Louis de 121
Sola-Morales, Manual de 208, 348–9; *Ciudades, Esquinas* 208
Soleri, Paolo 35, 175, 179; *The City in the Image of Man* 175; his designs 35, 177, *179*, 192, *193*
Solversbörg, Sweden: Klisters Härads Tinghus *235*
Songdo, Korea *338*, 338–9, 357

Index

space syntax analysis 208
Speer, Albert 102–4, 160, 234
Spirn, Anne 211; *The Granite Garden* 211, 357
Staatliches Bahaus Weimar *see* Bauhaus
Stein, Clarence 115, 118, 121, 214, 352; *Toward New Towns for America* 206
Stern, Robert A. M. 300; *Paradise Planned: The Garden Suburb and the Modern Metropolis* with others 68
Stockholm, Sweden: Hasmmarby Sjöstadt 294, 315, 318–19, *319*; Valingby 219
streets/street design/street layouts 2, *2*, 19, 47, 68, 79, 81, 85, 101–2, 112, 122, 126, 133, 159, 168, 205, 218, 297, 370; pedestrian 165, 218, 227–9, *229*; as seams for urban life 159, 205, 266, 349, 352, 370; strip development 167; *see also woonerf*
Stübben, Josef 77, 85, 92, 95, 110, 131; *Der Städtebau* 92, 95
Stuttgart, Germany: Weissenhofsiedlung 145–6, *147*
suburbs/suburbia 19, 20, 21, 65–76, 165, 168, 170, 257; Bedford Park, London 69; and Broadacre City 118; Civil Lines, Delhi 69, 72, 72–3, 75, 125; Forest Hills, New York 69, 73–4, *74*, 75, 132, 293; Gardenstadt Perlach, Munich 69, *71*, 71–2; Humberstone, England 69; Levittown 294; Margarethenhöhe, Essen 61, 69, 71–3, *73*; pragmatic 65, 168, *169*; Residence Park, New Rochelle, New York 69; Riverside, Illinois 59, 66, 69–70, *70*, 75, 293, 300; St John's Wood, London 66, *67*; Yorkship Township, Camden New Jersey 99
superblocks 122, 165, 182, 206, 351; Asaid Village 232, *232*; Barbican 194–5, *195*; Brasília's *superquadras* 187–9, *188*; Ciudad Guasare proposal 226, 227, *228*; definition 122; Fort Worth plan 215, *216*; GSFC Township 227, *228*; Karle town center 336, *337*; La Défense 195–6, *196*; pedestrian pockets 215–16, *216*; Radburn 122–3, *123*, 206; town centers 227, *228*
sustainable cities/sustainable design 310–30, 362; definition 310; examples 311, *311*, 312, *312*, 313, *316*, 318, *318*, *319*, 321, *322*, 323–4, *324*, *325*, 325–6, *326*, *327*, 327–8, *328*; limitations of current thinking 356–7; looking ahead 362–3
Sydney, Australia: Breakfast Point 220; Goods Line 317; Market Street in 1910 *91*; Opera House 249, 264, 339; Rouse Hill Centre 301–2, *302*, 306; St Leonards TOD 229, *230*

Tafuri, Manfredo: *Architecture and Utopia* 172
Taller de Aquitectura Bofill 241; projects 241, *241*, 243, *243*, 250
Tallinn, Estonia 99

Tange, Kenzo 172, 180, 181
Taut, Bruno 51, 69, 115, 117, 118, 125, 158; *Crown City* 117, *117*, 125
Tbilisi, Georgia: Minavtodor building 159
Team 10 171, 173, 177, 178, 190, 350; *Doorn Manifesto* 174; members 173; projects 190–3, *191*, *192*
technological innovations and urban design 88, 132, 163, 254, 332; future possibilities 8, 331
Tel Aviv, Palestine (now Israel): Geddes' plan 125, 126–7, *127*; as a smart city 335
Tendenza, La 176, 198–200; members 198; projects *198*, 199
Teotihuacán, Mexico 29, 30, *31*, 190
Terry, Quinlan 248, 252
Thessaloniki, Greece 103; Hébrard's plan *106*, 106–7
Tianjin, China *259*
Tokyo, Japan: Kohn Pedersen Fox proposal *269*; Nagakagin Capsule Tower 193; Tokyo Bay proposals, Metabolists' proposal *180*, *193*
Toronto, Ontario, Canada: Downsview Park proposal 318, 324
Townscape movement 21, 206, 219, *220*; *see also* Cullen, Gordon
Transit-Oriented Development (TOD) 209, 215–17, *218*, 229, *230*
Tschumi, Bernard 235, 238, 242, 245, 250, 251, 282, 355; *Architecture and Disjunction* 238
Tsukuba Civic Center, Tsukuba, Japan 247–8, *248*, 251
Turner, John 213; *Housing by People* 213

Ulaanbaatar, Mongolia: Sukhbaatar Square 269
Umbumbulu, South Africa: eThekwini Center 301, 305, *306*
Unité d' habitation 172, 178, *178*, 182, *183*, 191, 201, 350; influence of 187, 189, 202; locations of 182
university campuses 19, 257; M. S. Ramaiah Medical College, Bengaluru 247, *247*, 251; Punjab University, Chandigarh 186–7, *188*; Universidad Nacional Autónoma, Mexico City 194, *194*; Universität Bielefeld 183–4; University of Minnesota, St Paul 99; University of Texas, Austin 102, *103*
Unwin, Raymond 68, 70, 114, 119, 205; *The Art of Designing Cities and Suburbs* with Barry Parker 9, 114; *Town Planning in Practice* 68, 76, 92
urban composition/structure models 214, *223*
urban design: empiricist 12–13, 110–30, 204–33; the nature of 6–8; the philosophical bases of 9–13; pragmatic 9–10, 19–20, 90–1, 132, 164–70, 171, 258–61, 342–3; as project design and as public policy 7–8; rational 10–13, 123–60, 171–203; self-conscious and unselfconscious 10, 16

422

Index

Utrecht, The Netherlands: pedestrianization of 227, *228*

Vadodara, India: GSFC Township 227, *228*
Van den Boek and Bakema 166
Vaux, Calvert 70, 111
Venice, Italy 339; flood control 311
Venturi, Robert 14, 252, 301; *Complexity and Contradiction* 14, 236; and Denise Scott Brown 235, 237; and *Learning from Las Vegas* with Steve Izenour 235, 237
Versailles, France 43, 95
vertical segregation of traffic modes 115–16, 165–7, *166*, 200, 203; La Défense 195–7, *196*; Minneapolis's Skyway system 167, *167*; Wright's model for New York 112, *114*
Vienna, Austria 18, 41, 77, *342*; Franz Joseph I's 47–8, 133; Heldenplatz 47, *48*; Karl-Marx-Hof 144, 156, *158*, 159, 271; Maria-Thereseien-Platz 47, *48*; Ringstrasse 48, 52, 83, 157; Sitte's Central Vienna design *83*, 83–4; walls of 18, 48, 52, 83; Whonpark Neue Danau 271, *272*
Villanueva, Carlos Raúl 184
Villeurbanne, France: Le Quartier de Gratte-ciel 155–7, *157*, 228
Vinci, Leonardo da 13, 201
Vitruvius 24, 201

Wagner, Otto 40, 133, 142, 248; *Grossstadt* 133, 138, *139*
Waldheim, Charles 311
Warsaw, Poland: World War Two destruction *162*
Washington, DC, USA 47; Crystal City proposal 113, *114*, 348; Dupont Circle area *2*; L'Enfant's plan 48–9, *49*, 95, 100; McMillan plan 100–1, *102*

Weisbaden, Germany: Eglise Catholique 81, *82*
Welwyn Garden City, England 117, 121, *121*, 204, 293
West Wycombe Park, England *12*
Wollstonecraft, Mary 55, 172
woonerf 219
World's Fairs 19, 257; London 1851 19, 97; Louisiana Purchas Exposition 101, *102*; Paris 1889 97; World's Columbian Exposition, Chicago 19, *96*, 97
World War One: impact of 89–90, *89*, 156, 172
World War Two 90; bombing of cities *162*; impact of 204; recovery from 90, 102, 163
Wren, Christopher: plan for London 41, *42*
Wright, Frank Lloyd 13, 70, 86, 89, 110, 112, 115, 118, 127, 142, 172, 311, 346, 348; and Ayn Rand's Howard Roark 192; his background 110, 346; *The Living City* 115
Wright, Henry 122

Xi'an, China 29

Za'atari refugee camp, Jordan 3, *3*, 4
Zaha Hadid Architects 238, 257, 282, 315; designs by 279–80, *280*, *284*, 285–6, *286*, 286–9, *288*, 315–16, *316*
Zamość, Poland 45, *45*, 52
Zhuhai, China: Opera House complex *269*
Zion, City of *see* Mormon design philosophy
zoning laws and building codes 56, 112, 266, 350; tax increment zoning 271

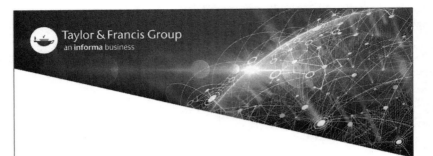

Taylor & Francis eBooks

www.taylorfrancis.com

A single destination for eBooks from Taylor & Francis with increased functionality and an improved user experience to meet the needs of our customers.

90,000+ eBooks of award-winning academic content in Humanities, Social Science, Science, Technology, Engineering, and Medical written by a global network of editors and authors.

TAYLOR & FRANCIS EBOOKS OFFERS:

- A streamlined experience for our library customers
- A single point of discovery for all of our eBook content
- Improved search and discovery of content at both book and chapter level

REQUEST A FREE TRIAL
support@taylorfrancis.com